Development of Psychopathology

To my family: Michelle, Noah, and Jacob.
Thank you for your love, support, laughter, intelligence, and flexibility.

To my many academic mentors, especially Lyn Abramson:
Thank you for teaching, challenging, and guiding me professionally and personally.

— Benjamin L. Hankin

To my mentors: Martin E. P. Seligman,
David C. Zuroff, Robert J. DeRubeis, and
Philip G. Levendusky. Thank you for investing
in me, believing in me, and constantly challenging me. I owe where
I am today, in large part, to you. I will be forever grateful for your support.

— John R. Z. Abela

Development of Psychopathology

A Vulnerability-Stress Perspective

Edited by

Benjamin L. Hankin

University of South Carolina

John R. Z. Abela

McGill University

For information:

Sage Publications, Inc.
2455 Teller Road
Thousand Oaks, California 91320
E-mail: order@sagepub.com

Sage Publications Ltd.
1 Oliver's Yard
55 City Road
London EC1Y 1SP
United Kingdom

Sage Publications India Pvt. Ltd.
B-42, Panchsheel Enclave
Post Box 4109
New Delhi 110 017 India

Printed in the United States of America.

Library of Congress Cataloging-in-Publication Data

Development of psychopathology: a vulnerability-stress perspective / editors Benjamin L. Hankin, John R. Z. Abela.
p. cm.
Includes bibliographical references and index.
ISBN 1-4129-0490-0 (pbk.)
1. Mental illness—Risk factors. 2. Psychology, Pathological—Etiology. 3. Developmental psychology. 4. Stress (Psychology) I. Hankin, Benjamin L. II. Abela, John R. Z.
RC455.4.R56D48 2005
616.89—dc22

2004025359

This book is printed on acid-free paper.

05 06 07 08 09 10 9 8 7 6 5 4 3 2 1

Acquisitions Editor:	Jim Brace-Thompson
Editorial Assistant:	Karen Ehrmann
Production Editor:	Tracy Alpern
Copy Editor:	Rachel Hile Bassett
Typesetter:	C&M Digitals (P) Ltd.
Indexer:	Mary Mortensen
Cover Designer:	Edgar Abarca

Contents

Preface

A VULNERABILITY-STRESS PERSPECTIVE ON THE DEVELOPMENT OF PSYCHOPATHOLOGY

Stress has long been implicated in the etiology of a wide range of psychological disorders including depression, anxiety disorders, eating disorders, schizophrenia, substance abuse, personality disorders, and externalizing disorders. At the same time, although an etiological link clearly exists between the occurrence of stressful life events and the onset of symptoms of psychopathology, it is apparent that the majority of individuals who experience stressors do not develop such symptoms.

In order to better understand why stressful life events appear to be linked to symptoms of psychopathology in some individuals but not in others, researchers have increasingly begun to conceptualize the development of psychopathology from a vulnerability-stress perspective. Vulnerability factors represent relatively stable aspects of an individual that make him or her more likely than others to develop symptoms of psychopathology following stressful life events. Vulnerability factors may include, but are not necessarily limited to, genetic factors, biological processes, cognitive structures, maladaptive ways of interacting with others, insecure attachment styles, and deficits in emotion regulation. Within vulnerability-stress models, individuals who possess vulnerability factors are only more likely than other individuals to experience symptoms of psychopathology in the presence of stressful life events. In the absence of such events, individuals who possess vulnerability factors are no more likely than others to exhibit symptoms of psychopathology.

A large number of vulnerability-stress theories have been proposed in recent years in order to explain the development of various forms of psychopathology including depression, schizophrenia, externalizing disorders, and substance-use disorders. Vulnerability-stress theories have also recently gained momentum as frameworks for understanding the development of personality disorders, anxiety disorders, and eating disorders. Increased interest in vulnerability-stress models has led to a rapid accumulation of empirical studies examining their central tenets. For some disorders, such as schizophrenia and depression, central tenets of prevailing models have been buttressed by a large body of empirical findings. For other disorders, such as personality and eating disorders, preliminary findings support the applicability of vulnerability-stress models to understanding the development of symptoms.

The goal of the current volume is to present cutting-edge theory and research examining the development of psychopathology from a vulnerability-stress perspective. The current volume is intended to advance our understanding of vulnerability-stress theories in three ways.

First, the majority of theory and research examining vulnerability to psychopathology have conceptualized and examined vulnerability within specific, limited content domains such as the biological, cognitive, or interpersonal domains. Although such a narrow focus has led to substantial leaps in our understanding of the relationship between specific types of vulnerability factors and the development of specific types of psychopathology, it has also blocked our progress in understanding how vulnerability factors across different content domains relate to one another to lead to the development of psychopathology. It is entirely possible that certain disorders, such as depression and schizophrenia, are heterogeneous in nature, with some individuals developing symptoms primarily as the result of genetic or biological factors and other individuals developing symptoms as the result of cognitive or environmental factors. At the same time, such purity in etiology is likely to be the exception rather than the rule. As research accumulates implicating specific types of vulnerability factors in the development of specific types of psychopathology, theorists and researchers must begin to tackle more challenging questions by examining how vulnerability factors across different biopsychosocial domains interact with one another to influence the onset and maintenance of symptoms. The current volume aims to present conceptualizations of vulnerability factors within six different content domains: genetic, biological, emotion regulation, cognitive, interpersonal, and attachment. In addition, the current volume aims to provide an overview of empirical findings connecting such vulnerability factors to a diverse array of psychopathologies.

Second, although early pioneering theory and research examining the development of schizophrenia from a vulnerability-stress perspective have had profound impacts on subsequent models of the etiology of a multitude of psychopathologies, subsequent theory and research have been relatively disorder specific in terms of accumulation of knowledge. It is important to highlight that an advance in the understanding of the development of any given type of psychopathology not only increases our understanding of the development of that particular form of psychopathology, but also suggests possible avenues of inquiry for theorists and researchers examining the development of other forms of psychopathology. As vulnerability-stress models become increasingly used as frameworks for understanding the development of various psychopathologies, forums are needed for monitoring theoretical and empirical progress across a wide array of disorders. The current volume consequently presents current theory and research examining various forms of psychopathology from a vulnerability-stress perspective including, but not limited to, depression, anxiety disorders, eating disorders, personality disorders, externalizing disorders, and substance-use disorders. In addition, for each disorder presented, literature pertinent to multiple types of vulnerability factors is presented.

Last, the majority of theories of vulnerability to psychopathology have been developed by researchers working with adult populations. Further, researchers testing "adult models" of vulnerability to psychopathology in child and adolescent populations have typically taken a "one size fits all" approach, paying little attention to how developmental differences may influence (a) the operationalization and assessment of vulnerability factors, and (b) the transactional associations between vulnerabilities and stressors. Such an experimental psychopathology approach, as opposed to a developmental psychopathology approach, has led to premature claims rejecting the applicability of certain vulnerability-stress theories to younger populations. Because "top-down" rather than "bottom-up" approaches have characterized the majority of theory and research examining vulnerability to psychopathology, our understanding of the etiology, maintenance, and treatment of psychopathology in children and adolescents has lagged far behind our understanding of the etiology, maintenance, and treatment of psychopathology in adults. The current volume aims to provide a critical analysis of prevailing theories of vulnerability to psychopathology by placing such theories within a developmental psychopathology framework. Because the current volume represents one of the first attempts to bridge the gap between developmental psychopathology frameworks and vulnerability-stress models of psychological disorders, more questions are posed than answers given. At the same time, the current volume aims to serve as a springboard toward the development of more holistic, developmentally sensitive models of the development of psychopathology from a vulnerability-stress perspective.

Acknowledgments

We would like to thank Jim Brace-Thompson, Senior Editor, Sage Publications, for believing in our vision and providing us and our contributors with the opportunity to share it with our colleagues in our field. We would like to thank Karen Ehrmann, Editorial Assistant, Sage Publications, for her high level of dedication to this project during the past 14 months. Without her assistance, the book would never have been completed in such a timely fashion. Finally, we would like to thank Tracy Alpern, Production Editor, Sage Publications, for her fastidious work in editing the final versions of the chapters.

Sage Publications wishes to thank the following reviewers: Irving I. Gottesman, PhD, University of Minnesota; Carolyn Black Becker, Trinity University; Terri L. Weaver, Saint Louis University; Robin J. Lewis, PhD, Old Dominion University; and Linda Guthrie, Tennessee State University.

Part I

OVERVIEW AND FOUNDATIONS

CHAPTER 1

Conceptualizing the Role of Stressors in the Development of Psychopathology

KATHRYN E. GRANT AND SUSAN D. MCMAHON

Stressors occupy a central role in the field of developmental psychopathology. At the theoretical level, most prevailing models of psychopathology recognize the potential importance of environmental stressors in the etiology and maintenance of psychological disorder (e.g., Cicchetti & Toth, 1997; Haggerty, Roghmann, & Pless, 1993; Rutter, 1989). Stressors represent the environmental contribution of risk, which interacts with multiple forms of vulnerability (e.g., genetic, biological, cognitive, interpersonal, and personality) to lead to psychopathology (Mash & Barkley, 2003; Monroe & Hadjiyannakis, 2002).

In spite of the potential significance of stressors, recent reviews (Grant et al., 2003; Grant, Compas, Thurm, McMahon, & Gipson, 2004; McMahon, Grant, Compas, Thurm, & Ey, 2003) acknowledge that the past decades have yielded only limited and incremental progress in the field. What makes this conclusion particularly notable is that a vast number of studies have been conducted in this area—more than 1,500 in the past 15 years on child and adolescent stress alone. Two related problems have been identified as reasons for this lack of progress: (a) conceptualization problems, and (b) measurement problems (Grant et al., 2003).

DEFINING STRESS

Few constructs in mental health have been as important, yet at the same time as difficult to define, as the concept of *stress* (S. Cohen, Kessler, & Gordon, 1995). Prevailing definitions all focus on environmental circumstances or conditions that threaten, challenge, exceed, or harm the psychological or biological capacities of the individual (S. Cohen et al., 1995). These demands may occur in the form of change in the social environment or in persistent environmental conditions that present ongoing threats and challenges. In this sense, all definitions of stress include an environmental component.

Definitions of stress differ, however, in the degree to which they emphasize psychological processes that occur in response to the environment.

The most widely accepted definition of stress has been the one offered by Lazarus and Folkman (1984): "Psychological stress involves a particular relationship between the person and the environment that is *appraised* by the person as taxing or exceeding his or her resources and endangering his or her well being" (p. 19). This definition has been cited frequently as the conceptual basis for research on stress in young people and adults.

Although the transactional theory that Lazarus and Folkman (1984) proposed helped to advance the field of psychology and the understanding of stress processes, there are some inherent problems with including appraisal in the definition of stress. First, a definition of stress that relies on cognitive appraisal processes is problematic for research on children and adolescents (Grant et al., 2003). Results of research on stress during infancy indicate there are clear negative effects of maternal separation, abuse, and neglect on infants (e.g., Field, 1995; Perry, Pollard, Blakley, Baker, & Vigilante, 1995). These negative effects occur, presumably, without the cognitive appraisal component that is central to the transactional definition.[1] In addition, preliminary research indicates that cognitive appraisal processes that play a significant role later in development do not play the same role for young children exposed to stressors (Nolen-Hoeksema, Girgus, & Seligman, 1992; J. E. Turner & Cole, 1994).

Further, in recent years, theoretical models of the etiology of developmental psychopathology have become more sophisticated, and there is greater emphasis on moderating and mediating processes that influence or explain the relation between stressors and psychopathology across development (Cicchetti & D. J. Cohen, 1995; Pearlin, 1999). Reliance on a definition of stress that "lumps" together potential mediating or moderating processes, such as cognitive appraisal processes, with stressors is conceptually unclear and empirically problematic (Reiss & Oliveri, 1991). To understand fully how stressful experiences, moderating factors, and mediating processes relate to one another in the prediction of psychopathology, it is important to discretely define and measure each of these variables (Aneshensel, 1999). This is particularly true in child and adolescent research, because the role of specific mediating and moderating processes is likely to shift across development.

A final reason for moving beyond a transactional definition of stress is that the individually based focus of such an approach may accentuate confounding of multiple vulnerabilities in stress research. From a transactional perspective, whether an experience is defined as a stressor is based on whether the individual appraises it as such. Appraisal processes, however, may reflect genetic or other vulnerability contributions to risk, thereby exacerbating potential confounding of vulnerabilities and environmental contributions to symptomatology (Brown, 1990; B. P. Dohrenwend & Shrout, 1986; Skodol, B. P. Dohrenwend, Link, & Shrout, 1990). Although any self-report method is susceptible to some degree of such confounding, methods that emphasize objective definitions of stressors are better equipped to assess the unique contribution of environmental risk to the development of psychopathology.

The single essential element of stress research—distinct from moderators and mediators, psychological symptoms, and other sources of risk or vulnerability—is external, an environmental threat to the individual (S. Cohen et al., 1995). For this reason, Grant and colleagues (2003) propose that *stress* be defined as "environmental events or chronic conditions that objectively threaten the physical and/or psychological health or well-being of individuals of a particular age in a particular society" (p. 449). Such a definition is consistent with traditional "stimulus-based" definitions of stress (Holmes & Rahe, 1967) and more recent definitions of *stressors* (McCubbin & Patterson, 1983) and *objective stress* (Brown & Harris, 1989; B. P. Dohrenwend & Shrout, 1985; Hammen, 1997).[2]

Development of a clear working definition of stressors, distinct from moderating and mediating variables, is an important first step toward fully defining the construct. Nonetheless, it remains a first step. Much additional research is needed to determine which specific environmental changes, events, and situations are "objectively threatening" to individuals. In this way, conceptualization of stressors is integrally linked with measurement and with the broader notion of a stressor classification system or taxonomy.

MEASURING STRESSORS

Stressor Checklists

The most widely used method for assessing stressors is the self-report checklist. Checklists are relatively easy to administer and allow investigators to collect data on large samples, thus increasing statistical power to detect relations among stressors, mediating and moderating variables, and psychological outcomes. Checklists vary in the extent to which they focus on breadth or depth. General checklists assess a broad range of stressful experiences, whereas specialized checklists assess specific types or domains of stressful events.

General Checklists of Stressful Events

Advances have been made in the development and refinement of general stressor checklists for adolescents and adults, but less progress has been made in the development of checklists for children. General checklists are all similar in that they present respondents with a sample of negative and, in some cases, positive events that are representative of the types of events that researchers deem relevant. None of the inventories is designed to be exhaustive; rather, they are intended to offer a sufficiently broad sampling to be representative of stressful events and experiences. Test-retest reliability and concurrent validity of several general life events checklists for adolescents and adults have been established (e.g., Burnett & Fanshawe, 1997; Cheng, 1997; L. H. Cohen & Park, 1992; Compas, Davis, Forsythe, & Wagner, 1987; B. S. Dohrenwend, Krasnoff, Askenasy, & B. P. Dohrenwend, 1978; Vagg & Spielberger, 1998; Williams & Cooper, 1998).

In contrast to self-report measures for adolescents and adults, checklists for the assessment of children's life events are often designed for parents to complete, on the assumption that preadolescents may not be reliable informants (e.g., Coddington, 1972). Little attention has been paid to the reliability and validity of child measures, however, and the implications of relying on external reports of parents as opposed to self-reports have not been examined (Grant et al., 2004). Much research is also needed on the developmental progression of children's ability to accurately report on stressful experiences (Stone & Lemanek, 1990).

Specialized Checklists

Specialized stressor checklists have generally been developed with two related issues in mind—the need for specific measures for specific populations, and the need for measures of specific types of events.

With some notable exceptions (e.g., Allison et al., 2004; Cheng, 1997; Gil, Vega, & Dimas, 1994; Loo et al., 2001; Nyborg & Curry, 2003; Richters & Martinez, 1993), measures of cumulative life stressors have been developed on European American middle-class samples. These measures have been criticized for lacking items pertinent to individuals of color, particularly those living in disadvantaged urban communities (Miller, Webster, & MacIntosh, 2002). A small number of measures have been developed to address this issue. For example, Hastings and Kelley (1997) developed a scale to assess exposure to violence in a sample of low-income urban adolescents (Hastings & Kelley). In the adult literature, measures have been developed to assess issues such as race-related stressors for Asian American Vietnam veterans (Loo et al.), race-related stressors encountered by African Americans (Utsey, 1999), and acculturative stressors for international students (Sandhu & Asrabadi, 1994).

A small number of measures have been developed on predominantly white middle-class samples exposed to specific stressors, including measures of events related to parental divorce (Roosa, Beals, Sandler, & Pillow, 1990) and parental alcoholism (Roosa, Sandler, Gehring, & Beals, 1988) affecting children and adolescents, and occupational stressors affecting adults (Greiner, Ragland, Krause, Syme, & Fisher, 1997; Vagg & Spielberger, 1998; Williams & Cooper, 1998). These measures contain events and chronic stressors that characterize these broader stressful experiences. Measures developed for specific populations offer the advantage of being more comprehensive and sensitive in measuring the types of stressors experienced by these groups. On the other hand, the limited range of events included on these measures prohibits their use in comparative studies across samples exposed to various types of stressful events and circumstances (Grant et al., 2004).

Critiques of the Checklist Approach

Although most stressor checklists are consistent with an objective conceptualization of environmental stress, the degree to which stressor checklists actually assess objective threat is unclear. The items included on stressor checklists have typically been selected by researchers based on their personal opinion, general consensus about the nature of threatening experiences, or information generated in small focus groups. Thus, the items themselves have not been empirically generated relative to objective threat. In addition, because cumulative stressor checklists include a list of brief items (e.g., death of a parent), it is unclear to what degree each item assesses the same experience for different individuals. For example, the death of a grandparent who has had little contact with a child represents less threat and disruption than the death of a grandparent who has served as that child's primary caregiver (Duggal et al., 2000)

Another critique of stressor checklists is that they do not require respondents to provide information about the date of occurrence or timing of the events (Duggal et al., 2000). Most checklists focus on a particular period of time (e.g., events that have occurred in the previous 6 months) without specifying at what point during that period the event took place. This limits the usefulness of checklists in determining the role of the occurrence of stressors in relation to the onset and remission of psychiatric disorders, as well as physical and psychological symptoms.

Finally, most stressor checklists have been criticized for failing to distinguish between stressors that are independent of the individual's behavior (e.g., fateful events, such as death of a partner or parent) and those that are not independent of behavior (e.g., job loss or school failure) (Hammen, 1997). Independent events are generally considered less confounded with psychopathology and are therefore seen as representing "cleaner" markers of environmental effects. On the other hand, there is increasing evidence of a reciprocal relation between stressors and psychological symptoms (discussed further below), indicating the importance of also examining stressors that may be dependent on an individual's behavior.

Stressor Interviews

Stressor interviews were developed in part to address the methodological shortcomings of stressor checklists. The most extensive structured interview work on adult samples has been conducted by Brown, B. P. Dohrenwend, and Monroe and their colleagues (e.g., Brown & Harris, 1989; B. P. Dohrenwend, Raphael, Schwartz, Stueve, & Skodol, 1993; McQuaid, Monroe, Roberts, Kupfer, & Frank, 2000; Monroe, Kupfer, & Frank, 1992; Wethington, Brown, & Kessler, 1997). Child and adolescent researchers, such as Garber, Goodyer, Frank, and Hammen and their colleagues, have modified and built upon adult work with these methodologies for use with children and adolescents (e.g., Adrian & Hammen, 1993; Duggal et al., 2000; Garber, Keiley, & Martin, 2002; Garber & Robinson, 1997; Goodyer & Altham, 1991; Hammen, 1995, 1997; Rudolph & Hammen, 1999; Rudolph, Hammen, & Burge, 1997; Williamson, Duchmann, Barker, & Bruno, 1998).

Stressor interviews are designed to provide relatively objective indices of the degree of contextual threat that is associated with stressful events and conditions. Interviews are used to generate a list of stressful events that have been encountered and the conditions that have surrounded these events. Probes for each event that has occurred include a description of what happened, when it happened (using a calendar to establish the dates of occurrence), who was involved, and the objective consequences of the event (Rudolph & Hammen, 1999; Rudolph et al., 1997). External raters then evaluate the level of threat associated with each event and condition or the severity of impact of each event. These ratings are then summed (or consensus is achieved among raters) to form an objective index of stressors that each child or adolescent has encountered. Interrater reliability of these ratings has typically been quite high (Adrian & Hammen, 1993; Garber & Robinson, 1997; Rudolph & Hammen; Rudolph et al., 1997).

Although many potential advantages of stressor interviews have been identified, there have been relatively few empirical comparisons of the relative merits of interviews and checklists, at least in the child and adolescent literature. In the adult literature, there have been a number of studies that have compared the number and types of stressors assessed by the two methods (e.g., Lewinsohn, Rohde, & Gau, 2003; Oei & Zwart, 1986; Zimmerman, Pfohl, & Stangl, 1986). A number of these studies have concluded that checklist and interview methods differ in the stressors they assess. For example, Oei and Zwart found significantly more reports of problems with work, education, illness, and marriage using the checklist method, whereas the interview led to more reports of deaths; they suggest that the anonymity of the checklist may facilitate reporting events of a more personal nature.

Gorman (1993) reviewed 11 studies that compared checklist with interview methods, and he concluded that checklists are more likely to suffer from overreporting of trivial events. Several of these studies also suggest that stressor checklists are associated with higher error rates (e.g., Zimmerman et al., 1986). For example, McQuaid, Monroe, Roberts, Johnson, and Brussel (1992) compared the Bedford College Life Events and Difficulties Schedule interview (LEDS; Brown & Harris, 1989) with the Psychiatric Epidemiology Research Interview Life Events Scale (PERI; B. S. Dohrenwend et al., 1978) and found that individuals reported the same event twice under different headings 4.5% of the time and events outside of the time period 7.6% of the time on the PERI (McQuaid et al., 1992). The extent to which these error rates represent unacceptably "high" levels is unclear, however.

In contrast to these findings, Abela, Wagner, and Brozina (2004) found that there was a strong association between interviews and checklists in terms of both numbers of events reported and objective and subjective severity ratings. They found no evidence of systematic bias in the checklist approach for either parents or children.

There have been fewer comparisons of interview and checklist methods in the prediction of psychopathology (e.g., Katschnig, 1986; Shrout et al., 1989), particularly in children and adolescents. We highlight three studies that illustrate the pattern of findings in this small literature. The first two were conducted on adolescents, the third on adults. Duggal and colleagues (2000) administered the LEDS interview modified for adolescents (Monck & Dobbs, 1985) and the Life Events Checklist (Johnson & McCutcheon, 1980) to a sample of 35 depressed and 35 control adolescents. Comparisons between the two measures revealed that a similar total number of stressors was identified by each, but that different events were tapped by the two measures. In fact, 68% of the events identified as severe by objective coders of the LEDS were not identified on the stressor checklist. Nonetheless, the two methods were equally effective at distinguishing between depressed adolescents and controls. This research is consistent with Lewinsohn's more recent work on older adolescents, which also demonstrates a high correlation between the checklist and the interview and equivalence of these approaches in predicting depression (Lewinsohn, Roberts, Hops, & Andrews, 1991; Lewinsohn et al., 2003).

McQuaid and colleagues (2000) administered the LEDS and PERI interviews to a sample of 91 outpatient adults enrolled in a treatment program for recurrent major depression. Comparisons between the two measures revealed that severe events on the LEDS were predictive of higher initial depressive symptoms and lower likelihood of remission, whereas PERI severe events were predictive of fewer previous episodes of depression and not predictive of remission.

It is unclear whether the two adolescent studies yielded such different results from the adult study because of developmental differences between the two samples, differences in research design, or differences between the checklists used or the scoring methods employed. The differences in findings highlight, however, the need for standardized measures of stressors that are more directly comparable across the life span in order to facilitate integration of stress research across developmental periods. This recommendation is discussed further below.

Critiques of the Interview Approach

Despite their potential advantages, stressor interviews have been used much less frequently than stressor checklists. This is likely because of the increased time demands and person power associated with interview administration, which bring substantially increased costs to the researcher and the participants. Given this reduced cost-effectiveness, interviews do not offer a complete solution to the problems identified with existing checklist measures. Complete reliance on stressor interviews would limit the field by reducing the participation of some researchers and by reducing the sample sizes of those studies that are conducted.

Beyond concerns about cost-effectiveness, interviews have been criticized as less likely to elicit information that may be embarrassing or have potential negative consequences if reported (Oei & Zwart, 1986; Singleton & Straits, 1999). This may be of particular concern with child and adolescent samples. For example, children and adolescents may be less likely to answer truthfully questions about physical or sexual abuse in an interview format (to an interviewer who may be required to report such abuse) than they would in an anonymous survey.

Nonetheless, there are research questions for which stressor interviews are essential.

In particular, interviews are recommended to better understand the complexity of the relation between the temporal course of psychological symptoms/disorders and stressors. For example, identifying the onset, course, duration, severity, and remission of psychological symptoms in relation to the specific nature, duration, and severity of stressors would be more easily accomplished through an interview process. In addition, interviews can be particularly helpful when considering diagnoses based on criteria from the *Diagnostic and Statistical Manual of Mental Disorders,* 4th edition (*DSM-IV*; American Psychiatric Association [APA], 1994), especially given the emphasis on the onset, course, duration, and remission of a disorder (e.g., diagnostic criteria that require a change in symptom level and functioning for a minimum of the past 2 weeks). In these cases, researchers need to document the timing of stressful events in relation to changes in the individual's symptoms and functioning. This requires the use of measures of both stressful events and psychopathology that are sensitive to timing and duration and research designs that are able to identify the specific timing of events in relation to the onset or termination of an episode of disorder (S. Cohen et al., 1995). Interviews have been designed to identify the date and timing of stressful events so they can be linked to the timing of the onset and remission of a disorder. Although it might be possible to design a checklist that assesses timing information, such checklists have not yet been developed.

General Critiques of Stressor Measurement Strategies

In addition to critiques that are specific to either survey or interview methods, two significant problems apply to both approaches to measurement. A first general concern involves possible confounding of stressors and symptoms of psychopathology due to similar items appearing on measures of both constructs (e.g., B. P. Dohrenwend & Shrout, 1985). For example, fights or conflicts with others and worries or concerns about one's life situation have been included on some measures of stressors, but they are also symptoms of some forms of psychopathology (e.g., disruptive behavior disorders and anxiety). The development of an empirically based taxonomy of stressors, including only stressors that are not overly confounded with symptoms, could address this problem (discussed further below). In the meantime, researchers should evaluate existing stressor measures for degree of overlap with symptomatology.

A second area of concern centers on the lack of standardization of stressor measurement. For example, a recent review of measurement strategies in child and adolescent stress research revealed that fewer than 10% used a well-validated measure (i.e., a measure that has well-documented and sound psychometric properties), and no single measure was used in more than 3% of studies (Grant et al., 2003). Almost half of the studies used measures created by the author (psychometric data and methods of measurement development were not typically provided), and the remaining studies used 1 of the roughly 50 available cumulative stressor measures. Although we are not aware of a comparable review of stressor measurement used with adult samples, a quick perusal of the adult literature reveals considerable variability in measurement strategy. In addition, theoretical and methodological critiques published in the adult literature were the first to level many of the critiques more recently leveled at the child literature (e.g., Brown, 1989, 1990, 1993; B. S. Dohrenwend, B. P. Dohrenwend, Dodson, & Shrout, 1984; B. P. Dohrenwend, Link, Kern, Shrout, & Markowitz, 1990; B. P. Dohrenwend & Shrout, 1986; Link, Mesagno, Lubner, & B. P. Dohrenwend, 1992; McQuaid et al., 1992; Monroe & McQuaid, 1994; Monroe &

Roberts, 1990; Raphael, Cloitre, & B. P. Dohrenwend, 1991; Skodol et al., 1990).

Lack of standardization highlights a central difference between the state of the field of stressor measurement and the state of the field of psychopathology measurement. Specifically, taxonomies of psychopathology (e.g., the *DSM-IV*; APA, 1994), and the Achenbach System of Empirically Based Assessment (ASEBA; Achenbach & Rescorla, 2001) have been developed, but no such taxonomy exists for stressors. The development of such psychopathology taxonomies represents an important achievement in the past half century and has dramatically improved the ability of researchers to communicate with one another and to replicate one another's work.

The progress made in stressor measurement over the past 15 years suggests it might be possible to develop a taxonomy of stressors. In particular, the development of reliable and valid stressor interviews indicates that it is possible to achieve agreement about events and conditions that pose threat to individuals in our society. Evidence for the reliability and validity of stressor checklists has also emerged, in spite of the fact that these measures have been developed independent of empirically based objective threat ratings. These achievements suggest that a standardized measure of stressors, which would build on the strengths of checklist and interview methodologies, could be developed (Grant et al., 2004).

RECOMMENDED NEXT STEPS IN CONCEPTUALIZATION AND MEASUREMENT OF STRESSORS

Development of a Taxonomy of Stressors

Standardization of measures, the generation of normative data on the occurrence of stressors, and the development of a taxonomy of stressors are recommended as the next steps in stress measurement research. There are at least two promising avenues for the development of a taxonomy of stressors. Both depend on an objective definition of stressors and the use of narrative interview methodology as a first step. The first approach uses the deductive method and builds on the tradition of the *DSM-IV* (APA, 1994). It focuses on applying conceptually based categories and dimensions of stressors (e.g., valence, fatefulness, predictability, centrality, magnitude) to in-depth analysis of existing transcripts of narrative stressor interviews. B. P. Dohrenwend and colleagues have begun such work with adult samples faced with poverty, racism, and war (personal communication, January 27, 2004), with the goal of developing a stressor taxonomy that can be assessed using intensive narrative interviews.

The second approach, building on the inductive method and the tradition of Achenbach's ASEBA (Achenbach & Rescorla, 2001) would proceed in three phases. The first phase would involve quantitative coding of stressors generated by individuals who have been exposed to heightened rates of stressors (e.g., individuals living in urban poverty) and individuals who have been underrepresented in stress research (e.g., individuals of color) in order to generate a comprehensive and representative list of stressors. Each identified stressor would be coded for objective threat based on the coding protocol of a well-validated stressor interview (e.g., Hammen & Rudolph, 1996), and the contextual descriptors that lead to the judges' objective threat rating for each stressor would be identified. The list of stressors generated on an underrepresented sample would be compared with existing stressor measures (developed on white, middle-class samples) to ensure that it is comprehensive. The second phase would involve inductive qualitative analysis of stressor interview transcripts in conjunction with objective impact ratings (Harper et al., in press; Patton, 1990). The goal of the qualitative analysis would be to condense an initial list of individual stressors and their relevant contextual descriptors to a nonredundant list of stressors (of a length conducive to use in checklist research) that includes contextual descriptors associated with significant variation in objective impact ratings. Once reliability and validity were established, the final step would be to administer the stressor taxonomy checklist to a large, nationally representative sample for the purpose of establishing stressor base rates, norms, and risk cutpoints relative to clinically significant symptomatology (Achenbach & Rescorla, 2001; Grant et al., 2004). Grant and colleagues (2004) have begun phase 1 of this research with a sample of low-income urban adolescents. In contrast with B. P. Dohrenwend's goal to develop a deductively based taxonomy that can be assessed using interview methods, the goal of Grant's research is to develop an inductively based taxonomy that can be assessed using a checklist standardized on a large nationally representative sample.

It will be important for adult, adolescent, and child researchers as well as researchers focused on interview-based and checklist-based taxonomies to collaborate toward the development of a life-span taxonomy of stressors that can be assessed through an integrated system of checklist and interview methods. B. P. Dohrenwend and Grant have begun to collaborate on integrating their respective work on adults and adolescents, interviews and checklists. To our knowledge, no one has yet begun to tackle the development of a taxonomy of stressors for young children. Creating such a taxonomy will involve labor-intensive efforts including observations, reports of parents and guardians, and physiological measures of stress reactivity in young children not yet able to report on stressful experiences. Until a taxonomy of stressors is developed, stress researchers must pay more attention to measurement issues in stress research by using currently available stressor measures with good psychometric properties and providing detailed information about stressor measures utilized in their research.

Integration of Macro- and Microenvironmental Processes

In the long run, it will be useful to test the limits of Grant and colleagues' (2003) definition and the taxonomies that emanate from it with an eye toward possible integration of broader notions of ecological influence (Bronfenbrenner, 1977; Cicchetti & Toth, 1997; B. P. Dohrenwend, 1998; Pearlin, 1999). A definition that requires evidence of objective threat would capture broad stressors such as poverty and specific experiences and overt conditions related to "isms" such as sexism, racism, and homophobia, but it would not capture broader, more implicit, societal values related to such "isms," because individuals reporting on stressors might not "see" these influences as stressful, and judges might have difficulty quantifying them as threatening. For example, the ways in which particular groups of individuals are portrayed in our society have typically been conceptualized as cultural or societal values. The extent to which some of these portrayals might also constitute a measurable threat remains an empirical question. In the future, it might be possible for judges to analyze media images of women and girls, for example, and evaluate the ways in which they are portrayed (including their physical measurements relative to the measurements of the average adolescent girl) and determine whether societal pressures around appearance constitute a threat to the physical and emotional health of adolescent girls (Hankin & Abramson, 2001). Developing methods for determining variability in exposure to potential cultural toxins such as these would present the next challenge in such research.

Another area for long-term investigation falls at the opposite end of the continuum from societally based threat, and that is the notion of daily hassles. Daily hassles have historically occupied an important place in stress research, and some research has demonstrated that major events lead to hassles, which in turn lead to emotional distress. However, stressor definitions that focus on objectively threatening experiences are unlikely to include minor events, because achieving agreement across judges about the objective threat of such events is difficult (Monroe & McQuaid, 1994). Once a reliable and valid taxonomy of objectively threatening stressors is developed, however, it may be possible to expand the taxonomy to include more minor events. For example, it might be possible to use average physiological response (e.g., electroencephalogram, startle, and heart rate) to minor events as a means of quantifying the degree to which these events might be threatening to individuals.

In the long run, to fully understand environmental effects on mental health, it will be important to examine the degree to which broader ecological influences and microevents might also pose threats to individuals in our society. In the short run, however, we believe that the lack of consensus around operationalization of stressors and their role in the etiology of psychopathology, including concerns about confounding in stress research (B. P. Dohrenwend & Shrout, 1985), demand that we begin with a rigorous, focused definition of stressors (i.e., events and circumstances that are objectively threatening) and that we proceed with the development of a taxonomy based upon such a definition.

CONCEPTUALIZING THE ROLE OF STRESSORS IN THE DEVELOPMENT OF PSYCHOPATHOLOGY

A Proposed Model

Grant and colleagues (Grant et al., 2003) have proposed a general conceptual model of the role of stressors in the etiology of developmental psychopathology. This model builds on previously proposed specific models of psychopathology (e.g., Albano, Chorpita, & Barlow, 1996; Asarnow & Asarnow, 1996; Hammen & Rudolph, 1996) and mechanisms of stress (e.g., Pearlin, 1999) and includes five central propositions: (a) stressors contribute to psychopathology; (b) moderators influence the relation between stressors and psychopathology; (c) mediators explain the relation between stressors and psychopathology; (d) there is specificity in the relations among stressors, moderators, and mediators; and (e) relations among stressors, moderators, mediators, and psychopathology are reciprocal and dynamic. None of these propositions is mutually exclusive. All may operate at once or in dynamic interaction.

The first proposition of this conceptual model, that stressors contribute to psychopathology, provides the most basic conceptual basis for all studies of the relation between stressors and psychopathology. Indeed, this provides part of the foundation for the current volume exploring vulnerabilities and stressors in a developmental psychopathology perspective. Grant and colleagues (2004) recently reviewed the evidence for prospective effects in 60 studies conducted with children and adolescents. They found consistent evidence that stressful life experiences predict psychological problems in children and adolescents over time (Grant et al., 2004). Cumulative measures of stressors and particular stressful experiences (e.g., poverty, divorce) were both found to predict psychological symptoms, and positive associations were reported for both interviews (e.g., Hammen, Burge, & Adrian, 1991) and checklists (e.g., DuBois, Felner, Brand, Adan, & Evans, 1992). In addition, stressful events were found to predict both internalizing problems, such as depression and anxiety, as well as externalizing symptoms, such as aggression and delinquency (e.g., Robinson, Garber, & Hilsman, 1995), though the associations were typically stronger with internalizing than externalizing problems (Compas, Howell, Phares, Williams, & Ledoux, 1989), and externalizing symptoms were examined less frequently.

We are not aware of a recent review of prospective studies of the effects of stressors on adult mental health. Nonetheless, there have been a number of individual studies that have established this relation in adult samples (e.g., Alspaugh, Stephens, Townsend, Zarit, & Greene, 1999; Halligan, Michael, Clark, & Ehlers, 2003; Hankin, Abramson, Miller, & Haeffel, 2004; Monroe, 1982, 1983; Ritsher, Warner, Johnson, & Dohrenwend, 2001; Ritter, Hobfol, Lavin, Cameron, & Hulsizer, 2000; Tein, Sandler, & Zautra, 2000; Wilcox et al., 2003).

The notion that moderators influence the relation between stressors and psychopathology has been examined in numerous studies of children, adolescents, and adults. Moderators may be conceptualized as vulnerabilities or protective factors, because they represent preexisting characteristics (in existence prior to exposure to the stressor) that increase or decrease the likelihood that stressors will lead to psychopathology (Baron & Kenny, 1986; Holmbeck, 1997). Moderators may also be viewed as the mechanisms that explain variability in processes and outcomes ranging from equifinality to multifinality (i.e., the mechanisms that explain why varying processes may lead to similar outcomes, and similar processes may lead to varying outcomes; Sameroff, Lewis, & Miller, 2000). Potential moderating variables include demographic variables (e.g., age, sex, race, ethnicity, gender, education, marital status, socioeconomic status), social factors (e.g., social support; parent, peer, and romantic relationships; and work, school, and neighborhood contexts), and "fixed" cognitive/relational styles (e.g., temperament, personality, attributions, coping). Moderating variables may be the result of genetic vulnerabilities (or protective factors), nonstressor environmental influences (e.g., societal, parental, or peer influences), or, in some cases, stressful experiences. For example, exposure to severe and chronic stressors may lead to the development of a stable attributional style that interacts with future stressors to predict psychopathology (Grant et al., 2004). In terms of social moderators, researchers have been more likely to consider parenting issues for children, peer influences for adolescents, and significant others for adults. Research on personality moderators may focus on temperamental characteristics, such as impulsivity or difficulty concentrating, in childhood or early adolescence, whereas in adulthood, neuroticism and conscientiousness have been found to increase risk (Chassin, Collins, Ritter, & Shirley, 2001). Part II of this volume discusses in greater detail various potential moderating vulnerabilities, their potential interactions with stressors, and the evidence for vulnerabilities as they are implicated in the development of psychopathology.

In a recent review of the literature on moderators of the association between stressors and psychological problems in young people (Grant et al., 2004), few consistent moderating effects emerged. However, most studies simply included variables, such as age or sex, in more general analyses without reference to conceptual models of developmental psychopathology (Grant et al., 2004). Those that tested a specific theory-based hypothesis were more likely to report positive findings. One expected pattern of results was that boys were more likely to exhibit externalizing symptoms, and girls were more likely to exhibit internalizing symptoms, in response to stressors (Grant et al., 2004). We are not aware of any recent reviews of moderator studies with adult samples. Nonetheless, there have been a number of moderator studies with adults that have tested specific conceptual models of the relation between stressors and psychopathology, and evidence has emerged for a number of these specific moderators (e.g., Bartone,

1999; Chang & Rand, 2000; Chassin et al., 2001; Corning, 2002; Dormann & Zapf, 1999; Fischer & Shaw, 1999; Frese, 1999; Lay & Nguyen, 1998; Lester, Nebel, & Baum, 1994; McNally, Malcarne, & Hansdottir, 2001; Moradi & Subich, 2004; Schat & Kelloway, 2003; Smith, McCullough, & Poll, 2003; Tein et al., 2000; Wrosch, Schulz, & Heckhausen, 2002).

Although some variables may serve either a moderating or mediating function (e.g., cognitive attributions, coping), mediators are conceptually distinct from moderators in that they are "activated," "set off," or "caused by" the current stressful experience and serve to account, conceptually and statistically, for the relation between stressors and psychopathology (Baron & Kenny, 1986; Holmbeck, 1997). Whereas moderators are characteristics of the individual or his or her social network prior to the stressor, mediators become characteristics of the individual or his or her social network in response to the stressor. In some cases, the individual may possess some of the mediating characteristics prior to exposure, but the characteristic increases (or decreases) substantially in response to the stressor.

Mediators, conceptually and empirically, explain how and why stressors are predictive of psychopathology. Broadly conceptualized, mediators include biological processes, psychological processes, and social processes. Biological mediators of the relation between stressors and psychopathology might include overactivation of hormones designed to help protect individuals from external threats (i.e., allostatic load; McEwen, 1998). Psychological processes might include cognitive changes in views of the world (e.g., benign vs. threatening), others (e.g., trustworthy vs. dangerous), and the self (e.g., competent vs. incompetent, lovable vs. unlovable) as well as changes in coping strategies (DuBois, Felner, Sherman, & Bull, 1994; Sandler, Tein, & West, 1994). Social mediators might emanate from the individual as a result of increased biological or cognitive vulnerability (e.g., individual may withdraw from others or become more irritable with others as a result of cognitive changes or negative coping in response to the stressor) (Cole & J. D. Turner, 1993; Spaccarelli, Coatsworth, & Bowden, 1995). Stressors might also act directly upon the social environment. For example, economic stressors, loss of a loved one, or divorce might lead to reductions in social support from family members also affected by the stressful experience (Pearlin, 1999).

Grant and colleagues (2004) recently reviewed the literature on mediators of the association between stressors and psychological problems in young people and reported promising evidence of mediating effects. Studies of mediators of the relation between stressors and child and adolescent psychopathology represent one of the few areas in child and adolescent stress research that has consistently tested specific theoretical models of the etiology of child and adolescent psychopathology. Within this area, the most frequently examined conceptual model has been one in which negative parenting mediates the relation between poverty/ economic stressors and child and adolescent psychopathology. Results have generally been supportive of this model (see Grant et al., 2004).

We are not aware of any recent reviews of mediator studies with adult samples, yet there have been a number of mediator studies with adults that have tested specific conceptual models of the relation between stressors and psychopathology. Evidence has emerged for a number of these specific mediators (e.g., Charney et al., 1990; Koss, Figueredo, & Prince, 2002; Sharkansky et al., 2000; Tein et al., 2000; R. J. Turner & Roszell, 1994). For example, a diminished sense of mastery or control has been found to mediate the relation between health problems and depression in older adults (Mirowsky & Ross, 1999). Additionally, emotional abuse in childhood has been found to predict various mediating vulnerabilities in adulthood, including more insecure attachment, greater exposure to stressors, and cognitive vulnerability. These mediators, in turn, predicted depression in adults (Hankin, in press).

The fourth proposition of Grant and colleagues' (2004) broad conceptual model is that there is specificity in relations among particular stressors, moderators, mediators, and psychological outcomes. According to this proposition, a particular type of stressor (e.g., interpersonal rejection) is linked with a particular type of psychological problem (e.g., depression) via a particular mediating process (e.g., ruminative coping) in the context of a particular moderating variable (e.g., female gender, adolescent age).

McMahon and colleagues (2003) recently reviewed the literature on specificity in the relation between particular stressors and particular psychological outcomes in children and adolescents and failed to discover any studies that had examined a "full specificity model" including specific mediating and moderating processes in the relation between particular stressors and particular outcomes. A number of studies examined more than one stressor and more than one outcome, thereby allowing for the examination of specific associations between particular stressors and particular outcomes (McMahon et al., 2003). With a few notable exceptions (e.g., Eley & Stevenson, 2000; Sandler, Reynolds, Kliewer, & Ramirez, 1992), these studies did not define themselves as "specificity" studies, nor did they test a specificity theory. A consistent pattern of specific effects failed to emerge, with the exception of sexual abuse. Several studies demonstrated that sexual abuse was specifically associated with internalizing outcomes, posttraumatic stress disorder (PTSD), and sexual acting out. However, results from studies examining the relations between other stressors (exposure to violence, physical abuse, neglect, divorce, marital conflict, poverty, illness, and cumulative stress) and psychological outcomes were more consistent with tenets of equifinality and multifinality (McMahon et al., 2003). This lack of consistent effects may be due to high co-occurrence rates for psychological problems and for particular types of stressful experiences. The degree to which a more comprehensive specificity model (i.e., one that also includes specific moderators and mediators) might prove valid has yet to be investigated in young people.

Although there have not been any recent reviews of specificity studies with adult samples, theoretical models that provide the basis for specificity analyses have emerged from the adult literature. Hankin and Abramson (2001), in their life-span developmental psychopathological model, proposed that stress would operate as a nonspecific risk factor for psychopathology, but that certain vulnerabilities (e.g., cognitive) would interact with stress to contribute to the development of depression specifically. Consistent with this hypothesis, general stressors have been found to predict both anxiety and depression in adults (Hankin, Abramson, et al., 2004) as well as depression and externalizing behaviors in adolescence (Hankin & Abramson; Quiggle, Garber, Panak, & Dodge, 1992), but cognitive vulnerability interacting with these stressors particularly predicted depression. In addition, there is greater evidence of specific associations between particular stressors and particular types of psychopathology for adults, particularly in the area of loss events and depression (e.g., Bifulco, Brown, & Harris, 1987; Brown, 1998; Brown, Harris, & Copeland, 1977; Finlay-Jones & Brown, 1981; Harris, Brown, & Bifulco, 1990; Lloyd, 1980;

Matussek & Neuner, 1981; Monroe, Rohde, Seeley, & Lewinsohn, 1999; Shrout et al., 1989), with more limited evidence for specific associations between future harm/danger events and anxiety (Kendler, Hettema, Butera, Gardner, & Prescott, 2003; Kendler, Karkowski, & Prescott, 1998; Lee & Lee, 1999).

The final proposition that relations among stressors, moderators, mediators, and psychopathology are reciprocal and dynamic broadly encompasses the following specific hypotheses: (a) each variable in the model influences the other (with some exceptions, e.g., fixed moderators such as age will not be influenced by other variables); (b) the role of specific variables within the model may vary across specific stressors and shift over time (e.g., a mediator that developed in response to a particular stressor may become a fixed pattern of responding and may thus interact as a moderator with subsequent stressors); and (c) reciprocal and dynamic relations among stressors, moderators, and mediators will predict not only the onset of psychological problems, but also the exacerbation of symptoms and the movement along a continuum from less to more severe forms of psychopathology (e.g., shifts from depressive symptoms to depressive disorder).

The proposition that relations among stressors, moderators, mediators, and psychopathology are reciprocal and dynamic has received the least research attention. Longitudinal research that measures stressors and potential mediators, moderators, and psychological outcomes at each of several time points is needed for a full examination of reciprocal and dynamic relations among these variables over time. Extant research has generally focused on the hypothesis that psychopathology predicts additional stressful experiences (Hammen, 1991). Grant and colleagues (2004) recently reviewed studies examining this hypothesis in children and adolescents. Results of this review suggest that symptoms do predict increased exposure to stressors, indicating that at least some children and adolescents are caught in a continuing cycle in which stressful experiences contribute to increases in symptoms of internalizing or externalizing problems, and these problems contribute to disrupted interpersonal relationships, failures in achievement tasks, and other types of stressors. For example, findings from multiwave prospective research with adolescents show that greater depressive symptoms at one time predict increases in stressors, especially interpersonal stressors, at a later time point, even after accounting for the stability of both depression and stressors over time (Hankin, Roesch, Mermelstein, & Flay, 2004). There have also been studies conducted with adult samples that have demonstrated that symptoms lead to additional stressors and that adults generate stressful experiences in their lives (e.g., Magnus, Diener, Fujita, & Payot, 1994; Monroe & Simons, 1991; Rudolph et al., 2000; Simons, Angell, Monroe, & Thase, 1993; Sobolewski, Strelau, & Zawadzki, 2001).

Additional research is needed to test for reciprocal and dynamic relations among particular stressors, particular moderating and mediating processes, and particular outcomes. Little research has been conducted on reciprocal and dynamic relations among these variables, but at least three studies exemplify the type of research needed in this area. Davila and colleagues (1995) tested the hypothesis that interpersonal stressors function both as predictors of depressive symptoms and as mediators of the relation between initial and later depressive symptoms in a sample of late adolescents. The authors found support for their hypothesis in a series of reciprocal relations, thus illustrating the dynamic relations among stressors, psychopathology, and mediating processes. Nolen-Hoeksema and colleagues (1992) found that stressors predicted a pessimistic explanatory style in youth that was associated with depression but that did not remit with the remittance of depressive symptoms. This phenomenon, which the authors labeled a "scar," suggests that pessimistic explanatory style may initially play a mediating role in response to stressors in the prediction of depression but, over time, may become a fixed pattern of responding and may eventually function as a moderator in relation to future stressors. Lakdawalla and Hankin (in press) found that the personality trait of neuroticism predicted greater exposure to stressors over time and was associated with elevated cognitive vulnerability, and in turn, the interaction of cognitive vulnerability with more stressors predicted increases in depressive symptoms. This finding suggests that moderating variables may also serve as predictors of stressors. Additional studies testing hypotheses such as these are needed to determine the ways in which relations among stressors, mediators, moderators, and psychological problems may be reciprocal and dynamic.

Research on reciprocal and dynamic processes in the relations among stressors, moderators, mediators, and psychopathology represents an especially promising area of inquiry for stress research across the life span. For example, some developmental psychopathologists (Cole & Turner, 1993; Shirk, 2004) have theorized that cognitive mediational processes may be more salient than cognitive moderational processes at younger ages (see Gibb & Coles, Chapter 5 of this volume, for greater discussion of cognitive vulnerabilities). Cognitive attributions and coping styles are not likely to be well developed in young children; thus, these types of variables are more likely to serve mediational functions in younger samples. Across development, however, these cognitive processes may develop into stable attributional or coping styles, which are better conceptualized as moderators (Grant et al., 2003). Thus, from a life-span perspective, it will be useful to examine the ways in which mediators may develop into moderators (or predictors of additional stressors and symptoms) across development.

It would also be useful to investigate the ways in which stressors experienced at varying points in development may be related to varying types of psychopathology. As the brain develops, the capacity for particular types of cognitive mediation also develops, thereby providing the mediational link between stressors and emerging manifestations of particular types of disorder (Mash & Barkley, 2003). The ways in which development constrains or fosters potential mediating cognitions, the degree to which stressors might operate within a developmental context to further facilitate or inhibit the development of particular cognitive processes, and the degree to which developmental influences on cognitive mediation might explain developmental variation in the manifestation of psychopathology represent interrelated and promising avenues for future research.

Another promising area of inquiry is investigation of the degree to which uncontrollable stressors experienced in early childhood may set the stage for controllable, self-generated stressors later in life. For example, abuse experienced in childhood may lead to avoidance, which may become a fixed pattern of responding that is predictive of additional stressors and distress. Thus, stressors experienced in childhood may predict both maladaptive coping strategies and psychopathology, which in turn set the stage for additional stressful experiences at older ages (Gibb, 2002; Hankin, in press; Magnus et al., 1994; Monroe & Simons, 1991; Simons et al., 1993; Sobolewski et al., 2002).

RECOMMENDATIONS FOR FUTURE RESEARCH ON CONCEPTUALIZING THE ROLE OF STRESSORS IN THE DEVELOPMENT OF PSYCHOPATHOLOGY

Although Grant and colleagues' (2003) general model is simpler than many of the models it builds upon, completing the task of testing its basic tenets across the life span will not be simple. The first step is to disaggregate this generic model into one of the numerous specific models it comprises. For example, although many studies have tested whether the association between stressors and outcome varies as a function of age or sex, few have done so in the context of a specific theory-based model of moderation. Research testing such a model might (a) examine the influence of a particular moderator on the relation between a particular stressor and a particular outcome (e.g., test the hypothesis that some stressors, such as exposure to violence, have a larger impact on boys than they do on girls, at least in relation to some outcomes, such as aggression); (b) examine the influence of a particular moderator on the relation between a particular stressor and a particular mediator (e.g., test the hypothesis that girls are more likely to respond to a particular stressor, such as dissolution of a relationship, with a particular response, such as ruminative coping); or (c) examine the influence of a particular moderator on the relation between a particular stressor and a particular outcome via a particular mediator (e.g., test the hypothesis that the association between exposure to violence and aggression might be stronger for boys because boys are more likely to respond with distraction and avoidant coping). In addition, reciprocal and dynamic relations between a particular moderator and a particular stressor, outcome, or mediating process could be examined. For example, one might test the hypothesis that psychological problems (e.g., aggressive behavior) lead to the development of a moderating context (e.g., hostility from classmates at school), which in turn exacerbates the association between a particular stressor (e.g., a violent attack at school) and additional psychological symptoms.

Similarly, specific models of mediating mechanisms could be tested. Research testing such models might examine the hypotheses that (a) a particular mediator (e.g., avoidant coping) explains the relation between a particular stressor (e.g., sexual assault) and a particular psychological outcome (e.g., PTSD); or that (b) a particular stressor (e.g., severe sexual abuse) "pulls for" a particular mediating process (e.g., avoidant coping), which interacts with a particular moderator (e.g., early childhood) to lead to a new moderator (e.g., avoidant coping that has become a fixed pattern of responding), which in turn interacts with additional stressors (e.g., interpersonal loss) to lead to ongoing psychological distress (e.g., depression, anxiety).

As illustrated in the examples above, the propositions that stressors contribute to psychopathology and that associations among particular stressors, moderators, mediators, and outcomes are reciprocal, dynamic, and specific are easily examined within the context of research on moderating and mediating mechanisms. Alternatively, they could serve as the conceptual starting point. For example, research on specificity would, ideally, include examination of specific mediators and moderators of the association between a specific stressor and a specific psychological outcome.

In the long run, once each of the propositions of the simple, general stress model has been supported or rejected, it will be important to integrate this simple model with a larger ecological model of environmental influences on mental health. A number of researchers, working predominantly with adults, have developed ecological and sociological models of environmental influence that shed light on stress research and point toward future, more sophisticated and integrative areas for investigation (e.g., Cicchetti & Toth, 1997; Dohrenwend, 1998; Pearlin, 1999). These approaches explicitly recognize the ecology of broad, societally based influences on individual development, as well as contextual strains and problems with person-environment fit.

For example, Bronfenbrenner's (e.g., 1977) work provides a framework for understanding environmental influences across a variety of systems (i.e., macrosystem, exosystem, mesosystem, and microsystem), and B. P. Dohrenwend (1998) nests proximal life events within broad pervasive influences associated with socioeconomic status (SES), gender, or race/ethnicity. Pearlin (1999) offers a model for integration of a more focused stress model with broader ecological models, because his model includes basic variables of stressors, moderators, mediators, and outcomes but also explicitly defines stress broadly (e.g., unequal distribution of resources, such as those associated with race, gender, SES, age, occupation).

There is clearly overlap between more comprehensive ecological theories and models that more simply outline the relation between stressors and psychopathology with specific moderators and mediators. In some ways, the more simple representation is subsumed as a part of the larger ecological models. Although these broad ecological models are more comprehensive and better represent the complexity of reality, methodology has not kept pace with theory. There are few measures that assess negative environmental influences at broader ecological levels, and the complexity of these models makes them difficult to test. As we begin to develop a taxonomy of stressors, we can incorporate some aspects of broader environmental influence. For example, testing models in which specific moderators include contextual factors, such as school climate or sense of community, can help us begin to understand the broader ecological picture of environmental influence on the relation between stressors and psychological outcomes. Perhaps, as we obtain more agreement regarding how specific stressors influence specific outcomes, we can move toward assessment of more comprehensive models.

Nonetheless, given the state of the field, including the general lack of consensus around a definition of stressors and their role in the etiology of psychopathology, the lack of a stressor taxonomy, inconsistent measurement of stressors, and the lack of conclusive evidence for some of the basic tenets of a simple model (i.e., moderating effects, specificity effects, reciprocal and dynamic effects), we recommend beginning with the simpler model. In this way, we can shift the pattern that has characterized stress research in the past two decades: limited incremental progress relative to volumes of studies published in the field.

SUMMARY, INTEGRATION, AND DIRECTIONS FOR FUTURE RESEARCH

In recent decades, research on the effects of stressors on children and adolescents has followed in the footsteps of research on the effects of stressors on adults, with little concerted effort at collaboration or integration. In the past few years, however, there has been a concerted effort on the part of child and adolescent stress researchers to "catch up" with their adult counterparts. Recent reviews of stress research on children and adolescents (Grant et al., 2003; Grant et al., 2004; McMahon et al., 2003) have resulted in: (a) a working definition of stressors that builds on research with both adults and younger samples, (b) a proposed conceptual model applicable across the life span, and (c) a clearer picture of the state of the field, including strong evidence of prospective effects of stressors on psychopathology. In addition, child and adolescent stress researchers have built on adult research (Brown & Harris, 1989) to develop a narrative interview methodology for young people (Adrian & Hammen, 1993; Goodyer & Altham, 1991; Hammen, 1995, 1997; Rudolph & Hammen, 1999) and have begun to use this methodology to develop a taxonomy of stressors for children and adolescents.

A recommended next step is to integrate better the work conducted on adult and child/adolescent samples. Whereas there is value to examining specific developmental periods and the etiology of specific disorders within certain populations (i.e., certain disorders tend to be exhibited in childhood, whereas others have onsets in adulthood), a life-span approach can lead us to consider both continuity and change in the relation between stressors and outcomes from a developmental perspective (Cicchetti & Toth, 1997). With the advent of developmental psychopathology, there has been a greater interest in integration of research across the life span. However, few researchers currently practice such integration, which is a necessary step toward advancing the field (Ingram & Price, 2001).

There is a need for a conceptual bridge and a common language to facilitate longitudinal investigations of the impact of stressors across the life span. To develop a common language, we recommend collaboration between adult and child/adolescent researchers toward the development of a taxonomy of stressors that is comparable across the life span. To build a conceptual bridge, we recommend that studies of the role of stressors in the development of psychopathology in children, adolescents, and adults build upon a simple, general conceptualization like that proposed by Grant and colleagues (2003). A general model such as this one includes the most consistently described elements of stress research proposed in both the child and adult literatures (e.g., Aneshensel, 1999; Chorpita, 2003; DeBellis, 2001; Fletcher, 2003; Hammen & Rudolph, 2003; Pearlin, 1999; Rubin, Burgess, Kennedy, & Stewart, 2003; Sher, 1991; Zuckerman, 1999). Once each of the propositions of the simple, general stress model has been supported or rejected, it will be important to integrate this simple model with a larger ecological model of environmental influences. To understand fully environmental effects on mental health, it will be important to examine the degree to which broader ecological influences and minor events might also pose threats to individuals in our society.

In conclusion, stressors remain a construct of central importance to the field of developmental psychopathology. Definition and measurement problems have limited incremental progress in stress research, as has the lack of conceptually driven studies. We believe that the lack of consensus around operationalization of stressors and their role in the etiology of psychopathology requires the following in response: (a) a rigorous, focused definition of stressors; (b) the development of a taxonomy based upon such a definition; (c) incremental research based on a relatively simple generic model; and (d) a developmental approach that integrates theory and research across the life span. These approaches, we hope, will lead us to the next generation of stress research, characterized by consistent measurement, incremental progress, a clearer understanding of the direct role of stressors in the etiology of psychopathology, an enhanced picture of the moderating and mediating influences that vulnerabilities and stressors may have on the development of psychopathology, and ultimately a better road map to effective interventions and policy initiatives across the life span.

NOTES

1. If cognitive appraisal processes are involved in the negative effects of stressors on infants, we are unable to measure these processes with currently available instruments.

2. Given the historical association of the term *stress* with a wide array of psychological phenomena (i.e., from environmental stressors to mediating and moderating processes to psychological responses to environmental stressors), Grant and colleagues (2003) recommend use of the word *stressor* to refer to the environmental experiences that should be the defining feature of stress research. The broader term *stress* is more useful as an inclusive term that refers not only to the environmental stressors themselves but also to the range of processes set in motion by exposure to environmental stressors. Thus, *stress research* refers to the body of literature that examines environmental stressors as well as reciprocal and dynamic processes among stressors, mediators, moderators, and psychological symptoms (Grant et al., 2003).

REFERENCES

Abela, J. R. Z., Wagner, C., & Brozina, K. (2004). *A comparison of the self-report checklist and the clinician-rated interview in measurement of stressful life events in children and adolescents.* Manuscript in preparation.

Achenbach, T. M., & Rescorla, L. A. (2001). *Manual for the ASEBA school-age forms and profiles.* Burlington: University of Vermont, Research Center for Children, Youth, and Families.

Adrian, C., & Hammen, C. (1993). Stress exposure and stress generation in children of depressed mothers. *Journal of Consulting & Clinical Psychology, 61,* 354–359.

Albano, A. M., Chorpita, B. F., & Barlow, D. H. (1996). Childhood anxiety disorders. In E. J. Mash & R. A. Barkley (Eds.), *Child psychopathology* (pp. 196–241). New York: Guilford Press.

Allison, S., Martin, G., Bergen, H. A., & Roeger, L. (2004). Depression in young adolescents: Investigations using 2 and 3 factor versions of the Parental Bonding Instrument. *Journal of Nervous & Mental Disease, 192,* 650–657.

Alspaugh, M. E., Stephens, M. A. P., Townsend, A. L., Zarit, S. H., & Greene, R. (1999). Longitudinal patterns of risk of depression in dementia caregivers: Objective and subjective primary stress as predictors. *Psychology & Aging, 14,* 24–43.

American Psychiatric Association. (1994). *Diagnostic and statistical manual of mental disorders* (4th ed.). Washington, DC: Author.

Aneshensel, C. S. (1999). Outcomes of the stress process. In A. V. Horwitz & T. L. Scheid (Eds.), *A handbook for the study of mental health: Social contexts, theories, and systems* (pp. 211–227). Cambridge, UK: Cambridge University Press.

Arsanow, J., & Arsanow, R. (1996). Childhood-onset schizophrenia. In E. J. Mash & R. A. Barkley (Eds.), *Child psychopathology* (pp. 340–361). New York: Guilford Press.

Baron, R., & Kenny, D. (1986). The moderator-mediator variable distinction in social psychological research: Conceptual, strategic, and statistical considerations. *Journal of Personality and Social Psychology, 51,* 1173–1182.

Bartone, P. T. (1999). Hardiness protects against war-related stress in Army Reserve forces. *Consulting Psychology Journal: Practices & Research, 51,* 72–82.

Bifulco, A. T., Brown, G. W., & Harris, T. O. (1987). Childhood loss of parent, lack of adequate parental care and adult depression: A replication. *Journal of Affective Disorders, 12,* 115–128.

Bronfenbrenner, U. (1977). Toward an experimental ecology of human development. *American Psychologist, 32,* 513–531.

Brown, G. W. (1989). Life events and measurement. In G. W. Brown & T. Harris (Eds.), *Life events and illness* (pp. 3–45). New York: Guilford Press.

Brown, G. W. (1990). What about real world? Hassles and Richard Lazarus. *Psychological Inquiry, 1,* 19–22.

Brown, G. W. (1993). The role of life events in the aetiology of depressive and anxiety disorders. In C. S. Stanford & P. Salmon (Eds.), *Stress: From synapse to syndrome* (pp. 23–50). San Diego, CA: Academic Press.

Brown, G. W. (1998). Loss and depressive disorders. In B. P. Dohrenwend (Ed.), *Adversity, stress, and psychopathology* (pp. 358–370). San Diego, CA: Academic Press.

Brown, G. W., & Harris, T. (Eds.). (1989). *Life events and illness.* New York: Guilford Press.

Brown, G. W., Harris, T. O., & Copeland, J. R. (1977). Depression and loss. *British Journal of Psychiatry, 130,* 1.

Burnett, P., & Fanshawe, P. (1997). Measuring school-related stressors in adolescents. *Journal of Youth & Adolescence, 26,* 415–428.

Chang, E., & Rand, K. L. (2000). Perfectionism as a predictor of subsequent adjustment: Evidence for a specific diathesis-stress mechanism among college students. *Journal of Counseling Psychology, 47,* 129–137.

Charney, D. S., Woods, S. W., Nagy, L. M., Southwich, S. M., Krystal, J. H., & Heniger, G. P. (1990). Noradrenergic function in panic disorder. *Journal of Clinical Psychology, 51,* 5–11.

Chassin, L., Collins, R. L., Ritter, J., & Shirley, M. C. (2001). Vulnerability to substance use disorders across the lifespan. In E. R. Ingram & J. M. Price (Eds.), *Vulnerability to psychopathology* (pp. 165–172). New York: Guilford Press.

Cheng, C. (1997). Assessment of major life events for Hong Kong adolescents: The Chinese Adolescent Life Event Scale. *American Journal of Community Psychology, 25,* 17–33.

Chorpita, B. F. (2003). The frontier of evidence-based practice. In A. E. Kazdin (Ed.), *Evidence-based psychotherapies for children and adolescents* (pp. 42–59). New York: Guilford Press.

Cicchetti, D., & Cohen, D. J. (1995). Perspectives of developmental psychopathology. In D. Cicchetti & D. J. Cohen (Eds.), *Developmental psychopathology: Vol. 1. Theory and methods* (pp. 3–20). Oxford, UK: John Wiley & Sons.

Cicchetti, D., & Toth, S. L. (1997). Transactional ecological systems in developmental psychopathology. In S. S. Luthar & J. A. Burack (Eds.), *Developmental psychopathology: Perspectives on adjustment, risk, and disorder* (pp. 317–349). Cambridge, UK: Cambridge University Press.

Coddington, R. D. (1972). The significance of life events as etiologic factors in the diseases of children: II. A study of a normal population. *Journal of Psychosomatic Research, 16,* 205–213.

Cohen, L. H., & Park, C. (1992). Religious beliefs and practices and the coping process. In B. N. Carpenter (Ed.), *Personal coping: Theory, research, and application* (pp. 185–198). Westport, CT: Praeger/Greenwood.

Cohen, S., Kessler, R. C., & Gordon, L. U. (1995). *Measuring stress: A guide for health and social scientists.* London: Oxford Press.

Cole, D. A., & Turner, J. D. (1993). Models of cognitive mediation and moderation in child depression. *Journal of Abnormal Psychology, 102,* 271–281.

Compas, D. E., Davis, G. E., Forsythe, C. J., & Wagner, B. M. (1987). Assessment of major and daily stressful events during adolescence: The Adolescent Perceived Events Scale. *Journal of Consulting and Clinical Psychology, 55,* 534–541.

Compas, B. E., Howell, D. C., Phares, V., Williams, R. A., & Ledoux, N. (1989). Parent and child stress and symptoms: An integrative analysis. *Developmental Psychology, 25,* 550–559.

Corning, A. F. (2002). Self-esteem as a moderator between perceived discrimination and psychological distress among women. *Journal of Counseling Psychology, 49,* 117–126.

Davila, J., Hammen, C., Burge, D., Paley, B., & Daley, S. E. (1995). Poor interpersonal problem solving as a mechanism of stress generation in depression among adolescent women. *Journal of Abnormal Psychology, 104,* 592–600.

DeBellis, M. D. (2001). Developmental traumatology: The psychobiological development of maltreated children and its implications for research, treatment, and policy. *Development and Psychopathology, 13,* 539–564.

Dohrenwend, B. P. (1998). *Adversity, stress, and psychopathology.* London: Oxford University Press.

Dohrenwend, B. P., Link, B. G., Kern, R., Shrout, P. E., & Markowitz, J. (1990). Measuring life events: The problem of variability within event categories. *Stress Medicine, 6,* 179–187.

Dohrenwend, B. P., Raphael, K. G., Schwartz, S., Stueve, A., & Skodol, A. (1993). The structured event probe and narrative rating method for measuring stressful life events. In L. Goldberger & S. Breznitz (Eds.), *Handbook of stress: Theoretical and clinical aspects* (pp. 174–199). New York: Free Press.

Dohrenwend, B. P., & Shrout, P. E. (1985). "Hassles" in the conceptualization and measurement of life stress variables. *American Psychologist, 40,* 780–785.

Dohrenwend, B. P., & Shrout, P. E. (1986). A discriminant rule for screening cases of diverse diagnostic types: Preliminary results. *Journal of Consulting and Clinical Psychology, 54,* 314–319.

Dohrenwend, B. S., Dohrenwend, B. P., Dodson, M., & Shrout, P. E. (1984). Symptoms, hassles, social supports, and life events: Problems of confounding measures. *Journal of Abnormal Psychology, 93,* 222–230.

Dohrenwend, B. S., Krasnoff, L., Askenasy, A. R., & Dohrenwend, B. P. (1978). Exemplification of a method for scaling life events: The PERI Life Events Scale. *Journal of Health & Social Behavior, 19,* 205–229.

Dormann, C., & Zapf, D. (1999). Social support, social stressors at work, and depressive symptoms: Testing for main and moderating effects with structural equations in a three-way longitudinal study. *Journal of Applied Psychology, 84,* 874–884.

DuBois, D. L., Felner, R. D., Brand, S., Adan, A., & Evans, E. (1992). A prospective study of life stress, social support, and adaptation in early adolescence. *Child Development, 63,* 542–557.

DuBois, D. L., Felner, R. D., Sherman, M. D., & Bull, C. A. (1994). Socioenvironmental experiences, self-esteem, and emotional/behavioral problems in early adolescence. *American Journal of Community Psychology, 22,* 371–397.

Duggal, S., Malkoff-Schwartz, S., Birmaher, B., Anderson, B. P., Matty, M. K., Houck, P. R., et al. (2000). Assessment of life stress in adolescents: Self-report versus interview methods. *Journal of the American Academy of Child & Adolescent Psychiatry, 39,* 445–452.

Eley, T. C., & Stevenson, J. (2000). Specific life events and chronic experiences differentially associated with depression and anxiety in young twins. *Journal of Abnormal Psychology, 28,* 383–394.

Field, T. M. (1995). Psychologically depressed parents. In M. H. Bornstein (Ed.), *Handbook of parenting: Vol. 4. Applied and practical parenting* (pp. 85–99). Hillsdale, NJ: Lawrence Erlbaum.

Finlay-Jones, R., & Brown, G. W. (1981). Types of stressful life events and the onset of anxiety and depressive disorders. *Psychological Medicine, 11,* 803–815.

Fischer, A. R., & Shaw, C. M. (1999). African Americans' mental health and perceptions of racist discrimination: The moderating effects of racial socialization experiences and self-esteem. *Journal of Counseling Psychology, 46,* 395–407.

Fletcher, K. E. (2003). Childhood posttraumatic stress disorder. In E. J. Mash & R. A. Barkley (Eds.), *Child psychopathology* (2nd ed., pp. 330–371). New York: Guilford Press.

Frese, M. (1999). Social support as a moderator of the relationship between work stressors and psychological dysfunctioning: A longitudinal study with objective measures. *Journal of Occupational Health and Psychology, 4,* 179–192.

Garber, J., Keiley, M. K., & Martin, N. C. (2002). Developmental trajectories of adolescents' depressive symptoms: Predictors of change. *Journal of Consulting and Clinical Psychology, 70,* 79–95.

Garber, J., & Robinson, N. S. (1997). Cognitive vulnerability in children at risk for depression. *Cognition & Emotion, 11,* 619–635.

Gibb, B. E. (2002). Childhood malnutrition and negative cognitive styles: A quantitative and qualitative review. *Clinical Psychology Review, 22,* 223–246.

Gil, A. G., Vega, W. A., & Dimas, J. M. (1994) Acculturative stress and personal adjustment among Hispanic adolescent boys. *Journal of Community Psychology, 22,* 43–54.

Goodyer, I. M., & Altham, P. M. (1991). Lifetime exit events and recent social and family adversities in anxious and depressed school-age children and adolescents: II. *Journal of Affective Disorders, 21,* 229–238.

Gorman, D. M. (1993). A review of studies comparing checklist and interview methods of data collection in life event research. *Behavioral Medicine, 19,* 66–73.

Grant, K. E., Compas, B. E., Stuhlmacher, A. F., Thurm, A. E., McMahon, S. D., & Halpert, J. A. (2003). Stressors and child and adolescent psychopathology: Moving from markers to mechanisms of risk. *Psychological Bulletin, 129,* 447–466.

Grant, K. E., Compas, B. E., Thurm, A. E., McMahon, S. D., & Gipson, P. Y. (2004). Stressors and child and adolescent psychopathology: Measurement issues and prospective effects. *Journal of Clinical Child & Adolescent Psychology, 334,* 412–425.

Greiner, B. A., Ragland, D. R., Krause, N., Syme, S. L., & Fisher, J. M. (1997). Objective measurement of occupational stress factors: An example with San Francisco urban transit operators. *Journal of Occupational Health and Psychology, 2,* 325–342.

Haggerty, R. J., Roghmann K. J., & Pless, I. B. (1993). *Child health and the community.* New Brunswick, NJ: Transaction.

Halligan, S. L., Michael, T., Clark, D. M., & Ehlers, A. (2003). Posttraumatic stress disorder following assault: The role of cognitive processing, trauma, memory, and appraisals. *Journal of Consulting & Clinical Psychology, 71,* 419–431.

Hammen, C. (1995). The social context of risk for depression. In K. D. Craig & K. S. Dobson (Eds.), *Anxiety and depression in adults and children* (pp. 82–96). Thousand Oaks, CA: Sage.

Hammen, C. (1997). Children of depressed parents: The stress context. In S. H. Wolchik & I. N. Sandler (Eds.), *Handbook of children's coping: Linking theory and intervention. Issues in clinical child psychology* (pp. 131–157). New York: Plenum Press.

Hammen, C., Burge, D., & Adrian, C. (1991). Timing of mother and child depression in a longitudinal study of children at risk. *Journal of Consulting and Clinical Psychology, 59,* 341–345.

Hammen, C., & Rudolph, K. D. (1996). Childhood depression. In E. J. Mash & R. A. Barkley (Eds.), *Child psychopathology* (pp. 143–195). New York: Guilford Press.

Hammen, C., & Rudolph, K. D. (2003). Childhood mood disorders. In E. J. Mash & R. A. Barkley (Eds.), *Child psychopathology* (2nd ed., pp. 233–278). New York: Guilford Press.

Hankin, B. L. (in press). Childhood maltreatment and psychopathology: Prospective tests of attachment, cognitive vulnerability, and stress as mediating processes. *Cognitive Therapy and Research.*

Hankin, B. L., & Abramson, L. Y. (2001). Development of gender differences in depression: An elaborated cognitive vulnerability-transactional stress theory. *Psychological Bulletin, 127,* 773–796.

Hankin, B. L., Abramson, L. Y., Miller, N., & Haeffel, G. J. (2004). Cognitive vulnerability-stress theories of depression: Examining affective specificity in the prediction of depression versus anxiety in 3 prospective studies. *Cognitive Therapy and Research, 28,* 309–345.

Hankin, B. L., Roesch, L., Mermelstein, R., & Flay, B. (2004, July). *Depression, stressors, and gender differences in adolescence: Examination of a transactional stress generation hypothesis in a multi-wave study.* Paper presented at the World Congress of Behavioural and Cognitive Therapies, Kobe, Japan.

Harper, G. W., Lardon, C., Rappaport, J., Bangi, A. K., Contreras, R., & Pedraza, A. (2004). Community narratives: The use of narrative ethnography in participatory community research. In L. A. Jason & C. B. Keys (Eds.), *Participatory community research: Theories and methods in action* (pp. 199–217). Washington, DC: American Psychological Association.

Harris, T., Brown, G. W., & Bifulco, A. T. (1990). Loss of parent in childhood and adult psychiatric disorder: A tentative overall model. *Development and Psychopathology, 2,* 311–328.

Hastings, T. L., & Kelley, M. L. (1997). Development and validation of Screen for Adolescent Violence Exposure (SAVE). *Journal of Abnormal Child Psychology, 25,* 511–520.

Holmbeck, G. N. (1997). Toward terminological, conceptual, and statistical clarity in the study of mediators and moderators: Examples from the child-clinical and pediatric psychology literatures. *Journal of Consulting & Clinical Psychology, 65,* 599–610.

Holmes, T., & Rahe, T. (1967). The social readjustment rating scale. *Journal of Psychosomatic Research, 11,* 213–218.

Ingram, E. R., & Price, J. M. (2001). *Vulnerability to psychopathology*. New York: Guilford Press.

Johnson, J. H., & McCutcheon, S. M. (1980). Assessing life stress in older children and adolescents: Preliminary findings with the Life Events Checklist. In I. G. Sarason & C. D. Spielberger (Eds.), *Stress and anxiety* (Vol. 7, pp. 111–125). Washington, DC: Hemisphere.

Katschnig, H. (1986). Measuring life-stress: A comparison of the checklist and the panel technique. In H. Katschnig (Ed.), *Life events and psychiatric disorders: Controversial issues* (pp. 74–106). Cambridge, UK: Cambridge University Press.

Kendler, K. S., Hettema, J. M., Butera, F., Gardner, C. O., & Prescott, C. A. (2003). Life event dimensions of loss, humiliation, entrapment, and danger in the prediction of onsets of major depression and generalized anxiety. *Archives of General Psychiatry, 60,* 789–796.

Kendler, K. S., Karkowski, L. M., & Prescott, C. A. (1998). Stressful life events and major depression: Risk period, long-term contextual threat, and diagnostic specificity. *Journal of Nervous and Mental Disease, 186,* 661–669.

Koss, M. P., Figueredo, A. J., & Prince, R. J. (2002). Cognitive mediation of rape's mental, physical and social health impact: Tests of four models in cross-sectional data. *Journal of Consulting & Clinical Psychology, 70,* 926–941.

Lakdawalla, Z., & Hankin, B. (2004). *Personality and psychopathology: Prospective tests of cognitive vulnerability and stress as mediating processes.* Manuscript submitted for publication.

Lay, C., & Nguyen, T. (1998). The role of acculturation-related and acculturation non-specific daily hassles: Vietnamese-Canadian students and psychological stress. *Canadian Journal of Behavioral Sciences, 30,* 172–181.

Lazarus, R. S., & Folkman, S. (1984). *Stress, appraisal and coping.* New York: Springer.

Lee, K. R., & Lee, Y. H. (1999). The effects of affectivity and types of stress on common and specific symptoms of depression and anxiety. *Korean Journal of Clinical Psychology, 17,* 69–86.

Lester, N., Nebel, L. E., & Baum, A. (1994). Psychophysiological and behavioral measurement of stress: Applications to mental health. In W. R. Avison & I. H. Gotlib (Eds.), *Stress and mental health: Contemporary issues and prospects for the future* (pp. 291–314). New York: Plenum Press.

Lewinsohn, P. M., Roberts, R. E., Hops, H., & Andrews, J. A. (1991). The Oregon adolescent depression project: Overview and preliminary results. In S. Suzuki & R. E. Roberts (Eds.), *Methods and applications in mental health surveys: The Todai Health Index* (pp. 249–278). Tokyo: University of Tokyo Press.

Lewinsohn, P. M., Rohde, P., & Gau, J. M. (2003). Comparability of self-report checklist and interview data in the assessment of stressful life events in young adults. *Psychological Reports, 93,* 459–471.

Link, B. G., Mesagno, F. P., Lubner, M. E., & Dohrenwend, B. P. (1990). Problems in measuring role strains and social functioning in relation to psychological symptoms. *Journal of Health & Social Behavior, 31,* 354–369.

Lloyd, C. (1980). Life events and depressive disorders reviewed: I. Events as predisposing factors. *Archives of General Psychiatry, 37,* 529–539.

Loo, C. M., Fairbank, J. A., Scurfield, R. M., Ruch, L. O., King, D. W., Adams, L. J., et al. (2001). Measuring exposure to racism: Development and validation of a Race-Related Stressor Scale (RRSS) for Asian American Vietnam veterans. *Psychological Assessment, 13,* 503–520.

Magnus, K., Diener, E., Fujita, F., & Payot, W. (1993). Extraversion and neuroticism as predictors of objective life events: A longitudinal analysis. *Journal of Personality & Social Psychology, 109,* 1046–1053.

Mash, E. J., & Barkley, R. A. (2003). *Child psychopathology* (2nd ed.). New York: Guilford Press.

Matussek, P., & Neuner, R. (1981). Loss events preceding endogenous and neurotic depressions. *Acta Psychiatrica Scandinavica, 64,* 340–350.

McCubbin, H. I., & Patterson, J. M. (1983). The family stress process: The double ABCX model of adjustment and adaptation. *Marriage & Family Review, 6,* 7–37.

McEwen, B. S. (1998). Protective and damaging effects of stress mediators. *New England Journal of Medicine, 338,* 171–179.

McMahon, S. D., Grant, K. E., Compas, B. E., Thurm, A. E., & Ey, S. (2003). Stress and psychopathology in children and adolescents: Is there evidence of specificity? *Journal of Child Psychology & Psychiatry & Allied Disciplines, 44,* 107–133.

McNally, R. J., Malcarne, V. L., & Hansdottir, I. (2001). Vulnerability to anxiety disorders across the lifespan. In E. R. Ingram & J. M. Price (Eds.), *Vulnerability to psychopathology* (pp. 322–325). New York: Guilford Press.

McQuaid, J. R., Monroe, S. M., Roberts, J. E., Johnson, S. L., & Brussel, J. A. (1992). Towards the standardization of life stress assessment: Definitional discrepancies and inconsistencies in methods. *Stress Medicine, 8,* 47–56.

McQuaid, J. R., Monroe, S. M., Roberts, J. E., Kupfer, D. J., & Frank, E. (2000). A comparison of two life stress assessment approaches: Prospective prediction of treatment outcome in recurrent depression. *Journal of Abnormal Psychology, 109,* 787–791.

Miller, D. B., Webster, S. E., & MacIntosh, R. (2002). What's there and what's not: Measuring daily hassles in urban African American adolescents. *Research on Social Work Practice, 12,* 375–388.

Mirowsky, J., & Ross, C. E. (1999). Well-being across the life course. In A. V. Horwitz & T. L. Scheid (Eds.), *A handbook for the study of mental health: Social contexts, theories, and systems* (pp. 328–347). Cambridge, UK: Cambridge University Press.

Monck, E., & Dobbs, R. (1985). Measuring life events in an adolescent population: Methodological issues and related findings. *Psychological Medicine, 15,* 841–850.

Monroe, S. M. (1982). Life events and disorders: Event-symptom association and the course of disorders. *Journal of Abnormal Psychology, 91,* 14–24.

Monroe, S. M. (1983). Major and minor life events as predictors of psychological distress: Further issues and findings. *Journal of Behavioral Medicine, 6,* 189–205.

Monroe, S. M., & Hadjiyannakis, K. (2002). The social environment of depression: Focusing on severe life stress. In I. H. Gotlib & C. L. Hammen (Eds.), *Handbook of depression* (pp. 314–340). New York: Guilford Press.

Monroe, S. M., Kupfer, D. J., & Frank, E. F. (1992). Life stress and treatment course of recurrent depression: Response during index episode. *Journal of Consulting & Clinical Psychology, 60,* 718–724.

Monroe, S. M., & McQuaid, J. R. (1994). Measuring life stress and assessing its impact on mental health. In W. R. Avison & I. H. Gotlib (Eds.), *Stress and mental health: Contemporary issues and prospects for the future. The Plenum series on stress and coping* (pp. 43–73). New York: Plenum.

Monroe, S. M., & Roberts, J. E. (1990). Conceptualizing and measuring life stress: Problems, principles, procedures, progress. *Stress Medicine, 6,* 209–216.

Monroe, S. M., Rohde, P., Seeley, J. R., & Lewinsohn, P. M. (1999). Life events and depression in adolescence: Relationship loss as a prospective risk factor for first onset of major depressive disorder. *Journal of Abnormal Psychology, 108,* 606–614.

Monroe, S. M., & Simons, A. D. (1991). Diathesis stress theories in the context of life stress research: Implications for the depressive disorders. *Psychological Bulletin, 110,* 406–425.

Moradi, B., & Subich, L. M. (2004). Examining the moderating role of self-esteem in the link between experiences of perceived sexist events and psychological distress. *Journal of Counseling Psychology, 51, 50–56.*

Nolen-Hoeksema, S., Girgus, J. S., & Seligman, M. E. P. (1992). Predictors and consequences of childhood depressive symptoms: A 5-year longitudinal study. *Journal of Abnormal Psychology, 101,* 405–422.

Nyborg, V. M., & Curry, J. F. (2003). The impact of perceived racism: Psychological symptoms among African American adolescents. *Journal of Clinical Child & Adolescent Psychology, 32,* 258–266.

Oei, T. I., & Zwart, F. M. (1986). The assessment of life events: Self-administered questionnaire versus interview. *Journal of Affective Disorders, 10,* 185–190.

Patton, M. Q. (1990). *Qualitative evaluation and research methods.* Thousand Oaks, CA: Sage.

Pearlin, L. I. (1999). Stress and mental health: A conceptual overview. In A. V. Horwitz & T. L. Scheid (Eds.), *A handbook for the study of mental health: Social contexts, theories, and systems* (pp. 161–175). Cambridge, UK: Cambridge University Press.

Perry, B. D., Pollard, R. A., Blakley, T. L., Baker, W. L., & Vigilante, D. (1995). Childhood trauma, the neurobiology of adaptation, and "use-dependent" development of the brain: How "states" become "traits." *Infant Mental Heath Journal, 16,* 271–289.

Quiggle, N. L., Garber, J., Panak, W. F., & Dodge, K. A. (1992). Social information processing in aggressive and depressed children. *Child Development, 63,* 1305–1320.

Raphael, K. G., Cloitre, M., & Dohrenwend, B. P. (1991). Problems of recall and misclassification with checklist methods of measuring stressful life events. *Health Psychology, 10,* 62–74.

Reiss, D., & Oliveri, M. E. (1991). The family's conception of accountability and competence: A new approach to the conceptualization and assessment of family stress. *Family Process, 30,* 193–214.

Richters, J. E., & Martinez, P. (1993). Children as victims of and witnesses to violence in a Washington, D.C. neighborhood. In L. A. Leavitt & N. A. Fox (Eds.), *The psychological effects of war and violence on children* (pp. 243–278). Hillsdale, NJ: Lawrence Erlbaum.

Ritsher, J. E., Warner, V., Johnson, J. G., & Dohrenwend, B. P. (2001). Intergenerational longitudinal study of social class and depression: A test of social causation and social selection models. *British Journal of Psychiatry, 178,* s84–s90.

Ritter, C., Hobfol, S. E., Lavin, J., Cameron, R. P., & Hulsizer, M. R. (2000). Stress, psychosocial resources, and depressive symptomatology during pregnancy in low-income, inner-city women. *Health Psychology, 19, 576–585.*

Robinson, N. S., Garber, J., & Hilsman, R. (1995). Cognitions and stress: Direct and moderating effects on depressive versus externalizing symptoms during the junior high school transition. *Journal of Abnormal Psychology, 104,* 453–463.

Roosa, M. W., Beals, J., Sandler, I. N., & Pillow, D. R. (1990). The role of risk and protective factors in predicting symptomatology in adolescent self-identified children of alcoholic parents. *American Journal of Community Psychology, 18,* 725–741.

Roosa, M. W., Sandler, I. N., Gehring, M., & Beals, J. (1988). The children of alcoholics life-events schedule: A stress scale for children of alcohol-abusing parents. *Journal of Studies on Alcohol, 49,* 422–429.

Rubin, K. H., Burgess, K. B., Kennedy, A. E., & Stewart, S. L. (2003). Social withdrawal in childhood. In E. J. Mash & R. A. Barkley (Eds.), *Child psychopathology* (2nd ed., pp. 372–406). New York: Guilford Press.

Rudolph, K. D., & Hammen, C. (1999). Age and gender as determinants of stress exposure, generation and reactions in youngsters: A transactional perspective. *Child Development, 70,* 660–677.

Rudolph, K. D., Hammen, C., & Burge, D. (1997). A cognitive-interpersonal approach to depressive symptoms in preadolescent children. *Journal of Abnormal Child Psychology, 25,* 33–45.

Rudolph, K. D., Hammen, C., Burge, D., Lindberg, N., Herzberg, D., & Daley, S. E. (2000). Toward an interpersonal life-stress model of depression: The developmental context of stress generation. *Development & Psychopathology, 12,* 215–234.

Rutter, M. (1989). Psychosocial risk trajectories and beneficial turning points. In S. Doxiadis & S. Stewart (Eds.), *Early influences shaping the individual* (pp. 229–239). New York: Plenum.

Sameroff, A. J., Lewis, M., & Miller, S. M. (2000). *Handbook of developmental psychopathology.* Dordrecht, The Netherlands: Kluwer Academic Publishers.

Sandhu, D. S., & Asrabadi, B. R. (1994). Development of an acculturative stress scale for international students: Preliminary findings. *Psychological Reports, 75,* 435–448.

Sandler, I. N., Reynolds, K. D., Kliewer, W., & Ramirez, R. (1992). Specificity of the relation between life events and psychological symptomatology. *Journal of Clinical Child Psychology, 21,* 240–248.

Sandler, I. N., Tein, J., & West, S. G. (1994). Coping, stress, and psychological symptoms of children of divorce: A cross-sectional and longitudinal study. *Child Development, 65,* 1744–1763.

Schat, A. C. H., & Kelloway, E. K. (2003). Reducing the adverse consequences of workplace aggression and violence: The buffering effects of organizational support. *Journal of Occupational Health Psychology, 8,* 110–122.

Sharkansky, E. J., King, D. W., King, L. A., Wolfe, J., Erickson, D. J., & Stokes, L. R. (2000). Coping with gulf war combat stress: Mediating and moderating effects. *Journal of Abnormal Psychology, 109,* 188–197.

Sher, K. J. (1991). *Children of alcoholics: A critical appraisal of theory and research.* Chicago: University of Chicago Press.

Shirk, S. R. (2004). Dissemination of youth ESTs: Ready for prime time? *Clinical Psychology: Science and Practice, 11,* 308–312.

Shrout, P. E., Link, B. G., Dohrenwend, B. P., Skodol, A. E., Stueve, A., & Mirotznik, G. (1989). Characterizing life events as risk factors for depression: The role of fateful loss events. *Journal of Abnormal Psychology, 98,* 460–467.

Simons, A. D., Angell, K. L., Monroe, S. M., & Thase, M. E. (1993). Cognition and life stress in depression: Cognitive factors and the definition, rating, and generation of negative life events. *Journal of Abnormal Psychology, 102,* 584–591.

Singleton, R. A., & Straits, B. C. (1999). *Approaches to social research.* London: Oxford University Press.

Skodol, A. E., Dohrenwend, B. P., Link, B. G., & Shrout, P. E. (1990). The nature of stress: Problems of measurement. In J. D. Noshpitz & R. D. Coddington (Eds.), *Stressors and the adjustment disorders* (pp. 3–20). Oxford, UK: John Wiley & Sons.

Smith, T. B., McCullough, M. E., & Poll, J. (2003). Religiousness and depression: Evidence for a main effect and the moderating influence of stressful life events. *Psychological Bulletin, 129,* 614–636.

Sobolewski, A., Strelau, J., & Zawadzki, B. (2001). The temperamental determinants of stressors as life changes. *European Psychologist, 6,* 287–295.

Spaccarelli, S., Coatsworth, J., & Bowden, B. (1995). Exposure to serious family violence among incarcerated boys: Its association with violent offending and potential mediating variables. *Violence & Victims, 10,* 163–182.

Stone, W. L., & Lemanek, K. L. (1990). Developmental issues in children's self-reports. In A. LaGreca (Ed.), *Through the eyes of the child: Obtaining self-reports from children and adolescents* (pp. 18–56). Needham Heights, MA: Allyn & Bacon.

Tein, J. Y., Sandler, I. N., & Zautra, A. J. (2000). Stressful life events, psychological distress, coping, and parenting of divorced mothers: A longitudinal study. *Journal of Family Psychology, 14,* 27–41.

Turner, J. E., & Cole, D. A. (1994). Developmental differences in cognitive diatheses for child depression. *Journal of Abnormal Child Psychology, 22,* 15–32.

Turner, R. J., & Roszell, P. (1994). Psychosocial resources and the stress process. In W. R. Avison & I. H. Gotlib (Eds.), *Stress and mental health: Contemporary issues and prospects for the future* (pp. 179–210). New York: Plenum.

Utsey, S. O. (1999). Development and validation of a short form of the Index of Race-Related Stress (IRRS)—Brief version. *Measurement & Evaluation in Counseling & Development, 32,* 149–167.

Vagg, P. R., & Spielberger, C. D. (1998). Occupational stress: Measuring job pressure and organizational support in the workplace. *Journal of Occupational Health Psychology, 3,* 294–305.

Wethington, E., Brown, B. W., & Kessler, R. C. (1997). Interview measurement of stressful life events. In S. Cohen & R. C. Kessler (Eds.), *Measuring stress: A guide for health and social scientists* (pp. 59–79). London: Oxford University Press.

Wilcox, S., Evenson, K. R., Aragaki, A., Wassertheil-Smoller, S., Mouton, C. P., & Loevinger, B. L. (2003). The effects of widowhood on physical and mental health, health behaviors, and health outcomes: The woman's health initiative. *Health Psychology, 22,* 513–522.

Williams, S., & Cooper, C. L. (1998). Measuring occupational stress: Development of the Pressure Management Indicator. *Journal of Occupational Health Psychology, 3,* 306–321.

Williamson, D. A., Duchmann, E. G., Barker, S. E., & Bruno, R. M. (1998). Anorexia nervosa. In V. B. Van Hasselt & M. Hersen (Eds.), *Handbook of psychological treatment protocols for children and adolescents* (pp. 413–434). Mahwah, NJ: Lawrence Erlbaum.

Wrosch, C., Schulz, R., & Heckhausen, J. (2002). Health stresses and depressive symptomatology in the elderly: The importance of health engagement control strategies. *Health Psychology, 21,* 340–348.

Zimmerman, M., Pfohl, B., & Stangl, D. (1986). Life events assessment of depressed patients: A comparison of self-report and interview formats. *Journal of Human Stress, 11,* 13–19.

Zuckerman, M. (1999). *Vulnerability to psychopathology.* Washington, DC: American Psychological Association.

CHAPTER 2

Vulnerability-Stress Models

Rick E. Ingram and David D. Luxton

Early models of psychopathology typically identified processes operating during the course of the disorder as reflecting the key determinants of the onset of psychopathology (e.g., irrational beliefs; Ellis, 1962). Such models have led to important advances in understanding important features of psychopathology. For example, in the cognitive arena, schema models initially focused almost exclusively on understanding cognitive variables functioning in the disordered state. This conceptual approach, as well as the empirical research motivated by these models, has led to a number of significant insights into depression (Ingram, Miranda, & Segal, 1998), anxiety (e.g., McManus & Clark, 2002), personality disorders (Beck, 1999), and even problematic marital interactions (Beck, 1989). Schema models thus represent a clear example of the power of such constructs as they apply to the description of psychopathology.

Stress has also been recognized as an important contributor to the development and course of psychopathology, so much so that a variety of models have featured stress as a primary determinant of disordered functioning (Brown & Harris, 1978, 1989). Such models suggest that severe enough negative events could precipitate psychological disorders even without reference to individual psychological or biological characteristics. For example, the link between an adverse social environment and the onset of depression has long been recognized. The majority of research investigating possible links consistently finds a relationship between the experience of stressful life events and the onset of depression, with some data suggesting that approximately 50% of individuals diagnosed with depression have experienced severe stress before onset (Mazure, 1998). More recent perspectives suggest the possibility that life stress may engender a specific subtype of depression (Monroe & Hadjiyannakis, 2002).

Despite advancing understanding, the limitations of these approaches have become increasingly apparent. For instance, models that place primary emphasis on stress as a key cause of a disorder have difficulty dealing with data showing that even extreme stress is not linked to psychopathology in all individuals (Monroe & Hadjiyannakis, 2002); after all, approximately 50% of individuals do *not* show evidence of a disorder such as depression following significant life stress. Hence, although data convincingly show that stress plays a role in depression, they just as convincingly show that other factors also play a critical role.

The fact that not all individuals who experience significant stress develop a disorder has led, in part, to the recognition that vulnerability processes are important components of psychopathology; such factors predispose some individuals to psychopathology when stress is encountered. Notions about vulnerability have also begun to address questions about whether variables operating within the disordered state are antecedents of the state, or whether they can reasonably be considered to be consequences of the state (e.g., Barnett & Gotlib, 1988). By definition, vulnerability to a disorder must serve as an antecedent of the disorder. Although vulnerability ideas have been a central part of some of the earliest models of psychopathology (e.g., Beck, 1967), the emphasis on their essential nature in the onset of psychopathology has seen a remarkable resurgence (Segal & Ingram, 1994).

Although vulnerability and stress can be reasonably considered to be conceptually distinct constructs, separately, their power to describe key aspects of psychopathology is limited. Thus, most modern models of psychopathology explicitly combine vulnerability and stress in their descriptions of the functional processes leading to disorder. This chapter focuses on the interaction of vulnerability and stress as essential for understand ing the development of psychopathology. To serve as a background for exploring their interactive role, we briefly provide definitions of *vulnerability* and *stress* and then briefly discuss the origins of these constructs. We then examine general principles that characterize most diathesis-stress models and, finally, explore different models of vulnerability-stress interactions. Finally, we comment on some issues that are pertinent to conceptualizations of stress and conceptualizations of diatheses in the context of the diathesis-stress relationship.

DEFINITIONS

Numerous discussions of vulnerability (e.g., Ingram et al., 1998) and stress (e.g., Grant & McMahon, Chapter 1 of this volume) can be found in the literature. Detailed examination of these ideas can be found in these sources. For purposes of context, in this chapter we briefly note ideas about the individual constructs that form diathesis-stress models. We start with stress.

Stress

Definitions of stress encompass a number of facets. In general, however, stress falls into a limited number of broad categories. One major category of stress is conceptualized as the occurrence of significant life events that are interpreted by the person as undesirable (Lazarus & Folkman, 1984; Luthar & Zigler, 1991; Monroe & Peterman, 1988; Monroe & Simons, 1991). The accumulation of minor events or hassles represents another kind of stress (Dohrenwend & Shrout, 1985; Lazarus, 1990). Socioeconomic factors have also been implicated in stress, in that variables such as low maternal educational status or membership in an ethnic minority group may reflect stressful living circumstances (Luthar & Zigler).

Although it is clear from these descriptions that the definitions of *stress* are many, we can view *stress* in the context of this chapter as the life events (major or minor) that disrupt those mechanisms that maintain the stability of individuals' physiology, emotion, and cognition. Indeed, Selye's (1963) classic description of stress notes that such events represent a strain on the person's adaptive capability that cause an interruption of the person's routine or habitual functioning. Stress thus reflects those factors that interfere with the system's physiological and psychological homeostasis.

Even though stress is frequently conceptualized as the occurrence of "externally" ordained processes, two sets of factors suggest an important role for "internal" forces in the occurrence of stress. First, although some stressful events may simply befall people, several researchers have persuasively argued, and empirically demonstrated, that other events are the results of individuals' own actions (Depue & Monroe, 1986; Hammen, 1991; Monroe & Simons, 1991; Rutter, 1986). For instance, a person with social skills deficits (e.g., inappropriately critical of others) may engender tumultuous relationships with acquaintances, coworkers, and romantic partners that result in the generation of significant stress. Vulnerable individuals, or those in a disordered state, may therefore play a role in creating their own stresses (Ingram et al., 1998). Later in this chapter, we expand on the implications of this idea as it pertains to diathesis-stress models.

A second factor is the influence of appraisal processes on what is perceived to be stressful (Monroe, 1989; Monroe & Simons, 1991). That is, stress is not independent of the individual's appraisals of events. Even though there are a number of events that are undoubtedly universally appraised as stressful (e.g., the death of a loved one), even in these cases individual differences may determine the degree of stress that is perceived and experienced. In other cases, events that are perceived as stressful by some individuals may be perceived and experienced as not stressful, or at the least as minimally stressful, by other individuals. Indeed, a multitude of other factors can affect the determination and degree of stress.

Diatheses

We employ the terms *diathesis* and *vulnerability* interchangeably. A diathesis, or vulnerability, is typically conceptualized as a predispositional factor, or set of factors, that makes possible a disordered state. The earliest psychopathology models featuring vulnerability suggested that these redispositional factors constituted genetic or biological factors. In more recent years, the term has been broadened to include psychological factors, such as cognitive and interpersonal variables, that make a person susceptible to psychopathology (Monroe & Simons, 1991).

Intuitive ideas about vulnerability imply an increased susceptibility to emotional pain and to the occurrence of psychopathology of some type. Yet, as intuitively straightforward as this concept has been, and despite extensive discussion in the literature about vulnerability, few precise definitions are available in the scientific literature. Ingram et al. (1998) noted several core features of vulnerability that appear to constitute the common themes that emerge in discussions of vulnerability and that can thus help establish a working definition of the construct. These ideas suggest that vulnerability is a trait, is stable but can change, is endogenous to individuals, and is usually latent.

Most discussions regard vulnerability as an enduring trait. For example, Zubin and Spring (1977) argued that "we regard [vulnerability] as a relatively permanent, enduring trait" (p. 109). They continue, "The one feature that all schizophrenics have . . . is the everpresence of their vulnerability" (p. 122). Such assumptions of permanence seem likely to be rooted in the genetic level of analysis employed by researchers who pioneered this concept, as can be seen among schizophrenia researchers who point to the genetic endowment of individuals who are at risk for this disorder. Meehl's (1962) idea of schizotaxia represents an inherited neural deficit, whereas other researchers, such as Zubin and Spring, Nicholson and Neufeld (1992), and McGue and Gottesman (1989), explicitly argue that genetic endowment determines one's level of vulnerability (at least to schizophrenia). Hence, little change is theoretically possible.

Although vulnerability may in many cases be permanent and enduring, this need not always be true. For example, when the level of vulnerability analysis is psychological rather than genetic in nature, change may be possible. Even though assumptions of genetic vulnerability offer little possibility for modification of vulnerability, most psychological approaches rely on assumptions of dysfunctional learning as the genesis of vulnerability. Given such assumptions, vulnerability levels may fluctuate as a function of new learning experiences.

The traitlike nature of vulnerability suggests that vulnerability tends to be, at the least, stable. It is important to note, however, that stability does not necessarily mean permanence. That is, even though the idea of stability suggests a resistance to change, it does not presume that change is never possible. Under some circumstances, positive changes in an otherwise stable variable may very well occur. Indeed, the notion of therapy is based on just this premise. It is also the case, however, that some experiences (e.g., trauma) might serve to strengthen vulnerability. It thus seems reasonable to conceptualize vulnerability as stable but not immutable.

Following from the traitlike characteristics of vulnerability, another core feature of the construct is that vulnerability is an endogenous process. In particular, whether stemming from genetically or biologically acquired characteristics or acquired through psychological or learning processes, vulnerability resides within the person. This serves to explicitly distinguish vulnerability from "external" stress or life events. Finally, because diatheses are often not easily recognized, they are frequently considered to be latent, requiring activation in some fashion before psychopathology can occur. Although not all researchers agree with this position (e.g., Just, Abramson, & Alloy, 2001), there is widespread consensus among many researchers concerning the latent nature of many vulnerability characteristics. This is particularly the case with "unseen" genetic or biological factors that may predispose to disorder, but it also includes more psychologically based vulnerability processes.

Risk and Diatheses/Vulnerability

Terms such as *risk* and *vulnerability* (or *diatheses*) are often used interchangeably, and in fact there is little doubt that these constructs overlap substantially. However, it is important to note that although we use the terms *diathesis* and *vulnerability* interchangeably, we do not view vulnerability and risk as interchangeable. As several investigators have argued (e.g., Ingram et al., 1998; Luthar & Zigler, 1991; Rutter, 1987), *risk* describes factors that are associated, or correlated, with an increased likelihood of experiencing a disorder. Nevertheless, the presence of risk suggests only an increased probability of the occurrence of a disorder; it does not specify what causes the disorder. Risk factors are thus not informative about the actual mechanisms that bring about a state of psychopathology. For example, female gender is a well-established risk factor for many disorders, but this knowledge alone is uninformative about *why* women are more likely to experience a range of disorders. Alternatively, *vulnerability* is usually defined in such a way that it reflects statements about causal mechanisms.[1] Risk is certainly an important predictive variable that can be seen as acting in concert with vulnerability (Rutter, 1988), but these constructs are not synonymous.

DIATHESIS-STRESS ORIGINS CONSIDERED

To understand fully diathesis-stress interactions, it is useful to briefly consider the historical context in which these ideas emerged. Monroe and Simons (1991) note that the diathesis concept has a long history in medical terminology. The concept dates back to the ancient Greeks; the word *diathesis* derives from the ancient Greek idea of disposition, which is related to the humoral (body fluids) theory of temperament and disease (Zuckerman, 1999). By the 1800s, the term had become part of the psychiatric language of the day (e.g., Beard, 1881). Likewise, although the role of stress had long been considered an important factor in the development of mental disorders, it was theories of schizophrenia proposed during the 1960s (e.g., Meehl, 1962) that highlighted stress and brought the diathesis and stress concepts together. More specifically, the particular terminology of the diathesis-stress interactions was developed by Bleuler (1963) and Rosenthal (1963).

Beyond these pioneering approaches, somewhat more contemporary and detailed conceptualizations of the nature of vulnerability and the role of stress have been proposed that specify under what circumstances a disorder will ensue. For example, Audy (1971) suggested that the preservation of health requires the maintenance of a dynamic equilibrium against insults coming from chemical, physical, infectious, psychological, and social environment factors. A disorder occurs when the equilibrium is disturbed by an inability to maintain homeostasis. Vulnerability factors influence the ease and frequency with which these factors will challenge homeostasis; such factors therefore determine the probability that the disorder will occur. Thus, the highly vulnerable person is one in whom numerous circumstances can elicit an episode.

GENERAL PRINCIPLES OF DIATHESIS-STRESS MODELS

According to Monroe and Simons (1991) and Monroe and Hadjiyannakis (2002), most diathesis-stress models of psychopathology suggest that all people have some level of predisposing factors (diatheses) for any given mental disorder. However, individuals have their own point at which they will develop a given disorder, a point that depends on the interaction between the degree to which these risk factors exist and the degree of stress experienced by the individual. Because diathesis-stress models address the interactions between premorbid risk factors and situational stressors, they are useful for describing who will develop a disorder and who will not. Many—perhaps most—psychopathologists have recognized the conceptual and empirical utility of combining diathesis and stress constructs, and accordingly, models of psychopathology tend to be explicit diathesis-stress models.

A variety of diathesis-stress models have been proposed for various types of psychopathology (see Ingram & Price, 2001). Depending upon the particular theory, these models suggest specific variables that combine in some fashion to produce the disorder. Beyond the description of particular variables in particular disorders, however, these ideas about psychopathology also illustrate different ways that the structure of a diathesis-stress interaction can be conceptualized. Examination of these models suggests several general principles that characterize hypothesized diathesis-stress interactions.

Additivity

On the surface, diathesis-stress models represent straightforward, linear, dose-response–type relationships, or additive relationships. Hence, at the most basic level, many models suggest that whether or not a disorder will develop depends on the combined effects of stress and the loading of the diathesis. One model, for example, may suggest that relatively minor stressors may precipitate the onset of the disorder for a person who is highly vulnerable, whereas another model might suggest that a major stressful event might cause a similar reaction in a person low in vulnerability. Although various models may accord a stronger role for one component over the other, this idea presupposes *additivity,* that is, the idea that diatheses and stress add together in some way to produce the disorder.

Ipsative Models

Monroe and Hadjiyannakis (2002) note that many diathesis-stress models reflect an ipsative approach to the relationship between the constructs. Ipsative models posit an inverse relationship between factors such that the greater the presence of one factor, the less of the other factor is needed to bring about the disorder. Ipsative models are not necessarily distinct from additive approaches and can thus be considered an additional quality of many diathesis-stress models of psychopathology. More specifically, these models suggest that the diathesis and stress sum together to cause psychopathology, and that whatever this sum is, it reflects an inverse relationship. Thus, the degree of effect of diathesis or stress can be offset or compensated by the other in the summation that is needed for psychopathology.

Mega Diathesis-Stress Models

Although ipsative (and additive) models are prevalent, Monroe and Hadjiyannakis (2002) also note that other possibilities exist. One such possibility is a model that suggests that disorder results from the combination of significant life stress *and* a heightened vulnerability. For the sake of simplicity, we refer to this as a *mega* diathesis-stress model to denote that both the diathesis and the stress must be considerable before a disorder occurs. Thus, cognitive models of depression that conceptually rely on diathesis-stress interactions would suggest that not only is the presence of a depressogenic schema needed, but substantial life stress must *also* occur before the process eventuates in depression. This differs from an ipsative model, which suggests that minimal stress is needed for depression to occur in individuals with a strongly depressogenic schema.

Static Versus Dynamic Diathesis-Stress Relationships

Comparison of ipsative and mega models reveals a neglected aspect of many diathesis-stress models of psychopathology, specifically the idea that the relationship between the diathesis and stress can change over time. This changing interaction can be illustrated by reference to the idea of kindling. In response to data showing that repeated episodes of depression within some individuals begin to appear with decreasing stress, Post (1992) proposed the idea of kindling. Kindling suggests that repeated instances of a disorder cause neuronal changes that result in more sensitivity to stress. With heightened sensitivity, less stress becomes necessary to activate the requisite processes that lead to psychopathology. Applying these ideas to diathesis-stress models suggests that the precise relationship between these constructs is not necessarily static. More specifically, this also suggests that as the relationship changes with recurrence or relapse, mega processes may become more ipsative. That is, whereas the mega model suggests that high levels of both stress and diatheses are needed, the kindling theory suggests that at some point diatheses are changed (and presumably strengthened) so that less stress becomes necessary to activate the vulnerability factors. Of course, other changes are also possible. Recall that we noted that in at least some models, diatheses are viewed as stable although not necessarily immutable. It is therefore possible that the relationship between diatheses and stress may change if the diathesis becomes weaker.

We believe that consideration of the static versus dynamic relationship between diatheses and stress has potentially important implications for the conceptualization of diathesis-stress ideas. In general, varying relations between diatheses and stress models over time may affect the accuracy of the model at any given moment, but they may also have considerable implications for models that seek to understand the function of these processes in remission, recovery, relapse, and recurrence. As we have noted, few contemporary models, at least explicitly, take into theoretical account potential changes over time of the relationship between diatheses and stress, but clearly the nature of the relationship over time is an important factor to consider.

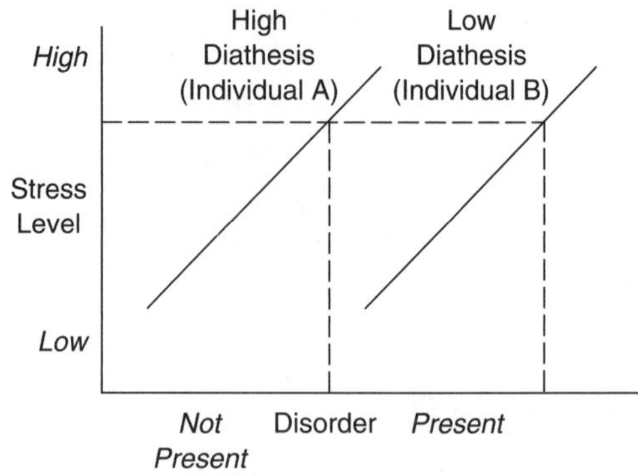

Figure 2.1 Additive Model of Diathesis-Stress Interaction With a Dichotomous Diathesis for Disorder

DIATHESIS-STRESS MODELS

With the caveat that dynamic relationships may be quite significant, our focus is on more "static" models of the diathesis-stress processes. At present, most diathesis-stress models are ipsative, although several permutations are possible. Hence, different investigators have described these models in somewhat varying terms. The models we describe here illustrate these different terms. In particular, we discuss the *interactive model with dichotomous diatheses,* the *quasi-continuous diathesis models, threshold models,* and *risk-resilience continuum models.* Before doing so, it is important to acknowledge that these models tend to vary in emphasis rather than in basic structure. Thus, there is considerable overlap in how these approaches view the relationship between diatheses and stress.

Interactive Model With Dichotomous Diatheses

As noted, vulnerability-stress models originated from schizophrenia theory and research, starting with Meehl's (1962) groundbreaking ideas. In his first model of schizophrenia, Meehl described the diathesis as a single dominant "schizogene," which produces a schizotaxic brain pathology (e.g., neural integrative defect) that eventuates in a schizotypic personality. According to Meehl, however, only some people with schizotypic personality will develop clinical schizophrenia. Most at-risk individuals will not, because the schizotypic personality, although necessary for the development of schizophrenia, is not sufficient in and of itself for the development of schizophrenia. Instead, an environmental stressor is required to produce schizophrenia. Meehl suggested that the stress produced by a schizophrenogenic-type mother who is "ambivalent and inconsistently aversive to the schizotypic" is the most important type of stress that may produce the disorder. Alternatively, if the schizogene is absent, no amount of stress or type of rearing will produce schizophrenia. In sum, Meehl's theory suggested that the onset of schizophrenia is a joint function of both biological and psychological factors.

Meehl's (1962) first model for schizophrenia, which arguably launched the idea of diatheses and stress, can thus be described as an interactive model with dichotomous diatheses (see Figure 2.1). *Dichotomous diathesis* suggests that one either has the diathesis or does not; if the diathesis is absent, there is no effect for stress. Hence, even severe stress will not lead to the development of the disorder. On the other hand, when the diathesis is present, the expression of disorder will be conditional on the degree of stress. That is, as stress increases, so does the risk for the disorder in those who possess the diathesis.

We note Meehl's (1962) original model for historical context, but it is also important to note that this model has been updated to the extent that it no longer resembles the earlier model. Hence, to better clarify the interaction between diathetic characteristics and environmental stressors, Meehl (1989, 1990) revised his original model to describe another pathway that could lead to schizophrenia, called the SHAITU genophenocopy (Meehl, 1989, 1990). SHAI stands for personality trait extremes—submissive, hypohedonic, anxious, and introverted—of polygenic origins, which may increase the potential for schizotaxia to develop into schizotypic personality and subsequently lead to clinical schizophrenia. TU stands for environmental risk factors; T stands for major or frequent minor traumas during development, whereas U stands for unlucky events in adult life, which also increase the risk for schizophrenia. In Meehl's original 1962 model, the dominant schizogene and the resulting schizotaxic brain pathology were necessary but not sufficient causes of schizophrenia. In contrast, the SHAITU genophenocopy not only plays a role in the schizotaxic type of schizophrenia, but it can produce a schizophrenic disorder even in the absence of the schizogene. As such, however, the revised diathesis-stress model is no longer an example of an interactive model with dichotomous diathesis conceptualization.

Although Meehl's (1962) original model of schizophrenia illustrates the idea of an interactive model with dichotomous diathesis, a more contemporary example can be seen in the posttraumatic stress disorder (PTSD) theory proposed by McKeever and Huff (2003). They suggest two types of diatheses: One type consists of ecological variables and revolves around factors such as child abuse and cognitive distortions. Another type is biological and includes variables such as neurophysiological dysregulation. Individuals with higher degrees of these premorbid vulnerability factors (diatheses) would not need to experience as severe a stressor to reach the threshold and develop PTSD symptomatology. In contrast, individuals without the diatheses might not display any signs or symptoms of PTSD even after experiencing a traumatic event. Even to the extent that signs or symptoms are experienced, however, they would not be indicative of a clinical disorder.

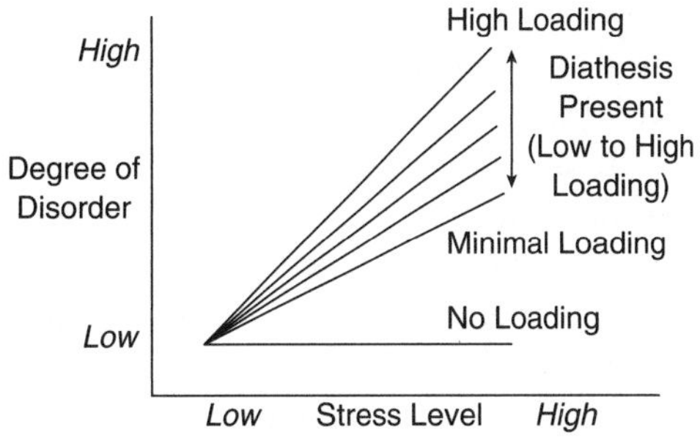

Figure 2.2 Interactive Model of Diathesis-Stress Interaction With Quasi-Continuous Diathesis

Quasi-Continuous Diathesis Models

Dichotomous models suggest that when the diathesis is absent, there is no effect for stress. That is, regardless of the amount of stress experienced by the individual, the disorder will not occur if the individual does not have the diathesis. However, many disorders suggest polygenic models that allow for varying degrees of diatheses (such as the level of a particular neurotransmitter) (Zuckerman, 1999). Thus, instead of being dichotomous, the diathesis is "quasi-continuous" (Monroe & Simons, 1991). As illustrated in Figure 2.2, in the quasi-continuous model there is a point beyond which a disorder will occur, but there is also a continuous effect of the diathesis once the threshold is passed. In other words, a very minimal level of diathesis may be insufficient to produce the disorder even under high stress, but the probability of disorder increases as a function of both level of stress and strength of the diathesis beyond a minimal level (Zuckerman).

Few models of psychopathology are explicitly framed in terms of a continuous or quasi-continuous vulnerability model, but it is easy to see how this diathesis-stress conceptualization could be applied to psychopathology models. Moreover, this idea could also help clarify or refine these models. For example, schema models of depression are typically conceptually stated as dichotomous models; if the individual possesses a depressogenic schema, then he or she is at risk for depression when events occur that activate this schema (see Beck, 1967, for the original description of the role of depressogenic schemata in depression). However, various discussions of the properties of schemata suggest how schemata could be conceptualized in more continuous terms (e.g., the relative density and strength of negative connections; see Segal, 1988). Some descriptions of these processes have been implicitly, but rarely explicitly, suggested (see Ingram et al., 1998). To the extent that schemata could explicitly be considered to represent a more continuous variable, such that some individuals may possess schemata that are "strongly" depressogenic, whereas others may possess only "weak" or mild depressive schemata, then a more continuous diathesis-stress model may not only be applicable to depression, but may also suggest refinement of key elements of the theory that were not previously considered.

Threshold Models

Some models suggest that the synergism between the diathesis and stress yields an effect beyond their combined separate effects (Monroe & Simons, 1991; Rothman, 1976). Moreover, complex diathesis-stress models that represent additive and interactional relationships between variables, as well as threshold effects for the diathesis, have also been proposed (Monroe & Simons). These ideas can be illustrated by what we would term a *threshold model.*

To illustrate a threshold model, consider the integrative model of schizophrenia proposed by Zubin and Spring (1977). Zubin and Spring suggest that *every* person has a degree of vulnerability that represents a threshold for the development of schizophrenia. At the most basic level, this model suggests that as the intensity of the trauma (stressor) increases, so too do the risks for psychopathology. The diathetic threshold is the point at which the people who fall below the threshold will not develop the disorder, whereas those above this level cross the threshold into disorder (see Bebbington, 1987; Monroe & Simons, 1991). Thus, the threshold for triggering schizophrenia may vary from one person to the next depending on the degree of vulnerability and the level of stress experienced. For a person who is highly vulnerable, relatively minor stressors may cause the threshold to be crossed. On the other hand, a major stressful event might cause a similar reaction even for a person low in vulnerability.

Risk-Resilience Continuum Models

Invulnerability, competence, protective factors, and *resilience* are terms often used to describe the opposite of vulnerability (Ingram & Price, 2001). Resilience can be thought of as factors that make a person resistant to the deleterious effects of stressors. Examples of resilience features could include particular personality traits, social skills, and coping responses. Resilience and vulnerability represent, therefore, opposite ends of a vulnerability continuum, although models typically do not specify if resilience simply reflects the lack of vulnerability

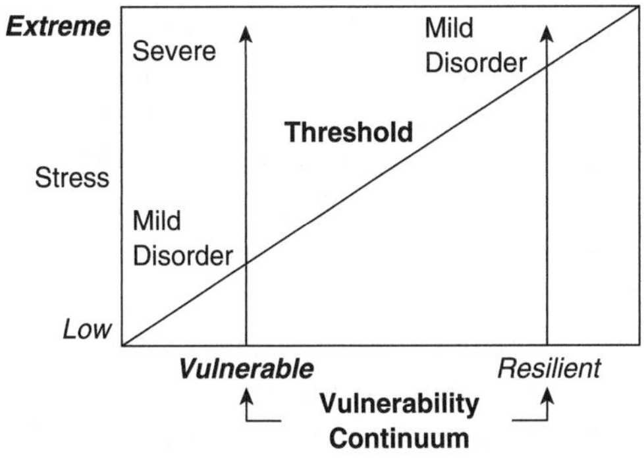

Figure 2.3 The Vulnerability-Resilience Model

factors or instead encompasses specific factors that confer resilience.

As in other models, the diathesis continuum interacts with a continuum of stress to produce the possibility that a disordered state will occur. At the most extreme vulnerability end of the spectrum, little life stress is necessary to trigger disorder. At the resilient end, however, a great deal of stress is needed before psychopathology develops. A vulnerability-resilience relationship is presented in Figure 2.3. As this figure illustrates, with decreasing resilience, and hence increasing vulnerability, the probability that stress will result in a disorder increases. Conversely, when resilience increases, the risk of disorder goes down but does not vanish entirely. That is, resilience may be the opposite of vulnerability, suggesting a resistance to disorder but not immunity from it entirely (Ingram et al., 1998). Of course, although not specified by most models, the idea of resilience can easily be incorporated into diathesis-stress interactions.

Like a threshold model, a risk-resilience model also notes a threshold at which a particular disorder will be encountered. However, this model can also take into account the severity of psychopathology that is experienced. Hence, even the most resilient people can be at risk for developing significant symptomatology with enough stress, although the symptomatology will likely be less severe than that experienced by individuals who experience stress and who are vulnerable. On the other hand, highly vulnerable people who encounter significant stress are proposed to experience a more severely disordered state. This model therefore takes into account not only the continuum of vulnerability, ranging from vulnerable to resilient, but also a continuum of disorder severity.

SOME ISSUES FOR CONSIDERATION IN DIATHESIS-STRESS MODELS

While maintaining the same basic structure, the models we have described reflect the different approaches that investigators have taken to understanding psychopathology. Beyond these basic models, there are, however, a number of issues that need to be considered as efforts continue to more fully understand how diatheses and stress interact to produce psychopathology. Although artificial in some respects, for discussion purposes we divide these into diathesis issues and stress issues.

Diathesis Issues in Diathesis-Stress Models: Single Versus Multiple Diatheses Factors

For models suggesting genetic diatheses, evidence of the polygenic aspect of psychopathological disorders suggests a combination of genes that may be required for disorder. Thus, individuals inheriting any particular gene defect will be normal if they do not possess the other gene defects needed to produce a disorder such as schizophrenia. Of course, genetic diatheses are not the only approach to understanding psychopathology. Hence, models featuring psychosocial factors may also need to highlight more than one diathetic factor. For example, an interpersonal and cognitive model of depression (Gotlib & Hammen, 1992) extended to vulnerability would need to specify the multiple diathesis factors that fall into their respective cognitive and interpersonal categories, and the link between them, to provide a more complete model. Likewise, models that highlight biological and psychological factors (e.g., Goodman & Gotlib, 1999) would also need to specify the link between various processes and how they would work in concert to produce the disorder when life stress is encountered.

Development and Stress Issues in Diathesis-Stress Models

The nature of the diathesis-stress interaction described in various models is often ambiguous (Monroe & Hadjiyannakis, 2002). As we have noted in our description of schema models of depression, diatheses are often portrayed as discontinuous and categorical (people either have a given diathesis or they do not). Alternatively, stress is frequently portrayed as nonspecific and continuous, varying only in degree but not in type. However, diatheses can often become continuous once a certain threshold has been reached. Moreover, because diatheses and stress are rarely completely independent of each other, the interactions between the diathesis and stress can be quite complex (Monroe & Simons, 1991).

Early formulations of the diathesis-stress model were based on biological factors (e.g., Meehl, 1962) that inferred temporal precedence and assumed that the diathesis was inactive in the developmental scheme of things. Thus, the interpretation of a significant interaction seemed relatively clear-cut: Stress activated the diathesis, which in turn brought about the onset of disorder. This interpretation suggests that until the diathesis is activated by stress, the diathesis is inconsequential. The complementary influence of the diathesis on stress was typically disregarded in these early models (Monroe & Simons, 1991).

The influence of diatheses on stress also received little attention in early formulations of this relationship, but there are several ways in which the constructs may not be as independent as they seem at first glance. For example, it may be that likelihood of incurring a stressor increases with the loading of the diathesis. To the extent that the diathesis influences the incidence of the requisite forms of stress, the more likely it is that highly predisposed people will develop a disorder. For a young person in the early stages of schizophrenia onset, for example, abnormal or socially withdrawn behavior that results from diathesis may create tension in the young person's interpersonal life at home and at school. The additional interpersonal stress, which is directly influenced by the diathesis, may exacerbate stress and subsequently increase the likelihood of the onset of full-blown schizophrenia.

This idea is similar to proposals regarding stress generation. As we have previously noted, stress is typically seen as operating externally to the individual, although it does appear that at least some people may also play a part in creating the stressful environment that acts to trigger pathology. That is, the diathesis may influence the manner in which a person deals with life and thus the nature of the stressors to which he or she is exposed. Indeed, a number of researchers have argued that many stressors may constitute the results of one's own actions (Depue & Monroe, 1986; Hammen, 1991, 1992; Monroe & Simons, 1991; Rutter, 1986). For example, people who have doubts about their self-worth may seek reassurance in an effort to counter these doubts (Luxton & Wenzlaff, in press), but repeated efforts may result in rejection from others, therefore precipitating a depressive disorder. Beyond the exacerbation of stress that may occur as the result of the emergent activation of diatheses, vulnerable individuals may thus play a role in creating their own stresses, which may then activate the diatheses and precipitate disorder.

Some models have proposed that the vulnerability factor itself affects the perception of stress (e.g., Zubin & Spring, 1977), suggesting that stress is not independent from vulnerability. In this sense, the vulnerability does not "cause" the stress in this case, but rather the vulnerability is part of the stress. In other cases, stress may affect the development of the diathesis. For example, there is evidence to suggest that stress may play a role in the etiology of schizophrenia as early as the prenatal period, when the fetus is exposed to a possible range of developmental insults that in turn produces the diathesis (Brennan & Walker, 2001). In depression theory and research, the "scar" hypothesis (Rohde, Lewinsohn, & Seeley, 1990) suggests that a first episode of depression may leave cognitive scars in the form of negative thinking patterns that may not have been previously present. If such scars subsequently serve as a diathesis for additional episodes of depression, then this may be understood as a stress-induced diathesis.

Not only may a disorder be the result of both diathesis and stress, but the diatheses may precipitate stress that combines with stress not related to the diatheses (Monroe & Simons, 1991). For example, "external" stressors (e.g., a death in the family, alcoholic parent, socioeconomic strife) may or may not be substantial enough to trigger the disorder. However, if the diathesis plays a direct role in creating "other" kinds of stress by, for example, increasing tension in the person's interpersonal life, the combined state of affairs may subsequently increase the likelihood of the onset of a full-blown disorder.

Typically, diathesis-stress models refer to stressful events that are proximal to the onset of disorder. However, it should be noted that stressors earlier in life may also influence how later stressful events are responded to and thus increase future susceptibility to disorder. For example, maladaptive methods of coping with stress in childhood and throughout development may be detrimental to the development of effective coping competencies; lacking effective coping skills, in turn, can compromise resilience and encourage vulnerability (Hammen, 1992). Thus, maladaptive cognitions about the self and others and ineffective coping competencies may contribute to the occurrence of stressful events and circumstances—and these in turn may trigger depressive reactions.

SUMMARY AND CONCLUSIONS

Individually, vulnerability and stress are important concepts, but their real power lies in their interaction. Diathesis-stress models thus describe the interactions between these constructs and are useful for understanding the development of psychopathology. In this chapter, we described some basic principles that characterize diatheses-stress models, such as the idea that models tend to be additive and ipsative. We also noted that mega diathesis-stress models are also possible, although uncommon, and emphasized the importance of considering varying relationships between diatheses and stress over time. We also described the interactive model with dichotomous diatheses approach to diathesis-stress conceptualizations, the quasi-continuous diathesis model, threshold models, and risk-resilience continuum models. In describing these different models, however, we also noted that these models tend to vary not in basic structure but rater in the emphasis that different investigators give to different components. Finally, within the context of diathesis-stress interactions, we noted some outstanding issues that reflect on conceptualizations of diatheses and conceptualizations of stress.

The development of psychopathology is obviously complex and involves numerous vulnerability factors and interactions between those factors and stress. Diathesis-stress models are excellent heuristic devices (Monroe & Simons, 1991) that enable us to potentially understand how predispositional factors from various domains may increase susceptibility to psychopathology and subsequently create the sufficient conditions for the onset of disorder. Furthermore, diathesis-stress models help describe how diatheses and stressors can be better conceptualized and more precisely measured empirically with respect to specific forms of psychopathology. Such models are necessary if psychopathologists ever hope to be able to understand the multifactoral complexity of psychopathology, including developmental experiences, biological vulnerabilities, psychological susceptibilities, and socioenvironmental variables.

NOTE

1. Because possessing vulnerability places one at higher risk for developing a disorder, vulnerability is probably most accurately seen as a subcategory of risk.

REFERENCES

Audy, J. R. (1971). *Measurement and diagnosis of health.* San Francisco: George Williams Hooper Foundation for Medical Research, University of California.

Barnett, P. A., & Gotlib, I. H. (1988). Psychosocial functioning in depression: Distinguishing among antecedents, concomitants, and consequences. *Psychological Bulletin, 104,* 97–126.

Beard, G. M. (1881). *American nervousness, its causes and consequences.* New York: Putnam.

Bebbington, P. (1987). Misery and beyond: The pursuit of disease theories of depression. *International Journal of Social Psychiatry, 33,* 13–20.

Beck, A. T. (1967). *Depression: Causes and treatment.* Philadelphia: University of Pennsylvania Press.

Beck, A. T. (1989). *Love is never enough.* New York: Perennial.

Beck, A. T. (1999). Cognitive aspects of personality disorders and their relation to syndromal disorder: A psychoevolutionary approach. In R. C. Cloninger (Ed.), *Personality and psychopathology* (pp. 411–429). Washington, DC: American Psychiatric Association.

Bleuler, M. (1963). Conception of schizophrenia within the last fifty years and today. *Proceedings of the Royal Society of Medicine, 56,* 945–952.

Brennan, P. A., & Walker, E. F. (2001). Vulnerability to schizophrenia: Risk factors in childhood and adolescence. In R. E. Ingram & J. M. Price (Eds.), *Vulnerability to psychopathology: Risk across the lifespan* (pp. 329–354). New York: Guilford Press.

Brown, G. W., & Harris, T. O. (1978). *Social origins of depression.* New York: Free Press.

Brown, G. W., & Harris, T. O. (1989). *Life events and illness.* New York: Guilford Press.

Depue, R. A., & Monroe, S. M. (1986). Conceptualization and measurement of human disorder and life stress research: The problem of chronic disturbance. *Psychological Bulletin, 99,* 36–51.

Dohrenwend, B. P., & Shrout, P. E. (1985). "Hassles" in the conceptualization and measurement of life stress variables. *American Psychologist, 40,* 780–785.

Ellis, A. (1962). *Reason and emotion in psychotherapy.* Oxford, UK: Lyle Stuart.

Goodman, S. H., & Gotlib, I. H. (1999). Risk for psychopathology in the children of depressed mothers: A developmental model for understanding mechanisms of transmission. *Psychological Review, 106,* 458–490.

Gotlib, I. H., & Hammen, C. (1992). *Psychological aspects of depression: Toward a cognitive-interpersonal integration.* Oxford, UK: Wiley.

Hammen, C. (1991). Generation of stress in the course of unipolar depression. *Journal of Abnormal Psychology, 100,* 555–561.

Hammen, C. (1992). Cognitive, life stress, and interpersonal approaches to a developmental psychopathology model of depression. *Development and Psychopathology, 4,* 189–206.

Ingram, R. E., Miranda, J., & Segal, Z. V. (1998). *Cognitive vulnerability to depression.* New York: Guilford Press.

Ingram, R. E., & Price, J. M. (Eds.). (2001). *Vulnerability to psychopathology: Risk across the lifespan.* New York: Guilford Press.

Just, N., Abramson, L. Y., & Alloy, L. B. (2001). Remitted depression studies as tests of the cognitive vulnerability hypothesis of depression: A critique and conceptual analysis. *Clinical Psychology Review, 21,* 63–83.

Lazarus, R. S. (1990). Theory-based stress measurement. *Psychological Inquiry, 1,* 3–13.

Lazarus, R. S., & Folkman, S. (1984). *Stress, appraisal, and coping.* New York: Springer.

Luthar, S. S., & Zigler, E. (1991). Vulnerability and competence: A review of research on resilience in childhood. *American Journal of Orthopsychiatry, 61,* 6–22.

Luxton, D. D., & Wenzlaff, R. M. (in press). Self-esteem uncertainty and depression vulnerability. *Cognition & Emotion.*

Mazure, C. (1998). Life stressors as risk factors in depression. *Clinical Psychology: Science and Practice, 5,* 291–313.

McGue, M., & Gottesman, I. I. (1989). Genetic linkage in schizophrenia: Perspectives from genetic epidemiology. *Schizophrenia Bulletin, 15,* 453–464.

McKeever, V. M., & Huff, M. E. (2003). A diathesis-stress model of posttraumatic stress disorder: Ecological, biological, and residual stress pathways. *Review of General Psychology, 7,* 237–250.

McManus, F., & Clark, D. M. (2002). Information processing in social phobia. *Biological Psychiatry, 51,* 92–100.

Meehl, P. E. (1962). Schizotaxia, schizotypy, schizophrenia. *American Psychologist, 17,* 827–838.

Meehl, P. E. (1989). Schizotaxia revisited. *Archives of General Psychiatry, 46,* 935–944.

Meehl, P. E. (1990). Toward an integrated theory of schizotaxia, schizotypy, and schizophrenia. *Journal of Personality Disorders, 4,* 1–99.

Monroe, S. M. (1989). Stress and social support: Assessment issues. In N. Schneiderman, S. M. Weiss, & P. G. Kaufman (Eds.), *Handbook of research in cardiovascular behavioral medicine* (pp. 511–526). New York: Plenum Press.

Monroe, S. M., & Hadjiyannakis, H. (2002). The social environment and depression: Focusing on severe life stress. In I. H. Gotlib & C. L. Hammen (Eds.), *Handbook of depression* (pp. 314–340). New York: Guilford Press.

Monroe, S. M., & Peterman, A. M. (1988). Life stress and psychopathology. In L. Cohen (Ed.), *Research on stressful life events: Theoretical and methodological issues* (pp. 31–63). Newbury Park, CA: Sage.

Monroe, S. M., & Simons, A. D. (1991). Diathesis-stress theories in the context of life-stress research: Implications for the depressive disorders. *Psychological Bulletin, 110,* 406–425.

Nicholson, I. R., & Neufeld, R. W. (1992). A dynamic vulnerability perspective on stress and schizophrenia. *American Journal of Orthopsychiatry, 62,* 117–130.

Post, R. M. (1992). Transduction of psychosocial stress into the neurobiology of recurrent affective disorder. *American Journal of Psychiatry, 149,* 999–1010.

Rohde, P., Lewinsohn, P. M., & Seeley, J. R. (1990). Are people changed by the experience of having an episode of depression? A further test of the scar hypothesis. *Journal of Abnormal Psychology, 99,* 264–271.

Rosenthal, D. (1963). A suggested conceptual framework. In D. Rosenthal (Ed.), *The Genian quadruplets* (pp. 505–516). New York: Basic Books.

Rothman, K. J. (1976). Causes. *American Journal of Epidemiology, 104,* 587–592.

Rutter, M. (1986). Meyerian psychobiology, personality development, and the role of life experiences. *American Journal of Psychiatry, 143,* 1077–1087.

Rutter, M. (1987). Psychosocial resilience and protective mechanisms. *American Journal of Orthopsychiatry, 57,* 316–331.

Rutter, M. (1988). Longitudinal data in the study of causal processes: Some uses and some pitfalls. In M. Rutter (Ed.), *Studies of psychosocial risk: The power of longitudinal data* (pp. 1–28). Cambridge, UK: Cambridge University Press.

Segal, Z. V. (1988). Appraisal of the self-schema construct in cognitive models of depression. *Psychological Bulletin, 103,* 147–162.

Segal, Z. V., & Ingram, R. E. (1994). Mood priming and construct activation in tests of cognitive vulnerability to unipolar depression. *Clinical Psychology Review, 14,* 663–695.

Selye, H. (1963). A syndrome produced by diverse noxious agents. *Nature, 138,* 32.

Zubin, J., & Spring, B. (1977). Vulnerability: A new view of schizophrenia. *Journal of Abnormal Psychology, 86,* 103–126.

Zuckerman, M. (1999). *Vulnerability to psychopathology: A biosocial model.* Washington, DC: American Psychological Association.

Part II
VULNERABILITIES

CHAPTER 3

The Role of Emotion Regulation in the Development of Psychopathology

TARA M. CHAPLIN AND PAMELA M. COLE

An 8-year-old boy begins to take a test. He looks at the first question. He doesn't understand it! He tenses, looks harder, but cannot see a solution. He can't think straight now. His eyes dart around the page, but without really taking in the questions and planning answers. He feels agitated. He covers his face with his hands, then looks at the first question again—and again—but he doesn't know what to do. He sneaks a glance at the other students, then at the teacher—*Oh no—she is watching him!* His cheeks reddening, his heart racing, he tries to look like he's working. He begins to kick the legs of his desk. The teacher comes over, tells him to stop kicking. She can see his panic, so she softly encourages him, offers help. It's too much! He jumps up, kicking over the desk, and runs out of the room. The teacher finds him pounding his fist against a locker in the hallway. The boy tells her what she can do with her stupid test. He cannot recover and is sent to the principal's office; he does not take the test.

Emotions have long been linked to psychopathology. Western philosophers, for example, viewed madness as the result of an excess of emotion that interferes with reason (Cicchetti, Ackerman, & Izard, 1995). Eastern philosophies regard emotions as human limitations that are obstacles to achieving enlightenment (Goleman, 2003). The view of emotions as dangerous culprits that threaten health and adjustment also appeared in the first formal psychological theories (Greenberg & Safran, 1987). Freud contended that pent-up emotional energy caused psychopathology. He argued that early childhood stress typically created unacceptably intense feelings in children, feelings that required psychological defenses to remove them from conscious awareness. In the process, these transformed emotions still expended energy, producing psychological symptoms. In sum, throughout history, emotions have captured the minds of great thinkers who strove to understand human behavior, and from the very first, emotions have been implicated in models of human frailty, deviance, and psychopathology.

In the more recent past, emotions have reemerged as an important area of study, including as a factor in models of adult and child psychopathology and treatment (e.g., Cole, Michel, & Teti, 1994; Davidson, Scherer, & Goldsmith, 2003; Greenberg & Safran, 1987). Contemporary emotion theories, building upon Darwin's (1872) view that the capacity to be emotional is crucial to adaptation, describe emotions as psychological processes that serve the function of achieving goals for maintaining well-being (e.g., Barrett & Campos, 1987; Ekman, 1992; Frijda, 1986; Izard, 1977; LeDoux, 1996; Panksepp, 1982; Plutchik, 1962; Sroufe, 1996; Tomkins, 1962–1991). Yet, emotions are also thought to play a significant role in the nature and development of psychopathology. Hence emerges a conundrum.

The concept of emotion regulation solves this seeming contradiction. It is not emotions themselves that create psychological vulnerability. Rather, it is the manner in which emotions are managed that determines whether a person's adjustment or functioning is jeopardized (Cicchetti et al., 1995; Cole, Michel, et al., 1994; Davidson, 1998; Garber & Dodge, 1991; Gross, 1999; Keenan, 2000; Thompson & Calkins, 1996). In general, emotion regulation patterns that are flexible, allowing a person to access the full range of human emotions and yet modulate the experience and expression in accordance with the ever-changing demands of life, are associated with healthy functioning (Cole, Michel, et al.).

The emotional presentations associated with psychopathology often involve poorly regulated responses, such as overwhelming emotion (e.g., rage), restricted emotion (e.g., inability to enjoy previously preferred activities), inappropriate affect (e.g., laughing at another's pain), and poorly timed or attuned emotion (e.g., affective lability and affective instability). In the example above, the boy was understandably frustrated, embarrassed, and nervous, but he ended up overwhelmed with frustration, shame, and anxiety; he was unable to use external resources (the teacher's solace) or internal mechanisms (self-talk, distraction) to manage those emotions in a way that would allow him to solve the immediate problem of the confusing question.

Our view of the role of emotion regulation in psychopathology begins with the premise that emotional processes are fundamentally adaptive, providing a means of positioning oneself in relation to circumstances in order to achieve well-being. With a generally intact nervous system and reasonably decent relationships, our emotions—each and all of them—serve these goals and do not create vulnerability for psychopathology. Vulnerability to psychopathology emerges when the manner of emotion regulation, although achieving some immediate goal, interferes with other proximal or distal goals of development (taking the test, passing the test, preserving a good relationship with the teacher, gaining the respect of your peers, knowing how to avoid storming out of the office of your boss when you feel confused in later years; see also Cicchetti, Ganiban, & Barnett, 1991). In addition, context determines whether a particular way of regulating emotion is competent or deviant, appropriate or dysregulated (Campos, Mumme, Kermonian, & Campos, 1994; Cole, Michel, et al., 1994; Markus & Kitayama, 1991; Saarni, 1999; Shields, 2002). Finally, risk for developing a disorder does not arise in one moment alone. Rather, vulnerability for psychopathology exists when stable, stylized patterns of emotion regulation that lack the flexibility and situational sensitivity necessary for dealing with a complex world of goals and relationships are the dominant mode of responding (Izard & Malatesta, 1987; Magai & McFadden, 1995; Malatesta & Wilson, 1988).

In this chapter, we suggest that early patterns of emotional dysregulation create vulnerability to the development of psychopathology. Although any psychological process can create risk, emotions are central candidates because they are the fuel behind behavior (Cicchetti et al., 1995; Izard, 1977; Tomkins, 1962–1991). We suggest that patterns of emotion regulation may precede the emergence of formal disorders. In reviewing studies of children and adolescents with known problems, we generate hypotheses about the types of early emotional experience and expression that might predispose a child, particularly a child faced with stressful life circumstances, to develop symptoms and eventually a disorder.

We organize the discussion around particular emotion families, linking them to behavioral approach and avoidance motivations (i.e., anger, joy, empathy, sadness, fear, guilt, and shame). In this way, we attempt to tie the tradition of emotion theories, which classify subjective feeling states, with contemporary advances in affective neuroscience that shed light on how the brain supports motivated behavior under emotional conditions. The literature linking emotional processes to child and adolescent psychopathology has tended to rely on the proverbial basic emotions—anger, joy, empathy, fear, sadness, shame, and guilt. Throughout our discussion, we relate these findings to the motivational approach and avoidance systems. Moreover, our focus is on how emotions are experienced and expressed. We refer readers to excellent reviews focusing on the role of general emotional competence in the development of disorders (e.g., Casey, 1996; Halberstadt, Denham, & Dunsmore, 2001; Saarni, 1999).

EMOTIONS AND THE ADAPTIVE CAPACITIES TO APPROACH AND WITHDRAW

Emotions are motivational systems that function to help achieve goals (Barrett & Campos, 1987; Izard & Ackerman, 2000). The basic emotions, which are generally regarded as specific motivational states, appear to have important relations to the two overarching motivational systems: approach and withdrawal systems. Approach systems (Fowles, 1980; Gray, 1987) subserve our capacity to act upon the environment. Happiness, anger, and empathy are regarded as approach-oriented emotions (Coan & Allen, 2004; Davidson, 1998), although there is some debate about whether anger is an approach or withdrawal emotion (Harmon-Jones, 2003). Here, we treat anger as an approach emotion, given the theoretical argument that anger motivates action to overcome obstacles (Barrett & Campos). Withdrawal systems orient us away from the environment, toward avoiding dangers and relinquishing goals. Withdrawal systems lead to (temporary) inaction and often elicit support from others. Withdrawal system emotions include sadness, fear, and some social emotions, such as shame and possibly guilt (Davidson, 1998; Gray; LeDoux, 1996; M. Lewis, 2000).

The ability to both approach and withdraw from circumstances is essential to human survival (Abe & Izard, 1999; Barrett & Campos, 1987; Izard & Ackerman, 2000; Keltner & Gross, 1999). Emotions signal specific orientations toward perceived circumstances (Barrett & Campos). An infant's smile signals a desire to approach, which serves the critical role of inviting and maintaining caregiver interest, care, and affection. The tears of a child signal the giving up of a goal, eliciting comfort and care from others and possibly solutions to attaining the goal. Anger signals a negatively valenced approach; anger supports persistence, power, and dominant behavior, warning others of a readiness to act against their goals. Each serves adaptive functions, but poorly regulated joy, sadness, anger, and other emotions can interfere with healthy development and create vulnerability for the development of psychopathology.

ANGER, JOY, AND EMPATHY: THE CAPACITY TO APPROACH AND VULNERABILITY TO PSYCHOPATHOLOGY

Anger: Approaching Obstacles

The angry emotions involve appraising that one's goals for well-being are blocked, thwarted, or unjustly removed and that they still can and should be achieved, and readying to act to overcome the obstacles and achieve the goal (Barrett & Campos, 1987; Frijda, 1986). The anger-related emotions support asserting one's best interests, as one perceives them, and aid in establishing one's dominant status, autonomy, and identity.

In the course of development, what must the pattern of anger regulation appear like to indicate vulnerability to psychopathology? Irritability, rage, rudeness, aggression, and hostility describe symptoms in both the international and U.S. diagnostic manuals for classifying mental disorders (American Psychiatric Association [APA], 1994; World Health Organization [WHO], 1993). They indicate pervasive anger, reactive and intense anger, and anger expressed against others in socially unacceptable ways. Clinical conceptualizations of these problems describe such anger as underregulated. In other words, attempts to maintain a sense of control or dominance are no longer regulated in ways that take into account the needs of relationships and situational constraints (e.g., when a teenager acts out rather than coping with the disappointments in her family life). Angry emotions, however, can also be overregulated, also creating risk for psychopathology. A person may be unable to experience and communicate justified anger that would be useful in signaling an acute need and solving problems (e.g., when a youngster cannot stand up for himself with other persons).

The Underregulation of Angry Emotions

The underregulation of angry emotions is the most studied aspect of emotional processes in the development of psychopathology. It is most often associated with "externalizing" symptoms, that is, symptoms that disrupt or disturb others (see Hankin, Abela, Auerbach, McWhinnie, & Skitch, Chapter 14 of this volume, for greater discussion of externalizing problems). Anger is not exclusively linked to externalizing, however. Irritability and other forms of intense or reactive anger are also seen in individuals with anxious and depressive symptoms.

There is a wealth of studies showing relations between higher levels of anger, measured in various ways, and externalizing behavior problems, as reported by teachers or parents among both preschool and school-age children (e.g., Casey, 1996; Cole, Zahn-Waxler, & Smith, 1994; Eisenberg et al., 1994; Eisenberg et al., 2001; Gilliom, Shaw, Beck, Schonberg, & Lukon, 2002; Zeman, Shipman, & Suveg, 2002). Research with adolescents has also shown the relation (Keltner, Moffitt, & Stouthamer-Loeber, 1995), although fewer studies have been conducted with this age group (Sheeber, Allen, Davis, & Sorenson, 2000). Children with externalizing problems are often persistent, defiant, oppositional, or aggressive in their efforts to achieve goals, at the cost of disrupting their relationships.

Relations between underregulated anger and symptomatic behavior are context specific and may vary as a function of situation, a person's gender, or cultural display rules. Anger displays in boys may be viewed as more acceptable than anger in girls, which may contribute to boys' greater rates of overt aggression (Brody & Hall, 1993; Keenan & Shaw, 1997). Young girls with externalizing symptoms, on the other hand, may overregulate anger expressions in certain interpersonal contexts (Cole et al., 1994). Thus, relations between symptoms and particular emotions, such as angry defiance, are complex and must be considered in terms of context.

Anger has been most clearly articulated as a risk factor for externalizing disorders in Patterson's (1986) coercive cycle model. In a coercive cycle, a young child defies the parent, who then becomes angry, leading to an escalation of child and parental anger until one party yields. In other words, these parent-child dyads escalate, rather than modulate, each other's anger in their attempts to influence each other. The model has withstood empirical tests. In children as young as preschool age, mutually angry interactions are associated with early externalizing problems (Cole, Teti, & Zahn-Waxler, 2003; Dumas, LaFreniere, & Serketich, 1995; Denham et al., 2000), and reciprocal anger between parents and youth is also correlated with conduct disorder in adolescents (Dadds, Sanders, Morrison, & Rebgetz, 1992; Sanders, Dadds, Johnston, & Cash, 1992). Moreover, high levels of anger expression are not merely correlates of externalizing problems; they forecast continuing problems. Longitudinal studies that began when participants were infants or preschoolers, for example, show that early indications of anger underregulation pre dispose children to later disruptive behavior problems (Bates, Pettit, Dodge, & Ridge, 1998; Chaplin, Cole, & Zahn-Waxler, in press; Cole et al., 2003; Cole, Zahn-Waxler, Fox, Usher, & Welsh, 1996; Eisenberg et al., 1997; Gilliom et al., 2002).

In a review of the adult literature, Kring and Bachorowski (1999) discussed links between the biologically based approach motivational system and antisocial personality disorder. They suggested that the underregulation of approach behavior, involving physiological responses to angry emotions, may predispose a youth to acting without regard for others. Anger has been theoretically linked to both approach and withdrawal areas of the brain (Coan & Allen, 2004; Harmon-Jones, 2003), and research is needed to better understand how anger and approach and withdrawal are related. Nonetheless, it is clear that dysregulated anger is a risk factor for psychopathology, and particularly for externalizing disorders.

Although links between underregulated anger and externalizing symptoms are clear, there is not an isomorphic relation between them. For example, children with elevated depressive symptoms reveal hostile interpretations of events (Quiggle, Garber, Panak, & Dodge, 1992), a form of underregulation of anger appraisal. Interestingly, what distinguishes children with high depressive symptoms from those with high externalizing symptoms is that, despite angry ideas organizing their perceptions and perhaps their feelings, depressed children are less likely than externalizing children to act aggressively. Thus, the regulation of angry experience and expression both need to be considered.

The Overregulation of Angry Emotions

Although the underregulation of angry emotions has received the lion's share of empirical attention, the overregulation of anger is also considered a risk factor in the development of psychopathology. Many individuals with depressed and anxious symptoms report intense and recurrent angry emotional experiences (Clark & Watson, 1991; Hankin & Abramson, 2001), although others report feeling unable to experience anger. Still others seem angry but are unable to recognize their anger. Every clinician has experience with a client who furiously insists, "I'm NOT angry." A pattern of experiencing high levels of frustration and irritation but regularly trying to suppress or to mask them is argued to create vulnerability for depression (Biaggio & Godwin, 1987; Gross, 1999; Gross & John, 2003; Zahn-Waxler, 2001).

Angry emotions support self-assertion and maintenance of one's individuality, autonomy, and dominance. Difficulties in establishing a firm sense of autonomy or mastery may reflect anger overregulation and are related to depressive symptoms in adolescents (Allen, Hauser, Eickholt, Bell, & O'Connor, 1994; Burhans & Dweck, 1995; Kobak & Ferenz-Gillies, 1995). A young child who experiences barriers to, and attendant frustration at, getting goals met but who, for various reasons, develops a pattern of stifling frustration, injustice, or protest may be vulnerable to psychopathology and perhaps prone to depression. Suppression of outward anger implies that the anger is still felt (Gross & John, 2003), and in many clinical cases, that suppressed anger is turned inward. In children, the suppression of strongly felt anger may lead to self-criticism and blame, commonly associated with depression (Abraham, 1924/1968; Izard, 1972).

Girls may be particularly vulnerable to this style of anger regulation (Zahn-Waxler, 2001). In one study, intropunitive, oversocialized traits in 7-year-olds were predictive of adolescent depression in girls, whereas aggressive, undercontrolled traits were predictive of later depressive symptoms for boys (Block, Gjerde, & Block, 1991). It may be that girls in stressful conditions are prone to exaggerate their interpersonally oriented gender role and therefore be at particular risk for depression, in contrast to boys, whose role orientation is not focused on concern about the effect of their anger on others (Zahn-Waxler, Klimes Dougan, & Slattery, 2000). Females' propensity for focusing on others' needs, above their own, has been linked to depression in females (Leadbeater, Kuperminc, Blatt, & Hertzog, 1999).

Most discussion of the overregulation of anger focuses on individuals who experience high levels of angry emotions but do not feel entitled to express or even feel them. Reports of high levels of anger and self-directed hostility feelings are correlated with depressive symptoms and diagnoses of depression in children and adolescents (Blumberg & Izard, 1985; Carey, Finch, & Carey, 1991). Less research has examined whether children and adolescents at risk for depression actually suppress their feelings of anger, although studies showing a tendency for depressed children to have hostile feelings but not act on them are consistent with overregulation of anger being associated with depression (Quiggle et al., 1992). Higher levels of angry emotions generally, coupled with *lower* levels of observed anger in a specific frustrating situation, accounted for depressive symptoms in college students (Chaplin, 2004). Observed suppression of aggression toward mothers was associated with increases in levels of depression for adolescent girls 1 year later (Davis, Sheeber, Hops, & Tildesley, 2000).

There are few prospective studies of early anger patterns. The few that exist show that later depression can be predicted by overcontrolled and intropunitive traits in early childhood (Block et al., 1991; Caspi, Henry, McGee, Moffitt, & Silva, 1995). Suppression of anger may be implicated in those traits, but more research is needed.

Happiness: Approaching the Environment

Like anger, happiness involves an approach-oriented motivational stance. The family of happy emotions motivates humans to reach out into their environment in order to promote personal growth and growth of harmony with family, friends, and community (Izard & Ackerman, 2000). Also, happy feelings appear to involve activation of the left prefrontal cortex, an area of the brain associated with approach-oriented goals and behavior (Davidson, 2000). Poorly regulated expressions and feelings of happy emotions are linked with the impulsivity and expansiveness symptomatic of disorders such as attention deficit/hyperactivity disorder (ADHD) and mania (Barkley, 1997, 2003). On the other hand, difficulty experiencing joy in situations that previously made one happy defines anhedonia and associated conditions, symptoms of depressive disorders (Clark & Watson, 1991; Henriques & Davidson, 1991; Izard, 1972; Hankin & Abramson, 2001).

Generally, expressions and feelings of pleasure and happiness reflect the satisfaction of goals for well-being. Such satisfaction, however, can come at another's expense. Relatively little research has examined phenomena such as gleeful aggression and happy victimization. Yet, some examples of conduct problems and antisocial behavior involve enjoyment at another's expense. Preschoolers who expressed joy while aggressing against a peer were in fact more aggressive, less accepted by peers, and rated by teachers as less socially competent than preschoolers who did not express joy under such circumstances (Arsenio, Cooperman, & Lover, 2000).

The Underregulation of Happy Emotions

The underregulation of happiness creates risk when it overtakes behavior and creates problems for one's own well-being or the well-being of others. The creativity of some famous artists, perhaps reflecting the openness to experience associated with happiness, has been attributed to manic phases (Jamison, 1993). Another potentially problematic pattern is a presentation of cheerfulness that is not felt (Hochschild, 1983; Zahn-Waxler, 2001; Zahn-Waxler, Cole, & Barrett, 1991). Thus, abundant joy, when it overtakes goals of effective personal action or social propriety, is dysregulated.

Theorists and clinicians have noted that children with ADHD often express exuberant joy, even in inappropriate situations (Barkley, 1997; Saarni, 1999; Whalen & Henker, 1985). Barkley (1997) proposed that ADHD involves a failure to inhibit emotion expressions and to understand how to coordinate expressions to situations. Boys with ADHD report more "pleasurable" reactions to startling sounds than boys without ADHD, suggesting that they feel happy when others feel discomfort (Ornitz et al., 1997).

At the same time, ADHD often co-occurs with anxiety and major depression, suggesting that some children with ADHD may also experience strong negative emotions. Thus, children with ADHD may show general deficits in emotion regulation rather than dysregulation involving a specific set of emotions. One study found concurrent relations between ineffective emotion regulation in a frustrating task (difficulty maintaining focus and effort and not displaying disruptive emotions such as anger) and ADHD in boys, particularly those with aggressive behavior (Melnick & Hinshaw, 2000). Future research should explore these relations longitudinally, including an examination of the degree to which earlier attentional and emotional difficulties forecast the development of ADHD symptoms in preschool and school age.

In bipolar disorders, euphoric states that overtake the best interest of the individual as well as others are observed. Bipolar disorder in adults, and somewhat in children, is characterized by mood lability, particularly alternations between depression and elation (Nottelmann et al., 2001). The euphoric moods are associated with behaviors such as unrestrained spending, risk taking, and sexual promiscuity. There is surprisingly little research on the developmental origins of dysregulated joy. Recent studies have shown that high levels of elated mood in children and early adolescents are related to concurrent bipolar disorder diagnoses (Geller et al., 2002). Interestingly, Geller and colleagues (1998) find that elated mood may be specific to children with bipolar disorder and may differentiate them from children with ADHD. However, much more remains to be known about the role of underregulated joy and the development of different disorders and more broadly about emotional lability.

Lack of Happy Emotions

Difficulty experiencing joy or happiness is related to psychopathology, notably unipolar depressive disorders (APA, 1994; WHO, 1993; see Hankin & Abela, Chapter 10 of this volume, for greater discussion about depression). Even when circumstances are difficult, the up-regulation of positive emotion is thought to be a sign of health (Folkman & Moskowitz, 2000). Although depression typically does not emerge until adolescence, difficulty generating and experiencing happiness and joy can be present early in childhood. Without an adequate reserve of happiness to motivate seeking out experiences and companionship with others, particularly in the presence of life circumstances that do not compensate for difficulty up-regulating positive emotions, children may be at risk for depression. Children who are low in happiness may appear unhappy or affectively flat. Others may cover anhedonia with inauthentic happy expressions despite persistently feeling unhappy.

Empirical evidence on relations between a lack of happiness and actual symptoms of clinical depression has been found in research using both physiological and self-report measures of emotion experience. Studies of brain activity show that depressed adults, as compared to nondisordered adults, have lower activation of the left prefrontal cortex, the area associated with approach-related positive emotion (e.g., Davidson, 2000; Henriques & Davidson, 1991). Young children of depressed mothers show similar patterns of neural activity (Dawson et al., 1999; Dawson et al., 2001). Consistent with these findings, children's and adolescents' reports of low levels of happiness are correlated with self-reported depressive symptoms (Blumberg & Izard, 1985; Carey et al., 1991; Chaplin, 2004; Hammen & Rudolph, 1996). This correlation remains even after controlling for item overlap between self-reports of emotion and depressive symptoms (Blumberg & Izard; Chaplin). Also, low self-reported happiness is more characteristic of depressive disorders than elevated sadness, and in fact, low levels of happiness distinguish depressive disorders from anxiety disorders (Clark & Watson, 1991; Mineka, Watson, & Clark, 1998).

False cheeriness, when unhappy children try to appear cheerful, may constitute risk for psychopathology. Some children express happiness even when they are not feeling it in order to please others or to keep harmony in relations with others (Zahn-Waxler, 2001). Even infants can be "overly cheery" to regulate interactions with an unresponsive caregiver (Cassidy, 1994). This may be more common for females, because girls are socialized to focus on the needs of others (Gilligan, 1982). False cheeriness that becomes a style of dealing with an averse or unresponsive environment may occur at the cost of honest emotional expression and assertion and potential vulnerability to internalizing disorders including depression. Further research is needed to identify whether overly cheerful expressions in early childhood may create vulnerability for the development of depression and gender differences in depression later in development.

Empathy: Approaching Others in Distress

Empathy is typically classified as a *social* emotion, reflecting a motivational orientation toward acting for the welfare of persons in distress (Miller & Eisenberg, 1988; Zahn-Waxler, 2001). Authors have distinguished two forms of empathy (e.g., Eisenberg et al., 1988; Zahn-Waxler): empathic concern and personal distress. Empathic concern may be considered an approach-oriented emotion, motivating inquiry and aid. Personal distress, however, involves fear or anxiety and withdrawal from the discomfort (Eisenberg et al., 1988). In this chapter, we consider personal distress as fear based; in this section we focus on empathic concern.

Concern for others' distress is considered a milestone of prosocial development. Empathic concern fosters caring relationships and a sense of conscience or morality (Hoffman, 1982; Kochanska, DeVet, Goldman, Murray, & Putnam, 1994). When, then, does empathic concern contribute to vulnerability for psychopathology? Risk arises if a child feels empathy for others to the exclusion of taking care of his or her own needs; such a pattern is thought to create risk for the development of internalizing disorders, including depression and anxiety (Zahn-Waxler, 2001; Zahn-Waxler et al., 1991). Alternately, if children show a chronic underexperience of empathy when seeing others in distress, they may be at risk for conduct disorder in childhood or adolescence and could be at elevated risk for later antisocial personality disorder in adulthood (Miller & Eisenberg, 1988).

The Overregulation of Empathic Concern

The inability to up-regulate empathy is thought to be a risk factor for conduct disorder and antisocial personality disorder (Feshbach & Feshbach, 1969; Miller & Eisenberg, 1988). The main feature of antisocial personality disorder, for example, is "a persistent disregard for and violation of the rights of others" (APA, 1994). This includes stealing, lying, or violence. Impoverished empathic concern may be one factor that enables such callous acts, which disregard the pain and suffering of others. It is as yet unknown whether individuals are born without a capacity to experience empathy or whether abusive or neglectful early environments interfere with the normal development of empathic concern (Frick, Cornell, Barry, Bodin, & Dane, 2003).

Low levels of reported and observed empathic responding have been correlated with aggression and greater rates of externalizing problems in children, particularly in middle childhood and adolescence (e.g., Hughes, White, Sharpen, & Dunn, 2000; for meta-analysis, see Miller & Eisenberg, 1988). Studies also indicate that physiological underarousal while observing others in distress is associated with low empathic concern (e.g., Liew et al., 2003). It is not clear whether this develops in early childhood or is present at birth.

Children who lack empathic concern early in life may be at elevated risk for later conduct problems. A study of preschoolers who were at risk for the development of conduct problems, by virtue of elevated externalizing symptoms at age 4 to 5 years, did not differ in empathic concern (Zahn-Waxler, Cole, Welsh, & Fox, 1995). On follow-up, however, early concern for others predicted *decreases* in previously elevated externalizing problems (Hastings, Zahn-Waxler, Robinson, Usher, & Bridges, 2000). Moreover, externalizing preschoolers showed decreased concern for others by 6 to 7 years of age.

Lack of Empathic Concern

Whereas low levels of empathic concern for others in distress are associated with conduct problems, high levels of empathic concern can create vulnerability to psychopathology, particularly for internalizing disorders. Overly empathic children, especially if they also experience significant guilt, may put others' needs above their own (Zahn-Waxler, 2001; Zahn-Waxler et al., 1991; Zahn-Waxler et al., 2000). An exaggerated sense of responsibility for others can interfere with the development of a strong sense of self and autonomy and lead to the passivity and low self-esteem of depression. Zahn-Waxler has also argued that the gender difference in empathy may be related to the preponderance of internalizing disorders among girls.

The theorized link between excessive empathic concern and internalizing disorders has only begun to be tested empirically. Most research focuses on high empathy as facilitating positive development. However, the potential cost of being "overly" prosocial has some empirical support. Hay and Pawlby (2003) found that extreme worry about others, a feature symptom of generalized anxiety disorder, was correlated with prosocial behavior. The nature of difficulties in empathic concerns and how they contribute to the development of psychopathology is an interesting topic that requires more research focused on thorough analysis of the emotional components prior to the onset of formal disorder.

SADNESS, FEAR, GUILT, AND SHAME: THE CAPACITY TO WITHDRAW AND VULNERABILITY TO PSYCHOPATHOLOGY

Sadness: Relinquishing Goals

Sadness orients one toward withdrawal. It allows one to relinquish control over situations one cannot change or control (Barrett & Campos, 1987). Yet poorly regulated sadness may contribute to vulnerability for psychopathology. Intense or frequent sadness, particularly to the exclusion of other emotions, will lead to relinquishing control and withdrawing from challenges, behaviors that are common in depression. However, a rigid refusal to allow sad feelings or expressions may also create risk for psychopathology. Some individuals who turn to alcohol or drugs to cope may be trying to block out experiencing sadness (Wills, Sandy, & Yaeger, 2002).

The Underregulation of Sad Emotions

Persistent sadness is a feature of depression. A pattern of recurrent and intense sadness may exist in some children before they appear to be depressed (Blumberg & Izard, 1985). Such a pattern, in a context where children are stressed and unable to overcome those stresses, may lead to a predominant style of reacting to challenge with sadness and risk for depression. Hankin and Abramson (2001) argue that depression in adolescence is set in motion by initial negative affect (including sadness, but also anger and fear), which they theorize is caused by persistent negative life events (also see Abela, 2001; Abramson, Metalsky, & Alloy, 1989). The greater tendency for experiencing or expressing sadness in females (Broderick, 1998; Stapley & Haviland, 1989) may help to explain the gender difference in depression (Hankin & Abramson, 2001; Nolen-Hoeksema & Girgus, 1994). Nolen-Hoeksema and others have proposed that rumination, including thinking about and talking about one's depressive symptoms (including sadness) may actually amplify the symptoms, creating increased sad feelings and increases of depression. Initial findings show that rumination is related to depressive symptoms in adolescents and in adults, particularly in the presence of stressful life events (Kraaij et al., 2003; Nolen-Hoeksema, Larson, & Grayson, 1999).

Subjective feelings of sadness are related to depressive symptoms in childhood (Blumberg & Izard, 1985; Carey et al., 1991) and late adolescence and adulthood (Chaplin, 2004; Kasch, Rottenberg, Arnow, & Gotlib, 2002). They are also associated with activation of the right prefrontal cortex (Davidson, 1998; Davidson & Fox, 1988). The offspring of depressed mothers, even infants, have higher relative activation in the right frontal brain area, although it is unclear whether this is due to heightened right activation (indicating sadness) or reduced left activation (associated with reduced joy) (Dawson et al., 1999; Field, Fox, Pickens, & Nawrocki, 1995; Jones, Field, Fox, Davalos, & Gomez, 2001). Moreover, infants of depressed mothers are more responsive to sad than to happy expressions by their mothers, suggesting a bias toward responding to sadness (Lundy, Field, Cigales, & Cuadra, 1997). Such a bias could prime children to develop a pattern of amplifying or ruminating on sad feelings. Typically developing children, with no known risks, do not like feeling sad and will say that other children feel sad in appropriate contexts but that they themselves do not (Glasberg &

Aboud, 1982). Thus, the process of feeling very sad may constitute risk.

In addition to feelings of sadness, the *expression* of sadness is assumed to be related to depression. One criterion for diagnosing major depression is sad or tearful appearance, although children and adolescents may appear irritable rather than sad (APA, 1994; WHO, 1993). Empirical studies, however, have failed to find relations between sad expressions and depressive symptoms (Chaplin, 2004; Rottenberg, Gross, Willhelm, Najmi, & Gotlib, 2002). Sanders and colleagues (1992) found that adolescents with depression, conduct disorder, or both appeared sadder during a family interaction than did normally developing adolescents. Casey (1996) reported similar findings for children with internalizing and externalizing disorders. Sadness experience may be related specifically to depression, but appearing sad, among other negative emotional expressions, may be a general aspect of psychopathology.

The Overregulation of Sad Emotions

Theory and research have not considered the risk of low levels of sad affect, in keeping with an emphasis on *reducing* negative affect. Cole, Michel et al. (1994) argued that the emotionally well-regulated person has access to the full range of emotions, including sadness. Wills and colleagues (2002) proposed that avoidance and distraction from one's sadness may predispose adolescents to substance use problems. A failure to appreciate lost objectives, to experience and convey sadness in close relationships, and to cope realistically with such loss may be signs of risk for maladjustment. Male gender roles that condemn the expression of submissive emotions (e.g., sadness) may place males at risk for overregulation (Nolen-Hoeksema & Girgus, 1994). Chaplin et al. (in press) found that preschool-age boys showed less sadness to their parents than girls during a difficult game. The overregulation of sadness could predispose children to persist in anger and to fail to realistically appraise situations in which they cannot or should not have control.

Fear: Withdrawing From Danger

The fearful emotions are our means of appraising danger to well-being and preparing to act swiftly and certainly to retreat and flee (Barrett & Campos, 1987; Izard & Ackerman, 2000). Persistent fearfulness, for example, behavioral inhibition (Kagan, Reznick, & Snidman, 1987) or chronic exposure to trauma (Cicchetti & Toth, 1997), may create vulnerability, especially for the development of anxiety disorders. Alternatively, fearlessness constitutes behavioral risk. Individuals who do not learn from punishment or failure, that is, individuals who behave as if they do not fear those outcomes, are at risk for the development of psychopathy.

The Underregulation of Fear Emotions

Generalized anxiety disorder involves excessive worrying (APA, 1994). Social phobia involves intense fear of negative evaluation by others (e.g., humiliation, embarrassment) to the point that one either avoids social situations or endures them with marked discomfort (APA). Both disorders are seen in children (see Williams, Reardon, Murray, & Cole, Chapter 11 in this volume) and are thought to have origins in early emotional functioning (Lonigan, Vasey, Phillips, & Hazen, 2004; Vasey & Dadds, 2001).

Proneness to fear and behavioral inhibition, both of which reflect fearfulness, have been linked to the development of anxiety disorders (Kagan et al., 1987; Rothbart & Bates, 1998). A predisposition to respond to novelty fearfully by stopping action (inhibition) or by avoiding (withdrawal) does not by itself cause anxiety disorder. Coupled with certain styles of caregiving or circumstances that overtax the fear system, a child may not develop flexible coping skills to deal with this temperamental tendency (Lonigan et al., 2004; Rothbart, Posner, & Hershey, 1995; see Tackett & Krueger, Chapter 8 in this volume, for discussion of temperament).

The physiological reactions of temperamentally fearful children parallel those of individuals with anxiety disorders (Davidson, 2000; Kagan, Reznick, & Snidman, 1988). The evidence suggests that fearful individuals experience more activation of the biological fear system and difficulty regulating such arousal (Davidson, 2000; Davidson & Fox, 1988; Davidson, Marshall, Tomraken, & Henriques, 2000; Rauch et al., 1996; see Pihl and Nantel-Vivier, Chapter 4 in this volume, for review of biological vulnerabilities to psychopathology). Very young children identified as fear prone or behaviorally inhibited are more likely to develop anxiety disorders than other children (Biederman et al., 1990; Hirschfeld et al., 1992; Kagan, 1994).

Physiological evidence linking underregulated fear with anxiety disorders is supported by personality research that uses self-report instruments. These find that whereas general negative affectivity is predictive of both anxiety and depression (Clark, Watson, & Mineka, 1994), self-reported fear (termed *autonomic hyperarousal*) is specifically related to anxiety symptoms in adults (Brown, Chorpita, & Barlow, 1998) and in children (Chorpita, Albano, & Barlow, 1998; Ollendick, Yule, & Ollier, 1991). Thus, early fearfulness may specifically forecast later anxiety disorders, rather than general internalizing disorders, although there is a lack of longitudinal research (Lonigan et al., 2004).

The Overregulation of Fear Emotions

Overregulation of fear is associated with antisocial behaviors and traits. Insufficient fearfulness in the face of real danger leads to acting without caution and without appreciation of known consequences (Barkeley, 2004; Fowles, 1980; Lahey, Hart, Pliszka, Applegate, & McBurnett, 1993; Lykken, 1995). It is not known whether such persons overregulate fear or are unable to up-regulate fear in appropriate situations.

Children and adults with severe conduct problems show lower sympathetic arousal in situations that would normally involve increases in arousal, and they have lower resting heart rates (for review, see Lahey et al., 1993). Moreover, Raine, Venables, and Mednick (1997) found that low resting heart rate in 3-year-olds, one component of a fear reaction, predicted more severe aggressive conduct problems at age 11. In sum, there is evidence that antisocial behaviors may be a result of an underactive or overregulated fear response (see also Hankin et al., Chapter 14 of this volume), which, notably, may correspond to lower personal distress, one component of empathy.

Shame and Guilt: Withdrawing in the Eyes of Others

Shame and guilt, like empathy, are social emotions, considered to develop over time as children interact with their environment (H. B. Lewis, 1971) and possibly as children develop the cognitive ability to evaluate the self (M. Lewis, 2000). Shame is an aversive emotion that occurs when one perceives that the self is inadequate in some way and does not measure up to the ideal self (Higgins, 1987; M. Lewis, 2000; Tangney, 1993). Guilt is a related emotion but is thought to refer more specifically to a behavior than to the self, for example, regret about a specific transgression that violates moral values (Tangney).

Shame and guilt motivate a person to care about socially determined values, and the capacity to experience them should be related to the development of moral behavior and conscience (Kochanska et al., 1994). Shame, at least in the cultural context of U.S. society, is often seen as creating more vulnerability for maladjustment than guilt, because it involves a negative evaluation about one's entire self, not just a particular action, and can undermine self-esteem (M. Lewis, 2000; Tangney, 1993). It is noteworthy that many Asian peoples believe that shame is a necessary and healthy emotion that should be cultivated in a person (Kitayama, Markus, & Matsumoto, 1995).

Excessive shame, beyond what is expected in a society, is associated with withdrawal in situations that involve being evaluated by others. In college student samples, it is related to eating disorders (Reimer, 1996; Sanftner, Barlow, Marschall, & Tangney, 1995) and depressive symptoms (Tangney, Wagner, & Gramzow, 1992). Intense shame may also be turned against others, perhaps as a defensive reaction, creating feelings of rage and hostility that are related to conduct disorder, antisocial personality disorder, and narcissistic personality disorder (H. B. Lewis, 1971; Tangney, Wagner, Fletcher, & Gramzow, 1992; Wright, O'Leary, & Balkin, 1989). Feeling guilt even when one has not done anything wrong may also create risk for psychopathology. A proclivity toward guilt can lead to excessive self-blame, feelings of hopelessness, and depression (Zahn-Waxler, 2001; Zahn-Waxler & Robinson, 1995). Low levels of guilt (and some forms of shame), like low levels of empathic concern, may contribute to risk for conduct problems and aggressive behavior (Cimbora & McIntosh, 2003).

The Underregulation of Shame and Guilt

A pattern of exaggerated and intense shame and guilt may be implicated in the development of internalizing disorders (e.g., Tangney, 1993; Zahn-Waxler et al., 1991; see Cooper, Chapter 12 in this volume, for a review of eating disorders). Self-reports of feeling guilt and shame are correlated with depressive symptoms in children, adolescents, and adults (Blumberg & Izard, 1985; Izard, 1972; Tangney, Wagner, & Gramzow, 1992). Preschoolers with depressed mothers report more distorted and less resolved narratives about guilt (Zahn-Waxler, Kochanska, Krupnick, & McKnew, 1990). One possibility is that being exposed to maternal anhedonia and irritability, particularly when a young child does not have the cognitive resources to understand that a mother's problems are not his or her fault, leads to unresolved guilt. An exaggerated sense of personal responsibility and guilt or shame might create risk for later depression.

Excessive feelings of shame have also been linked to the development of eating disorders (Reimer, 1996). Shame involves a perception that one's self does not match up to an internalized standard, which could include standards about body shape. In college samples, self-reports of shame, but not guilt, are related to eating disorder symptoms (Sanftner et al., 1995). Eating disorders are more common among females, and the greater tendency of girls to endorse feelings of shame and guilt suggests consideration of these early emotional patterns as gender-related vulnerabilities for such problems (Tangney, 1993). The female tendency to feel shame may be exacerbated during puberty, particularly because girls have more negative evaluations of their bodily changes than boys at this time (Brooks-Gunn, 1988). Again, longitudinal research is needed.

The Overregulation of Shame and Guilt

Children with serious conduct problems and adults with antisocial personality disorder are often thought to lack guilt or shame (Damon, 1988). Young children who do not experience guilt in response to their misbehaviors may not internalize moral standards and a sense of conscience, which in turn could lead to acting out against others (Hoffman, 1982; Zahn-Waxler & Robinson, 1995). This pattern is a potential formula for conduct disorder and, later, antisocial personality disorder. Indeed, children with conduct problems are more likely to report that transgressors do not feel guilt while committing aggressive acts than are children without conduct problems (Cimbora & McIntosh, 2003; Eisikovits & Sagi, 1982).

The relation between shame and conduct problems may be more complex. One study found that embarrassment (a self-conscious emotion similar to shame) was less likely to occur in adolescent males with conduct disorder (Keltner et al., 1995). However, other research shows relations between shame and anger-proneness, resentment, and aggression, particularly indirect aggression (Tangney, Wagner, Fletcher, et al., 1992; Wicker, Payne, & Morgan, 1983). Thus, shame may engender two responses: an embarrassed response involving hiding from others, which may protect one from externalizing problems, and a rage response involving directing negative feelings toward others, which may lead to externalizing problems or relational aggression (Crick & Zahn-Waxler, 2003).

EMOTION REGULATION PATTERNS AND VULNERABILITY TO PSYCHOPATHOLOGY: A TRANSACTIONAL PERSPECTIVE

A central premise of our discussion is that maladaptive patterns of emotion regulation in childhood contribute to the development of psychopathology. It is not our position that all forms of psychopathology are caused by emotional problems. Rather, emotional functioning is an aspect of all psychological functioning, and, we believe, early signs of deviation in emotional functioning may precede the development of a formal disorder. Before children reach first grade, they have had thousands of emotional experiences and have developed consistent patterns of regulating emotions. With origins in early childhood and the tendency for patterns of emotional reactions and regulation to become fairly automatic, emotion regulation often occurs out of a person's awareness. In fact, clinicians expend considerable thought and effort helping clients understand or modify such highly patterned responses (Greenberg & Safran, 1987; Russell & Shirk, 1998).

Although much remains to be known about how emotion regulation early in life might lead to psychopathology, considerable research is under way to explore these links. The transactional model is particularly useful for conceptualizing the role of emotion regulation in the development of psychopathology (Cummings, Davies, & Campbell, 2000; Sameroff, 1975, 2000). From this perspective, environmental stresses (see Grant & McMahon, Chapter 1 in this volume, for discussion of stress) interact with an individual's regulatory style in reciprocal fashion to determine outcomes such as adjustment or psychopathology. Stressors (a) influence emotion regulation style (e.g., a child hitting another child at school after seeing his parents hit each other), (b) are influenced by an individual's emotion regulation style (e.g., a child who tends to be angry or irritable elicits more physical punishment from his or her parents), and (c) interact with an individual's emotion regulation style over time (e.g., a child copes with his or her parents' divorce by expressing extreme anger and acting out, leading to an expression of externalizing problems).

In infancy and early childhood, one major stressor is caregiver dysfunction (Goodman & Gotlib, 1999). A caregiver's capacity to be emotionally available and exert developmentally sensitive control is clearly crucial to a child's healthy development (Collins, Maccoby, Steinberg, & Hetherington, 2000; Parke, 2004). Moreover, a caregiver's skillfulness must be sensitive to the particular needs of the child (Kochanska, 1995; Thomas & Chess, 1977). That is, children enter their worlds with different styles and needs and require different treatment from their caregivers. A transactional model assumes that there must be an adequate fit between the caregiving context and the child to lead to positive developmental outcomes. For example, temperamental difficultness is less likely to lead to externalizing symptoms in the presence of caregivers who set flexible, appropriate limits on child misbehavior (Bates et al., 1998).

A child may face any number of stressors in the course of development. Within the family, research has focused on marital conflict and divorce (Davies & Cummings, 1994), domestic violence between parents (Jouriles, Norwood, McDonald, & Peters, 2001), death of a parent (Garmezy & Rutter, 1984), poverty (McLoyd, 1998), and physical and sexual abuse or neglect of children (Cicchetti & Toth, 1997). These stressors have direct consequences for a child's ability to engage in flexible emotion regulation. For example, physically abused children are more hypersensitive than other children to angry facial displays (Pollak & Tolley-Schell, 2003). This sensitivity is adaptive in a family where anger leads to danger, but it can also lead to other problems, such as overinterpretation of peers' behavior as hostile (Crick & Dodge, 1994).

At the start of adolescence, there are new stressors, including the onset of puberty and associated bodily changes and the transition to junior high school, which can lead to adjustment problems or the emergence of disorders for certain youth (Brooks-Gunn, 1988; Eccles et al., 1993). The adolescent must also negotiate the transition to adulthood in terms of roles and relationships (Arnett, 2000). Each of these potential stressors during adolescence may reciprocally influence and be influenced by emotion regulation patterns, helping to shape an adolescent's emotional style and possibly exacerbating emotional risk factors, leading to psychopathology.

SUMMARY

In sum, emotional regulation is central to conceptualizations of the development of psychopathology. The key to a healthy emotional life is balance and the capacity to modulate one's emotional experience and behavior with situational demands and constraints in culturally acceptable ways. Dysregulated emotional functioning, involving difficulty engaging in flexible regulation of emotion that coordinates the individual's goals with the needs of others and the standards of one's social group, is one pathway to the development of psychopathology. Biological stressors and challenging life experiences strain the preadapted system of emotional functioning and can set the stage for vulnerability. These strains can affect one, but often more than one, emotion system. They can also exacerbate preexisting emotional vulnerabilities, such as temperamental proneness to anger or fear. We are confident that future research on the role of emotion will advance our understanding of how child-environment transactions influence the development of psychopathology. The evidence that exists suggests that psychological impairment is closely tied to early patterns of emotion regulation that are exaggerated, inflexible, or otherwise poorly regulated.

REFERENCES

Abe, J. A., & Izard, C. E. (1999). The developmental functions of emotions: An analysis in terms of differential emotions theory. *Cognition and Emotion, 13,* 523–549.

Abela, J. R. Z. (2001). The hopelessness theory of depression: A test of the diathesis-stress and causal mediation components in third and seventh grade children. *Journal of Abnormal Child Psychology, 29,* 241–261.

Abraham, K. (1968). The influence of oral-eroticism on character-formation. In *Selected papers of Karl Abraham* (D. Bryan & A. Strachey, Trans.). London: Hogarth Press. (Original work published 1924)

Abramson, L. Y., Metalsky, L. B., & Alloy, L. B. (1989). Hopelessness depression: A theory-based subtype of depression. *Psychological Review, 96,* 358–372.

Allen, J. P., Hauser, S. T., Eickholt, C., Bell, K. L., & O'Connor, T. (1994). Autonomy and relatedness in family interactions as predictors of expressions of negative adolescent affect. *Journal of Research on Adolescence, 4,* 535–552.

American Psychiatric Association. (1994). *Diagnostic and statistical manual of mental disorders* (4th ed.). Washington, DC: Author.

Arnett, J. J. (2000). Emerging adulthood: A theory of development from the late teens through the twenties. *American Psychologist, 55,* 469–480.

Arsenio, W. F., Cooperman, S., & Lover, A. (2000). Affective predictors of preschoolers' aggression and peer acceptance: Direct and indirect effects. *Developmental Psychology, 36,* 438–448.

Barkley, R. A. (1997). Behavioral inhibition, sustained attention, and executive functions: Constructing a unified theory of ADHD. *Psychological Bulletin, 121,* 65–94.

Barkley, R. A. (2003). Attention-deficit/hyperactivity disorder. In E. J. Mash & R. A. Barkley (Eds.), *Child psychopathology* (2nd ed., pp. 75–143). New York: Guilford Press.

Barkley, R. A. (2004). Attention-deficit/hyperactivity disorder and self-regulation: Taking an evolutionary perspective on executive functioning. In R. F. Baumeister & K. D. Vohs (Eds.), *Handbook of self-regulation: Research, theory, and applications* (pp. 301–323). New York: Guilford Press.

Barrett, K. C., & Campos, J. J. (1987). Perspectives on emotional development: II. A functionalist approach to emotions. In J. Osofsky (Ed.), *Handbook of infant development* (pp. 555–578). New York: Wiley.

Bates, J. E., Pettit, G. S., Dodge, K. A., & Ridge, B. (1998). The interaction of temperamental resistance to control and restrictive parenting in the development of externalizing behavior. *Developmental Psychology, 34,* 51–67.

Biaggio, M. K., & Godwin, W. H. (1987). Relation of depression to anger and hostility constructs. *Psychological Reports, 61,* 87–90.

Biederman, J., Rosenbaum, J. F., Hirshfeld, D. R., Faraone, S., Bouldec, E. A., Gersten, M., et al. (1990). Psychiatric correlates of behavioral inhibition in young children of parents with and without psychiatric disorders. *Archives of General Psychiatry, 47,* 21–26.

Block, J., Gjerde, P. F., & Block, J. H. (1991). Personality antecedents of depressive tendencies in 18-year-olds: A prospective study. *Journal of Personality and Social Psychology, 60,* 726–738.

Blumberg, S., & Izard, C. E. (1985). Affective and cognitive characteristics of depression in 10- and 11-year-old children. *Journal of Personality and Social Psychology, 49,* 194–202.

Broderick, P. C. (1998). Early adolescent gender differences in the use of ruminative and distracting coping strategies. *Journal of Early Adolescence, 18,* 173–191.

Brody, L. R., & Hall, J. A. (1993). Gender and emotion. In M. Lewis & J. M. Haviland (Eds.), *Handbook of emotions* (pp. 447–460). New York: Guilford Press.

Brooks-Gunn, J. (1988). Antecedents and consequences of variations in girls' maturational timing. *Journal of Adolescent Health Care, 9,* 365–373.

Brown, T. A., Chorpita, B. F., & Barlow, D. H. (1998). Structural relationships among dimensions of the DSM-IV anxiety and mood disorders and dimensions of negative affect, positive affect, and autonomic arousal. *Journal of Abnormal Psychology, 107,* 179–192.

Burhans, K. K., & Dweck, C. S. (1991). Helplessness in early childhood: The role of contingent worth. *Child Development, 66,* 1719–1738.

Campos, J. J., Mumme, D. L., Kermonian, R., & Campos, R. G. (1994). A functionalist perspective on the nature of emotion. In N. A. Fox (Ed.), The development of emotion regulation and dysregulation: Biological and behavioral considerations. *Monographs of the Society for Research in Child Development, 59*(2–3, Serial No. 240), 7–24.

Carey, T. C., Finch, A. J., & Carey, M. P. (1991). Relation between differential emotions and depression in emotionally disturbed children and adolescents. *Journal of Consulting and Clinical Psychology, 59,* 594–597.

Casey, R. J. (1996). Emotional competence in children with externalizing and internalizing disorders. In M. Lewis & M. W. Sullivan (Eds.), *Emotional development in atypical children* (pp. 161–183). Mahwah, NJ: Lawrence Erlbaum.

Caspi, A., Henry, B., McGee, R. O., Moffitt, T. E., & Silva, P. A. (1995). Temperamental origins of child and adolescent behavior problems: From age three to fifteen. *Child Development, 66,* 55–68.

Cassidy, J. (1994). Emotion regulation: Influences of attachment relationships. In N. A. Fox (Ed.), The development of emotion regulation: Biological and behavioral considerations. *Monographs of the Society for Research in Child Development, 59*(2–3, Serial No. 240), 73–100.

Chaplin, T. M. (2004). *Relations between emotional style and depressive symptoms in older adolescents.* Unpublished manuscript.

Chaplin, T. M., Cole, P. M., & Zahn-Waxler, C. (in press). Parental socialization of emotion expression: Gender differences and relations to child adjustment. *Emotion.*

Chorpita, B. F., Albano, A. M., & Barlow, D. H. (1998). The structure of negative emotions in a clinical sample of children and adolescents. *Journal of Abnormal Psychology, 107,* 74–85.

Cicchetti, D., Ackerman, B. P., & Izard, C. E. (1995). Emotions and emotion regulation in developmental psychopathology. *Development and Psychopathology, 7,* 1–10.

Cicchetti, D., Ganiban, J., & Barnett, D. (1991). Contributions from the study of high-risk populations to understanding the development of emotion regulation. In J. Garber & K. Dodge (Eds.), *The development of emotion regulation and dysregulation* (pp. 15–48). New York: Cambridge University Press.

Cicchetti, D., & Toth, S. (Eds.). (1997). *Rochester symposium on developmental psychology: Vol. 8. Developmental perspectives on trauma: Theory, research, and intervention.* Rochester, NY: University of Rochester Press.

Cimbora, D. M., & McIntosh, D. N. (2003). Emotional responses to antisocial acts in adolescent males with conduct disorder: A link to affective morality. *Journal of Clinical Child and Adolescent Psychology, 32,* 296–301.

Clark, L. A., & Watson, D. (1991). Tripartite model of anxiety and depression: Psychometric evidence and taxonomic implications. *Journal of Abnormal Psychology, 100,* 316–336.

Clark, L. A., Watson, D., & Mineka, S. (1994). Temperament, personality, and the mood and anxiety disorders. *Journal of Abnormal Psychology, 103,* 103–116.

Coan, J. A., & Allen, J. J. B. (2004). Frontal EEG asymmetry as a moderator and mediator of emotion. *Biological Psychiatry, 67,* 183–218.

Cole, P. M., Michel, M. K., & Teti, L. O. (1994). The development of emotion regulation and dysregulation: A clinical perspective. In N. A. Fox (Ed.), The development of emotion regulation: Biological and behavioral considerations. *Monographs of the Society for Research in Child Development, 59*(2–3, Serial No. 240), 73–100.

Cole, P. M., Teti, L. O., & Zahn-Waxler, C. (2003). Mutual emotion regulation and the stability of conduct problems between preschool and early school age. *Development and Psychopathology, 15,* 1–18.

Cole, P. M., Zahn-Waxler, C., Fox, N. A., Usher, B. A., & Welsh, J. D. (1996). Individual differences in emotion regulation and behavior problems in preschool children. *Journal of Abnormal Psychology, 105,* 518–529.

Cole, P. M., Zahn-Waxler, C., & Smith, K. D. (1994). Expressive control during a disappointment: Variations related to preschoolers' behavior problems. *Developmental Psychology, 30,* 835–846.

Collins, W. A., Maccoby, E. E., Steinberg, L., & Hetherington, E. M. (2000). Contemporary research on parenting: The case for nature and nurture. *American Psychologist, 55,* 218–232.

Crick, N., & Dodge, K. A. (1994). A review and reformulation of social information–processing mechanisms in children's social adjustment. *Psychological Bulletin, 115,* 74–101.

Crick, N., & Zahn-Waxler, C. (2003). The development of psychopathology in males and females: Current progress and future challenges. *Development and Psychopathology, 15,* 719–742.

Cummings, E. M., Davies, P. T., & Campbell, S. B. (Eds.). (2000). *Developmental psychopathology and family process: Theory, research, and clinical implications.* New York: Guilford Press.

Dadds, M. R., Sanders, M. R., Morrison, M., & Rebgetz, M. (1992). Childhood depression and conduct disorder: II. An analysis of family interaction patterns in the home. *Journal of Abnormal Psychology, 101,* 505–513.

Damon, W. (1988). Socialization and individuation. In G. Handel (Ed.), *Childhood socialization* (pp. 3–10). Hawthorne, NY: Aldine de Gruyter.

Darwin, C. (1872). *The expression of emotions in man and animals.* Chicago: University of Chicago Press.

Davidson, R. J. (1998). Affective style and affective disorders: Perspectives from affective neuroscience. *Cognition and Emotion, 12,* 307–320.

Davidson, R. J. (2000). Affective style, psychopathology, and resilience: Brain mechanisms and plasticity. *American Psychologist, 55,* 1196–1214.

Davidson, R. J., & Fox, N. A. (1988). Cerebral asymmetry and emotion: Development and individual differences. In S. Segalowitz & D. Molfese (Eds.), *Developmental implications of brain lateralization* (pp. 191–206). New York: Guilford Press.

Davidson, R. J., Marshall, J. R., Tomraken, A. J., & Henriques, J. B. (2000). While a phobic waits: Regional brain electrical and autonomic activity in social phobics during anticipation of public speaking. *Biological Psychiatry, 47,* 85–95.

Davidson, R. J., Scherer, K. R., & Goldsmith, H. H. (2003). *Handbook of affective sciences*. Oxford, UK: Oxford University Press.

Davies, P. T., & Cummings, E. M. (1994). Marital conflict and child adjustment: An emotional security hypothesis. *Psychological Bulletin, 116,* 387–411.

Davis, B., Sheeber, L., Hops, H., & Tildesley, E. (2000). Adolescent responses to depressive parental behaviors in problem-solving interactions: Implications for depressive symptoms. *Journal of Abnormal Child Psychology, 28,* 451–465.

Dawson, G., Ashman, S. B., Hessl, D., Spieker, S., Frey, K., Panagiotides, H., et al. (2001). Autonomic and brain electrical activity in securely- and insecurely-attached infants of depressed mothers. *Infant Behavior and Development, 24,* 135–149.

Dawson, G., Frey, K., Panagiotides, H., Yamada, E., Hessl, D., & Osterling, J. (1999). Infants of depressed mothers exhibit atypical frontal electrical brain activity during interactions with mother and with a familiar, nondepressed adult. *Child Development, 70,* 1058–1066.

Denham, S. A., Workman, E., Cole, P. M., Weissbrod, C., Kendziora, K. T., & Zahn-Waxler, C. (2000). Prediction of externalizing behavior problems from early to middle childhood: The role of parental socialization and emotion expression. *Development and Psychopathology, 12,* 23–45.

Dumas, J. E., LaFreniere, P. J., & Serketich, W. J. (1995). "Balance of power": A transactional analysis of control in mother-child dyads involving socially competent, aggressive, and anxious children. *Journal of Abnormal Psychology, 104,* 104–113.

Eccles, J., Midgley, C., Buchanan, C. M., Wigfield, A., Reuman, D., & MacIver, D. (1993). Development during adolescence: The impact of stage/environment fit. *American Psychologist, 48,* 90–101.

Eisenberg, N., Cumberland, A., Spinrad, T. L., Fabes, R. A., Shepard, S. A., Reiser, M., et al. (2001). The relations of regulation and emotionality to children's externalizing and internalizing problem behavior. *Child Development, 72,* 1112–1134.

Eisenberg, N., Fabes, R. A., Minore, D., Mathy, R., Hanish, L. D., & Brown, B. (1994). Children's enacted interpersonal strategies: Their relations to social behavior and negative emotionality. *Merrill-Palmer Quarterly, 40,* 212–232.

Eisenberg, N., Fabes, R. A., Shepard, S. A., Murphy, B. C., Guthrie, I. K., Jones, S., et al. (1997). Contemporaneous and longitudinal prediction of children's social functioning from regulation and emotionality. *Child Development, 68,* 642–664.

Eisenberg, N., Schaller, M., Fabes, R., Bustamante, D., Mathy, R., Shell, R., et al. (1988). Differentiation of personal distress and sympathy in children and adults. *Developmental Psychology, 24,* 766–775.

Eisikovits, Z., & Sagi, A. (1982). Moral development and discipline encounter in delinquent and nondelinquent adolescents. *Journal of Youth and Adolescence, 11,* 217–230.

Ekman, P. (1992). An argument for basic emotions. *Cognition and Emotion, 6,* 169–200.

Feshbach, N. D., & Feshbach, S. (1969). The relationship between empathy and aggression in two age groups. *Developmental Psychology, 1,* 102–107.

Field, T., Fox, N., Pickens, J., & Nawrocki, R. (1995). Relative right frontal activation in 3- to 6-month-old infants of "depressed" mothers. *Developmental Psychology, 31,* 358–363.

Folkman, S., & Moskowitz, J. T. (2000). Stress, positive emotion, and coping. *Current Directions in Psychological Science, 9,* 115–118.

Fowles, D. C. (1980). The three arousal model: Implications of Gray's two-factor learning theory for heart rate, electrodermal activity, and psychopathy. *Psychophysiology, 17,* 87–104.

Frick, P. J., Cornell, A. H., Barry, C. T., Bodin, S. D., & Dane, H. E. (2003). Callous unemotional traits and conduct problems in the prediction of conduct problem severity, aggression, and self-report of delinquency. *Journal of Abnormal Child Psychology, 31,* 457–470.

Frijda, N. (1986). *The emotions: Studies in emotion and social interaction.* New York: Cambridge University Press.

Garber, J., & Dodge, K. A. (1991). *The development of emotion regulation and dysregulation.* New York: Cambridge University Press.

Garmezy, N., & Rutter, M. (Eds.). (1984). *Stress, coping, and development in children.* Baltimore: Johns Hopkins University Press.

Geller, B., Williams, M., Zimerman, B., Frazier, J., Beringer, L., & Warner, K. L. (1998). Prepubertal and early adolescent bipolarity differentiate from ADHD by manic symptoms, grandiose delusions, ultra-rapid or ultradian cycling. *Journal of Affective Disorders, 51,* 81–91.

Geller, B., Zimerman, B., Williams, M., DelBello, M. P., Frazier, J., & Beringer, L. (2002). Phenomenology of prepubertal and early adolescent bipolar disorder: Examples of elated mood, grandiose behaviors, decreased need for sleep, racing thoughts and hypersexuality. *Journal of Child & Adolescent Psychopharmacology, 12,* 3–9.

Gilligan, C. (1982). *In a different voice: Psychological theory and women's development.* Cambridge, MA: Harvard University Press.

Gilliom, M., Shaw, D. S., Beck, J. E., Schonberg, M. A., & Lukon, J. L. (2002). Anger regulation in disadvantaged preschool boys: Strategies, antecedents, and the development of self-control. *Developmental Psychology, 38,* 222–235.

Glasberg, R., & Aboud, F. E. (1982). Keeping one's distance from sadness: Children's self-reports of emotional experience. *Developmental Psychology, 18,* 287–293.

Goleman, D. (2003). *Destructive emotions: How we can overcome them.* New York: Bantam.

Goodman, S. H., & Gotlib, I. H. (1999). Risk for psychopathology in the children of depressed mothers: A developmental model for understanding mechanisms of transmission. *Psychological Review, 106,* 458–490.

Gray, J. A. (1987). The neuropsychology of emotion and personality. In S. M. Stahl & S. D. Iverson (Eds.), *Cognitive neurochemistry* (pp. 171–190). London: Oxford University Press.

Greenberg, L. S., & Safran, J. D. (1987). *Emotion in psychotherapy: Affect, cognition, and the process of change.* New York: Guilford Press.

Gross, J. J. (1999). Emotion regulation: Past, present and future. *Cognition and Emotion, 13,* 551–573.

Gross, J. J., & John, O. P. (2003). Individual differences in two emotion regulation processes: Implications for affect, relationships, and well-being. *Journal of Personality and Social Psychology, 85,* 348–362.

Halberstadt, A. G., Denham, S. A., & Dunsmore, J. C. (2001). Affective social competence. *Social Development, 10,* 79–119.

Hammen, C., & Rudolph, K. (1996). Childhood depression. In E. J. Mash & R. A. Barkley (Eds.), *Child psychopathology* (pp. 153–195). New York: Guilford Press.

Hankin, B. L., & Abramson, L. Y. (2001). Development of gender differences in depression: An elaborated cognitive vulnerability-transactional stress theory. *Psychological Bulletin, 127,* 773–796.

Harmon-Jones, E. (2003). Anger and the behavioral approach system. *Personality and Individual Differences, 35,* 995–1005.

Hastings, P. D., Zahn-Waxler, C., Robinson, J., Usher, B., & Bridges, D. (2000). The development of concern for others in children with behavior problems. *Developmental Psychology, 36,* 531–546.

Hay, D. F., & Pawlby, S. (2003). Prosocial development in relation to children's and mothers' psychological problems. *Child Development, 74,* 1314–1327.

Henriques, J. B., & Davidson, R. J. (1991). Left frontal hypoactivation in depression. *Journal of Abnormal Psychology, 100,* 535–545.

Higgins, E. T. (1987). Self-discrepancy: A theory relating self and affect. *Psychological Review, 94,* 319–340.

Hirschfeld, D. R., Rosenbaum, J. F., Biederman, J., Bolduc, E. A., Faraone, S. V., & Snidman, N. (1992). Stable behavioral inhibition and its association with anxiety disorder. *Journal of the American Academy of Child and Adolescent Psychiatry, 31,* 103–111.

Hochschild, A. R. (1983). *The managed heart.* Berkeley: University of California Press.

Hoffman, M. L. (1982). Development of prosocial motivation: Empathy and guilt. In N. Eisenberg (Ed.), *The development of prosocial behavior* (pp. 281–313). New York: Academic Press.

Hughes, C., White, A., Sharpen, J., & Dunn, J. (2000). Antisocial, angry, and unsympathetic: "Hard-to-manage" preschoolers' peer problems and possible cognitive influences. *Journal of Child Psychology and Psychiatry, 41,* 169–179.

Izard, C. E. (1972). *Patterns of emotions: A new analysis of anxiety and depression.* New York: Academic Press.

Izard, C. E. (1977). *Human emotions.* New York: Plenum Press.

Izard, C. E., & Ackerman, B. P. (2000). Motivational, organizational and regulatory functions of discrete emotions. In M. Lewis & J. M. Haviland (Eds.), *Handbook of emotions* (2nd ed., pp. 253–264). New York: Guilford Press.

Izard, C. E., & Malatesta, C. Z. (1987). Perspectives on emotional development: I. Differential emotions theory of early emotional development. In J. D. Osofsky (Ed.), *Handbook of infant development* (2nd ed., pp. 494–554). New York: Wiley-Interscience.

Jamison, K. R. (1993). *Touched with fire: Manic-depressive illness and the artistic temperament.* New York: Free Press.

Jones, N. A., Field, T., Fox, N. A., Davalos, M., & Gomez, C. (2001). EEG during different emotions in 10-month-old infants of depressed mothers. *Journal of Reproductive and Infant Psychology, 19,* 295–312.

Jouriles, E. N., Norwood, W. D., McDonald, R., & Peters, B. (2001). Domestic violence and child adjustment. In J. H. Grych & F. D. Fincham (Eds.), *Interparental conflict and child development: Theory, research, and applications* (pp. 315–336). New York: Cambridge University Press.

Kagan, J. (1994). On the nature of emotion. In N. A. Fox (Ed.), The development of emotion regulation and dysregulation: Biological and behavioral considerations. *Monographs of the Society for Research in Child Development, 59*(2–3, Serial No. 240), 7–24.

Kagan, J., Reznick, J. S., & Snidman, N. (1987). The physiology and psychology of behavioral inhibition in children. *Child Development, 58,* 1459–1473.

Kagan, J., Reznick, J. S., & Snidman, N. (1988). Biological bases of childhood shyness. *Science, 240,* 167–171.

Kasch, K. L., Rottenberg, J., Arnow, B. A., & Gotlib, I. H. (2002). Behavioral activation and inhibition systems and the severity and course of depression. *Journal of Abnormal Psychology, 111,* 589–597.

Keenan, K. (2000). Emotion dysregulation as a risk factor for child psychopathology. *Clinical Psychology: Science and Practice, 7,* 418–434.

Keenan, K., & Shaw, D. (1997). Developmental and social influences on young girls' early problem behaviors. *Psychological Bulletin, 121,* 95–113.

Keltner, D., & Gross, J. J. (1999). Functional accounts of emotions. *Cognition and Emotion, 13,* 467–480.

Keltner, D., Moffitt, T. E., & Stouthamer-Loeber, M. (1995). Facial expressions of emotion and psychopathology in adolescent boys. *Journal of Abnormal Psychology, 104,* 644–652.

Kitayama, S., Markus, H. R., & Matsumoto, H. (1995). Culture, self, and emotion: A cultural perspective on "self-conscious" emotions. In J. P. Tangney & K. W. Fischer (Eds.), *Self conscious emotions: The psychology of shame, guilt, embarrassment, and pride* (pp. 439–464). New York: Guilford Press.

Kobak, R., & Ferenz-Gillies, R. (1995). Emotion regulation and depressive symptoms during adolescence: A functionalist perspective. *Development & Psychopathology, 7,* 183–192.

Kochanska, G. (1995). Children's temperament, mothers' discipline, and security of attachment: Multiple pathways to emerging internalization. *Child Development, 66,* 597–615.

Kochanska, G., DeVet, K., Goldman, M., Murray, K., & Putnam, S. P. (1994). Maternal reports of conscience development and temperament in young children. *Child Development, 65,* 852–868.

Kraaij, V., Garnefski, N., de Wilde, E. J., Dijkstra, A., Gebhardt, W., Maes, S., et al. (2003). Negative life events and depressive symptoms in late adolescence: Bonding and cognitive coping as vulnerability factors? *Journal of Youth and Adolescence, 32,* 185–193.

Kring, A. M., & Bachorowski, J. (1999). Emotions and psychopathology. *Cognition and Emotion, 13,* 575–599.

Lahey, B. B., Hart, E. L., Pliszka, S., Applegate, B., & McBurnett, K. (1993). Neurophysiological correlates of conduct disorder: A rationale and a review of research. *Journal of Clinical Child Psychology, 22,* 141–153.

Leadbeater, B. J., Kuperminc, G. P., Blatt, S. J., & Hertzog, C. (1999). A multivariate model of gender differences in adolescents' internalizing and externalizing problems. *Developmental Psychology, 35,* 1268–1282.

LeDoux, J. (1996). *The emotional brain: The mysterious underpinnings of emotional life.* New York: Simon & Schuster.

Lewis, H. B. (1971). *Shame and guilt in neurosis.* New York: International Universities Press.

Lewis, M. (2000). Self-conscious emotions: Embarrassment, pride, shame, and guilt. In M. Lewis and J. M. Haviland-Jones (Eds.), *Handbook of emotions* (pp. 573–691). New York: Guilford Press.

Liew, J., Eisenberg, N., Losoya, S. H., Fabes, R. A., Guthrie, I. K., & Murphy, B. C. (2003). Children's physiological indices of empathy and their socioemotional adjustment: Does caregivers' expressivity matter? *Journal of Family Psychology, 17,* 584–597.

Lonigan, C. J., Vasey, M. W., Phillips, B. M., & Hazen, R. A. (2004). Temperament, anxiety, and the processing of threat-relevant stimuli. *Journal of Clinical Child and Adolescent Psychology, 33,* 8–20.

Lundy, B., Field, T., Cigales, M., & Cuadra, A. (1997). Vocal and facial expression matching in infants of mothers with depressive symptoms. *Infant Mental Health Journal, 18,* 265–273.

Lykken, D. T. (1995). *The antisocial personalities.* Hillsdale, NJ: Lawrence Erlbaum.

Magai, C., & McFadden, S. (1995). *The role of emotion in social and personality development.* New York: Plenum.

Malatesta, C. Z., & Wilson, A. (1988). Emotion cognition interaction in personality development: A discrete emotions functionalist analysis. *British Journal of Social Psychology, 27,* 91–112.

Markus, H. R., & Kitayama, S. (1991). Culture and the self: Implications for cognition, emotion, and motivation. *Psychological Review, 98,* 224–253.

McLoyd, V. C. (1998). Socioeconomic disadvantage and child development. *American Psychologist, 53,* 185–204.

Melnick, S. M., & Hinshaw, S. P. (2000). Emotion regulation and parenting in ADHD and comparison boys: Linkages with social behaviors and peer preference. *Journal of Abnormal Child Psychology, 28,* 73–86.

Miller, P. A., & Eisenberg, N. (1988). The relation of empathy to aggressive and externalizing/antisocial behavior. *Psychological Bulletin, 103,* 324–344.

Mineka, S., Watson, D., & Clark, L. (1998). Comorbidity of anxiety and unipolar mood disorders. *Annual Review of Psychology, 49,* 377–412.

Nolen-Hoeksema, S., & Girgus, J. S. (1994). The emergence of gender differences in depression during adolescence. *Psychological Bulletin, 115,* 424–443.

Nolen-Hoeksema, S., Larson, J., & Grayson, C. (1999). Explaining the gender difference in depressive symptoms. *Journal of Personality and Social Psychology, 77,* 1061–1072.

Nottelmann, E. D., Biederman, J., Birmaher, B., Carlson, G. A., Chang, K. D., Fenton, W. S., et al. (2001). National Institute of Mental Health Research Roundtable on Prepubertal Bipolar Disorder. *Journal of the American Academy of Child and Adolescent Psychiatry, 40,* 871–878.

Ollendick, T. H., Yule, W., & Ollier, K. (1991). Fears in British children and their relationship to manifest anxiety and depression. *Journal of Child Psychology and Psychiatry and Allied Disciplines, 32,* 321–331.

Ornitz, E. M., Gabikian, P., Russel, A. T., Guthrie, D., Hirano, C., & Gehricke, J. (1997). Affective valence and arousal in ADHD and normal boys during a startle habituation experiment. *Journal of the American Academy of Child and Adolescent Psychiatry, 36,* 1698–1705.

Panksepp, J. (1982). Toward a general psychobiological theory of emotions. *Behavioral and Brain Sciences, 5,* 407–467.

Parke, R. D. (2004). Development in the family. *Annual Review of Psychology, 55,* 365–399.

Patterson, G. (1986). Performance models for antisocial boys. *American Psychologist, 41,* 432–444.

Plutchik, R. (1962). *The emotions: Facts, theories, and a new model.* New York: Random House.

Pollak, S. D., & Tolley-Schell, S. A. (2003). Selective attention to facial emotion in physically abused children. *Journal of Abnormal Psychology, 112,* 323–338.

Quiggle, N. L., Garber, J., Panak, W. F., & Dodge, K. A. (1992). Social information processing in aggressive and depressed children. *Child Development, 63,* 1305–1320.

Raine, A., Venables, P. H., & Mednick, S. A. (1997). Low resting heart rate at age 3 years predisposes to aggression at age 11 years: Evidence from the Mauritius Child Health Project. *Journal of the Academy of Child and Adolescent Psychiatry, 36,* 1457–1465.

Rauch, S. L., van der Kolk, B. A., Fisler, R. E., Alpert, N. M., Orr, S. P., Savage, C. R., et al. (1996). A symptom provocation study of posttraumatic stress disorder using positron emission tomography and script-driven imagery. *Archives of General Psychiatry, 53,* 380–387.

Reimer, M. S. (1996). "Sinking into the ground": The development and consequences of shame in adolescence. *Developmental Review, 16,* 321–363.

Rothbart, M. K., & Bates, J. E. (1998). Temperament. In W. Damon (Series Ed.) & N. Eisenberg (Vol. Ed.), *Handbook of child psychology: Vol. 3. Social, emotional, and personality development* (5th ed., pp. 105–176). Mahwah, NJ: Lawrence Erlbaum.

Rothbart, M. K., Posner, M. I., & Hershey, K. (1995). Temperament, attention, and developmental psychopathology. In D. Cicchetti & J. D. Cohen (Eds.), *Manual of developmental psychopathology* (Vol. 1, pp. 315–340). New York: Wiley.

Rottenberg, J., Gross, J. J., Wilhelm, F. H., Najmi, S., & Gotlib, I. H. (2002). Crying threshold and intensity in major depressive disorder. *Journal of Abnormal Psychology, 111,* 302–312.

Russell, R. L., & Shirk, S. R. (1998). Child psychotherapy process research. *Advances in Clinical Child Psychology, 20,* 93–124.

Saarni, C. (1999). *The development of emotional competence.* New York: Guilford Press.

Sameroff, A. J. (1975). Transactional models in early social relations. *Human Development, 18,* 65–69.

Sameroff, A. J. (2000). Developmental systems and psychopathology. *Development and Psychopathology, 12,* 297–312.

Sanders, M. R., Dadds, M. R., Johnston, B. M., & Cash, R. (1992). Childhood depression and conduct disorder: I. Behavioral, affective, and cognitive aspects of family problem-solving interactions. *Journal of Abnormal Psychology, 101,* 495–504.

Sanftner, J. L., Barlow, D. H., Marschall, D. E., & Tangney, J. P. (1995). The relation of shame and guilt to eating disorder symptomatology. *Journal of Social and Clinical Psychology, 14,* 315–324.

Sheeber, L., Allen, N., Davis, B., & Sorenson, E. (2000). Regulation of negative affect during mother-child problem-solving interactions: Adolescent depressive status and family processes. *Journal of Abnormal Child Psychology, 28,* 467–479.

Shields, S. (2002). *Speaking from the heart: Gender and the social meaning of emotion.* Cambridge, UK: Cambridge University Press.

Sroufe, A. L. (1996). *Emotional development: The organization of emotional life in the early years.* New York: Cambridge University Press.

Stapley, J. C., & Haviland, J. M. (1989). Beyond depression: Gender differences in normal adolescents' emotional experiences. *Sex Roles, 20,* 295–308.

Tangney, J. P. (1993). Shame and guilt. In C. G. Costello (Ed.), *Symptoms of depression* (pp. 161–180). Oxford, UK: Wiley.

Tangney, J. P., Wagner, P., Fletcher, C., & Gramzow, R. (1992). Shamed into anger? The relation of shame and guilt to anger and self-reported aggression. *Journal of Personality and Social Psychology, 62,* 669–675.

Tangney, J. P., Wagner, P., & Gramzow, R. (1992). Proneness to shame, proneness to guilt, and psychopathology. *Journal of Abnormal Psychology, 101,* 469–478.

Thomas, A., & Chess, S. (1977). *Temperament and development.* Oxford, UK: Brunner/Mazel.

Thompson, R. A., & Calkins, S. D. (1996). The double-edged sword: Emotional regulation for children at risk. *Development and Psychopathology, 8,* 163–182.

Tomkins, S. S. (1962–1991). *Affect, imagery, and consciousness* (Vols. 1–3). New York: Springer.

Vasey, M. W., & Dadds, M. R. (2001). *The developmental psychopathology of anxiety.* London: Oxford University Press.

Whalen, C. K., & Henker, B. (1985). The social worlds of hyperactive children. *Clinical Psychology Review, 5,* 447–478.

Wicker, F. W., Payne, G. C., & Morgan, R. D. (1983). Participant descriptions of guilt and shame. *Motivation and Emotion, 7,* 25–39.

Wills, T. A., Sandy, J. M., & Yaeger, A. M. (2002). Moderators of the relation between substance use level and problems: Test of a self-regulation model in middle adolescence. *Journal of Abnormal Psychology, 111,* 3–21.

World Health Organization. (1993). *The ICD-10 classification of mental and behavioral disorders: Diagnostic criteria for research.* Geneva, Switzerland: Author.

Wright, F., O'Leary, J., & Balkin, J. (1989). Shame, guilt, narcissism, and depression: Correlates and sex differences. *Psychoanalytic Psychology, 6,* 217–230.

Zahn-Waxler, C. (2001). The development of empathy, guilt, and internalization of distress: Implications for gender differences in internalizing and externalizing problems. In R. Davidson (Ed.), *Anxiety, depression, and emotion: Wisconsin Symposium on Emotion* (Vol. 1, pp. 222–265). New York: Oxford Press.

Zahn-Waxler, C., Cole, P. M., & Barrett, K. C. (1991). Guilt and empathy: Sex differences and implications for the development of depression. In J. Garber & K. A. Dodge (Eds.), *The development of emotion regulation and dysregulation* (pp. 243–272). Cambridge, UK: Cambridge University Press.

Zahn-Waxler, C., Cole, P. M., Welsh, J. D., & Fox, N. A. (1995). Psychophysiological correlates of empathy and prosocial behaviors in preschool children with behavior problems. *Development & Psychopathology, 7,* 27–48.

Zahn-Waxler, C., Klimes Dougan, B., & Slattery, M. J. (2000). Internalizing problems of childhood and adolescence: Prospects, pitfalls, and progress in understanding the development of anxiety and depression. *Development and Psychopathology, 12,* 443–466.

Zahn-Waxler, C., Kochanska, G., Krupnick, J., & McKnew, D. (1990). Patterns of guilt in children of depressed and well mothers. *Developmental Psychology, 26,* 51–59.

Zahn-Waxler, C., & Robinson, J. (1995). Empathy and guilt: Early origins of feelings of responsibility. In J. P. Tangney & K. W. Fischer (Eds.), *Self-conscious emotions: The psychology of shame, guilt, embarrassment, and pride* (pp. 143–173). New York: Guilford Press.

Zeman, J., Shipman, K., & Suveg, C. (2002). Anger and sadness regulation: Predictions to internalizing and externalizing symptoms in children. *Journal of Clinical Child and Adolescent Psychology, 31,* 393–398.

CHAPTER 4

Biological Vulnerabilities to the Development of Psychopathology

ROBERT O. PIHL AND AMÉLIE NANTEL-VIVIER

The history of psychopathology is replete with a fascination with biological explanations for various disorders. From the trepanations of early cave dwellers, in which holes were gouged in the skull; to the humoral theories of Hippocrates, circa 400 BCE; the custodial, animal-like treatment of the mentally ill of the Renaissance; the enlightened humanists period; the time of influential theorists such as Kraeplin, Freud, and Jung; and on to the present, the belief in biological mechanisms underlying pathology has existed. Nevertheless, today is not yesterday. Generally lacking even just 30 years ago was credible scientific evidence to support this specific and persistent belief. In fact, a sort of antibiological movement grew through the 1950s–1960s, and remnants of this view, which persist today, view mental illnesses as socially learned disorders treatable solely by behavioral interventions. Today, of course, the well-known vulnerability-stress model predominates as an explanation for the etiology of most disorders, representing an obvious interaction of these two historical views.

The relatively recent resurgence of biological explanations, however, has not been predicated on historical influence but rather has exploded from a cascading body of evidence driven by growth in the neurosciences. This growth, in turn, has benefited directly from powerful new scientific methodologies able to delineate the vulnerability component of the vulnerability-stress model. Discriminating biological vulnerabilities is the focus of this chapter.

NEW TECHNOLOGIES

The essence of biological studies of mental disorders is that there is an ascertainable relationship between a particular disorder and brain functioning. Measuring brain functioning is then basic. This, however, is not a simple task, and for centuries only nonfunctional measures, from the bizarre (phrenology) to the imprecise (X-rays) existed. Advances in pharmacology, neuropsychology, electrophysiology, and brain imaging are at the forefront of technologies that are prime contributors to new investigations of biological variables. Pharmacology has been the traditional route for developing biological explanations for psychopathology. Unfortunately, "miracle drugs," which implicated specific chemical systems in various disorders, seemed over time to lose their luster, as did the implicated theory as well. Recently, the manipulation of neurotransmitters in both experimental and clinical subjects by regulating amino acid precursors has resulted in the ability, for example, to dramatically decrease brain serotonin (Young, Smith, Pihl, & Ervin, 1985). Similar procedures exist for dopamine, although like many pharmacological manipulations, which are improving, specificity is an issue. Parallel developments in new drugs that are more targeted in their effects on specific aspects of a neurotransmitter system have lent support to biochemical theories, as have drugs currently in pharmaceutical company pipelines that will affect the action of genes or target a single aspect of a neurosystem's function. Neuropsychology has benefited greatly from advances in neuroimaging, because many tests have been refined to assess specific abilities—be they cognitive, motor, or perceptual—and then validated by concomitant activity in particular brain areas. Neuropsychology has been at the forefront in determining behavioral deficits in frontal lobe functioning, which is implicated in many disorders. This evolutionary "new brain" seems to have a key role in working memory, learning, response inhibition, and coordinating sensory input with responding. Further, perhaps as Luria (1980) suggested, it is this part of the brain that projects the integration of the past, present, and future so basic to controlled responding. Many neuropsychological findings have been validated by imaging technology, which in combination can determine the endophenotypes that underlie and are the precursors to various clinical disorders.

Relatively recently, there has been a dramatic growth in noninvasive methods to monitor the brain and its functioning, all of which are dependent upon the rapid processing of complex information, an impossible task before the development of microprocessors. This includes measuring the brain's electrophysiology and advanced brain imaging technologies that can show structural aspects of the brain and the level and site of activity when the individual is presented with various stimuli. Electrophysiology, involving the measurement of brain oscillations, particularly in response to prescribed tasks, has determined differential patterns of action for various pathologies. More specifically, these patterns have been shown to represent localized activity and to be heritable and linked to a range of behaviors. Nuclear magnetic resonance imaging (MRI) is a noninvasive technique that involves measuring atoms in order to obtain a detailed structural picture of the brain and specific areas. A blood oxygenation signal measured by a functional MRI (fMRI) allows the assessment of neural activity without requiring the use of radioactive substances, which are needed with positron emission tomography (PET), also a valuable, but a more invasive, procedure for measuring activity to specific brain areas. More powerful technologies are rapidly coming online. Diffusion tension imaging, for example, is an MRI procedure uniquely suited to study white matter.

Burgeoning findings in other areas also direct one to the level of biology. One example is the increasing recognition that numerous psychopathological disorders run in families; this implies the existence of genetic vulnerabilities and biological mechanisms. Questions regarding which genes or genetic material affect which biochemical processes have drawn our attention first (see Lemery & Doelger, Chapter 7 in this volume, for details on genetic vulnerabilities). Subsequent concerns about brain development and functioning and the interactions of these biological factors with stressful environmental events represent the next critical step.

NORMAL FUNCTIONING OF BRAIN AREAS AND PATHWAYS

Decades of neuropsychological research, especially with the recent technological advances, have elucidated the normal function and purpose of various brain areas and the pathways that integrate these functions together. Here, we briefly review central brain areas, pathways, and the normal psychological functions that modern neuroscience believes they serve. Understanding how these brain areas and pathways normally function and what thoughts, behaviors, and emotions they are associated with is critically important for elucidating how deficits and dysfunctions in these brain areas may create biological vulnerabilities for the development of different psychopathologies.

The frontal lobes have been broadly associated with executive cognitive functioning, which is generally understood to refer to the "ability to plan, initiate, and maintain or alter goal-directed behaviours" (Pihl, Vant, & Assaad, 2003, p. 173). This ability is dependent upon specific cognitive functions, such as attention and working memory. The prefrontal cortex area is believed to subserve the representation of goals and the means to achieve them (Miller & Cohen, 2001). More specifically, through its connections with other brain areas, the prefrontal cortex is part of an important circuitry that underlies the emergence of appropriate responses and the simultaneous inhibition of inappropriate actions (Miller & Cohen). Connections to the basal ganglia, an agglomeration of nuclei within the forebrain believed to be important in motor control, contribute to the organism's ability to show appropriate motor response and inhibition (Carlson, 2001). Simultaneous connections to temporal limbic structures ensure the affective appropriateness of the response. Davidson and colleagues (Davidson, Pizzagalli, Nitschke, & Putnam, 2002) describe this process as "affect-guided planning and anticipation" (p. 548), whereby actions expected to provide "rewards" will be pursued, and actions known to lead to "punishment" will be inhibited. Davidson et al. (2002) proposed that the left prefrontal cortex may be particularly important for the anticipation of positive outcomes and approach behaviors, whereas the right prefrontal cortex may be crucial for appropriate inhibition and withdrawal. They report that imaging studies have found the left orbital and ventral regions to be sensitive to rewards, whereas the same areas in the right hemisphere were found to be particularly sensitive to cues of punishment (Davidson et al., 2002).

As mentioned above, the frontal lobes show strong connections with temporal limbic areas such as the amygdala and the hippocampus, which are believed to be crucial for emotional responses (Carlson, 2001). The amygdala has been shown to be important for promoting vigilance and attention to novel or affectively salient stimuli, both positive and negative (Davidson et al., 2002). The amygdala is intrinsically connected to the hippocampus, which has been found to subserve memory, contextual conditioning, and stress response (Davidson et al., 2002). Upon stress, the hypothalamus, a group of nuclei located at the base of the brain (Carlson, 2001), secretes corticotropin releasing factor (CRF), which in turn triggers synthesis and release of adrenocorticotropin (ACTH) by the pituitary. ACTH then stimulates synthesis and release of glucocorticoids by the adrenal cortex (Nestler et al., 2002). The hypothalamic-pituitary-adrenal (HPA) axis has reciprocal feedback connections with the hippocampus and the amygdala (Nestler et al.), so that glucocorticoids release triggers inhibition of the HPA axis by the hippocampus. High, chronic levels of glucocorticoids have been suggested to lead to hippocampal damage in the form of reduced dendritic branching and glutamatergic dendritic spines, as well as reduced genesis of granule cell neurons (Nestler et al.). A vicious cycle may thus operate, as decreased HPA axis inhibition due to hippocampal damage would lead to increasing glucocorticoid levels, which in turn may lead to further hippocampal damage (Nestler et al.).

The prefrontal cortex, basal ganglia, and limbic structures, together with other brain areas, thus constitute an intrinsic system underlying our ability to appropriately respond to our environment. As will be described in sections of this chapter pertaining to specific disorders, functional or anatomical anomalies of these regions and their interconnections may contribute to difficulties in different spheres of functioning, such as impairments in regulating responses (e.g., motor, affective) to the environment.

CAVEATS

Unfortunately, the road to clarity of understanding is neither straight nor paved. The powerful methodologies briefly mentioned above cannot override definitional and philosophical issues seemingly fundamental to the study of mental disorders. Psychopathologies are laden with noise, replete with debate, and lacking in specificity. This issue is exemplified by Andreasen (1999), who in proposing a model for schizophrenia wrote,

> At present the most important problem in schizophrenia research is not finding the gene or localizing it in the brain and understanding its neural circuits. Our most important problem is identifying the correct target at which to aim our powerful new scientific weapons. Our most pressing problem is at the clinical level: defining what schizophrenia is. (p. 781)

Similar statements can and should be repeatedly made about most if not all definitions of mental disorders (see chapters in Part III of this volume for discussion of definitions and classifications of disorders). It is axiomatic in this area that names are bestowed, not discovered, and names have been growing at a prodigious rate. The number of disorders in the different versions of the American Psychiatric Association's (APA) *Diagnostic and Statistical Manual of Mental Disorders* (*DSM*) has grown from around 100 in 1952 to more than 360 in today's *DSM-IV-TR* (APA, 2000). That is a threefold increase, which clearly points to rampant inflation in mental disorders. Of course, an increase in definitions is expected as knowledge is gained and specificities refined. However, the fundamental question is, "Just how many disorders are there?" It is almost certain that there are not exactly 360 psychological disorders in nature. A factor analysis of 10 common mental disorders from the large, representative National Comorbidity Survey (NCS; Krueger, 1999) resulted in a three-factor fit, respectively labeled Anxious-Misery, Fear, and Externalizing. Similar results were obtained in a large, representative sample of children and adolescents (Lahey, Applegate, Waldman, Hankin, & Rick, 2004). Further, who gets hospitalized, both voluntarily and involuntarily, is less a function of diagnostic label than of the display of aggression, be it self- or other-directed (Pihl, 1995). Finally, there is the issue of comorbidity. In the two broad surveys of mental illness, more than one disorder was present in an individual 60% of the time in the National Institutes of Mental Health study (Robins & Regier, 1991) and 56% of the time in the NCS study (Kessler et al., 1994). Comorbidity is the rule with mental disorders, not the exception. This fact raises the possibility that, instead of many disorders existing, there may be a relatively small number of underlying biological processes that, through environmental interactions, result in many diverse behavioral forms.

A conundrum thus remains. In the *DSM-IV-TR,* and presumably in the *DSM-V* when it arrives, mental disorders are defined on a behavioral level, whereas disorders in general are seen in the definition of mental disorders as residing within the individual (APA, 2000). Thus, the necessary recrafting of current definitions of mental disorders must include biological factors if the unacceptable variability in current definitions is to be reduced and terminology become more meaningful. It is also axiomatic that nosology necessarily precedes etiology. Thus, it is necessary to determine which biological variables, as well as those vulnerabilities from other levels of analyses (see other chapters in Part II of this volume), are relevant to the definition of a disorder.

Studying individuals likely to develop a disorder, which should be the basis of risk research in psychopathology, provides a contemporaneous recording of events. This design thus controls for a major error in studies of psychopathologies in which findings with patients often reflect having a disorder rather than a causative factor. Put bluntly, by studying already diagnosed and treated individuals, we may learn more about the explosion than the triggering mechanisms. Studying vulnerable individuals also allows for the study of "escape" from risk processes, which can illustrate the importance of interacting variables, and heterogeneity of outcomes, where for example similar underlying biological conditions may have varying trajectories to divergent disorders depending upon interacting factors. This research also allows for the discrimination of the significance of age of onset, which is of critical importance, because most disorders are age sensitive. Finally, by assessing the development of disorders through the study of vulnerabilities, we are provided with the opportunity to elucidate feedback mechanisms, circular processes, and chain effects typically important in causation.

There are also caveats of import regarding the "new" methodologies. In the case of neuroimaging, these range from the general issue of inference to specific concerns regarding how a region of interest is selected. Regarding inference, mental and physical states are seldom measured simultaneously, because a label is hardly a mental state, and thus any connections to a disorder represent speculation. Even when testing for specific cognitive states, converging evidence of that state is required; these states are often altered with experience and context. Even specific paradigms, such as an attentional go-stop procedure, have multiple neural functioning explanations (Schall, 2004). Another problem is that the brain is active in general, and PET and fMRI results simply point to one or more areas being relatively more active than other areas. The area highlighted is labeled the region of interest. Because there is widespread activation in the brain, strong preexperiment rationale is required for selection of a specific area versus contrasting areas. Further, because the typical design in psychopathology involves group comparisons between psychiatric patients and controls, resolution is further distorted because of imperfect registration, because individual brains differ both in anatomy and function. Finally, it is important to remember that the brain is dynamic and ever-changing. The deterioration of neuroanatomy with age is well known, and more recently the negative ramifications of emotional states, pain, and drugs have been documented. In the case of stress, the release of emotion-correlated glucocorticoid hydrocortisone has been shown to be related to significant hippocampal atrophy in patients with depression (Sheline, Wang, Gado, Csernansky, & Vannier, 1996) and with posttraumatic stress disorder (Bremner et al., 1995). It thus seems likely that there are other neuropathological consequences of stress, and perhaps other emotional states. Longitudinal neuroimaging studies, for example, show progressive deterioration in brains of some schizophrenics over time, yet debate rages as to whether or not this is a primary feature of the disorder (Mathalon, Rapoport, Davis, & Krystal, 2003). From one perspective, these changes may reflect the basis of the chronicity of the disorder, whereas for others it represents concomitants such as medication histories, comorbid drug use, incidental head injury, and so forth.

The good news is that new technology is begetting newer technology at an exponential rate. MRI studies, for example, must continually be reevaluated in light of the development of increasingly more powerful scans. For example, in the future, temporal and spatial resolution will be at the level of individual neurons. Thus, the following representative reviews of biological vulnerabilities for attention deficit/hyperactivity disorder (ADHD), conduct disorder, depression, and substance abuse should be seen as current state-of-the art knowledge and theory, yet likely ephemeral and open to change with new developments. What the reviews do underscore, however, is that currently, "the brain is the game," and there exist substantial biological vulnerabilities to psychopathologies.

ATTENTION DEFICIT/ HYPERACTIVITY DISORDER

ADHD is the most prevalent of the childhood-onset psychiatric disorders. Estimated to affect between 3% and 7% of school-age children, with affected boys outnumbering affected girls by a ratio of approximately three to one (APA, 2000), it represents 50% of all referrals to child health professionals (Hale, Hariri, & McCracken, 2000; Wicks-Nelson & Israel, 2000). ADHD is a heterogeneous syndrome, with the current psychiatric nomenclature recognizing three subtypes: inattentive, hyperactive/impulsive, and combined. Comorbidity with other psychiatric disorders has been well established, with at least 50% of ADHD children receiving an additional diagnosis of oppositional defiant disorder, conduct disorder (CD), depression, anxiety, or learning disability (APA, 2000). Once considered a childhood-limited condition, ADHD is increasingly perceived as chronic, with symptoms persisting in as many as 75% of affected individuals through adulthood (Wilens, Biederman, & Spencer, 2002).

British pediatrician George Still (1902) first described ADHD symptomatology using the label of "defective moral control," which he believed was caused by subtle anomalies in the structure and activity of neurons resulting from physical illness or heredity, with minimal environmental contribution. Since then, although inattention, hyperactivity, and impulsivity have been the object of numerous categorizations and conceptualizations (Baumeister & Hawkins, 2001), brain anomalies have remained at the core of etiological models of the disorder. Researchers have sought to confirm the biological roots of ADHD using a variety of methods, such as behavioral and molecular genetics, neuropsychology, drug challenges, and investigation of environmental factors likely to affect brain structure and functioning. Although numerous neurobiological theories of ADHD have been put forward, most have focused on dysfunctions of the frontal lobes, as well as the basal ganglia and the cerebellum. This emphasis logically follows from the well-established association between frontal lobe lesions or deficits with impulsivity and executive function deficits (i.e., problems regulating responses because of impairments in attention, working memory, self-monitoring, and planning) as well as the known importance of the basal ganglia for the regulation of motor activity (Anderson, Polcari, Lowen, Renshaw, & Teicher, 2002). These impairments are congruent with the impulsivity, difficulty in planning and concentrating, and context-inappropriate hyperactive behaviors displayed by individuals described as having

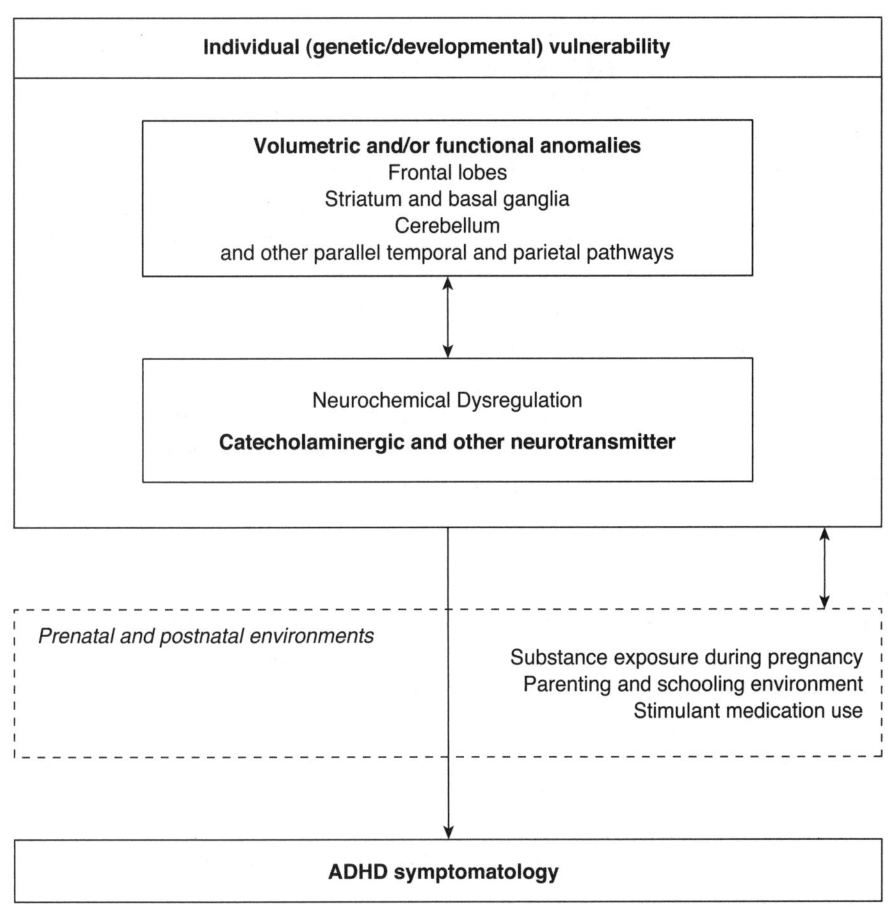

Figure 4.1 Attention Deficit/Hyperactivity Disorder

ADHD. Together with the cerebellum, the frontal lobes and the basal ganglia form a pathway that is subserved by the mesolimbic and mesocortical dopaminergic systems, neurotransmitter systems directly affected by stimulant medication (Anderson et al., 2002). Figure 4.1 summarizes the interactions between the fronto-striatal-cerebellar pathway, the dopaminergic system, and pre/postnatal moderating influences in leading to ADHD symptomatology. However, it is only within the last two decades that the available neuroimaging technologies have enabled researchers to directly investigate the specific nature of the brain anomalies putatively responsible for the disorder.

Brain Structural and Functional Abnormalities Associated With ADHD

In the largest structural imaging study of ADHD patients to date, Castellanos and colleagues (2002) investigated brain volumetric changes over time, with repetitive MRI scans at 2- to 3-year intervals, in 152 both medicated and unmedicated patients and 139 matched controls. Results indicated that at initial scan, patients exhibited smaller whole-brain volumes (see also Hill et al., 2003; Mostofsky, Cooper, Kates, Denckla, & Kaufmann, 2002, for other supportive evidence, but Filipek et al., 1997; Lyoo et al., 1996, for negative findings).

This difference was most significant for unmedicated patients. Unmedicated patients were found to have smaller total white matter volumes than medicated patients and controls. They also exhibited smaller cerebellar, temporal gray matter, and total cerebral volumes than controls. Medicated patients and controls were not significantly different on white matter volumes, but they differed for all measured gray matter regions, with ADHD patients exhibiting smaller volumes. At follow-up, differences in total and regional volumes between the groups were found to persist over time, except for the caudate nucleus, which was originally smaller in patients but did not differ in size by adolescence. Except for the caudate nucleus, growth curves were found to be lower in patients but to follow the same shape as in controls. No significant differences were found between males and females.

The study by Castellanos and colleagues (2002) is very important because it attempts to provide answers to important questions left lingering by previous research. First, the vast majority of studies on ADHD have used samples of male participants, so less information has been available on the possible sex differences in the biological underpinnings of the disorder (e.g., Baving, Laucht, & Schmidt, 1999; Ernst et al., 1994). Results by Castellanos et al. (2002) suggest that patterns of brain volumetric abnormalities in ADHD patients are similar in boys and in girls. Second, because the vast majority of patients participating in imaging studies have been exposed to stimulant medication, it becomes difficult to disentangle which brain anomaly may be attributed to the disorder and which may be attributed to medication use. Castellanos et al. (2002) suggest that stimulant medication use is not responsible for the reduced total and regional brain volumes observed in ADHD children. It may be that medication contributes to a normalization of brain volumes in ADHD children. Such findings are consistent with a growing literature suggesting that stimulant medication may help normalize metabolic activity in frontostriatal regions of ADHD patients (Hale et al., 2000). Last, there has been debate as to whether ADHD constitutes a form of developmental delay whose severity may lessen over time, or whether the disorder should be characterized as involving a stable biological vulnerability. Castellanos et al. (2002) showed, using a longitudinal design, that brain volumetric anomalies found in ADHD children are present early on and are stable over time, which is consistent with a vulnerability perspective and the increasing evidence that significant symptoms may persist through adulthood for a great number of individuals.

The structural and functional imaging literature provides support for the presence of frontal-striatal-cerebellar anomalies in ADHD patients. The majority of functional imaging studies have found evidence for frontal hypofunction in ADHD patients (Baving et al., 1999; Durston et al., 2003; Lou, Henriksen, & Bruhn, 1984; Sieg, Gaffney, Preston, & Hellings, 1995; Silberstein et al., 1998; Zametkin et al., 1990). Most investigations of the basal ganglia have focused on the caudate nucleus. Abnormalities of caudate volumes have been reported, with ADHD patients exhibiting reduced volumes (Castellanos et al., 1996; Filipek et al., 1997; Hynd et al., 1993; Mataro, Garcia-Sanchez, Junque, Estevez-Gonzalez, & Pujol, 1997). PET and fMRI studies have shown striatal activity to be reduced in ADHD patients (Durston et al.; Lou, Henriksen, Bruhn, Borner, & Nielsen, 1989; Lou, Henriksen, & Bruhn, 1990; Vaidya et al., 1998). Volumetric abnormalities of the cerebellum have been found in ADHD patients, but there are inconsistencies concerning the specific localization of these abnormalities (Berquin et al., 1998; Castellanos et al., 1996; Hill et al., 2003). In addition to the evidence showing that

ADHD stems from a dysfunction of the fronto-striatal-cerebellar pathway, ADHD is also influenced by other parallel circuits involving association areas (e.g., temporal, parietal, and occipital lobes) important to the integration of information (Sowell et al., 2003).

Neurochemistry of ADHD

In light of evidence from neuroimaging studies of frontal-striatal-cerebellar anatomic and functional anomalies in ADHD patients, as well as the neuropharmacology of stimulant medications (Kirley et al., 2002), great attention has been given to the contribution of dopaminergic functioning to the presentation of ADHD. A number of studies using single-photon emission computed tomography technology found evidence of increased striatal dopamine transporter density in ADHD patients (Dougherty et al., 1999; Krause, Dressel, Krause, Lung, & Tatsch, 2000). The evidence, however, has been somewhat mixed, with some studies finding no differences (van Dyck et al., 2002). PET studies labeling catecholamine terminals have found reduced uptake in the left medial prefrontal cortex in adults with ADHD but have also found increased uptake in the right midbrain of ADHD adolescents (Ernst, Zametkin, Matochik, Jons, & Cohen, 1998; Ernst et al., 1999). Animal studies have found that both hypo- and hyperdopaminergic states are positively linked with hyperactive behaviors (Castellanos & Tannock, 2002; Denckla, 2003). The pattern of findings thus suggests that dysregulation of the catecholaminergic system is involved in ADHD, although the nature of the dysregulation is not well defined. It is also possible that other neurotransmitter systems are involved in the etiology of the disorder. Stimulant medications, as a group, increase synaptic levels of all catecholamines. Methylphenidate, for one, inhibits reuptake of dopamine and noradrenaline (Denckla). As well, the noradrenergic system has been shown to be essential to executive functions and may be especially important for inattention symptoms (Denckla). Serotonin also may be implicated, especially for comorbid aggression. It has also been shown to play a role in executive functioning (Denckla). However, medications that affect catecholaminergic functioning are generally found to be effective, whereas those that affect primarily the serotonergic system have not (Wilens et al., 2002). In a meta-analysis of 20 genes for dopaminergic, serotonergic, and noradrenergic metabolism by Comings and colleagues (2000), noradrenergic genes were found to account for a greater proportion of the variance in the ADHD phenotype than dopamine and serotonin genes combined. It has been suggested that an anomalous balance between levels of different neurotransmitters, rather than anomalies in one neurotransmitter system per se, may contribute to the etiology of ADHD (Oades, 2002).

Conduct Disorder

One of the most common comorbid conditions observed in children with a diagnosis of ADHD is CD (see Hankin, Abela, Auerbach, McWhinnie, & Skitch, Chapter 14 of this volume, for greater discussion and description), which is defined as a persistent and recurrent disregard for social rules and the basic rights of others. In contrast to ADHD, CD, as a diagnosis, has not received as much attention from the field of brain neuroimaging. Instead, research has focused on the neuroimaging correlates of the most disruptive symptoms of CD, aggression and violence, in both normative adult samples and in individuals who show the most extreme forms of antisocial behaviors, namely murderers and psychopaths. Special attention has also been given to the contribution of serotonergic functioning, testosterone, cortisol, and sympathetic arousal to

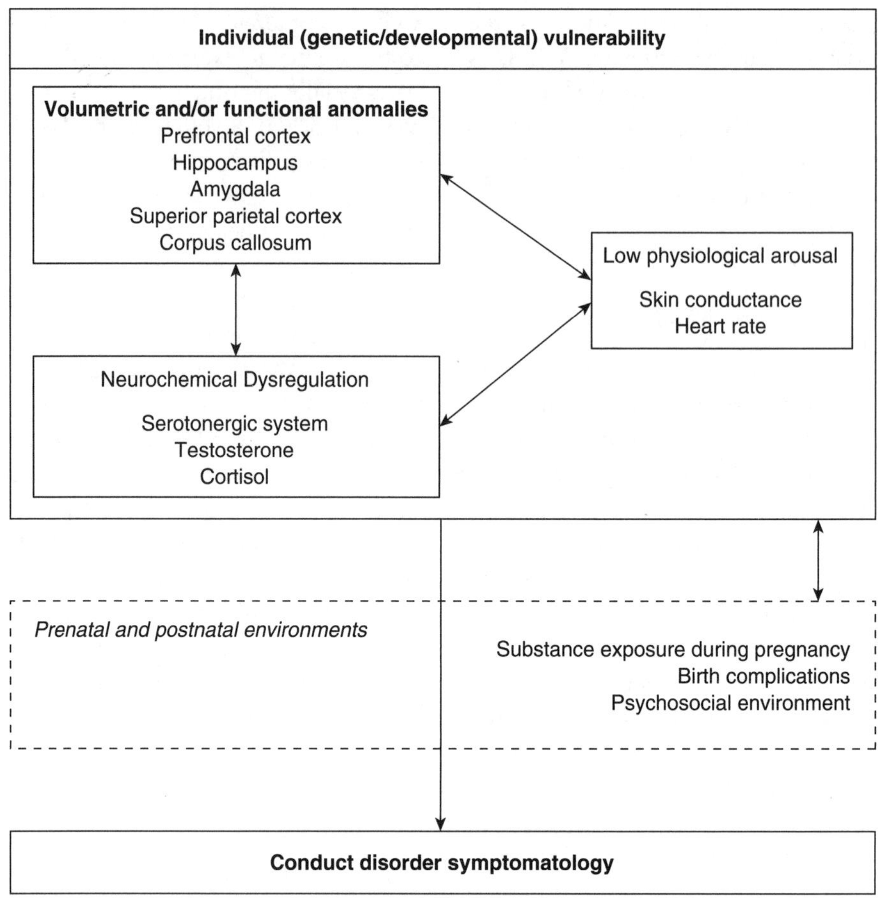

Figure 4.2 Conduct Disorder

aggression, as well as the potential role of abnormal prenatal brain development. Current conceptualizations of antisocial behavior point to dysfunctions in areas and neurochemical systems important to the regulation of impulsivity and aggression (e.g., prefrontal cortex, serotonin), as well as affect-guided anticipation (e.g., amygdala, hippocampus). Davidson, Putnam, and Larson (2000), for example, suggest that impulsive aggression results from anomalies in the threshold for activating negative affective states and the anticipation of negative consequences of aggression. Figure 4.2 illustrates how these dysfunctions interact with pre- and postnatal moderating factors in leading to symptoms of CD.

THE BRAIN AND AGGRESSION

Lesion studies have provided evidence for a link between damage to specific brain regions and behavioral symptoms similar to conduct disorders and associated antisocial behaviors. One of the earliest cases—and perhaps the most famous case—is that of Phineas Gage, who, upon an explosion at his work site, had an iron rod blown through his inferior frontal cortex, more specifically the ventromedial region. Previously a conservative and friendly young man, Gage became highly irritable and impulsive, showing little consideration for the consequences of his actions (Stuss, Gow, & Hetherington, 1992). This pattern of impulsivity, antisocial behaviors, and inability to inhibit responses resulting from damage to the inferior frontal temporal lobes has been labeled by some as "acquired sociopathy" (Damasio, Tranel, & Damasio, 1990). Damage to the amygdala, in turn, has been found to lead to symptoms reminiscent of psychopathy, such as reduced emotionality and understanding of emotions, as well as disturbed fear processing (Hoptman, 2003).

In his recent review of the neuroimaging literature of antisocial and violent behaviors, Hoptman (2003) notes that anger induction in healthy adults has been linked with increased blood flow to the left orbitofrontal cortex, the right ventral anterior cingulate cortex, and bilaterally to the anterior temporal poles, as well as to the thalamus. In violent patients and offenders, aggression levels are associated with reduced metabolism of the anterior, inferior, and medial frontal and temporal lobes, as well as of the thalamus (Hoptman). In a series of studies by Raine and colleagues (Raine et al., 1994; Raine et al., 1998; Raine, Buchsbaum, & LaCasse, 1997), accused murderers were found to have reduced metabolism of the prefrontal and superior parietal cortex, as well as the angular gyrus and corpus callosum. Abnormal functional asymmetry of the amygdala, thalamus, and medial temporal lobe were also observed. Reductions of prefrontal activity were more pronounced in individuals whose crime could be described as impulsive (Raine et al., 1998). It has been suggested that hypometabolism may be most pronounced in criminals with a positive psychosocial background (e.g., from relatively affluent socioeconomic conditions, intact homes, with absence of deprivation or abuse) (Combalbert, Bret-Dibat, & Favard, 2002; Raine, 2002). More recently, Soderstrom et al. (2002) observed a negative correlation between right frontal and temporal blood flow and scores on the personality dimension of a psychopathy interview (Factor 1 of the Psychopathy Checklist-Revised) in violent offenders. Raine and colleagues (2003) observed increased interhemispheric connectivity in a study of the corpus callosum in psychopathic, antisocial individuals. The functional anomalies observed in violent, antisocial individuals appear to be accompanied by structural anomalies. Raine, Lencz, Bihrle, LaCasse, and Colletti (2000) found that individuals with antisocial personality disorder exhibited an 11% reduction of prefrontal gray matter volumes. As well, hippocampal volumetric reductions have been negatively associated with psychopathy levels (Laakso et al., 2001). In a recent study of successful and unsuccessful psychopaths, Raine and colleagues (2004) noted that unsuccessful psychopaths exhibit a greater asymmetry of the hippocampus than successful psychopaths and controls. This greater asymmetry was caused by decreased left hippocampal and increased right hippocampal volumes.

Lesion and imaging studies have thus pointed to a number of brain anomalies as potentially underlying violent and antisocial behavior. Studies investigating the relationship between perinatal complications, prenatal exposure to toxins, and aggression suggest that these brain anomalies may in part be caused by disrupted prenatal brain development due to very early exposure to stressors. Alcohol and nicotine exposure during pregnancy have been shown to increase the risk of later conduct disorders (Raine, 2002). Birth complications also increase the risk of CD; delinquency; and impulsive, violent offending, through causing brain damage to the frontal lobes and other regions, such as the hippocampus, which have been found to be abnormal in certain types of offenders (Combalbert et al., 2002; Raine). Exposures to toxins and birth complications interact in predicting conduct outcomes (Combalbert et al.; Raine). Consistent with a vulnerability-stress perspective, Brennan, Grekin, and Mednick (1999) found that whereas children whose mothers smoked 20 cigarettes per day during pregnancy had a twofold increase in violent offending as adults, children who were exposed to both nicotine and delivery complications exhibited a fivefold increase in violent offending as adults. Thus, it appears that exposure to toxins and obstetric complications interact with the postnatal psychosocial environment in predicting later aggression and violence in children (Raine).

Aggression and Arousal

Low resting heart rate has been shown to be characteristic of antisocial individuals, especially those who come from privileged social backgrounds (Raine, 2002). A similar pattern is generally found for skin conductance (Raine). Both indices of reactivity appear to have some predictive value, because lower heart rate and skin conductance at age 3 have been shown to predict violence levels at age 11 (Combalbert et al., 2002). In turn, higher physiological arousal may serve a protective function, because individuals who desist from adolescent antisocial behavior have been shown to have increased electrodermal and cardiovascular activity (Raine). Increased heart rate and skin conductance have also been observed in individuals with criminal fathers who do not themselves commit crimes (Combalbert et al.). Although the specific mechanism through which low physiological arousal may lead to conduct problems is still unclear, it has been hypothesized that lowered physiological arousal may result from prefrontal damage and may predispose individuals to low levels of fear, high levels of stimulation seeking, or both, which may in turn cause them to act out (Raine).

The Neurochemistry of Aggression

The contribution of serotonergic functioning to aggression has been studied in rodents, nonhuman primates, and humans using a variety of methods, such as lesions, measurement of serotonin metabolites in CSF and plasma, tryptophan depletion and supplementation, platelet serotonin uptake, and prolactin response to serotonergic agonists (Krakowski, 2003). In rodents, increased levels of aggression have been observed following serotonin depletion or neuronal destruction. In nonhuman primates, low serotonin levels have been associated with severe, unrestrained, dysfunctional aggression, whereas no relationship with more positive, assertive types of aggression has been observed (Krakowski). More specifically, low serotonin early in life has been linked with later violence and death, and experimental manipulations of serotonin levels have confirmed this inverse relationship between aggression and serotonin (Krakowski). In human studies, negative correlations have been found between lifetime aggression in individuals with personality disorders and serotonin levels, and low serotonin levels are associated with impulsive violence and recidivism in offenders (Krakowski). Experimental studies have shown reduction of irritability and aggression in patients with personality disorders upon treatment with selective serotonin reuptake inhibitors (SSRIs) (e.g., Cherek, Lane, Pietras, & Steinberg, 2002). Furthermore, tryptophan depletion and supplementation have been shown to yield changes in aggression levels in the expected directions, although these changes may occur only in individuals who have a preexisting vulnerability (e.g., family history of alcoholism, high hostility) (Krakowski). In a recent meta-analysis (Moore, Scarpa, & Raine, 2002), reduced 5-HIAA levels in antisocial individuals were found compared with nonantisocial individuals. However, age was found to be a significant moderator: Individuals younger than 30 years of age exhibited significantly lower 5-HIAA levels. The attenuation with age of decreased serotonergic levels may contribute to the observed age-related decline in crime (Moore et al.).

Age differences have also been found with regard to the relationship between testosterone and aggression. High testosterone levels have been associated with increased levels of aggression in adults. Patterns are less clear in children and adolescents, for whom the relationship between testosterone and aggression has sometimes been found to be reversed or absent (Raine, 2002). Raine has suggested that inverse relationships between testosterone and aggression in younger and older individuals may be attributed to the differing social experiences of these age groups. Aggressive children and adolescents usually exhibit poor academic and social functioning, and it may be these aversive experiences that decrease their testosterone levels. However, as they get older and are perhaps able to use their aggression to obtain dominance and success, their testosterone levels rise to their naturally high levels (Raine). Activity of the HPA axis has also been proposed as influencing aggression and conduct problems. Individuals with a diagnosis of CD who show significant levels of anxiety have greater levels of cortisol, show less aggression, and have fewer police contacts (Pihl et al., 2003). It is likely that testosterone and cortisol interact together in contributing to aggression and conduct disorders. Finally, it is also most likely that neurochemical functioning interacts with psychosocial experiences in predicting the presence or absence of antisocial behaviors. Caspi and colleagues (2002), for example, found that polymorphism of the *MAOA* gene, located on the X chromosome, interacts with childhood maltreatment in predicting adult criminal behaviors. The *MAOA* gene encodes an enzyme that metabolizes a number of neurotransmitters, including serotonin. Although low activity of the *MAOA* gene was not found to predict adult criminal behavior by itself, its combination with childhood maltreatment was significantly related to the presence of antisocial behaviors during adulthood (Caspi et al.).

DEPRESSION

The *DSM-IV-TR* (APA, 2000) defines major depressive episode as being characterized by affective (e.g., depressed mood, anhedonia), cognitive (e.g., worthlessness or guilt, diminished concentration), and vegetative symptoms (e.g., changes in sleeping or eating) (see Hankin & Abela, Chapter 10 in this volume, for greater description and discussion about depression). Faced with the increasing prevalence of depression and its progressively earlier onset, researchers are focusing more and more on the factors that render individuals vulnerable to depression. This endeavor, however, is not novel, because proposals regarding the etiological role of both innate and environmental factors have been present since the first descriptions of the disorder more than 2,000 years ago (Nestler et al., 2002). However, it is only with the use of increasingly sophisticated imaging technology that researchers have been able to begin describing the specific brain anomalies potentially associated with the disorder. Davidson and colleagues (2002) proposed a model whereby hypoactivation of the left prefrontal cortex and anterior cingulate cortex and hyperactivation of the right prefrontal cortex would lead to decreased approach behaviors and increased withdrawal and anxiety, which are often seen in depressed patients. Decreased activity of the left prefrontal cortex could in turn lead to a decreased inhibition of the amygdala and thus persistent negative affective states. Abnormalities of the hippocampus were also suggested to contribute to an absence of appropriate contextual modulation of emotions (Davidson et al., 2002). Figure 4.3 summarizes brain areas and neurochemical systems found to be involved in depressive affective states and their interactions with various psychosocial moderating factors.

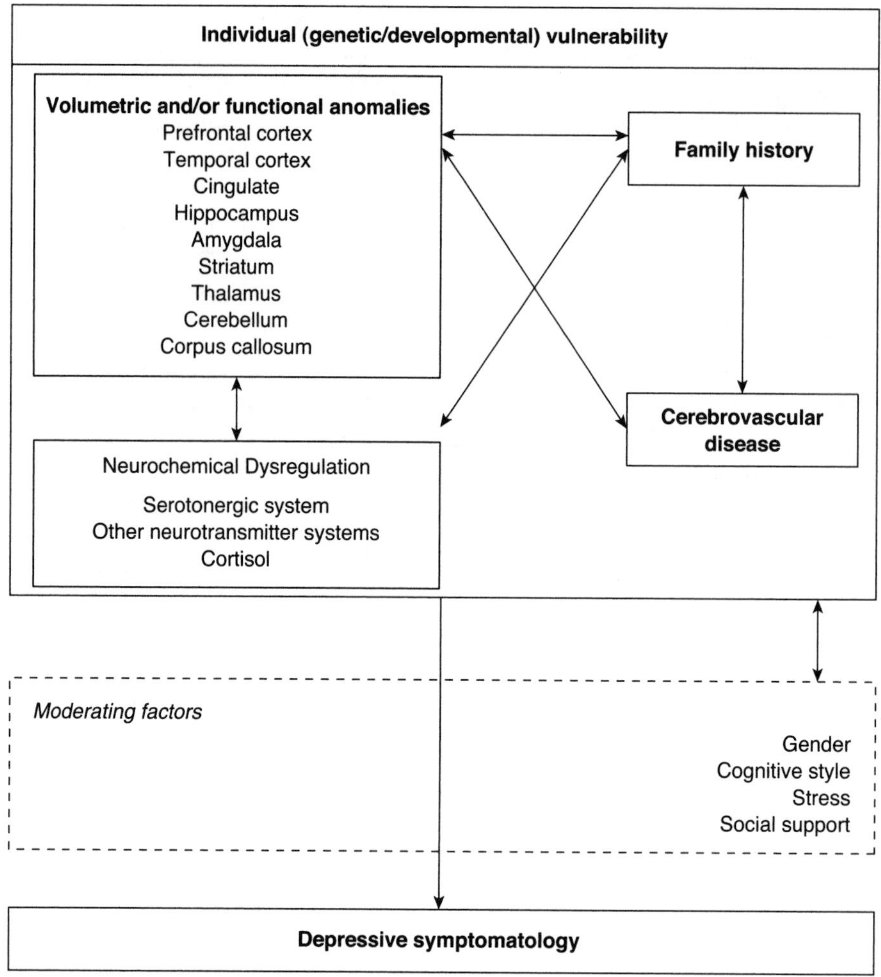

Figure 4.3 Depression

Functional and Structural Anomalies

Little evidence has been provided for differences in overall whole-brain volumes in depressed patients when compared with healthy controls (Strakowski, Adler, & DelBello, 2002). However, consistent with the model proposed by Davidson et al. (2002), differences in metabolism and volumes have been reported for a number of subregions, such as the prefrontal and cingulate cortex, the hippocampus, and the amygdala (Nestler et al., 2002). Total frontal lobe volumes have been found to be reduced by approximately 7% in depressed patients. The subgenual prefrontal cortex appears to be particularly reduced, with studies finding reductions of approximately 48% (Drevets et al., 1997). As well, reduction of the right-greater-than-left asymmetry of the frontal lobes usually found in controls has also been observed. The extent of total frontal lobe volumetric reduction and decreased asymmetry has been associated with severity of symptoms (Beyer & Krishnan, 2002; Strakowski et al., 2002). Imaging and postmortem studies have provided support for the presence of volumetric anomalies in the orbital region, more specifically bilateral volume reductions and decreased cortical thickness, as well as decreased neuronal size and density (Lai, Payne, Byrum, Steffens, & Krishnan, 2000; Rajkowska et al., 1999). It is important to note, however, that a number of studies have not found evidence for significant volumetric differences in these brain regions between depressed patients and healthy controls (Nestler et al.).

Decreased bilateral or left prefrontal cortex activation is one of the most often reported functional anomalies in the imaging literature on depression (Davidson et al., 2002). Resting state imaging studies have shown hypometabolism of the frontal lobes, more specifically of the dorsolateral and dorsomedial prefrontal cortex (Davidson et al., 2002; Drevets, 2000; Liotti & Mayberg, 2001). Specificity of reduced activity to the left hemisphere has been replicated numerous times by electroencephalogram (EEG) studies, although negative evidence has also been found (Davidson et al., 2002). Partial support has been provided for an increase in dorsolateral and dorsomedial activity with antidepressant use, more specifically to the left hemisphere (Davidson et al., 2002; Drevets). However, although the dorsolateral and dorsomedial prefrontal regions have been found to be hypoactive in some studies, evidence for hyperactivity of other prefrontal regions in depression has also been provided. Increased activity in the subgenual prefrontal cortex, as well as bilateral posterior orbital cortex, left ventrolateral prefrontal cortex, and anterior insula has been found, together with a body of findings suggesting that antidepressant treatment may lead to a reduction of activity in these regions (Drevets).

Evidence for volumetric anomalies of the temporal lobes and limbic structures has been somewhat mixed (Beyer & Krishnan, 2002). Patients suffering from major depression have been found to have decreased temporal cortical volumes when compared with healthy controls in some studies, although a number of investigations have reported null findings (Strakowski et al., 2002). Structural imaging studies have reported reductions of hippocampal volumes in patients with major depression, a finding also reported in patients with bipolar disorder, posttraumatic stress disorder, and borderline personality disorder (Davidson et al., 2002; Strakowski et al.). Hippocampal volumetric reductions for patients with major depression have been estimated to range from 8% to 19% (Davidson et al., 2002). Decreased hippocampal activity has also been reported using PET technology (Davidson et al., 2002). Findings for volumetric anomalies of the amygdala have been inconsistent, with different studies reporting increased, decreased, or no differences in volumes in depressed patients compared with controls (Davidson et al., 2002). Studies have also reported a left-greater-than-right asymmetry of the amygdala found in patients but not in controls (Davidson et al., 2002). Functional studies have reported increased activity of the amygdala in depressed patients, an increase evaluated by some to be of a magnitude of 44% (Davidson et al., 2002). As well, although remission of major depressive symptoms is associated with a reduction of activity levels of the amygdala, relapse is associated with increased amygdala activation (Davidson et al., 2002). It is interesting to note that increased amygdala activity has also been associated with bipolar disorder and anxiety disorders (Davidson et al., 2002). Bilateral reductions in anterior cingulate activity have also been noted and have been found to correlate with the extent of gray matter reduction, which is consistent with the finding that antidepressant treatment does not generally lead to a normalization of activity in this region (Davidson et al., 2002; Drevets, 2000).

Reduced volumes of the basal ganglia have been noted in depressed patients, most specifically of the caudate nucleus and the putamen, in the context, however, of numerous null findings (Beyer & Krishnan, 2002; Strakowski et al., 2002). Limited research has been done on the presence of cerebellar and corpus callosum structural anomalies in depression (Beyer & Krishnan). A number of studies have found decreased volumes of the cerebellum (Strakowski et al.), whereas some evidence has been provided for increased volumes of some subregions of the corpus callosum in depressed patients (Beyer & Krishnan). Research on thalamic structural anomalies has been limited and inconsistent. Volume reductions have been observed in some studies, but it has been suggested that thalamic volumetric reductions may be more common in bipolar disorder (Strakowski et al.). Increased, decreased, and no change of thalamic activity in depressed patients have all been reported (Liotti & Mayberg, 2001).

The imaging literature on the brain structural and functional correlates of depression has thus produced a number of heterogeneous findings, with partial empirical support provided for an involvement of the frontal and temporal lobes, the amygdala, the hippocampus, the basal ganglia and thalamus, and the cerebellum and corpus callosum. The equivocal nature of evidence for volumetric and functional anomalies in depression has been attributed by some to the heterogeneity of the disorder. More specifically, it has been suggested that some brain anomalies may characterize specific subtypes of patients (Davidson et al., 2002). For example, patients with a family history of major depression have been shown to be more likely to have increased activity of the amygdala, orbital cortex, and medial thalamus and decreased activity in specific subregions of the prefrontal cortex, as well as volumetric anomalies of the basal ganglia (Drevets, 2000). As well, patients with a family history of major depression do not exhibit the reduced amygdala activity usually associated with remission of symptoms, suggesting that amygdala hyperactivity may constitute a marker of a depressive trait rather than a depressive state in this subpopulation (Davidson et al., 2002). Patients with a late onset of the disorder have also been shown to exhibit a specific pattern of anomalies (Drevets, 2000). They exhibit sulcal and ventricular enlargement, as well as reduced volumes of the frontal lobes and the basal ganglia. Infarction to the frontal lobes or striatum has been associated with increased risk of depression, and there has been suggestion that late-onset depression may develop as a result of cerebrovascular disease (Strakowski et al., 2002). Some brain functional and structural anomalies may thus be specific to familial or late-onset depression cases (Strakowski et al.). Overlap in some of the observed regional anomalies may confer a common vulnerability to both subtypes, although different causal mechanisms are at play (Drevets).

Neurochemical Anomalies

Evidence for a serotonergic contribution to the physiology and treatment of depression comes from several lines of evidence. All pharmacological treatments of depression to date have focused on the monoamines, and the latest generation of antidepressants, the SSRIs, has been shown to be effective in reducing symptoms (Stockmeier, 2003). As well, depletion of tryptophan, a serotonergic precursor, has been shown to cause recurrence of symptoms in unmedicated patients in remission (Young & Leyton, 2002). Reduced levels of serotonergic metabolites in the cerebrospinal fluids of depressed patients with a history of suicide attempts have also been found, as well as decreased neuroendocrine response to serotonin stimuli (Stockmeier). In his recent review, Stockmeier reported a number of anomalies in serotonergic receptor binding sites associated with depression. Serotonin-1A receptor binding was found to be reduced in a number of regions, such as the medial temporal cortex, the temporal pole, the orbitofrontal cortex, the anterior cingulate cortex, the insula, and the dorsolateral prefrontal cortex. Alternatively, serotonin-2A receptor binding was found to be increased in the prefrontal cortex (Stockmeier). However, it is most likely that serotonin is not acting alone in the neurochemistry of depression. Norepinephrine receptor and transporter anomalies have been noted in depressed patients (Stockmeier). As well, depressed patients have been shown to have cortical levels of the inhibitory neurotransmitter GABA that are half that of healthy controls, levels that are restored by antidepressant medications (Stockmeier). Antagonists of substance P, a peptide neurotransmitter, have been shown by some researchers to be as effective as SSRIs in alleviating symptoms of major depression and anxiety (Stockmeier). In certain brain regions, nearly half of serotonergic neurons are colocalized with substance P neurons, and substance P antagonists have been shown to increase firing activity of serotonergic neurons in certain brain areas (Stockmeier). Interactions of a number of neurochemical systems are thus most likely involved in the etiology and treatment of depression.

Neurochemical explanations of depression have also focused on possible hyperactivity of the HPA axis. Research has shown that abnormally elevated HPA activity may be present in approximately 50% of depressed patients, most importantly those with a family history of major depression, and that these anomalies may be corrected with antidepressant administration (Nestler et al., 2002). Thus, hyperactivity of the HPA axis may contribute to depression through hippocampal damage, which is consistent with reduced hippocampal volumes sometimes found in depressed patients (Nestler et al.). As well, hippocampal volume reductions have been positively associated with duration of illness, which concurs with exposure to chronically elevated glucocorticoid levels (Davidson et al., 2002). Furthermore, centrally administered CRF has been shown to trigger symptoms found in depression such as anxiety and neurovegetative symptoms. This suggests that the contribution of the HPA axis hyperactivity to depression may not be limited to the hippocampus, but may also extend to other brain regions such as the hypothalamus (Nestler et al.).

The vast majority of studies on the biological bases of depression have focused on adult depression, using cross-sectional designs. This has made difficult a clear understanding of the role biology plays in the emergence of the disorder and how biological contributions to depression evolve over time. Research with children and adolescents has pointed to possible anomalies of the frontal lobes. Steingard and colleagues (2002), for example, have noted smaller white matter volume but greater gray matter volumes in depressed adolescents. Nolan and colleagues (2002) found that although depressed children and adolescents with no family history of major depression (MD) had larger left prefrontal volumes than depressed individuals with a family MD and normal controls, depressed children and adolescents with a family history of MD and controls did not significantly differ in terms of prefrontal volumes. Furthermore, a study focusing on depressed preschoolers has pointed to a possible contribution of the stress system to childhood-onset depression (Luby et al., 2003). Depressed preschoolers exhibited increased cortisol levels in response to both situations of separation and frustration. Nondepressed preschoolers, however, showed decreased cortical levels in separation situations and increased cortisol levels when frustrated. A longitudinal study by Goodyer, Herbert, and Tamplin (2003) has suggested that anomalies in steroid levels may precede the onset of the disorder. Adolescents who developed persistent depressive symptoms within 2 years initially showed a higher morning cortisol/dehydroepiandrosterone ratio. More longitudinal studies focusing on individuals at risk of developing depression are required in order to disentangle the biological roots of the emergence and development of the disorder.

SUBSTANCE ABUSE AND DEPENDENCE

Of the many "fat" words in psychopathology, perhaps the most obese is substance abuse/dependence (see Kassel, Weinstein, Mermelstein, Skitch, & Veilleux, Chapter 13 in this volume, for greater description and discussion). The size (the large number of differential drug diagnoses) and obtuseness (the myriad of paths to the end point) of the diagnosis make this diagnosis highly prevalent but often meaningless. Nevertheless, depending on the survey, substance abuse remains the most prevalent form of mental disorder, with alcohol abuse and dependence accounting for a majority of diagnoses (Pihl, 1999). Until recently, there has been a dearth of knowledge concerning etiology.

It is now clear that some individuals, for varying reasons, are more likely than others to develop problems with drugs. To understand reasons for abuse, it is no longer necessary to look at each drug individually; instead, the focus is on what a drug or group of drugs does for a specific individual. By adopting this perspective, one can get a glimpse of how genetic, biochemical, physiological, neuropsychological, and experiential facts interact. Two major drug groupings are the stimulant drugs and the depressant drugs, although there are obvious additional groupings (e.g., pain relief, hallucinogenics). Further, this dual, broad classification also suffers from the fact that some drugs have, for example, both stimulant and depressive effects. The most notable substance displaying this characteristic is alcohol, because for most individuals, on the rising limb of the blood alcohol curve, approximately 30 minutes postingestion of the drug, one reacts as if stimulated, whereas later on the blood alcohol curve, depressant brain effects are normative.

Stimulant Drugs

Research with rats and monkeys had clearly demonstrated in the 1960s and 1970s that certain parts of the brain, when stimulated electrically or chemically, produced reinforcing effects. That is, animals would work to receive this stimulation and would learn new responses based on pairing some behavior with the stimulation of the mesolimbic brain area, particularly the ventral tegmental area and specifically the nucleus accumbens. Dopamine has been implicated in this response in that these effects are directly related to the density of dopamine neurons. Further, drugs that blocked these neurons reduced these effects (Fibiger & Phillips, 1988). Stimulant drugs such as cocaine and amphetamines have been shown not only to directly release dopamine as well as other neurotransmitters but also to block the reuptake process, thus prolonging dopamine's effects (Koob & Blume, 1988). Some other drugs that increase dopamine flow into the nucleus accumbens are alcohol, marijuana, and opiates. At issue is whether these various drugs have a direct or indirect effect, but it is clear that the dopaminergic system, which is related to psychostimulation, is affected. Recently, Boileau and colleagues (2003) used PET technology to show increased dopamine release in the nucleus accumbens in humans after consuming an alcohol challenge. In addition, the study provided clues to the critical issue of why some individuals develop drug problems, whereas a large percentage of individuals who try various legal and illegal stimulant drugs do not develop abuse or dependency problems (i.e., a vulnerability to substances). Specifically, individuals who had previously demonstrated an accelerated heart rate response to alcohol were significantly more likely to show this dopamine release than individuals who did not previously show an accelerated heart rate response to alcohol. Although many situations, physical and psychological, affect heart rate, this intoxicated heart rate response has been shown to distinguish individuals who self-report positive subjective feelings to alcohol (Conrod, Peterson, & Pihl, 2001) and those for whom alcohol is positively reinforcing on a memory task (Bruce, Shestowksy, Mayerovitch, & Pihl, 1999). Thus, some individuals at risk for developing problems with alcohol are characterized by this elevated heart rate response on the rising limb of the blood alcohol curve, which has also been shown to be characteristic of individuals who reflect externalizing behaviors such as CD (Pihl et al., 2003) and pathological gambling (Brunelle, Assaad, Pihl, Tremblay, & Vitaro, 2003). The fact that these groups seem to respond with this response as well as having a propensity to develop stimulant substance abuse problems suggests particularities in baseline biological functioning. In rats selectively bred to prefer alcohol, increased functioning of the dopamine system has been demonstrated (McBride, Murphy, Lumeng, & Li, 1990). In these particular strains, alcohol facilitates stimulant-like behaviors, such as increased motor activity. In addition, rats selectively bred to self-administer opiates and cocaine demonstrate heightened place learning when administered these drugs, reminiscent of the early electrical stimulation studies (Guitart, Beitnes-Johnson, & Nestler, 1992). These findings suggest some preexisting genetic vulnerability. Indeed, there is a large literature showing that children of alcoholics, particularly sons—who are at four to nine times increased risk to develop the disorder—have discernible neuropsychological, electrophysiological, and behavioral responses to alcohol characteristics (Pihl, Peterson, & Finn, 1990). Further, sensitization (i.e., the fact that the use of one drug makes other similar drugs more reinforcing) has been shown to be potentiated by environmental stimuli such as stress (Deminiere, Piazza, Le Moal, & Simon, 1989). However, these effects are not only the result of biologically determined vulnerability but also are affected by using certain drugs. Some drugs per se do produce long-term potentiation of dopamine-releasing cells in the ventral tegmental area of the brain. Further, cross-sensitization with stress means that stress can reinstate drug taking, perhaps accounting for the difficulties in treatment and the high probability of relapse. This pattern is called neural adaptation and occurs by raising the excitatory neurotransmitter glutamate, which stimulates specific receptors on dopamine cells (Saal, Dong, Bonci, & Malenka, 2003). Similar effects are likely to occur with other stimulant drugs, such as nicotine, where withdrawal has been associated with a significant decrease in dopamine levels. Recent research shows that treating smokers with a drug designed to increase dopamine levels is more effective than typical nicotine replacement therapy (George & O'Malley, 2004).

The precise nature of the reward when dopamine is released in this particular brain area is also open to some debate. It appears not to be reinforcement in the classical sense, because the behavior affected does not satiate. Consequently, we have referred to this system as the "cue for reward system" (Pihl & Peterson, 1995) in that it stimulates locomotor activity and feelings of pleasure as if something is about to happen or is happening. Thus, commonalities are found in behavior among individuals who are sensation seekers, conduct disordered, and generally externalizing, and the abuse of stimulant drugs (Pihl & Peterson). These characteristics are particularly reminiscent of individuals at risk for type 2 alcoholism, which involves high heritability, early onset, and associated antisocial behavior (Pihl et al., 1990). Further, it has been recently demonstrated that the risk for ADHD and CD is 3.8 and 6.6 times greater, respectively, among children whose parents were alcohol dependent compared with controls. Twin studies have shown that shared genetic factors are largely responsible for this comorbidity

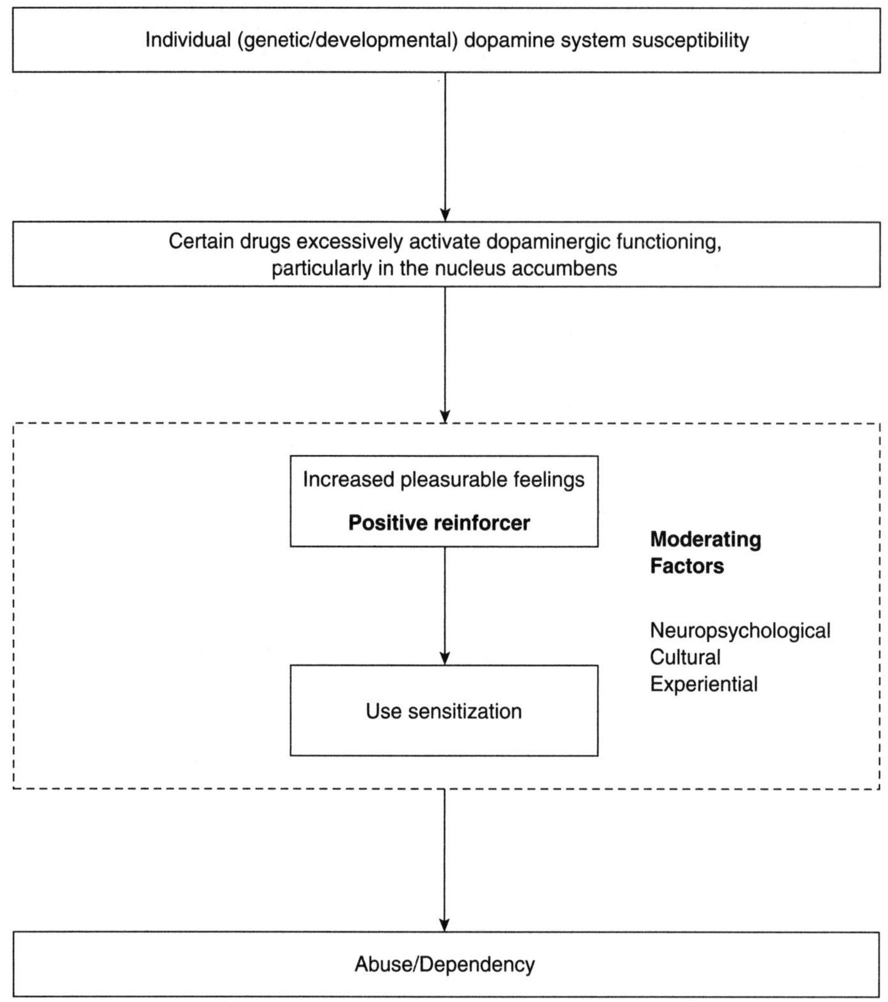

Figure 4.4 Substance Abuse

(Kendler, Prescott, Myers, & Neale, 2003). Commonalities between these groups in neuropsychological and electrophysiological findings have also been reported. In particular, cognitive deficits associated with the functioning of the prefrontal cortex, specifically involving problems in attention, planning, and foresight, have been well documented in both populations, as have particular EEG and event-related potential responses. Further, it has been shown that this particular response pattern, as well as the neuropsychological deficit, precedes onset of heavy drinking and dependence (Harden & Pihl, 1995). More recent electrophysiological work in individuals at risk for alcoholism has also shown a genetic linkage, which has focused on the neurotransmitter GABA, and specifically on the *GABA2* gene, which is thought to modulate the level of neural excitation (Edenberg et al., 2004). This *GABA-A* receptor gene on chromosome 4 has further been shown to be related to P300, N100, N400, and beta frequency EEG abnormalities in individuals at risk for alcoholism (Porjesz et al., 2002).

Depressant Drugs

Negative reinforcement (i.e., when an aversive situation is reduced) is another reward response that can also explain drug abuse. Drugs that reduce anxiety, fear, and dysphoric pain are frequently abused. Individuals with phobias, for example, are 2.5 times more likely to abuse alcohol and individuals with panic disorder four times more likely (Weissman, 1988). "Stress response dampening" is a phrase used to characterize the effect of some drugs on these and otherwise vulnerable individuals. The implied mechanism for abuse is thus seen as a form of self-medication that reduces the intensity of an aversive state. Although some experimental results in this area have been contradictory to this explanation (e.g., Steele & Josephs, 1990), like most studies in psychopathology the choice of subjects is critical. Vulnerable subjects are required, and one particularly vulnerable group is anxiety-sensitive individuals. In the paradigmatic study, these individuals are first shown stimuli when sober, which results in heightened physiological reactivity, which then is greatly diminished when they are alcohol intoxicated (Stewart & Pihl, 1994). Alcohol in this case is acting as an antianxiolytic, putatively by potentiating the action of the inhibitory neurotransmitter GABA. These drugs and other sedatives operate on selective GABA-A and benzodiazepine receptor sites. There are actually three subunits of the GABA-A receptors and 14 variants of the subunits. What is notable is that alcohol and benzodiazepines act on one specific subunit (Suzdak et al., 1986). It is also known that when measured in plasma, baseline levels of GABA are heritable and that individuals at risk for developing alcoholism, like alcoholics, have lower levels (Song et al., 2003). PET studies with offspring of alcoholics have also shown a reduced GABA response to a drug challenge, supporting the notion of reduced gabanergic activity. This conclusion is reinforced by numerous animal studies on selectively bred alcohol-preferring rats; these studies have shown that such rats have dense gabanergic innervation in the nucleus accumbens, that GABA chronically inhibits this system, that alcohol inhibits the action of the gabanergic inhibitory system, and that this inhibitory action accounts for the reward these rats receive from alcohol (McBride et al., 1990). Thus, it is suggested that at high doses needed to produce intoxication (Stewart, Finn, & Pihl, 1995), alcohol might directly potentiate inhibition of certain neurons.

Similar autonomic reactivity and dampening in children of alcoholics, particularly sons, have been reported, perhaps as a result of the same mechanisms just described, but not from fear or anxiety. This response, however, likely results from an overreactivity to novelty, the latter likely resulting from the aforementioned frontal neuropsychological deficits (Pihl & Peterson, 1995). Consequently, both highly anxious and externalizing individuals can display dampening and negative reinforcement, albeit for divergent reasons: those high on anxiety to self-medicate and those with externalizing problems possibly to improve focus.

CONCLUSION

Studies of the biological bases of psychopathology have pointed to subtle anatomical, functional, and neurochemical anomalies being associated with disorders such as attention deficit/hyperactivity disorder, conduct disorder, major depressive disorder, and substance abuse. Generally, results to date for most disorders have been inconsistent and of small magnitude, with a great overlap in distributions observed between patients and controls. As well, few biological findings have been found to be specific to a single disorder. Therefore, our understanding of biological vulnerabilities must be refined before we can use such vulnerabilities as markers or diagnostic tools for psychiatry and psychopathology. However, current psychiatry and diagnostic systems are the problem. The use of broad, heterogeneous, behavioral definitions as classification measures is undoubtedly the major contributor to the observed lack of consistency. The assumption that diagnostic categories are distinct, when in fact psychiatric disorders show very high comorbidity with each other, is simply spurious. It must be recognized that psychiatric nomenclatures represent the ways in which mental health researchers and professionals have carved out the edges of psychopathology in a way that is meaningful to them and that supposedly allows communication between them, but these are not the true frontiers of psychopathology. It may be that many disorders that we think of as distinct in fact share similar biological etiological mechanisms and that the same phenotype may result from a number of etiological mechanisms, with multiple pathways.

In keeping with the need to consider the multicausal nature of psychopathology, biological vulnerability must be considered in the context of the environment in which the human organism evolves. The environment provides the context in which psychosocial risk and protective factors interact with biological vulnerability in determining whether psychopathology will emerge or not, as well as the prognosis for each individual. The scientific literature is replete with examples of how biology interacts with events in the environment in creating or preventing psychopathology, as well as in determining its outcome. Research on antisocial behaviors, for example, has shown that adolescent boys whose fathers have been convicted of various crimes, but who do not commit crimes themselves, show higher sympathetic arousal, pointing perhaps to a protective effect of biology (Raine, 2002). Furthermore, low sympathetic arousal is often more characteristic of criminals from advantaged than disadvantaged psychosocial backgrounds, suggesting that biological vulnerability may add little to the risk associated with an upbringing in low socioeconomic circumstances. In contrast, minor physical anomalies have been found to predict violence only in individuals growing up in unstable and stressful family environments (Raine). Additionally, the provision of firm structure, combined with warmth by parents or teachers, has been found to be particularly important for behavioral management of children with a diagnosis of ADHD (Denckla, 2003; Wicks-Nelson & Israel, 2000). Not all individuals exposed to psychosocial stress or biological vulnerability will go on to develop signs of psychopathology, and biological or environmental risks are often not sufficient in themselves to trigger onset of psychiatric disorders or to determine their course. It is the interaction of both types of contributors that determines psychopathology. Biological and psychosocial research must thus take into account contributors from each field in order to create a more complete etiological picture of each psychopathology.

However, it may be in many ways impossible to attempt to distinguish the separate contributions of biological and psychosocial factors to psychopathology, because both types of factors are in constant interaction, and the boundaries between them are at best blurry. For example, smoking during pregnancy could be considered as a stressor that confers risk, through biological processes, for the development of later psychopathology through disruption of early brain development (potentially a biological vulnerability). However, women who smoke during pregnancy may be likely to create a postnatal environment for their child that is very different from that created by women who refrain from smoking (i.e., a more stressful environment). This postnatal environment may then contribute to the emergence of different psychopathological symptoms, such as disruptive behaviors observed in children with ADHD or CD. Parents with a history of antisocial behaviors are more likely to have children who will grow up displaying some forms of antisocial behaviors as well. The extent to which this familial aggregation of socially inappropriate behaviors is due to genetic or biological transmission, the creation of a disruptive environment during upbringing, both, or some interactive combination is, however, unclear. Divisions between different vulnerabilities, especially biological, are thus artificial ones, because all behaviors, thoughts, and emotions ultimately have biological substrates. A multicausal approach to psychopathology, such as embodied in this volume, is the approach that will provide the most complete understanding of psychiatric disorders and their etiology.

REFERENCES

American Psychiatric Association. (2000). *Diagnostic and statistical manual of mental disorders* (4th ed., text revision). Washington, DC: Author.

Anderson, C. M., Polcari, A., Lowen, S. B., Renshaw, P. F., & Teicher, M. H. (2002). Effects of methylphenidate on functional magnetic resonance relaxometry of the cerebellar vermis in boys with ADHD. *American Journal of Psychiatry, 159,* 1322–1328.

Andreasen, N. C. (1999). A unitary model of schizophrenia. *Archives of General Psychiatry, 56,* 781–787.

Baumeister, A. A., & Hawkins, M. F. (2001). Incoherence of neuroimaging studies of attention deficit/hyperactivity disorder. *Clinical Neuropharmacology, 24*(1), 2–10.

Baving, L., Laucht, M., & Schmidt, M. H. (1999). Atypical frontal brain activation in ADHD: Preschool and elementary school boys and girls. *Journal of the American Academy of Child and Adolescent Psychiatry, 38,* 1363–1371.

Berquin, P. C., Giedd, J. N., Jacobsen, L. K., Hamburger, S. D., Krain, A. L., Rapoport, J. L., et al. (1998). Cerebellum in attention-deficit hyperactivity disorder: A morphometric MRI study. *Neurology, 50,* 1087–1093.

Beyer, J. L., & Krishnan, K. R. R. (2002). Volumetric brain imaging findings in mood disorders. *Bipolar Disorders, 4,* 89–104.

Boileau, I., Assaad, J. M., Pihl, R. O., Benkelfat, C., Leyton, M., Diksic, M., et al. (2003). Alcohol promotes dopamine release in the human nucleus accumbens. *Synapse, 49,* 226–231.

Bremner, J., Randall, P., Scott, R., Bronen, A., Seibyl, J., Southwick, G., et al. (1995). MRI-based measurement of hippocampal volume in patients with combat-related posttraumatic stress disorder. *American Journal of Psychiatry, 152,* 973–981.

Brennan, P. A., Grekin, E. R., & Mednick, S. A. (1999). Maternal smoking during pregnancy and adult male criminal outcome. *Archives of General Psychiatry, 56,* 215–219.

Bruce, K., Shestowksy, J., Mayerovitch, J., & Pihl, R. (1999). Concomitant psychomotor stimulation and differentially-enhanced consolidation of emotionally charged memory following alcohol consumption. *Alcoholism: Clinical and Experimental Research, 23,* 693–701.

Brunelle, C., Assaad, J. M., Pihl, R. O., Tremblay, R., & Vitaro, F. (2003). Exaggerated ethanol-induced cardiac reactivity as an indicator of increased risk for gambling. *Psychology of Addictive Behaviors, 17,* 83–86.

Carlson, N. R. (2001). *Physiology of behavior* (7th ed.). Boston: Allyn & Bacon.

Caspi, A., McClay, J., Moffitt, T. E., Mill, J., Martin, J., Craig, I. W., et al. (2002). Role of genotype in the cycle of violence in maltreated children. *Science, 297,* 851–854.

Castellanos, F. X., Giedd, J. N., Marsh, W. L., Hamburger, S. D., Vaituzis, A. C., Dickstein, D. P., et al. (1996). Quantitative brain magnetic resonance imaging in attention-deficit hyperactivity disorder. *Archives of General Psychiatry, 53,* 607–616.

Castellanos, F. X., Lee, P. P., Sharp, W., Jeffries, N. O., Greenstein, D. K., Clasen, L. S., et al. (2002). Developmental trajectories of brain volume abnormalities in children and adolescents with attention-deficit/hyperactivity disorder. *Journal of the American Medical Association, 288,* 1740–1748.

Castellanos, F. X., & Tannock, R. (2002). Neuroscience of attention-deficit/hyperactivity disorder: The search for endophenotypes. *Nature Reviews Neuroscience, 3,* 617–628.

Cherek, D. R., Lane, S. D., Pietras, C. J., & Steinberg, J. K. (2002). Effects of chronic paroxetine administration on measures of aggressive and impulsive responses of adult males with a history of conduct disorder. *Psychopharmacology, 159,* 266–274.

Combalbert, N., Bret-Dibat, J. L., & Favard, A. M. (2002). Biological approach for the study of violent behaviours: Interest and limits. *Annales Médico Psychologiques, 160,* 640–648.

Comings, D. E., Gade-Andavolu, R., Gonzalez, N., Wu, S., Muhleman, D., Blake, H., et al. (2000). Comparison of the role of dopamine, serotonin, and noradrenaline genes in ADHD, ODD and conduct disorder: Multivariate regression analysis of 20 genes. *Clinical Genetics, 57,* 178–196.

Conrod, P., Peterson, J., & Pihl, R. (2001). Reliability and validity of alcohol-induced heart rate increase as a measure of sensitivity to the stimulant properties of alcohol. *Psychopharmacology, 157,* 20–30.

Damasio, A. R., Tranel, D., & Damasio, H. (1990). Individuals with sociopathic behavior caused by frontal damage fail to respond autonomically to social stimuli. *Behavioural Brain Research, 41,* 81–94.

Davidson, R. J., Pizzagalli, D., Nitschke, J. B., & Putnam, K. (2002). Depression: Perspectives from affective neuroscience. *Annual Review of Psychology, 53,* 545–574.

Davidson, R. J., Putnam, K. M., & Larson, C. L. (2000). Dysfunction in the neural circuitry of emotion regulation: A possible prelude to violence. *Science, 289,* 591–594.

Deminiere, J. M., Piazza, P. V., Le Moal, M., & Simon, H. (1989). Experimental approach to individual vulnerability to psychostimulant addiction. *Neuroscience and Biobehavioral Review, 13,* 141–147.

Denckla, M. B. (2003). ADHD: Topic update. *Brain and Development, 25,* 383–389.

Dougherty, D. D., Bonah, A. A., Spencer, T. J., Rauch, S. L., Madras, B. K., & Fischman, A. J. (1999). Dopamine transporter density in patients with attention deficit hyperactivity disorder. *Lancet, 354,* 2132–2133.

Drevets, W. C. (2000). Neuroimaging studies of mood disorders. *Biological Psychiatry, 48,* 813–829.

Drevets, W. C., Price, J. L., Simpson, J. R., Todd, R. D., Reich, T., Vannier, M., et al. (1997). Subgenual prefrontal cortex abnormalities in mood disorders. *Nature, 386,* 824–827.

Durston, S., Tottenham, N. T., Thomas, K. M., Davidson, M. C., Eigsti, I. M., Yang, Y., et al. (2003). Differential patterns of striatal activation in young children with and without ADHD. *Biological Psychiatry, 53,* 871–878.

Edenberg, H., Dick, D., Xuei, X., Tian, H., Almasy, L., Bauer, L., et al. (2004). *Variations in GABRA2 encoding the alpha 2 sub unit of the GABA$_A$ receptor, are associated with alcohol dependence and with brain oscillations.* Unpublished manuscript.

Ernst, M., Liebenauer, L. L., King, A. C., Fitzgerald, G. A., Cohen, R. M., & Zametkin, A. J. (1994). Reduced brain metabolism in hyperactive girls. *Journal of the American Academy of Child and Adolescent Psychiatry, 33,* 858–868.

Ernst, M., Zametkin, A. J., Matochik, J. A., Jons, P. H., & Cohen, R. M. (1998). DOPA decarboxylase activity in attention deficit hyperactivity disorder in adults: A FDOPA positron emission tomographic study. *Journal of Neuroscience, 18,* 5901–5907.

Ernst, M., Zametkin, A. J., Matochik, J. A., Pascualvaca, D., Jons, P. H., & Cohen, R. M. (1999). High midbrain [^{18}F]DOPA accumulation in children with ADHD. *American Journal of Psychiatry, 156,* 1209–1215.

Fibiger, H. C., & Phillips, A. G. (1988). Mesocorticolimbic dopamine systems and reward. *Annals of the New York Academy of Science, 537,* 206–215.

Filipek, P. A., Semrud-Clikeman, M., Steingard, R. J., Renshaw, P. F., Kennedy, D. N., & Biederman, J. (1997). Volumetric MRI analysis comparing subjects having attention-deficit hyperactivity disorder with normal controls. *Neurology, 48,* 589–601.

George, T. P., & O'Malley, S. S. (2004). Current pharmacological treatments for nicotine dependence. *Trends in Pharmacological Science, 25,* 42–48.

Goodyer, I. M., Herbert, J., & Tamplin, A. (2003). Psychoendocrine antecedents of persistent first-episode major depression in adolescents: A community-based longitudinal enquiry. *Psychological Medicine, 33,* 601–610.

Guitart, X., Beitnes-Johnson, D., & Nestler, E. (1992). Fischer and Lewis rat strains differ in basal levels of neurofilament proteins and in their regulation by chronic morphine. *Synapse, 12,* 242–243.

Hale, T. S., Hariri, A. R., & McCracken, J. T. (2000). Attention-deficit/hyperactivity disorder: Perspectives from neuroimaging. *Mental Retardation and Developmental Disabilities Research Reviews, 6,* 214–219.

Harden, P., & Pihl, R. (1995). Cognitive deficits and autonomic reactivity in boys at high risk for alcoholism. *Journal of Abnormal Psychology, 104,* 94–103.

Hill, D. E., Yeo, R. A., Campbell, R. A., Hart, B., Vigil, J., & Brooks, W. (2003). Magnetic resonance imaging correlates of attention-deficit/hyperactivity disorder in children. *Neuropsychology, 17,* 496–506.

Hoptman, M. J. (2003). Neuroimaging studies of violence and antisocial behavior. *Journal of Psychiatric Practice, 9,* 265–278.

Hynd, G. W., Hern, K. L., Novey, E. S., Eliopulos, D., Marshall, R., Gonzalez, J. J., et al. (1993). Attention deficit-hyperactivity disorder and asymmetry of the caudate nucleus. *Journal of Child Neurology, 8,* 339–347.

Kendler, K., Prescott, C., Myers, J., & Neale, M. (2003). The structure of genetic and environmental risk factors for common psychiatric and substance use disorders in men and women. *Archives of General Psychiatry, 60,* 929–937.

Kessler, R. C., McGonagle, K. A., Zhao, S., Nelson, C. B., Hughes, M., Eshleman, S., et al. (1994). Lifetime and 12-month prevalence of DSM-III-R psychiatric disorders in the United States: Results from the National Comorbidity Survey. *Archives of General Psychiatry, 51,* 8–19.

Kirley, A., Hawi, Z., Daly, G., McCarron, M., Mullins, C., Millar, N., et al. (2002). Dopaminergic system genes in ADHD: Toward a biological hypothesis. *Neuropsychopharmacology, 27,* 607–619.

Koob, G. F., & Bloom, F. E. (1988). Cellular and molecular mechanisms of drug dependence. *Science, 242,* 715–723.

Krakowski, M. (2003). Violence and serotonin: Influence of impulse control, affect regulation, and social functioning. *Journal of Neuropsychiatry and Clinical Neurosciences, 15,* 294–305.

Krause, K. H., Dressel, S. H., Krause, J., Lung, H. F., & Tatsch, K. (2000). Increased striatal dopamine transporter in adult patients with attention deficit hyperactivity disorder: Effects of methylphenidate as measured by single photon emission computed tomography. *Neuroscience Letter, 285,* 107–110.

Krueger, R. F. (1999). The structure of common mental disorders. *Archives of General Psychiatry, 56,* 921–926.

Laakso, M. P., Vaurio, O., Koivisto, E., Savolainen, L., Eronen, M., Aronen, H. J., et al. (2001). Psychopathy and the posterior hippocampus. *Behavioural Brain Research, 118,* 187–193.

Lahey, B. B., Applegate, B., Waldman, I., Hankin, B. L., & Rick, J. (2004). The structure of child and adolescent psychopathology: Generating new hypotheses. *Journal of Abnormal Psychology, 113,* 358–385.

Lai, T.-J., Payne, M. E., Byrum, C. E., Steffens, D. C., & Krishnan, K. R. (2000). Reduction of orbital frontal cortex volume in geriatric depression. *Biological Psychiatry, 48,* 971–975.

Liotti, M., & Mayberg, H. S. (2001). The role of functional neuroimaging in the neuropsychology of depression. *Journal of Clinical and Experimental Neuropsychology, 23,* 121–136.

Lou, H. C., Henriksen, L., & Bruhn, P. (1984). Focal cerebral hypoperfusion in children with dysphasia and/or attention deficit disorder. *Archives of Neurology, 41,* 825–829.

Lou, H. C., Henriksen, L., & Bruhn, P. (1990). Focal cerebral dysfunction in developmental learning disabilities. *Lancet, 335,* 8–11.

Lou, H. C., Henriksen, L., Bruhn, P., Borner, H., & Nielsen, J. B. (1989). Striatal dysfunction in attention deficit and hyperkinetic disorder. *Archives of Neurology, 46,* 48–52.

Luby, J. L., Heffelfinger, A., Mrakotsky, C., Brown, K., Hessler, M., & Spitznagel, E. (2003). Alterations in stress cortisol reactivity in depressed preschoolers relative to psychiatric and no-disorder comparison groups. *Archives of General Psychiatry, 60,* 1248–1255.

Luria, A. R. (1980). *Higher cortical functions in man.* (B. Haigh, Trans.) (2nd ed.). New York: Basic Books.

Lyoo, I. K., Noam, G. G., Lee, C. K., Lee, H. K., Kennedy, B. P., & Renshaw, P. F. (1996). The corpus callosum and lateral ventricles in children with attention-deficit hyperactivity disorder: A brain magnetic resonance imaging study. *Biological Psychiatry, 40,* 1060–1063.

Mataro, M., Garcia-Sanchez, C., Junque, C., Estevez-Gonzalez, A., & Pujol, J. (1997). Magnetic resonance imaging measurement of the caudate nucleus in adolescents with attention deficit hyperactivity disorder and its relationship with neuropsychological and behavioral measures. *Archives of Neurology, 54,* 963–968.

Mathalon, D., Rapoport, J., Davis, K., & Krystal, J. (2003). Neurotoxicity, neuroplasticity, and magnetic resonance imaging morphometry. *Archives of General Psychiatry, 60,* 846–848.

McBride, W. J., Murphy, J. M., Lumeng, L., & Li, T. K. (1990). Serotonin, dopamine and GABA involvement in alcohol drinking of selectively bred rats. *Alcohol, 7,* 199–205.

Miller, E. K., & Cohen, J. D. (2001). An integrative theory of prefrontal cortex function. *Annual Review of Neuroscience, 24,* 167–202.

Moore, T. M., Scarpa, A., & Raine, A. (2002). A meta-analysis of serotonin metabolite 5-HIAA and antisocial behavior. *Aggressive Behavior, 28,* 299–316.

Mostofsky, S. H., Cooper, K. L., Kates, W. R., Denckla, M. B., & Kaufmann, W. E. (2002). Smaller prefrontal and premotor volumes in boys with attention-deficit/hyperactivity disorder. *Biological Psychiatry, 52,* 785–794.

Nestler, E. J., Barrot, M., Dileone, R. J., Eisch, A. J., Gold, S. J., Monteggia, L. M. (2002). Neurobiology of depression. *Neuron, 34,* 13–25.

Nolan, C. L., Moore, G. J., Madden, R., Farchione, T., Bartoi, M., Lorch, E., et al. (2002). Prefrontal cortical volume in childhood-onset major depression: Preliminary findings. *Archives of General Psychiatry, 59,* 173–179.

Oades, R. D. (2002). Dopamine may be "hyper" with respect to noradrenaline metabolism, but "hypo" with respect to serotonin metabolism in children with attention-deficit hyperactivity disorder. *Behavioural Brain Research, 130,* 97–102.

Pihl, R. O. (1995). Violent behavior. *Journal of Psychiatry & Neuroscience, 20,* 101–103.

Pihl, R. O. (1999). Substance abuse. In T. Miller, P. Blaney, & R. D. Davis (Eds.), *Oxford textbook of psychopathology* (pp. 249–276). New York: Oxford University Press.

Pihl, R. O., & Peterson, J. B. (1995). Alcoholism: The role of different motivational systems. *Journal of Psychiatry and Neuroscience, 20,* 372–396.

Pihl, R. O., Peterson, J. B., & Finn, P. R. (1990). The inherited predisposition to alcoholism: Characteristics of sons of male alcoholics. *Journal of Abnormal Psychology, 99,* 291–301.

Pihl, R. O., Vant, J., & Assaad, J. M. (2003). Neuropsychological and neuroendocrine factors. In C. A. Essau (Ed.), *Conduct and oppositional defiant disorders: Epidemiology, risk factors, and treatment* (pp. 163–189). Mahwah, NJ: Lawrence Erlbaum.

Porjesz, B., Almasy, L., Edenberg, H., Wang, K., Charlian, D., Forud, T., et al. (2002). Linkage disequilibrium between the beta frequency of the human EEG and a $GABA_A$ receptor gene locus. *Proceedings of the National Academy of Science, 99,* 3729–3733.

Raine, A. (2002). Biosocial studies of antisocial and violent behaviour in children and adults: A review. *Journal of Abnormal Child Psychology, 30,* 211–236.

Raine, A., Buchsbaum, M. S., & LaCasse, L. (1997). Brain abnormalities in murderers indicated by positron emission tomography. *Biological Psychiatry, 42,* 495–508.

Raine, A., Buchsbaum, M. S., Stanley, J., Lottenberg, S., Abel, L., & Stoddard, J. (1994). Selective reductions in prefrontal glucose metabolism in murderers. *Biological Psychiatry, 36,* 365–373.

Raine, A., Ishikawa, S. S., Arce, E., Lencz, T., Knuth, K. H., Bihrle, S., et al. (2004). Hippocampal structural asymmetry in unsuccessful psychopaths. *Biological Psychiatry, 55,* 185–191.

Raine, A., Lencz, T., Bihrle, S., LaCasse, L., & Colletti, P. (2000). Reduced prefrontal gray matter volume and reduced autonomic activity in antisocial personality disorder. *Archives of General Psychiatry, 57,* 119–127.

Raine, A., Lencz, T., Taylor, K., Hellige, J. B., Bihrle, S., LaCasse, L., et al. (2003). Corpus callosum abnormalities in psychopathic antisocial individuals. *Archives of General Psychiatry, 60,* 1134–1142.

Raine, A., Meloy, J. R., Bihrle, S., Stoddard, J., LaCasse, L., & Buchsbaum, M. S. (1998). Reduced prefrontal and increased subcortical brain functioning assessed using positron emission tomography in predatory and affective murderers. *Behavioral Sciences and the Law, 16,* 319–332.

Rajkowska, G., Miguel-Hidalgo, J. J., Wei, J., Dilley, G., Pittman, S. D., Meltzer, H. Y., et al. (1999). Morphometric evidence for neuronal and glial prefrontal cell pathology in major depression. *Biological Psychiatry, 45,* 1085–1098.

Robins, L. N., & Regier, D. A. (1991). *Psychiatric disorders in America: The Epidemiologic Catchment Area Study.* New York: Free Press.

Saal, D., Dong, Y., Bonci, A., & Malenka, R. (2003). Drugs of abuse and stress trigger a common synaptic adaptation in dopamine neurons. *Neuron, 37,* 577–582.

Schall, J. D. (2004). On building a bridge between brain and behavior. *Annual Review of Psychology, 55,* 23–50.

Sheline, Y., Wang, P., Gado, M., Csernansky, J., & Vannier, M. (1996). Hippocampal atrophy in recurrent major depression. *Proceedings of the National Academy of Science, 93,* 3908–3913.

Sieg, K. G., Gaffney, G. R., Preston, D. F., & Hellings, J. A. (1995). SPECT brain imaging abnormalities in attention deficit hyperactivity disorder. *Clinical Nuclear Medicine, 20,* 55–59.

Silberstein, R. B., Farrow, M., Levy, F., Pipingas, A., Hay, D. A., & Jarman, F. C. (1998). Functional brain electrical mapping in boys with attention-deficit/hyperactivity disorder. *Archives of General Psychiatry, 55,* 1105–1112.

Soderstrom, H., Hultin, L., Tullberg, M., Wikkelso, C., Ekholm, S., & Forsman, A. (2002). Reduced frontotemporal perfusion in psychopathic personality. *Psychiatry Research Neuroimaging, 114,* 81–94.

Song, J., Koller, D. L., Foroud, T., Carr, K., Zhao, J., Rice, J., et al. (2003). Association of GABA(A) receptors and alcohol dependence and the effects of genetic imprinting. *American Journal of Medical Genetics, 117B*(1), 39–45.

Sowell, E. R., Thompson, P. M., Welcome, S. E., Henkenius, A. L., Toga, A. W., & Peterson, B. S. (2003). Cortical abnormalities in children and adolescents with attention-deficit hyperactivity disorder. *Lancet, 362,* 1699–1707.

Steele, C. M., & Josephs, R. A. (1990). Alcohol myopia: Its prized and dangerous effects. *American Psychologist, 45,* 921–933.

Steingard, R. J., Renshaw, P. F., Hennen, J., Lenox, M., Cintron, C. B., Young, A. D., et al. (2002). Smaller frontal lobe white matter volumes in depressed adolescents. *Biological Psychiatry, 52,* 413–417.

Stewart, S., Finn, P., & Pihl, R. (1995). A dose response study of the effects of alcohol on the perception of pain and discomfort due to electric shock in men at high risk for alcoholism. *Psychopharmacology, 119,* 261–267.

Stewart, S., & Pihl, R. (1994). Effects of alcohol administration on psychophysiological and subjective-emotional responses to aversive stimulation in anxiety sensitive women. *Psychology of Addictive Behaviors, 8,* 29–42.

Still, G. F. (1902). Some abnormal conditions in children: Lectures I, II, and III. *Lancet, 1,* 1008–1012, 1077–1082, 1163–1168.

Stockmeier, C. A. (2003). Involvement of serotonin in depression: Evidence from postmortem and imaging studies of serotonin receptors and the serotonin transporter. *Journal of Psychiatric Research, 37,* 357–373.

Strakowski, S. M., Adler, C. M., & DelBello, M. P. (2002). Volumetric MRI studies of mood disorders: Do they distinguish unipolar and bipolar disorder. *Bipolar Disorders, 4,* 80–88.

Stuss, D. T., Gow, C. A., & Hetherington, C. R. (1992). "No longer Gage": Frontal lobe dysfunction and emotional changes. *Journal of Consulting and Clinical Psychology, 60,* 349–359.

Suzdak, P., Glewa, J., Crawley, J., Schwartz, R., Skolnick, P., & Paul, S. (1986). A selective imidazobenzodiazepine antagonist of ethanol in the rat. *Science, 234,* 1243–1247.

Vaidya, C. J., Austin, G., Kirkirian, G., Ridlehuber, H. W., Desmond, J. E., Glover, G. H., et al. (1998). Selective effects of methylphenidate in attention deficit hyperactivity disorder: A functional magnetic resonance study. *Proceedings of the National Academy of Science USA, 95,* 14494–14499.

van Dyck, C. H., Quinlan, D. M., Cretella, L. M., Staley, J. K., Malison, R. T., Baldwin, R. M., et al. (2002). Unaltered dopamine transporter availability in adult attention deficit hyperactivity disorder. *American Journal of Psychiatry, 159,* 309–312.

Weissman, M. (1988). Anxiety of alcoholism. *Journal of Clinical Psychiatry, 49,* 17–19.

Wicks-Nelson, R., & Israel, A. C. (2000). *Behavior disorders of childhood.* Toronto, Ontario, Canada: Prentice Hall Canada.

Wilens, T. E., Biederman, J., & Spencer, T. J. (2002). Attention deficit/hyperactivity disorder across the lifespan. *Annual Review of Medicine, 53,* 112–131.

Young, S. N., & Leyton, M. (2002). The role of serotonin in human mood and social interaction: Insight from altered tryptophan levels. *Pharmacology, Biochemistry & Behavior, 71,* 857–865.

Young, S., Smith, S., Pihl, R., & Ervin, F. (1985). Tryptophan depletion lowers mood in normal males. *Psychopharmacology, 87,* 173–177.

Zametkin, A. J., Nordahl, T. E., Gross, M., King, A. C., Semple, W. E., Rumsey, J., et al. (1990). Cerebral glucose metabolism in adults with hyperactivity of childhood onset. *New England Journal of Medicine, 323,* 1361–1366.

CHAPTER 5

Cognitive Vulnerability-Stress Models of Psychopathology

A Developmental Perspective

BRANDON E. GIBB AND MEREDITH E. COLES

Since their introduction, cognitive vulnerability-stress theories of psychopathology (e.g., Abramson, Seligman, & Teasdale, 1978; Beck, 1967; Dodge, 1986; Williams, Watts, MacLeod, & Mathews, 1988) have spurred an enormous amount of research. These theories share the general hypothesis that one's characteristic way of attending to, interpreting, and remembering negative events contributes vulnerability to the development of psychopathology in the presence of negative life events. In this chapter, we focus on biases in attention and interpretation, given the relative paucity of research examining memory biases as vulnerability factors (for recent reviews of the role of memory in psychopathology, see Clark, Beck, & Alford, 1999; Coles & Heimberg, 2002; Gotlib & Neubauer, 2000). Specifically, we review studies evaluating whether these biases, both alone and interacting with the occurrence of negative life events, contribute to the development of three specific types of psychopathology: depression, anxiety, and aggression. In doing so, we first review the relevant theoretical models and discuss studies testing their vulnerability hypotheses. Next, we discuss the role of development, in terms of both its impact upon the development of cognitive vulnerability itself and upon the proposed vulnerability-stress interactions. Throughout this chapter, we discuss the cognitive vulnerability-stress theories from a developmental psychopathology perspective, emphasizing prospective, longitudinal studies. To facilitate exploration of developmental differences, we have specified the ages of participants included in the studies reviewed whenever possible. Although this can be cumbersome at times, we want to emphasize any potential differences between studies that may be due to developmental factors.

DEFINITION OF COGNITIVE VULNERABILITIES

Depression

Cognitive vulnerability to depression has generally been defined as biased processing of information reflecting themes of loss and failure (see, e.g., Clark et al., 1999). For example, in the theory of Beck and colleagues (Beck, 1967, 1987; Clark et al.), cognitive vulnerability to depression is defined by the presence of maladaptive self-schemata reflecting themes of helplessness and unlovability that become activated by schema-congruent negative life events or negative moods. Although early statements of the theory (e.g., Beck, 1967) focused on the presence of dysfunctional attitudes as representations of these negative self-schemata, more recent statements (e.g., Beck, 1987; Clark et al.) have focused on sociotropy and autonomy, cognitive-personality types that are hypothesized to confer vulnerability to depression following negative events in the interpersonal and achievement domains, respectively (for a similar theory regarding the personality styles of dependency and self-criticism, see Blatt, 1974, 2004). Despite the shift in emphasis from dysfunctional attitudes to sociotropy and autonomy, Beck has been consistent in proposing that once activated, these schemata contribute to the expression of biases in attention, interpretation, and memory. Specifically, Beck has proposed that individuals who are cognitively vulnerable to depression will exhibit negative interpretation biases as well as preferential attention and memory for depression-relevant stimuli (i.e., stimuli reflecting themes of helplessness, unlovability, etc.).

Further elaborating the role of attentional biases in depression, Nolen-Hoeksema (1987, 1991) suggested that depression-prone individuals might be characterized by a specific form of attentional bias—rumination—which has been described as perseverative self-focused attention. Specifically, Nolen-Hoeksema (1987, 1991) proposed that individuals who tend to ruminate in response to initial dysphoric moods (e.g., focusing on how bad one feels and the implications or consequences of negative moods) would develop a more severe and longer-lasting depression. In contrast, individuals who tend to distract themselves from dysphoric moods (e.g., through pleasant activities) are hypothesized to recover from dysphoric moods more quickly.

Finally, in the reformulated theory of learned helplessness (Abramson et al., 1978) and its more recent incarnation, the hopelessness theory of depression (Abramson, Metalsky, & Alloy, 1989), cognitive vulnerability is defined as a specific type of interpretation bias—attributions for the causes of negative events. In revising the original theory of learned helplessness (see Maier & Seligman, 1976), Abramson et al. (1978) sought to explain why only some individuals become depressed following the occurrence of negative life events. Abramson and colleagues (1978) proposed that a tendency to attribute negative events to internal, stable, and global causes (negative attributional style) would contribute vulnerability to the development of depression following the occurrence of negative life events. In further refining the theory, Abramson et al. (1989) de-emphasized the internality dimension of causal attributions and introduced components for the negative consequences and self-characteristics inferred from the occurrence of negative life events. Therefore, in the hopelessness theory, cognitive vulnerability (negative inferential style) is defined as the tendency to attribute negative events to stable, global causes and to infer negative consequences and negative self-characteristics following the events' occurrence. In both the reformulated theory of learned helplessness and the hopelessness theory, these cognitive vulnerabilities (negative attributional and inferential styles) are hypothesized to contribute vulnerability to depression in the presence, but not absence, of negative life events.

Anxiety

Cognitive models of anxiety also emphasize attention and interpretation biases as vulnerability factors. For example, Beck, Emery, and Greenberg (1985) defined vulnerability to anxiety in terms of the presence of schemata reflecting themes of threat or danger. Specifically, Beck et al. proposed that individuals who are cognitively vulnerable to anxiety would exhibit preferential attention and memory, as well as schema-congruent interpretation biases, for anxiety-relevant stimuli (i.e., stimuli reflecting themes of threat or danger). Beck et al. further hypothesized specificity in terms of the content of the information-processing biases related to each anxiety disorder. For example, individuals vulnerable to panic are hypothesized to exhibit preferential attention to physiological symptoms and interpretation biases characterized by catastrophic misinterpretation of these bodily sensations.

Building upon Beck's theory, Riskind and colleagues (e.g., Riskind, 1997; Riskind & Williams, in press; Riskind, Williams, Gessner, Chrosniak, & Cortina, 2000) have provided detailed hypotheses regarding the type of schema likely to contribute vulnerability to anxiety, which they have termed the *looming maladaptive style.* Whereas earlier models of anxiety (e.g., Beck et al., 1985) focused on static perceptions of threat, Riskind and colleagues proposed that cognitive vulnerability to anxiety may be best characterized as a cognitive style reflecting dynamic perceptions of rapidly escalating threat. The looming maladaptive style, therefore, is hypothesized to give rise not only to attentional biases for threat-relevant information, but also to interpretation biases of threat-relevant stimuli as rapidly approaching and accelerating in their approach, which then increase the perceived probability and cost of the threat. These attention and interpretation biases are hypothesized to mediate the link between the looming maladaptive style and both the development and maintenance of anxiety (see Riskind; Riskind & Williams). Although the looming maladaptive style has been proposed as a cognitive vulnerability common to all anxiety disorders, Riskind hypothesized that vulnerability to each anxiety disorder would be characterized by a unique cognitive content (e.g., perceptions of rapidly spreading germs among individuals vulnerable to obsessive-compulsive disorder).

In a third cognitive model of anxiety, Williams and colleagues (Williams et al., 1988; Williams, Watts, MacLeod, & Mathews, 1997) built upon Beck's theory by integrating it with network theories of human information processing (Bower, 1981). In doing so, they distinguished between strategic and automatic stages of information processing. Thus, for example, rather than proposing general attentional biases toward threat-relevant information, Williams et al. (1988, 1997) hypothesized that cognitive vulnerability to anxiety may be characterized by an automatic initial attentional bias toward threatening stimuli, followed by a rapid attentional shift away from the stimuli, which would limit further strategic processing of the threat. In addition to the interpretation biases proposed by Beck et al. (1985), this vigilance-avoidance pattern of attentional bias is hypothesized to contribute to the development of anxiety in the presence of threat-relevant stimuli (Mathews & MacLeod, 2002).

Finally, Chorpita and Barlow (1998) proposed that a specific form of interpretation bias—low perceived control—may contribute vulnerability to the development of anxiety. Specifically, providing a vulnerability-stress framework for understanding the development of anxiety, Chorpita and Barlow suggested that it is not merely the occurrence of negative events that contributes vulnerability to the development of anxiety, but rather the person's characteristic tendency to interpret these events as uncontrollable. In contrast to the other theories, however, Chorpita and Barlow hypothesized that low perceived control may contribute to the development of depression as well as anxiety. Specifically, citing Alloy, Kelly, Mineka, and Clements (1990), Chorpita and Barlow suggested that perceptions of low control over desired outcomes may initially contribute to anxiety, but as the individuals' perceptions of control diminish into a sense of hopelessness regarding the occurrence of desired outcomes, anxiety will give way to depression (cf. Bowlby, 1973, 1980).

Aggression

Cognitive models of aggression and externalizing disorders focus on information-processing biases associated with perceived attacks or transgressions (e.g., Beck, 1976). The most well-researched cognitive model of aggression and externalizing disorders (e.g., conduct disorder) is Dodge's (1986, 1993; Crick & Dodge, 1994) social information–processing model. This model is also relatively unique in that it is one of the few cognitive vulnerability-stress models of psychopathology developed specifically for children and adolescents rather than being a downward extension of a theory developed for adults. In this model, Crick and Dodge proposed that the occurrence of negative life events (e.g., rejection) activates a series of cognitive processes: (a) encoding and (b) interpretation of event cues; (c) selection of a desired outcome for the situation; (d) generation of possible responses based upon past experience; and (e) selection of a response, followed by a behavioral reaction. These processes are hypothesized to operate in a continuous cycle (with feedback loops), interacting at each step with the child's memory and social schemata. In this model, cognitively vulnerable individuals are hypothesized to exhibit biased attention to, and encoding of, hostile situation cues; a hostile attributional bias for these situations (tendency to attribute hostile intent to the others' behavior); preferential generation of aggressive responses to the event; and a tendency to anticipate positive outcomes for aggressive behavior (thereby making them more likely to choose an aggressive response). Dodge (1991; Dodge, Lochman, Harnish, Bates, & Pettit, 1997) has also hypothesized specific processing biases thought to differentiate reactive from proactive aggression. Specifically, reactive forms of aggression are hypothesized to be most strongly related to biases in attention, encoding, interpretation, and generation of possible responses, whereas proactive aggression is hypothesized to be most strongly associated with the tendency to anticipate positive outcomes of aggression.

Conclusions

In summary, information-processing biases in depression, anxiety, and aggression are hypothesized to center on themes of helplessness and loss, perceived threat or danger, and perceptions of being attacked or wronged, respectively (Beck, 1976; Beck et al., 1985; Clark et al., 1999). Each of the models proposes similar cognitive processes (e.g., attention and interpretation biases) that confer vulnerability to psychopathology. The key differences are the stimuli that elicit these information-processing biases as well as the specific cognitive content of each vulnerability factor. It should be kept in mind that each of the theories reviewed presents cognitive vulnerability-stress models for the development of psychopathology. That is, individuals hypothesized to be at highest risk for developing the disorder are those exhibiting the respective cognitive vulnerability who also experience corresponding forms of negative life events. We now turn to a review of studies evaluating each of the models' vulnerability hypotheses.

EVIDENCE FOR THE COGNITIVE VULNERABILITY-STRESS MODELS OF PSYCHOPATHOLOGY

Depression

By far, the largest number of studies examining cognitive models of psychopathology has focused on depression. A variety of study designs have been used to evaluate the cognitive models of depression, including cross-sectional, retrospective, and remitted depression designs (for reviews, see Abramson et al., 2002; Clark et al., 1999; Gladstone & Kaslow, 1995; Gotlib & Neubauer, 2000; Haaga, Dyck, & Ernst, 1991; Ingram, Miranda, & Segal, 1998; Joiner & Wagner, 1995; Peterson & Seligman, 1984; Sweeney, Anderson, & Bailey, 1986). However, none of these three study designs allows an adequate test of the vulnerability-stress hypothesis, because they cannot determine whether the cognitive vulnerability temporally preceded the onset of depression (for a discussion of other limitations of remitted depression designs, see Just, Abramson, & Alloy, 2001). In this section, therefore, we will focus on results from prospective longitudinal studies, which provide the most powerful test of the cognitive theories' vulnerability-stress hypotheses.

Schemata

Prospective studies have provided mixed support for Beck's (1967, 1987; Clark et al., 1999) hypothesis that depressive schemata (as evidenced by dysfunctional attitudes, sociotropy, and autonomy) interact with negative life events to predict the development and maintenance of depression. Specifically, although the majority of prospective studies have supported the hypothesis that dysfunctional attitudes moderate the relation between negative life events and the development of both symptoms and diagnoses of depression (e.g., Brown, Hammen, Craske, & Wickens, 1995; Hankin, Abramson, Miller, & Haeffel, 2004; Joiner, Metalsky, Lew, & Klocek, 1999; Kwon & Oei, 1992; Lewinsohn, Joiner, & Rohde, 2001; Reilly-Harrington, Alloy, Fresco, & Whitehouse, 1999), other studies found only mixed support (e.g., Abela & D'Allesandro, 2002; Abela & Sullivan, 2003; Dykman & Johll, 1998; Voyer & Cappeliez, 2002), and some have provided no support (e.g., Alloy, Reilly-Harrington, Fresco, Whitehouse, & Zechmeister, 1999; Barnett & Gotlib, 1988, 1990; Kuiper & Dance, 1994).

Similar results have been found in studies examining sociotropy/dependency and autonomy/self-criticism. Specifically, the majority of prospective studies have provided either full (e.g., Fresco, Sampson, Craighead, & Koons, 2001; Hammen, Ellicott, & Gitlin, 1989; Hammen & Goodman-Brown, 1990; Robins, Hayes, Block, Kramer, & Villena, 1995) or partial (e.g., Abela & Taylor, 2003; Hammen, Marks, Mayol, & deMayo, 1985; Little & Garber, 2000; Shahar, Joiner, Zuroff, & Blatt, 2004) support for the moderating role of these vulnerability factors in the development of depression (but see also Hammen, Marks, deMayo, & Mayol, 1985; Shahar, Blatt, Zuroff, Kuperminc, & Leadbeater, 2004). In terms of Beck's (1987; Clark et al., 1999) and Blatt's (1974, 2004) event congruency hypothesis, there is some evidence that sociotropy/dependency confers vulnerability to depression following interpersonal but not achievement events, whereas autonomy/self-criticism follows the opposite pattern (Abela & Taylor; Brown et al., 1995; Hammen et al., 1989; Hammen & Goodman-Brown; Hammen, Marks, Mayol, et al.; but see also Dykman & Johll, 1998; Little & Garber; Voyer & Cappeliez, 2002). In contrast, however, some studies have found that both forms of vulnerability interacted with both interpersonal and achievement events or with schema-noncongruent events to predict depressive symptom changes (e.g., Fresco et al.; Robins et al.).

A number of points should be made about these studies. The most notable is that there are few prospective longitudinal studies examining the schema vulnerability-stress hypothesis, particularly among children and adolescents. Despite the relatively small number of studies conducted in younger samples, these studies have provided preliminary support for the vulnerability-stress hypothesis. Given the developmental focus of this chapter, however, we should also note that there is some evidence for age-related differences in the findings. Specifically, of the four prospective studies we found in relatively younger samples (i.e., children in elementary or middle school) one study found unequivocal support for the vulnerability-stress hypothesis (Hammen & Goodman-Brown, 1990), one found no support (Shahar, Blatt, et al., 2004), and the remainder found mixed support.[1] In contrast, among studies including older participants, we found 11 providing full support (Brown et al., 1995; Fresco et al., 2001; Hammen et al., 1989; Hammen, Marks, Mayol, et al., 1985; Hankin et al., 2004, studies 1, 2, and 3; Joiner et al., 1999; Kwon & Oei, 1992; Reilly-Harrington et al., 1999; Robins et al., 1995) compared with only 6 providing no support (Alloy et al., 1999; Barnett & Gotlib, 1988, 1990; Hammen, Marks, deMayo, et al., 1985; Kuiper & Dance, 1994; Lewinsohn et al., 2001). Despite this general pattern, however, there is variability in the observed results across all age groups. Given Beck's hypothesis that schemata remain latent until primed by a negative event or negative mood, it is possible that some of the nonsignificant results were due to a failure to activate the schema prior to the assessment. This possibility must remain speculative, however, because we are aware of no prospective studies to directly compare the predictive ability of primed versus unprimed schema in the development of depression (but see Abela & Brozina, 2004; Abela, Brozina, & Seligman, 2004; and Beevers & Carver, 2003, for priming studies of interpretation and attentional biases).

Interpretation Biases

Studies focusing more specifically on the role of interpretation biases have also provided tentative support for the hypothesis that they moderate the relation between negative life events and the development of depressive symptoms. One group of these studies has focused on children's perceptions of their competence in a variety of domains and has suggested that negative self-perceptions of competence contribute to the development of depressive symptoms (Cole, Martin, & Powers, 1997; Hoffman, Cole, Martin, Tram, & Seroczynski, 2000; Tram & Cole, 2000; but see also McGrath & Repetti, 2002). However, it appears that perceptions of competence may mediate rather than moderate the link between negative life events and the development of depressive symptoms (Tram & Cole).

There is also evidence that attributional/inferential styles moderate the link between negative life events and the development of depressive symptoms. These studies are fairly evenly split, however, between those providing full support for the vulnerability-stress hypothesis (Alloy & Clements, 1998; Alloy et al., 1999; Hankin et al., 2004; Hilsman & Garber, 1995; Joiner, 2000; Metalsky, Halberstadt, & Abramson, 1987; Metalsky & Joiner, 1992, 1997; Needles & Abramson, 1990; Reilly-Harrington et al., 1999) and those providing partial support (Abela, 2001, 2002; Abela & Brozina, 2004; Abela et al., 2004; Abela & Payne, 2003; Abela & Sarin, 2002; Abela & Seligman, 2000; Alloy, Just, & Panzarella, 1997; Conley,

Haines, Hilt, & Metalsky, 2001; Dixon & Ahrens, 1992; Hankin, Abramson, & Siler, 2001; Houston, 1995a, 1995b; Hunsley, 1989; Metalsky, Joiner, Hardin, & Abramson, 1993; Nolen-Hoeksema, Girgus, & Seligman, 1986, 1992; Panak & Garber, 1992; Priester & Clum, 1992; Prinstein & Aikins, 2004; N. S. Robinson, Garber, & Hilsman, 1995). There are also some studies, however, that have failed to support the vulnerability-stress hypothesis entirely (Bennett & Bates, 1995; Follette & Jacobson, 1987; Hammen, Adrian, & Hiroto, 1988; Lewinsohn et al., 2001; Ralph & Mineka, 1998; Spence, Sheffield, & Donovan, 2002; Swendsen, 1997).

Similar to studies examining depressive schemata, there is some evidence that the predictive ability of the attributional/inferential vulnerability-stress interaction may be stronger among adults compared with children. Specifically, whereas we found only two studies with younger participants (i.e., elementary or middle school–aged children) that fully supported the attributional/inferential vulnerability-stress hypothesis (Hilsman & Garber, 1995; Joiner, 2000), three others provided no support (Bennett & Bates, 1995; Hammen et al., 1988; Spence et al., 2002). In contrast, we found 10 studies among adults supporting the vulnerability-stress hypothesis (Alloy & Clements, 1998; Alloy et al., 1999; Hankin et al., 2004, studies 1, 2, and 3; Metalsky et al., 1987; Metalsky & Joiner, 1992, 1997; Needles & Abramson, 1990; Reilly-Harrington et al., 1999), compared to only 4 providing no support (Follette & Jacobson, 1987; Lewinsohn et al., 2001; Ralph & Mineka, 1998; Swendsen, 1997). Further support for age-related differences comes from a 5-year longitudinal study of third and fourth graders in which life events and depressive symptoms were assessed every 6 months (Nolen-Hoeksema et al., 1992). In this study, the attributional vulnerability-stress interaction significantly predicted depressive symptom changes at four of the last five follow-ups, but none of the first four follow-ups. Although far from conclusive, these studies provide some evidence that the predictive ability of the attributional/inferential vulnerability-stress interaction may increase with age.

There is also some evidence that the mixed results obtained in studies examining the attributional/inferential vulnerability-stress hypothesis may be due, at least in part, to variations in levels of self-esteem among the participants. Specifically, there is a growing body of research suggesting that levels of self-esteem may moderate the attributional/inferential vulnerability-stress interaction in predicting changes in depressive symptoms (Abela, 2002; Abela & Payne, 2003; Conley et al., 2001; Metalsky et al., 1993; Ralph & Mineka, 1998; N. S. Robinson et al., 1995). That is, individuals at highest risk for developing depression may be those with negative attributional/inferential styles combined with high levels of negative life events *and* low levels of self-esteem. It should also be noted that these findings have been consistently obtained in children and adults. Future studies are needed to determine whether there is something unique about self-esteem or whether the presence of any number of cognitive vulnerabilities may augment the predictive ability of the attributional/inferential vulnerability-stress interaction.

Complementing the results of studies examining the development of depressive symptoms, there is also research supporting the cognitive models in predicting the onset of depressive disorders. For example, individuals in the Temple-Wisconsin Cognitive Vulnerability to Depression (CVD) Project (Alloy & Abramson, 1999) at high cognitive risk for depression as defined by *both* Beck's (1967, 1987) theory and the hopelessness theory (Abramson et al., 1989) were more likely to exhibit first onsets as well as recurrences of major depression over a 2- to 5-year follow-up than were those at low cognitive risk (Alloy et al., 2000, 2004). Further, these results were maintained even after statistically controlling for participants' initial depressive symptom levels. Because analyses of CVD Project data, to date, have been limited to the main effects of cognitive risk status, however, they have not yet provided a full test of the cognitive theories' vulnerability-stress hypothesis. Indeed, we were able to find only two published prospective studies examining the hypothesis that attributional/inferential styles moderate the relation between negative life events and the onset of depressive disorders (Hankin et al., 2004; Lewinsohn et al., 2001). Although both studies found support for the vulnerability-stress hypothesis, they obtained different patterns for the interaction. Consistent with the cognitive theories of depression (e.g., Abramson et al., 1989), Hankin et al. (2004) found that inferential styles were most strongly related to the onset of depressive disorders (major depression or dysthymia) among undergraduates reporting relatively *high*, compared to low, levels of negative life events during a 2-year follow-up. Contrary to predictions, however, Lewinsohn et al. (2001) found that attributional styles were most strongly related to the onset and recurrence of major depression over a 14-month follow-up among adolescents reporting relatively *low*, rather than high, levels of negative life events during the follow-up.[2] Despite this latter unexpected result, there is a growing body of research suggesting that negative attributional/inferential styles moderate the relation between negative life events and the development of both depressive symptoms and diagnoses.

Attention Biases

Studies have also supported the hypothesis that attentional biases may contribute vulnerability to depression. For example, there is increasing evidence that rumination (i.e., self-focused perseverative attention) contributes vulnerability to both the development and maintenance of depression. Although the majority of these studies have focused on adult samples (e.g., Just & Alloy, 1997; Nolen-Hoeksema, 2000; Nolen-Hoeksema & Morrow, 1991; Nolen-Hoeksema, Morrow, & Fredrickson, 1993; Spasojevic & Alloy, 2001; but see also Lara, Klein, & Kasch, 2000), there is also preliminary evidence that rumination contributes vulnerability to depression in adolescents (Schwartz & Koenig, 1996) and children (Abela, Brozina, & Haigh, 2002; Abela, Vanderbilt, & Rochon, 2004) as well.

A limitation of each of the studies discussed thus far is that the assessment of cognitive vulnerability (both interpretation and attentional biases) was based upon participants' self-report. The problem with this is the reliance upon participants' awareness of their depressive cognitions, many of which are hypothesized to operate outside the person's awareness (particularly attentional biases; Gotlib & Neubauer, 2000). Given this, relatively recent research has focused on measures of attentional bias that do not rely on participants' conscious report of the process. A common paradigm for measuring attentional biases is the dot-probe task (MacLeod, Mathews, & Tata, 1986), in which participants' reaction times to identify probes (e.g., dots) following emotional versus neutral stimuli (e.g., words or faces) are measured (see Gotlib & Neubauer, 2000, for a review). Results from dot-probe studies of attention mirror results found in studies using self-report methods to examine cognitive vulnerability to depression. Specifically, studies of adults using dot-probe tasks have generally found that depressed individuals exhibit preferential attention to depression-relevant information compared to neutral information (Bradley, Mogg, & Lee, 1997; Gotlib, Krasnoperova, Yue, & Joorman,

2004; Mathews, Ridgeway, & Williamson, 1996; Westra & Kuiper, 1997; but see also Hill & Dutton, 1989; MacLeod et al., 1986). However, this relationship has not been observed in children (Neshat-Doost, Moradi, Taghavi, Yule, & Dalgleish, 2000).

Despite the strengths of studies employing the dot-probe paradigm to examine attentional biases, the majority have been limited by their cross-sectional design and by the fact that they have not considered the potential effects of negative life events. Therefore, they do not address the hypothesis that attentional biases will interact with the experience of negative life events to predict the development of depression. To our knowledge, only one study has prospectively examined whether attentional biases to depression-relevant material assessed using reaction times interact with negative life events to predict changes in depressive symptoms (Beevers & Carver, 2003). In this study, initially nondepressed undergraduates' attentional biases were assessed before and after a mood induction using the dot-probe task (with depression-relevant vs. neutral words as the stimuli). Consistent with Beck's (1967, 1987; Clark et al., 1999) theory, attentional biases assessed following, but not prior to, the mood induction interacted with levels of negative life events reported over a 1-week follow-up to predict changes in depressive symptom levels over this time (even after statistically controlling for pre–mood induction attentional bias scores). Thus, in contrast to the hypothesis of Williams et al. (1988, 1997), there is some evidence that attentional biases may contribute vulnerability to depression in the presence of negative life events.

Anxiety

In contrast to studies of depression, prospective cognitive vulnerability-stress studies examining the development of anxiety are rare. In addition, the majority of work has examined either the impact of the cognitive vulnerability or stress, separately, with few studies looking at their interaction. However, the data that do exist are largely consistent with cognitive conceptualizations of vulnerability to anxiety.

Schemata

Studies examining the looming vulnerability model of anxiety (Riskind et al., 2000) have provided fairly consistent support for its role in anxiety. Specifically, these studies have suggested that the looming maladaptive style is distinct from other anxious cognitions (e.g., anxiety sensitivity and worry) and that it is related specifically to anxiety, rather than depression (for a review, see Riskind & Williams, in press). In addition, there is evidence that a looming maladaptive style prospectively predicts the development of anxiety (Riskind et al.). Supporting its role as a danger schema, there is also evidence that it may contribute to the expression of anxiety-related attentional and interpretation processing biases (Riskind & Williams; Riskind et al.)

Interpretation Biases

Studies have also supported the role of interpretation biases in anxiety. For example, retrospective studies have supported the link between low perceived control and the presence of both symptoms and diagnoses of posttraumatic stress disorder (PTSD) following traumatic experiences (i.e., war-related traumas and motor vehicle accidents; Ginzburg, Solomon, Dekel, & Neria, 2003; Hickling, Blanchard, Buckley, & Taylor, 1999). There is also evidence from prospective longitudinal studies that cognitive appraisals of traumatic events, and one's responses to the trauma, prospectively predict changes in PTSD symptoms over time (Dunmore, Clark, & Ehlers, 2001). Finally, there is a relatively large body of research indicating that the tendency to interpret physical symptoms as threatening (i.e., anxiety sensitivity) prospectively predicts subsequent panic attacks (Hayward, Killen, Kraemer, & Taylor, 2000; Maller & Reiss, 1992; Schmidt & Lerew, 2002; Schmidt, Lerew, & Jackson, 1997). Indeed, Schmidt and colleagues (1997) found that anxiety sensitivity uniquely predicted the development of panic symptoms, over trait anxiety, during a period of heightened stress (military basic training).

A final line of evidence supporting the role of interpretation biases in the development and maintenance of anxiety comes from studies in which these processing biases are induced. In these studies, computerized experimental paradigms are used to induce interpretation biases by requiring the participant to repeatedly make threatening interpretations of ambiguous stimuli. Researchers have found that these experimentally induced interpretation biases predict subsequent responses to stress such that participants with the induced biases for threat exhibited greater anxiety following stress than did participants induced to make benign interpretations (Mathews & Mackintosh, 2000; Mathews & MacLeod, 2002).

Attentional Biases

Studies supporting the role of attentional biases in anxiety have primarily been cross-sectional in design. Despite the limitations of cross-sectional designs, these studies have consistently shown that both adults and children with either elevated anxiety symptom levels or diagnosed anxiety disorders exhibit preferential attention to threat-relevant stimuli compared with nonanxious controls (for reviews, see Vasey & MacLeod, 2001; Williams et al., 1997). In addition, paralleling the findings from induced interpretation biases, participants in whom attentional biases for threat have been induced exhibit heightened anxious responses to subsequent stress compared with participants trained to attend to neutral stimuli (MacLeod, Rutherford, Campbell, Ebsworthy, & Holker, 2002; Mathews & MacLeod, 2002). Finally, studies have also provided preliminary evidence that attentional biases for threat-relevant information predict changes in anxiety from before to after the occurrence of negative life events (MacLeod & Hagan, 1992; Verhaak, Smeenk, van Minnen, & Kraaimaat, 2004).

Aggression

Studies have also provided consistent support for Dodge's (1986, 1993; Crick & Dodge, 1994) social information–processing model of aggression and externalizing disorders (for reviews, see Crick & Dodge; Yoon, Hughes, Gaur, & Thompson, 1999). Although the majority of these studies have been cross-sectional comparisons of aggressive and nonaggressive children's information processing, there is also some evidence that these social information–processing biases (e.g., hostile attributional biases) prospectively predict the development of aggression (e.g., Dodge, Pettit, Bates, & Valente, 1995). Studies have also supported Dodge's (1991) hypothesis that reactive forms of aggression would be most strongly related to biases hypothesized to occur in earlier stages of information processing, whereas proactive aggression would be related to later-stage processing biases. Specifically, as hypothesized, it appears that reactive aggression is more strongly related to biases in attending to, encoding, and interpreting event cues, whereas proactive aggression is more strongly related to the tendency to predict positive outcomes for aggressive responses (for reviews, see Crick & Dodge; Dodge, 1993; see also Crick & Dodge, 1996; Dodge et al., 1997).

Conclusions

In summary, studies have generally supported the cognitive vulnerability-stress models of depression, anxiety, and aggression. Despite this, however, there are some notable gaps in the literature. First, few studies have provided prospective tests of the cognitive models of anxiety and aggression, and even fewer studies have tested the vulnerability-stress hypotheses. Second, although Beck (1967, 1987; Clark et al., 1999) proposed that schemata remain latent until primed by a negative mood or negative life event, few studies have examined this hypothesis. Among studies of cognitive vulnerability to depression, however, there is some evidence that cognitive vulnerabilities assessed after a priming procedure (e.g., mood induction) exhibit greater predictive utility than do assessments of the cognitive style prior to the priming (e.g., Abela & Brozina, 2004; Abela et al., 2004; Beevers & Carver, 2003). Some of the mixed results reviewed, therefore, may have been due, at least in part, to variations in the degree to which participants' cognitive styles were naturally primed during their participation. Given the small number of prospective studies to test the priming hypothesis, however, this possibility remains speculative and should be explored in future studies. Third, there are relatively few prospective evaluations of the cognitive theories in children. The only exceptions to this are studies testing Dodge's (1986, 1993; Crick & Dodge, 1994) social information–processing model and studies testing the reformulated learned helplessness and hopelessness models of depression (Abramson et al., 1978, 1989). Prospective studies of the helplessness/hopelessness theories in children have provided less consistent support for the vulnerability-stress hypotheses than have studies of adults. Possible reasons for this pattern of findings among children will be discussed below (see section on "Developmental Differences in the Expression of the Vulnerability-Stress Relation").

DEVELOPMENT OF COGNITIONS IN CHILDREN

A limitation of many of the cognitive vulnerability-stress models of psychopathology is that they were developed for adults (Dodge's [1986, 1993; Crick & Dodge, 1994] social information–processing model of aggression is a notable exception). Although this in itself is not a problem, many of these models have been applied to the development of childhood psychopathology without a thorough consideration of the potential need for revisions to the theory. It is likely, however, that many of the vulnerabilities featured in the cognitive models develop over time as a function of both the accumulation of experience as well as increasing cognitive capacities. Although a comprehensive review of the cognitive development literature is beyond the scope of this chapter, we will briefly discuss two aspects of cognitive development that are particularly relevant to cognitive models of psychopathology—developmental differences in cognitive capacities and the increasing rigidity of cognitive processes over time (see also Crick & Dodge, 1994). We also highlight the likely interplay between experience and development in influencing cognitive processing.

In terms of cognitive capacities, there is evidence that children's ability to make internal and stable attributions for events increases across development. There is a large body of work showing that children's interpretations of behavior become increasingly internal, or psychological, with age (Barenboim, 1981; Shirk, 1988). Indeed, Barenboim proposed a developmental sequence of person perception, starting with behavioral comparisons and progressing through psychological constructs to psychological comparisons. In support of this model, research with children from ages 6 through 19 has shown that older children are more likely to attribute behaviors to inferred stable attributes. Research also shows that self-concepts develop with age, starting with the development of self-representation and theory of mind around age 4 (Nelson & Fivush, 2004; Nelson et al., 2003). Theory of mind is conceptualized as a child's ability to recognize a causal relationship between mental states and actions and to recognize that beliefs can be false. Development of theory of mind serves as a foundation for inferring internal and stable attributions for behavior and for associated developments, such as the emergence of autobiographical memory (Nelson & Fivush).

In addition to the increasing internality of attributions, there is also evidence that attributions become more stable across childhood (Ruble & Rholes, 1981). This may be because stable attributions require the ability to integrate information across time, a skill that is not well developed in younger children (see Rose & Abramson, 1992). In addition, younger children are less likely to incorporate experiences into working knowledge that informs predictions (Rholes, Blackwell, Jordan, & Walters, 1980). Instead, young children appear to be more reactive to current circumstances, tending to focus on current or recent states (for a review, see Shirk, 1988). This is contrasted with research suggesting that by middle childhood, children recognize the enduring effects of emotional events (Shirk).

Finally, in addition to the development of cognitive capacities, theorists have hypothesized that cognitive processes may become more generalized and rigid across development (e.g., Crick & Dodge, 1994; Gotlib & MacLeod, 1997). Support for increasing rigidity of processing over time comes from the literature on the self-perpetuating nature of interpretation biases (e.g., Hill, Lewicki, Czyzewska, & Boss, 1989; Hill, Lewicki, & Neubauer, 1991; Lewicki, Hill, & Sasaki, 1989). These studies have demonstrated that once an unconscious interpretative bias is acquired, new information is then interpreted in a manner consistent with this bias. The repetition of interpreting new material in this same way thereby strengthens the bias over time. Regarding the increasing generalizability of cognitive processes, we are not aware of any studies specifically testing this hypothesis. However, this type of investigation could have important implications for cognitive models of psychopathology. Indeed, it seems likely that attention and interpretation biases for specific stimuli generalize over time to entire classes of stimuli (cf. Crick & Dodge; Gotlib & MacLeod). For example, a child with a physically abusive parent may initially exhibit preferential attention to the parents' facial expressions of anger, hoping to avoid further abuse. Over time, however, this attentional bias may generalize to people other than the child's parents (e.g., peers), and, when any anger is perceived, the child may interpret the other person as exhibiting a hostile intent toward the child. With repetition, these attention and interpretation biases may become more resistant to disconfirmatory evidence. Though speculative, this is clearly an important line of future research.

DEVELOPMENT OF COGNITIVE VULNERABILITY

Given evidence for the cognitive models of psychopathology, researchers have begun investigating how cognitive vulnerabilities develop. In this section, we review studies that have examined the development of these vulnerabilities.

Depression

Arguably the most well-developed model for the development of cognitive vulnerability to depression is that proposed by Rose and Abramson (1992). In this model, Rose and Abramson provided a developmental framework by which negative events in childhood may contribute to the development of a cognitive vulnerability to depression. Specifically, they suggested that when negative events occur (e.g., father yelling at the child), the child initially makes hopefulness-inducing attributions and inferences about its occurrence (e.g., "He must just be in a bad mood today"). However, with the repeated occurrence of these negative events (e.g., chronic maltreatment), the child's hopefulness-inducing attributions are repeatedly disconfirmed, and the child may begin to make hopelessness-inducing attributions and inferences (e.g., "I'm a bad kid and I deserve it"). Further, Rose and Abramson hypothesized that over time, these event-specific attributions and inferences would generalize to other forms of negative life events and eventually culminate in a general negative attributional/inferential style for negative events. Finally, Rose and Abramson proposed that experiences of childhood emotional maltreatment or other forms of verbal victimization (e.g., teasing) would be more likely to contribute to the development of a cognitive vulnerability to depression than would other types of negative life events, because with emotional maltreatment and verbal victimization, the negative cognitions (e.g., "I'm worthless") are directly supplied to the child by the abuser. In contrast, with other negative life events, the child must supply his or her own explanations for the events and, therefore, may have greater opportunity to make more benign attributions and inferences for their occurrence.

A number of studies have supported Rose and Abramson's (1992) developmental model. For example, there is growing evidence that negative events in childhood may contribute to the development of a cognitive vulnerability to depression (e.g., Garber & Flynn, 2001; Nolen-Hoeksema et al., 1992). In addition, a number of studies have supported the relation between reports of childhood maltreatment, particularly childhood emotional maltreatment, and the presence of negative attributional/inferential styles (for a review, see Gibb, 2002; see also Gibb, Abramson, & Alloy, 2004), dysfunctional attitudes (Gibb, Alloy, & Abramson, 2003), autonomy (Mendelson, Robins, & Johnson, 2002), and other forms of self-referent information-processing biases (e.g., Steinberg, Gibb, Alloy, & Abramson, 2003). Further, there is evidence that levels of verbal victimization by peers, parents, or both prospectively predict changes in children's attributional styles (Gibb, Alloy, et al., 2004). Finally, consistent with Rose and Abramson's model, there is evidence that negative cognitive styles mediate the relation between childhood emotional, but not physical or sexual, maltreatment and the development of both symptoms and diagnoses of depression (e.g., Gibb, Alloy, et al., 2004; Gibb et al., 2001; Gibb, Alloy, Abramson, & Marx, 2003; Hankin, 2004).

Building from the "scar hypothesis" (Lewinsohn, Steinmertz, Larson, & Franklin, 1981), studies have also examined the possibility that childhood experiences with depression may contribute to the development of negative cognitive styles. According to the scar hypothesis, episodes of depression may lead to lasting psychological changes, such as increasingly negative attributional styles. Consistent with this prediction, studies focusing on child and adolescent samples have found consistent support for the hypothesis that elevations in depressive symptoms contribute to the development of negative attributional styles (e.g., Bennett & Bates, 1995; Gibb, Alloy, et al., 2004; Nolen-Hoeksema et al., 1986, 1992) as well as perceived competence (Hoffman et al., 2000).

Finally, another commonly discussed hypothesis for the development of negative attributional/inferential styles is that children may follow the model of either their parents' own attributional styles or their parents' attributions for events in the children's lives. However, there is little support for this hypothesis. First, there is little consistent evidence for a relationship between children's and their parents' attributional styles (e.g., Alloy et al., 2001; Seligman et al., 1984; but see also Garber & Flynn, 2001; Kaslow, Rehm, Pollack, & Siegel, 1988; Oliver & Berger, 1992). Second, although studies have supported the cross-sectional relationship between children's attributional styles and their parents' attributional styles for child-relevant events (e.g., Alloy et al., 2001; Garber & Flynn; Gibb, Alloy, et al., 2004; Turk & Bry, 1992), there is no evidence that parents' attributions for children's events prospectively predict changes in children's attributional styles (Garber & Flynn; Gibb, Alloy, et al., 2004).

Anxiety

Although there is mounting evidence that cognitive vulnerabilities may contribute to the development of anxiety, little is known about how these cognitive vulnerabilities develop. However, limited bodies of work have examined the etiology of low perceived control and other specific cognitive styles characteristic of anxiety disorders (e.g., anxiety sensitivity, inflated responsibility beliefs). For example, there are some data to suggest that certain parenting styles (i.e., overprotection and excessive criticism) may contribute to the development of control-related beliefs (i.e., low perceived control), a hypothesized vulnerability to anxiety. Indeed, patients with panic disorder and generalized anxiety disorder have been shown to rate their parents as more overprotective than do control subjects (Silove, Parker, Hadzi-Pavlovic, Manicavasagar, & Blaszynski, 1991). Further, other work has demonstrated a relationship between parental overprotection and the presence of an anxiety disorder (Bennet & Stirling, 1998). Studies with unselected child samples also support a link between parenting style and control beliefs. For example, Chandler and colleagues (Chandler, Wolf, Cook, & Dugovics, 1980) found that fifth graders who demonstrated high levels of internal locus of control had parents who were more accepting and rewarding of independence. Similarly, using a behavioral observation task, second graders who were classified as high on internal locus of control had mothers who were rated as warmer, less critical, and more supportive of working independently than mothers of children high on external locus of control (Gordon, Nowicki, & Wichern, 1981). Finally, parents whose reactions are contingent on their child's behavior and whose reactions are enacted in a consistent manner, have children with higher levels of internal locus of control (for a review, see Chorpita & Barlow, 1998). Consistent with Chorpita and Barlow's hypothesis, therefore, these findings suggest that high levels of parental overprotection or criticism may provide early experiences with a lack of control, contributing to the development of a cognitive style characterized by interpretations of an external locus of control, which then contributes vulnerability to the development of anxiety. These findings are also consistent with the work of Beck and colleagues (1985), in that experiences with parental overprotection may contribute to core beliefs of vulnerability.

Whereas low perceived control is hypothesized to contribute vulnerability to anxiety generally, other work has focused on the origins of cognitive biases hypothesized to be associated with specific anxiety disorders. For example, recent empirical work has examined the origins of anxiety sensitivity, a cognitive vulnerability to panic. These studies have provided evidence for both genetic (Stein, Jang, & Livesley, 1999) and environmental (Schmidt, Lerew, & Joiner, 2000; Stein et al.; Watt, Stewart, & Cox, 1998) contributions to the development of anxiety sensitivity. Specifically, two of the three components of anxiety sensitivity—physical and social concerns—appear to have a strong heritable component. However, preliminary data suggest that the third component of anxiety sensitivity—psychological concerns (e.g., worry about physical symptoms reflecting mental illness, feeling scared to be nervous)—is not significantly influenced by genetic factors but is influenced by shared and nonshared environmental factors (Stein et al.). Evidence for the influence of environmental factors on anxiety sensitivity shows that both general stress and the specific stress of a panic attack contributed to increased levels of anxiety sensitivity (Schmidt et al., 2000). Schmidt and colleagues (2000) discuss a transactional interplay between stress, anxiety, and anxiety sensitivity that could increase over time and lead to the development of panic disorder.

Finally, theoretical work has begun to address the origins of specific cognitive biases associated with obsessive-compulsive disorder (OCD). For example, given the centrality of beliefs reflecting inflated responsibility in OCD (see Salkovskis & Forrester, 2002), Salkovskis, Shafran, Rachman, and Freeston (1999) hypothesized five specific pathways to the development of inflated responsibility beliefs: (a) heightened responsibility as a child; (b) rigid and extreme codes of conduct as a child; (c) lack of experience with responsibility (i.e., overprotection) as a child; (d) incidents where one's actions or inactions contribute to a serious misfortune; and (e) incidents where it appears that one's actions, inactions, or thoughts contribute to a serious misfortune. In a preliminary test of this hypothesis, all five proposed pathways were significantly correlated with OCD symptoms in an undergraduate sample (Coles & Horng, 2004). Further, there was initial evidence for the specificity of some of the pathways to OCD symptoms in constrast to depressive symptoms.

Aggression

In discussing the development of social information–processing biases (e.g., encoding and interpretation of cues, as well as generation and selection of responses), Dodge and colleagues have emphasized the role of early adverse interpersonal experiences (particularly childhood physical maltreatment and rejection or aggression from peers; see Crick & Dodge, 1994; Dodge, 1993; Dodge et al., 2003; Dodge et al., 1995). Supporting this hypothesis, studies have supported the link between the presence of social information–processing biases and a history of either harsh physical discipline (Weiss, Dodge, Bates, & Pettit, 1992) or physical abuse (Dodge et al., 1995) during childhood. Similarly, physically abused children have been shown to exhibit both attention and interpretation biases for angry facial stimuli compared with nonabused children (Pollak & Kistler, 2002; Pollak & Tolley-Schell, 2003). Studies have also suggested that experiences of peer rejection prospectively predict the development of these social information–processing biases (e.g., Dodge et al., 2003). Supporting the distinction between reactive and proactive aggression, there is some evidence that these negative interpersonal experiences are more strongly related to the development of reactive than proactive aggression (Dodge et al., 1997). Finally, studies have supported the hypothesis that these information-processing biases partially mediate the relation between early adverse experiences and the development of aggression (Dodge et al., 1995, 2003; Weiss et al.). Indeed, there is also evidence for a transactional relationship between interpersonal difficulties and social information processing such that early biases (e.g., hostile attributional bias) contribute to peer rejection, which then exacerbates the processing biases, contributing to the development of aggressive behavior (Dodge et al., 2003).

Conclusions

In summary, studies have identified a number of developmental antecedents of cognitive vulnerability to depression, anxiety, and aggression. Not surprisingly, these studies have focused almost exclusively on childhood events, particularly childhood maltreatment and maladaptive styles of parenting. To date, however, there are relatively few studies prospectively examining the development of these vulnerability factors. In addition, little is known about the specificity of developmental pathways. Specifically, more research is needed to determine whether certain childhood experiences are more strongly related to the development of one form of cognitive vulnerability versus another. Studies should also examine whether certain factors may moderate the relation between childhood experiences and the development of these vulnerabilities. For example, experiences of childhood emotional maltreatment may be most likely to contribute to the development of a cognitive vulnerability to depression among children who also have a genetic vulnerability to depression (e.g., a depressed parent).

DEVELOPMENTAL DIFFERENCES IN THE EXPRESSION OF THE VULNERABILITY-STRESS RELATION

Depression

As reviewed earlier, there is some evidence that ability of cognitive styles to moderate the relation between negative life events and the development of depression increases with age. Although far from conclusive, this pattern of findings has been observed across a range of cognitive vulnerability factors (e.g., dysfunctional attitudes, attributions, attentional biases). In addition to the general factors noted above that could contribute to mixed findings across all age groups (e.g., failure to adequately prime the vulnerabilities before assessment), there are at least three potential reasons for mixed findings of studies examining the cognitive vulnerability-stress theories of depression in children. First, as Cole and Turner (1993; Turner & Cole, 1994) have suggested, there may be a point in children's cognitive development before which their cognitive patterns have not yet stabilized into traitlike "styles." While these cognitive styles are still developing, children's cognitions may mediate rather than moderate the effects of negative life events upon the development of depression. Thus, although there is no evidence for age-related differences in the cross-sectional relationship between attributional styles and depressive symptoms (see Garber, Weiss, & Shanley, 1993), there may be differences in the extent to which attributional styles moderate the effects of negative life events. Supporting this hypothesis, Cole and Turner (1993; Turner & Cole, 1994) found that attributional styles mediated the cross-sectional relation between negative life events and depressive symptoms among fourth and sixth graders and served as a moderator only for eighth graders. Similarly, Tram and Cole (2000) found that ninth graders' levels of perceived competence across a variety of domains (academics, social acceptance, athletics, physical appearance, and behavioral conduct) mediated, rather than moderated, the relation between negative life events and the development of depressive symptoms over a 6-month follow-up. In addition, although not formally testing the mediation hypothesis, there is evidence that a variety of cognitive variables (e.g., sociotropy, autonomy, and attributional styles) predict changes in depressive symptoms even after statistically controlling for the influence of negative life events (Abela & Payne, 2003; Conley et al., 2001; Little & Garber, 2000; Nolen-Hoeksema et al., 1986, 1992; Panak & Garber, 1992; N. S. Robinson et al., 1995; Spence et al., 2002). However, an equal number of studies have not found significant main effects for the cognitive variables (Abela, 2001; Abela & Sarin, 2002; Abela & Sullivan, 2003; Abela & Taylor, 2003; Bennett & Bates, 1995; Dixon & Ahrens, 1992; Hammen et al., 1988; Hankin et al., 2001; Hilsman & Garber, 1995; Joiner, 2000). Therefore, although there is some support for Cole and Turner's developmental hypothesis, the evidence is far from conclusive and is in need of further investigation. Specifically, longitudinal studies are needed in which the mediational versus moderational role of the cognitive variables is explicitly examined as a function of children's age.

A second hypothesis for mixed results in child samples has been offered by Abela (e.g., Abela & Payne, 2003; Abela & Sarin, 2002), who suggested that various forms of cognitive vulnerability may develop at different rates for different children. According to this "weakest link" hypothesis, until the different forms of cognitive vulnerability coalesce into a more global negative cognitive style, children's cognitive vulnerability to depression is determined by their most negative cognitive style (e.g., inferences about causes, consequences, or self-characteristics). Supporting this hypothesis, Abela and Sarin found that although seventh-graders' inferential styles (combination of inferences for causes, consequences, and self-characteristics) did not interact with negative life events to predict changes in depressive symptoms over a 10-week follow-up, their "weakest link" (most negative score on measures of the three types of inferences considered individually) did. Similar results were obtained in a 6-week prospective study of third and seventh graders, although the vulnerability-stress interaction was further moderated by children's sex and levels of self-esteem such that the vulnerability-stress effects were strongest among boys with low self-esteem and among girls with high self-esteem (Abela & Payne). Abela and Payne also reported that the bias identified as the children's weakest link varied across development. Specifically, attributions were more likely to be the weakest link for seventh graders than for third graders, whereas inferences about the self were more likely to be the weakest link for third graders than for seventh graders. This suggests that attributional styles for causes may develop as a vulnerability factor later than do inferences about self-characteristics, and this finding supports the hypothesis that previous mixed findings of studies evaluating the attribution vulnerability-stress hypothesis may have been due to differences across studies in the proportion of children for whom attributional styles for causes were the weakest link.

A third possible reason for mixed findings in child samples is the way in which children's cognitive styles are typically measured. Specifically, the majority of studies evaluating the helplessness/hopelessness theories (Abramson et al., 1978, 1989) in children have used the Children's Attributional Style Questionnaire (CASQ; Kaslow & Nolen-Hoeksema, 1991; Seligman et al., 1984). Despite the strengths of this measure, it also exhibits fairly low reliability (e.g., α's of .45 to .61; Thompson, Kaslow, Weiss, & Nolen-Hoeksema, 1998). This low reliability limits researchers' ability to detect significant effects even when they are present (i.e., it increases type II errors). Supporting this hypothesis, recent investigations using more reliable measures of children's attributional styles have found more support for the cognitive theories' vulnerability-stress hypothesis (e.g., Brozina & Abela, 2003; Conley et al., 2001; Hankin & Abramson, 2002).

Anxiety

There is also mounting support for the cognitive vulnerability-stress theories of anxiety, particularly for the hypothesis that attention or interpretation biases can confer vulnerability to the development of anxiety. However, it is important to consider that the expression of such cognitive vulnerabilities may differ across developmental levels. For example, paralleling data from the depression literature, there is evidence that the cognitive vulnerability of control beliefs may *mediate* the relationship between parenting and anxiety earlier in development but *moderate* the relationship later in development. Specifically, in a sample of children from ages 6 to 15, Chorpita, Brown, and Barlow

(1998) found that levels of perceived control *mediated* the relationship between parental control and negative affect (anxiety and depression). In contrast, using an older sample (ages 11 to 14), Muris, Meesters, Schouten, and Hoge (2004) found that perceived control *moderated,* rather than mediated, the relationship between parental style and anxiety. Muris and colleagues propose that the age differences between their study and that of Chorpita et al. may reflect developmental differences in the stability of cognitive constructs and thereby explain the divergent findings. These findings are notably similar to the depression review described above, suggesting the possibility that during childhood, cognitive biases may be more of a consequence or reflection of negative life events than a stable vulnerability factor.

In addition, differences in the observation of cognitive biases in anxious children may reflect how these biases are typically measured. For example, the reliability and validity of specific tasks assessing information-processing biases are likely to vary with age and developmental level (Vasey, Dalgleish, & Silverman, 2003). Reliability may be influenced by developmental differences in susceptibility to fatigue and the ability to comprehend instructions, whereas validity may be influenced by factors such as developmental differences in the content of fears or reliance on cognitive skills required to perform the task (e.g., inhibitory skills). For example, attentional biases in anxiety (as measured by the Stroop emotional task) are more consistently observed in older children than younger children (Vasey & MacLeod, 2001). Existing data suggest that this relative inconsistency of observing attentional biases to threat in young children may be influenced by the extent to which the task requires the capacity to inhibit attention to distracting information, a skill that is not well developed in young children (see Vasey & MacLeod). Future efforts should seek to clarify whether information-processing biases are less easy to detect in younger samples because such biases are not yet developed or because the tasks that are being used are not sensitive enough to detect existing biases (Vasey & MacLeod).

Aggression

In contrast to studies testing cognitive models of depression and anxiety, the majority of studies evaluating Dodge's (1986, 1993; Crick & Dodge, 1994) model of aggression have been conducted among a fairly narrow age range of children (i.e., 9- to 12-year-olds; Crick & Dodge). This said, the results of a recent meta-analysis suggested that the strength of the relation between social information–processing biases and aggression did not differ significantly between younger (kindergarten through sixth-grade) and older (sixth- through twelfth-grade) children (Yoon et al., 1999). Thus, it appears that the association between social information–processing biases and aggression may be relatively stable across development. Despite this, however, it may be that developmental differences would be observed in more fine-grained analyses. Specifically, as Crick and Dodge suggested, it may be that developmental differences would be observed for social information–processing biases elicited by developmentally relevant social tasks (e.g., the importance of empathy and social comparisons should increase as children age; cf. Crick & Dodge). Future longitudinal studies are needed to test these more fine-grained hypotheses.

Conclusions

In summary, studies have suggested important avenues of future research on the impact of development upon cognitive vulnerabilities and their potential interaction with negative life events. First, though far from conclusive, there is some evidence that before a certain age, the vulnerabilities featured in the cognitive models may be more reflective of reactions to negative life events than a stable risk factor that would interact with the events' occurrence to predict the onset of psychopathology. Relatedly, the different cognitive vulnerabilities may develop at different rates depending on the salience of particular developmentally relevant experiences. Future research is needed to clarify the impact of development on the vulnerability-stress relationship. These studies should focus on repeated assessments of the hypothesized vulnerability factors and experiences of negative life events, as well as symptoms of psychopathology, across time. Studies should seek to follow the same individuals across development to examine the hypothesized increasing stability of information-processing biases and whether there is a shift from mediating to moderating the relation between negative life events and the development of psychopathology.

A second important line of future research is developing developmentally appropriate measures of cognitive vulnerability in children (cf. Conley et al., 2001; Hankin & Abramson, 2002). Specifically, reliable and valid measures of the hypothesized vulnerability factors are needed before adequate tests of the cognitive vulnerability-stress theories can be conducted in child samples. Paradigms and measures used in adult samples will likely need modifications for use in younger samples. For example, stimuli (e.g., words) used in adult studies of attentional bias may be too complex or may not tap the appropriate target constructs for children (cf. Neshat-Doost, Moradi, Taghavi, Yule, & Dalgleish, 1999). Only when developmentally appropriate measures and paradigms are utilized can researchers begin to clarify the existence and stability of children's information-processing styles and their relationship to psychopathology.

CONCLUSIONS AND FUTURE DIRECTIONS

In this chapter, we have provided an overview of research evaluating cognitive models of depression, anxiety, and aggression. By reviewing studies of multiple forms of psychopathology together in the same chapter, our goal was to highlight similarities in findings across domains and to delineate common areas for future research. In general, our review showed that studies have provided considerable support for these theories' vulnerability hypotheses. Specifically, there is increasing evidence that individuals' characteristic ways of attending to and interpreting negative life events contribute vulnerability to the development of psychopathology. Despite this evidence, however, there are a number of important lines of future research.

The most important area of future research is the need for more prospective longitudinal studies of the cognitive vulnerability-stress models. These studies should take a developmental perspective and evaluate the adequacy of existing models across the range of development, so that we can better determine what modifications may be needed to the theories to make them developmentally appropriate. For example, finer-grained studies are needed to determine how the cognitive vulnerabilities develop and the process by which event-specific cognitions or a single "weakest link" generalizes into a general maladaptive cognitive style or schema. On the opposite end of the spectrum, more research is needed among older adults to determine the adequacy of current cognitive models of psychopathology among this segment of the population (cf. Mazure & Maciejewski, 2003).

Another important line of future research is the examination of interactions among the different vulnerabilities proposed. For example, do attentional and interpretation biases interact to increase risk for the development of psychopathology, or do they act relatively independently? As mentioned above, there is growing evidence that, in the presence of negative life events, levels of self-esteem interact with other forms of cognitive vulnerability to predict the onset of depressive symptoms (Abela, 2002; Abela & Payne, 2003; Conley et al., 2001; Metalsky et al., 1993; N. S. Robinson et al., 1995). There is also preliminary evidence that levels of rumination may interact with other cognitive vulnerabilities to predict onset of depression (e.g., M. S. Robinson & Alloy, 2003). Future research is needed to determine whether other forms of information-processing biases interact to predict not only depression but also other forms of psychopathology.

A related question is whether, as Beck (1967; Clark et al., 1999) has suggested, the activation of maladaptive schemata also activate the entire range of information-processing biases (i.e., attention, interpretation, and memory; see Riskind et al., 2000), or are certain biases more likely than others to be activated for certain individuals? At present, there is some evidence for the interrelationships of these biases. For example, studies have shown that people induced to ruminate (an attentional bias) also exhibit more interpretation and memory biases (Lyubomirsky, Caldwell, & Nolen-Hoeksema, 1998; Lyubomirsky & Nolen-Hoeksema, 1995) compared with individuals induced to distract. Similarly, individuals at high cognitive risk for depression (defined by high levels of dysfunctional attitudes and negative inferential styles) have been shown to be more likely to exhibit self-referent information-processing biases than individuals at low cognitive risk for depression (Alloy, Abramson, Murray, Whitehouse, & Hogan, 1997). If these results are maintained and replicated for other forms of cognitive vulnerability, it would then be important to know when in development this coordination of activation occurs.

A final area for future research is to explore the ability of cognitive models to explain the occurrence of symptom and diagnostic comorbidity. That is, although the cognitive vulnerabilities featured in these models have demonstrated relatively good specificity for the disorder of interest (see, for example, Alloy et al., 2000, 2004; Hankin et al., 2004; Riskind & Williams, in press; Riskind et al., 2000), it is unclear how these models would be adapted for the prediction of comorbid forms of psychopathology. For example, are there specific cognitive patterns that predict symptom and diagnostic comorbidity, or is symptom and diagnostic comorbidity best predicted by the presence of comorbid vulnerabilities?

In conclusion, therefore, studies have provided strong initial support for the cognitive vulnerability-stress theories of psychopathology. Despite the weight of evidence accumulated thus far, however, prospective longitudinal studies remain rare, particularly those taking a developmental perspective in terms of the development of the cognitive vulnerability as well as the nature of the vulnerability-stress relation. We feel that this developmental focus should be an integral component of future research and that it is essential to the further refinement of our theories.

NOTES

1. Although we recognize that the cutoff used is somewhat arbitrary, it provides a useful way of comparing studies given that most, if not all, of the studies reviewed in this chapter included participants on one side or the other of the middle school–high school transition.

2. It is possible that the pattern of results observed in the study by Lewinsohn et al. (2001) is due to the presence of suppressor effects (cf. Cohen & Cohen, 1983). Supporting this hypothesis, the zero-order relationship between attributional styles and onsets of major depression during the follow-up was positive (though nonsignificant). However, the valence of the relation became negative once attributional

styles were included in the regression model, predicting onsets of depression along with other variables. A similar reversal was also found for the relationship between a past history of depression and the prediction of new depressive episodes. Specifically, whereas the correlation analyses supported the well-replicated finding that individuals with a prior history of depression are more likely to experience depression in the future (for a review, see Boland & Keller, 2002), results from the regression analyses in which history of depression was entered along with a number of other predictor variables suggested that those with a history of depression were actually less likely to experience new depressive episodes. This reversal of effects can be a sign of suppression, suggesting that the results may reflect an artifact of the predictor's relation with other variables in the model.

REFERENCES

Abela, J. R. Z. (2001). The hopelessness theory of depression: A test of the diathesis-stress and causal mediation components in third and seventh grade children. *Journal of Abnormal Child Psychology, 29,* 241–254.

Abela, J. R. Z. (2002). Depressive mood reactions to failure in the achievement domain: A test of the integration of the hopelessness and self-esteem theories of depression. *Cognitive Therapy and Research, 26,* 531–552.

Abela, J. R. Z., & Brozina, K. (2004). The use of negative events to prime cognitive vulnerability to depression. *Cognitive Therapy and Research, 28,* 209–227.

Abela, J. R. Z., Brozina, K., & Haigh, E. P. (2002). An examination of the response styles theory of depression in third- and seventh-grade children: A short-term longitudinal study. *Journal of Abnormal Child Psychology, 30,* 515–527.

Abela, J. R. Z., Brozina, K., & Seligman, M. E. P. (2004). A test of the integration of the activation hypothesis and the diathesis-stress component of the hopelessness theory of depression. *British Journal of Clinical Psychology, 43,* 111–128.

Abela, J. R. Z., & D'Alessandro, D. U. (2002). Beck's cognitive theory of depression: A test of the diathesis-stress and causal mediation components. *British Journal of Clinical Psychology, 41,* 111–128.

Abela, J. R. Z., & Payne, A. V. L. (2003). A test of the integration of the hopelessness and self-esteem theories of depression in school children. *Cognitive Therapy and Research, 27,* 519–535.

Abela, J. R. Z., & Sarin, S. (2002). Cognitive vulnerability to hopelessness depression: A chain is only as strong as its weakest link. *Cognitive Therapy and Research, 26,* 811–829.

Abela, J. R. Z., & Seligman, M. E. P. (2000). The hopelessness theory of depression: A test of the diathesis-stress component in the interpersonal and achievement domains. *Cognitive Therapy and Research, 24,* 361–378.

Abela, J. R. Z., & Sullivan, C. (2003). A test of Beck's cognitive diathesis-stress theory of depression in early adolescents. *Journal of Early Adolescence, 23,* 384–404.

Abela, J. R. Z., & Taylor, G. (2003). Specific vulnerability to depressive mood reaction in schoolchildren: The moderating role of self-esteem. *Journal of Clinical Child and Adolescent Psychology, 32,* 408–418.

Abela, J. R. Z., Vanderbilt, E., & Rochon, A. (2004). A test of the integration of the response styles and social support theories of depression in third and seventh grade children. *Journal of Social and Clinical Psychology, 23,* 653–674.

Abramson, L. Y., Alloy, L. B., Hankin, B. L., Haeffel, G. J., MacCoon, D. G., & Gibb, B. E. (2002). Cognitive vulnerability-stress models of depression in a self-regulatory and psychobiological context. In I. H. Gotlib & C. L. Hammen (Eds.), *Handbook of depression* (pp. 268–294). New York: Guilford Press.

Abramson, L. Y., Metalsky, G. I., & Alloy, L. B. (1989). Hopelessness depression: A theory-based subtype of depression. *Psychological Review, 96,* 358–372.

Abramson, L. Y., Seligman, M. E. P., & Teasdale, J. D. (1978). Learned helplessness in humans: Critique and reformulation. *Journal of Abnormal Psychology, 87,* 49–74.

Alloy, L. B., & Abramson, L. Y. (1999). The Temple-Wisconsin Cognitive Vulnerability to Depression (CVD) Project: Conceptual background, design and methods. *Journal of Cognitive Psychotherapy, 13,* 227–262.

Alloy, L. B., Abramson, L. Y., Hogan, M. E., Whitehouse, W. G., Rose, D. T., Robinson, M. S., et al. (2000). The Temple-Wisconsin Cognitive Vulnerability to Depression Project: Lifetime history of Axis I psychopathology in individuals at high and low cognitive risk for depression. *Journal of Abnormal Psychology, 109,* 403–418.

Alloy, L. B., Abramson, L. Y., Murray, L. A., Whitehouse, W. G., & Hogan, M. E. (1997). Self-referent information-processing in individuals at high and low cognitive risk for depression. *Cognition and Emotion, 11,* 539–568.

Alloy, L. B., Abramson, L. Y., Tashman, N. A., Berrebbi, D. S., Hogan, M. E., Whitehouse, W. G., et al. (2001). Developmental origins of cognitive vulnerability to depression: Parenting, cognitive, and inferential feedback styles of the parents of individuals at high and low cognitive risk for depression. *Cognitive Therapy and Research, 25,* 397–423.

Alloy, L. B., Abramson, L. Y., Whitehouse, W. G., Hogan, M. E., Panzarella, C., & Rose, D. T. (2004). *Prospective incidence of first onsets and recurrences of depression in individuals at high and low cognitive risk for depression.* Manuscript submitted for publication.

Alloy, L. B., & Clements, C. M. (1998). Hopelessness theory of depression: Tests of the symptom component. *Cognitive Therapy and Research, 22,* 303–335.

Alloy, L. B., Just, N., & Panzarella, C. (1997). Attributional style, daily life events, and hopelessness depression: Subtype validation by prospective variability and specificity of symptoms. *Cognitive Therapy and Research, 21,* 321–344.

Alloy, L. B., Kelly, K. A., Mineka, S., & Clements, C. M. (1990). Comorbidity of anxiety and depressive disorders: A helplessness-hopelessness perspective. In J. D. Maser & C. R. Cloninger (Eds.), *Comorbidity of mood and anxiety disorders* (pp. 499–543). Washington, DC: American Psychiatric Press.

Alloy, L. B., Reilly-Harrington, N., Fresco, D. M., Whitehouse, W. G., & Zechmeister, J. S. (1999). Cognitive styles and life events in subsyndromal unipolar and bipolar disorders: Stability and prospective prediction of depressive and hypomanic mood swings. *Journal of Cognitive Psychotherapy, 13,* 21–40.

Barenboim, C. (1981). The development of person perception in childhood and adolescence: From behavioral comparisons to psychological constructs to psychological comparisons. *Child Development, 52,* 129–144.

Barnett, P. A., & Gotlib, I. H. (1988). Dysfunctional attitudes and psychosocial stress: The differential prediction of future psychological symptomatology. *Motivation and Emotion, 12,* 251–270.

Barnett, P. A., & Gotlib, I. H. (1990). Cognitive vulnerability to depressive symptoms among men and women. *Cognitive Therapy and Research, 14,* 47–61.

Beck, A. T. (1967). *Depression: Clinical, experimental, and theoretical aspects.* New York: Harper & Row.

Beck, A. T. (1976). *Cognitive therapy and the emotional disorders.* New York: International Universities Press.

Beck, A. T. (1987). Cognitive models of depression. *Journal of Cognitive Psychotherapy, 1,* 5–37.

Beck, A. T., Emery, G., & Greenberg, R. L. (1985). *Anxiety disorders and phobias: A cognitive perspective.* New York: Basic Books.

Beevers, C. G., & Carver, C. S. (2003). Attentional bias and mood persistence as prospective predictors of dysphoria. *Cognitive Therapy and Research, 27,* 619–637.

Bennet, A., & Stirling, J. (1998). Vulnerability factors in the anxiety disorders. *British Journal of Medical Psychology, 71,* 311–321.

Bennett, D. S., & Bates, J. E. (1995). Prospective models of depressive symptoms in early adolescence: Attributional styles, stress, and support. *Journal of Early Adolescence, 15,* 229–315.

Blatt, S. J. (1974). Levels of object representation in anaclitic and introjective depression. *Psychoanalytic Study of the Child, 29,* 107–157.

Blatt, S. J. (2004). *Experiences of depression: Theoretical, clinical, and research perspectives.* Washington, DC: American Psychological Association.

Boland, R. J., & Keller, M. B. (2002). Course and outcome of depression. In I. H. Gotlib & C. L. Hammen (Eds.), *Handbook of depression* (pp. 43–60). New York: Guilford Press.

Bower, G. H. (1981). Mood and memory. *American Psychologist, 36,* 129–148.

Bowlby, J. (1973). *Attachment and loss: Vol. 2. Separation: Anxiety and anger.* New York: Basic Books.

Bowlby, J. (1980). *Attachment and loss: Vol. 3. Loss: Sadness and depression.* New York: Basic Books.

Bradley, B. P., Mogg, K., & Lee, S. C. (1997). Attentional biases for negative information in induced and naturally occurring dysphoria. *Behaviour Research and Therapy, 35,* 911–927.

Brown, G. P., Hammen, C. L., Craske, M. G., & Wickens, T. D. (1995). Dimensions of dysfunctional attitudes as vulnerabilities to depressive symptoms. *Journal of Abnormal Psychology, 104,* 431–435.

Brozina, K., & Abela, J. R. Z. (2003, November). *The Youth Attributional Style Questionnaire versus the Children's Attributional Style Questionnaire: A prospective examination of vulnerability to depression.* Poster session presented at the annual meeting of the Association for Advancement of Behavior Therapy, Boston.

Chandler, T. A., Wolf, F. M., Cook, B., & Dugovics, D. A. (1980). Parental correlates of locus of control in fifth graders: An attempt at experimentation in the home. *Merrill-Palmer Quarterly, 26,* 183–195.

Chorpita, B. F., & Barlow, D. H. (1998). The development of anxiety: The role of control in the early environment. *Psychological Bulletin, 124,* 3–21.

Chorpita, B. F., Brown, T. A., & Barlow, D. H. (1998). Perceived control as a mediator of family environment in etiological models of childhood anxiety. *Behavior Therapy, 29,* 457–476.

Clark, D. A., Beck, A. T., & Alford, B. A. (1999). *Scientific foundations of cognitive theory and therapy of depression.* New York: Wiley.

Cohen, J., & Cohen, P. (1983). *Applied multiple regression/correlation analysis for the behavioral sciences* (2nd ed.). Hillsdale, NJ: Lawrence Erlbaum.

Cole, D. A., Martin, J. M., & Powers, B. (1997). A competency-based model of child depression: A longitudinal study of peer, parent, teacher, and self-evaluation. *Journal of Child Psychology and Psychiatry, 38,* 505–514.

Cole, D. A., & Turner, J. E., Jr. (1993). Models of cognitive mediation and moderation in child depression. *Journal of Abnormal Psychology, 102,* 271–281.

Coles, M. E., & Heimberg, R. G. (2002). Memory biases in the anxiety disorders: Current status. *Clinical Psychology Review, 22,* 587–627.

Coles, M. E., & Horng, B. (2004, March). *Examining pathways to pathological anxiety: The etiology of inflated responsibility beliefs in obsessive-compulsive disorder.* Paper presented at the meeting of the Anxiety Disorders Association of America, Miami, Florida.

Conley, C. S., Haines, B. A., Hilt, L. M., & Metalsky, G. I. (2001). The Children's Attributional Style Interview: Developmental tests of cognitive diathesis-stress theories of depression. *Journal of Abnormal Child Psychology, 29,* 445–463.

Crick, N. R., & Dodge, K. A. (1994). A review and reformulation of social information–processing mechanisms in children's social adjustment. *Psychological Bulletin, 115,* 74–101.

Crick, N. R., & Dodge, K. A. (1996). Social information-processing mechanisms on reactive and proactive aggression. *Child Development, 67,* 993–1002.

Dixon, J. F., & Ahrens, A. H. (1992). Stress and attributional style as predictors of self-reported depression in children. *Cognitive Therapy and Research, 16,* 623–634.

Dodge, K. A. (1986). A social information processing model of social competence in children. In M. Perlmutter (Ed.), *The Minnesota symposium on child psychology* (Vol. 18, pp. 77–125). Hillsdale, NJ: Lawrence Erlbaum.

Dodge, K. A. (1991). The structure and function of reactive and proactive aggression. In D. J. Pepler & K. H. Rubin (Eds.), *The development and treatment of childhood aggression* (pp. 201–218). Hillsdale, NJ: Lawrence Erlbaum.

Dodge, K. A. (1993). Social-cognitive mechanisms in the development of conduct disorder and depression. *Annual Review of Psychology, 44,* 559–584.

Dodge, K. A., Lansford, J. E., Burks, V. S., Bates, J. E., Pettit, G. S., Rontaine, R., et al. (2003). Peer rejection and social information–processing factors in the development of aggressive behavior problems in children. *Child Development, 74,* 374–393.

Dodge, K. A., Lochman, J. E., Harnish, J. D., Bates, J. E., & Pettit, G. S. (1997). Reactive and proactive aggression in school children and psychiatrically impaired chronically assaultive youth. *Journal of Abnormal Psychology, 106,* 37–51.

Dodge, K. A., Pettit, G. S., Bates, J. E., & Valente, E. (1995). Social information–processing patterns partially mediate the effect of early physical abuse on later conduct problems. *Journal of Abnormal Psychology, 104,* 632–643.

Dunmore, E., Clark, D. M., & Ehlers, A. (2001). A prospective investigation of the role of cognitive factors in persistent posttraumatic stress disorder (PTSD) after physical or sexual assault. *Behaviour Research and Therapy, 39,* 1063–1084.

Dykman, B. M., & Johll, M. (1998). Dysfunctional attitudes and vulnerability to depressive symptoms: A 14 week longitudinal study. *Cognitive Therapy and Research, 22,* 337–352.

Follette, V. M., & Jacobson, N. S. (1987). Importance of attributions as a predictor of how people cope with failure. *Journal of Personality and Social Psychology, 52,* 1205–1211.

Fresco, D. M., Sampson, W. S., Craighead, L. W., & Koons, A. N. (2001). The relationship of sociotropy and autonomy to symptoms of depression and anxiety. *Journal of Cognitive Psychotherapy, 15,* 17–31.

Garber, J., & Flynn, C. (2001). Predictors of depressive cognitions in young adolescents. *Cognitive Therapy and Research, 25,* 353–376.

Garber, J., Weiss, B., & Shanley, N. (1993). Cognitions, depressive symptoms, and development in adolescents. *Journal of Abnormal Psychology, 102,* 47–57.

Gibb, B. E. (2002). Childhood maltreatment and negative cognitive styles: A quantitative and qualitative review. *Clinical Psychology Review, 22,* 223–246.

Gibb, B. E., Abramson, L. Y., & Alloy, L. B. (2004). Emotional maltreatment by parents, verbal peer victimization, and cognitive vulnerability to depression. *Cognitive Therapy and Research, 28,* 1–21.

Gibb, B. E., Alloy, L. B., & Abramson, L. Y. (2003). Global reports of childhood maltreatment versus recall of specific maltreatment experiences: Relationships with dysfunctional attitudes and depressive symptoms. *Cognition and Emotion, 17,* 903–915.

Gibb, B. E., Alloy, L. B., Abramson, L. Y., & Marx, B. P. (2003). Childhood maltreatment and maltreatment-specific inferences: A test of Rose and Abramson's (1992) extension of the hopelessness theory. *Cognition and Emotion, 17,* 917–931.

Gibb, B. E., Alloy, L. B., Abramson, L. Y., Rose, D. T., Whitehouse, W. G., Donovan, P., et al. (2001). History of childhood maltreatment, depressogenic cognitive style, and episodes of depression in adulthood. *Cognitive Therapy and Research, 25,* 425–446.

Gibb, B. E., Alloy, L. B., Walshaw, P. D., Comer, J. S., Chang, G. H., & Villari, A. G. (2004). *Development of negative attributional styles in children.* Manuscript submitted for publication.

Ginzburg, K., Solomon, Z., Dekel, R., & Neria, Y. (2003). Battlefield functioning and chronic PTSD: Associations with perceived self efficacy and causal attribution. *Personality and Individual Differences, 34,* 463–476.

Gladstone, T. R. G., & Kaslow, N. J. (1995). Depression and attributions in children and adolescents: A meta-analytic review. *Journal of Abnormal Child Psychology, 23,* 597–606.

Gordon, D., Nowicki, S., & Wichern, F. (1981). Observed maternal and child behaviors in a dependency producing task as a function of children's locus of control orientation. *Merrill-Palmer Quarterly, 27,* 43–51.

Gotlib, I. H., Krasnoperova, E., Yue, D. N., & Joorman, J. (2004). Attentional biases for negative interpersonal stimuli in depression. *Journal of Abnormal Psychology, 113,* 127–135.

Gotlib, I. H., & MacLeod, C. (1997). Information processing in anxiety and depression: A cognitive-developmental perspective. In J. A. Burack & J. T. Enns (Eds.), *Attention, development, and psychopathology* (pp. 350–378). New York: Guilford Press.

Gotlib, I. H., & Neubauer, D. L. (2000). Information-processing approaches to the study of cognitive biases in depression. In S. L. Johnson, A. M. Hayes, T. M. Field, N. Schneiderman, & P. M. McCabe (Eds.), *Stress, coping, and depression* (pp. 117–143). Mahwah, NJ: Lawrence Erlbaum.

Haaga, D. A. F., Dyck, M. J., & Ernst, D. (1991). Empirical status of cognitive theory of depression. *Psychological Bulletin, 110,* 215–236.

Hammen, C., Adrian, C., & Hiroto, D. (1988). A longitudinal test of the attributional vulnerability model in children at risk for depression. *British Journal of Clinical Psychology, 27,* 37–46.

Hammen, C., Ellicott, A., & Gitlin, M. (1989). Vulnerabilities to specific life events and the prediction of course of disorder in unipolar depressed patients. *Canadian Journal of Behavioral Science, 21,* 377–388.

Hammen, C., & Goodman-Brown, T. (1990). Self-schemas and vulnerability to specific life stress in children at risk for depression. *Cognitive Therapy and Research, 14,* 215–227.

Hammen, C., Marks, T., deMayo, R., & Mayol, A. (1985). Self-schemas and risk for depression: A prospective study. *Journal of Personality and Social Psychology, 49,* 1147–1159.

Hammen, C., Marks, T., Mayol, A., & deMayo, R. (1985). Depressive self-schemas, life stress, and vulnerability to depression. *Journal of Abnormal Psychology, 94,* 308–319.

Hankin, B. L. (in press). Childhood maltreatment and psychopathology: Prospective tests of attachment, cognitive vulnerability, and stress as mediating processes. *Cognitive Therapy and Research.*

Hankin, B. L. & Abramson, L. Y. (2002). Measuring cognitive vulnerability to depression in adolescence: Reliability, validity, and gender differences. *Journal of Child and Adolescent Clinical Psychology, 31,* 491–504.

Hankin, B. L., Abramson, L. Y., Miller, N., & Haeffel, G. J. (2004). Cognitive vulnerability-stress theories of depression: Examining affective specificity in the prediction of depression versus anxiety in three prospective studies. *Cognitive Therapy and Research, 28,* 309–345.

Hankin, B. L., Abramson, L. Y., & Siler, M. (2001). A prospective test of the hopelessness theory of depression in adolescence. *Cognitive Therapy and Research, 25,* 607–632.

Hayward, C., Killen, J. D., Kraemer, H. C., & Taylor, C. B. (2000). Predictors of panic attacks in adolescents. *Journal of the American Academy of Child and Adolescent Psychiatry, 39,* 207–214.

Hickling, E. J., Blanchard, E. B., Buckley, T. C., & Taylor, A. E. (1999). Effects of responsibility for motor vehicle accidents on severity of PTSD symptoms, ways of coping, and recovery over six months. *Journal of Traumatic Stress, 12,* 345–353.

Hill, A. B., & Dutton, F. (1989). Depression and selective attention to self-esteem threatening words. *Personality and Individual Differences, 10,* 915–917.

Hill, T., Lewicki, P., Czyzewska, M., & Boss, A. (1989). Self-perpetuating development of encoding biases in person perception. *Journal of Personality and Social Psychology, 57,* 373–387.

Hill, T., Lewicki, P., & Neubauer, R. M. (1991). The development of depressive encoding dispositions: A case of self-perpetuation of biases. *Journal of Experimental Social Psychology, 27,* 392–409.

Hilsman, R., & Garber, J. (1995). A test of the cognitive diathesis-stress model of depression in children: Academic stressors, attributional style, perceived competence, and control. *Journal of Personality and Social Psychology, 69,* 370–380.

Hoffman, K. B., Cole, D. A., Martin, J. M., Tram, J., & Seroczynski, A. D. (2000). Are discrepancies between self- and others' appraisals of competence predictive or reflective of depressive symptoms in children and adolescents: A longitudinal study, part II. *Journal of Abnormal Psychology, 109,* 651–662.

Houston, D. M. (1995a). Surviving a failure: Efficacy and a laboratory based test of the hopelessness model of depression. *European Journal of Social Psychology, 25,* 545–558.

Houston, D. M. (1995b). Vulnerability to depressive mood reactions: Retesting the hopelessness model of depression. *British Journal of Social Psychology, 34,* 293–302.

Hunsley, J. (1989). Vulnerability to depressive mood: An examination of the temporal consistency of the reformulated learned helplessness model. *Cognitive Therapy and Research, 13,* 599–608.

Ingram, R. E., Miranda, J., & Segal, Z. V. (1998). *Cognitive vulnerability to depression.* New York: Guilford Press.

Joiner, T. E., Jr. (2000). A test of the hopelessness theory of depression in youth psychiatric inpatients. *Journal of Clinical Child Psychology, 29,* 167–176.

Joiner, T. E., Jr., Metalsky, G. I., Lew, A., & Klocek, J. (1999). Testing the causal mediation component of Beck's theory of depression: Evidence for specific mediation. *Cognitive Therapy and Research, 23,* 401–412.

Joiner, T. E., Jr., & Wagner, K. D. (1995). Attributional style and depression in children and adolescents: A meta-analytic review. *Clinical Psychology Review, 15,* 777–798.

Just, N., Abramson, L. Y., & Alloy, L. B. (2001). Remitted depression studies as tests of the cognitive vulnerability hypotheses of depression onset: A critique and conceptual analysis. *Clinical Psychology Review, 21,* 63–83.

Just, N., & Alloy, L. B. (1997). The response styles theory of depression: Tests and an extension of the theory. *Journal of Abnormal Psychology, 106,* 221–229.

Kaslow, N. J., & Nolen-Hoeksema, S. (1991). *Children's Attributional Style Questionnaire–Revised.* Unpublished manuscript, Emory University, Atlanta, GA.

Kaslow, N. J., Rehm, L. P., Pollack, S. L., & Siegel, A. W. (1988). Attributional style and self-control behavior in depressed and non-depressed children and their parents. *Journal of Abnormal Child Psychology, 16,* 163–175.

Kuiper, N. A., & Dance, K. A. (1994). Dysfunctional attitudes, role stress evaluations, and psychological well-being. *Journal of Research in Personality, 28,* 245–262.

Kwon, S., & Oei, T. P. (1992). Differential causal roles of dysfunctional attitudes and automatic thoughts in depression. *Cognitive Therapy and Research, 16,* 309–328.

Lara, M. E., Klein, D. N., & Kasch, K. L. (2000). Psychosocial predictors of the short-term course and outcome of major depression: A longitudinal study of a nonclinical sample with recent-onset episodes. *Journal of Abnormal Psychology, 109,* 644–650.

Lewicki, P., Hill, T., & Sasaki, I. (1989). Self-perpetuating development of encoding biases. *Journal of Experimental Psychology: General, 118,* 323–337.

Lewinsohn, P. M., Joiner, T. E., Jr., & Rohde, P. (2001). Evaluation of cognitive diathesis-stress models in predicting major depressive disorder in adolescents. *Journal of Abnormal Psychology, 110,* 203–215.

Lewinsohn, P. M., Steinmertz, J., Larson, D., & Franklin, J. (1981). Depression related cognitions: Antecedents or consequences? *Journal of Abnormal Psychology, 90,* 213–219.

Little, S. A., & Garber, J. (2000). Interpersonal and achievement orientations and specific stressors predicting depressive and aggressive symptoms in children. *Cognitive Therapy and Research, 24,* 651–670.

Lyubomirsky, S., Caldwell, N. D., & Nolen-Hoeksema, S. (1998). Effects of ruminative and distracting responses to depressed mood on retreival of autobiographical memories. *Journal of Personality and Social Psychology, 75,* 166–177.

Lyubomirsky, S., & Nolen-Hoeksema, S. (1995). Effects of self-focused rumination on negative thinking and interpersonal problem solving. *Journal of Personality and Social Psychology, 69,* 176–190.

MacLeod, C., & Hagan, R. (1992). Individual differences in selective processing of threatening information, and emotional responses to a stressful life event. *Behaviour Research and Therapy, 30,* 151–161.

MacLeod, C., Matthews, A., & Tata, P. (1986). Attentional biases in the emotional disorders. *Journal of Abnormal Psychology, 95,* 15–20.

MacLeod, C., Rutherford, E., Campbell, L., Ebsworthy, G., & Holker, L. (2002). Selective attention and emotional vulnerability: Assessing the causal basis of their association through the experimental manipulation of attentional bias. *Journal of Abnormal Psychology, 111,* 107–123.

Maier, S. F., & Seligman, M. E. P. (1976). Learned helplessness: Theory and evidence. *Journal of Experimental Psychology: General, 105,* 3–46.

Maller, R. G., & Reiss, S. (1992). Anxiety sensitivity in 1984 and panic attacks in 1987. *Journal of Anxiety Disorders, 6,* 241–247.

Mathews, A., & Mackintosh, B. (2000). Induced emotional interpretation bias and anxiety. *Journal of Abnormal Psychology, 109,* 602–615.

Mathews, A., & MacLeod, C. (2002). Induced processing biases have causal effects on anxiety. *Cognition and Emotion, 16,* 331–354.

Mathews, A., Ridgeway, V., & Williamson, D. A. (1996). Evidence for attention to threatening stimuli in depression. *Behaviour Research and Therapy, 34,* 695–705.

Mazure, C. M., & Maciejewski, P. K. (2003). A model of risk for major depression: Effects of life stress and cognitive style vary by age. *Depression and Anxiety, 17,* 26–33.

McGrath, E. P., & Repetti, R. L. (2002). A longitudinal study of children's depressive symptoms, self-perceptions, and cognitive distortions about the self. *Journal of Abnormal Psychology, 111,* 77–87.

Mendelson, T., Robins, C. J., & Johnson, C. S. (2002). Relations of sociotropy and autonomy to developmental experiences among psychiatric patients. *Cognitive Therapy and Research, 26,* 189–198.

Metalsky, G. I., Halberstadt, L. J., & Abramson, L. Y. (1987). Vulnerability to depressive mood reactions: Toward a more powerful test of the diathesis-stress and causal mediation components of the reformulated theory of depression. *Journal of Personality and Social Psychology, 52,* 386–393.

Metalsky, G. I., & Joiner, T. E., Jr. (1992). Vulnerability to depressive symptomatology: A prospective test of the diathesis-stress and causal mediation components of the hopelessness theory of depression. *Journal of Personality and Social Psychology, 63,* 667–675.

Metalsky, G. I., & Joiner, T. E., Jr. (1997). The Hopelessness Depression Symptom Questionnaire. *Cognitive Therapy and Research, 21,* 359–384.

Metalsky, G. I., Joiner, T. E., Jr., Hardin, T. S., & Abramson, L. Y. (1993). Depressive reactions to failure in a naturalistic setting: A test of the hopelessness and self-esteem theories of depression. *Journal of Abnormal Psychology,, 102,* 101–109.

Muris, P., Meesters, C., Schouten, E., & Hoge, E. (2004). Effects of perceived control on the relationship between perceived parental rearing behaviors and symptoms of anxiety and depression in nonclinical preadolescents. *Journal of Youth and Adolescence, 33,* 51–58.

Needles, D. J., & Abramson, L. Y. (1990). Positive life events, attributional style, and hopefulness: Testing a model of recovery from depression. *Journal of Abnormal Psychology, 99,* 156–165.

Nelson, K., & Fivush, R. (2004). The emergence of autobiographical memory: A social cultural developmental theory. *Psychological Review, 111,* 486–511.

Nelson, K., Plesa, D., Goldman, S., Henseler, S., Presler, N., & Walkenfeld, F. (2003). Entering a community of minds: An experiential approach to theory of minds. *Human Development, 46,* 24–46.

Neshat-Doost, H. T., Moradi, A. R., Taghavi, M. R., Yule, W., & Dalgleish, T. (1999). The development of a corpus of emotional words produced by children and adolescents. *Personality and Individual Differences, 27,* 433–451.

Neshat-Doost, H. T., Moradi, A. R., Taghavi, M. R., Yule, W., & Dalgleish, T. (2000). Lack of attentional bias for emotional information in depressed children and adolescents on the dot-probe task. *Journal of Child Psychology and Psychiatry, 41,* 363–368.

Nolen-Hoeksema, S. (1987). Sex differences in unipolar depression: Evidence and theory. *Psychological Bulletin, 101,* 259–282.

Nolen-Hoeksema, S. (1991). Responses to depression and their effects on the duration of depressive episodes. *Journal of Abnormal Psychology, 100,* 569–582.

Nolen-Hoeksema, S. (2000). The role of rumination in depressive disorders and mixed anxiety/depressive symptoms. *Journal of Abnormal Psychology, 109,* 504–511.

Nolen-Hoeksema, S., Girgus, J. S., & Seligman, M. E. P. (1986). Learned helplessness in children: A longitudinal study of depression, achievement, and explanatory style. *Journal of Personality and Social Psychology, 51,* 435–442.

Nolen-Hoeksema, S., Girgus, J. S., & Seligman, M. E. P. (1992). Predictors and consequences of childhood depressive symptoms: A 5-year longitudinal study. *Journal of Abnormal Psychology, 101,* 405–422.

Nolen-Hoeksema, S., & Morrow, J. (1991). A prospective study of depression and posttraumatic stress symptoms after a natural disaster: The 1989 Loma Prieta Earthquake. *Journal of Personality and Social Psychology, 61,* 115–121.

Nolen-Hoeksema, S., Morrow, J., & Fredrickson, B. L. (1993). Response styles and the duration of episodes of depression. *Journal of Abnormal Psychology, 102,* 20–28.

Oliver, J. M., & Berger, L. S. (1992). Depression, parent-offspring relationships, and cognitive vulnerability. *Journal of Social Behavior and Personality, 7,* 415–429.

Panak, W. F., & Garber, J. (1992). Role of aggression, rejection, and attributions in the prediction of depression in children. *Development and Psychopathology, 4,* 145–165.

Peterson, C., & Seligman, M. E. P. (1984). Causal explanations as a risk factor for depression: Theory and evidence. *Psychological Review, 91,* 347–374.

Pollak, S. D., & Kistler, D. J. (2002). Early experience is associated with the development of categorical representations for facial expressions of emotion. *Proceedings of the National Academy of Sciences USA, 99,* 9072–9076.

Pollak, S. D., & Tolley-Schell, S. A. (2003). Selective attention to facial emotion in physically abused children. *Journal of Abnormal Psychology, 112,* 323–338.

Priester, M. J., & Clum, G. A. (1992). Attributional style as a diathesis in predicting depression, hopelessness, and suicidal ideation in college students. *Journal of Psychopathology and Behavioral Assessment, 14,* 111–122.

Prinstein, M. J., & Aikins, J. W. (2004). Cognitive moderators of the longitudinal association between peer rejection and adolescent depressive symptoms. *Journal of Abnormal Child Psychology, 32,* 147–158.

Ralph, J. A., & Mineka, S. (1998). Attributional style and self-esteem: The prediction of emotional distress following a midterm exam. *Journal of Abnormal Psychology, 107,* 203–215.

Reilly-Harrington, N. A., Alloy, L. B., Fresco, D. M., & Whitehouse, W. G. (1999). Cognitive styles and life events interact to predict bipolar and unipolar symptomatology. *Journal of Abnormal Psychology, 108,* 567–578.

Rholes, W. S., Blackwell, J., Jordan, C., & Walters, C. (1980). A developmental study of learned helplessness. *Developmental Psychology, 16,* 616–624.

Riskind, J. H. (1997). Looming vulnerability to threat: A cognitive paradigm for anxiety. *Behaviour Research and Therapy, 35,* 685–702.

Riskind, J. H., & Williams, N. L. (in press). A unique vulnerability common to all anxiety disorders: The looming maladaptive style. In L. B. Alloy & J. H. Riskind (Eds.), *Cognitive vulnerability to emotional disorders.* Mahwah, NJ: Lawrence Erlbaum.

Riskind, J. H., Williams, N. L., Gessner, T. L., Chrosniak, L. D., & Cortina, J. M. (2000). The looming maladaptive style: Anxiety, danger, and schematic processing. *Journal of Personality and Social Psychology, 79,* 837–852.

Robins, C. J., Hayes, A. M., Block, P., Kramer, R. J., & Villena, M. (1995). Interpersonal and achievement concerns and the depressive vulnerability and symptom hypothesis: A prospective study. *Cognitive Therapy and Research, 19,* 1–20.

Robinson, M. S., & Alloy, L. B. (2003). Negative cognitive styles and stress-reactive rumination interact to predict depression: A prospective study. *Cognitive Therapy and Research, 27,* 275–291.

Robinson, N. S., Garber, J., & Hilsman, R. (1995). Cognitions and stress: Direct and moderating effects on depressive versus externalizing symptoms during the junior high school transition. *Journal of Abnormal Psychology, 104,* 453–463.

Rose, D. T., & Abramson, L. Y. (1992). Developmental predictors of depressive cognitive style: Research and theory. In D. Cicchetti & S. Toth (Eds.), *Rochester symposium of developmental psychopathology* (Vol. 4, pp. 323–349). Rochester, NY: University of Rochester Press.

Ruble, D. N., & Rholes, W. S. (1981). The development of children's perceptions and attributions about their social world. In J. H. Harvey, W. Ickes, & R. F. Kidd (Eds.), *New directions in attribution research* (Vol. 3, pp. 4–40). Hillsdale, NJ: Lawrence Erlbaum.

Salkovskis, P. M., & Forrester, E. (2002). Responsibility. In R. O. Frost & G. Steketee (Eds.), *Cognitive approaches to obsessions and compulsions: Theory, assessment, and treatment* (pp. 337–360). New York: Pergamon.

Salkovskis, P., Shafran, R., Rachman, S., & Freeston, M. H. (1999). Multiple pathways to inflated responsibility beliefs in obsessional problems: Possible origins and implications for therapy and research. *Behaviour Research and Therapy, 37,* 1055–1072.

Schmidt, N. B., & Lerew, D. R. (2002). Prospective evaluation of perceived control, predictability, and anxiety sensitivity in the pathogenesis of panic. *Journal of Psychopathology and Behavioral Assessment, 24,* 207–214.

Schmidt, N. B., Lerew, D. R., & Jackson, R. J. (1997). The role of anxiety sensitivity in the pathogenesis of panic: Prospective evaluation of spontaneous panic attacks during acute stress. *Journal of Abnormal Psychology, 106,* 355–364.

Schmidt, N. B., Lerew, D. R., & Joiner, T. E., Jr. (2000). Prospective evaluation of the etiology of anxiety sensitivity: Test of a scar model. *Behaviour Research and Therapy, 38,* 1083–1095.

Schwartz, J. A. J., & Koenig, L. J. (1996). Response styles and negative affect among adolescents. *Cognitive Therapy and Research, 20,* 13–36.

Seligman, M. E. P., Peterson, C., Kaslow, N. J., Tanenbaum, R. L., Alloy, L. B., & Abramson, L. Y. (1984). Attributional style and depressive symptoms among children. *Journal of Abnormal Psychology, 93,* 235–238.

Shahar, G., Blatt, S. J., Zuroff, D. C., Kuperminc, J. P., & Leadbeater, B. J. (2004). Reciprocal relations between depressive symptoms and self-criticism (but not dependency) among early adolescent girls (but not boys). *Cognitive Therapy and Research, 28,* 85–103.

Shahar, G., Joiner, T. E., Jr., Zuroff, D. C., & Blatt, S. J. (2004). Personality, interpersonal behavior, and depression: Co-existence of stress-specific moderating and mediating effects. *Personality and Individual Differences, 36,* 1583–1596.

Shirk, S. R. (1988). Causal reasoning and children's comprehension of therapeutic interpretations. In S. R. Shirk (Ed.), *Cognitive development and child psychotherapy* (pp. 53–89). New York: Plenum Press.

Silove, D., Parker, G., Hadzi-Pavlovic, D., Manicavasagar, V., & Blaszynski, A. (1991). Parental representations of patients with panic disorders and general anxiety disorder. *British Journal of Psychiatry, 159,* 835–841.

Spasojevic, J., & Alloy, L. B. (2001). Rumination as a common mechanism relating depressive risk factors to depression. *Emotion, 1,* 25–37.

Spence, S. H., Sheffield, J., & Donovan, C. (2002). Problem-solving orientation and attributional style: Moderators of the impact of negative life events on the development of depressive symptoms in adolescence? *Journal of Clinical Psychology, 31,* 219–229.

Stein, M. B., Jang, K. L., & Livesley, W. J. (1999). Heritability of anxiety sensitivity: A twin study. *American Journal of Psychiatry, 156,* 246–251.

Steinberg, J. A., Gibb, B. E., Alloy, L. B., & Abramson, L. Y. (2003). Childhood emotional maltreatment, cognitive vulnerability to depression, and self-referent information processing in adulthood: Reciprocal relations. *Journal of Cognitive Psychotherapy, 17,* 347–358.

Sweeney, P. D., Anderson, K., & Bailey, S. (1986). Attributional style in depression: A meta-analytic review. *Journal of Personality and Social Psychology, 50,* 974–991.

Swendsen, J. D. (1997). Anxiety, depression, and their comorbidity: An experience sampling test of the helplessness-hopelessness theory. *Cognitive Therapy and Research, 21,* 97–114.

Thompson, M., Kaslow, N. J., Weiss, B., & Nolen-Hoeksema, S. (1998). Children's Attributional Style Questionnaire–Revised: Psychometric Examination. *Psychological Assessment, 10,* 166–170.

Tram, J. M., & Cole, D. A. (2000). Self-perceived competence and the relation between life events and depressive symptoms in adolescence: Mediator or moderator? *Journal of Abnormal Psychology, 109,* 753–760.

Turk, E., & Bry, B. H. (1992). Adolescents' and parents' explanatory styles and parents' causal explanations about their adolescents. *Cognitive Therapy and Research, 16,* 349–357.

Turner, J. E., Jr., & Cole, D. A. (1994). Developmental differences in cognitive diatheses for child depression. *Journal of Abnormal Child Psychology, 22,* 15–32.

Vasey, M. W., Dalgleish, T., & Silverman, W. K. (2003). Research on information-processing factors in child and adolescent psychopathology: A critical commentary. *Journal of Clinical Child and Adolescent Psychology, 32,* 81–93.

Vasey, M. W., & MacLeod, C. (2001). Information-processing factors in childhood anxiety: A developmental perspective. In M. W. Vasey & M. R. Dadds (Eds.), *The developmental psychopathology of anxiety* (pp. 253–277). New York: Oxford University Press.

Verhaak, C. M., Smeenk, J. M. J., van Minnen, A., & Kraaimaat, F. W. (2004). Neuroticism, perattentive and attentional biases towards threat, and anxiety before and after a stressor: A prospective study. *Personality and Individual Differences, 36,* 767–778.

Voyer, M., & Cappeliez, P. (2002). Congruence between depressogenic schemas and life events for the prediction of depressive relapse in remitted older patients. *Behavioral and Cognitive Psychotherapy, 30,* 165–177.

Watt, M. C., Stewart, S. H., & Cox, B. J. (1998). A retrospective study of the learning history origins of anxiety sensitivity. *Behaviour Research and Therapy, 36,* 505–525.

Weiss, B., Dodge, K. A., Bates, J. E., & Pettit, G. S. (1992). Some consequences of early harsh discipline: Child aggression and a maladaptive social information processing style. *Child Development, 63,* 1321–1335.

Westra, H. A., & Kuiper, N. A. (1997). Cognitive content specificity in selective attention across four domains of maladjustment. *Behaviour Research and Therapy, 35,* 349–365.

Williams, J. M. G., Watts, F. N., MacLeod, C., & Mathews, A. (1988). *Cognitive psychology and emotional disorders.* New York: Wiley.

Williams, J. M. G., Watts, F. N., MacLeod, C., & Mathews, A. (1997). *Cognitive psychology and emotional disorders* (2nd ed.). New York: Wiley.

Yoon, J., Hughes, J., Gaur, A., & Thompson, B. (1999). Social cognition in aggressive children: A metaanalytic review. *Cognitive and Behavioral Practice, 6,* 320–331.

CHAPTER 6

Interpersonal Factors as Vulnerability to Psychopathology Over the Life Course

KIMBERLY VAN ORDEN, LARICKA R. WINGATE, KATHRYN H. GORDON, AND THOMAS E. JOINER

> *"There is almost always trouble to be found in the terrain of interpersonal relationships with people who are or will become psychologically distressed." (Segrin, 2001, p. 11)*

An interpersonal perspective on psychopathology highlights the importance of human interactions and relationships for both well-being and psychopathology (e.g., Joiner, Coyne, & Blalock, 1999; Segrin, 2001). The context of human development includes layers of social influences, ranging from direct social contacts such as family members, neighbors, and peers, to indirect social influences such as local government or the workplace (Bronfenbrenner, 1986). Each of the layers has the potential both to nurture and to impede development and psychological functioning. Kowalski (2003) reports that respondents to a survey indicated that interpersonal relationships were the most important contributor to a sense of meaning in their lives. These same individuals also reported that interpersonal relationships were the greatest source of stress and disappointment in their lives. The pervasive influence of interpersonal factors on the human experience makes our connections and interactions with others both our greatest asset and potentially our greatest liability.

Interpersonal relationships can buffer us from the effects of stressful life events in the form of social support, or conversely, interpersonal relationships can themselves become a source of stress when relationships become distressed or dissatisfying (Segrin, 2001). Garbarino (1997) goes further by suggesting that some social environments should be classified as "socially toxic" in that, for some children, "the social context in which they grow up has become poisonous to their development" (p. 141). He suggests that one form of social toxin involves interpersonal turmoil, especially familial disruptions. We conceptualize interpersonal vulnerability as an aspect of an individual's interpersonal context that increases the likelihood for interpersonal turmoil and as a result increases the likelihood of the development of psychopathology. These aspects of the interpersonal context can be framed as beliefs an individual brings to a social situation, behaviors an individual engages in while in social situations, or interpersonal processes set in motion by an individual that then exert influence on the individual through the reactions and behaviors of others. Thus, we suggest that interpersonal vulnerabilities for a multitude of disorders may be conceptualized as primarily belonging to one of three categories (although we make no claims that these categories are mutually exclusive or necessarily exhaustive): (a) maladaptive interpersonal beliefs, (b) maladaptive interpersonal behaviors, and (c) interpersonal self-propagatory processes (Joiner, 2002). We briefly conceptualize each of the three categories of interpersonal vulnerabilities below.

Interpersonal beliefs are cognitions that involve the relation between the self and others (e.g., Aron, 2003). How we think about our world (i.e., schemata) and how we plan to act in it (i.e., scripts) have consequences for psychological well-being and health (e.g., Singer & Salovey, 1991). For example, schemata may continue to guide information processing even in the face of disconfirming evidence and may even bias attention away from disconfirming evidence and toward confirming evidence (Singer & Salovey). Thus, erroneous interpersonal schemata may underlie biased, and potentially maladaptive, information processing, which may give rise to maladaptive interpersonal behaviors. Self-schemata involve beliefs people hold about themselves. These cognitive structures make up the self-concept and guide processing of information relevant to the self (e.g., Markus, 1977). Researchers of the self-concept generally contend that the self is socially constructed (e.g., Baldwin & Sinclair, 1996). Baldwin and Sinclair argue that self-construal (i.e., the process of gleaning information about the self) operates through the activation of relational schemata—associative networks of knowledge structures about typical interpersonal situations and the beliefs (self- and other schemata) and feelings that are activated or experienced in those situations. Thus, beliefs about the self, others, and social interactions may be interpersonally based, and, when maladaptive (i.e., resulting in social disruptions), may confer vulnerability to psychopathology.

Interpersonal behaviors are the ways individuals attempt to communicate with one another, including verbalizations (i.e., what individuals say) as well as nonverbal behaviors such as tone of voice, eye contact, rate of speech, posture, and gestures (Segrin, 2001). Segrin notes that it is these behaviors that set up individuals' interpersonal contexts. Thus, the beliefs and behaviors an individual brings to the interpersonal sphere influence the reactions of others. Sometimes, the beliefs and behaviors individuals bring to their social interactions can set in motion processes that both result from individuals' psychopathology and maintain or exacerbate these individuals' psychopathology. These processes, which involve a set of interpersonal beliefs and interpersonal behaviors that "take on a life of their own" in the interpersonal sphere, are termed *self-propagatory processes*. Joiner (2000) explains that the label self-propagatory "is used in the sense that depression and its sequellae induce one another and thus propagate themselves" (p. 205). Although depression is a clear example of the influence of self-propagatory processes, we will present evidence that these processes are equally relevant for the development of other forms of psychopathology.

This conceptualization of a self-propagatory process, which integrates the behaviors and reactions of all individuals involved in a social situation, is compatible with the conceptualization of transactional models of risk in the developmental psychopathology literature. For example, Cicchetti and Toth (1987) describe a transactional model as a conceptualization of development that focuses on all components of individuals' social sphere (both functional and nonfunctional) and the reciprocal influences among all individuals and the characteristics of the environment. In both types of models, self-propagatory and transactional, cause and effect cease to be unidirectional: Vulnerabilities have bidirectional influence, and all components of the interpersonal sphere mutually interact.

In our discussion, we begin with the more intrapersonally based form of interpersonal vulnerabilities—maladaptive interpersonal beliefs. Then, we move to the border of the individual with maladaptive interpersonal behaviors, and finally to the interaction of the individual with the interpersonal environment in the form of self-propagatory processes. For each of the three categories of interpersonal vulnerabilities, we provide examples of interpersonal factors, describe the processes involved, and present evidence linking the interpersonal vulnerabilities to various forms of psychopathology.

MALADAPTIVE INTERPERSONAL BELIEFS

Above, we began to suggest that the self plays a central role in our interpersonal worlds. In the following section, we focus on two forms of interpersonally based self-beliefs: self-discrepancies and perceptions of unmet interpersonal needs. Both involve discordance in the self-concept. In contrast, research on the development of the self-concept in children often focuses on the development of the self-concept into a cohesive, concordant collection of "me attributes." For example, the categorical self is an early emergence of the self-concept in the toddler years; it involves categorizing the self on dimensions along which people differ, such as "goodness" (e.g., "I'm a good girl") or physical attractiveness (e.g., "I'm pretty"; Stipek, Gralinski, & Kopp, 1990). However, as cognitive sophistication increases, complete concordance is rarely possible (e.g., Harter & Monsour, 1992), nor would it necessarily be desirable. The occurrence of discrepant self-views can be normal and adaptive in some circumstances when discrepancies are framed as goals for self-improvement (Higgins, 1989). However, there are inherent trade-offs: Goals can motivate us, yet having goals also opens us up to failure. Thus, in some circumstances, possessing discrepant self-views may lead to emotional discomfort when goals are not met (Higgins, 1989; Vieth et al., 2003).

Self-discrepancy theory (Higgins, 1987) posits that discrepancies between self-schema components (i.e., self-state representations) relate to emotional vulnerabilities. Self-discrepancies can be intrapersonally based (i.e., involving personal views of the self vs. personal standards) or interpersonally based (i.e., involving personal views of the self vs. standards for the self from the standpoint of significant others). Self-discrepancy theory posits that there are three domains of the self: the actual self-concept (a schematic representation of the attributes an individual believes he or she actually possesses), the ideal self-guide (a representation of the self an individual wishes or aspires to become), and the ought self-guide (a representation of the self an individual believes he or she is obligated or required to become). Although the previous examples were framed in the "own" standpoint, self-guides can be held in relation to one of two standpoints, "own" or "other." Thus, individuals can have discrepancies between the actual self-guide and the ideal or ought *own* self-guides, or between the actual self-guide and the ideal or ought *other* self-guides.

Other self-guides represent the desired or required self from the standpoint of significant others in an individual's interpersonal sphere (e.g., the self an individual believes his or her spouse wishes or requires that he or she become in the future). These interpersonally based self-beliefs (which form the structure of self-discrepancies) can take many forms: an actual-self versus an ideal other-self involves a discrepancy between the actual self-concept and the state an individual believes a significant other hopes or wishes that he or she would attain, whereas an actual-self versus an ought other-self involves the state an individual believes a significant other considers it to be his or her obligation or duty to attain. Consequently, individuals can believe they fall short of what others desire them to be or what others require them to be. These two types of interpersonally based self-beliefs have been found to relate to forms of emotional distress involved in many psychological disorders, such as depression and anxiety (e.g., Higgins, 1987).

Self-discrepancy theory (Higgins, 1987) suggests that socialization factors may explain why some individuals develop primarily ideal self-discrepancies, whereas others may develop primarily ought self-discrepancies, and when those discrepancies may lead to problematic levels of emotional distress. Individuals possessing actual-versus-ought discrepancies may have had parental interactions characterized primarily by the presence of negative outcomes (e.g., parents who criticized, punished, or rejected children for not being the people they ought to have been). Individuals possessing actual-versus-ideal self-discrepancies may have had parental interactions characterized primarily by the absence of positive outcomes (e.g., parents who withdrew from, abandoned, or paid little attention to their children for not being the people they ideally could have been).

Manian, Strauman, and Denney (1998) tested the developmental postulates of self-discrepancy theory (although the design was retrospective). The authors report that undergraduate students' use of a style of self-regulation primarily focused on the ideal-self domain was associated with memories of their parents' styles of interacting with them as warm. In contrast, undergraduates' use of a style of self-regulation primarily focused on the ought-self domain was associated with memories of their parents' styles of interacting with them as rejecting. For children whose parents were nurturing and warm, self-standards may have been internalized as ideal goals it would be desirable for them to attain. For children whose parents were rejecting, self-standards may have been internalized as ought goals it was necessary for them to attain (because otherwise rejection would be forthcoming). The consequences of not meeting self-standards would then be associated with the emotional distress that resulted from parental criticism or withdrawal. In this case, the activation of self-discrepancies later in life could be quite painful. To extend this developmental scheme into a diathesis-stress framework, it is plausible that when faced with a stressor that activates self-discrepancies, individuals with histories of parental criticism or withdrawal could become especially emotionally distressed and unable to cope with the stressors—thus opening a window for the development of psychopathology.

Research on self-discrepancy theory (Higgins, 1987) has garnered evidence that self-discrepancies (interpersonally based cognitive structures) are related to depressive, as well as anxious, symptoms. Particularly relevant to interpersonal vulnerabilities for psychopathology are discrepancies between individuals' actual selves and the selves they believe *others* desire or require they become (i.e., ideal and ought self-guides from the "other" standpoint). Self-discrepancies between the actual/own and ideal/other self-guides are associated with depressive feelings, such as "feeling lonely," "feeling blue," and "feeling no interest in things" (Higgins, 1987). Self-discrepancies between the actual/own and ought/other self-guides are associated with anxious symptoms, such as experiencing "spells of terror and panic," "feeling suddenly scared for no reason," and feeling "so concerned with how or what I feel that it's hard to think of much else" (Higgins, 1987; see Hankin, Roberts, & Gotlib, 1997, for evidence in youth). Self-discrepancy theory posits that individuals are motivated to achieve a state of self-consistency by resolving discrepancies between the actual self and relevant self-guides; thus, self-guides serve as standards and goals, like a metaphorical "to do" list for self-improvement. However, the presence of self-discrepancies may not always be advantageous, as suggested by the relation between discrepancies and emotional discomfort. Discrepancies may become problematic when they are extremely large in magnitude or when individuals do not experience a sense of progress in resolving the discrepancies (Vieth et al., 2003).

Duval, Duval, and Mulilis (1992) report that increases in the magnitude of self-discrepancies relate to increased attempts to conform the self to standards (i.e., resolve self-discrepancies) when individuals perceive their rate of progress as adequate, whereas increases in the magnitude of self-discrepancies relate to increased attempts to *withdraw* from attempts to conform the self to standards when individuals perceive their rate of progress as inadequate. Without motivation to resolve discrepancies, individuals may be left with intensified emotional reactions from the corresponding type of discrepancy (hopeless or overanxious feelings). However, the evidence for the relation between self-discrepancies and emotional discomfort provided thus far could be interpreted as support for the hypothesis that self-discrepancies are vulnerabilities for the experience of "normal" levels of sadness or anxiety, but not necessarily as vulnerabilities for clinical levels of depression and anxiety. However, research on self-discrepancies using clinical samples has yielded evidence in support of the latter hypothesis. Strauman (1989) demonstrated that a greater magnitude of ideal self-discrepancies are reported by individuals meeting criteria for major depressive disorder (according to the *Diagnostic and Statistical Manual of Mental Disorders* [*DSM-III-R*], American Psychiatric Association [APA], 1987) than individuals meeting criteria for social phobia (also according to *DSM-III-R*) or individuals with no psychiatric diagnosis. In contrast, a greater magnitude of ought self-discrepancies were reported by individuals with social phobia than individuals with depression or individuals with no psychiatric diagnosis. Scott and O'Hara (1993) replicated these findings with a more heterogeneous clinical population, including individuals meeting the *DSM-III-R* (APA, 1987) criteria for a depressive disorder, individuals meeting criteria for an anxiety disorder, and individuals meeting criteria for *both* a depressive and an anxiety disorder. This result suggests that the relation between ought self-discrepancies and anxiety is not limited to individuals with social phobia but may generalize to other anxiety disorders, especially those relating to self-evaluation. Thus, self-discrepancies that are large in magnitude and that are not perceived as "in progress" toward resolution may function as vulnerabilities for the development of both depressive and anxious symptoms. However, the studies reviewed above are cross-sectional and thus do not preclude the possibility that depression and anxiety lead to the development of differential forms of self-discrepancies.[1]

Self-discrepancies are also implicated in the development of suicidality. The first step toward suicide in Baumeister's (1990) theory of "suicide as escape from self" involves the experience of an extreme self-discrepancy. The self becomes aware of some aspect of behavior that does not meet self-standards, resulting in increased salience for a discrepancy between the actual self-concept and personal goals or expectations (Vohs & Baumeister, 2000). Escape theory posits that self-discrepancies may start an individual down a pathway to suicidality when the magnitude of discrepancies is especially large. In addition to self-discrepancies, the suicidal pathway involves the experience of aversive self-awareness and negative affect, both of which result from attending to self-discrepancies: Because of unmet standards, individuals experience negative emotions and then wish to escape these negative emotions. This is accomplished by escaping to a state of cognitive deconstruction with less meaningful and integrative forms of thought—this lower-level cognitive state prevents awareness of self-discrepancies and thus prevents aversive self-awareness and unpleasant emotions. However, this escape will never be entirely successful; thus, individuals desire increasingly more complete forms of escape, culminating in the "ultimate" escape through death. This desire for escape from mental pain, combined with reduced inhibitions and a short-term focus resulting from a deconstructed state, makes suicide a possible outcome of emotional distress.

How might the self-discrepancies in escape theory develop, and what form might they take? Cornette, Abramson, and Bardone (2000) use Higgins's (1987) self-discrepancy theory to begin to answer these questions. They suggest that views of the self that fall below ideal or ought self-standards and that are both cognitively accessible and large in magnitude lead to states of negative affect (depression, anxiety, or both), which are in turn associated with suicidality. Cornette and colleagues argue that the link between self-discrepancies and suicidality is consistent with the finding that negative self-conceptions are associated with suicidal ideation (Beck & Weishaar, 1990). The relation between self-discrepancies and suicidality appears grounded in theory, yet it awaits direct empirical support, thus representing a promising area for future research that could help elucidate sources of negative emotions in suicidality as well as highlight a point in the causal chain that could be amenable to intervention.

Self-discrepancies have also been investigated as potential vulnerabilities for eating disorders. In a meta-analytic review, Cash and Deagle (1997) found that groups of eating-disordered women (anorexic and bulimic) had significantly greater ideal self-discrepancies than did non–eating-disordered control groups. In an application of self-discrepancy theory (Higgins, 1987) to eating-disordered behavior, Strauman, Vookles, Berenstein, Chaiken, and Higgins (1991) found that the magnitude of ought self-discrepancies from the "other" domain (i.e., actual/own vs. ought/other) was related to anorexic-related attitudes and behaviors, whereas the magnitude of ideal self-discrepancies from the "own" domain (i.e., actual/own vs. ideal/own) was more closely related to bulimic-related behaviors in two samples of college undergraduates (one sample included men). They proposed that ought/other self-discrepancies were more closely related to anorexia nervosa because the disorder typically involves immense motivation to live up to others' demands (i.e., standards framed as duties and responsibilities). In contrast, they suggested that ideal/own self-discrepancies were more characterized by feelings frequently associated with bulimia nervosa, such as disappointment and dissatisfaction. Thus, anorexic behaviors seem particularly related to maladaptive interpersonal beliefs because of the association between anorexic behaviors and unmet standards from the standpoint of significant others. Strauman and colleagues suggest that self-discrepancies may function as a vulnerability to psychopathology irrespective of the *content* of the discrepancies: The *structure* of self-beliefs alone may confer vulnerability. The relations described between disordered eating behaviors and ideal and ought discrepancies remained significant even after discrepancies involving weight and body concerns were excluded. This suggests that the presence of incompatible self-beliefs in the form of an inability to achieve matches between the actual self and ideal or ought self-guides may operate as a vulnerability for the development of eating disorders.

Harrison (2001) argued that body-specific self-discrepancies mediated the relationship between thin-ideal media exposure and disordered eating. She found that exposure to thin-ideal television activated ideal self-discrepancies, whereas exposure to fat-negative media tended to activate ought self-discrepancies in both male and female adolescents. Activation of both ought and ideal self-discrepancies appeared to lead to negative affect, which has been associated with eating disorders. Thus, Harrison proposed that individuals who have self-discrepancies that are both large in magnitude and easily accessible will be the most likely to experience negative affect about their body weight and thus be more susceptible to the development of eating disorder symptoms. For example, if an individual's ideal or ought self is thinner than the actual self, the individual might attempt to restrict his or her eating in order to reduce self-discrepancies and negative affect. If this restrained eating (dieting) goes awry, it might lead to the onset of an eating disorder. In fact, excessive dieting has been identified as a risk factor for eating disorder development (see Stice, 2002, for a meta-analytic review of risk factors). In addition, if an individual is unable to reduce self-discrepancies through restrictive eating behavior, the individual may experience increased negative affect about the failure to reach the goal weight. In this connection, Heatherton and Baumeister's (1991) escape theory of binge eating and Bardone, Abramson, Vohs, Heatherton, and Joiner's (2004) expanded escape theory of binge eating predict that individuals will binge-eat as a means of escaping distress about their inability to change for the better (i.e., inability to achieve their ought or ideal self).

We have provided evidence that discrepancies in the self-concept may function as vulnerabilities for depression, anxiety, and eating disorders. Another type of interpersonal discrepancy involves the perception that one's interpersonal needs are not being met. Joiner's (2004) interpersonal-psychological theory of attempted and completed suicide posits interpersonal vulnerabilities for suicidal desire, including a thwarted sense of belongingness that involves perceptions of an unmet need to belong (Baumeister & Leary, 1995).[2] Although the theory describes this unmet need as a vulnerability for suicidal desire, we suggest that a thwarted need to belong is relevant to the development of other forms of psychopathology as well.

A thwarted sense of belongingness results from an unmet need to belong (Baumeister & Leary, 1995). In order to satisfy this fundamental need, individuals must have frequent, affectively positive interactions with others. An individual with a strong sense of belongingness (i.e., his or her need to belong is fully met) has frequent social interactions with people he or she deems significant and feels cared about. An unmet need to belong, in contrast, results in numerous negative outcomes, including problems with health, happiness, and adjustment. Baumeister and Leary argue that social ties (which would increase belongingness) are associated with decreased risk of suicide, possibly because they may restrain people from following through on suicidal desires. Joiner (2004) argues that belongingness may operate as more than a protective factor: A lack of belongingness may in fact directly contribute to a desire for suicide. Thus, suicide may be one of many negative outcomes of an unmet need to belong. Loneliness may be one manifestation of an unmet need to belong, and in support of this hypothesis, many studies have found an association between loneliness and suicidality (e.g., Bonner & Rich, 1987; Dieserud, Roysamb, Ekeberg, & Kraft, 2001; Waern, Rubenowitz, & Wilhelmson, 2003).

Keeping in mind the association between loneliness and suicidality, and thus the potential deleterious outcome of loneliness, peer rejection has been found to predict loneliness in childhood and adolescence (Cassidy & Asher, 1992; Crick & Ladd, 1993; Parkhurst & Asher, 1992), though the association is modest (McDougall, Hymel, Vaillancourt, & Mercer, 2001). Leary (2001) suggests that interpersonal rejection is one pathway to a thwarted need to belong. Thus, peer rejection may represent a thwarted need to belong in children and may function as a developmental vulnerability for forms of psychopathology (see McDougall et al. for a review). Parker and Asher's (1987) influential review of peer rejection as a vulnerability for later adjustment problems suggested that peer rejection may predict externalizing problems; the only form of these problems they considered was delinquency and criminality.

Research on the development of conduct-disordered behavior by Patterson and his colleagues (e.g., Patterson, DeBaryshe, & Ramsey, 1989) suggests that the relation between peer rejection and future externalizing problems (i.e., conduct-disordered behavior) may be indirect. Thus, although a thwarted need to belong is likely a key component in the development of conduct disorder, its role is to set a deleterious process in motion. The model of Patterson and colleagues begins with a child whose parents do not provide adequate supervision and who are noncontingent in their application of both rewards and punishments. The child is not consistently rewarded for prosocial behaviors and is not consistently punished for antisocial behaviors, and thus the child enters the peer group with both antisocial symptoms and a lack of social skills. This child is likely to be rejected from the peer group early on. This initial peer rejection then serves as a vulnerability for externalizing problems that is activated by the stress of the entry into adolescence. McDougall and colleagues (2001) suggest that the child's need to belong in this stressful time may account for the proposal of Patterson et al. that the peer-rejected child gravitates toward similar peers in adolescence and thus becomes a part of a deviant peer group. It is in this peer environment that the adolescent learns the attitudes and behaviors requisite for, as well as encounters the opportunities for, antisocial acts. Thus, a thwarted need to belong in childhood may place someone on a road toward antisocial behaviors. When the stress of hitting a bump along that road is encountered (e.g., the stresses of adolescence), the vulnerability may be activated, and externalizing psychopathology may appear.

Peer rejection may also predict future internalizing problems, including loneliness (as mentioned above; McDougall et al., 2001). Hershberger, Pilkington, and D'Augelli (1997) present evidence that a loss of friends after disclosing one's sexual orientation is one of the strongest predictors of suicide attempts among gay, lesbian, and bisexual youth. Thus, peer rejection in the midst of a stressful event such as disclosing sensitive personal information may elevate young people's risk for suicide attempts. This supports the hypothesis that a thwarted need to belong can be a powerful predictor of psychological pain and a vulnerability for the development of psychopathology.

MALADAPTIVE INTERPERSONAL BEHAVIORS

The previous section provided a framework for the role interpersonal beliefs might play in the development of psychopathology. The following section describes possible forms of interpersonal behaviors that may play a role in the development of psychopathology. We suggest that interpersonal behaviors become maladaptive and thus operate as vulnerabilities for psychopathology when they contribute to the thwarting of the basic psychological need to belong.

In addition to its proposed relationship to suicidal desire, a thwarted need to belong may play a role in the development of other forms of psychopathology. We suggest that a thwarted need to belong may result from a lack of social skills. There is evidence to suggest that having poor social skills is related to depression, alcoholism, social anxiety, and schizophrenia (Segrin & Flora, 2000). *Social skills,* defined as the ability to communicate and interact with others in an appropriate and effective manner, include such skills as remaining sensitive to others, controlling behaviors and emotions, and attending to social cues (Segrin & Flora, 2000). Segrin and Flora (2000) found that lower social skills in high school students about to enter college predicted increases in depressive and socially anxious symptomatology during the first semester of college. In addition, social skill levels and negative life events were found to function in a diathesis-stress manner, such that low social skills led to an increase in depressive symptomatology when participants experienced stressful negative life events.

Another form of social skills, nonverbal communication, also affects the quality of interpersonal interactions and may result in a thwarted need to belong. Communication behaviors provide insights into a person's psychological state, and more important, communication behaviors are what help to create the interpersonal context in which a mentally distressed person finds himself or herself (Segrin, 2001). Differences between depressed and nondepressed individuals are an illustration of the potential role maladaptive communication behaviors may play in the development of psychopathology (for a review, see Joiner, 2002). For example, depressed individuals (compared with nondepressed individuals) display different vocal patterns in conversational speech: Depressed people speak slowly, softly, and with less inflection; exhibit longer pauses; and take longer to respond to others (e.g., Youngren & Lewinsohn, 1980; see Joiner, 2002, for a review). Depressed individuals also engage in less eye contact than nondepressed individuals during social interactions (Youngren & Lewinsohn).

Individuals with social phobias have also been found to exhibit longer and more frequent silent pauses in speech, as well as more filled pauses (Hofmann, Gerlach, Wender, & Roth, 1997). Social phobics have also been found to exhibit less eye contact during conversations in the laboratory than nonclinical individuals and have been rated by observers as less adequate in speech fluency and overall social performance compared with clinically anxious and nonclinical individuals (Baker & Edelmann, 2002). Higher levels of social anxiety have been shown to relate to problems with relationships (Davila & Beck, 2002), and there is ample evidence for relationship difficulties in depression. For example, voices of depressed individuals are perceived negatively by others (e.g., Tolkmitt, Helfrich, Standke, & Scherer, 1982); the social interactions of depressed individuals are particularly likely to involve negative content when the interaction is with an intimate partner as opposed to strangers or nonintimate acquaintances (e.g., Segrin & Flora, 1998); and the occurrence of disruptions in marital relationships is related to depression (e.g., Beach & O'Leary, 1993).

These findings, that the interpersonal relations of depressed and socially anxious individuals may often be negatively tinged, suggests that the interpersonal behaviors of depressed and socially anxious individuals may not lead to social interactions that meet the belongingness needs of either partner: As stated earlier, for a relationship to contribute to an individual's belongingness needs, the interactions must be positively valenced. An unmet need to belong results in numerous negative outcomes, including problems with health, happiness, and adjustment, and is theorized to be a vulnerability for the development of suicidal desire. Social behavior styles may also function as interpersonal vulnerabilities for psychopathology. For example, Joiner, Katz, and Lew (1997) found that shyness, a form of interpersonal inhibition (i.e., social behaviors involving withdrawal and submission as opposed to interpersonal excesses involving excessive dependency or clinginess), may be a vulnerability for the development of depression. Participants who reported shyness and low social support during an initial assessment were more likely than other participants to experience increases in depressive symptoms at a second assessment point. This effect was partially mediated by loneliness, suggesting that unmet belongingness needs may be a reason why shyness may be a maladaptive interpersonal behavioral style. Shy individuals with low social support may be caught in a vicious depressogenic cycle—they withdraw or avoid the situations (i.e., social interactions) that could provide the social support they need by alleviating their loneliness and increasing belongingness. Instead, when faced with low social support, shy individuals become vulnerable to depression.

Most researchers investigating antecedent interpersonal characteristics associated with eating disorders have done so retrospectively. For example, Troop and Bifulco (2002) conducted retrospective interviews with 43 women with a history of eating disorders and 20 women without a history of eating disorders about feelings and experiences of shyness in childhood and adolescence. They found that women with a history of anorexia with a binge-purge subtype or bulimia nervosa reported significantly higher levels of shyness in adolescence than did women with no history of an eating disorder. No significant difference emerged between groups with regard to levels of shyness in childhood. However, Fairburn, Welch, Doll, Davies, and O'Connor (1997) utilized a retrospective community-based case-control design and found that bulimic women were more likely to report having no close friends during childhood (18%) than were general psychiatric controls (10%) and healthy controls (5%). Although the difference between women with bulimia nervosa and general psychiatric control subjects was not significant, the direction of findings suggests that interpersonal problems may be greater in bulimia nervosa than in some other psychiatric illnesses.

Grissett and Norvell (1992) explored the effects of social skills in a study comparing 21 bulimic women with 21 control subjects, all of whom completed self-report measures assessing social skills as well as other important variables, such as comorbid symptoms. Bulimic women reported less social competence and more negative interactions and conflict than did control participants, differences that remained after controlling for overall symptom severity. In addition, bulimic women were rated as less socially effective than control participants by observers unaware of their group membership. This study affirmed the co-occurrence of bulimia nervosa and social skills problems both as perceived by women suffering from bulimia nervosa and as observed by others. However, this association may reflect the extent to which bulimia nervosa impairs social skills rather than the influence of social skills deficits on the development of bulimia nervosa.

Keel, Mitchell, Miller, Davis, and Crow (2000) examined social adjustment among

177 women who had been diagnosed with bulimia more than a decade earlier. At follow-up assessment, measures of social adjustment suggested continued impairment in interpersonal relationships. In addition, interpersonal problems did not differ between women recovered from bulimia nervosa and those still suffering from an eating disorder. The authors concluded that continued difficulties in social adjustment may reflect an underlying vulnerability from which disordered eating developed and that treatments for bulimia may benefit from including interpersonal skills training. Supporting these interpretations, social adaptation, interpersonal trust, and social support represent useful prognostic indices in treatment (e.g., Blouin, Schnarre, Carter, & Blouin, 1995; Steiger, Leung, & Thibaudeau, 1993); poor psychosocial relating prior to eating disorder onset predicted relapse in eating disorders (Strober, Freeman, & Morrell, 1997); and interpersonal psychotherapy represents an effective treatment for bulimia nervosa at long-term follow-up (e.g., Fairburn, Norman, Welch, O'Connor, & Doll, 1995). Therefore, future research (particularly prospective) that investigates the interpersonal aspects of the development, maintenance, and course of eating disorders could provide valuable information about the etiology and treatment for these pernicious mental health disorders.

We have provided evidence that social skills deficits may act as vulnerabilities for depression, social anxiety, and eating disorders. There is also evidence that this form of interpersonal vulnerability may begin to exert influence early on. Cole, Jacquez, and Maschman (2001) report that children's social competence is a contributor to overall levels of perceived competence, which in turn prospectively predict levels of depressive symptoms. Higher levels of self-perceived competence relate to lower levels of depressive symptoms over time. Thus, children with lower levels of social competence were more likely to experience increases in depressive symptoms over time. An inability to engage in positive social interactions with others may represent a vulnerability to psychopathology that manifests itself early on and continues to increase the likelihood of the development of many kinds of psychopathology in adulthood, including depression, social anxiety, and eating disorders.

SELF-PROPAGATORY PROCESSES

We have described beliefs and behaviors individuals bring to their social interactions that may function as vulnerabilities for psychopathology. Some of these beliefs and behaviors can also set in motion processes that both result from individuals' psychopathology and maintain or exacerbate psychopathology. As mentioned above, this is called a *self-propagatory process* because the components in the process induce one another such that an antecedent is also a consequence, and vice versa. These processes often serve as maintaining agents for disorders such that disorders are more likely to continue and exacerbate and less likely to remit. Below, we discuss four forms of self-propagatory processes: negative feedback seeking, excessive reassurance seeking, stress generation, and blame maintenance.

Negative feedback seeking is one example of an interpersonally based self-propagatory process. Derived from self-verification theory (e.g., Swann, 1990), negative feedback seeking involves the tendency for individuals with negative self-views (i.e., negatively valenced self-schemata) to seek out negative feedback from others. Negative feedback can be elicited in two ways: first, by selecting relational partners who will verify individuals' negative self-views by providing criticism, or second, by interpreting evaluative information in a manner consistent with the self-concept (i.e., as negatively valenced). Why would individuals seek out information that will make them feel bad about themselves? Research on self-verification theory suggests that individuals have needs for both positive feelings (positivity strivings) and consistent self-views (verification strivings; e.g., Swann, Wenzlaff, Krull, & Pelham, 1992). Individuals are motivated to confirm self-perceptions—even if they are negative—because confirming feedback fosters a sense of prediction and control, whereas disconfirming feedback threatens individuals' most basic knowledge base—their own self-concepts. Disconfirming feedback about the self may leave individuals wondering, "If I don't know myself, what *do* I know?" Self-verification theory also posits that individuals are motivated to confirm self-perceptions out of pragmatic concerns: Social interactions in which one partner sees him- or herself in the same manner as the others see him or her are more likely to proceed smoothly. Although soliciting verifying feedback may confer advantages when individuals have negative self-views (and thus are seeking out negative feedback), negative consequences also occur. For disorders such as depression, in which low self-esteem is a symptom, the confirmation of negative self-views becomes a vulnerability for psychopathology.

Clinical depression, according to the criteria of the fourth edition of the *Diagnostic and Statistical Manual of Mental Disorders* (*DSM-IV*; APA, 1994), involves feelings of worthlessness and low self-esteem, and thus depressed individuals should be more likely to engage in negative feedback seeking than nondepressed individuals, especially those individuals with high self-esteem. An empirical investigation of this hypothesis with clinically depressed individuals, nondepressed individuals with low self-esteem, and nondepressed individuals with high self-esteem found support for this hypothesis (Giesler, Josephs, & Swann, 1996). Participants were given a choice about whether they wished to review a personality profile that seemed positive (e.g., "This person seems well adjusted and self-confident") or a profile that seemed negative (e.g., "This person seems unconfident and uncomfortable around others") and were asked to rate the extent to which they wished to review each profile. The percentage of participants who chose the negative feedback varied across the three groups in the pattern predicted by self-verification theory: 82% of clinically depressed participants selected the negative feedback; 64% of nondepressed, low–self-esteem participants chose the negative feedback; and only 25% of nondepressed, high–self-esteem participants chose the negative feedback. This quasi dose-response relationship between level of negative self-feelings and preference for negative feedback suggests a pathway for the development of clinical levels of depression: Once negative self-schemata are in place, negative feedback seeking becomes more likely. Increased negative feedback seeking may then confirm as well as magnify the negativity of self-schemata, thus contributing to the development of clinically relevant levels of low self-esteem and worthlessness.

There is some preliminary evidence suggesting that the interpersonal functioning of eating-disordered individuals may resemble that of depressed individuals. For example, similar to depression, self-esteem deficits have been linked to eating disorders (e.g., Bulik, Wade, & Kendler, 2000; Button, Songua-Barke, & Thompson, 1996; Fisher, Pastore, Schneider, Pegler, & Napolitano, 1994; Tomori & Rus-Makovec, 2000). Thus, similar to depressed individuals, self-verification theory would predict that eating disorder patients have a tendency toward negative feedback seeking (i.e., to confirm their negative views of themselves). Joiner (1999a) empirically investigated negative feedback–seeking tendencies and bulimic symptoms in a sample of undergraduate women. The results were consistent with self-verification predictions, such that bulimic symptoms were positively correlated with desire for negative feedback in multiple domains (i.e., physical attractiveness, artistic-musical, intellectual, and social). Furthermore, Joiner (1999a) found that negative feedback seeking predicted an increase in bulimic symptoms 5 weeks later. Joiner (1999a) found that this relationship was mediated by body dissatisfaction, such that expressed interest in negative feedback predicted an increase in body dissatisfaction, which in turn predicted an increase in bulimic symptoms. Therefore, he speculated that bulimic women may perpetuate their own symptoms by soliciting negative feedback and that this may play a role in the chronic course of bulimia nervosa (e.g., Joiner, Heatherton, & Keel, 1997).

There is evidence that the self-propagatory process of negative feedback seeking may occur in children. A group of inpatient youth completed self-report questionnaires on depression and interest in negative feedback from others. Chart diagnoses and peer rejection ratings were also examined. Joiner, Katz, et al. (1997) found that interest in negative feedback was associated with depression and was predictive of peer rejection in longer peer relationships. Thus, negative feedback seeking may be an interpersonal vulnerability that begins to exert influence early in life.

Excessive reassurance seeking is another example of a self-propagatory process that has been found to function as an interpersonal vulnerability to psychopathology (e.g., Joiner & Metalsky, 2001). Research on this process grew out of Coyne's (1976) interpersonal characterization of depression, which posits that the common assumption in many theories of depression is that depressed individuals misinterpret or misuse the information from their social contexts or are unable to use interpersonal support offered to them. In other words, the problem of depression lies within the person. Most theories assume that the responses of depressed individuals are somehow incongruent with their environments; in contrast, Coyne (1976) argued that depressed individuals play an active role in the formation of their interpersonal environments and that a transactional process ensues in which the individual and environment reciprocally interact to maintain depression. This alternative conceptualization of depression provided by Coyne (1976) posits that depressed individuals do not necessarily misuse or misinterpret information from their social contexts and are not necessarily unable to use the support provided to them; rather, depressed individuals interact with their environments in maladaptive patterns that elicit depressogenic feedback and negate the offering of support. The downward cycle is hypothesized to begin when depression-prone individuals seek reassurance of their worth in response to negative feelings but then doubt the sincerity of others' supportive feedback, thus feeling compelled to seek further reassurance. At this point, the individual enters into a vicious cycle of seeking reassurance, which can never be satisfied and induces negative feelings and responses in others. The frustration, irritation, and possibly depression elicited in others increase the likelihood that others will really reject depression-prone individuals. Armed with feedback that could confirm feelings of low self-worth, depression-prone individuals now need to seek reassurance once again, and the cycle continues (for a more detailed description of the process, see Joiner, 2000).

This process relies not just on processes within depression-prone individuals, but on the responses of others and how the two interact—this is the essence of an interactional-interpersonal approach to psychopathology. Coyne's 1999 reflection on his 1976 interpersonal conceptualization of depression argues that a key contribution of an interactional perspective on depression (but his ideas are equally applicable to other forms of psychopathology) is that it prevents "the fundamental attributional error in depression theory and research" (Coyne, 1999, p. 369). Many conceptualizations of depression attribute causality for the symptoms of depression to "the person" rather than "the situation," when in fact, Coyne (1999) argues, many processes in depression may be best understood as resulting from exchanges between a depressed person and his or her environment or from features of a depressed person's environment. Investigations of the process of excessive reassurance seeking (e.g., Joiner, Metalsky, Katz, & Beach, 1999) have elaborated Coyne's (1976) interactional perspective on depression. This line of research illustrates the benefit of using an interactional approach while also integrating the interpersonal perspective with a social-cognitive perspective. Although Coyne's (1976) original conceptualization in its strictest interpretation would not allow for this blend, we suggest that using a social-cognitive framework (by conceptualizing problematic behaviors in psychopathology as functions of interpersonal scripts) will be advantageous because it allows researchers to use the knowledge and paradigms from the social-cognitive realm, including information-processing paradigms (e.g., accessibility of beliefs), memory, and attention (see Baldwin & Sinclair, 1996, for a similar discussion for the construct of self-esteem). Joiner, Metalsky, et al. (1999) posit that excessive reassurance seeking is a key construct in Coyne's (1976) formulation of depression and functions as the "interpersonal vehicle that transmits the distress and desperation of depression from one person to another" and thus perpetuates a vicious interpersonal cycle and maintains depression (Joiner, Metalsky, et al., 1999, p. 270).

Excessive reassurance seeking involves excessively and persistently seeking out feedback from others that the self is worthy and deserving of love, regardless of whether assurance has already been provided. These behaviors may be a function of an interpersonal script for reassurance seeking that is activated by feelings of doubt related to self-worth. For example, for an individual with the excessive reassurance-seeking vulnerability (i.e., a highly accessible reassurance-seeking script), situations in which his or her feelings of self-worth are called into question may activate a cognitive script such as "If I feel bad, then I ask my friends if they like me." We do not want to argue that these scripts are under conscious control (i.e., we do not imagine individuals consciously thinking through the if-then scenario described above). In fact, one of the goals in a form of cognitive-behavioral treatment for depression, Cognitive Behavioral Analysis System Psychotherapy (CBASP; e.g., McCullough, 2003), is to help clients become aware of interpersonal situations in which they act in maladaptive ways in order to come up with more adaptive interpersonal behaviors (i.e., a new interpersonal script). For an individual who engages in excessive reassurance seeking, CBASP would help the client realize that persistently asking others about his or her self-worth does not lead to increased positive feelings about the self. The client and the therapist would then devise an alternative interpersonal plan for dealing with low feelings of self-worth that would be more likely to lead to a desirable outcome.

Depressive symptoms are empirically related to reassurance-seeking behaviors: Joiner and Metalsky (2001) found that participants diagnosed with clinical depression endorsed higher levels of reassurance-seeking behaviors on a measure of excessive reassurance seeking than participants diagnosed with other disorders. Participants who developed depressive symptoms over the course of the study (after entering the study symptom free) obtained elevated reassurance-seeking scores at baseline but did not obtain elevated scores on other interpersonal variables, suggesting that excessive reassurance seeking may play a specific role in the development, as well as maintenance, of depressive symptoms.

Excessive reassurance seeking has also been found to moderate the relationship between depression and social rejection in adults such that depression results in social rejection most often when individuals engage in excessive reassurance seeking (Joiner, Alfano, & Metalsky, 1992; Joiner & Metalsky, 1995; Katz & Beach, 1997). The relationship between depression, reassurance seeking, and social rejection was also examined with children (Joiner, 1999b) in a cross-sectional study of youth psychiatric inpatients. An index of social rejection using items from the Children's Depression Inventory (Kovacs, 1992) was devised for this study. This measure of rejection was found to be predicted by the interaction of depressive symptoms (as measured by a lack of positive affect) and reassurance seeking. The form of the interaction indicated that children with higher depression scores (i.e., low positive affect) but low reassurance-seeking scores did not report elevated social rejection scores. The combination of depression and reassurance seeking was necessary to obtain the effect of elevated social rejection. Thus, reassurance seeking seems to operate as an interpersonal vulnerability in children that may be activated by stress related to the experience of depression. As shown above, peer rejection in turn predicts negative outcomes, such as conduct-disordered behavior as well as increased depression.

Excessive reassurance seeking may be relevant to the development and maintenance of eating disorders as well. To date, excessive reassurance seeking has been investigated in only one study. Perez, Wingate, and Joiner (2004) found that undergraduate women who exhibited high levels of excessive reassurance seeking (and were thus viewed as more interpersonally dependent) and experienced stressful events tended to have an increase in bulimic symptoms over a 3-week period. Notably, these effects remained stable after controlling for depression symptoms. Perez et al. speculated that women who have highly dependent tendencies may resort to bulimic behavior as a coping mechanism in the face of general life stress. These preliminary findings suggest that excessive reassurance-seeking tendencies may serve as a diathesis that interacts with life stress to predict an increase in bulimic symptoms.

Stress generation is a self-propagatory process that involves actively contributing to the occurrence of negative life events in one's life. The stress generation literature suggests that many depressed people actively do things to generate the stressors that befall them. Stress generation was first studied in a 1-year longitudinal study among groups of women with bipolar disorder, depression, medical illness, or no disorder (Hammen, 1991). The results of this study supported the conclusion that depressed people did in fact engage in stress generation and caused more negative life events to happen to them. This finding of stress generation was specific to those with depression and was not supported among women with bipolar disorder, medical illness, or no disorder. Support has been found for the occurrence of stress generation in married couples (Davila, Bradbury, Cohan, & Tochluk, 1997), men and women (Hammen, Davila, Brown, Ellicott, & Gitlin, 1992), adolescent women (Daley, Hammen, Burge, & Davila, 1997; Davila, Hammen, Burge, & Paley, 1995), black adolescents (Wingate & Joiner, in press), and children (Adrian & Hammen, 1993). A key theme to the study of stress generation is a focus on contingent negative life events. These are events that a person is actively involved in (e.g., a breakup), as opposed to independent stressful events in which a person is not directly involved (e.g., a natural disaster). Contingent negative life events are often interpersonal in nature, as it is suggested in the description that in order to be contingent, it must involve the person. Interpersonal stress lengthens episodes of disorders and increases risk of relapse (Joiner, 2000).

Blame maintenance is a self-propagatory process that occurs when depressed persons' relationship partners develop mental representations of them that bias subsequent perceptions of the depressed person, regardless of whether depression has remitted (Sacco & Dunn, 1990). These representations become relatively autonomous once they are initiated so that they actually become independent of a person's symptomatology. Research has shown that social-cognitive processes selectively guide attention and expectancies to confirm the representation (Fiske, 1993). These processes may occur outside of the awareness of the partner (Lewicki, Hill, & Czyzewska, 1992) and may be particularly salient regarding negative behaviors. It appears that depression erodes others' views of formerly depressed people, in that negative depressive behaviors, including those discussed in this chapter (e.g., excessive reassurance seeking, negative feedback seeking) maintain others' negative views of the depressed person, but the positive behaviors often go unnoticed or misattributed (Joiner, 2000). There is evidence that blaming communications predict depressive chronicity, and blame maintenance processes are clearly related to recurrence (Hooley & Teasdale, 1989; Lara, Leader, & Klein, 1997).

Blame maintenance is a self-propagatory process that can be used to elaborate on the interpersonal processes described above. Mentally ill people tend to engage in processes that others view as negative and offensive, such as negative feedback seeking and excessive reassurance seeking, and display inappropriate communication behaviors and social skills. Others will then view the affected person in relation to the negative interpersonal behaviors that they display. So, although it is not necessarily conscious, people may view the affected person as someone who is irritating (because he or she continually seeks negative feedback or reassurance) or is a bad communicator (because he or she does not make eye contact and lacks appropriate skills, etc.). This image of the person is then instilled in the minds of others, and it is difficult to change—even when the person's behaviors have changed. Blame maintenance essentially enables the interpersonal vulnerabilities to continue to affect the mentally ill person negatively.

INTERPERSONAL RELATIONS AS BOTH VULNERABILITY AND PROTECTIVE FACTORS

When examining interpersonal vulnerabilities in a developmental psychopathology framework, it is important to focus on how interpersonal vulnerabilities affect individuals and over the life span. The focus is on both the changes and the continuities in interpersonal behavior over time. The research presented suggests that over time, social networks of people with mental illnesses will likely dwindle. This is likely to occur with the culmination of several of the interpersonal vulnerabilities. For example, a person may display a particular interpersonal vulnerability (e.g., excessive reassurance seeking) and the negative behaviors associated with it, whereas others react negatively to the behaviors (e.g., rejection) and hold negative thoughts about the person that are resistant to change (i.e., blame maintenance). As these vulnerabilities interact over time and people weaken their social network, these individuals may become increasingly isolated over time.

A significant finding in the literature is that social isolation is one of the strongest risk factors for suicide. In fact, the finding that those who die by suicide experience isolation and withdrawal prior to their deaths is among the clearest in all the literature on suicide (Trout, 1980). These interpersonal interactions could be part of a causal chain linking mental disorders to suicide by way of social isolation. Interpersonal vulnerabilities could operate in a person over time, so that a person is suffering with isolation and rejection over a number of years. When considering the developmental perspective, suicide, and how disorders evolve over time, it is interesting to note that the highest rates of suicide occur in older adults. Older age is a time period in the life span when people are particularly affected by social isolation. In terms of the interactional vulnerabilities, many older people, because of their interpersonal styles, have experienced years of interpersonal distress, social isolation, and rejection, leading to social isolation. It is also at this point in the lifetime that children are no longer living at home and peers are beginning to pass away. The link between psychiatric disorders, interpersonal vulnerabilities, social isolation, and suicide may culminate and be particularly disturbing in older age.

Of course, children have commonly been a focus of developmental psychology, because it is important to examine how a disorder manifests itself over time, including throughout childhood. Interpersonal processes have been documented in children, and one particular area of focus has been the intergenerational transmission of depression from depressed women to their children. Hammen (1999) stated that maternal depression is probably the strongest predictor of depression (as well as of other psychopathology) in children and adolescents (Downey & Coyne, 1990; Hammen, Burge, Burney, & Adrian, 1990). Hammen (1999) argues that interpersonal interactions between the mother and the child are significant in the risk for the child's depression. Both the mother's and the child's negative moods and behaviors can interactionally affect the other person, so that the process becomes cyclical and could possibly elicit some of the mother's critical or avoidant style of interaction (Burge & Hammen, 1991; Conrad & Hammen, 1989; Hammen, 1999). This is suggestive of an interactional style that could possibly be passed on from generation to generation, either leading to or passing on psychopathology over each generation.

Although the work discussed has been demonstrated with specific reference to depression, mothers with psychological disorders in general are more likely to have children with psychological disorders, and interpersonal processes may play a significant role in this relationship. It is quite possible to imagine that findings regarding interpersonal interactions between mothers and children may be dysfunctional if the mother displays the interpersonal vulnerabilities. A mother could possibly engage in negative feedback seeking or excessive reassurance seeking with her children and thereby disaffect them. It is also quite possible for the stress that a mother generates (through stress-generation mechanisms) to negatively affect her child in either a direct or indirect way. Processes such as blame maintenance may also occur in a relationship between a mother and child, in which the child grows to hold a steadfastly negative view of his or her mother. Even if these interpersonal processes did not occur explicitly between mother and child, the child could still be negatively affected, because the mother serves as a model for the child's behavior. Therefore, although a child may not have expressed a psychopathology, the child may through modeling begin to imitate the mother's maladaptive behavior. This could include the child's learning inappropriate communication styles (e.g., lack of eye contact and little tonal variation) or scripts such as negative feedback seeking. These behaviors could possibly lead to other disordered behaviors or psychopathology.

Haines, Metalsky, Cardamone, and Joiner (1999) described interpersonal pathways into the origins of attributional style from a developmental perspective. The authors suggested that childhood depression research implicates interpersonal experiences as significant antecedents to a negative attributional style. Their proposed model identifies three interpersonal domains that are likely to significantly affect the development of attributional style: (a) family experiences and parent-child relationships, (b) peer relationships, and (c) teacher-child relationships. In terms of developmental sequencing, early parent-child relationships precede peer and teacher relationships, and these relational experiences interact with cognitive development to influence attributional style. They suggest that consistent, chronic, and intense negative experience across interpersonal domains will increase the likelihood of a child's developing a negative attributional style. The authors described possible risk factors in each domain that could lead to a negative attributional style. One risk factor in the domain of family experiences is the possibility that children may acquire attributional style from their mothers either by learning it through observation or from the causal explanations that parents share with their children about the children's behavior.

In support of this hypothesis, significant correlations between mothers' and children's attributional styles have been found (Peterson & Seligman, 1984). In the domain of peer relationships, there is a significant relationship between peer rejection and depression (Cole, 1990; Lefkowitz & Tesiny, 1984). Panak and Garber (1992) more specifically suggest that aggression and peer rejection may put children at risk for developing depressive symptoms only if they perceive the rejection and attribute it to a personal flaw. Finally, a possible risk factor in the domain of teacher-child relationships is the suggestion that children may learn attributional style from the type of feedback they receive from teachers (Peterson & Seligman). This research and model are suggestive of the idea of contingent self-worth, which occurs when a child believes that his or her worth is contingent on the feedback of significant others (parents, peers, teachers; Burhans & Dweck, 1995). Contingent self-worth leads children to seek positive feedback from others, and their self-worth is associated with helpless responses when they receive negative feedback. The authors suggest this may be similar to the reassurance seeking described earlier. This model, like many of the other models of interpersonal vulnerabilities, was conceptualized with a focus on depression. However, akin to the other models, it is likely generalizable to other psychological disorders and related interpersonal consequences.

We have provided evidence that maladaptive interpersonal beliefs, maladaptive interpersonal behaviors, and interpersonal self-propagatory processes function as vulnerabilities for psychopathology. Many of these processes seem to operate as vulnerabilities throughout the life span, with evidence that children who engage in these processes are at risk for psychopathology at a young age (e.g., social skill deficits leading to peer rejection, excessive reassurance seeking leading to depression). Conceptualizing these processes as diatheses that are activated by the stresses of life transitions helps place interpersonal vulnerabilities into a life-span perspective. For example, Patterson and colleagues' (1989) model of the development of antisocial behavior involves the vulnerability of early-childhood peer rejection, which becomes activated in the face of the transition to adolescence, at which point antisocial behaviors begin to appear.

Interpersonal factors, in addition to serving as vulnerabilities for psychopathology when maladaptive, can also function as protective factors. Werner and Smith's (1982) longitudinal study investigating resilient children found that children who recovered from or adjusted easily to extreme life stress often had the ability (often seen as early as infancy) to gain the positive attention of others. These resilient children were able to connect with others and meet their needs to belong. Werner (1984) suggests that as long as the balance between vulnerability and protective factors in children's lives remains manageable, children will be able to cope. This suggests that although interpersonal problems may tip the balance toward the development of psychopathology, it also follows that helping children connect with others and develop interpersonal skills may be a strong protective factor against the development of psychopathology.

NOTES

1. Strauman and Higgins (1988) used a longitudinal design, with actual-versus-ideal and actual-versus-ought other-generated self-discrepancies discriminatively predicting dejection and agitation levels, respectively, 2 months later. However, initial levels of dejection and agitation were not measured or controlled for, rendering the design unable to support temporal precedence for self-discrepancies.

2. Joiner's (2004) theory also posits an additional vulnerability for serious suicidal desire, a thwarted sense of interpersonal effectiveness, which involves perceptions of burdensomeness on others, although we do not elaborate on that vulnerability in this chapter.

REFERENCES

Adrian, C., & Hammen, C. (1993). Stress exposure and stress generation in children of depressed mothers. *Journal of Consulting and Clinical Psychology, 61,* 354–359.

American Psychiatric Association. (1987). *Diagnostic and statistical manual of mental disorders* (3rd ed.). Washington, DC: Author.

American Psychiatric Association. (1994). *Diagnostic and statistical manual of mental disorders* (4th ed.). Washington, DC: Author.

Aron, A. (2003). Self and close relationships. In M. R. Leary & J. P Tangney (Eds.), *Handbook of self and identity* (pp. 442–461). New York: Guilford Press.

Baker, S. R., & Edelmann, R. J. (2002). Is social phobia related to lack of social skills? Duration of skill-related behaviours and ratings of behavioural adequacy. *British Journal of Clinical Psychology, 41,* 243–257.

Baldwin, M. W., & Sinclair, L. (1996). Self-esteem and "if . . . then" contingencies of interpersonal acceptance. *Journal of Personality and Social Psychology, 71,* 1130–1141.

Bardone, A. M., Abramson, L. Y., Vohs, K. D., Heatherton, T. F., & Joiner, T. E., Jr. (2004). *The expanded escape theory of binge eating.* Manuscript in preparation.

Baumeister, R. F. (1990). Suicide as escape from self. *Psychological Review, 97,* 90–113.

Baumeister, R. F., & Leary, M. R. (1995). The need to belong: Desire for interpersonal attachments as a fundamental human motivation. *Psychological Bulletin, 117,* 497–529.

Beach, S. R., & O'Leary, D. K. (1993). Marital discord and dysphoria: For whom does the marital relationship predict depressive symptomatology? *Journal of Social & Personal Relationships, 10,* 405–420.

Beck, A. T., & Weishaar, M. E. (1990). Suicide risk assessment and prediction. *Crisis, 11,* 22–30.

Blouin, J. H., Schnarre, K., Carter, J., & Blouin, A. (1995). Factors affecting dropout rate from cognitive-behavioral group treatment for bulimia nervosa. *International Journal of Eating Disorders, 17,* 323–329.

Bonner, R. L., & Rich, A. L. (1987). Toward a predictive model of suicidal ideation and behavior: Some preliminary data in college students. *Suicide and Life-Threatening Behavior, 17,* 50–63.

Bronfenbrenner, U. (1986). Ecology of the family as a context for human development: Research perspectives. *Developmental Psychology, 22,* 723–742.

Bulik, C. M., Wade, T. D., & Kendler, K. S. (2000). Characteristics of monozygotic twins discordant for bulimia nervosa. *International Journal of Eating Disorders, 29,* 1–10.

Burge, D., & Hammen, C. (1991). Maternal communication: Predictors of outcome at follow-up in a sample of children at high and low risk for depression. *Journal of Abnormal Psychology, 100,* 174–180.

Burhans, K. K., & Dweck, C. S. (1995). Helplessness in early childhood: The role of contingent worth. *Child Development, 66,* 1719–1738.

Button, E. J., Songua-Barke, E. J., & Thompson, M. (1996). A prospective study of self-esteem in the prediction of eating problems in adolescent schoolgirls: Questionnaire findings. *British Journal of Clinical Psychology, 35,* 193–203.

Cash, D. F., & Deagle, E. A. (1997). The nature and extent of body-image disturbances in anorexia nervosa and bulimia nervosa: A meta-analysis. *International Journal of Eating Disorders, 22,* 107–125.

Cassidy, J., & Asher, S. R. (1992). Loneliness and peer relations in young children. *Child Development, 63,* 350–365.

Cicchetti, D., & Toth, S. (1987). The application of a transactional risk model to intervention with multi-risk maltreating families. *Zero to Three, 5,* 1–8.

Cole, D. A. (1990). Relation of social and academic competence to depressive symptoms in childhood. *Journal of Abnormal Psychology, 99,* 422–429.

Cole, D., Jacquez, F., & Maschman, T. (2001). Social origins of depressive cognitions: A longitudinal study of self-perceived competence in children. *Cognitive Therapy and Research, 25,* 377–395.

Conrad, M., & Hammen, C. (1989). Role of maternal depression in perceptions of child maladjustment. *Journal of Consulting & Clinical Psychology, 57,* 663–667.

Cornette, M. M., Abramson, L. Y., & Bardone, A. M. (2000). Toward an integrated theory of suicidal behaviors: Merging the hopelessness, self-discrepancy, and escape theories. In T. E. Joiner & D. M. Rudd (Eds.), *Suicide science: Expanding the boundaries* (pp. 43–66). Boston: Kluwer Academic Press.

Coyne, J. C. (1976). Toward an interactional description of depression. *Psychiatry, 39,* 28–40.

Coyne, J. C. (1999). Thinking interactionally about depression: A radical restatement. In T. Joiner & J. Coyne (Eds.), *The interactional nature of depression* (pp. 365–392). Washington, DC: American Psychological Association.

Crick, N. R., & Ladd, G. W. (1993). Children's perceptions of their peer experiences: Attributions, loneliness, social anxiety, and social avoidance. *Developmental Psychology, 29,* 244–254.

Daley, S. E., Hammen, C., Burge, D., & Davila, J. (1997). Predictors of the generation of episodic stress: A longitudinal study of late adolescent women. *Journal of Abnormal Psychology, 106,* 251–259.

Davila, J., & Beck, G. J. (2002). Is social anxiety associated with impairment in close relationships? A preliminary investigation. *Behavior Therapy, 33,* 427–446.

Davila, J., Bradbury, T. N., Cohan, C. L., & Tochluk, S. (1997). Marital functioning and depressive symptoms: Evidence for a stress generation model. *Journal of Personality and Social Psychology, 73,* 849–861.

Davila, J., Hammen, C., Burge, D., & Paley, B. (1995). Poor interpersonal problem solving as a mechanism of stress generation in depression among adolescent women. *Journal of Abnormal Psychology, 104,* 592–600.

Dieserud, G., Roysamb, E., Ekeberg, O., & Kraft, P. (2001). Toward an integrative model of suicide attempt: A cognitive psychological approach. *Suicide and Life-Threatening Behavior, 31,* 153–168.

Downey, G., & Coyne, J. C. (1990). Children of depressed parents: An integrative review. *Psychological Bulletin, 108,* 50–76.

Duval, S. T., Duval, V. H., & Mulilis, J. P. (1992). Effects of self-focus, discrepancy between self and standard, and outcome expectancy favorability on the tendency to match self to standard or to withdraw. *Journal of Personality and Social Psychology, 62,* 340–348.

Fairburn, C. G., Norman, P. A., Welch, S. L., O'Connor, M. E., & Doll, H. A. (1995). A prospective study of outcome in bulimia nervosa and the long-term effects of three psychological treatments. *Archives of General Psychiatry, 52,* 304–312.

Fairburn, C. G., Welch, S. L., Doll, H. A., Davies, B. A., & O'Connor, M. E. (1997). Risk factors for bulimia nervosa: A community-based case-control study. *Archives of General Psychiatry, 54,* 509–517.

Fisher, M., Pastore, D., Schneider, M., Pegler, C., & Napolitano, B. (1994). Eating attitudes in urban and suburban adolescents. *International Journal of Eating Disorders, 16,* 67–74.

Fiske, S. T. (1993). Social cognition and social perception. *Annual Review of Psychology, 44,* 155–194.

Garbarino, J. (1997). Growing up in a socially toxic environment. In D. Cicchetti & S. L. Toth (Eds.), *Rochester symposium on developmental psychopathology—Developmental perspectives on trauma: Theory, research, and intervention* (Vol. 8, pp. 141–154). Rochester, NY: University of Rochester Press.

Giesler, R. B., Josephs, R. A., & Swann, W. B., Jr. (1996). Self-verification in clinical depression: The desire for negative evaluation. *Journal of Abnormal Psychology, 105,* 358–368.

Grissett, N. I., & Norvell, N. K. (1992). Perceived social support, social skills, and quality of relationships in bulimic women. *Journal of Consulting & Clinical Psychology, 60,* 293–299.

Haines, B. A., Metalsky, G. I., Cardamone, A. L., & Joiner, T. E. (1999). Interpersonal and cognitive pathways into the origins of attributional style: A developmental perspective. In T. Joiner & J. Coyne (Eds.), *The interactional nature of depression* (pp. 65–92). Washington, DC: American Psychological Association.

Hammen, C. (1991). Generation of stress in the course of unipolar depression. *Journal of Abnormal Psychology, 100,* 555–561.

Hammen, C. (1999). The emergence of an interpersonal approach to depression. In T. Joiner & J. Coyne (Eds.), *The interactional nature of depression* (pp. 21–35). Washington, DC: American Psychological Association.

Hammen, C., Burge, D., Burney, E., & Adrian, C. (1990). Longitudinal study of diagnoses in children of women with unipolar and bipolar affective disorder. *Archives of General Psychiatry, 47,* 1112–1117.

Hammen, C., Davila, J., Brown, G., Ellicott, A., & Gitlin, M. (1992). Psychiatric history and stress: Predictors of severity of unipolar depression. *Journal of Abnormal Psychology, 101,* 45–52.

Hankin, B. L., Roberts, J., & Gotlib, I. H. (1997). Elevated self-standards and emotional distress during adolescence: Emotional specificity and gender differences. *Cognitive Therapy and Research, 21,* 663–681.

Harrison, K. (2001). Ourselves, our bodies: Thin-ideal media, self-discrepancies, and eating disorders symptomatology in adolescents. *Journal of Social & Clinical Psychology, 20,* 289–323.

Harter, S., & Monsour, A. (1992). Developmental analysis of conflict caused by opposing attributes in the adolescent self-portrait. *Developmental Psychology, 28,* 251–260.

Heatherton, T. F., & Baumeister, R. F. (1991). Binge eating as escape from self-awareness. *Psychological Bulletin, 110,* 86–108.

Hershberger, S. L., Pilkington, N. W., & D'Augelli, A. R. (1997). Predictors of suicide attempts among gay, lesbian, and bisexual youth. *Journal of Adolescent Research, 12,* 477–497.

Higgins, E. T. (1987). Self-discrepancy: A theory relating self and affect. *Psychological Review, 94,* 319–340.

Higgins, E. T. (1989). Knowledge accessibility and activation: Subjectivity and suffering from unconscious sources. In J. Uleman & J. Bargh (Eds.), *Unintended thought* (pp. 75–123). New York: Guilford Press.

Hofmann, S. G., Gerlach, A. L., Wender, A., & Roth, W. T. (1997). Speech disturbances and gaze behavior during public speaking in subtypes of social phobia. *Journal of Anxiety Disorders, 11,* 573–585.

Hooley, J. M., & Teasdale, J. D. (1989). Predictors of relapse in unipolar depressives: Expressed emotion, marital distress, and perceived criticism. *Journal of Abnormal Psychology, 98,* 229–235.

Joiner, T. E., Jr. (1999a). Self-verification and bulimic symptoms: Do bulimic women play a role in perpetuating their own dissatisfaction and symptoms? *International Journal of Eating Disorders, 26,* 145–151.

Joiner, T. E., Jr. (1999b). A test of interpersonal theory of depression among youth psychiatric inpatients. *Journal of Abnormal Child Psychology, 27,* 75–84.

Joiner, T. E., Jr. (2000). Depression's vicious scree: Self-propagatory and erosive processes in depression chronicity. *Clinical Psychology: Science and Practice, 7,* 203–218.

Joiner, T. E., Jr. (2002). Depression in its interpersonal context. In I. H. Gotlib & C. L. Hammen (Eds.), *Handbook of depression* (pp. 295–313). New York: Guilford Press.

Joiner, T. E., Jr. (2004). *An interpersonal-psychological theory of attempted and completed suicide.* Manuscript submitted for publication.

Joiner, T. E., Jr., Alfano, M., & Metalsky, G. (1992). When depression breeds contempt: Reassurance seeking, self-esteem, and rejection of depressed college students by their roommates. *Journal of Abnormal Psychology, 101,* 165–173.

Joiner, T. E., Jr., Coyne, J. C., & Blalock, J. (1999). Overview and synthesis. In T. E. Joiner & J. Coyne (Eds.), *The interactional nature of depression* (pp. 3–20). Washington, DC: American Psychological Association.

Joiner, T. E., Jr., Heatherton, T. F., & Keel, P. K. (1997). Ten-year stability and predictive validity of five bulimia-related indicators. *American Journal of Psychiatry, 154,* 1133–1138.

Joiner, T. E., Jr., Katz, J., & Lew, A. (1997). Self-verification and depression in youth psychiatric inpatients. *Journal of Abnormal Psychology, 106,* 608–618.

Joiner, T. E., Jr., & Metalsky, G. (1995). A prospective test of an integrative interpersonal theory of depression: A naturalistic study of college roommates. *Journal of Personality & Social Psychology, 67,* 778–788.

Joiner, T. E., & Metalsky, G. I. (2001). Excessive reassurance-seeking: Delineating a risk factor involved in the development of depressive symptoms. *Psychological Science, 12,* 371–378.

Joiner, T. E., Jr., Metalsky, G. I., Katz, J., & Beach, S. R. H. (1999). Depression and excessive reassurance-seeking. *Psychological Inquiry, 10,* 269–278.

Katz, J., & Beach, S. R. H. (1997). Romance in the crossfire: When do women's depressive symptoms predict partner relationship dissatisfaction? *Journal of Social and Clinical Psychology, 16,* 243–258.

Keel, P. K., Mitchell, J. E., Miller, K. B., Davis, T. L., & Crow, S. J. (2000). Social adjustment over 10 years following diagnosis with bulimia nervosa. *International Journal of Eating Disorders, 27,* 21–28.

Kowalski, R. M. (2003). *Complaining, teasing, and other annoying behaviors.* New Haven, CT: Yale University Press.

Kovacs, M. (1992). *Children's Depression Inventory CDI Manual.* Toronto, Ontario, Canada: Multi-Health Systems Inc.

Lara, M. E., Leader, J., & Klein, D. N. (1997). The association between social support and course of depression: Is it confounded with personality? *Journal of Abnormal Psychology, 106,* 478–482.

Leary, M. R. (Ed.). (2001) *Interpersonal rejection.* Oxford, UK: Oxford University Press.

Lefkowitz, M. M., & Tesiny, E. P. (1984). Rejection and depression: Prospective and contemporaneous analyses. *Developmental Psychology, 20,* 776–785.

Lewicki, P., Hill, T., & Czyzewska, M. (1992). Nonconscious acquisition of information. *American Psychologist, 47,* 796–801.

Manian, N., Strauman, T., & Denney, N. (1998). Temperament, recalled parenting styles, and self-regulation: Testing the developmental postulates of self-discrepancy theory. *Journal of Personality & Social Psychology, 75,* 1321–1332.

Markus, H. (1977). Self-schemata and processing information about the self. *Journal of Personality and Social Psychology, 35,* 63–78.

McCullough, J. P. (2003). Treatment for chronic depression: Cognitive behavioral analysis system of psychotherapy (CBASP). *Journal of Psychotherapy Integration, 13,* 241–263.

McDougall, P., Hymel, S., Vaillancourt, T., & Mercer, L. (2001). The consequences of childhood peer rejection. In M. R. Leary (Ed.), *Interpersonal rejection* (pp. 3–20). Oxford, UK: Oxford University Press.

Panak, W. F., & Garber, J. (1992). Role of aggression, rejection, and attributions in the prediction of depression in children. *Development and Psychopathology, 4,* 145–165.

Parker, J., & Asher, S. (1987). Peer relations and later personal adjustment: Are low-accepted children at risk? *Psychological Bulletin, 102,* 357–389.

Parkhurst, J. T., & Asher, S. R. (1992). Peer rejection in middle school: Subgroup differences in behavior, loneliness, and interpersonal concerns. *Developmental Psychology, 28,* 231–241.

Patterson, G. R., DeBaryshe, B. D., & Ramsey, E. (1989). A developmental perspective on antisocial behavior. *American Psychologist, 44,* 329–335.

Perez, M., Wingate, L. R., & Joiner, T. E., Jr. (2004). *Does the interaction between excessive reassurance-seeking and life stress constitute a risk for bulimic symptoms?* Manuscript submitted for publication.

Peterson, C., & Seligman, M. E. P. (1984). Causal explanations as a risk factor for depression: Theory and evidence. *Psychological Review, 91,* 347–374.

Sacco, W., & Dunn, V. (1990). Effect of actor depression on observer attributions: Existence and impact of negative attributions toward the depressed. *Journal of Personality & Social Psychology, 59,* 517–524.

Scott, L., & O'Hara, M. W. (1993). Self-discrepancies in clinically anxious and depressed university students. *Journal of Abnormal Psychology, 102,* 282–287.

Segrin, C. (2001). *Interpersonal processes in psychological problems.* New York: Guilford Press.

Segrin, C., & Flora, J. (1998). Depression and verbal behavior in conversations with friends and strangers. *Journal of Language & Social Psychology, 17,* 492–503.

Segrin, C., & Flora, J. (2000). Poor social skills are a vulnerability factor in the development of psychosocial problems. *Human Communication Research, 26,* 489–514.

Singer, J. L., & Salovey, P. (1991). Organized knowledge structures and personality: Person schemas, self schemas, prototypes, and scripts. In M. J. Horowitz (Ed.), *Person schemas and maladaptive interpersonal patterns* (pp. 33–79). Chicago: University of Chicago Press.

Steiger, H., Leung, F., & Thibaudeau, J. (1993). Prognostic value of pretreatment social adaptation in bulimia nervosa. *International Journal of Eating Disorders, 14,* 269–276.

Stice, E. (2002). Risk and maintenance factors for eating pathology: A meta-analytic review. *Psychological Bulletin, 128,* 825–848.

Stipek, D. J., Gralinski, J. H., & Kopp, C. B. (1990). Self-concept development in the toddler years. *Developmental Psychology, 26,* 972–977.

Strauman, T. J. (1989). Self-discrepancies in clinical depression and social phobia: Cognitive structures that underlie emotional disorders? *Journal of Abnormal Psychology, 98,* 14–22.

Strauman, T. J., & Higgins, E. T. (1988). Self-discrepancies as predictors of vulnerability to distinct syndromes of chronic emotional distress. *Journal of Personality, 56,* 685–707.

Strauman, T. J., Vookles, J., Berenstein, V., Chaiken, S., & Higgins, E. T. (1991). Self-discrepancies and vulnerability to body dissatisfaction and disordered eating. *Journal of Personality & Social Psychology, 61,* 946–956.

Strober, M., Freeman, R., & Morrell, W. (1997). The long-term course of severe anorexia nervosa in adolescents: Survival analysis of recovery, relapse, and outcome predictors over 10–15 years in a prospective study. *International Journal of Eating Disorders, 22,* 339–360.

Swann, W. B., Jr. (1990). To be known or to be adored: The interplay of self-enhancement and self-verification. In E. T. Higgins & R. M. Sorrentino (Eds.), *Handbook of motivation and cognition* (Vol. 2, pp. 408–448). New York: Guilford Press.

Swann, W. B., Jr., Wenzlaff, R. A., Krull, D. S., & Pelham, B. W. (1992). Allure of negative feedback: Self-verification strivings among depressed persons. *Journal of Abnormal Psychology, 101,* 293–306.

Tolkmitt, F., Helfrich, H., Standke, R., & Scherer, K. R. (1982). Vocal indicators of psychiatric treatment effects in depressives and schizophrenics. *Journal of Communication Disorders, 15,* 209–222.

Tomori, M., & Rus-Makovec, M. (2000). Eating behavior, depression, and self-esteem in high school students. *Journal of Adolescent Health, 26,* 361–367.

Troop, N. A., & Bifulco, A. (2002). Childhood social arena and cognitive sets in eating disorders. *British Journal of Clinical Psychology, 41,* 205–212.

Trout, D. L. (1980). The role of social isolation in suicide. *Suicide & Life-Threatening Behavior, 10,* 10–23.

Vieth, A. Z., Strauman, T. J., Kolden, G. C., Woods, T. E., Michels, J. L., & Klein, M. H. (2003). Self-System Therapy (SST): A theory-based psychotherapy for depression. *Clinical Psychology: Science and Practice, 10,* 245–268.

Vohs, K., & Baumeister, R. F. (2000). Escaping the self consumes regulatory resources: A self-regulatory model of suicide. In T. E. Joiner & D. M. Rudd (Eds.), *Suicide science: Expanding the boundaries* (pp. 33–41). Boston: Kluwer Academic Press.

Waern, M., Rubenowitz, E., & Wilhelmson, K. (2003). Predictors of suicide in the old elderly. *Gerontology, 49,* 328–334.

Werner, E. E. (1984). Resilient children. *Young Children, 40,* 68–72.

Werner, E. E., & Smith, R. S. (1982). *Vulnerable, but invincible: A longitudinal study of resilient children and youth.* New York: McGraw-Hill.

Wingate, L. R., & Joiner, T. (in press). Depression-related stress generation: A longitudinal study of black adolescents. *Behavior Therapy.*

Youngren, M. A., & Lewinsohn, P. M. (1980). The functional relation between depression and problematic interpersonal behavior. *Journal of Abnormal Psychology, 89,* 333–341.

CHAPTER 7

Genetic Vulnerabilities to the Development of Psychopathology

KATHRYN S. LEMERY AND LISA DOELGER

Developmental psychology textbooks have declared that the nature-versus-nurture debate is resolved and that the field has now demonstrated that psychological traits, behaviors, and psychopathologies arise from a complex interaction of both genes and the environment. The complexities of the interaction extend across multiple environmental levels, from the subatomic to the macroenvironment, and our methods cannot separate these influences for a given individual. This declaration makes sense, for certainly genes are equipped to code for proteins, and environmental conditions are quite necessary for any gene expression. Although few would argue with the truth of this statement, it does not address the tremendous contributions made by studying *individual differences* and using genetically informative designs to understand the development of psychopathology. We view genes as general risk factors that influence underlying endophenotypes (the mediators) to influence human health and behavior.

In this chapter we introduce behavior-genetic methods, from twin-family designs to associating the influence of particular genetic variants (e.g., the long and short alleles of the serotonin transporter gene) to liability for psychopathology. An extensive review is included of twin study results on the heritability of depression, anxiety, oppositional defiant/conduct disorder/antisocial personality disorder, and attention deficit/hyperactivity disorder (ADHD) from the preschool through adult years. We also introduce behavioral genomics methods and six genes with known influence on the brain that have also been associated with psychopathology. Finally, we emphasize the importance of a developmental vulnerability-stress perspective and suggest promising future directions.

Progress in identifying specific genes, particularly in the Human Genome Project, has made possible research dissecting the genetic contribution to human mental and physical diseases. Even before that, behavior geneticists were indirectly estimating genetic and environmental components from the resemblance of relatives. The basic linear model of quantitative genetics parses the phenotypic variances into the variance due to genetic influences and that due to environmental influences. Symbolically, $V_P = V_G + V_E + 2Cov(G)(E) + V_{G \times E}$, where V_P is the phenotypic variance (the sum of the individual's squared deviations from the mean, divided by the number of individuals), V_G is the genetic (G) variance, V_E is the environmental (E) variance, 2Cov(G)(E) is the covariance between G and E, and $V_{G \times E}$ represents any nonadditive effect of G and E. If relatives are more similar to each other than are individuals picked randomly from the population on a particular trait, then there is phenotypic covariation for that trait, which is then parsed into genetic and environmental influences. Even more powerfully, multivariate designs allow a decomposition of the covariance between two or more traits. For example, Dick, Rose, Viken, and Kaprio (2000) reported that the same genetic factor influenced the age when teens started smoking and drinking (genetic r = 1.0), but once these behaviors were initiated, the genetic influences on frequency of smoking and drinking were substance specific (genetic r = .25).

Both GE interaction and GE correlation provide support for the vulnerability-stress model. GE interactions are statistical interactions and refer to the same environment's having different effects, depending on the genotype of the individual. A behaviorally inhibited child (behavioral inhibition being a genetically influenced temperament trait) reacts differently to a novel environment than a sociable child does. GE interactions are easiest to identify using molecular genetic techniques, which are reviewed below. However, adoption designs are also conducive to testing for GE interactions if good measures of birth parents are used. The biological parents' phenotypes (e.g., diagnosis) are taken as estimates of the offspring's genotype, depending on the heritability of the trait or disorder. The adoptive parents' phenotypes can then be taken as estimates of environmental influence. Main effects represent independent effects of genotype or environment, and statistical interactions are measures of GE interaction.

GE correlations occur when genetic predispositions influence environment selection. For example, genetics affect lifestyle selection, dietary preferences, and exercise habits, which in turn influence obesity and body mass, which are associated with poor health outcomes. The literature identifies three types of GE covariance: passive, reactive or evocative, and active (Plomin, DeFries, & Loehlin, 1977). Passive GE correlations arise because a child's genotype is correlated with the environment of his or her parents and siblings (who have similar genotypes). Reactive, or evocative, GE correlation occurs when others react to a particular individual on the basis of some of the individual's inherited characteristics. The environment becomes correlated with genetic differences when an inattentive child, for example, is taught less material in a less effective manner in school. An active GE correlation is present when an individual seeks out environments that are conducive to further developing his or her genetic tendencies. Aggressive youths, for example, may seek to associate with peers who are also easily frustrated and prone to attribute hostile intent to benign actions of others. In fact, Rose (2002) recently reported that sixth-grade twins actively select their friends from among their classmates. Genetic dispositions play some role in selection of friends, with genetically identical co-twins making highly similar friendship selections. These three types of GE correlation may all contribute to many developmental pathways.

BEHAVIOR-GENETIC METHODOLOGICAL CONSIDERATIONS

Defining the phenotype and understanding the heritability statistic and assumptions of behavior-genetic designs are important methodological considerations.

Some definitions of the disorder, or the phenotype, will mask associations with genes, whereas others will enhance them. The diagnosis should be reasonably reproducible and can be refined by administering the measure multiple times and incorporating other useful information, such as family history, severity of disorder, and age of onset. Factor analysis, principal components analysis, and latent class analysis are techniques among others that can be used to reduce the number of correlated traits that make up many complex disorders.

Behavior-genetic designs can be used to help define phenotypes and determine a taxonomic system that best captures individual similarities and differences. For example, there is considerable debate about whether psychopathology can be viewed as the extreme on one or more quantitatively distributed personality traits, or whether psychopathology is qualitatively distinct from traits. With these designs, we can consider whether the genetic influence on the phenotype differs for the disordered extreme. Does the same genetic factor that influences acting-out behaviors in children contribute to a conduct disorder diagnosis? Or do genetic influences become more important in the extreme? These designs can also inform our taxonomy by examining the effect on diagnosis when multisource data are employed. In addition, we can identify both shared and independent genetic and environmental influences on comorbid disorders and components of a single heterogeneous disorder. Adding a developmental perspective, genetic influence on putative underlying processes (e.g., baseline levels of the stress hormone cortisol) can be examined, and links with disorder can be decomposed into genetic and environmental components. Individuals with the same diagnosis who differ on measures of these endophenotypes can yield useful information on forming more homogeneous subgroups. Overall, defining the phenotype is a central issue when studying psychopathology, and the behavior-genetic design holds considerable power for advancing our knowledge.

Heritability is a statistic that is often reported but seldom explained. It is the proportion of the phenotypic variance due to genetic variance among individuals in a population. Because heritability is a proportion, estimates of heritability will be different in different environments. Systematic environmental factors may play a larger role in societies where between-family disparity in socioeconomic status is substantial, for example. Heritability decreases when the relevant environment varies a lot from individual to individual, and heritability increases if the environment is nearly the same for all individuals. Conversely, heritability is greater if the population has greater variability in the relevant genes, and it decreases if the population shares nearly all genes that affect a particular phenotype. Thus, a heritability estimate is specific to the population studied and can be generalized only to groups that share a distribution of relevant genes and environments.

A third methodological consideration is testing the assumptions of behavior-genetic designs. Twin, adoption, and family designs have testable, defensible assumptions. The main assumptions of a twin design are first, that twins are representative of the normal population, and second, that environmental similarity does not differ for identical (monozygotic, MZ) pairs and fraternal (dizygotic, DZ) pairs for the trait under study. Data on singletons with the same assessment procedure can be compared with the twin data to test the first assumption. The second assumption may be examined by measuring putative relevant environments. With children, we sometimes compare the data from parents who believe they have DZ twins but who really have MZ twins with data from parents who correctly believe their twins are MZ (or vice versa; as many as 30% of parents can be mistaken in their beliefs about their twins' zygosity; Goldsmith, 1991). The adoption design has assumptions concerning the absence of selective placement and that adoptive family environments are representative of general family environments. Selective placement is the tendency of adoption agencies to match children and families on some trait, usually physical characteristics. By measuring both biological and adoptive parents, selective placement can be accounted for in statistical analyses. Similarly, measures of family environment can be compared, and of course, these differences would apply only if they affect the behavior under study. The largest drawback with the family design is that it confounds shared environment and genetic similarity. These assumptions can be minimized by including biological, nontwin siblings in twin designs, parents in twin designs, and biological siblings in adoption designs.

ESTIMATES OF HERITABILITY FROM ADOPTION AND FAMILY STUDIES

This review will focus on criteria from the *Diagnostic and Statistical Manual of Mental Disorders,* 4th edition (*DSM-IV,* American Psychiatric Association [APA], 1994) for internalizing and externalizing disorders seen both in children and adults. The internalizing category refers to mood disorders, such as depression and anxiety, whereas the externalizing category encompasses disorders characterized by acting-out behaviors, such as oppositional defiant disorder (ODD), conduct disorder (CD), antisocial personality disorder (APD), and ADHD. The vast majority of the studies utilized population-based samples, rather than clinical samples, and most recruited participants through a twin registry, which included all sets of twins born in a particular area. Although there was some overlap, age ranges, measures, and the use of either parent or twin report of symptomatology differ among the studies.

Child Depression

A number of twin studies have reported heritability estimates for childhood depression (see Hankin & Abela, Chapter 10 of this volume, for greater detail on depression). These studies are summarized in Table 7.1. Although the heritability estimates vary across studies, a significant genetic influence is apparent for depression in both children and adolescents. However, the range in estimates is substantial, from 0% to 80%, which is too large to come to any clear conclusion about how much variation in depression is due to genetic factors. Considering only parent report in studies with very large sample sizes ($n > 900$), the range narrows (23%–72%), but it is still broad enough to be inconclusive. Population differences could account for some differences, plus age and sex effects and measurement differences. Estimates for a^2 (additive genetic influence), c^2 (shared environment, or those aspects of the environment that tend to make twins similar to one another), and e^2 (nonshared environment, or those aspects of the environment that tend to make twins dissimilar) have been shown to differ between children and adolescents (Eley & Stevenson, 1999; Gjone & Stevenson, 1997; Scourfield et al., 2003). A number of studies have combined children and adolescents in the same analysis (Eaves et al., 1997; Edelbrock, Rende, Plomin, & Thompson, 1995; Eley, 1997; Gjone, Stevenson, Sundet, & Eilertsen, 1996; Silberg et al., 1994; Thapar & McGuffin, 1997), which could lead to varying heritability estimates. There is also the question of sex differences. There are two testable explanations for the nature of sex differences: (a) that such differences result from the magnitude of the

Table 7.1 Summary of Twin Studies of Childhood Depression

Study	Number of Twin Pairs	Age (Years)	Sample Origin	Measure	Reporter	a^2		c^2		e^2	
						Male	*Female*	*Male*	*Female*	*Male*	*Female*
Eaves et al. (1997)	1,412	8–16	American	CAPA	Mother	.64	.66	—	—	.36	.34
					Father	.72	.54	—	—	.28	.46
					Self	.11	.19	—	—	.89	.81
Edelbrock et al. (1995)	181 same sex	7–15	American	CBCL Internalizing	Parent	.50		.25		.25	
Eley (1997)	395 same sex	8–16	British	CDI	Self	.48		.10		.42	
Eley and Stevenson (1999)	490		British	CDI	Self						
		8–11			Young	.08	.23	.36	.37	.56	.40
		12–16			Old	.57	.02	.01	.56	.42	.42
Gjone and Stevenson (1997)	915		Norwegian	CBCL Internalizing	Parent						
		5–9			Young	.44	.38	.25	.34	.31	.29
		12–15			Old	.26	.33	.50	.45	.24	.21
Glowinski et al. (2003)	1,708	13–19	American	C-SSAGA	Self		.40		—		.60
Happonen et al. (2002)	1,366	11–12	Finnish	CDI	Self	.45		—		.55	
				MPNI	Parent	.43		.19		.38	
				MPNI	Teacher	.28	.42	.39	.39	.34	.20
				MPNI	Peer	.71		—		.29	
Hudziak et al. (2000)	492 same sex	8–12	American	CBCL Anexiety/ Depression	Parent	.65	.61	—	—	.35	.39
Murray and Sines (1996)	364 same sex		American	MCBC	Mother						
		4–6			Younger	—		.29		.71	
		7–12			Older	.46		—		.54	

(Continued)

Table 7.1 (Continued)

Study	*Number of Twin Pairs*	*Age (Years)*	*Sample Origin*	*Measure*	*Reporter*	a^2		c^2		e^2	
						Male	*Female*	*Male*	*Female*	*Male*	*Female*
Schmitz et al. (1995)	463	2–3 7 (mean)	American	CBCL/2–3 Internalizing CBCL/4–18 Internalizing	Mother	.17 .37		.45 .26		.38 .37	
Scourfield et al. (2003)	670		British	MFQ	Parent						
		5–10			Child	—	.41	.49	.35	.51	.24
		11–17			Adolescent	.68	.80	—	—	.32	.20
					Self						
					Adolescent	.66		—		.34	
Silberg et al. (1994)	1,263	8–16	American	CBCL Internalizing	Mother	.23		.36		.41	
Thapar and McGuffin (1997)	172 same sex	8–16	British	MFQ	Mother	.75		—		.25	

NOTES: CAPA = Child and Adolescent Psychiatric Assessment (Angold et al., 1995); CBCL = Child Behavior Checklist (Achenbach, 1991); CDI = Child Depression Inventory (Kovacs, 1992); C-SSAGA = Child Semi-Structured Assessment for the Genetics of Alcoholism (adapted from the Diagnostic Interview for Children & Adolescents; Reich, 1996); MFQ = Mood and Feelings Questionnaire (Angold et al., 1987); MCBC = Missouri Children's Behavior Checklist (Sines, 1986); MPNI = Multidimensional Peer Nomination Inventory (Pulkkinen, Kaprio, & Rose, 1999).

parameter estimates that differ between males and females, in other words, a quantitative difference in the amount of influence from the same genes or the same environments; or (b) that they result from actually different genetic or environmental influences for males and females. Both can be tested with twin models, but again, the results as they pertain to childhood depression have varied among studies. Some studies have shown evidence of sex differences, whereas others have not. Measurement issues can also explain varying estimates of heritability. Measures that rely on symptom report versus diagnostic criteria for depression can differ in heritability estimates. Also, different reporters of depression have been shown to yield different estimates (Happonen et al., 2002).

Age and Environmental Influences on Depression

In general, it would appear that heritability estimates increase with age, whereas estimates for the influence of the shared environment decrease. Increasing heritability estimates with age are consistent with a genetic explanation for the increase in prevalence rates during adolescence (Birmaher et al., 1996). The question then becomes whether the influence of the same genes simply increases, or if different genes begin influencing depression during adolescence. However, although the general trend is an increase in heritability estimates with age, it has not always been supported. Only one study included in this review examined internalizing disorder, measured by the Child Behavior Checklist (CBCL, Achenbach, Edelbrock, & Howell, 1987) in very young children (2 to 3 years), and they found a significant c^2 of .45, with an a^2 of only .17 (Schmitz, Fulker, & Mrazek, 1995). All of the studies that included children between the ages of 4 and 10 reported a significant value of c^2 within the range of .25 to .49 (Eley & Stevenson, 1999; Murray & Sines, 1996; Schmitz et al., 1995; Scourfield et al., 2003). Samples that studied slightly older children (7 to 12 years) had much lower or no shared environmental influences (Happonen et al., 2002; Hudziak, Rudiger, Neale, Heath, & Todd, 2000; Murray & Sines), with the exception of Eley and Stevenson, who relied on self-report from 8- to 11-year-olds. However, some of these children may have been too young to be considered reliable reporters (Ezpeleta, Polaino, E. Domenech, & J. M. Domenech, 1990). Among studies that used parental and self-report for adolescents (12 to 19 years), there appeared to be mostly no shared environment influence and heritability estimates that ranged from .40 to .80 (Eley & Stevenson; Glowinski, Madden, Bucholz, Lynskey, & Heath, 2003; Scourfield et al.). But there was one study that used parental report on the CBCL for 12- to 15-year-olds, and this study reported considerable shared environment estimates, .50 and .45 for boys and girls, respectively (Gjone & Stevenson, 1997). Also, Eley and Stevenson found a significant c^2 for females only with self-report on the Child Depression Inventory (CDI; Kovacs, 1992).

If we distinguish studies that consider age differences cross-sectionally or longitudinally, the results are conflicting. Three studies (Murray & Sines, 1996; Schmitz et al., 1995; Scourfield et al., 2003) showed that heritability increased and shared environment decreased with age, and Eley and Stevenson (1999) found the same pattern only for boys in their sample. For girls, the opposite was true: Heritability decreased with age, whereas the shared environment increased, and this pattern was also seen in Gjone and Stevenson (1997). Thus, depression in children is heritable, but research to date has not elucidated the magnitude of this influence. Additional longitudinal investigations are necessary to further differentiate the nature of the genetic influence and its changes with age. The study of Scourfield et al. was the only one to examine these distinctions, reporting that new genetic influences emerged in adolescence.

Sex Differences in Heritability of Depression

At the onset of adolescence, along with an increase in the prevalence of depression overall, a sex difference emerges, with higher rates of depression in girls (Hankin & Abramson, 2001; Nolen-Hoeksema, Girgus, & Seligman, 1992). Seven of the studies included in this review found no evidence of sex differences in heritability estimates. Of those that did report significant sex differences, the ranges of the parameter estimates by sex for these studies were almost identical (Eaves et al., 1997; Eley & Stevenson, 1999; Gjone & Stevenson, 1997; Hudziak et al., 2000; Scourfield et al., 2003). The range of heritability estimates among these studies was 0 to .72 for boys and .02 to .80 for girls. Within each study, the estimates were very similar across the sexes, with the exception of the studies of Eley and Stevenson and of Scourfield et al. Among the studies that included adolescents, all reported sex differences in parameter estimates (Eley & Stevenson; Gjone & Stevenson; Scourfield et al.). The only exception was self-report in the Scourfield et al. study. The differences were in the amount of genetic and environmental influences, rather than the source. Although some of these studies tested the latter type of model with nonsignificant results, this null finding could be due to insufficient sample sizes, which underscores the need for more large-scale twin studies.

Measurement Issues for Depression

Symptom reporting versus diagnosis of major depressive disorder may influence parameter estimates (Gotlib, Lewinsohn, & Seeley, 1998). Many of the studies reviewed in this chapter used parent report on the CBCL, which asks parents to report frequencies of a large number of behaviors listed in alphabetical order (Achenbach, 1991). Subscales are pooled and yield an internalizing score for the child. The CDI is a self-report measure that taps depression in a similar way and was used in some of the studies. Other studies used structured clinical interviews such as the Child and Adolescent Psychiatric Assessment (CAPA; Angold et al., 1995) or the Child Semi-Structured Assessment for the Genetics of Alcoholism (C-SSAGA, adapted from the Diagnostic Interview for Children & Adolescents; Reich, 1996), based on *DSM-IV* criteria. The Mood and Feelings Questionnaire (MFQ; Angold, Costello, Pickles, & Winder, 1987), also used in some of the studies, takes a similar approach but uses a pencil-and-paper format. A few differences can be noted. Heritability estimates were lower and shared environment estimates were higher with the CBCL and CDI symptom measures compared with studies that relied on the CAPA, C-SSAGA, and MFQ. If reliable, these differences could be due to differences in the measures or samples. What is needed is careful measurement work and multiple measures used with the same sample to better understand relations among these measures.

Differences in Heritability by Reporter for Depression

All of the studies relied on either parent report for both twins (usually the mother), self-report, or both; only one study also included measures from teachers and peers (Happonen et al., 2002). However, much has been written about how different reporters yield different responses. This could arise because they are reporting different behaviors from different contexts or because of unreliable reporting (Happonen et al.). Another problem arises in twin studies when the same reporter is relied on for both twins, which is the case when parent report is used. This can lead to rater assimilation or contrast effects, in which the reporter compares the twins, which leads to scoring the twins as more similar than they really are (assimilation) or more dissimilar (contrast) (Hudziak et al., 2000). It has been reported elsewhere that self-report tends to yield lower heritability estimates than does parent report (Rice, Harold, & Thapar, 2002). However, the ranges of parameter estimates for the studies we reviewed were very similar for parent and self-report. Only two of the six studies using self-report had low heritability estimates (Eaves et al., 1997; Eley & Stevenson, 1999). Also, only one of the self-report studies found significant shared environmental influences (Eley & Stevenson); the rest found small or no such influences (Eaves et al.; Eley, 1997; Glowinski et al., 2003; Happonen et al.; Scourfield et al., 2003). However, this difference could be due to the fact that self-report was taken from adolescents, at which point c^2 can be lower (Scourfield et al.). Also, c^2 can be overestimated when parents rate twins as more similar (Hudziak et al.). The only study to include teachers and peer report along with self and parent found very different estimates among reporters (Happonen et al.), which emphasizes the importance of including multiple raters in a study design.

Importantly, as Rice et al. (2002) point out in their review of childhood depression, there has not yet been a twin study of depressive disorder in childhood; all of the studies reviewed here were with population-based samples (see Rice et al. for a discussion of analyses with extreme groups). Certainly, more twin studies investigating childhood and adolescent depression are needed to give us a clear understanding of the influence of genes. Longitudinal analyses with multiple raters would be the most helpful in answering this question.

Adult Depression

The most obvious difference between twin studies of child and adult depression is the lack of shared environmental influences for adults (see Table 7.2). Only 1 of the 13 adult studies reviewed had a significant c^2 estimate (Gatz, Pedersen, Plomin, Nesselroade, & McClearn, 1992). Thus, shared environment seems not to contribute to variation in adult depression. By adulthood, twins' environments are much more separate than during childhood. A lack of a shared environmental influence on adult depression suggests that current environment is more influential than shared environmental influences from childhood. However, this in no way means that the environment has no influence on adult depression, because there were still significant contributions of the nonshared environment, which often surpassed the heritability estimate and accounted for the majority of the variance.

All of the studies investigating adult depression used self-report either from a structured clinical interview or a symptom questionnaire. Most of the studies were conducted with population-based samples; only one used a clinical sample (McGuffin, Katz, Watkins, & Rutherford, 1996). The range of heritability estimates across the samples was quite large, .16 to .57. At least three of the hypotheses concerning the genetic influences that underlie adult depression cannot be consistently supported when comparing the results from the studies included here (Carmelli et al., 2000; Kendler, Gardner, Neale, & Prescott, 2001; McGuffin et al.). The first hypothesis proposes different magnitudes of genetic influence for males versus females, based on the much greater prevalence of depression among adult women. For studies that did find sex differences, heritability estimates were always larger for women (Bierut et al., 1999; Kendler et al.; McGue & Christensen, 2003). However, at least six of the studies found no evidence of sex differences (Gatz et al., 1992; Johnson, McGue, Gaist, Vaupel, & Christensen, 2002; Kendler & Prescott, 1999; McGue & Christensen, 1997; McGuffin et al.; Roy, Neale, Pederson, Mathe, & Kendler, 1995),

Table 7.2 Summary of Twin Studies of Adult Depression

Study	Number of Twin Pairs	Age (Years)	Sample Origin	Measure	Reporter	a^2		c^2		e^2	
						Male	*Female*	*Male*	*Female*	*Male*	*Female*
Bierut et al. (1999)	2,662	28–89	Australian	SSAGA	Self						
				DSM-III-R		.24	.44	—	—	.76	.56
				DSM-IV		.31	.31	—	—	.69	.69
				Severe *DSM-IV*		—	.38	—	—	1.00	.63
Carmelli et al. (2000)	167		American	CES-D	Self						
		59–70			Time 1	.25		—		.75	
		69–80			Time 2	.55		—		.45	
Gatz et al. (1992)	481	29–87	Swedish	CES-D	Self	.16		.27		.55	
Johnson et al. (2002)	2,169 same sex	45–95	Danish	CAMDEX	Self	.29		—		.71	
Kendler et al. (1992a, 1992b)	1,033	17–55	American	SCID	Self		.42		—		.58
Kendler et al. (1993)	860	17–55	American	Health and Personality Questionnaire, SCID	Time 1		.49		—		.51
					Time 2		.35		—		.65
					Accounting for measurement error		.71		—		.29
Kendler and Prescott (1999)	3,790	18–60	American	Structured clinical interview	Self	.39		—		.61	

Study	Number of Twin Pairs	Age (Years)	Sample Origin	Measure	Reporter	a^2		c^2		e^2	
						Male	*Female*	*Male*	*Female*	*Male*	*Female*
Kendler et al. (2001)	3,336	18 and over (mean approx. 35)	American	Structured psychiatric interview based on SCID	Self *DSM-III-R* criteria	.44	.57	—	—	.56	.43
McGue and Christensen (1997)	406 same sex	75 and over (mean approx. 80)	Danish	CAMDEX	Self	.34		—		.66	
McGue and Christensen (2003)	1,050	70 and over	Danish	CAMDEX	Self Time 1 Time 2 Time 3 Time 4 **Level**	 .32 .28 .22 .26 .64	 .33 .33 .37 .33 .69	 — — — — —	 — — — — —	 .68 .72 .78 .74 .36	 .67 .67 .63 .63 .31
McGuffin et al. (1996)	177 same sex, clinical sample	18–65	British	PSE, hospital charts	Self *DSM-IV* without missing	 .75 .80		 — —		 .25 .20	
Rijsdijk et al. (2003)	1,950 Time 1 360 Time 2	18–79	British	GHQ	Self Time 1 Time 2		 .42 .39		 —		 .58 .61
Roy et al. (1995)	742	26–74	Swedish	Questionnaire based on SCID	Self Narrow criteria Broad criteria	 .51 .62		— —		 .49 .38	

NOTES: CAMDEX = Cambridge Mental Disorders of the Elderly Examination (Roth et al., 1986); CES-D = Center for Epidemiologic Studies, Depression scale (Radloff, 1977); *DSM-III-R* = *Diagnostic and Statistical Manual of Mental Disorders*, 3rd edition, revised (APA, 1987); *DSM-IV* = *Diagnostic and Statistical Manual of Mental Disorders*, 4th edition (APA, 1994); GHQ = General Health Questionnaire (Goldberg, 1972); PSE = Present State Examination (Wing, Cooper, & Sartorius, 1974); SCID = Structured Clinical Interview for *DSM-III-R* (Spitzer & Williams, 1985); SSAGA = Semi-Structured Assessment for the Genetics of Alcoholism (Bucholz et al., 1994).

and across all of the studies the heritability ranges (including studies that examined men or women exclusively) were only slightly higher for women, with a range of .22 to .64 for men and .33 to .71 for women.

The second hypothesis is the idea that heritability estimates increase with age, and that for the very old, the heritability of depression is much higher than at other ages in adulthood. Carmelli et al. (2000) found a significant increase in heritability estimates longitudinally, from .25 to .55 over a 10-year period, but their sample included only 167 twin pairs. Many of the samples included all ages and found no significant age differences (Bierut et al., 1999; Gatz et al., 1992; Kendler, Neale, Kessler, Heath, & Eaves, 1992b; Kendler, Neale, Kessler, Heath, & Eaves, 1993; Kendler & Prescott, 1999; Kendler et al., 2001; Rijsdijk et al., 2003), and samples that focused exclusively on older adults did not have higher estimates than samples that included younger adults (Johnson et al., 2002; McGue & Christensen, 1997, 2003).

A third hypothesis that has received attention is higher heritability estimates for clinical lifetime diagnoses of major depressive disorder than for current symptoms of depression (McGuffin et al., 1996). This could be a measurement issue, that is, some of the self-report symptom measures used in these studies may not be truly capturing people with the disorder, because symptoms may fluctuate over time. Lower heritability estimates would be expected if we were comparing twins on their depression symptoms at only one particular moment in time. If the difference is in the measures, then better measures are needed to be sure that scores reflect those afflicted with the disorder. The only study to use a clinical sample (McGuffin et al.) did have a much higher heritability estimate than the other studies (.75), but their sample was very small, and this finding would need to be replicated. Roy et al. (1995) reported evidence to the contrary, because their heritability estimate decreased when more narrow criteria (presumably capturing clinical diagnoses) were used to determine presence of depression. Longitudinal studies are helpful in answering this question, and more are needed to show how genetic influence contributes to stability and change in depression over time. McGue and Christensen (2003) have addressed the stability of depression and shown that in the elderly, symptoms of depression over an 8-year period had a common genetic factor, with a much higher heritability estimate than each occasion-specific heritability estimate.

Childhood Anxiety

Many of the issues with childhood depression can also be applied to childhood anxiety (see Williams, Reardon, Murray, & Cole, Chapter 11 of this volume, for greater detail on anxiety disorders). Fewer studies have investigated anxiety, and at least two are studies of both depression and anxiety, measured with the CBCL (Edelbrock et al., 1995; Hudziak et al., 2000). Almost all of the studies (see Table 7.3) show that a genetic influence exists for anxiety, but its strength is still unclear, with heritability estimates ranging from 0% to 72%. However, contrary to depression, self-report tends to yield lower estimates than mother or father report (Eaves et al, 1997; Eley & Stevenson, 1999; Thapar & McGuffin, 1995). Many of the studies included mother or self-report only, but the importance of using multiple raters cannot be overlooked, because different raters tend to disagree in their ratings of problem behaviors (Simonoff et al., 1995). The role of the shared environment is also unclear, with some studies finding no evidence of influence of shared environment and others showing an increase with age (Eaves et al.; Eley & Stevenson; Thapar & McGuffin; Topolski et al., 1997; van Beijsterveldt, Verhulst, Molenaar, & Boomsma, 2004). There is a significant contribution of the nonshared environment to anxiety problems, but more studies with large

Table 7.3 Summary of Twin Studies of Childhood and Adult Anxiety

Childhood Anxiety											
						a^2		c^2		e^2	
Study	*Number of Twin Pairs*	*Age (Years)*	*Sample Origin*	*Measure*	*Reporter*	*Male*	*Female*	*Male*	*Female*	*Male*	*Female*
Eaves et al. (1997)	1,412	8–16	American	CAPA	Mother Father Self	.57 .72 0	.52 .69 .37	— — .33	— — —	.43 .28 .67	.48 .31 .55
Edelbrock et al. (1995)	181 same sex	7–15	American	CBCL Anxiety/ Depression	Parent	.34		.30		.36	
Eley and Stevenson (1999)	490	 8–11 12–16	British	STAIC	Self Young Old	 .19 .15	 .15 .25	 .19 .30	 .30 .35	 .62 .55	 .55 .40
Hudziak et al. (2000)	492 same sex	8–12	American	CBCL Anxiety/ Depression	Parent	.65	.61	—	—	.35	.39
Thapar and McGuffin (1995)	367 same sex	8–16 12–16	British	RCMAS	Mother Self Adolescent	.59 —		— .55		.41 .45	
Topolski et al. (1997)	1,412	 8–10 11–13 14–16	American	RCMAS	Self Young Middle Old	 .29 .01 .23	 .57 .40 .57	 — .44 —	 — .03 —	 .71 .55 .77	 .43 .57 .44
van Beijsterveldt et al. (2004)	7,600	5	Dutch	DCB	Mother Father	.53 .43		.19 .28		.28 .29	

(Continued)

Table 7.3 (Continued)

Adult Anxiety											
						a^2		c^2		e^2	
Study	*Number of Twin Pairs*	*Age (Years)*	*Sample Origin*	*Measure*	*Reporter*	*Male*	*Female*	*Male*	*Female*	*Male*	*Female*
Rijsdijk et al. (2003)	1,950 Time 1 360 Time 2	18–79	British	GHQ	Self Time 1 Time 2		.40 .50		— —		.60 .50
Roy et al. (1995)	742	26–74	Swedish	Questionnaire based on SCID	Self Narrow Broad	.14 .49		— —		.86 .51	
Scherrer et al. (2000)	3,362	36–55	American	DIS-III-R	Self	.38		—		.62	

NOTES: CAPA = Child and Adolescent Psychiatric Assessment (Angold et al., 1995); CBCL = Child Behavior Checklist (Achenbach, 1991); DCB = Devereux Child Behavior Rating Scale (Spivack & Spotts, 1966); DIS-III-R = Diagnostic Interview Schedule, Version 3–Revised (Robins, Helzer, Cottler, & Goldring, 1988); GHQ = General Health Questionnaire (Goldberg, 1972); RCMAS = Revised Child Manifest Anxiety Scale (Reynolds & Richmond, 1978); SCID = Structured Clinical Interview for *DSM-III-R* (Spitzer & Williams, 1985); STAIC = State-Trait Anxiety Inventory for Children (Spielberger, 1973).

enough sample sizes for sufficient power will be helpful to describe anxiety's etiology.

Adult Anxiety

Just like childhood anxiety, only a handful of twin studies have investigated pure adult generalized anxiety disorder (GAD), because of high comorbidity rates of GAD with depression (Flint, 1994). Hettema, Neale, and Kendler (2001) estimated an additive genetic influence for anxiety of .32 for both males and females and a common environmental influence of .17 for women. This was determined through a meta-analysis including two large twin studies measuring anxiety: the study by Roy et al. (1995) of males from the Vietnam Era Twin Registry and the Hettema, Prescott, and Kendler (2001) study of males and females from the Virginia Twin Registry. Rijsdijk et al. (2003) had slightly higher estimates, between .40 and .50, for genetic liability and found no evidence of common environmental influences using the Anxiety scale from the General Health Questionnaire (Goldberg, 1972) with a sample of volunteer females. However, they did not make an attempt to measure individuals with anxiety alone. Overall, the additive genetic influence on anxiety appears to be slightly lower than what is usually estimated for depression. One exception is a more recent study by Kendler, Prescott, Jacobson, Myers, and Neale (2002), which incorporated a multiple-rater model of ratings from both the twin and the co-twin. When the multiple-rater model was applied, the estimate for genetic influences for GAD increased dramatically to .98 with no common environmental influence; however, the estimated measurement error rates were also high.

Comorbidity of Depression and Anxiety

As mentioned above, the high comorbidity rate between GAD and depression leads to difficulties in measuring pure GAD without depression. Genetically informative designs have addressed the high co-occurrence of GAD and depression with the use of bivariate genetic designs to determine what contributes to the association between the two. Two separate studies found very similar results in adults. Kendler, Neale, Kessler, Heath, and Eaves (1992a) and Roy et al. (1995) both demonstrated a shared genetic liability for GAD and depression. Although neither found influences from the common environment for GAD or depression, only part of the nonshared environmental influences overlapped between GAD and depression, demonstrating some environmental influences specific to each disorder. Similarly, Eley and Stevenson (1999) demonstrated a shared genetic liability for anxiety and depression symptoms in children and adolescents ages 8 to 16 years.

Summary of Twin Studies of Internalizing

For depression, heritability estimates increase across childhood and adulthood, and shared environmental influences decrease. On the other hand, for anxiety there is some evidence that the influence of the shared environment increases during childhood and adolescence but is negligible by adulthood. There is still inconclusive evidence as to why the two are so highly associated with one another. As Eley and Stevenson (1999) discuss, there are at least four explanations for their relationship: (a) they share the same etiological factors; (b) comorbid anxiety and depression is a distinct disorder, with its own etiological factors; (c) they are temporally associated; or (d) they are causally related, such that having one puts a person at risk for developing the other. Work in this area should test these hypotheses and should continue to elucidate the developmental trajectories of these disorders.

Child Oppositional and Conduct Disorders

Although externalizing problem behaviors such as ODD and CD are often measured and treated separately in the literature, it is clear that they are highly related, and it is not uncommon to group them together (see Hankin, Abela, Auerbach, McWhinnie, & Skitch, Chapter 14 of this volume, for greater detail on externalizing, behavioral problems, and discussion of this issue). Although the *DSM-IV* treats ODD and CD as two separate disorders, a distinction between the two may be unwarranted. Behavioral genetics has contributed to our understanding of the relationship between the two by demonstrating a common genetic liability for ODD and CD through the use of bivariate genetic models that decompose the covariance (Eaves et al., 2000). The presence of this underlying shared genetic factor suggests that they may be manifestations of the same disorder.

The studies included in Table 7.4 provide evidence for the existence of a genetic influence on externalizing problem behaviors, although the magnitude varied among studies from .13 to .71. When externalizing was measured with the CBCL (Achenbach, 1991), there was most often a significant shared environmental influence as well, ranging from .22 to .62 (Gjone et al., 1996; Schmitz et al., 1995; Silberg et al., 1994). However, for studies that reported separate estimates for the Aggression and Delinquency scales, which comprise the CBCL Externalizing composite, the shared environmental influence was higher for the Delinquency scale (Edelbrock et al., 1995; Eley, Lichtenstein, & Stevenson, 1999). On the other hand, studies using structured clinical interviews usually did not demonstrate a shared environmental influence (Eaves et al., 1997; Slutske et al., 1997).

In contrast to childhood depression, externalizing behavior problems and related disorders are much more prevalent in boys than girls; however, this sex difference tapers off during adolescence (Keenan, Loeber, & Green, 1999; McGee, Feehan, Williams, & Anderson, 1992). Twin studies can examine whether there are entirely separate or differing magnitudes of genetic influence for males and females. The general idea is that externalizing behaviors should be more heritable in males than females because of the higher prevalence rates for males, but also perhaps because the genetic influences are of a different nature. Many of the studies included in this review found no sex differences in parameter estimates of a^2, c^2, and e^2. Only one research group demonstrated qualitative differences in genetic liabilities for the sexes (Silberg et al., 1994; Silberg et al., 1996). However, their results contradicted each other: The former study found qualitative sex differences only for the younger children in the sample (ages 8 to 11 years), for whom the CBCL was completed by the mother; for the latter study, the Rutter Parent Scale (Rutter, Tizard, & Whitmore, 1970) was used instead, and significant sex differences emerged for the older group (ages 12 to 16 years). A number of studies demonstrate quantitative differences in the magnitude of heritability estimates for boys and girls, and although results differ, there is some evidence that externalizing problem behaviors are more heritable for boys (Hudziak et al., 2000; Nadder, Silberg, Eaves, & Maes, 1998).

There is also a sex difference in the types of behaviors displayed, with boys showing more overt (e.g., fighting, violence) and girls showing more covert (e.g., lying, stealing) antisocial behaviors (Zoccolillo, 1993). The Aggression and Delinquency scales on the CBCL discriminate among overt and covert antisocial behaviors, respectively, and heritability estimates from two different studies suggest that aggression is much more heritable than delinquency (Edelbrock et al., 1995; Eley et al., 1999). Studies also need to test whether overt and covert behaviors have different genetic liabilities, which might be a better explanation for the sex differences we see in prevalence

Table 7.4 Summary of Twin Studies of Childhood Externalizing, Oppositional Defiant, and Conduct Disorders and Adult Antisocial Personality Disorder

Study	*Number of Twin Pairs*	*Age (Years)*	*Sample Origin*	*Measure*	*Reporter*	a^2		c^2		e^2	
						Male	*Female*	*Male*	*Female*	*Male*	*Female*
Eaves et al. (1997) CD	1,412	8–16	American	CAPA	Mother	.69		—		.31	
					Father	.27	.58	.37	.09	.36	.33
					Self	.36	.23	—	—	.64	.77
OOD					Mother	.53	.51	—	—	.47	.49
					Father	.65	.49	—	—	.36	.51
					Self	.21	.23	—	—	.79	.77
Edelbrock et al. (1995)	181 same sex	7–15	American	CBCL Externalizing	Parent	.51		.28		.21	
Eley, Lichtenstein, and Stevenson (1999)	1,022	7–9	Swedish	CBCL Aggression	Parent	.70		.07		.23	
				Delinquency		.30	.41	.44	.37	.26	.22
Eley, Lichtenstein, and Stevenson (1999)	501	8–16	British	CBCL Aggression	Parent	.69		.04		.27	
				Delinquency		.00	.47	.64	.27	.36	.26
Gjone and Stevenson (1997)	915		Norwegian	CBCL Externalizing	Parent						
		5–9			Young	.47	.38	.47	.50	.07	.12
		12–15			Old	.57	.65	.33	.23	.10	.12
Goldstein et al. (2001)	558	Mean 38	American		Self						
				Onset < 15 years			.38		—		.62
				Onset < 19 years			.41		—		.58
Hudziak et al. (2000)	492 same sex	8–12	American	CBCL Aggression	Parent	.77	.70	—	—	.23	.30

(Continued)

Table 7.4 (Continued)

Study	*Number of Twin Pairs*	*Age (Years)*	*Sample Origin*	*Measure*	*Reporter*	a^2		c^2		e^2	
						Male	*Female*	*Male*	*Female*	*Male*	*Female*
Lyons et al. (1995)	3,226	36–55	American	DIS-III-R Onset < 15 years	Self	.07		.31		.62	
Schmitz et al. (1995)	463	2–3 mean 7	American	CBCL/2–3 years CBCL/4–18 years	Mother Young Old	.34 .57		.32 .22		.34 .21	
Silberg et al. (1994)	1,263	8–11 12–16	American	CBCL Externalizing	Mother Young Old	.38 .24	.13	.46 .57	.62	.16 .19	.25
Silberg et al. (1996) CD	1,197	8–11 12–16	American	RPS	Mother Young Old	.57 .66	.25 .48	.10 .04	.42 .23	.33 .30	.23 .29
Slutske et al. (1997)	2,682	27–90	Australian	SSAGA *DSM-III-R* Multiple Threshold	Self	.71 .53	.71 .53	— —	— .12	.29 .47	.29 .35
van Beijsterveldt et al. (2004)	7,600	5	Dutch	DCB Aggression	Parent	.48	.47	.25	.29	.27	.25
Young et al. (2000) CD	334	12–18	American	DISC-IV	Self	.34		—		.66	
Adult Antisocial Personality Disorder											
Goldstein et al. (2001)	558	Mean 38	American		Self		—		.38		.62
Lyons et al. (1995)	3,226	36–55	American	DIS-III-R	Self	.43		.05		.52	

NOTES: CAPA = Child and Adolescent Psychiatric Assessment (Angold et al., 1995); CBCL = Child Behavior Checklist (Achenbach, 1991); CD = conduct disorder; DCB = Devereux Child Behavior Rating Scale (Spivack & Spotts, 1966); DISC-IV = Diagnostic Interview Schedule for Children-IV (Shaffer, Fisher, & Lucas, 1997); DIS-III-R = Diagnostic Interview Schedule, Version 3–Revised (Robins et al., 1988); *DSM-III-R* = *Diagnostic and Statistical Manual of Mental Disorders*, 3rd edition, revised (APA, 1987); ODD = oppositional defiant disorder; SSAGA = Semi-Structured Assessment for the Genetics of Alcoholism (Bucholz et al., 1994); RPS = Rutter Parent Scale (Rutter, Tizard, & Whitmore, during childhood. However, another explanation could be found in the lifetime-persistent and adolescent-limited pathways to conduct problems (Moffitt, Caspi, Dickson, Silva, & Stanton, 1996). The lifetime-persistent course tends to be dominated by aggressive behaviors, and because it is more stable, it perhaps has a stronger genetic liability. However, there has not been any consistent evidence of this difference, and more important, none of the studies included in this review was longitudinal, which would be most helpful in testing the hypothesis concerning these two demonstrated pathways for conduct problems.

Adult Antisocial Personality Disorder

Among the outcomes for children and adolescents with ODD and CD, the most serious is a diagnosis of antisocial personality disorder (APD) in adulthood (Burke, Loeber, & Lahey, 2003). Approximately 25% of CD diagnoses lead to APD, and in fact part of the *DSM-IV* criteria for APD is a childhood diagnosis of CD, which is often determined retrospectively (Robins, Tipp, & Przybeck, 1991). Genetically informative designs have likewise used the approach of retrospective reports of CD when investigating both CD and APD. However, there are certainly a number of methodological limitations with relying on retrospective data, including those identified in a study by Rueter, Chao, and Conger (2000), which showed that young adults retrospectively reported more or fewer CD symptoms than their contemporaneous reporting 7 years earlier depending on whether their problems had worsened or improved. Results from genetically informative designs have suggested that APD is moderately heritable and that the behaviors comprising APD lie on a continuum, rather than depicting a qualitatively distinct group of antisocial individuals (McGuffin & Thapar, 1998). Lyons et al. (1995) compared APD and retrospective reports of CD with a sample of males taken from the Vietnam Era Twin Registry and showed that the genetic influence for juvenile CD and adult APD was entirely shared. However, juvenile CD, which was based on symptoms present before the age of 15 years, had an extremely low genetic influence, paired with a moderate shared environmental influence, whereas just the opposite occurred for the adult APD ratings. Goldstein, Prescott, and Kendler (2001) conducted a similar study with females recruited from the Virginia Twin Registry. Unlike the findings for males in the Lyons et al. study, the best-fitting model for CD symptoms in females included additive genetic and nonshared environmental effects, and the parameter estimates were quite similar whether the onset was before the age of 15 or between the ages of 15 to 18 years. On the other hand, a model including shared and nonshared environmental effects but no genetic effects provided the best fit to the data for APD. The Goldstein et al. results were more in line with those of Slutske et al. (1997), who measured retrospective reports of CD only and found a substantial genetic influence for both males and females. Again, however, these studies all relied on retrospective reports of CD behaviors, and because of the limitations of this type of measurement, contemporaneous measurement of CD and then later APD symptoms would be a better approach.

Child ADHD

All of the studies summarized in Table 7.5 had strong heritability estimates for ADHD in childhood and adolescence, ranging from .55 to .81. There was no evidence for shared environmental influences, and modest influences were attributed to the nonshared environment. Because children are poor reporters of ADHD symptoms (Angold et al., 1995), these studies utilized parent report. However, rater contrast effects seem to occur more often with ADHD measures than with other measures of childhood disorders (Eaves et al., 2000; van Beijsterveldt et al., 2004). If

Table 7.5 Summary of Twin Studies of Childhood ADHD

ADHD											
						a^2		c^2		e^2	
Study	*Number of Twin Pairs*	*Age (Years)*	*Sample Origin*	*Measure*	*Reporter*	*Male*	*Female*	*Male*	*Female*	*Male*	*Female*
Eaves et al. (1997)	1,412	8–16	American	CAPA	Mother Father	.71 .78	.74 .55	— —	— —	.29 .22	.26 .45
Hudziak et al. (2000)	492 same sex	8–12	American	CBCL Attention Problems	Parent	.68	.60	—	—	.32	.40
Nadder et al. (1998)	900	7–13	American	Interview adapted from CAPA	Parent	.61		—		.39	
Neuman et al. (2001)	2,904	13–23	American	SSAGA Inattention	Parent		.62		—		.38
Silberg et al. (1996)	1,197	8–11 12–16	American	RPS	Mother Young Old	.70 .70	.67 .70	— —	— —	.27 .25	.32 .26
van Beijsterveldt et al. 2004	7,600	5	Dutch	DCB Attention Problems	Mother	.79	.81	—	—	.21	.19
					Father	.62		—		.38	

NOTES: ADHD = attention deficit/hyperactivity disorder; CAPA = Child and Adolescent Psychiatric Assessment (Angold et al., 1995); CBCL = Child Behavior Checklist (Achenbach, 1991); DCB = Devereux Child Behavior Rating Scale (Spivack & Spotts, 1966); RPS = Rutter Parent Scale (Rutter et al., 1970); SSAGA = Semi-Structured Assessment for the Genetics of Alcoholism (Bucholz et al., 1994).

the similarity of twins is exaggerated, it will raise the estimate of the shared environment, and if twins are contrasted, it can influence the heritability estimate (Eaves et al., 1997). Again, the importance of using multiple informants for child psychopathology symptoms is underscored.

Some of the most interesting work in this area is in explicating the high comorbidity rate that exists for ADHD and ODD or CD. About half of children with ADHD also meet diagnostic criteria for ODD or CD (Biederman, Faraone, & Lapey, 1992). Just why this association occurs is unclear at present, but it could be either environmentally or genetically mediated. In Burt, Krueger, McGue, and Iacono (2001), 753 twin pairs ranging in age from 10 to 12 were assessed for ADHD, ODD, and CD using the Diagnostic Interview for Children and Adolescents (Reich, 1996), which was administered to both mother and child, and the biggest source of the covariation among the three was a common shared environment influence. However, there has been more evidence to the contrary that genetic factors explain the covariation of ADHD with ODD/CD (Nadder, Rutter, Silberg, Maes, & Eaves, 2002; Silberg et al., 1996; Young, Stallings, Corley, Krauter, & Hewitt, 2000). For example, Nadder et al. (2002) investigated 1,098 twin pairs between the ages of 8 and 16 who were measured for ADHD, ODD, and CD with mother report on the CAPA and teacher report on the Rutter B and Conners scales and found genetic mediation. Understanding the comorbidity of ADHD with externalizing disorders can be enhanced by considering gene-environment correlations and interactions, subsumed within the genetic influence in most studies.

Summary of Twin Studies of Externalizing

Findings from genetic studies of externalizing behaviors have shown that ODD and CD share a genetic liability. The nature of the developmental trajectory from ODD/CD to APD in adulthood is still unclear, and longitudinal investigations should be able to show whether ODD/CD and APD share the same etiological factors. ADHD is another disorder highly related to ODD/CD, and studies suggest that they share a common genetic liability. From our reading of the literature, as of yet there are no twin studies of adult ADHD, which if investigated could show whether the strong association between ODD/CD and ADHD in childhood continues in adulthood, with a similar relationship between adult ADHD and APD.

BEHAVIORAL GENOMICS METHODOLOGY

The application of molecular genetics to behavior is the new field called *behavioral genomics*. Traits and disorders that are shown to be heritable through traditional family resemblance methods can now be explored further, and actual genes may be identified. Specific information about genotypes can be incorporated into behavior-genetic or pedigree models to test the importance of individual genes on behavior, or the effect of genes may be associated with behavior in samples of unrelated individuals. Once a gene is identified, we can track the corresponding protein and study how this protein affects behavior, elucidating genetic links between behaviors, genetic interactions, and correlations and tracing the etiology of developmental courses.

A gene that influences a complex, quantitative trait is called a *quantitative trait locus* (QTL) (Gelderman, 1975). Behavioral phenotypes, such as aggression, are most likely influenced by multiple genes. QTLs have varying effect sizes, and often much of the genetic variation is due to gene-gene interactive effects, in which more than one gene is responsible for a particular phenotype. In finding QTLs for complex traits, animal models are often used. Once QTLs are identified in animals, such as mice, then we search for these same QTLs in humans. Current methods of considering the genetic etiology of complex traits include the following: (a) examining phenotypic results of large crosses of known animal strains, (b) allele sharing, (c) linkage analysis, and (d) association studies. Detailed methodology is presented in Benjamin, Ebstein, and Belmaker (2002) and Plomin, DeFries, Craig, and McGuffin (2003), among others.

Using experimental animal crosses is a powerful design for identifying QTLs. Mice and rats are typically used, and entire genomes have been identified through systematic QTL mapping (Lander & Schork, 1994). Nongenetic noise can be minimized, genetic heterogeneity can be controlled through inbreeding, and large numbers of progeny can be obtained. Quantitative traits can be dissected into discrete genetic factors, and the action of modifier genes and the effects of knockout analysis can be examined. One issue with using animal models is the questionable applicability of animal models to humans in some cases. Disease-causing alleles may occur at many steps of a biological pathway, and animal models may not uncover the most frequently mutated link in humans. However, they are a powerful first step for techniques that can be done with humans.

Allele sharing involves seeking an association between particular alleles (i.e., gene variations) and a particular phenotype in pairs of affected relatives in many different families. Affected relatives should inherit identical copies of a particular gene more often than expected by chance. Siblings, for example, would show greater than the 50% expected allele sharing. The phenotype under study can also be sibling differences, in which case a less than 50% sharing would be desirable. Allelic sharing is a useful technique for detecting smaller effect sizes (Plomin, 1995). The frequency of an allele in a sample with the trait is compared with the frequency of the allele in a sample without the trait. This technique can be used for quantitative dimensions, such as temperament, as well as dichotomies, such as disorders. With quantitative traits, the phenotypic similarity between two relatives should be correlated with the number of shared alleles at a relevant locus.

Another method of behavioral genomics is linkage analysis. Linkage is an exception to Mendel's second law of independent assortment: Two genes are *not* inherited independently if they are close together on the same chromosome. Thus, we can map genes to chromosomes by examining whether or not a pair of genes (a DNA marker and a gene that affects the phenotype) are inherited together. One does this by constructing a model to explain the inheritance pattern (Lander & Schork, 1994). One compares a model with a specific association between a DNA marker and the gene influencing the phenotype to a null model positing no linkage between a marker and trait-influencing gene. Because humans are outbred, linkage studies must be done within a large family pedigree. Linkage is typically used for tracing the cotransmission of a DNA marker and a single-gene disorder, and it works very well for simple Mendelian traits. In order to have the power to detect an effect, investigators typically begin with traits that are highly genetically influenced. Large sample sizes are also needed. With complex polygenic traits, it is hard to find a model to explain the transmission pattern. Very homogeneous traits are needed, which poses a problem for psychopathological disorders, which are heterogeneous. In fact, in the late 1980s, reports on linkage for psychopathology were later retracted because of lack of replication. With quantitative traits, one wants to identify some of the QTLs that affect the trait. Comparing allele frequencies in extreme groups has proven to be useful. Like other model-fitting exercises, linkage analysis is powerful if one specifies the correct model. If one tests many models, one needs to use high significance levels, which of course decreases the power to detect a trait-relevant gene.

Allele sharing is more robust than linkage analysis; because it does not assume a model of transmission (i.e., because it is a nonparametric method), it is sensitive to incomplete penetrance, phenocopy, and genetic heterogeneity (Lander & Schork, 1994). On the other hand, when considering a highly genetically influenced trait, allele sharing can be less powerful than linkage analysis.

A fourth method is the association study. Unlike allele sharing and linkage analysis, association studies compare unrelated affected and unaffected individuals. Does a particular allele occur at a significantly higher frequency among affected individuals than unaffected individuals (Lander & Schork, 1994)? The control group selection is critical, and homogeneous populations must be studied, because some genes and some behaviors are more common in some ethnic groups. If an association between an allele and a disorder is found, this association could be an artifact of mixed ethnicity in the population studied; it could be that the gene is on the same chromosome as the gene that influences the trait; or it could be the gene that plays a causal role in the disorder. Studies in the early 1990s on a putative link between alcoholism and an allele at the dopamine D2 receptor (*DRD2*) illustrate the importance of control group selection. The initial study undertook a postmortem comparison of 35 alcoholics and 35 controls and found the A1 allele to be present in 69% of the alcoholics and 27% of the controls (Blum et al., 1990). However, this study did not control for ethnic ancestry other than race, and subsequent replication attempts yielded mixed results. The frequency of a particular allele can vary substantially among populations; thus, many investigators recommend using an internal control group, such as the parents of affected individuals (called an *affected family–based control*), to minimize the problem of mixed ethnicity. In conclusion, association studies test whether an allele and a trait have correlated occurrence within a population as contrasted to linkage studies, which test whether an allele and a trait have correlated transmission within a pedigree.

Those within the new field of behavioral genomics are still figuring out the most powerful sampling units (e.g., extremely discordant sibling pairs), genotyping issues such as which types of markers to use and how many, and methodological approaches. Despite the limitations of a new field, progress has been made in identifying the relation between some candidate genes and psychopathology.

LINKING AND ASSOCIATING SPECIFIC FUNCTIONAL GENETIC POLYMORPHISMS WITH PSYCHOPATHOLOGY

We will describe genetic regions involved in the control of the serotonin transporter, dopamine D4 receptor (*DRD4*), dopamine transporter (*DAT1*), monoamine oxidase inhibitor (*MAOA*), catechol-O-methyltransferase (*COMT*), and corticotropin-releasing hormone (*CRH*). Because this field is relatively new and methods are changing dramatically, we do not attempt to summarize all relevant studies, but rather focus on a few illustrative examples.

Because of serotonin's role in brain development and its influence on limbic brain systems, genetic variations affecting the serotonin transporter are likely to influence personality and health (Lesch, Greenberg, Higley, Bennett, & Murphy, 2002). A polymorphic repetitive element (*5-HTTLPR*) located upstream of the transcription start site modulates the transcriptional frequency of the serotonin transporter. Human cells with the long *5-HTTLPR* allele produce higher concentrations of serotonin transporter messenger RNA than cells with one or two copies of the short allele (Lesch et al., 2002). Serotonin has been found to influence both personality and psychopathology. For example, individuals with one or two copies of the short allele report higher levels of Neuroticism and Anxiety and lower levels of Agreeableness (Greenberg et al., 2000; Lesch et al., 1996). Furthermore, the serotonin transporter gene confers risk for common disorders such as ADHD and anxiety (Cadoret, Langbehn, & Caspers, 2003). It also interacts with an early rearing environment to predict aggression in rhesus monkeys (Barr et al., 2003). In young adult humans, those with the short allele had significantly more depressive symptoms, diagnoses of depression, and suicidality following stressful life events than those homozygous for the long allele (Caspi et al., 2003). These GE interactions underscore the importance of considering genetic vulnerability-stress models.

Dopamine genes (both *DRD4* and *DAT1*) have been linked to temperament (Lakatos, Nemoda, & Birkas, 2003; Van Gestel, Forsgren, & Claes, 2002), internalizing disorders (Rowe, Stever, & Gard, 1998), posttraumatic stress disorder (PTSD; Segman, Cooper-Kazaz, & Macciardi, 2002), obsessive compulsive disorder (Millet et al., 2003), and ADHD (Maher, Marazita, & Ferrell, 2002). *DRD4* is highly expressed in limbic areas (e.g., nucleus accumbens, amygdala, cingulate cortex) of the brain. *DRD4* has been considered along with the serotonin transporter gene in studies of infant temperament. The combined effect of the lack of a seven-repeat *DRD4* allele with the homozygous short serotonin transporter allele was associated with lower Orientation (Ebstein et al., 1998) and higher Distress to Limitations in neonates (Auerbach, Faroy, Ebstein, Kahana, & Levine, 2001). At 12 months, *DRD4* and the serotonin transporter gene predicted observed responses to the approach of a stranger in the lab (Lakotos et al., 2003). A variable-number tandem repeat in the untranslated region of the *DAT1* gene affects translational efficiency, and individuals homozygous for a 10-repeat allele showed significantly lower dopamine transporter binding than those with at least one nine-repeat allele (Jacobsen et al., 2002). *DAT1*-knockout mice display traits similar to ADHD in humans (DiMaio, Grizenko, & Joober, 2003), and a recent meta-analysis has confirmed that the 10-repeat allele confers a risk for ADHD (Fossella et al., 2002). Although the pathway linking *DAT1* to ADHD remains unclear, Loo et al. (2003) report that children with ADHD who had at least one copy of the 10-repeat allele exhibited poorer performance on a vigilance task.

The *MAOA* gene encodes the monoamine oxidase-A enzyme, which metabolizes neurotransmitters such as dopamine (DA), norepinephrine (NE), and serotonin. The promoter of the *MAOA* gene includes a variable-number tandem repeat polymorphism that is known to affect expression (Sabol, Hu, & Hamer, 1998). Shorter alleles (two to three copies) are transcribed less efficiently than longer alleles (Deckert et al., 1999). In knockout mice, increased levels of brain DA, NE, and serotonin were observed along with increased aggression (Cases et al., 1995). By restoring *MAOA* expression, aggression was normalized (Shih & Thompson, 1999). In humans, the evidence for an association with aggression is mixed (Jorm et al., 2000; Manuck, Flory, & Ferrell, 2000; Parsian & Cloninger, 2001). The *MAOA* gene has also been linked to mood disorders (Preisig et al., 2000) and ADHD (Lawson et al., 2003), although many of these findings have failed to replicate (Kunugi et al., 1999; Serretti et al., 2002). A vulnerability-stress perspective is helpful in elucidating the influence of the *MAOA* gene; Caspi et al.

(2002) reported a significant interaction between *MAOA* and childhood maltreatment in predicting aggression.

DA is critical for cognitive functioning, such as executive cognition and working memory subserved by the prefrontal cortex (Williams & Goldman-Rakic, 1995). Unlike the limbic region, concentrations of the DA transporter (the DAT protein) have minimal influence on DA levels in this region (Mazei, Pluto, Kirkbride, & Pehek, 2002), so metabolizing DA may be particularly important for inactivation. COMT is a key enzyme in the breakdown of DA (Boulton & Eisenhofer, 1998). The *COMT* gene has a common functional diallelic polymorphism that is associated with poor prefrontal function, executive cognition, and prefrontal cortex DA signaling in humans (Akil et al., 2003). Individuals homozygous for the *met* allele performed best on executive cognition tasks, *val/met* individuals were intermediate, and *val/val* individuals performed the worst (Egan et al., 2001). In addition, studies in mice have demonstrated that reduced DA signaling in the prefrontal cortex leads to hyperresponsivity of subcortically projecting midbrain DA neurons to stress stimuli (Harden, Ling, Finlay, & Grace, 1998). In *COMT*-knockout mice, DA levels in the prefrontal cortex are increased under certain conditions, but DA levels in the striatum are not modified (Huotari et al., 2002). Also, NE levels do not change, indicating the selective impact on DA of the COMT enzyme in the prefrontal cortex.

The hormone CRH mediates the stress response by influencing the hypothalamic-pituitary-adrenal (HPA) axis and limbic centers of the brain. Wuest, Federenko, Hellhammer, and Kirschbaum (2000) reported a significant heritability of cortisol levels after awakening, but not on a profile of measures across the day. Bartels, de Geus, Sluyter, Kirschbaum, and Boomsma (2002) reported a significant genetic contribution to morning and afternoon basal cortisol levels. Molecular genetic studies are beginning to illustrate the causal impact genotype has on HPA activity. Polymorphisms in the regulatory region of the *CRH* gene and the glucocorticoid-receptor gene have been identified, and their putative relationships to stress reactivity and disease susceptibility are being investigated. For example, Rosmond, Chagnon, Bouchard and Bjorntorp (2001) reported significantly increased basal and reactive (during physiologic stress) cortisol levels in middle-aged Swedish men who were carriers of the rarer variants of both genes. Glucocorticoids and the *CRH* gene are associated with (a) temperament, such as behavioral inhibition (although not in all studies); and (b) mental and physical health outcomes, including anticipatory anxiety, PTSD, melancholic depression, addictive behaviors, and allostatic load (see Schulkin, Gold, & McEwen, 1998, for a review). Smoller et al. (2003) reported the first evidence of a significant association between behavioral inhibition and a genetic marker in linkage disequilibrium with single-nucleotide polymorphisms at the *CRH* gene locus.

In summary, candidate gene studies hold great promise of elucidating the complex associations between the genetic and behavioral levels of analysis in psychopathology. However, the field is troubled by low rates of replication. One reason proposed for poor replication is that different behavioral assessment methods may tap different aspects of behavior and psychopathology. For example, Schmidt, Fox, Rubin, Hu, and Hamer (2002) reported a significant main effect for the *DRD4* long allele on parent reports of aggression but not on observed aggression. In contrast, Lakatos et al. (2003) found no association between parent ratings of infant response to novelty and *DRD4*, but they did report a significant relationship between *DRD4* and observed measures of response to novelty. The lack of correspondence among different assessment methods is a broader problem that characterizes the field of psychopathology.

Another reason for the low rate of replication is that most studies have focused on complex syndromes or heterogeneous disorders (see discussion of enhancing the definition of phenotypes, above). What is needed is an increased focus on multimodal assessments, subtypes, and cognitive and personality components of disorder. Heavy smoking and drinking frequency co-occur, and greater evidence of linkage was reported by combining these dependencies compared with studying tobacco dependence or alcohol dependence alone (Beirut et al., 2000). Several studies have examined personality constructs such as aggression, impulsivity, and novelty seeking with mixed results (Garpenstrand et al., 2002; Jorm et al., 2000; Koller, Bondy, & Preuss, 2003; Lakatos et al., 2003; Manuck et al., 2000; Rowe et al., 2001), owing in part to reliance on self or parent reports alone. Further, Langley, Marshall, and van den Bree (2004) found significant group differences (presence vs. absence of *DRD4* long allele) on various attentional tasks in children with ADHD. Although these findings also failed to replicate (Swanson, Flodman, & Kennedy, 2000), such process-oriented investigations represent an important step in elucidating the pathway from genetic to phenotypic variation.

A third reason many candidate gene studies do not replicate is the failure to account for unmeasured confounds or to use gene-environment interactional models. For example, Chotai, Serretti, Lattuada, Lorenzi, and Lilli (2003) found that season of birth interacted with tryptophan hydroxylase, serotonin transporter, and *DRD4* gene polymorphisms to predict unipolar and bipolar affective disorder and schizophrenia. Rose, Dick, Viken, and Kaprio (2001) reported greater genetic effects on adolescent alcohol use for those living in urban environments than those living in rural environments. Similarly, Koopmans, Slutske, van Baal, and Boomsma (1999) found greater genetic effects on women's alcohol use in those reared in nonreligious households than in those reared in religious households. The phenotype is ultimately influenced by interactions between genes and environments; therefore, models of development that do not consider moderators such as age, sex, family history, and socioeconomic status are ultimately simplistic.

UNDERSTANDING THE DEVELOPMENT OF PSYCHOPATHOLOGY USING VULNERABILITY-STRESS MODELS

Genetic vulnerability-stress developmental models are needed to advance this field beyond linear gene-phenotype associations. Already, these models are adding to our understanding of psychopathology. New research on the early environment, for example, is underscoring its importance in stress reactivity and psychopathology. There is evidence in both the animal and human literatures that early environment can alter DA, NE, serotonin, and HPA axis neurotransmitter systems (Luecken & Lemery, in press). These changes may dispose the organism to be hypersensitive to environmental stress, and they appear stable into adulthood and increase rates of psychopathology across the life span. For example, monkeys with a short serotonin transporter allele have impaired serotonergic function and are more severely affected by maternal deprivation (Bennett et al., 2000; Suomi, 2000). Those with the short allele, if peer reared, grew up to be socially anxious, easily emotionally aroused, fearful, aggressive, and impulsive, and they fell to the bottom of the dominance hierarchy. In contrast, monkeys with the short allele were behaviorally precocious and secure if reared by foster "super" mothers. Aspects of the early environment have also been shown to modify gene expression in humans (Fonagy, 2001; Post, Weiss, & Leverich, 1994). Caspi et al. (2002) reported that a childhood history of maltreatment combined with a low-activity *MAOA* genotype (GE interaction) predicted antisocial outcomes in young adulthood. Similarly, Caspi et al. (2003) reported that individuals with the short serotonin transporter allele were more depressed following stressful life events.

Incorporating measured aspects of the environment is important in fitting genetic vulnerability-stress models. In addition, measuring related phenotypes, such as temperament, and endophenotypes, such as HPA activation, can elucidate the gene-behavior pathway and ultimately inform our understanding of the development of psychopathology. Lemery (2000) decomposed the covariation between 5-year-old temperament and 7-year-old mood and behavioral disorder symptoms using the twin design. Model fitting suggested a shared genetic etiology between temperament and later symptoms. These results suggest that the genetic influence on child psychopathological symptoms is nonspecific. On the other hand, environmental influences on temperament and symptoms were for the most part independent. These two types of child behavior are either influenced by different environmental events or are influenced by the same environmental events in different ways. An obvious next step would be to also consider the interaction between candidate genes and specific environments to inform how genes and the environment work together to influence problem behaviors.

Endophenotypes exist along the pathway from genotype to disorder, and they may be endocrinological, biochemical, neurophysiological, neuroanatomical, neuropsychological, or cognitive (Gottesman & Gould, 2003). To be useful, endophenotypes should be heritable, as well as associated with one or more candidate genes and the disorder. Incorporating endophenotypes into our models can clarify our taxonomic system as well as elucidate pathways from genes to behavior. For example, nonaffected siblings of children with ADHD had deficits in response inhibition similar to their affected siblings, although their behavior was similar to controls (Slaats-Willemse, Swaab-Barneveld, deSonneville, van der Meulen, & Buitelaar, 2003), suggesting that response inhibition is a putative endophenotype for ADHD.

CONCLUSION

Developmental psychology textbooks are correct in moving away from a focus on the nature-versus-nurture debate and toward process-oriented, gene-environment interactional models. Genetic influences are probabilistic, and we should guard against explaining psychopathology in a reductionistic "genetic engineering" manner. Quantitative genetic liabilities to a specific temperament, disorder, or disease alter risk but rarely determine outcome. Genes are an important part of the developing system, influencing behavior indirectly through protein synthesis and its consequences. Genetically informative designs are powerful tools for understanding individual differences and the development of psychopathology. Specific aspects of the environment and candidate genes that have the greatest influence on behavior can be identified, and critical periods in which environmental influences are most malleable can be pinpointed. Once we gain a fuller understanding of GE interactions and development, interventions and preventions can target windows of opportunity and be tailored to specific groups of individuals to reduce the burden of psychopathology on individuals, communities, and countries.

REFERENCES

Achenbach, T. M. (1991). *Integrative guide for the 1991 CBCL/4–18, YSR, and TRF profiles.* Burlington: University of Vermont Department of Psychiatry.

Achenbach, T. M., Edelbrock, C. S., & Howell, C. T. (1987). Empirically-based assessment of the behavioral/emotional problems of 2- and 3-year-old children. *Journal of Abnormal Child Psychology, 15,* 629–650.

Akil, M., Kolachana, B. S., Rothmond, D. A., Hyde, T. M., Weinberger, D. R., & Kleinman, J. E. (2003). Catechol-O-methyltransferase genotype and dopamine regulation in the human brain. *Journal of Neuroscience, 23,* 2008–2013.

American Psychiatric Association. (1987). *Diagnostic and statistical manual of mental disorders* (3rd ed.). Washington, DC: Author.

American Psychiatric Association. (1994). *Diagnostic and statistical manual of mental disorders* (4th ed.). Washington, DC: Author.

Angold, A., Costello, E. J., Pickles, A., & Winder, F. (1987). *The development of a questionnaire for use in epidemiological studies of depression in children and adolescents.* London: Medical Research Council Child Psychiatry Unit.

Angold, A., Prendergast, M., Cox, A., Harrington, R., Simonoff, E., & Rutter, M. (1995). The Child and Adolescent Psychiatric Assessment (CAPA). *Psychological Medicine, 25,* 739–753.

Auerbach, J.G., Faroy, M., Ebstein, R., Kahana, M., & Levine, J. (2001). The association of the dopamine D4 receptor gene (DRD4) and the serotonin transporter promotor gene (5-HTTLPR) with temperament in 12-month-old infants. *Journal of Child Psychology & Psychiatry & Allied Disciplines, 42,* 777–783.

Barr, C. S., Newman, T. K., Becker, M. L., Parker, C. C., Champoux, M., Lesch, K. P., et al. (2003). The utility of the nonhuman primate: Model for studying gene by environment interactions in behavioral research. *Genes, Brain and Behavior, 2,* 336–340.

Bartels, M., de Geus, E. J. C., Sluyter, F., Kirschbaum, C., & Boomsma, D. I. (2002). *Heritability of daytime cortisol in children.* Manuscript submitted for publication.

Beirut, L., Rice, J., Goate, A., Foroud, T., Edenberg, H., Crowe, R., et al. (2000). Common and specific factors in the familial transmission of substance dependence. *American Journal of Medical Genetics, 96,* 459.

Benjamin, J., Ebstein, R. P., & Belmaker, R. H. (Eds.). (2002). *Molecular genetics and the human personality.* Washington, DC: American Psychiatric Publishing.

Bennett, A. J., Lesch, K. P., Heils, A., Long, J., Lorenz, J., Shoaf, S. E., et al. (2000). *Serotonin transporter gene variation, strain and early rearing environment affect CSF 5-HIAA concentrations in rhesus monkeys (Macaca mulatta).* Unpublished manuscript.

Biederman, J., Faraone, S. V., & Lapey, K. (1992). Comorbidity of diagnosis in attention-deficit hyperactivity disorders. In G. Weiss (Ed.), *Child and adolescent psychiatric clinics of North America: Attention-deficit hyperactivity disorder* (pp. 335–360). Philadelphia: Saunders.

Bierut, L. J., Heath, A. C., Bucholz, K. K., Dinwiddie, S. H., Madden, P. A. F., Statham, D. J., et al. (1999). Major depressive disorder in a community-based twin sample: Are there different genetic and environmental contributions for men and women? *Archives of General Psychiatry, 56,* 557–563.

Birmaher, B., Ryan, N. D., Williamson, D. E., Brent, D. A., Kaufman, J., Dahl, R. E., et al. (1996). Childhood and adolescent depression: A review of the past 10 years: Part I. *Journal of the American Academy of Child and Adolescent Psychiatry, 35,* 1427–1439.

Blum, K., Noble, E. P., Sheridan, P. J., Montgomery, A., Ritchie, T., Jagadeeswaran, P., et al. (1990). Allelic association of human dopamine D2 receptor gene in alcoholism. *Journal of the American Medical Association, 263,* 2055–2060.

Boulton, A. A., & Eisenhofer, G. (1998). Catecholamine metabolism. In D. S. Goldstein, G. Eisenhofer, & R. McCarty (Eds.), *Advances in pharmacology: Vol. 42. Catecholamines bridging basic science with clinical medicine* (pp. 273–292). San Diego, CA: Academic Press.

Bucholz, K. K., Cadoret, R., Cloninger, C. R., Dinwiddie, S. H., Hesselbrock, V. M., Nurnberger, J. I., Jr., et al. (1994). A new, semistructured psychiatric interview for use in genetic linkage studies: A report of the reliability of the SSAGA. *Journal of Studies on Alcoholism, 55,* 149–158.

Burke, J. D., Loeber, R., & Lahey, B. B. (2003). Course and outcomes. In C. A. Essau (Ed.), *Conduct and oppositional defiant disorders: Epidemiology, risk factors, and treatment* (pp. 61–94). Mahwah, NJ: Lawrence Erlbaum.

Burt, S. A., Krueger, R. F., McGue, M., & Iacono, W. G. (2001). Sources of covariation among attention-deficit/hyperactivity disorder, oppositional defiant disorder, and conduct disorder: The importance of shared environment. *Journal of Abnormal Psychology, 110,* 516–525.

Cadoret, R. J., Langbehn, D., & Caspers, K. (2003). Associations of the serotonin transporter promoter polymorphism with aggressivity, attention deficit, and conduct disorder in an adoptee population. *Comprehensive Psychiatry, 44,* 88–101.

Carmelli, D., Swan, G. E., Kelly-Hayes, M., Wolf, P. A., Reed, T., & Miller, B. (2000). Longitudinal changes in the contribution of genetic and environmental influences to symptoms of depression in older male twins. *Psychology and Aging, 15,* 505–510.

Cases, O., Seif, I., Grimsby, J., Gaspar, P., Chen, K., Pournin, S., et al. (1995). Aggressive behavior and altered amounts of brain serotonin and norepinephrine in mice lacking MAOA. *Science, 268,* 1763–1766.

Caspi, A., McClay, J., Moffitt, T. E., Mill, J., Martin, J., Craig, I. W., et al. (2002). Role of genotype in the cycle of violence in maltreated children. *Science, 297,* 851–854.

Caspi, A., Sugden, K., Moffitt, T. E., Taylor, A., Craig, I. W., Harrington, H., et al. (2003). Influence of life stress on depression: Moderation by a polymorphism in the 5-HTT gene. *Science, 301,* 386–389.

Chotai, J., Serretti, A., Lattuada, E., Lorenzi, C., & Lilli, R. (2003). Gene–environment interaction in psychiatric disorders as indicated by season of birth variations in tryptophan hydroxylase (TPH), serotonin transporter (5-HTTLPR) and dopamine receptor (DRD4) gene polymorphisms. *Psychiatry Research, 119,* 99–111.

Deckert, J., Catalano, M., Syagailo, Y., Bosi, M., Okladnova, O., Di Bella, D., et al. (1999). Excess of high activity monoamine oxidase A gene promoter alleles in female patients with panic disorder. *Human Molecular Genetics, 8,* 621–624.

Dick, D. M., Rose, R. J., Viken, R. J., & Kaprio, J. (2000). Pubertal timing and substance use: Associations between and within families across late adolescence. *Developmental Psychology, 36,* 180–189.

DiMaio, S., Grizenko, N., & Joober, R. (2003). Dopamine genes and attention-deficit hyperactivity disorder: A review. *Journal of Psychiatry and Neuroscience, 28,* 27–38.

Eaves, L., Rutter, M., Silberg, J. L., Shillady, L., Maes, H., & Pickles, A. (2000). Genetic and environmental causes of covariation in interview assessments of disruptive behavior in child and adolescent twins. *Behavior Genetics, 30,* 321–334.

Eaves, L., Silberg, J., Meyer, J. M., Maes, H. H., Simonoff, E., Pickles, A., et al. (1997). Genetics and developmental psychopathology: 2. The main effects of genetics and environment of behavioral problems in the Virginia twin study of adolescent behavioral development. *Journal of Child Psychology and Psychiatry, 38,* 965–980.

Ebstein, R. P., Levine, J., Geller, V., Auerbach, J., Gritsenko, I., & Belmaker, R. H. (1998). Dopamine D4 receptor and serotonin transporter promoter in the determination of neonatal temperament. *Molecular Psychiatry, 3,* 238–246.

Edelbrock, C., Rende, R. D., Plomin, R., & Thompson, L. A. (1995). A twin study of competence and problem behavior in childhood and early adolescence. *Journal of Child Psychology and Psychiatry and Allied Disciplines, 36,* 775–785.

Egan, M. F., Goldberg, T. E., Kolachana, B. S., Callicott, J. H., Mazzanti, C. M., Straub, R. E., et al. (2001). Effect of COMT Val 108/158 Met genotype on frontal lobe function and risk for schizophrenia. *Proceedings of the National Academy of Sciences USA, 98,* 6917–6922.

Eley, T. C. (1997). Depressive symptoms in children and adolescents: Etiological links between normality and abnormality: A research note. *Journal of Child Psychology and Psychiatry and Allied Disciplines, 38,* 861–865.

Eley, T. C., Lichtenstein, P., & Stevenson, J. (1999). Sex differences in the etiology of aggressive and nonaggressive antisocial behavior: Results from two twin studies. *Child Development, 70,* 155–168.

Eley, T. C., & Stevenson, J. (1999). Exploring the covariation between anxiety and depression symptoms: A genetic analysis of the effects of age and sex. *Journal of Child Psychology and Psychiatry, 40,* 1273–1282.

Ezpeleta, L., Polaino, A., Domenech, E., & Domenech, J. M. (1990). Peer nomination inventory of depression: Characteristic in a Spanish sample. *Journal of Abnormal Child Psychology, 18,* 373–391.

Flint, A. J. (1994). Epidemiology and comorbidity of anxiety disorders in the elderly. *American Journal of Psychiatry, 151,* 640–649.

Fonagy, P. (2001). The human genome and the representational world: The role of early mother-infant interaction in creating an interpersonal interpretive mechanism. *Bulletin of the Menninger Clinic, 65,* 427–448.

Fossella, J., Sommer, T., Fan, J., Yanhong, W., Swanson, J. M., Pfaff, D. W., et al. (2002). Assessing the molecular genetics of attention networks. *BMC Neuroscience, 3,* 14–27.

Garpenstrand, H., Longato-Stadler, E., af Klinteberg, B., Grigorenko, E., Damberg, M., Oreland, L., et al. (2002). Low platelet monoamine oxidase activity in Swedish imprisoned criminal offenders. *European Neuropsychopharmacology, 12,* 135–140.

Gatz, M., Pedersen, N. L., Plomin, R., Nesselroade, J. R., & McClearn, G. E. (1992). Importance of shared genes and shared environments for symptoms of depression in older adults. *Journal of Abnormal Psychology, 101,* 701–708.

Gelderman, H. (1975). Investigations on inheritance of quantitative characters in animals by gene markers: I. Methods. *Theoretical and Applied Genetics, 46,* 319–330.

Gjone, H., & Stevenson, J. (1997). The association between internalizing and externalizing behavior in childhood and early adolescence: Genetic or environmental common influences? *Journal of Abnormal Child Psychology, 25,* 277–296.

Gjone, H., Stevenson J., Sundet, J. M., & Eilertsen, D. E. (1996). Changes in heritability across increasing levels of behavior problems in young twins. *Behavior Genetics, 26,* 419–426.

Glowinski, A. L., Madden, P., Bucholz, K. K., Lynskey, M. T., & Heath, A. C. (2003). Genetic epidemiology of self-reported lifetime DSM-IV major depressive disorder in a population-based twin sample of female adolescents. *Journal of Child Psychology and Psychiatry, 44,* 988–996.

Goldberg, D. P. (1972). The detection of psychiatric illness by questionnaire. *Maudsley Monograph, 21.* Oxford, UK: Oxford University Press.

Goldsmith, H. H. (1991). A zygosity questionnaire for young twins: A research note. *Behavior Genetics, 21,* 257–269.

Goldstein, R. B., Prescott, C. A., & Kendler, K. S. (2001). Genetic and environmental factors in conduct problems and adult antisocial behavior among adult female twins. *Journal of Nervous and Mental Disease, 189,* 201–209.

Gotlib, I. H., Lewinsohn, P. M., & Seeley, J. R. (1995). Symptoms versus a diagnosis of depression: Differences in psychosocial functioning. *Journal of Consulting and Clinical Psychology, 63,* 90–100.

Gottesman, I. I., & Gould, T. D. (2003). The endophenotype concept in psychiatry: Etymology and strategic intentions. *American Journal of Psychiatry, 160,* 636–645.

Greenberg, B. D., Li, Q., Lucas, F. R., Hu, S., Sirota, L. A., Benjamin, J., et al. (2000). Association between the serotonin transporter promoter polymorphism and personality traits in a primarily female population sample. *American Journal of Medical Genetics, 96,* 202–216.

Hankin, B. L., & Abramson, L. Y. (2001). Development of gender differences in depression: An elaborated cognitive vulnerability-transactional stress theory. *Psychological Bulletin, 127,* 773–796.

Happonen, M., Pulkkinen, L., Kaprio, J., Van der Meere, J., Viken, R. J., & Rose, R. J. (2002). The heritability of depressive symptoms: Multiple informants and multiple measures. *Journal of Child Psychology and Psychiatry, 43,* 471–479.

Harden, D. G., Ling, D., Finlay, J. M., & Grace, A. A. (1998). Depletion of dopamine in the prefrontal cortex decreases the basal electrophysiological activity of mesolimbic dopamine neurons. *Brain Research, 794,* 96–102.

Hettema, J. M., Neale, M. C., & Kendler, K. S. (2001). A review and meta-analysis of the genetic epidemiology of anxiety disorders. *American Journal of Psychiatry, 158,* 1568–1578.

Hettema, J. M., Prescott, C. A., & Kendler, K. S. (2001). A population-based twin study of generalized anxiety disorder in men and women. *Journal of Nervous and Mental Disease, 189,* 413–420.

Hudziak, J. J., Rudiger, L. P., Neale, M. C., Heath, A. C., & Todd, R. D. (2000). A twin study of inattentive, aggressive, and anxious/depressed behaviors. *Journal of the American Academy of Child and Adolescent Psychiatry, 39,* 469–476.

Huotari, M., Gogos, J. A., Karayiorgou, M., Koponen, O., Forsberg, M., Raasmaja, A., et al. (2002). Brain catecholamine metabolism in catechol-O-methyltransferase (COMT)-deficient mice. *European Journal of Neuroscience, 15,* 246–256.

Jacobsen, L., Staley, J., Soghbi, S., Seibyl, J., Kosten, T., Innis, R., et al. (2002). Prediction of dopamine transporter binding availability by genotype: A preliminary report. *American Journal of Psychiatry, 157,* 1700–1703.

Johnson, W., McGue, M., Gaist, D., Vaupel, J. W., & Christensen, K. (2002). Frequency and heritability of depression symptomatology in the second half of life: Evidence from Danish twins over 45. *Psychological Medicine, 32,* 1175–1185.

Jorm, A. F., Henderson, A. S., Jacomb, P. A., Korten, A. E., Rodgers, B., Tan, X., et al. (2000). Association of a functional polymorphism of the monoamine oxidase A gene promoter with personality and psychiatric symptoms. *Psychiatric Genetics, 10,* 87–90.

Keenan, K., Loeber, R., & Green, S. (1999). Conduct disorder in girls: A review of the literature. *Clinical Child and Family Psychology Review, 2,* 3–19.

Kendler, K. S., Gardner, C. O., Neale, M. C., & Prescott, C. A. (2001). Genetic risk factors for major depression in men and women: Similar or different heritabilities and same or partly distinct genes? *Psychological Medicine, 31,* 605–616.

Kendler, K. S., Neale, M. C., Kessler, R. C., Heath, A. C., & Eaves, L. J. (1992a). Major depression and generalized anxiety disorder: Same genes, (partly) different environments? *Archives of General Psychiatry, 48,* 716–722.

Kendler, K. S., Neale, M. C., Kessler, R. C., Heath, A. C., & Eaves, L. J. (1992b). A population-based twin study of major depression in women: The impact of varying definitions of illness. *Archives of General Psychiatry, 49,* 257–266.

Kendler, K. S., Neale, M. C., Kessler, R. C., Heath, A. C., & Eaves, L. J. (1993). The lifetime history of major depression in women: Reliability of diagnosis and heritability. *Archives of General Psychiatry, 50,* 863–870.

Kendler, K. S., & Prescott, C. A. (1999). A population-based twin study of lifetime major depression in men and women. *Archives of General Psychiatry, 56,* 39–44.

Kendler, K. S., Prescott, C. A., Jacobson, K., Myers, J., & Neale, M. C. (2002). The joint analysis of personal interview and family history diagnoses: Evidence for validity of diagnosis and increased heritability estimates. *Psychological Medicine, 32,* 829–842.

Koller, G., Bondy, B., & Preuss, U. W. (2003). No association between a polymorphism in the promoter region of the MAOA gene with antisocial personality traits in alcoholics. *Alcohol and Alcoholism, 38,* 31–34.

Koopmans, J. R., Slutske, W. S., van Baal, G. C. M., & Boomsma, D. I. (1999). The influence of religion on alcohol use initiation: Evidence for genotype-environment interaction. *Behavior Genetics, 29,* 445–453.

Kovacs, M. (1992). *Children's Depression Inventory CDI Manual.* Pittsburgh, PA: Multi-Health Systems Inc.

Kunugi, H., Ishida, S., Kato, T., Tatsumi, M., Sakai, T., Hattori, M., et al. (1999). A functional polymorphism in the promoter region of monoamine oxidase-A gene and mood disorders. *Molecular Psychiatry, 4,* 393–395.

Lakatos, K., Nemoda, Z., & Birkas, E. (2003). Association of D4 dopamine receptor gene and serotonin transporter promoter polymorphisms with infant's response to novelty. *Molecular Psychiatry, 8,* 90–97.

Lander, E. S., & Schork, N. J. (1994). Genetic dissection of complex traits. *Science, 265,* 2037–2048.

Langley, K., Marshall, L., & van den Bree, M. (2004). Association of the dopamine D-sub-4 receptor gene 7-repeat allele with neuropsychological test performance of children with ADHD. *American Journal of Psychiatry, 161,* 1133–1138.

Lawson, D. C., Turic, D., Langley, K., Pay, H. M., Govan, C. F., Hamshere, M. L., et al. (2003). Association analysis of monoamine oxidase A and attention deficit hyperactivity disorder. *American Journal of Medical Genetics, 116,* 84–89.

Lemery, K. S. (2000). Exploring the etiology of the relationship between temperament and behavior problems in children. *Dissertation Abstracts International: Section B: The Sciences and Engineering, 61,* 1112.

Lesch, K. P., Bengel, D., Heils, A., Sabol, S. Z., Greenberg, B. D., Petri, S., et al. (1996). Association of anxiety-related traits with a polymorphism in the serotonin transporter gene regulatory region. *Science, 274,* 1527–1531.

Lesch, K. P., Greenberg, B. D., Higley, J. D., Bennett, A., & Murphy, D. L. (2002). Serotonin transporter, personality, and behavior: Toward a dissection of gene-gene and gene-environment interaction. In J. Benjamin, R. P. Ebstein, & R. H. Belmaker (Eds.), *Molecular genetics and the human personality* (pp. 109–135). Washington, DC: American Psychiatric Publishing.

Loo, S., Specter, E., Smolen, A., Hopfer, C., Teale, P. D., & Reite, M. L. (2003). Functional effects of the DAT1 polymorphism on EEG measures in ADHD. *Journal of the American Academy of Child & Adolescent Psychiatry, 42,* 986–993.

Luecken, L., & Lemery, K. S. (in press). Early caregiving and physiological stress responses. *Clinical Psychology Review.*

Lyons, M. J., True, W. R., Eisen, S. A., Goldberg, J., Meyer, J. M., Faraone, S. V., et al. (1995). Differential heritability of adult and juvenile antisocial traits. *Archives of General Psychiatry, 52,* 906–915.

Maher, B. S., Marazita, M. L., & Ferrell, R. E. (2002). Dopamine system genes and attention deficit hyperactivity disorder: A meta-analysis. *Psychiatric Genetics, 12,* 207–215.

Manuck, S. B., Flory, J. D., & Ferrell, R. E. (2000). A regulatory polymorphism of the monoamine oxidase-A gene may be associated with variability in aggression, impulsivity, and central nervous system serotonergic responsivity. *Psychiatry Research, 95,* 9–23.

Mazei, M. S., Pluto, C. P., Kirkbride, B., & Pehek, E. A. (2002). Effects of catecholamine uptake blockers in the caudate-putamen and subregions of the medial prefrontal cortex of the rat. *Brain Research, 936,* 58–67.

McGee, R., Feehan, M., Williams, S., & Anderson, J. (1992). DSM-III disorders from age 11 to 15 years. *Journal of the American Academy of Child and Adolescent Psychiatry, 31,* 50–59.

McGue, M., & Christensen, K. (1997). Genetic and environmental contributions to depression symptomatology: Evidence from Danish twins 75 years of age and older. *Journal of Abnormal Psychology, 106,* 439–448.

McGue, M., & Christensen, K. (2003). The heritability of depression symptoms in elderly Danish twins: Occasion-specific versus general effects. *Behavior Genetics, 33,* 83–93.

McGuffin, P., Katz, R., Watkins, S., & Rutherford, J. (1996). A hospital-based twin register of the heritability of DSM-IV uni-polar depression. *Archives of General Psychiatry, 53,* 129–136.

McGuffin, P., & Thapar, A. (1998). Genetics and antisocial personality disorder. In T. Millon, E. Simonsen, M. Birket-Smith, & R. D. Davis (Eds.), *Psychopathy: Antisocial, criminal, and violent behavior* (pp. 215–230). New York: Guilford Press.

Millet, B., Chabane, N., Delorme, R., Leboyer, M., Poirier, M. F., Bourdel, M. C., et al. (2003). Association between the dopamine receptor D4 (DRD4) gene and obsessive-compulsive disorder. *Behavior Genetics, 28,* 215–225.

Moffitt, T. E., Caspi, A., Dickson, N., Silva, P., & Stanton, W. (1996). Childhood-onset versus adolescent-onset antisocial conduct problems in males: Natural history from ages 3 to 18 years. *Development and Psychopathology, 8,* 399–424.

Murray, K. T., & Sines, J. O. (1996). Parsing the genetic and nongenetic variance in children's depressive behavior. *Journal of Affective Disorders, 38,* 23–34.

Nadder, T. S., Rutter, M., Silberg, J. L., Maes, H. H., & Eaves, L. J. (2002). Genetic effects on the variation and covariation of attention deficit-hyperactivity disorder (ADHD) and oppositional–defiant disorder/conduct disorder (ODD/CD) symptomatologies across informant and occasion of measurement. *Psychological Medicine, 32,* 39–53.

Nadder, T. S., Silberg, J. L., Eaves, L. J., & Maes, H. H. (1998). Genetic effects on ADHD symptomatology in 7- to 13-year-old twins: Results from a telephone survey. *Behavior Genetics, 81,* 322–326.

Neuman, R. J., Heath, A., Reich, W., Bucholz, K. K., Madden, P. A. F., Sun, L., et al. (2001). Latent class analysis of ADHD and comorbid symptoms in a population sample of adolescent female twins. *Journal of Child Psychology and Psychiatry and Allied Disciplines, 42,* 933–942.

Nolen-Hoeksema, S., Girgus, J. S., & Seligman, M. E. P. (1992). Predictors and consequences of childhood depressive symptoms: A 5-year longitudinal study. *Journal of Abnormal Psychology, 101,* 405–422.

Parsian, A., & Cloninger, C. R. (2001). Serotonergic pathway genes and subtypes of alcoholism: Association studies. *Psychiatric Genetics, 11,* 89–94.

Plomin, R. (1995). Molecular genetics and psychology. *Current Directions in Psychological Science, 4,* 114–117.

Plomin, R., DeFries, J. C., Craig, I. W., & McGuffin, P. (Eds.). (2003). *Behavioral genetics in the postgenomic era.* Washington, DC: American Psychological Association.

Plomin, R., DeFries, J. C., & Loehlin, J. L. (1977). Genotype-environment interaction and correlation in the analysis of human variation. *Psychological Bulletin, 84,* 309–322.

Post, R. M., Weiss, S. R. B., & Leverich, G. S. (1994). Recurrent affective disorder: Roots in developmental neurobiology and illness progression based on changes in gene expression. *Development and Psychopathology, 6,* 781–813.

Preisig, M., Bellivier, F., Fenton, B. T., Baud, P., Berney, A., Courtet, P., et al. (2000). Association between bipolar disorder and monoamine oxidase A gene polymorphisms: Results of a multicenter study. *American Journal of Psychiatry, 157,* 948–955.

Pulkkinen, L., Kaprio, J., & Rose, R. J. (1999). Peers, teachers and parents as assessors of the behavioral and emotional problems of twins and their adjustment: The Multidimensional Peer Nomination Inventory. *Twin Research, 2,* 274–285.

Radloff, L. S. (1977). A self-report depression scale for research in the general population. *Applied Psychological Measurement, 1,* 385–401.

Reich, W. (1996). *Diagnostic Interview for Children and Adolescents (DICA).* St. Louis, MO: Washington University Division of Child Psychiatry.

Reynolds, C. R., & Richmond, B. O. (1978). What I think and feel: A revised measure of children's manifest anxiety. *Journal of Abnormal Child Psychology, 6,* 271–280.

Rice, F., Harold, G., & Thapar, A. (2002). The genetic aetiology of childhood depression: A review. *Journal of Child Psychology and Psychiatry, 43,* 65–79.

Rijsdijk, F. V., Snieder, H., Ormel, J., Sham, P., Goldberg, D. P., & Spector, T. D. (2003). Genetic and environmental influences on psychological distress in the population: General Health Questionnaire analyses in UK twins. *Psychological Medicine, 33,* 793–801.

Robins, L., Helzer, J., Cottler, L., & Goldring, E. (1988). *NIMH diagnostic interview schedule version III revised (DIS-III-R).* St. Louis, MO: Department of Psychiatry, Washington University Medical School.

Robins, L. N., Tipp, J., & Przybeck, T. (1991). Antisocial personality. In L. N. Robins & D. A. Regier (Eds.), *Psychiatric disorders in America: The epidemiologic catchment area study* (pp. 258–290). New York: Free Press.

Rose, R. J. (2002). How do adolescents select their friends? A behavior-genetic perspective. In L. Pulkkinen & A. Caspi (Eds.), *Paths to successful development* (pp. 106–125). Cambridge, UK: Cambridge University Press.

Rose, R. J., Dick, D. M., Viken, R. J., & Kaprio, J. (2001). Gene-environment interaction in patterns of adolescent drinking: Regional residency moderates longitudinal influences on alcohol use. *Alcoholism: Clinical and Experimental Research, 25,* 637–643.

Rosmond, R., Chagnon, M., Bouchard, C., & Bjorntorp, P. (2001). A polymorphism in the regulatory region of the corticotrophin-releasing hormone gene in relation to cortisol secretion, obesity, and gene-gene interaction. *Metabolism, 50,* 1059–1062.

Roth, M., Tym, E., Mountjoy, C. Q., Huppert, F. A., Hendrie, H., Verma, S., et al. (1986). CAMDEX: A standardized instrument for the diagnosis of mental disorder in the elderly with special reference to the early detection of dementia. *British Journal of Psychiatry, 149,* 698–709.

Rowe, D. C., Stever, C., Chase, D., Sherman, S., Abramowitz, A., & Waldman, I. D. (2001). Two dopamine genes related to reports of childhood retrospective inattention and conduct disorder symptoms. *Molecular Psychiatry, 6,* 429–433.

Rowe, D. C., Stever, C., & Gard, J. M. C. (1998). The relation of the dopamine transporter gene (DAT1) to symptoms of internalizing disorders in children. *Behavior Genetics, 28,* 215–225.

Roy, M. A., Neale, M. C., Pederson, N. L., Mathe, A. A., & Kendler, K. S. (1995). A twin study on generalized anxiety disorder and major depression. *Psychological Medicine, 312,* 940–943.

Rueter, M. A., Chao, W., & Conger, R. D. (2000). The effect of systematic variation in retrospective conduct disorder reports on antisocial disorder diagnoses. *Journal of Consulting and Clinical Psychology, 68,* 307–312.

Rutter, M., Tizard, J., & Whitmore, K. (1970). *Education, health and behavior.* London: Longman.

Sabol, S. Z., Hu, S., & Hamer, D. (1998). A functional polymorphism in the monoamine oxidase A gene promoter. *Human Genetics, 103,* 273–279.

Scherrer, J. F., True, W. R., Xian, H., Lyons, M. J., Eisen, S. A., Goldberg, J., et al. (2000). Evidence for genetic influences common and specific to symptoms of generalized anxiety and panic. *Journal of Affective Disorders, 57,* 25–35.

Schmidt, L. A., Fox, N. A., Rubin, K. H., Hu, S., & Hamer, D. H. (2002). Molecular genetics of shyness and aggression in preschoolers. *Personality and Individual Differences, 33,* 227–238.

Schmitz, S., Fulker, D. W., & Mrazek, D. A. (1995). Problem behavior in early and middle childhood: An initial behavior genetic analysis. *Journal of Child Psychology and Psychiatry and Allied Disciplines, 32,* 1443–1458.

Schulkin, J., Gold, P. W., & McEwen, B. S. (1998). Induction of corticotrophin-releasing hormone gene expression by glucocorticoids: Implication for understanding the states of fear and anxiety and allostatic load. *Psychoneuroendocrinology, 23,* 219–243.

Scourfield, J., Rice, F., Thapar, A., Harold, G. T., Martin, N., & McGuffin, P. (2003). Depressive symptoms in children and adolescents: Changing aetiological influences with development. *Journal of Child Psychology and Psychiatry, 44,* 968–976.

Segman, R. H., Cooper-Kazaz, R., & Macciardi, F. (2002). Association between the dopamine transporter gene and posttraumatic stress disorder. *Molecular Psychiatry, 7,* 903–907.

Serretti, A., Cristina, S., Lilli, R., Cusin, C., Lattuada, E., Lorenzi, C., et al. (2002). Family-based association study of 5-HTTLPR, TPH, MAO-A, and DRD4 polymorphisms in mood disorders. *American Journal of Medical Genetics, 114,* 361–369.

Shaffer, D., Fisher, P., & Lucas, C. (1997). *The diagnostic interview schedule for children: IV.* New York: Columbia University, Ruane Center for Early Diagnosis, Division of Child Psychiatry.

Shih, J. C., & Thompson, R. F. (1999). Monoamine oxidase in neuropsychiatry and behavior. *American Journal of Human Genetics, 65,* 593–598.

Silberg, J. L., Erickson, M. T., Meyer, J. M., Eaves, L. J., Rutter, M. L., & Hewitt, J. K. (1994). The application of structural equation modeling to maternal ratings of twins' behavioral and emotional problems. *Journal of Consulting and Clinical Psychology, 62,* 510–521.

Silberg, J., Rutter, M., Meyer, J., Maes, H., Hewitt, J., Simonoff, E., et al. (1996). Genetic and environmental influences on the covariation between hyperactivity and conduct disturbance in juvenile twins. *Journal of Child Psychology and Psychiatry, 37,* 803–816.

Simonoff, E., Pickles, A., Hewitt, J., Silberg, J., Rutter, M., Loeber, R., et al. (1995). Multiple raters of disruptive child behavior: Using a genetic strategy to examine shared views and bias. *Behavior Genetics, 25,* 311–316.

Sines, J. O. (1986). Normative data for the revised Missouri Children's Behavior Checklist-Parent form (MCBC-P). *Journal of Abnormal Child Psychology, 14,* 89–94.

Slaats-Willemse, D., Swaab-Barneveld, H., deSonneville, L., van der Meulen, E., & Buitelaar, J. (2003). Deficient response inhibition as a cognitive endophenotype of ADHD. *Journal of the American Academy of Child and Adolescent Psychiatry, 42,* 1242–1248.

Slutske, W. S., Heath, A. C., Dinwiddie, S. H., Madden, P. A. F., Bucholz, K. K., Dunne, M. P., et al. (1997). Modeling genetic and environmental influences in the etiology of conduct disorder: A study of 2,682 adult twin pairs. *Journal of Abnormal Psychology, 106,* 266–279.

Smoller, J. W., Rosenbaum, J. F., Biederman, J., Kennedy, J., Dai, D., Racette, S. R., et al. (2003). Association of a genetic marker at the corticotrophin-releasing hormone locus with behavioral inhibition. *Biological Psychiatry, 54,* 1376–1381.

Spielberger, C. (1973). *Preliminary test manual for the State-Trait Anxiety Inventory for Children.* Palo Alto, CA: Consulting Psychologists Press.

Spitzer, R. L., & Williams, J. B. W. (1985). *Structured Clinical Interview for DSM-III-R (SCID).* New York: Biometrics Research Department, New York State Psychiatric Institute.

Spivack, G., & Spotts, J. (1966). *The Devereux Child Behavior (DCB) rating scale.* Devon, PA: Devereux Foundation.

Suomi, S. J. (2000). A biobehavioral perspective on developmental psychopathology: Excessive aggression and serotonergic dysfunction in monkeys. In A. J. Samaroff, M. Lewis, & S. Miller (Eds.), *Handbook of developmental psychopathology* (pp. 237–256). New York: Plenum.

Swanson, J. M., Flodman, P., & Kennedy, J. (2000). Dopamine genes and ADHD. *Neuroscience and Biobehavioral Reviews, 24,* 21–25.

Thapar, A., & McGuffin, P. (1995). Are anxiety symptoms in childhood heritable? *Journal of Child Psychology and Psychiatry and Allied Disciplines, 36,* 439–447.

Thapar, A., & McGuffin, P. (1997). Anxiety and depressive symptoms in childhood: A genetic study of comorbidity. *Journal of Child Psychology and Psychiatry and Allied Disciplines, 38,* 651–656.

Topolski, T. D., Hewitt, J. K., Eaves, L. J., Silberg, J. L., Meyer, J. M., Rutter, M., et al. (1997). Genetic and environmental influences on child reports of manifest anxiety and symptoms of separation anxiety and overanxious disorders: A community-based twin study. *Behavior Genetics, 27,* 15–28.

van Beijsterveldt, C. E. M., Verhulst, F. C., Molenaar, P. C. M., & Boomsma, D. I. (2004). The genetic basis of problem behavior in 5-year-old Dutch twin pairs. *Behavior Genetics, 34,* 229–242.

Van Gestel, S., Forsgren, T., & Claes, S. (2002). Epistatic effect of genes from the dopamine and serotonin systems on the temperament traits of novelty seeking and harm avoidance. *Molecular Psychiatry, 7,* 448–450.

Williams, G. V., & Goldman-Rakic, P. S. (1995). Modulation of memory fields by dopamine D1 receptors in prefrontal cortex. *Nature, 376,* 572–575.

Wing, J. K., Cooper, J. E., & Sartorius, N. (1974). *The measurement and classification of psychiatric symptoms.* New York: Cambridge University Press.

Wuest, S., Federenko, I., Hellhammer, D. H., & Kirschbaum, C. (2000). Genetic factors, perceived chronic stress, and the free cortisol response to awakening. *Psychoneuroendocrinology, 25,* 707–720.

Young, S. E., Stallings, M., Corley, R. P., Krauter, K. S., & Hewitt, J. K. (2000). Genetic and environmental influences on behavioral disinhibition. *American Journal of Medical Genetics, 96,* 684–695.

Zoccolillo, M. (1993). Gender and the development of conduct disorder. *Development and Psychopathology, 5,* 65–78.

CHAPTER 8

Interpreting Personality as a Vulnerability for Psychopathology

A Developmental Approach to the Personality-Psychopathology Relationship

JENNIFER L. TACKETT AND ROBERT F. KRUEGER

The goal of the present chapter is to review evidence regarding the role of personality as a diathesis for psychopathology within a developmental framework. Before discussing the personality-psychopathology relationship per se, a clear understanding of personality constructs is necessary. In particular, some continuity in definitions of personality constructs and personality structure across the life span is necessary to integrate and understand research extending from childhood to adulthood. Thus, we begin by defining *personality* and establishing a framework to help organize the personality-psychopathology literature reviewed here.

PERSONALITY

Personality can be described as the characteristic ways in which different individuals behave, think, and feel. Although researchers studying personality tend to focus on the same traits across the span of adulthood, conceptualizations of personality in children vary across studies and ages. Here, we briefly review approaches to conceptualizing personality in adults and children. Specifically, we focus on models of personality that have gained prominence in the field and that show convergence across the life span (early childhood to adulthood).

Defining Personality in Adults

Work on conceptualizations of personality in adults has an extensive history. Specifically, the five-factor model (FFM) has a long tradition in personality research and is often regarded as the most widely used trait model of the higher-order structure of adult personality. The factors in the FFM are Extraversion, Agreeableness, Neuroticism, Conscientiousness, and Openness to Experience. Extraversion is a trait represented by characteristics such as sociability, gregariousness, and positive energy. Agreeableness is indexed by characteristics such as warmth toward others and empathy. Neuroticism is related to experiencing feelings of anxiety, depression, and irritability. Conscientiousness reflects tendencies to be organized and self-disciplined. Finally, Openness to Experience is represented by characteristics such as interest in cultural events, creativity, and nontraditional beliefs.

Although the FFM is probably the most predominant trait model of adult personality, other popular models focus on three higher-order traits instead of five. Generally, three-trait models posit that the higher-order structure of personality consists of two factors that are strongly related to Extraversion and Neuroticism, whereas the third factor is related to both Conscientiousness and Agreeableness (Markon, Krueger, & Watson, 2004). Although there is some debate over exactly how to integrate these models, connections between three-factor models and the FFM have been well documented (Clark & Watson, 1999; Watson, Clark, & Harkness, 1994). Indeed, a three-factor model, a four-factor model (consisting of constructs resembling Extraversion, Conscientiousness, Neuroticism, and Agreeableness), and a five-factor model can be combined into an integrative, hierarchical model of personality (Markon et al.). Specifically, although the FFM trait of Neuroticism is represented similarly across five-trait and three-trait models, the FFM traits of Extraversion and Openness are best represented at a subordinate level to the second trait in three-trait models (i.e., Positive Emotionality), whereas the FFM traits of Agreeableness and Conscientiousness appear at a subordinate level to the third trait in three-trait models (i.e., Constraint).

Defining Personality in Children

In contrast to the work on adult personality, the literature on personality in children is newer and has been largely fragmented. A particularly thorny issue is the link between childhood personality and temperament (Halverson et al., 2003; Shiner & Caspi, 2003). Temperament is typically described as the study of traits that are biologically based and innate, such that they appear early in life (Goldsmith et al., 1987; Rothbart & Bates, 1998). In addition, most researchers describe temperament as making up the whole of personality in infancy and toddlerhood, but in early to middle childhood acting as the basis for the formation of more differentiated and complex personality traits (Rothbart & Ahadi, 1994; Shiner, 1998). Thus, temperament is typically described as a subset of later personality, such that personality encompasses a broader range of traits.

Much of the research on individual differences in children has focused on temperament traits, with no real consensus within the field on a universal model of temperament structure (Goldsmith et al., 1987). Alternatively, studies of personality in adolescents have largely relied on adult personality measures. Until recently, personality in early and middle childhood was not well defined, with some researchers applying temperament models upward to childhood and others applying adult models downward (Shiner, 1998). However, researchers have been moving forward in identifying the structure of personality in childhood and adolescence.

Recently, two provisional taxonomies were proposed for childhood personality (Halverson et al., 2003; Shiner & Caspi, 2003). These two articles, which were likely being prepared simultaneously, took two different approaches to developing a taxonomy, yet they showed notable convergence. Halverson et al. set out to develop a cross-cultural, cross-age measure of personality in children. Utilizing data from eight countries, the authors employed both empirical (e.g., factor analysis) and rational (e.g., sorting done by focus groups) techniques to develop a scale for children ages 3 to 12 years. The resulting measure consisted of five higher-order scales, four of which map directly onto four of the factors in the FFM. Specifically, the four higher-order scales that showed convergence with the FFM were Extraversion, Agreeableness, Conscientiousness, and Neuroticism. The fifth factor in the Halverson et al. study, labeled Intellect, appeared somewhat similar to facets of Openness to Experience, but it was not a clear analog to the FFM trait because it was narrower.

Shiner and Caspi (2003) took a different approach to developing a provisional taxonomy for childhood personality. The authors conducted a comprehensive review of the relevant literature and summarized and integrated existing work into a potential framework for childhood personality. The model proposed by Shiner and Caspi consists of four higher-order traits that map onto the same four FFM factors: Extraversion, Agreeableness, Conscientiousness, and Neuroticism. Thus, both of these taxonomies independently agreed on the higher-order structure of personality in children. Further support for this agreement comes from the different approaches utilized in defining the taxonomy: an empirical scale-construction approach by Halverson et al. (2003) versus a comprehensive literature review by Shiner and Caspi.

In summary, the FFM has proved to be a strong basis for understanding personality structure across the life span. In particular, the factors of Extraversion, Conscientiousness, Neuroticism, and Agreeableness are commonly reproduced in studies of adult personality (Clark & Livesley, 2002; Krueger & Tackett, 2003; Markon et al., 2004; Watson et al., 1994). In addition, these four factors have been identified in two recent provisional taxonomies of personality in childhood and adolescence. The role of Openness to Experience, the fifth trait in the FFM, in relation to adulthood psychopathology is unclear (Livesley, Jang, & Vernon, 1998; Widiger, 1998), and studies have suggested that the presence of Openness to Experience as a major personality trait may not be evident until later adolescence or adulthood (Lamb, Chuang, Wessels, Broberg, & Hwang, 2002; Halverson et al., 2003). Thus, in this chapter, we focus on a higher-order structure of Extraversion, Conscientiousness, Neuroticism, and Agreeableness to further promote the ability to communicate about personality across studies and ages. However, research utilizing other approaches to personality structure will be included when deemed particularly relevant. Specifically, we hope to emphasize the importance of integrating personality-related variables from other lines of research (e.g., behavioral inhibition) into existing structural models of personality to promote cohesion and communication within the field.

MODELS OF PERSONALITY AND PSYCHOPATHOLOGY

To date, work examining the relationship of personality and psychopathology has primarily consisted of correlational studies aimed at identifying associations between a particular personality trait and a particular disorder. Although a good deal of research has investigated the strength of potential relationships, much less attention has been paid to understanding how and why these relationships come about. However, recent years have shown increased interest in understanding personality-psychopathology relationships at a deeper level. In particular, four proposed models have shown some consensus among researchers to explain potential relationships: the vulnerability-predisposition model, the spectrum model, the scar model, and the pathoplasty-exacerbation model (Dolan-Sewell, Krueger, & Shea, 2001; Millon & Davis, 1996; Widiger, Verheul, & van den Brink, 1999).

Here, we focus on the first two of these: the vulnerability-predisposition model and the spectrum model, which are of particular relevance to the present chapter because they both inform a vulnerability-stress approach to psychopathology. The vulnerability-predisposition model states that certain personality traits may predispose an individual to developing certain types of psychopathology. For example, someone who is very high in Neuroticism may be predisposed to develop somatoform disorders (Kirmayer, Robbins, & Paris, 1994). The spectrum model is based on the hypothesis that personality traits and psychopathology (i.e., Axis I disorders) lie on a continuum, such that they are dimensionally related to one another. For example, schizophrenia is thought by some to represent a more severe variant of the same underlying pathology seen in schizotypal personality disorder (Siever & Davis, 1991).

It has been acknowledged that more than one model may describe any particular individual (Millon & Davis, 1996). Indeed, both the vulnerability-predisposition model and the spectrum model are commensurate with a diathesis-stress perspective, which we flesh out here. Here, we focus on research from children and adolescents to inform the developmental perspective of this book. These models have been reviewed elsewhere with respect to research in adults (e.g., Krueger & Tackett, 2003; Widiger et al., 1999).

Vulnerability-Predisposition Model

Externalizing Psychopathology

Externalizing problems in children and adolescents include aggressive behaviors, delinquent behaviors, inattentive and hyperactive behaviors, and substance-use problems (Achenbach & McConaughy, 1997). The most prevalent area of study from a vulnerability or risk factor perspective within externalizing psychopathology in children has focused on antisocial behaviors, including oppositional defiant disorder and conduct disorder (see Hankin, Abela, Auerbach, McWhinnie, & Skitch, Chapter 14 of this volume, for a review). Here, we review literature investigating certain personality traits, primarily focused on Conscientiousness and Neuroticism, as potential vulnerability factors for later externalizing psychopathology.

Observational ratings of negative affect in toddlers have been shown to predict aggressive behaviors in middle childhood (Renken, Egeland, Marvinney, Mangelsdorf, & Sroufe, 1989). In addition, measures of impulsivity or sensation-seeking behaviors have predicted antisocial behaviors across childhood (Hirshfeld et al., 1992; Raine, Reynolds, Venables, Mednick, & Farrington, 1998; Tremblay, Pihl, Vitaro, & Dobkin, 1994) and adolescence (Lynam et al., 2000). Some longitudinal studies have found predictive power across even greater time spans, with antisocial behavior in adulthood predicted by measurements of impulsivity as early as middle childhood (Farrington & West, 1993), adolescence (Sigvardsson, Bohman, & Cloninger, 1987; White, Bates, & Buyske, 2001), and even at 3 years of age (Caspi, 2000; Caspi, Moffitt, Newman, & Silva, 1996; Henry, Caspi, Moffitt, & Silva, 1996).

Within the realm of antisocial behavior, some studies have focused on personality traits that differentially predict different subtypes of antisocial behavior. Specifically, individuals engaging in life-course–persistent delinquency show greater disinhibition in adolescence and higher levels of negative emotionality in childhood than do individuals engaging in antisocial behavior only during adolescence (Moffitt, Caspi, Dickson, Silva, & Stanton, 1996; White et al., 2001). In addition, other researchers have shown that personality traits related to psychopathy, such as impulsivity and callousness, predict antisocial behavior across preadolescence (Frick, Cornell, Barry, Bodin, & Dane, 2003; Lynam, 1997; Tremblay et al., 1994).

The area of substance-use problems has also produced evidence for personality traits that may represent potential risk factors (see

Kassel, Weinstein, Mermelstein, Skitch, & Veilleux, Chapter 13 of this volume, for a review). Variables measured in early childhood that were related to disinhibition, or low Conscientiousness, as well as Neuroticism predicted drug usage in adolescence (J. Block, 1993; J. Block, J. H. Block, & Keyes, 1988; Masse & Tremblay, 1997). In addition, measures related to disinhibition and Neuroticism in middle childhood predicted problematic substance use in late adolescence (Shedler & J. Block, 1990) and into early adulthood (Cloninger, Sigvardsson, & Bohman, 1988). Low prosociality, which is related to low Agreeableness, in middle childhood predicted problem drinking in adulthood (Pulkkinen & Pitkanen, 1994).

In addition to studies that have focused on specific behavioral problems or disorders, many studies have also examined personality traits as predictors of externalizing behavior in general. There is some evidence that a measure reflecting Neuroticism, or negative emotionality, predicts externalizing behavior problems in middle childhood and adolescence (Gjone & Stevenson, 1997). Several studies have found that measures of disinhibition, or low Conscientiousness, predict externalizing behavior across early and middle childhood (Caspi, Henry, McGee, Moffitt, & Silva, 1995; Eisenberg et al., 2000; Eisenberg et al., 2004; Rende, 1993; Rubin, Burgess, Dwyer, & Hastings, 2003; Silverman & Ragusa, 1992; Young Mun, Fitzgerald, Von Eye, Puttler, & Zucker, 2001). In addition, impulsivity measured in childhood can predict externalizing behaviors in adolescence (Olson, Schilling, & Bates, 1999). Similarly, high levels of Conscientiousness, or inhibition, predict lower levels of externalizing behavior across middle childhood and adolescence (Schwartz, Snidman, & Kagan, 1996; Sigvardsson et al., 1987; Tremblay et al., 1994).

Fewer studies have extended outcome measurements of externalizing into adulthood. One study found that specific factors of sensation seeking in adolescence predict specific types of behavioral deviance in adulthood (Newcomb & McGee, 1991). Another study found that disinhibited children at age 3 were more likely to engage in a variety of health-risk behaviors in adulthood (Caspi et al., 1997).

In addition to the studies already reviewed, another group of studies examined a predictive factor referred to as "difficult," "resistant," or "hard to manage" temperament. The variables used in these studies measure traits similar to those that mark Neuroticism, or negative affect. Similar to the findings above, these measurements of Neuroticism-like traits predicted externalizing behavior across early and middle childhood (Bates, Pettit, Dodge, & Ridge, 1998; Campbell & Ewing, 1990; Deater-Deckard, Dodge, Bates, & Pettit, 1998; Olson, Bates, Sandy, & Schilling, 2002) as well as into later adolescence (Olson, Bates, Sandy, & Lanthier, 2000). It is important to note here that other studies have looked at "difficult" temperament as a predictor of later externalizing behaviors (e.g., Boudreault & Thivierge, 1986; Coon, Carey, Corley, & Fulker, 1992; Davies & Windle, 2001; Garrison, Earls, & Kindlon, 1984; Giancola & Mezzich, 2003; Maziade et al., 1985; Maziade et al., 1990). However, the definitions of *difficult temperament* vary from study to study, in most cases utilizing a conceptualization of *difficult temperament* that reflects some aspects of Neuroticism, or negative affect, as well as characteristics related to inhibition and physiological functions such as eating and sleeping patterns (e.g., Thomas, Chess, & Birch, 1968).

Internalizing Psychopathology

A construct labeled Behavioral Inhibition (BI) has been studied extensively in relation to the development of anxiety disorders (see Williams, Reardon, Murray, & Cole, Chapter 11 of this volume, for a review of anxiety). The construct of BI is typically defined as both shy-withdrawn behaviors and fearful-anxious behaviors (Kagan, 1998).

Thus, in relationship to the taxonomies of childhood personality outlined above, BI may be best conceptualized as a combination of low Extraversion and high Neuroticism. However, further work is needed to elucidate the construct of BI within a broad taxonomy of childhood personality.

A large literature has suggested that BI is an important personality construct for identifying later internalizing psychopathology (for a review, see Hirshfeld-Becker et al., 2003). BI measured in toddlerhood and early childhood predicts anxiety disorders across early and middle childhood (Biederman et al., 1993; Biederman et al., 1990; Caspi et al., 1995; Hirshfeld et al., 1992; Rosenbaum et al., 1993) and into adolescence (Hayward, Killen, Kraemer, & Taylor, 1998; Schwartz, Snidman, & Kagan, 1999).

In addition to anxiety disorders, a smaller group of studies have looked at personality characteristics as a vulnerability for depression (see Hankin & Abela, Chapter 10 of this volume, for a review of depression). There is some evidence that BI in early childhood predicts depression and, particularly in combination with traits marking low Conscientiousness, suicide attempts in early adulthood (Caspi, 2000; Caspi et al., 1996). Other studies have suggested that vulnerability for depression may show gender differences, such that boys who are undercontrolled in early to middle childhood are at greater risk for depression in late adolescence, whereas girls who are overcontrolled in early to middle childhood are at greater risk (J. Block, 1993; J. Block, Gjerde, & J. H. Block, 1991).

In addition to studies that have identified vulnerabilities to a specific group of disorders, other research has examined influences on internalizing psychopathology in general. Withdrawal, a characteristic associated with BI, in early childhood predicted internalizing problems in middle childhood (Young Mun et al., 2001). In addition, other studies have shown that characteristics related to Neuroticism, or Negative Emotionality, predict internalizing psychopathology across middle childhood and adolescence (Gjone & Stevenson, 1997; Mufson, Nomura, & Warner, 2002; Rende, 1993).

Spectrum Model

The work reviewed above has, for the most part, been conducted on the premise that particular personality traits may predispose an individual to developing psychopathology. However, research supporting the vulnerability model is also in agreement with a spectrum model explanation of the personality-psychopathology relationship. That is, the idea that personality traits and certain types of psychopathology lie on a similar dimension, or continuum, could be evidenced by early personality traits that later manifest as psychopathology by changing points on the continuum over time.

Childhood psychopathology is often conceptualized in dimensional terms. For example, the Child Behavior Checklist (CBCL; Achenbach, 1991), a commonly used assessment tool for childhood psychopathology, groups behavioral syndromes into broader Internalizing and Externalizing behavior dimensions based on observed phenotypic covariation of behavior problems. In addition, other researchers have emphasized the need to categorize childhood psychopathology from a hierarchical perspective, elucidating factors that are common to groups of disorders as well as factors that are specific to individual disorders (Lilienfeld, 2003; Weiss, Susser, & Catron, 1998). For example, research has suggested that conduct disorder, as described in the *Diagnostic and Statistical Manual of Mental Disorders,* 4th edition (American Psychiatric Association, 1994), may be better conceptualized as two correlated subfactors of an underlying dimension, distinguishing between aggressive and rule-breaking behaviors (e.g., Tackett,

Krueger, Sawyer, & Graetz, 2003). One hypothesis consistent with a spectrum model conceptualization is that personality traits are one set of common and specific factors in such a hierarchical model, such that personality traits may help to explain comorbidity among disorders. Also consistent with a spectrum model explanation is the idea that certain underlying predispositions (such as genetic influences) contribute to both personality traits and psychopathology that lie on the same dimension. Despite the increasingly common approach to childhood psychopathology from a dimensional perspective, much less work has been done to investigate the spectrum model directly than work investigating a vulnerability perspective. However, some lines of research that are gaining attention are relevant to evidence supporting a spectrum model approach.

Externalizing Psychopathology

Evidence for a dimensional model linking externalizing psychopathology with personality has primarily focused on the trait of Conscientiousness (specifically, low Conscientiousness) or disinhibition. Literature in this area often describes externalizing psychopathology as "disinhibitory psychopathology," with the idea that disinhibition is a common factor that ties externalizing disorders together.

Some evidence for a spectrum model explanation of externalizing disorders comes from psychobiological studies. Specifically, when certain psychobiological correlates are related to externalizing psychopathology and personality traits such as (lack of) Conscientiousness, it suggests that these types of psychopathology and personality traits may have common underlying influences. Multiple psychobiological correlates (e.g., psychophysiological measures, neurotransmitter functioning) thought to be related to disinhibition have also been connected with externalizing psychopathology in children and adolescents (see Beauchaine, 2001; Beauchaine, Katkin, Strassberg, & Snarr, 2001; Iacono, Carlson, Malone, & McGue, 2002; Iacono, Carlson, Taylor, Elkins, & McGue, 1999; Nigg, 2000; Quay, 1993).

In addition to studies examining psychobiological variables, a stronger test of the spectrum model is evidence from genetically informative studies. Specifically, if externalizing psychopathology does lie on a dimension with personality traits such as disinhibition, one would expect common genetic influences that suggest a predisposition for the dimension as a whole. Krueger et al. (2002) reported a latent "externalizing" factor that underlay substance dependence, antisocial behavior, and disinhibited personality and that was largely mediated by genetic influences. Similarly, in a study by Young, Stallings, Corley, Krauter, and Hewitt (2000), the authors found evidence for a highly heritable "behavioral disinhibition" trait that underlay symptoms of conduct disorder, attention deficit/hyperactivity disorder, substance use, and the personality trait of Novelty Seeking (which would be related to low levels of Conscientiousness). Other studies have investigated Externalizing behaviors as measured by the CBCL and a temperament dimension that reflects some measure of Neuroticism, or Negative Emotionality (specifically called Emotionality) in a longitudinal study of twins across toddlerhood, childhood, and early adolescence (Gjone & Stevenson, 1997; Schmitz et al., 1999). The results indicate that phenotypic correlations between Externalizing behaviors and Emotionality may be accounted for by similar underlying genetic influences.

Internalizing Psychopathology

Evidence for a dimensional model linking personality traits to internalizing disorders has come largely from investigations of the tripartite model in children and adolescents. The tripartite model, which developed out of work on adults, explains the high comorbidity between depression and anxiety with a hierarchical organization of personality traits and the internalizing disorders (Clark & Watson, 1991; Clark, Watson, & Mineka, 1994). Specifically, the tripartite model posits that the overlap between depression and anxiety is largely a result of negative affect, or Neuroticism. Furthermore, depression is uniquely related to low positive affectivity, or low Extraversion, whereas anxiety is uniquely related to somatic symptoms of hyperarousal.

Research has largely supported the applicability of the tripartite model in children and adolescents (Anthony, Lonigan, Hooe, & Phillips, 2002; Chorpita, Plummer, & Moffitt, 2000; Cole, Peeke, Martin, Truglio, & Seroczynski, 1998; Joiner, Catanzaro, & Laurent, 1996; Joiner & Lonigan, 2000; Laurent & Ettelson, 2001; Lonigan, Carey, & Finch, 1994; Lonigan, Hooe, David, & Kistner, 1999; Lonigan et al., 2003; Phillips, Lonigan, Driscoll, & Hooe, 2002). Although researchers have postulated that the tripartite model may likely be supported by behavioral-genetic studies investigating shared genetic effects on Neuroticism, anxiety, and depression, to date such research has largely been neglected in children (Axelson & Birmaher, 2001; Kovacs & Devlin, 1998). However, one study reviewed above found moderate phenotypic correlations between Internalizing behavior problems as measured by the CBCL and temperament dimensions of Shyness (likely similar to concepts of BI) and Emotionality (likely related to Neuroticism) in a longitudinal study of young twins (Schmitz et al., 1999). Furthermore, the phenotypic correlations between Internalizing problems with Emotionality and Internalizing problems with Shyness were largely accounted for by similar underlying genetic factors. However, another twin study investigating the relationship between Internalizing problems and Emotionality in an older sample (middle childhood to early adolescence) did not find evidence for common genetic influences (Gjone & Stevenson, 1997).

LINKING PERSONALITY, STRESS, AND PSYCHOPATHOLOGY

In this chapter, we have focused on the utility of vulnerability and spectrum models for conceptualizing the connection between personality and the development of psychopathology in children and adolescents. These models focus primarily on the person. That is, they focus on how certain personalities are at enhanced risk for psychopathology. They do not typically encompass the role of "extra-person" factors, such as stress, in an explicit way.

The role of stress in vulnerability and spectrum models is therefore intriguing to contemplate. Generally speaking, phenotypic connections between personality, stress, and psychopathology are often viewed through the lens of models of psychopathology that draw from a diathesis-stress framework. Often, these models are framed in terms of persons with certain vulnerabilities (e.g., personality styles) encountering certain stressors that then trigger psychopathology. The impact of the stressors may also be conceptualized in terms of correspondence with the vulnerability factors, a phenomenon Coyne and Whiffen (1995) refer to as the "congruency hypothesis." For example, a "sociotropic-dependent" personality style, involving high needs for connections with and reliance on other people, has been conceptualized as being especially vulnerable to stressors in the interpersonal domain (Coyne & Whiffen). That is, a sociotropic-dependent person is conceptualized as vulnerable to depression when he or she encounters interpersonal stressors, but relatively less vulnerable to, for example, disappointments in achievement strivings.

This perspective has clear utility for conceptualizing the way in which personality is connected to psychopathology, and it extends the vulnerability and spectrum models by incorporating stress into the framework. Nevertheless, it may also be worth considering the role people play in creating their own circumstances. It may be the case that putatively "extra-person" factors such as stress are less "outside of the person" than might initially be thought, and this consideration may help to link the biometrical-spectrum perspective we have focused on with literature on the role of stress in triggering psychopathology. For example, in outlining their elaborated cognitive vulnerability–transactional stress theory of depression, a theory that grew out of diathesis-stress models of depression, Hankin and Abramson (2001) note that neuroticism *predisposes* people to experience negative life events. That is, stressors do not occur randomly; they are encountered more frequently by persons with a vulnerability to psychopathology. Moreover, these connections may be attributable to genetic factors that undergird personality and that also lead to exposure to life stress. For example, Jang, Stein, Taylor, Asmundson, and Livesley (2003) presented evidence that relationships between personality and traumatic life events were partially genetically mediated.

Our viewpoint, therefore, is that genetically informative longitudinal studies of personality, stress, and psychopathology will be uniquely informative in linking a genetic spectrum perspective with work on how stress triggers personality diatheses. A recent review by Grant, Compas, Thurm, McMahon, and Gipson (2004) shows clearly that stress in children and adolescents is predictive of psychopathology, and, moreover, that these constructs show reciprocal relations, thereby emphasizing the importance of the person in contributing to his or her circumstances. In addition, genetically informative research in adolescent twin girls has demonstrated a close interplay between negative life events and genetic effects on depression and anxiety, such that genetic effects were enhanced in persons who had experienced recent negative life events (Silberg, Rutter, Neale, & Eaves, 2001). Connecting this research with the emerging structural framework for personality traits in childhood and adolescence outlined in this chapter represents a promising way to connect research on stress with vulnerability and spectrum models of the link between personality and psychopathology.

SUMMARY

Taken together, the research reviewed here suggests that evidence from studies of children and adolescents provides preliminary support for both a vulnerability model and a spectrum model conceptualization of the personality-psychopathology relationship. This review of the literature indicates that more attention has been devoted to tests of the vulnerability model than the spectrum model per se. However, as noted earlier, evidence for a vulnerability or diathesis perspective is difficult to disentangle from a spectrum model explanation, and it is possible that a combination of both perspectives may provide the best explanation. More direct tests of the spectrum model will help elucidate this relationship. Although the ample correlational research on connections between personality and psychopathology in children has been helpful in defining the strength and stability of these relationships, future work should move beyond basic correlational studies and move toward direct investigations of various models of personality-psychopathology relationships, as well as endeavor to connect these models with research on the role of stress in psychopathology.

Future research should directly test the models presented here in multivariate studies employing longitudinal and genetically informative designs. Specifically, longitudinal, biometric designs afford a rare opportunity to test both vulnerability and spectrum models, which will help researchers understand the relationships between various personality-psychopathology models. In addition, multivariate studies that assess multiple personality traits as well as multiple disorders are important for integrating structural models of personality with psychopathology, which will aid researchers in organizing related concepts and in tackling issues such as comorbidity (Watson et al., 1994), which is central to a spectrum model conceptualization. Although future studies have the opportunity to build these aspects into their design, existing studies can also provide informative tests of the personality-psychopathology relationship by approaching data with these questions in mind. Modern statistical methods such as item response theory or latent trait modeling may be particularly useful tools for investigating whether psychological characteristics (such as symptoms of psychopathology) can be conceptualized as falling along underlying continua (such as personality traits; see, e.g., Krueger et al., 2004).

REFERENCES

Achenbach, T. M. (1991). *Manual for the Child Behavior Checklist/4 and 1991 Profile.* Burlington: Department of Psychiatry, University of Vermont.

Achenbach, T. M., & McConaughy, S. H. (1997). *Empirically based assessment of child and adolescent psychopathology.* Thousand Oaks, CA: Sage.

American Psychiatric Association. (1994). *Diagnostic and statistical manual of mental disorders* (4th ed.). Washington, DC: Author.

Anthony, J. L., Lonigan, C. J., Hooe, E. S., & Phillips, B. M. (2002). An affect-based, hierarchical model of temperament and its relations with internalizing symptomatology. *Journal of Clinical Child and Adolescent Psychology, 31,* 480–490.

Axelson, D. A., & Birmaher, B. (2001). Relation between anxiety and depressive disorders in childhood and adolescence. *Depression and Anxiety, 14,* 67–78.

Bates, J. E., Pettit, G. S., Dodge, K. A., & Ridge, B. (1998). Interaction of temperamental resistance to control and restrictive parenting in the development of externalizing behavior. *Developmental Psychology, 34,* 982–995.

Beauchaine, T. P. (2001). Vagal tone, development, and Gray's motivational theory: Toward an integrated model of autonomic nervous system functioning in psychopathology. *Development and Psychopathology, 13,* 183–214.

Beauchaine, T. P., Katkin, E. S., Strassberg, Z., & Snarr, J. (2001). Disinhibitory psychopathology in male adolescents: Discriminating conduct disorder from attention-deficit/hyperactivity disorder through concurrent assessment of multiple autonomic states. *Journal of Abnormal Psychology, 110,* 610–624.

Biederman, J., Rosenbaum, J. F., Bolduc-Murphy, E. A., Faraone, S. V., Chaloff, J., Hirshfeld, D. R., et al. (1993). A 3-year follow-up of children with and without behavioral inhibition. *Journal of the American Academy of Child and Adolescent Psychiatry, 32,* 814–821.

Biederman, J., Rosenbaum, J. F., Hirshfeld, D. R., Faraone, S. V., Bolduc, E. A., Gersten, M., et al. (1990). Psychiatric correlates of behavioral inhibition in young children of parents with and without psychiatric disorders. *Archives of General Psychiatry, 47,* 21–26.

Block, J. (1993). Studying personality the long way. In D. C. Funder, R. D. Parke, C. Tomlinson-Keasey, & K. Widaman (Eds.), *Studying lives through time: Personality and development* (pp. 9–41). Washington, DC: American Psychological Association.

Block, J., Block, J. H., & Keyes, S. (1988). Longitudinally foretelling drug usage in adolescence: Early childhood personality and environmental precursors. *Child Development, 59,* 336–355.

Block, J., Gjerde, P. F., & Block, J. H. (1991). Personality antecedents of depressive tendencies in 18-year-olds: A prospective study. *Journal of Personality and Social Psychology, 60,* 726–738.

Boudreault, M., & Thivierge, J. (1986). The impact of temperament in a school setting: An epidemiological study. *Canadian Journal of Psychiatry, 31,* 499–504.

Campbell, S. B., & Ewing, L. J. (1990). Follow-up of hard-to-manage preschoolers: Adjustment at age 9 and predictors of continuing symptoms. *Journal of Child Psychology and Psychiatry and Allied Disciplines, 31,* 871–889.

Caspi, A. (2000). The child is father of the man: Personality continuities from childhood to adulthood. *Journal of Personality and Social Psychology, 78,* 158–172.

Caspi, A., Begg, D., Dickson, N., Harrington, H., Langley, J., Moffitt, T. E., et al. (1997). Personality differences predict health-risk behaviors in young adulthood: Evidence from a longitudinal study. *Journal of Personality and Social Psychology, 73,* 1052–1063.

Caspi, A., Henry, B., McGee, R. O., Moffitt, T. E., & Silva, P. A. (1995). Temperamental origins of child and adolescent behavior problems: From age three to age fifteen. *Child Development, 66,* 55–68.

Caspi, A., Moffitt, T. E., Newman, D. L., & Silva, P. A. (1996). Behavioral observations at age 3 years predict adult psychiatric disorders. *Archives of General Psychiatry, 53,* 1033–1039.

Chorpita, B. F., Plummer, C. M., & Moffitt, C. E. (2000). Relations of tripartite dimensions of emotion to childhood anxiety and mood disorders. *Journal of Abnormal Child Psychology, 28,* 299–310.

Clark, L. A., & Livesley, W. J. (2002). Two approaches to identifying the dimensions of personality disorder: Convergence on the five-factor model. In P. T. Costa & T. A. Widiger (Eds.), *Personality disorders and the five-factor model of personality* (2nd ed.). Washington, DC: American Psychological Association.

Clark, L. A., & Watson, D. (1991). Tripartite model of anxiety and depression: Psychometric evidence and taxonomic implications. *Journal of Abnormal Psychology, 100,* 316–336.

Clark, L. A., & Watson, D. (1999). Temperament: A new paradigm for trait psychology. In L. A. Pervin & O. P. John (Eds.), *Handbook of personality: Theory and research* (2nd ed., pp. 399–423). New York: Guilford Press.

Clark, L. A., Watson, D., & Mineka, S. (1994). Temperament, personality, and the mood and anxiety disorders. *Journal of Abnormal Psychology, 103,* 103–116.

Cloninger, C. R., Sigvardsson, S., & Bohman, M. (1988). Childhood personality predicts alcohol abuse in young adults. *Alcoholism: Clinical & Experimental Research, 12,* 494–505.

Cole, D. A., Peeke, L. G., Martin, J. M., Truglio, R., & Seroczynski, A. D. (1998). A longitudinal look at the relation between depression and anxiety in children and adolescents. *Journal of Consulting & Clinical Psychology, 66,* 451–460.

Coon, H., Carey, G., Corley, R., & Fulker, D. W. (1992). Identifying children in the Colorado Adoption Project at risk for conduct disorder. *Journal of the American Academy of Child and Adolescent Psychiatry, 31,* 503–511.

Coyne, J. C., & Whiffen, V. E. (1995). Issues in personality as diathesis for depression: The case of sociotropy-dependency and autonomy-self criticism. *Psychological Bulletin, 118,* 358–378.

Davies, P. T., & Windle, M. (2001). Interparental discord and adolescent adjustment trajectories: The potentiating and protective role of intrapersonal attributes. *Child Development, 72,* 1163–1178.

Deater-Deckard, K., Dodge, K. A., Bates, J. E., & Pettit, G. S. (1998). Multiple risk factors in the development of externalizing behavior problems: Group and individual differences. *Development and Psychopathology, 10,* 469–493.

Dolan-Sewell, R. T., Krueger, R. F., & Shea, M. T. (2001). Co-occurrence with syndrome disorders. In W. J. Livesley (Ed.), *Handbook of personality disorders* (pp. 84–104). New York: Guilford Press.

Eisenberg, N., Guthrie, I. K., Fabes, R. A., Shepard, S., Losoya, S., Murphy, B. C., et al. (2000). Prediction of elementary school children's externalizing problem behaviors from attentional and behavioral regulation and negative emotionality. *Child Development, 71,* 1367–1382.

Eisenberg, N., Spinrad, T. L., Fabes, R. A., Reiser, M., Cumberland, A., Shepard, S., et al. (2004). The relations of effortful control and impulsivity to children's resiliency and adjustment. *Child Development, 75,* 25–46.

Farrington, D. P., & West, D. J. (1993). Criminal, penal and life histories of chronic offenders: Risk and protective factors and early identification. *Criminal Behaviour and Mental Health, 3,* 492–523.

Frick, P. J., Cornell, A. H., Barry, C. T., Bodin, S. D., & Dane, H. E. (2003). Callous-unemotional traits and conduct problems in the prediction of conduct problem severity, aggression, and self-report of delinquency. *Journal of Abnormal Child Psychology, 31,* 457–470.

Garrison, W., Earls, F., & Kindlon, D. (1984). Temperament characteristics in the third year of life and behavioral adjustment at school entry. *Journal of Clinical Child Psychology, 13,* 298–303.

Giancola, P. R., & Mezzich, A. C. (2003). Executive functioning, temperament, and drug use involvement in adolescent females with a substance use disorder. *Journal of Child Psychology and Psychiatry, 44,* 857–866.

Gjone, H., & Stevenson, J. (1997). A longitudinal twin study of temperament and behavior problems: Common genetic or environmental influences? *Journal of the American Academy of Child and Adolescent Psychiatry, 36,* 1448–1456.

Goldsmith, H. H., Buss, A. H., Plomin, R., Rothbart, M. K., Thomas, A., & Chess, S. (1987). Roundtable: What is temperament? Four approaches. *Child Development, 58,* 505–529.

Grant, K. E., Compas, B. E., Thurm, A. E., McMahon, S. D., & Gipson, P. Y. (2004). Stressors and child and adolescent psychopathology: Measurement issues and prospective effects. *Journal of Clinical Child and Adolescent Psychology, 33,* 412–425.

Halverson, C. F., Havill, V. L., Deal, J., Baker, S. R., Victor, J. B., Pavlopoulos, V., et al. (2003). Personality structure as derived from parental ratings of free descriptions of children: The Inventory of Child Individual Differences. *Journal of Personality, 71,* 995–1026.

Hankin, B. L., & Abramson, L. Y. (2001). Development of gender differences in depression: An elaborated cognitive vulnerability-transactional stress theory. *Psychological Bulletin, 127,* 773–796.

Hayward, C., Killen, J., Kraemer, K., & Taylor, C. (1998). Linking self-reported childhood behavioral inhibition to adolescent social phobia. *Journal of the American Academy of Child and Adolescent Psychiatry, 37,* 1308–1316.

Henry, B., Caspi, A., Moffitt, T. E., & Silva, P. A. (1996). Temperamental and familial predictors of violent and nonviolent criminal convictions: Age 3 to age 18. *Developmental Psychology, 32,* 614–623.

Hirshfeld, D. R., Rosenbaum, J. F., Biederman, J., Bolduc, E. A., Faraone, S. V., Snidman, N., et al. (1992). Stable behavioral inhibition and its association with anxiety disorder. *Journal of the American Academy of Child and Adolescent Psychiatry, 31,* 103–111.

Hirshfeld-Becker, D. R., Biederman, J., Calltharp, S., Rosenbaum, E. D., Faraone, S. V., & Rosenbaum, J. F. (2003). Behavioral inhibition and disinhibition as hypothesized precursors to psychopathology: Implications for pediatric bipolar disorder. *Biological Psychiatry, 53,* 985–999.

Iacono, W. G., Carlson, S. R., Malone, S. M., & McGue, M. (2002). P3 event-related potential amplitude and the risk for disinhibitory disorders in adolescent boys. *Archives of General Psychiatry, 59,* 750–757.

Iacono, W. G., Carlson, S. R., Taylor, J., Elkins, I. J., & McGue, M. (1999). Behavioral disinhibition and the development of substance-use disorders: Findings from the Minnesota Twin Family Study. *Development and Psychopathology, 11,* 869–900.

Jang, K. L., Stein, M. B., Taylor, S., Asmundson, G. J. G., & Livesley, W. J. (2003). Exposure to traumatic events and experiences: Aetiological relationships with personality function. *Psychiatry Research, 120,* 61–69.

Joiner, Jr., T. E., Catanzaro, S. J., & Laurent, J. (1996). Tripartite structure of positive and negative affect, depression, and anxiety in child and adolescent psychiatric inpatients. *Journal of Abnormal Psychology, 105,* 401–409.

Joiner, Jr., T. E., & Lonigan, C. J. (2000). Tripartite model of depression and anxiety in youth psychiatric inpatients: Relations with diagnostic status and future symptoms. *Journal of Clinical Child Psychology, 29,* 372–382.

Kagan, J. (1998). *Galen's prophecy.* Boulder, CO: Westview Press.

Kirmayer, L. J., Robbins, J. M., & Paris, J. (1994). Somatoform disorders: Personality and the social matrix of somatic distress. *Journal of Abnormal Psychology, 103,* 125–136.

Kovacs, M., & Devlin, B. (1998). Internalizing disorders in childhood. *Journal of Child Psychology and Psychiatry and Allied Disciplines, 39,* 47–63.

Krueger, R. F., Hicks, B. M., Patrick, C. J., Carlson, S. R., Iacono, W. G., & McGue, M. (2002). Etiologic connections among substance dependence, antisocial behavior, and personality: Modeling the externalizing spectrum. *Journal of Abnormal Psychology, 111,* 411–424.

Krueger, R. F., Nichol, P. E., Hicks, B. M., Markon, K. E., Patrick, C. J., Iacono, W. G., et al. (2004). Using latent trait modeling to conceptualize an alcohol problems continuum. *Psychological Assessment, 16,* 107–119.

Krueger, R. F., & Tackett, J. L. (2003). Personality and psychopathology: Working toward the bigger picture. *Journal of Personality Disorders, 17,* 109–128.

Lamb, M. E., Chuang, S. S., Wessels, H., Broberg, A. G., & Hwang, C. P. (2002). Emergence and construct validation of the big five factors in early childhood:

A longitudinal analysis of their ontogeny in Sweden. *Child Development, 73,* 1517–1524.

Laurent, J., & Ettelson, R. (2001). An examination of the tripartite model of anxiety and depression and its application to youth. *Clinical Child and Family Psychology Review, 4,* 209–230.

Lilienfeld, S. O. (2003). Comorbidity between and within childhood externalizing and internalizing disorders: Reflections and directions. *Journal of Abnormal Child Psychology, 31,* 285–291.

Livesley, W. J., Jang, K. L., & Vernon, P. A. (1998). Phenotypic and genetic structure of traits delineating personality disorder. *Archives of General Psychiatry, 55,* 941–948.

Lonigan, C. J., Carey, M. P., & Finch, A. J., Jr. (1994). Anxiety and depression in children and adolescents: Negative affectivity and the utility of self-reports. *Journal of Consulting and Clinical Psychology, 62,* 1000–1008.

Lonigan, C. J., Hooe, E. S., David, C. F., & Kistner, J. A. (1999). Positive and negative affectivity in children: Confirmatory factor analysis of a two-factor model and its relation to symptoms of anxiety and depression. *Journal of Consulting and Clinical Psychology, 67,* 374–386.

Lonigan, C. J., Phillips, B. M., & Hooe, E. S. (2003). Relations of positive and negative affectivity to anxiety and depression in children: Evidence from a latent variable longitudinal study. *Journal of Consulting and Clinical Psychology, 71,* 465–481.

Lynam, D. R. (1997). Pursuing the psychopath: Capturing the fledgling psychopath in a nomological net. *Journal of Abnormal Psychology, 106,* 425–438.

Lynam, D. R., Caspi, A., Moffitt, T. E., Wisktrom, P. H., Loeber, R., & Novak, S. (2000). The interaction between impulsivity and neighborhood context on offending: The effects of impulsivity are stronger in poorer neighborhoods. *Journal of Abnormal Psychology, 109,* 563–574.

Markon, K. E., Krueger, R. F., & Watson, D. (2004). *Delineating the structure of normal and abnormal personality: An integrative hierarchical model.* Unpublished manuscript.

Masse, L. C., & Tremblay, R. E. (1997). Behavior of boys in kindergarten and the onset of substance use during adolescence. *Archives of General Psychiatry, 54,* 62–68.

Maziade, M., Caperaa, P., Laplante, B., Boudreault, M., Thivierge, J., Cote, R., et al. (1985). Value of difficult temperament among 7-year-olds in the general population for predicting psychiatric diagnosis at age 12. *American Journal of Psychiatry, 142,* 943–946.

Maziade, M., Caron, C., Cote, R., Merette, C., Bernier, H., Laplante, B., et al. (1990). Psychiatric status of adolescents who had extreme temperaments at age 7. *American Journal of Psychiatry, 147,* 1531–1536.

Millon, T., & Davis, R. (1996). *Disorders of personality: DSM-IV and beyond* (2nd ed.). New York: Wiley.

Moffitt, T. E., Caspi, A., Dickson, N., Silva, P., & Stanton, W. (1996). Childhood-onset versus adolescent-onset antisocial conduct problems in males: Natural history from ages 3 to 18 years. *Development and Psychopathology, 8,* 399–424.

Mufson, L., Nomura, Y., & Warner, V. (2002). The relationship between parental diagnosis, offspring temperament and offspring psychopathology: A longitudinal analysis. *Journal of Affective Disorders, 71,* 61–69.

Newcomb, M. D., & McGee, L. (1991). Influence of sensation seeking on general deviance and specific problem behaviors from adolescence to young adulthood. *Journal of Personality and Social Psychology, 61,* 614–628.

Nigg, J. T. (2000). On inhibition/disinhibition in developmental psychopathology: Views from cognitive and personality psychology and a working inhibition taxonomy. *Psychological Bulletin, 126,* 220–246.

Olson, S. L., Bates, J. E., Sandy, J. M., & Lanthier, R. (2000). Early developmental precursors of externalizing behavior in middle childhood and adolescence. *Journal of Abnormal Child Psychology, 28,* 119–133.

Olson, S. L., Bates, J. E., Sandy, J. M., & Schilling, E. M. (2002). Early developmental precursors of impulsive and inattentive behavior: From infancy to middle childhood. *Journal of Child Psychology and Psychiatry and Allied Disciplines, 43,* 435–447.

Olson, S. L., Schilling, E. M., & Bates, J. E. (1999). Measurement of impulsivity: Construct coherence, longitudinal stability, and relationship with externalizing problems in middle childhood and adolescence. *Journal of Abnormal Child Psychology, 27,* 151–165.

Phillips, B. M., Lonigan, C. J., Driscoll, K., & Hooe, E. S. (2002). Positive and negative affectivity in children: A multitrait-multimethod investigation. *Journal of Clinical Child and Adolescent Psychology, 31,* 465–479.

Pulkkinen, L., & Pitkanen, T. (1994). A prospective study of the precursors to problem drinking in young adulthood. *Journal of Studies in Alcohol, 55,* 578–587.

Quay, H. C. (1993). The psychobiology of undersocialized aggressive conduct disorder: A theoretical perspective. *Development and Psychopathology, 5,* 165–180.

Raine, A., Reynolds, C., Venables, P. H., Mednick, S. A., & Farrington, D. P. (1998). Fearlessness, stimulation-seeking, and large body size at age 3 years as early predispositions to childhood aggression at age 11 years. *Archives of General Psychiatry, 55,* 745–751.

Rende, R. (1993). Longitudinal relations between temperament traits and behavioral syndromes in middle childhood. *Journal of the American Academy of Child and Adolescent Psychiatry, 32,* 287–290.

Renken, B., Egeland, B., Marvinney, D., Mangelsdorf, S., & Sroufe, L. A. (1989). Early childhood antecedents of aggression and passive-withdrawal in early elementary school. *Journal of Personality, 57,* 257–281.

Rosenbaum, J. F., Biederman, J., Bolduc-Murphy, E. A., Faraone, S. V., Chaloff, J., Hirshfeld, D. R., et al. (1993). Behavioral inhibition in childhood: A risk factor for anxiety disorders. *Harvard Review of Psychiatry, 1,* 2–16.

Rothbart, M. K., & Ahadi, S. A. (1994). Temperament and the development of personality. *Journal of Abnormal Psychology, 103,* 55–66.

Rothbart, M. K., & Bates, J. E. (1998). Temperament. In W. Damon (Series Ed.) & N. Eisenberg (Vol. Ed.), *Handbook of child psychology: Vol. 3. Social, emotional, and personality development* (5th ed., pp. 105–176). New York: Wiley.

Rubin, K. H., Burgess, K. B., Dwyer, K. M., & Hastings, P. D. (2003). Predicting preschoolers' externalizing behaviors from toddler temperament, conflict and maternal negativity. *Developmental Psychology, 39,* 164–176.

Schmitz, S., Fulker, D. W., Plomin, R., Zahn-Waxler, C., Emde, R. N., & DeFries, J. C. (1999). Temperament and problem behaviour during early childhood. *International Journal of Behavioral Development, 23,* 333–355.

Schwartz, C. E., Snidman, N., & Kagan, J. (1996). Early childhood temperament as a determinant of externalizing behavior in adolescence. *Development and Psychopathology, 8,* 527–537.

Schwartz, C. E., Snidman, N., & Kagan, J. (1999). Adolescent social anxiety as an outcome of inhibited temperament in childhood. *Journal of the American Academy of Child and Adolescent Psychiatry, 38,* 1008–1015.

Shedler, J., & Block, J. (1990). Adolescent drug use and psychological health. *American Psychologist, 45,* 612–630.

Shiner, R. L. (1998). How shall we speak of children's personalities in middle childhood? A preliminary taxonomy. *Psychological Bulletin, 124,* 308–332.

Shiner, R., & Caspi, A. (2003). Personality differences in childhood and adolescence: Measurement, development, and consequences. *Journal of Child Psychology and Psychiatry, 44,* 2–32.

Siever, L., & Davis, K. (1991). A psychobiologic perspective on the personality disorders. *American Journal of Psychiatry, 148,* 1647–1658.

Sigvardsson, S., Bohman, M., & Cloninger, C. R. (1987). Structure and stability of childhood personality: Prediction of later social adjustment. *Journal of Child Psychology and Psychiatry and Allied Disciplines, 28,* 929–946.

Silberg, J., Rutter, M., Neale, M., & Eaves, L. J. (2001). Genetic moderation of environmental risk for depression and anxiety in adolescent girls. *British Journal of Psychiatry, 179,* 116–121.

Silverman, I., & Ragusa, D. (1992). A short-term longitudinal study of the early development of self-regulation. *Journal of Abnormal Child Psychology, 20,* 415–435.

Tackett, J. L., Krueger, R. F., Sawyer, M. G., & Graetz, B. W. (2003). Subfactors of *DSM-IV* conduct disorder: Evidence and connections with syndromes from the Child Behavior Checklist. *Journal of Abnormal Child Psychology, 31,* 647–654.

Thomas, A., Chess, S., & Birch, H. G. (1968). *Temperament and behavior disorders in children.* New York: New York University Press.

Tremblay, R. E., Pihl, R. O., Vitaro, F., & Dobkin, P. L. (1994). Predicting early onset of male antisocial behavior from preschool behavior. *Archives of General Psychiatry, 51,* 732–739.

Watson, D., Clark, L. A., & Harkness, A. R. (1994). Structures of personality and their relevance to psychopathology. *Journal of Abnormal Psychology, 103,* 18–31.

Weiss, B., Susser, K., & Catron, T. (1998). Common and specific features of childhood psychopathology. *Journal of Abnormal Psychology, 107,* 118–127.

White, H. R., Bates, M. E., & Buyske, S. (2001). Adolescence-limited versus persistent delinquency: Extending Moffitt's hypothesis into adulthood. *Journal of Abnormal Psychology, 110,* 600–609.

Widiger, T. A. (1998). Four out of five ain't bad. *Archives of General Psychiatry, 55,* 865–866.

Widiger, T. A., Verheul, R., & van den Brink, W. (1999). Personality and psychopathology. In L. A. Pervin & O. P. Johns (Eds.), *Handbook of personality: Theory and research* (pp. 347–366). New York: Guilford Press.

Young, S. E., Stallings, M. C., Corley, R. P., Krauter, K. S., & Hewitt, J. K. (2000). Genetic and environmental influences on behavioral disinhibition. *American Journal of Medical Genetics, 96,* 684–695.

Young Mun, E., Fitzgerald, H. E., Von Eye, A., Puttler, L. I., & Zucker, R. A. (2001). Temperamental characteristics as predictors of externalizing and internalizing child behavior problems in the contexts of high and low parental psychopathology. *Infant Mental Health Journal, 22,* 393–415.

CHAPTER 9

Attachment as Vulnerability to the Development of Psychopathology

Joanne Davila, Melissa Ramsay, Catherine B. Stroud, and Sara J. Steinberg

Without doubt, attachment theory, as proposed by Bowlby (1969, 1973, 1980) and Ainsworth et al. (Ainsworth, Blehar, Waters, & Wall, 1978) has had a profound effect on the understanding of human development and behavior, particularly with regard to normative processes of child development and, more recently, with regard to normative functioning in adult romantic relationships. However, as is also evident in the literature, attachment theory has been invoked as a way to understand the development and course of nonnormative and maladaptive behavior, including poor self-regulation, poor peer functioning, and poor romantic functioning. There is also a growing literature on how attachment theory can help to explain the development of psychopathology, and this topic is the focus of this chapter. In this chapter, we will discuss how principles of attachment theory can inform understanding of the development of psychopathology, with a particular emphasis on the circumstances under which attachment insecurity confers vulnerability to psychopathology. We will review the evidence for a link between attachment insecurity and psychopathology, focusing not only on specific disorders, but also on attachment-relevant maladaptive processes that cut across disorders. Finally, we will discuss how attachment insecurity can be conceptualized to confer risk for psychopathology within a vulnerability-stress perspective. Before doing so, however, we begin with a brief review of the basic principles of attachment theory and how they have been applied to the understanding of normative child and adult development.

PRINCIPLES OF ATTACHMENT THEORY

Attachment theory was proposed as a way to understand the role of the parent-child relationship in development. In line with psychoanalytic scholars, Bowlby (e.g., Bowlby,

1969, 1973, 1980) suggested that early parent-child relations set the stage for later functioning at the individual and interpersonal levels. Unlike his psychoanalytic predecessors (and contemporaries), however, Bowlby and his colleagues chose to directly observe and examine parent-child interaction and its subsequent correlates. Attachment theory is based on the notion that children will feel secure in their relationship with their parent to the extent that the parent provides consistent, warm, and sensitive care. When this happens, children learn to use the parent as a secure base, that is, they are willing to turn to the parent in times of need, the parent is available and responsive, and they are able to be comforted by the parent in a way that allows them to feel better and to return to other activities. This "secure base" hypothesis also suggests that when there is a lack of consistent, sensitive care, children will feel insecure in their relationship with their parent and consequently be unable to use the parent as a secure base.

Support for Bowlby's theory was provided by Mary Ainsworth and her colleagues (e.g., Ainsworth et al., 1978), who documented different patterns of secure base use among children and their parents using the "strange situation" procedure. This procedure involves separating children from their parents (presumably a stressor) and then observing how the children respond when reunited with the parents. In this procedure, children exhibited three primary sets of strategies. The first was classified as secure; that is, typical secure base behavior was displayed. Specifically, children went to the parents upon reunion, were able to be comforted by the parents, and then returned to independent play. The second strategy was classified as avoidant: Children did not approach the parents upon reunion—or actively avoided the parents—and continued with independent play. The third strategy was classified as ambivalent-resistant: Children simultaneously displayed approach toward the parents, but resistance to comfort, and ultimately were unable to be comforted. Each of the strategies was also shown to correlate with observed maternal behavior toward children in the home (see Weinfield, Sroufe, Egeland, & Carlson, 1999, for a review), thereby supporting the role of the parent-child relationship in the development of attachment patterns.

In addition to hypotheses about secure base functioning in childhood, attachment theory also predicts that childhood attachment patterns will predict subsequent child functioning with regard to the development of the sense of self, others, and interpersonal functioning. Bowlby proposed that early parent-child interactions will result in the development of "working models" or schemata about the self, others, and relationships that will guide functioning across the life span. Support for this hypothesis is strong, in that numerous studies have documented associations between childhood attachment security, views of the self and others, and interpersonal functioning (see Weinfield et al., 1999).

Bowlby's ideas about how security in parent-child relationships affects development have been extended into the realm of adult close relationships and development as well. For example, Hazan and Shaver (1987) proposed that attachment theory could be used to understand adult romantic love and relationships, suggesting that romantic relationships were the adult versions of attachment relationships and that security in those relationships would be associated with individual and interpersonal functioning in adulthood. For example, just as children turn to parents in times of stress and monitor their parents' availability in meeting their needs, adults do the same with their romantic partners, and the extent to which they perceive and experience the partner as available and responsive will affect both their intra- and interpersonal functioning (Hazan & Shaver, 1994; Waters, 1997). A large body of research supports this notion and shows, for example, that adult attachment security in romantic relationships is associated with numerous aspects of functioning in romantic relationships (see Feeney, 1999; Shaver & Hazan, 1993).

ATTACHMENT THEORY AND THE DEVELOPMENT OF PSYCHOPATHOLOGY

Although much of attachment theory focuses on normative development and the effect of attachment security on interpersonal functioning, Bowlby also considered attachment insecurity to be associated with the experience of significant emotional distress. Indeed, two volumes of his three-volume series (Bowlby, 1973, 1980) were dedicated to discussing how separation from attachment figures is related to anxiety and how loss of attachment figures is related to dysphoria. But the link between attachment insecurity and psychopathology should not be thought of as direct. Although it may be easy to equate insecurity with pathology, doing so is overly simplistic and will result in less, rather than more, clarity with regard to how attachment confers risk for psychopathology. Instead, as others have suggested, "insecure attachment is not a necessary and/or sufficient cause for the development of psychopathology" (Cicchetti, Toth, & Lynch, 1995, p. 59). Although insecure attachment itself may in some cases be severe enough to qualify as a disorder (e.g., reactive attachment disorder), in most other cases the role of attachment insecurity in psychopathology will either be moderated by other factors or only indirectly related to psychopathology through mediating factors. Interestingly, this has rarely been the approach taken in the literature. In the following sections, we will review the literature documenting associations between insecurity and different types of psychopathology in childhood and adulthood.

ASSOCIATIONS BETWEEN ATTACHMENT INSECURITY AND PSYCHOPATHOLOGY

As this section will describe, a growing body of literature exists documenting the association between attachment insecurity and various types of psychopathology (see also Dozier, Stovall, & Albus, 1999; Greenberg, 1999). As noted earlier, much of this research conceptualizes, or at least studies, the association as a direct one. Despite the problems with this, this literature can provide important information on the magnitude of the association between insecurity and the different types of psychopathology and can serve as a starting point for more conceptually refined models, such as the ones we will discuss later in this chapter. When research exists on moderators or mechanisms of the association between insecurity and psychopathology, these studies will be highlighted.

Furthermore, inherent in our review is an important limitation of the extant literature: the lack of clarity with regard to the conceptualization and measurement of the attachment construct. Studies vary widely in how they define and measure attachment insecurity, with some studies relying on relatively direct (or agreed-upon) measures of insecurity (e.g., the Adult Attachment Interview [AAI]: George, Kaplan, & Main, 1985; the Strange Situation: Ainsworth et al., 1978) and others relying on what may be best called "proxy" measures of insecurity, such as parenting style, child maltreatment, and parental bonding. Studies also vary in which system of attachment classifications they use. Some studies focus on Ainsworth's (Ainsworth et al.) original three categories of secure, avoidant (also called *dismissing*), and ambivalent-resistant (also called *preoccupied*). Others include a disorganized category, which was also described by Ainsworth et al. but not refined until more recently (Lyons-Ruth & Jacobvitz, 1999; Main

& Solomon, 1986). Still others focus on a more contemporary classification system described by Bartholomew (1990), which includes the original three categories plus a fourth called *fearful.* The fearful pattern is characterized by a desire for intimacy but a fear of rejection, which results in the avoidance of intimacy. Further complicating the clarity of the literature, other studies focus on dimensions of attachment security (e.g., avoidance of intimacy, anxiety about abandonment) rather than on classification systems. As the following review suggests, use of different classification systems and different measures can result in inconsistent findings. As such, an important direction for future research will be to define and measure the construct of insecurity in a precise manner and to clarify the role of insecurity and the proxy variables in our models of the development of psychopathology.

Depression

Bowlby (1980) suggested that early loss, both perceived and actual, occurring in a context where the loss is experienced as uncontrollable, is likely to result in the development of depression. Loss is conceptualized broadly and can include parental death, loss of attachment relationships, and unavailability of the caregiver. Bowlby asserted that loss of attachment relationships may occur when, despite persistent attempts by the child to form stable and secure relationships, such relationships are not formed, resulting in the perception of the self as a failure. This leads to the interpretation of subsequent losses as a reflection of the self as a failure. Similarly, when caregivers send messages of incompetence and unworthiness, the child may develop an internal working model that the self is unlovable and incompetent, leading to later expectations of others' hostility and rejection, increasing vulnerability to depression. Thus, loss of the attachment figure exerts its influence, in part, through the development of internal working models that can make people vulnerable to depression (Besser & Priel, 2003; Burge et al., 1997; Cole-Detke & Kobak, 1996; see Hankin & Abela, Chapter 10 of this volume, for discussion of depression).

In line with this idea, Cole-Detke and Kobak (1996) proposed that individuals characterized by a pattern of preoccupied attachment become overly focused on their negative views of the self and others, leading to ineffective coping methods and therefore perpetuating a cycle of self-blame, negative affect, and hopelessness. In a similar manner, Burge et al. (1997) proposed that negative working models of self and others serve as a risk factor in the development of depression through several mechanisms, namely by increasing individuals' vulnerability to interpersonal stressors and by influencing individuals to behave in interpersonal situations in ways that may generate stress (Hammen et al., 1995). Other theorists have suggested numerous additional factors that may help explain the mechanisms by which attachment security puts people at risk for depression, including agency of self (West & George, 2002), self-efficacy (Strodl & Noller, 2003), sociotropy and autonomy (Hammen et al.; Murphy & Bates, 1997; Strodl & Noller), and affect regulation (Sloman, Gilbert, & Hasey, 2003).

Recognizing the complexity of the relation between insecure attachment and depression as well as the wide array of factors likely to be involved in the development and maintenance of this disorder, Cummings and Cicchetti (1990) proposed a transactional model to explain the development of depression. In their model, the parent, child, and environment reciprocally influence each other across the life span, with the notion that factors in the model may have different effects on each other over time. Attachment (both historical and current) is conceptualized to exert influence across the life course via its role in the development of felt security, self-esteem, and perceptions of social support. Depression is thought to affect attachment over time as well.

Although theories about the association between attachment insecurity and depression tend to recognize some of the possible complexities in the association, most research has simply examined their direct association. As expected, this research has consistently documented an association between the two in childhood, adolescence, and adulthood, although it is unclear whether this association is specific to one type of insecurity. For example, Muris, Mayer, and Meesters (2000) found that 12-year-old children who self-reported having an avoidant or ambivalent attachment showed similar levels of depression. However, Graham and Easterbrooks (2000), using an observational measure of attachment pattern, found that 7- to 9-year-old children classified as disorganized reported significantly greater levels of depression as compared with children exhibiting the other three attachment patterns, with secure and avoidant children reporting similar levels of depression. Similarly, numerous studies document an association between general insecurity and depression in adolescence (e.g., Armsden, McCauley, Greenberg, Burke, & Mitchell, 1990; Burge et al., 1997; Muris, Meesters, van Melick, & Zwambag, 2001; Sund & Wichstrom, 2002), whereas others suggest that there may be a specific association between preoccupation and depression (e.g., Kobak, Sudler, & Gamble, 1991; Rosenstein & Horowitz, 1996). The same is true for research on adults. Many studies of both community and clinical samples, using self-report and interview-based assessments of attachment and focusing on both depression and dysthymia, support an association between insecurity and depression (e.g., Bifulco, Moran, Ball, & Bernazzani, 2002; Saltzman, 1996; West & George, 2002), but attempts to delineate a specific insecure style as a risk factor have produced inconsistent results.

For example, Cole-Detke and Kobak (1996) found an association between preoccupied attachment and depression using the AAI. Fonagy et al. (1996) found a similar association among depressed inpatients when using the three-way classification system of the AAI, but when the four-way classification system was used, depressed inpatients predominantly were classified as unresolved. Complicating the picture further, Murphy and Bates (1997), using a self-report measure, found that both preoccupied and fearful attachment styles were associated with depression, as did Carnelley, Pietromonaco, and Jaffe (1994). However, Carnelley et al. also found that, in a sample of married women recovering from clinical depression, only greater fearful avoidance was evident.

A few studies have tested more complex models of the association between insecurity and depression. A number of these studies have examined mediators of the association, particularly focusing on cognitive mediators. For example, Reinecke and Rogers (2001) found that dysfunctional attitudes partially mediated the association between insecure attachment and depressive symptoms. In a more extensive test of this notion, Roberts, Gotlib, and Kassel (1996) and Hankin, Kassel, and Abela (in press) found support for a model in which insecurity is associated with dysfunctional attitudes, which lead to low self-esteem and finally depressive symptoms. Hankin et al. also found evidence that interpersonal negative life events mediate the association between insecurity and depressive symptoms, and they suggest that insecurity may result in the generation of stress, which leads to increases in depression.

There are few studies of moderators of the association between insecurity and depression. However, one recent study found that working models of self and others interacted with self-criticism and dependency to predict depression (Besser & Priel, 2003). Individuals who showed high levels of self-criticism and low levels of positive self and other working models were most vulnerable to depression. Additionally, participants who exhibited low levels of dependency but high levels of positive self and other working models were less vulnerable to depression. Clearly, more studies are needed to investigate moderators.

Anxiety Disorders

Dating back to Freud (1940), disorganization in the face of anxiety, ways of dealing with anxiety, and the occurrence and magnitude of anxiety have been conceptually linked to early experiential history within relationships (Schneider-Rosen, 1990). Bowlby (1973) theorized that children's anxiety level is affected by their pattern of attachment to their caregiver, and he argued that common anxiety disorders (such as school phobia and separation anxiety) can be traced to concerns about the availability of the attachment figure. This conceptualization has produced an interest in delineating whether a specific relation between anxious pathology and different patterns of attachments exist. However, relatively few published reports document this hypothesized association, despite the observation that anxiety problems are some of the most common forms of psychopathology throughout the life span, with consequences for disrupted social relations and self-esteem (see Williams, Reardon, Murray, & Cole, Chapter 11 of this volume, for discussion of anxiety).

Of the studies that do exist, all have shown an association between anxiety and insecurity of one form or another at various ages across the life span. For example, Warren, Huston, Egeland, and Sroufe (1997) found a relation between ambivalent-resistant attachment in childhood (using the Strange Situation Procedure: Ainsworth et al., 1978) and anxiety disorders in childhood and adolescence, even when accounting for maternal anxiety and newborn temperament. Muris et al. (2000) found that, for 12-year-olds, self-reports of panic, generalized anxiety, social phobia, separation anxiety, and traumatic stress disorders were each associated with both avoidant and anxious self-reported attachment styles. Cooper, Shaver, and Collins (1998) found that ambivalent females (assessed via self-report) evidenced greater general anxiety at ages 13 to 14 than did other attachment types and male participants. However, this pattern changed in ages 15 to 19, by which time anxious symptoms appeared to have reduced. The authors concluded that this suggests that there may be different or differently timed developmental trajectories for each attachment style and their association with anxiety. Rosenstein and Horowitz (1996) reported that clinically referred adolescents with self-reported anxious traits were predominantly classified as preoccupied. Similarly, Kobak and Sceery (1988) interviewed college students and found that those with a preoccupied style were judged by peers to be the most anxious. Vivona (2000) and Burge et al. (1997) also studied college students and found, using self-report attachment measures, that insecurity of various types was associated with anxiety and worry. Finally, in adult samples, Fonagy et al. (1996) found that the majority of individuals with anxiety disorder diagnoses were classified as preoccupied (using three-way classification) or unresolved (using four-way classification), and Mickelson, Kessler, and Shaver (1997), in a nationally representative sample of adults, reported that both avoidant and ambivalent attachment styles were significantly associated with lifetime prevalence ratings of panic disorder, agoraphobia, social phobia, simple phobia, posttraumatic stress disorder, and generalized anxiety disorder.

The studies just described did not theorize about (or examine) whether associations between specific anxiety disorders and attachment insecurity might exist, but several studies have. Vertue (2003) has proposed that internal working models of the self and others that are established in the context of attachment relationships determine beliefs and expectations about social relationships and thus may contribute to social anxiety. In line with this, Eng, Heimberg, Hart, Schneier, and Liebowitz (2001) found that adults classified as preoccupied demonstrated more social fear and avoidance than did their secure counterparts.

A relation between attachment dimensions and agoraphobia has also been proposed and has received some research attention in recent years. Using self-report measures, Strodl and Noller (2003) reported that preoccupation was uniquely associated with agoraphobic behavior. In addition, de Ruiter and van Ijzendoorn (1992) conducted a meta-analysis to assess whether an ambivalent attachment style was a risk factor for the development of agoraphobia. Based on indirect support for their hypothesis (via measures of parental caregiving style and reports of childhood separation anxiety), the authors concluded that ambivalent attachment alone is not a specific risk factor for the development of agoraphobia. Instead, they proposed that this attachment style may play a more general etiological role in psychopathology.

Manassis, Bradley, Goldberg, Hood, and Swinson (1994) provided preliminary support for an association between insecure attachment (assessed using the AAI) and panic disorder. In this study of 18 women with an anxiety disorder, 14 met criteria for panic disorder, and all evidenced insecure attachment styles, particularly the preoccupied style. More specifically, these women reported a high level of unresolved loss and trauma associated with the constellation of insecure attachment and anxiety symptoms. However, although attachment insecurity appeared to be associated with panic disorder in this small sample, the association was not specific.

Attachment theory has also been hypothesized to be a useful framework in understanding the developmental antecedents of generalized anxiety disorder (Cassidy, 1995). However, at this time, empirical data exploring this relationship do not yet exist.

In sum, research demonstrates that there is a relation between attachment insecurity and anxiety disorders. However, the findings across studies fail to reveal a specific association between a particular insecure attachment style and anxiety. Future research is needed to better distinguish between different anxiety symptoms and their relation to specific attachment styles and to expand the limited literature on anxiety and attachment security.

Eating Disorders

Several authors have hypothesized about the relation between insecure attachment and the development of eating disorders (see Cooper, Chapter 12 of this volume, for discussion about eating disorders). In general, theories have focused on working models, maintaining proximity to caregivers during adolescence, and affect regulation. Extending Bowlby's (1980) conceptualizations of working models, Armstrong and Roth (1989) interpret the symptoms of eating disorders in adolescence as part of the continued development of working models, asserting that individuals with eating disorders believe that they must be thin in order to achieve the availability of attachment figures and avoid rejection. Therefore, the symptoms may function to alleviate separation distress occurring in adolescence by maintaining the availability of caregivers. In addition, it has been suggested that eating disorder symptoms, in particular bingeing, may function to regulate negative affect by decreasing awareness of anxious feelings about attachment figures (Armstrong & Roth; Brennan & Shaver, 1995; Strober & Humphrey, 1987).

Theories have also postulated that dismissing attachment may be a risk factor in the development of eating disorders, with the extreme focus on altering one's appearance representing an attempt to disengage from the attachment situation (Cole-Detke & Kobak, 1996). That is, individuals may be trying to improve attachment relationships by focusing on their appearance rather than on the relationship itself. Additionally, a dismissing attachment strategy may be conceptualized as a vulnerability that is moderated by sociocultural pressures in the development of eating disorders.

Focusing on the relation between insecure attachment and anorexia nervosa, O'Kearney (1996) asserted that anorexia may function to maintain proximity to attachment figures during the transition to adolescence. He focused on this transition as a time when changes in attachment relationships occur, with increased autonomy from caregivers coupled with increased importance of peer relationships. O'Kearney concluded that both avoidant (dismissing) and resistant (preoccupied) strategies could be related to anorexia. In the case of dismissing attachment, O'Kearney similarly posited that the symptoms of anorexia allow individuals to divert attention away from distressing attachment relationships during the transition. In the case of preoccupied attachment, the focus on appearance and body weight in anorexia may be seen as an intense focus on others, specifically criticism and disapproval. Similarly, Armstrong and Roth (1989) postulated that anorexia may function to establish and control the availability of attachment figures. Thus, theories of anorexia have focused on maintaining proximity to caregivers as the driving force behind the development of the disorder.

Theories of the development of bulimia nervosa have also focused on maintaining proximity to caregivers during adolescence and, additionally, have focused on symptoms as a mechanism of emotion regulation. O'Kearney (1996) postulated that the symptoms of bulimia may function to maintain proximity to attachment figures, particularly during the transition to adolescence. In his review, he concluded that specifying a type of insecure attachment may not be possible and posited that the symptomatic course of bulimia, with periods of chaos and bingeing followed by periods of control, may be parallel to an oscillation of insecure attachment patterns. Armstrong and Roth (1989) focused on the lack of internalization of effective emotion-regulation skills in individuals with emotionally unavailable caregivers who may not provide comfort during times of distress. Thus, extending Bowlby's (1980) formulations, the authors posit that the symptoms of bulimia may function to regulate negative affect.

Research thus far has consistently provided support for an association between eating disorders and insecure attachment, although little specificity exists (see Ward, Ramsay, & Treasure, 2000, for a review). For example, in a sample of in- and outpatients with eating disorders, patients showed a pattern of insecurity characterized by a combination of ambivalent and avoidant patterns (Ward, Ramsay, Turnbull, Benedettini, & Treasure, 2000). Broberg, Hjalmers, and Nevonen (2001) showed that individuals with bulimia, anorexia, and eating disorder NOS (not otherwise specified) manifested similar patterns of self-reported insecure attachment. Further, in a sample of young men and women with anorexia or eating disorder NOS, Ramacciotti and colleagues (2001) found that 70% of patients were classified as insecure. Similarly, work by Kenny and Hart (1992) showed that young adult inpatients with eating disorders described their relationships with their parents as more insecure than relationships described by a comparative sample of college women.

Some research does indicate that eating disorders may be related to specific types of insecurity, but support has been found for both dismissing and preoccupied styles. For example, in one study that used the AAI, more patients were classified as preoccupied than as dismissing (Fonagy et al., 1996). Similarly, Friedberg and Lyddon (1996) found that the secure and preoccupied attachment styles (as measured via self-report) significantly predicted classification into the nonclinical control group or the patient eating disorder group, respectively, in 75% of cases. However, Ward et al. (2001) classified 95% of the anorexic patients as insecure, with the majority (75%) classified as dismissing and only 20% classified as preoccupied.

The existence of comorbidity may help to clarify some of the inconsistencies of these findings. For instance, Cole-Detke & Kobak (1996) used the AAI to investigate attachment patterns in undergraduate women with depression only, eating disorders only, or comorbid depression and eating disorders. Women with eating disorders only were primarily classified as dismissing (67%). However, women with comorbid depressive symptoms were most often classified as preoccupied (53%). Thus, comorbid diagnoses may account for some of the different patterns of insecure attachment seen across studies.

Other research suggests it may be possible to link specific types of insecurity to specific symptoms rather than to eating disorder diagnoses. Candelori and Ciocca (1998), in a sample of 36 patients, found that those diagnosed with bulimia were most often classified (using an interview) as preoccupied (75%) but that the majority of patients diagnosed with anorexia exhibited either dismissing (33%) or preoccupied (30%) styles. Clearer patterns emerged when anorexic patients were further classified by subtype, restricting or bingeing/purging. Restricting patients were most often classified as dismissing (68%), whereas binge/purge patients, like bulimic patients, were most often classified as preoccupied (50%). Thus, a distinction emerged when individuals were classified by the presence or absence of bingeing and purging.

There are no known prospective studies documenting the development of eating disorders based on attachment patterns. However, a few studies have investigated the relation between insecure attachment and weight concerns, a risk factor for the development of eating disorders (Killen et al., 1994). Sharpe et al. (1998) found that insecurely attached adolescents reported significantly higher weight concerns than securely attached adolescents. Further, insecurely attached individuals were more likely to evidence weight concern scores that place them at risk for the development of eating disorders. Additionally, women with eating problems, particularly those with bulimic symptoms, exhibited higher relationship anxiety, lower comfort with closeness and intimacy, and lower feelings of others as trustworthy and dependable (Evans & Wertheim, 1998). These studies linking risk factors and premorbid symptoms to insecurity support the hypothesis that insecure attachment may be involved in the development of eating disorders.

Personality Disorders

In Bowlby's (1973, 1977) writings on attachment theory, attachment insecurity in the childhood years plays a central role in personality psychopathology (see Johnson et al., Chapter 15 of this volume, for discussion of personality disorder). Bowlby (1977) writes, "There is a strong causal relationship between an individual's experiences with his parents and his later capacity to make affectional bonds, and . . . certain common variations in that capacity, manifesting themselves . . . in neurotic symptoms and personality disorders, can be attributed to certain common variations in the ways that parents perform their roles" (p. 206). Conceptually, attachment styles and personality disorders (PDs) do overlap. For example, both can be described as enduring patterns of inner experience and behavior. Similarly, in the case of insecure attachment, both may lead to distress and impairment that affect interpersonal functioning (Brennan & Shaver, 1998; Meyer, Pilkonis, Proietti, Heape, & Egan, 2001). Indeed, recent conceptualizations of PDs frequently propose that the disturbed working models of attachment relationships play an etiological role in the development of personality pathology (Fonagy, 1991; Fossati et al., 2003; Westen, 1991). Thus, any inquiry into the role of attachment security in developmental psychopathology would be incomplete without addressing the topic of personality disorders.

However, at present there has been only a relatively limited exploration of the associations between attachment and many of the most commonly diagnosed PDs (Fossati et al., 2003). Instead, the majority of the research has focused on a single PD, often borderline and antisocial (likely because they are particularly impairing and costly). But by concentrating solely on one disorder, rather than taking into account the high rates of comorbidity among Axis II disorders, research may fail to capture the complex pattern of co-occurring PDs and specific attachment styles (Fossati et al., 2003; see also Livesley, Jackson, & Schroeder, 1992). Nevertheless, there is evidence that attachment theory can provide a framework for conceptualizing PDs (e.g., Lyddon & Sherry, 2001).

An increasing number of investigators have provided support for the conceptualization of PDs as disorders of attachment (e.g., Heard & Lake, 1986; Meyer et al., 2001; Shaver & Clark, 1994; West & Sheldon, 1988; West & Sheldon-Keller, 1994). In a study based on college students' self-reported attachment styles and PD symptoms, Brennan and Shaver (1998) found that people in the fearful and preoccupied groups were the most likely to have a PD (92.4% and 90.5%, respectively), with the dismissing group being next likely, and the secure group being least likely. They also found a number of specific associations. Schizoid PD was associated with both dismissing and fearful styles. Avoidant and paranoid PDs were associated with the fearful style. Dependent and histrionic PDs were associated with the preoccupied style.

Similar findings emerged in a mixed psychiatric sample with PD diagnoses based on semistructured interviews (Fossati et al., 2003). Specifically, the attachment dimension Avoidance of Intimacy correlated with avoidant, paranoid, schizoid, and schizotypal PDs, which are characterized by social anxieties, distrust of others, and social withdrawal. The attachment dimension Anxiety About Abandonment was associated with dependent, histrionic, and borderline PDs, which are all defined by an excessive need for the support of others, feelings of discomfort when alone, and intolerance of and excessive efforts to avoid abandonment. Nakashi-Eisikovits, Dutra, and Westen (2002) found similar results. However, Rosenstein and Horowitz (1996) found a number of different associations, although rates of PDs were low in their sample.

One of the most researched PDs is borderline personality disorder (BPD), a disorder commonly construed in terms of interpersonal theory, with particular emphasis on disrupted early relations (Benjamin, 1993). Given the characterization of BPD as a disorder typified by unstable representations of self and others, emotion dysregulation, and interpersonal dysfunction, an inquiry into the relationship between BPD and attachment style warrants attention. Similar to insecurely attached individuals with preoccupied and fearful styles, individuals suffering from BPD may experience preoccupying fears about abandonment in conjunction with extreme dependence, resulting in intense mood variations (Fonagy et al., 1996; Kobak & Sceery, 1988; Shapiro, 1978). For example, West, Keller, Links, and Patrick (1993) have proposed that in BPD, the underlying dysfunction of the attachment system is an exaggerated fear of loss that leads to oscillating behaviors of care seeking and angry withdrawal. As such, BPD should be associated with attachment insecurity, particularly a preoccupied style, and research generally supports this.

There is indirect evidence of an association between BPD and attachment insecurity based on high rates of early abuse and maltreatment among people with BPD (e.g., Greenman, Gunderson, Cane, & Saltzman, 1986; Herman, Perry, & van der Kolk, 1989; Soloff & Millward, 1983; Zanarini, Gunderson, Marion, & Schwartz, 1989). For example, Ludolph et al. (1990) found, among inpatient BPD-diagnosed adolescent girls, that disrupted attachment relationships—involving maternal neglect, maternal rejection, greater number of surrogate mothers and fathers, more time spent in foster care, and greater experiences with grossly inappropriate parental behavior—predict the BPD diagnosis. More direct evidence also exists. For example, Levy (2004) found that 92% of the BPD sample studied was classified as insecure using the AAI.

A number of studies have documented the link between BPD and preoccupied attachment insecurity. For example, Levy (2004), Fonagy et al. (1996), and Patrick, Hobson, Castle, Howard, and Maughan (1994) showed high rates of preoccupied attachment among their BPD samples. Community samples show a similar association. For example, Nickell, Waudby, and Trull (2002), using self-report measures, found that ambivalent attachment was uniquely associated with BPD features, even controlling for variables such as childhood adversity and symptoms of other disorders. Rosenstein and Horowitz (1996) also found that people with clinically significant borderline traits were more likely to have a preoccupied attachment pattern. However, they also found evidence of a dismissing style among a proportion of their participants. Sack, Sperling, Fagen, and Foelsch (1996) compared hospitalized BPD patients to college controls and also found that the BPD individuals endorsed both greater ambivalence and greater avoidance. As Rosenstein and Horowitz suggest, these findings may be due to heterogeneity among people diagnosed with BPD.

In sum, it seems clear that BPD is related to insecure attachment. What is less clear is the nature of the association between specific insecure patterns and BPD. However, the bulk of the evidence suggests that a preoccupied-ambivalent form of insecurity may be most common.

A second area of empirical exploration is the relation between attachment and antisocial PD (APD). Diagnostically, APD and its frequent precursor, conduct disorder (CD), are typically characterized by a disregard for the rights and feelings of others, often in the presence of intense anger and aggression (see Hankin, Abela, Auerbach, McWhinnie, & Skitch, Chapter 14 of this volume, for discussion of behavioral, disruptive problems). This anger, as described by Bowlby (1973), may arise from childhood separations from the parent(s) and, if separations continue, may elevate to a dysfunctional level and become directed at other, nonattachment targets. Moreover, Fonagy (1994) suggests that people who exhibit antisocial personality and behavior may not have acquired reflective capacity through their attachment relationships. This may manifest in a failure to envision the mental state of a potential victim and may allow for participation in criminal and violent offenses.

Despite these fairly specific hypotheses about how attachment insecurity may lead to APD and CD, research has not identified one insecure style that is specifically linked to antisocial behavior (possibly because these mechanisms may manifest in different attachment patterns). As indirect evidence of an association, some research supports a link between parental lack of care and APD (Enns,

Cox, & Clara, 2002; Zanarini et al., 1989). Some research supports a direct link between APD, CD, or antisocial behavior and insecurity in general. For example, Arbona and Power (2003) found that securely attached high school students had more positive sense of self-esteem and less involvement in antisocial behaviors. Evidence shows an association between both avoidant and ambivalent attachment styles with the development of CD and APD (as well as other disorders; Mickelson et al., 1997).

Other research supports a link between APD, CD, or antisocial behavior and avoidant attachment (see LaFreniere & Sroufe, 1985; Rosenstein & Horowitz, 1996; Sroufe, 1983). For example, Allen, Hauser, and Borman-Spurrell (1996) found that among adolescent inpatients, dismissing attachment (using the AAI) predicted criminal activity 10 years later. Renken, Egeland, Marvinney, Mangelsdorf, and Sroufe (1989) reported that nonaggressive avoidantly attached boys at 18 months were overrepresented in the subsequent aggressive group assessed at 24 and 48 months.

Some research also supports a link between APD, CD, or antisocial behavior and preoccupied attachment. For example, Fonagy et al. (1996) found, in a sample of individuals with comorbid APD and paranoid PD, that most were classified with the AAI as preoccupied and autonomous rather than dismissing. Cooper et al. (1998) found that ambivalently attached adolescents (assessed via self-report) experienced high levels of hostility and turned to delinquency and "acting-out" behaviors more so than did adolescents with other attachment styles. Although the avoidant group also had a high level of symptoms, they lacked the behavior problems experienced by the anxious-ambivalent group.

It is also important to note that a number of studies have not supported an association between insecurity and behavior problems or APD, particularly when examined over time. For example, although Lewis, Feiring, McGuffog, and Jaskir (1984) and Speltz, DeKlyen, and Greenberg (1999) found concurrent associations between insecurity and behavior problems, insecurity was not a strong predictor of behavior problems over time.

Some of the discrepant findings between behavioral problems and attachment insecurity may be partially attributable to the different attachment constructs themselves. That is, those categorized as dismissing may be described as having a defensive attachment style, including efforts to avoid emotion, idealize experiences, and derogate the importance of attachment relationships. In turn, dismissing individuals may be less likely to self-report difficulties and instead emphasize personal strength and independence (Pianta, Egeland, & Adam, 1996). In addition, there may be differences in the way aggression becomes expressed. For example, ambivalent-resistant children may engage in more physical and direct confrontation and disruptive activities, whereas avoidant people may engage in more subtle acts of noncompliance, as suggested by Sroufe (1983; see also Perry, Perry, & Boldizar, 1990). Finally, the inconsistent findings as to which subtype of insecure attachment is related to antisocial behavior may result from the heterogeneous nature of such behavior. For example, accumulating data support a distinction between life course–persistent and adolescence-limited antisocial behavior (see Moffitt, 1993). The life course–persistent subtype is distinguished from the adolescence-limited variety in part by the appearance of markedly disturbed behavior in the preschool years; impulsive, sensation-seeking, and aggressive behavioral features; and insecure attachment relationships (Aguilar, Sroufe, Egeland, & Carlson, 2000; Moffitt, Caspi, Harrington, & Milne, 2002). This distinction between age of onset and developmental course (Rutter & Sroufe, 2000) may be partly responsible for the variation in association that has been reported. Nevertheless, overall there appear to be consistent findings that children in high-social-risk environments characterized by insecure attachment relationships are at greater risk for aggression than are those with secure attachment styles (Greenberg, Speltz, & DeKlyen, 1993).

In conclusion, the findings from a number of studies using a variety of samples support the proposition that insecure attachment patterns in childhood and adulthood are associated with a diagnosis of one or more PDs. What is less evident is the specificity of certain attachment styles, above and beyond the other styles, to predict a given PD. It is likely that additional psychological, social, and biological variables may underlie the attachment-PD link (Fossati et al., 2003). The moderate effect sizes observed in even the most robust findings support this multimechanism perspective. Future research should explore *how* insecure attachment plays a role in personality pathology, rather than assuming that there is a causal process. It seems especially probable that, based on an identified overlap between patterns of insecure attachment styles and patterns of PDs, the two constructs may share similar developmental antecedents that combine with inborn temperaments and cultural variation to place individuals at risk for disordered relationship patterns (Brennan & Shaver, 1998). Investigators should assume that insecure attachments are not necessarily indicative of personality psychopathology and that attachment features do not constitute the whole of the attachment-psychopathology relationships that are found (Rutter & Sroufe, 2000). An example of one such approach is that of Paris (1998), who has proposed a predisposition-stress model for the pathogenesis of anxious-cluster (avoidant, dependent, and obsessive-compulsive) PDs whereby a vulnerability of anxious traits develops into pathology only in the presence of stressors, such as overprotective or unempathic parenting and insecure attachment relationships. However, the relationship between these variables may be nonspecific, with different outcomes from attachment relationships in different individuals based on temperamental factors.

CORE PROCESSES OF ATTACHMENT INSECURITY UNDERLYING PSYCHOPATHOLOGY

Beyond just thinking about how specific disorders relate to attachment insecurity, it may be useful to think about how different symptoms or processes that underlie many disorders may be related to insecurity. The high rates of comorbidity within Axis I disorders and between Axis I and II disorders suggest that core attachment processes may underlie diverse types of psychopathology. Although there are many ways to organize an inquiry into the relation between core processes of attachment and diverse psychopathology, we have chosen to focus on working models of self and others, affect regulation, and interpersonal functioning/social support.

Working Models of Self and Others

Bowlby (1969, 1980) conceptualized working models as mental representations of self and others that are developed based on early attachment experiences with primary caregivers and that serve to aid children in developing expectations about the availability and behavior of others (Cicchetti et al., 1995). According to Bowlby (1973), there are two primary features of working models: "(a) whether or not the attachment figure is judged to be the sort of person who in general responds to calls for support and protection, [and] (b) whether or not the self is judged to be the sort of person towards whom anyone, and the attachment figure in particular, is likely to respond in a helpful way" (p. 204).

Over time, these working models become stabilized cognitive representations and serve to guide psychosocial functioning across the life span. In this manner, working models provide a basis for continuity in how individuals view the self, others, and their interpersonal contexts.

Cognitions derived from attachment relationships may therefore be a key component of a variety of psychological disorders. This is consistent with cognitive models of psychopathology, which suggest that dysfunctional thoughts and maladaptive thought processes cause, exacerbate, and maintain psychopathology (see Gibb & Coles, Chapter 5 of this volume). Attesting to the pervasiveness of this idea, cognitive models have been proposed to explain disorders including depression, various anxiety disorders, eating disorders, and personality disorders, and these models often focus heavily on distorted cognitions about the self and others. The notion that maladaptive views of self and others are key components of psychopathology is central to many psychodynamic conceptualizations as well, including object relations theory and other contemporary relational approaches. As such, beliefs about the self and others may put people at risk for various types of disorders.

For example, the working models of self and others that characterize insecure attachment appear parallel to the cognitions about loss and unacceptability of self that depressed individuals experience (Cummings & Cicchetti, 1990). In this vein, it has been suggested that these depressogenic cognitions mediate the relation between early attachment experiences and depression (Hankin et al., in press; Reinecke & Rogers, 2001; Roberts et al., 1996). As another example, individuals with eating disorders are theorized to lack a coherent sense of self or to have developed a highly false self-image because of their failure to develop autonomy from overintrusive and overprotective caregivers. This lack of self-coherence may be manifested in low self-esteem and overreliance on weight and shape for self-evaluation, especially during times of separation distress such as adolescence (Bruch, 1973, 1978; O'Kearney, 1996).

Similarly, personality disorders can be understood from an attachment theory, working models perspective. For example, in the case of dependent personality disorder, individuals may have been led by an overprotective caregiver to believe that they are incapable of accomplishing things on their own (Lyddon & Sherry, 2001). Such individuals may then adopt a negative self-view characterized by feelings of inadequacy, which leads them to feel that they require excessive care by others (whom they view positively). Individuals with avoidant personality features endorse a negative self-view, perhaps because of engulfing or avoidant parenting behavior (Sperry & Mosak, 1993), yet they tend to see others in both positive and negative lights. That is, although such individuals may desire closeness, fears that they may be rejected or denied the intimacy they seek may lead them to avoid relationships rather than risk such rejection (Lyddon & Sherry). Furthermore, experiences of rejection and critical, persecutory parenting may lead to a widespread mistrust of others, characteristic of paranoid personality pathology, via negative working models of self and others (Lyddon & Sherry; Thompson-Pope & Turkat, 1993).

A hallmark of BPD is the presence of extreme oscillation in interpersonal relationships, from idealization to devaluation and denigration. This is mirrored by such individuals' incoherent discourse about early attachment relationships, which is thought to reflect disturbance in the formation of coherent representations (Patrick et al., 1994). Consistent with theory proposed by Bowlby (1973) and supported in research by Lynch and Cicchetti (1991), such individuals may exhibit multiple, inconsistent, and incompatible working models as a consequence of contradictory experiences in primary relationships. Further, as a means of coping with this early adverse situation, there may be a failure to conceive of the mind of another, that is, to gain a working model of another and therefore the self (Fonagy et al., 1996). The experience of early traumatic events, common to those with BPD, may fail to be processed because of a refusal to conceive of the mind of abusive caregivers (Patrick et al.). This early adaptive failure of reflective capacity carries over to adulthood through incoherent representations of self and others, disturbing subsequent intimate relationships (Fonagy et al.; Fonagy, 1999). This failure to understand the mental state of the self and of others may then become a characteristic response to interpersonal interactions in adulthood and may account for many aspects of the borderline personality (Fonagy, 1999).

The crystallization of working models is also a mechanism through which externalizing and aggressive difficulties may be understood (Greenberg et al., 1993). Hostility in response to relationships with caregivers that are characterized by anger, mistrust, rejection, and emotional unavailability may result in attributional biases in aggressive children (Dodge, 1980) and adults. This underlying anger becomes misdirected, aimed not at the original source but rather manifesting as aggressive, hostile, and antisocial behavior (Sroufe, 1983). Such skewed working models may represent an explanatory link between attachment difficulties and later externalizing troubles, whereby diverse antecedents are brought together to form a worldview characterized by alienation, threat, and unavailable others (Renken et al., 1989). Thus, based on attachment theory, internalized working models of the self and others are common components to both attachment security and numerous psychopathological conditions.

Affect Regulation

A central tenet of attachment theory is that caregivers provide children with a context in which they learn about and develop the ability to identify, tolerate, and express a range of emotions (Sroufe & Waters, 1977). In stable and consistent caregiver-child relationships, where the caregiver repeatedly demonstrates the ability to recognize and regulate the child's distress, the child will successfully develop emotion-regulation skills (see Chaplin & Cole, Chapter 3 of this volume, for discussion of emotion regulation). Therefore, the child's subsequent affect-regulation capacity will directly reflect the interactions of the caregiver with the child (Fonagy, 1999). However, when caregivers are unable to reflect upon and regulate their child's and their own emotional states, children do not have the opportunity to develop effective strategies to respond to their own emotions or the emotions of close others. As a consequence, individuals may learn to either exaggerate or inhibit negative emotions (Burge et al., 1997). These early dyadic experiences of emotion regulation then persist throughout the life span as an individual style for coping with difficulties (Sroufe, Carlson, Levy, & Egeland, 1999).

In the language of attachment theory, individuals who had a secure attachment to early caregivers are expected to be able to acknowledge negative emotions and subsequently employ effective coping strategies to deal with them. Individuals who had an avoidant attachment do not acknowledge their negative emotions, which may lead them to downplay their emotions, engage in behaviors that function to avoid their emotions, or even to act out their emotions without knowing why they are doing so. Conversely, individuals who had an ambivalent attachment with early caregivers experience strong emotions and are highly emotionally expressive but lack the ability to regulate their experience and expression of emotions and lack the ability to bring emotional behavior in line with personal and social interests (Cooper et al., 1998).

The failure to effectively manage emotional experiences in the ways described by attachment theory represents a common feature of many forms of psychopathology. Indeed, inherent in the definition of many disorders is the idea that individuals are unable to regulate their emotions successfully, thereby resulting in extreme or distorted affect. For example, both depression and generalized anxiety disorder are characterized by a failure to regulate and modulate intense and profuse feelings (Cassidy, 1995; Sloman et al., 2003). Both conditions are characterized by feelings of low self-efficacy and uncertainty about one's capacity to cope effectively in the environment and with one's own negative affective states (Warren et al., 1997). They are also both characterized by rumination and worry, which are unsuccessful coping strategies that result in the increase of negative emotion rather than the decrease.

Bulimia can also be understood from an emotion-regulation perspective. In particular, bingeing can be viewed as an attempt to regulate and soothe distressing and threatening emotions that originated in the context of an unavailable or insensitive caregiver but that now occur across diverse contexts (Strober & Humphrey, 1987). Similarly, an inability to tolerate distressing emotions may result in efforts toward avoidance or externalization that manifest in symptoms of substance abuse/dependence or conduct problems (Rosenstein & Horowitz, 1996).

Perhaps the disorder for which poor emotion regulation features most prominently is BPD. Current conceptualizations construe BPD as an attachment disorder and suggest that poor affect regulation is one of the core components of borderline pathology (e.g., Fonagy et al., 1996; Linehan, 1993). Furthermore, the intersection of strongly felt negative emotions that people with BPD experience, and the inability to tolerate such affect, has been attributed as a driving force behind the frequent cutting and parasuicidal behavior that these individuals exhibit (Favazza, 1998; Paris, 2004).

In summary, it appears that poor emotion regulation may result in enduring periods of negative affect and arousal, which in turn may underlie the development of a variety of psychological disorders (Bradley, 2000).

Interpersonal Functioning/ Social Support

As proposed by Bowlby (1973), the failure to establish a secure attachment relationship may mean that an individual develops a persistent perception that support is either inconsistently available or chronically unavailable. Consequently, distress may result from the perception that others are unavailable in times of need. It has therefore been suggested that attachment patterns are enacted in interpersonal relationships through the lifelong roles of care seeker and caregiver (Bowlby, 1982; Waters, 1997). From an attachment perspective, a competent care seeker seeks support from caregivers, accurately conveys his or her needs, and accepts support provided. As competent caregivers, individuals must be available and must effectively and consistently provide support to care seekers (Waters). Therefore, the competent care seeker/caregiver interaction may be compromised in any one of a number of situations when the attachment system is threatened. For example, as care seekers, individuals may behave in extreme behaviors in an attempt to elicit reassurance and support from others when they feel that their attachment figure is not available. Conversely, some individuals may fail to seek the care of others, fearing that support will be unavailable. Finally, as caregivers in close relationships, individuals may not provide a secure base (i.e., consistent and available support) for others if they have failed to internalize this working model of relationships.

A disrupted pattern of interpersonal behavior, particularly with regard to care seeking and caregiving, is evident across an array of psychological disorders. For example, in adolescence, the symptoms of eating disorders may demonstrate an effort to maintain proximity and connectedness (a form of care seeking) by making oneself more acceptable to attachment figures (Armstrong & Roth, 1989). Specifically, the behavior of individuals suffering from anorexia may function to inhibit change in the parent-child relationship during times of developmental transition (Kenny & Hart, 1992; O'Kearney, 1996). It is also possible that behaviors evident in childhood disruptive disorder, such as whining, noncompliance, and other negative attention-seeking behaviors, may reflect an attachment-driven effort that seeks to regulate caregiver patterns of attention after other strategies have proven to be ineffective or unavailable to the child (Greenberg et al., 1993). Furthermore, the internal working models of depressed individuals may lead them to have difficulty accepting supportive acts by others and may prompt these individuals to withdraw rather than to seek the support of others (Hammen et al., 1995). Depression may also be associated with poor caregiving because of the negative views of self and others that depressed people hold (e.g., Davila, Bradbury, Cohan, & Tochluk, 1999). Finally, others may withdraw support from depressed individuals who ineffectively seek reassurance, thereby perpetuating a cycle of reassurance seeking and rejection (Coyne, 1976).

Difficulties operating in the social environment are also common in the anxiety disorders. For example, both research and clinical observation document the difficulties that those experiencing social anxiety have depending on others and regulating fears of negative evaluation or abandonment (e.g., Eng et al., 2001). Given that these difficulties overlap with features of insecure attachment, attachment theory may provide a framework in which to better understand the experience of some socially anxious individuals. Bowlby's (1973) description of insecure attachment seems to reflect the experience and behavior of socially anxious people: "Through their eyes the world is seen as comfortless and unpredictable; and they respond either by shrinking from it or by doing battle with it" (p. 208). Thus, it may be that the discomfort, distress, and impairment of socially anxious individuals (Eng et al.), which lead them to avoid social interaction, constitute a defense against potential threats perceived to be inherent in interpersonal relationships (Mikulincer & Orbach, 1995). Similarly, these individuals may be thought of as "going to battle" with the social world in their hypervigilance and sensitivity to threat and loss (i.e., overly active defensive system) (Foa, Franklin, Perry, & Herbert, 1996).

Disruptions in interpersonal behavior are a hallmark of personality disorders marked by attachment-relevant problems, such as discomfort with closeness and intimacy, a high need for approval by others, and intense preoccupation with relationships (Burge et al., 1997). For example, the majority of borderline patients exhibit patterns of stormy interactions, including devaluation/manipulation/sadism and demandingness/entitlement, in their interpersonal relationships (Zanarini, Frankenburg, Hennen, & Silk, 2003). Furthermore, when individuals with BPD experience perceived or real threats to the attachment relationship, they often engage in desperate and extreme care-seeking efforts to maintaining relatedness with the caregiver. This may take the form of verbal pleas, excessive emotional displays, and parasuicidal and suicidal behaviors.

Adults who are dismissive of memories and emotions associated with attachment reveal less about themselves in their close relationships (Pianta et al., 1996). As suggested by Bowlby (1977), these individuals tend to act as though they are not concerned with others, even perhaps acting hostile and aggressive with others (Allen et al., 1996; Rosenstein & Horowitz, 1996). For example, those with schizoid personality disorder derogate the importance of close relationships (Brennan & Shaver, 1998; Duggan & Brennan, 1994), instead stressing self-sufficiency over attachment needs (West, Rose, & Sheldon-Keller, 1994). Conversely, others appear to become preoccupied with attachment-related experiences and emotions, in turn reporting greater symptoms, particularly anxiety, dysphoria, and symptoms in the interpersonal domain (Allen et al., 1996; Dozier, Stevenson, Lee, & Velligan, 1991; Kobak & Sceery, 1988; Pianta et al.; Rosenstein & Horowitz). For example, individuals diagnosed with histrionic personality disorder may have developed a low threshold for the perception of threatening environmental cues, which, when combined with mixed perceptions of support, leads to a chronic activation of the attachment system (Brennan & Shaver, 1998). Finally, individuals with avoidant personality symptoms may seek to avoid relationships, but they do so based on the conflict between a desire for closeness that becomes overridden by a fear of rejection, and thus these individuals are blocked from the very experiences they could benefit from (Bartholomew, 1990; Brennan & Shaver, 1998; Duggan & Brennan).

In conclusion, insecurely attached individuals appear to engage in deficient care-seeking behavior, including excessive efforts to secure support from others or an inability to communicate support needs to others. At the same time, caregiving behaviors may be lacking. For example, these individuals may provide ineffective support to others or may avoid closeness altogether. These deficiencies appear to be associated with an increased risk for the development of psychopathology. One way this may occur is via the increase in stress and interpersonal problems these individuals experience because of their maladaptive social patterns. This dysfunctional pattern can be seen parallel to findings that insecurely attached individuals exhibit greater rejection of treatment providers, engage in less self-disclosure in treatment settings, and overall have a lower use of treatment services (Dozier, 1990). These behaviors in the therapist-client context may be equivalent to failures to accept the support of others, inadequate communication of support needs, and a failure to seek the support of others in close relationships. Such behaviors may mean that not only do insecure individuals experience more interpersonal distress and problems, but that they may fail to seek and benefit from interventions that could ameliorate their difficulties, thus increasing their risk for psychopathology.

Summary

Core attachment processes regarding deficits in working models, affect regulation, and interpersonal functioning/support have been shown to be present in an array of disorders. Therefore, one may speculate that these mechanisms underlie the link between early attachment experiences and subsequent functioning. As such, insecure attachment may be thought of as a risk factor for some individuals in the development of psychopathology. The presence of common risk factors across many disorders may be one explanation for the observed high rates of comorbidity among disorders. As noted earlier, although insecure attachment may initiate a developmental pathway to psychopathology, it should not be thought of as a direct link between early adaptation and subsequent pathology (Warren et al., 1997). Instead, inquiry into the association between attachment and psychopathology should address mechanisms of this association in order to more fully understand the diverse processes at play in this relationship.

A VULNERABILITY-STRESS MODEL OF ATTACHMENT INSECURITY AND RISK FOR PSYCHOPATHOLOGY

As we have suggested throughout this chapter, perhaps the best way to conceptualize how attachment insecurity confers risk for psychopathology is through a vulnerability-stress model (see Ingram & Luxton, Chapter 2 of this volume), that is, a model that describes the circumstances under which some individuals are more likely than others to be at risk for the development of psychopathology in the face of attachment insecurity. There is no doubt, based on our review, that insecurity is associated with psychopathology, and we have identified some of the core attachment processes that may be most responsible for this association. But the questions remain: For whom will those processes be most likely to lead to symptomatic outcomes? What factors predict whether insecurity will point one down the path to psychopathology? A vulnerability-stress model can help to answer these questions, and it is consistent with how many theorists view the direction in which research on attachment and psychopathology needs to move (e.g., Cicchetti et al., 1995; Greenberg, 1999).

Within a vulnerability-stress model, attachment insecurity could be conceptualized as either the vulnerability or the stress. If insecurity is conceptualized as the vulnerability, then insecurity would lead to psychopathology in the face of another set of adverse circumstances (see Grant & McMahon, Chapter 1 of this volume). That is, insecurity would be most strongly associated with psychopathology among people facing some type of adversity. For example, an insecure person might be vulnerable because of negative working models, poor emotion regulation, or poor interpersonal functioning, as we suggested earlier in this chapter. However, these vulnerabilities might result in symptoms only when people are faced with challenging experiences that would require more adaptive behavior, such as more positive expectations, better coping ability and mood regulation, or better support seeking or provision. Of course, many circumstances demand such behaviors, which may be why insecurity is so consistently associated with psychopathology. Therefore, the experience of events that occur regularly over the life course, such as significant life stressors, developmental transitions, and interpersonal relationships, could interact with insecurity to increase risk for psychopathology (e.g., Hammen, 1991).

Insecurity could also be conceptualized as the stressor. For example, among people who are genetically predisposed to psychopathology (see Lemery & Doelger, Chapter 7 of this volume, for discussion of genetic vulnerability) or who have particular temperaments (see Tackett & Krueger, Chapter 8 of this volume, for discussion of temperament vulnerability) that put them at risk, attachment insecurity could be viewed as the stressor that allows the disorder to manifest. For instance, children who show behaviorally inhibited temperaments (e.g., who are shy, fearful, and not approach oriented) are at risk for anxiety disorders (e.g., Biederman, Rosenbaum, Bolduc-Murphy, & Faraone, 1993). This vulnerability, when combined with, for example, an attachment relationship characterized by poor secure-base functioning (e.g., caregiver unavailability, low proximity seeking, fear of rejection), could increase the likelihood that children would develop symptoms of social anxiety or avoidant personality disorders. This notion is consistent with Paris's (1998) model of how insecure attachment functions as a stressor to predict personality disorders in the face of early maladaptive traits. This notion is also consistent with research that suggests that match or fit between child temperament and parenting style best determines adaptive child development (e.g., Kochanska, 1995). Environmental factors could also function as vulnerabilities, and their impact on child outcome may be moderated by attachment security. For example, Graham and Easterbrooks (2000) found that attachment security moderated the association between economic risk and depression, with secure attachment protecting against the adverse effect of economic risk.

As noted throughout the chapter, a few studies have begun to test such models, but most have not. Perhaps the disorder for which the literature is most evolved is depression, where a few studies of vulnerability-stress models exist (e.g., Besser & Priel, 2003; Graham & Easterbrooks, 2000; Hammen et al., 1995) and where researchers have theorized about mechanisms of the association between insecurity and depression. Theory is somewhat more evolved with regard to personality disorders as well. However, much fewer studies exist. Clearly, then, our understanding of how attachment insecurity confers risk for psychopathology would benefit from more refined models of their association and from direct tests of those models.

Although it is tempting to try to provide a refined vulnerability-stress model that could be used to examine the conditions under which attachment insecurity and psychopathology are associated, it would be unwise to do so for a number of reasons. Most important, as we hope this chapter has made clear, there are numerous complexities involved in determining how, when, and what type of insecurity is related to which type of psychopathology, not only across disorders, but also within disorders. As such, no single vulnerability-stress model will apply to all circumstances. As our review highlights, attachment insecurity can put people at risk for various types of symptoms through a set of core maladaptive processes, which may render people unable to successfully manage stress or other challenges in their lives (or, which may cause stress and other challenges). From a vulnerability-stress perspective, researchers must now face the challenge of identifying which specific conditions will be most likely to interact with insecurity (and which type) to lead to risk for particular types of symptoms.

REFERENCES

Aguilar, B., Sroufe, L. A., Egeland, B., & Carlson, E. (2000). Distinguishing the early-onset/persistent and adolescence-onset antisocial behavior types: From birth to 16 years. *Development and Psychopathology, 12,* 109–132.

Ainsworth, M. D. S., Blehar, M. C., Waters, E., & Wall, S. (1978). *Patterns of attachment: A psychological study of the strange situation.* Hillsdale, NJ: Lawrence Erlbaum.

Allen, J. P., Hauser, S. T., & Borman-Spurrell, E. (1996). Attachment theory as a framework for understanding sequelae of severe adolescent psychopathology: An 11-year follow-up study. *Journal of Consulting and Clinical Psychology, 64,* 254–263.

Arbona, C., & Power, T. G. (2003). Parental attachment, self-esteem, and antisocial behaviors among African American, European American, and Mexican American adolescents. *Journal of Counseling Psychology, 50,* 40–51.

Armsden, G. C., McCauley, E., Greenberg, M. T., Burke, P. M., & Mitchell, J. R. (1990). Parent and peer attachment in early adolescent depression. *Journal of Abnormal Child Psychology, 18,* 683–697.

Armstrong, J. G., & Roth, D. M. (1989). Attachment separation difficulties in eating disorders: A preliminary investigation. *International Journal of Eating Disorders, 8,* 141–155.

Bartholomew, K. (1990). Avoidance of intimacy: An attachment perspective. *Journal of Social and Personal Relationships, 7,* 147–178.

Benjamin, L. S. (1993). *Interpersonal diagnosis and treatment of personality disorders.* New York: Guilford Press.

Besser, A., & Priel, B. (2003). A multisource approach to self-critical vulnerability to depression: The moderating role of attachment. *Journal of Personality, 71,* 515–555.

Biederman, J., Rosenbaum, J. F., Bolduc-Murphy, E. A., & Faraone, S. V. (1993). A 3-year follow-up of children with and without behavioral inhibition. *Journal of the American Academy of Child & Adolescent Psychiatry, 32,* 814–821.

Bifulco, A., Moran, P. M., Ball, C., & Bernazzani, O. (2002). Adult attachment style: I. Its relationship to clinical depression. *Social Psychiatry and Psychiatric Epidemiology, 37,* 50–59.

Bowlby, J. (1969). *Attachment and loss: Vol. 1. Attachment.* New York: Basic Books.

Bowlby, J. (1973). *Attachment and loss: Vol. 2. Separation: Anxiety and anger.* New York: Basic Books.

Bowlby, J. (1977) The making and breaking of affectional bonds. *British Journal of Psychiatry, 130,* 201–210, 421–431.

Bowlby, J. (1980). *Attachment and loss: Vol. 3. Loss.* New York: Basic Books.

Bowlby, J. (1982). Attachment and loss: Retrospect and prospect. *American Journal of Orthopsychiatry, 52,* 664–678.

Bradley, S. J. (2000). *Affect regulation and the development of psychopathology.* New York: Guilford Press.

Brennan, K. A., & Shaver, P. R. (1995). Dimensions of adult attachment, affect regulation, and romantic relationship functioning. *Personality and Social Psychology Bulletin, 21,* 267–283.

Brennan, K. A., & Shaver, P. R. (1998). Attachment styles and personality disorders: Their connections to each other and to parental divorce, parental death, and perceptions of parental caregiving. *Journal of Personality, 66,* 835–878.

Broberg, A. G., Hjalmers, I., & Nevonen, L. (2001). Eating disorders, attachment and interpersonal difficulties: A comparison between 18- to 24-year-old patients and normal controls. *European Eating Disorders Review, 9,* 381–396.

Bruch, H. (1973). *Eating disorders.* New York: Basic Books.

Bruch, H. (1978). *The golden cage: The enigma of anorexia nervosa.* Cambridge, MA: Harvard University Press.

Burge, D., Hammen, C., Davila, J., Daley, S. E., Paley, B., Lindberg, N., et al. (1997). The relationship between attachment cognitions and psychological adjustment in late adolescent women. *Development and Psychopathology, 9,* 151–167.

Candelori, C., & Ciocca, A. (1998). Attachment and eating disorders. In P. Bria, A. Ciocca, & S. De Risio (Eds.), *Psychotherapeutic issues in eating disorders: Models, methods, and results* (pp. 139–153). Rome: Società Editrice Universo.

Carnelley, K. B., Pietromonaco, P. R., & Jaffe, K. (1994). Depression, working models of others, and relationship functioning. *Journal of Personality and Social Psychology, 66,* 127–140.

Cassidy, J. (1995). Attachment and generalized anxiety disorder. In D. Cicchetti & S. Toth (Eds.), *Emotion, cognition, and representation* (pp. 343–370). Rochester, NY: University of Rochester Press.

Cicchetti, D., Toth, S. L., & Lynch, M. (1995). Bowlby's dream comes full circle: The application of attachment theory to risk and psychopathology. In T. H. Ollendick & R. J. Prinz (Eds.), *Advances in clinical child psychology* (Vol. 17, pp. 1–75). New York: Plenum Press.

Cole-Detke, H., & Kobak, R. (1996). Attachment processes in eating disorder and depression. *Journal of Consulting and Clinical Psychology, 64,* 282–290.

Cooper, M. L., Shaver, P. R., & Collins, N. L. (1998). Attachment styles, emotion regulation, and adjustment in adolescence. *Journal of Personality and Social Psychology, 74,* 1380–1397.

Coyne, J. C. (1976). Towards an interactional model of depression. *Psychiatry, 39,* 28–40.

Cummings, E. M., & Cicchetti, D. (1990). Toward a transactional model of relations between attachment and depression. In M. T. Greenberg, D. Cicchetti, & E. M. Cummings (Eds.), *Attachment in the preschool years: Theory, research, and intervention* (pp. 339–372). Chicago: University of Chicago Press.

Davila, J., Bradbury, T. N., Cohan, C. L., & Tochluk, S. (1997). Marital functioning and depressive symptoms: Evidence for a stress generation model. *Journal of Personality and Social Psychology, 73,* 849–861.

de Ruiter, C., & van Ijzendoorn, M. H. (1992). Agoraphobia and anxious-ambivalent attachment: An integrative review. *Journal of Anxiety Disorders, 6,* 365–381.

Dodge, K. A. (1980). Social cognition and children's aggressive behavior. *Child Development, 51,* 162–170.

Dozier, M. (1990). Attachment organization and treatment use for adults with serious psychopathological disorders. *Development and Psychopathology, 2,* 47–60.

Dozier, M., Stevenson, A. L., Lee, S. W., & Velligan, D. I. (1991). Attachment organization and familial overinvolvement for adults with serious psychopathological disorders. *Development and Psychopathology, 3,* 475–489.

Dozier, M., Stovall, K. C., & Albus, K. E. (1999). Attachment and psychopathology in adulthood. In J. Cassidy & P. R. Shaver (Eds.), *Handbook of attachment: Theory, research, and clinical applications* (pp. 497–519). New York: Guilford Press.

Duggan, E. S., & Brennan, K. A. (1994). Social avoidance and its relation to Bartholomew's adult attachment typology. *Journal of Social and Personal Relationships, 11,* 147–153.

Eng, W., Heimberg, R. G., Hart, T. A., Schneier, F. R., & Liebowitz, M. R. (2001). Attachment in individuals with social anxiety disorder: The relationship among adult attachment styles, social anxiety, and depression. *Emotion, 1,* 365–380.

Enns, M. W., Cox, B. J., & Clara, I. (2002). Parental bonding and adult psychopathology: Results from the US national comorbidity survey. *Psychological Medicine, 32,* 997–1008.

Evans, L., & Wertheim, E. H. (1998). Intimacy patterns and relationship satisfaction of women with eating problems and the mediating effects of depression, trait anxiety and social anxiety. *Journal of Psychosomatic Research, 44,* 355–365.

Favazza, A. R. (1998). The coming of age of self-mutilation. *Journal of Nervous and Mental Diseases, 186,* 259–268.

Feeney, J. A. (1999). Adult romantic attachment and couple relationships. In J. Cassidy & P. R. Shaver (Eds.), *Handbook of attachment: Theory, research, and clinical applications* (pp. 355–377). New York: Guilford Press.

Foa, E. B., Franklin, M. E., Perry, K. J., & Herbert, J. D. (1996). Cognitive biases in generalized social phobia. *Journal of Abnormal Psychology, 105,* 433–439.

Fonagy, P. (1991). Thinking about thinking: Some clinical and theoretical consideration in the treatment of a borderline patient. *International Journal of Psychoanalysis, 72,* 1–18.

Fonagy, P. (1994). The theory and practice of resilience. *Journal of Child Psychology and Psychiatry, 35,* 231–257.

Fonagy, P. (1999). Attachment, the development of the self, and its pathology in personality disorders. In J. Derksen, C. Maffei, & H. Groen (Eds.), *Treatment of personality disorders* (pp. 53–68). New York: Kluwer Academic.

Fonagy, P., Leigh, T., Steele, M., Steele, H., Kennedy, R., Mattoon, G., et al. (1996). The relation of attachment status, psychiatric classification, and response to psychotherapy. *Journal of Consulting and Clinical Psychology, 64,* 22–31.

Fossati, A., Feeney, J. A., Donati, D., Donini, M., Novella, L., Bagnato, M., et al. (2003). Personality disorders and adult attachment dimensions in a mixed psychiatric sample: A multivariate study. *Journal of Nervous and Mental Disease, 191,* 30–37.

Freud, S. (1940). An outline of psychoanalysis. In J. Strachey (Ed. & Trans.), *The standard edition of the complete psychological works of Sigmund Freud* (Vol. 23, pp. 137–207). London: Hogarth Press.

Friedberg, N. L., & Lyddon, W. J. (1996). Self-other working models and eating disorders. *Journal of Cognitive Psychotherapy: An International Quarterly, 10,* 193–203.

George, C., Kaplan, N., & Main, M. (1985). *Attachment interview for adults.* Unpublished manuscript, University of California, Berkeley.

Graham, C. A., & Easterbrooks, M. A. (2000). School-aged children's vulnerability to depressive symptomatology: The role of attachment security, maternal depressive symptomatology, and economic risk. *Development and Psychopathology, 12,* 201–213.

Greenberg, M. T. (1999). Attachment and psychopathology in childhood. In J. Cassidy & P. R. Shaver (Eds.), *Handbook of attachment: Theory, research, and clinical applications* (pp. 469–496). New York: Guilford Press.

Greenberg, M. T., Speltz, M. L., & DeKlyen, M. (1993). The role of attachment in the early development of disruptive behavior problems. *Development and Psychopathology, 5,* 191–213.

Greenman, D. A., Gunderson, J. G., Cane, M., & Saltzman, P. R. (1986). An examination of the borderline diagnosis in children. *American Journal of Psychiatry, 143,* 998–1003.

Hammen, C. (1991). The generation of stress in the course of unipolar depression. *Journal of Abnormal Psychology, 100,* 555–561.

Hammen, C. L., Burge, D., Daley, S. E., Davila, J., Paley, B., & Rudolph, K. D. (1995). Interpersonal attachment cognitions and prediction of symptomatic responses to interpersonal stress. *Journal of Abnormal Psychology, 104,* 436–443.

Hankin, B. L., Kassel, J. D., & Abela, J. R. Z. (2005). Adult attachment styles and specificity of emotional distress: Prospective investigations of cognitive risk and interpersonal stress generation as mediating mechanisms. *Personality and Social Psychology Bulletin, 31,* 136–151.

Hazan, C., & Shaver, P. R. (1987). Romantic love conceptualized as an attachment process. *Journal of Personality and Social Psychology, 52,* 511–524.

Hazan, C., & Shaver, P. (1994). Attachment as an organizational framework for research on close relationships. *Psychological Inquiry, 5,* 1–22.

Heard, D. H., & Lake, B. (1986). The attachment dynamic in adult life. *British Journal of Psychiatry, 149,* 430–438.

Herman, J. L., Perry, J. C., & van der Kolk, B. A. (1989). Childhood trauma in borderline personality disorder. *American Journal of Psychiatry, 146,* 490–495.

Kenny, M. E., & Hart, K. (1992). Relationship between parental attachment and eating disorders in an inpatient and a college sample. *Journal of Counseling Psychology, 39,* 521–526.

Killen, J. D., Taylor, C. B., Hayward, C., Wilson, D. M., Hammer, L. D., Robinson, T. N., et al. (1994). The pursuit of thinness and onset of eating disorder symptoms in a community sample of adolescent girls: A three-year prospective analysis. *International Journal of Eating Disorders, 16,* 227–238.

Kobak, R. R., & Sceery, A. (1988). Attachment in late adolescence: Working models, affect regulation, and representations of self and others. *Child Development, 59,* 135–146.

Kobak, R. R., Sudler, N., & Gamble, W. (1991). Attachment and depressive symptoms during adolescence: A developmental pathways analysis. *Development and Psychopathology, 3,* 461–474.

Kochanska, G. (1995). Children's temperament, mother's discipline, and security of attachment: Multiple pathways to emerging internalization. *Child Development, 66,* 597–615.

LaFreniere, P. J., & Sroufe, L. A. (1985). Profiles of peer competence in the preschool: Interrelations between measures, influence of social ecology, and relation to attachment history. *Developmental Psychology, 21,* 56–69.

Levy, K. N. (2004, April). *Change in relationship representations in treated patients diagnosed with borderline personality disorder.* Presented in the Relationship Concentration Colloquia, Department of Psychology, State University of New York at Stony Brook.

Lewis, M., Feiring, C., McGuffog, C., & Jaskir, J. (1984). Predicting psychopathology in six-year-olds from early social relations. *Child Development, 55,* 123–136.

Linehan, M. (1993). *Cognitive-behavioral treatment of borderline personality disorder.* New York: Guilford Press.

Livesley, W. J., Jackson, D. N., & Schroeder, M. L. (1992). Factorial structure of traits delineating personality disorders in clinical and general population samples. *Journal of Abnormal Psychology, 101,* 432–440.

Ludolph, P. S., Westen, D., Misle, B., Jackson, A., Wixon, J., & Wiss, F. C. (1990). The borderline diagnosis in adolescents: Symptoms and developmental history. *American Journal of Psychiatry, 147,* 470–476.

Lyddon, W. J., & Sherry, A. (2001). Development of personality styles: An attachment theory conceptualization of personality disorders. *Journal of Counseling and Development, 79,* 405–414.

Lynch, M., & Cicchetti, D. (1991). Patterns of relatedness in maltreated and nonmaltreated children: Connections among multiple representational models. *Development and Psychopathology, 3,* 207–226.

Lyons-Ruth, K., & Jacobvitz, D. (1999). Attachment disorganization: Unresolved loss, relational violence, and lapses in behavioral and attentional strategies. In J. Cassidy & P. R. Shaver (Eds.), *Handbook of attachment: Theory, research, and clinical applications* (pp. 520–554). New York: Guilford Press.

Main, M., & Solomon, J. (1986). Discovery of a new, insecure-disorganized/disoriented attachment pattern. In T. B. Brazelton & M. W. Yogman (Eds.), *Affective development in infancy* (pp. 95–124). Norwood, NJ: Ablex.

Manassis, K., Bradley, S., Goldberg, S., Hood, J., & Swinson, R. P. (1994). Attachment in mothers with anxiety disorders and their children. *Journal of the American Academy of Child and Adolescent Psychiatry, 33,* 1106–1113.

Meyer, B., Pilkonis, P. A., Proietti, J. M., Heape, C., & Egan, M. (2001). Attachment styles and personality disorders as predictors of symptom course. *Journal of Personality Disorders, 15,* 371–389.

Mickelson, K. D., Kessler, R. C., & Shaver, P. R. (1997). Adult attachment in a nationally representative sample. *Journal of Personality and Social Psychology, 73,* 1092–1106.

Mikulincer, M., & Orbach, I. (1995). Attachment styles and repressive defensiveness: The accessibility and architecture of affective memories. *Journal of Personality and Social Psychology, 68,* 917–925.

Moffitt, T. E. (1993). Adolescence-limited and life-course-persistent antisocial behavior: A developmental taxonomy. *Psychological Review, 100,* 674–710.

Moffitt, T. E., Caspi, A., Harrington, H., & Milne, B. J. (2002). Males on the life-course-persistent and adolescence-limited antisocial pathways: Follow-up at age 26 years. *Development and Psychopathology, 14,* 179–207.

Muris, P., Mayer, B., & Meesters, C. (2000). Self-reported attachment style, anxiety, and depression in children. *Social Behavior and Personality, 28,* 157–162.

Muris, P., Meesters, C., van Melick, M., & Zwambag, L. (2001). Self-reported attachment style, attachment quality, and symptoms of anxiety and depression in young adolescents. *Personality and Individual Differences, 30,* 809–818.

Murphy, B., & Bates, G. W. (1997). Adult attachment style and vulnerability to depression. *Personality and Individual Differences, 22,* 835–844.

Nakashi-Eisikovits, O., Dutra, L., & Westen, D. (2002). Relationship between attachment patterns and personality pathology in adolescents. *Journal of the American Academy of Child and Adolescent Psychiatry, 41,* 1111–1123.

Nickell, A. D., Waudby, C. J., & Trull, T. J. (2002). Attachment, parental bonding and borderline personality disorder features in young adults. *Journal of Personality Disorders, 16,* 148–159.

O'Kearney, R. (1996). Attachment disruption in anorexia nervosa and bulimia nervosa: A review of theory and empirical research. *International Journal of Eating Disorders, 20,* 115–127.

Paris, J. (1998). Anxious traits, anxious attachment, and anxious-cluster personality disorders. *Harvard Review of Psychiatry, 6,* 142–148.

Paris, J. (2004). Half in love with easeful death: The meaning of chronic suicidality in borderline personality disorder. *Harvard Review of Psychiatry, 12,* 42–48.

Patrick, M., Hobson, R. P., Castle, D., Howard, R., & Maughan, B. (1994). Personality disorder and the mental representation of early social experience. *Development and Psychopathology, 6,* 375–388.

Perry, D. G., Perry, L. C., & Boldizar, J. P. (1990). Learning and aggression. In M. Lewis & S. M. Miller (Eds.), *Handbook of developmental psychopathology* (pp. 135–144). New York: Plenum Press.

Pianta, R. C., Egeland, B., & Adam, E. K. (1996). Adult attachment classification and self-reported psychiatric symptoms as assessed by the Minnesota Multiphasic Personality Inventory-2. *Journal of Consulting and Clinical Psychology, 64,* 273–281.

Ramacciotti, A., Sorbello, M., Pazzagli, A., Vismara, L., Mancone, A., & Pallanti, S. (2001). Attachment processes in eating disorders. *Eating and Weight Disorders, 6,* 166–170.

Reinecke, M. A., & Rogers, G. M. (2001). Dysfunctional attitudes and attachment style among clinically depressed adults. *Behavioural and Cognitive Psychotherapy, 29,* 129–141.

Renken, B., Egeland, B., Marvinney, D., Mangelsdorf, S., & Sroufe, L. A. (1989). Early childhood antecedents of aggression and passive-withdrawal in early elementary school. *Journal of Personality, 57,* 257–281.

Roberts, J. E., Gotlib, I. H., & Kassel, J. D. (1996). Adult attachment security and symptoms of depression: The mediating roles of dysfunctional attitudes and low self-esteem. *Journal of Personality and Social Psychology, 70,* 310–320.

Rosenstein, D. S., & Horowitz, H. A. (1996). Adolescent attachment and psychopathology. *Journal of Consulting and Clinical Psychology, 64,* 244–253.

Rutter, M., & Sroufe, L. A. (2000). Developmental psychopathology: Concepts and challenges. *Development and Psychopathology, 12,* 265–296.

Sack, A., Sperling, M. B., Fagen, G., & Foelsch, P. (1996). Attachment style, history, and behavioral contrasts for a borderline and normal sample. *Journal of Personality Disorders, 10,* 88–102.

Saltzman, J. (1996). Primary attachment in female adolescents: Association of depression, self-esteem, and maternal identification. *Psychiatry, 59,* 20–33.

Schneider-Rosen, K. (1990). The developmental reorganization of attachment relationships: Guidelines for classification beyond infancy. In M. T. Greenberg & D. Cicchetti (Eds.), *Attachment in the preschool years: Theory, research, and intervention* (pp. 185–220). Chicago: University of Chicago Press.

Shapiro, E. R. (1978). The psychodynamics and developmental psychology of the borderline patient: A review of the literature. *American Journal of Psychiatry, 135,* 1305–1315.

Sharpe, T. M., Killen, J. D., Bryson, S. W., Shisslak, C. M., Estes, L. S., Gray, N., et al. (1998). Attachment style and weight concerns in preadolescents and adolescent girls. *International Journal of Eating Disorders, 23,* 39–44.

Shaver, P. R., & Clark, C. L. (1994). The psychodynamics of adult romantic attachment. In J. M. Masling & R. F. Bornstein (Eds.), *Empirical perspective on object relations theory* (pp. 105–156). Washington, DC: American Psychological Association.

Shaver, P. R., & Hazan, C. (1993). Adult romantic attachment: Theory and evidence. *Advances in Personal Relationships, 4,* 29–70.

Sloman, L., Gilbert, P., & Hasey, G. (2003). Evolved mechanisms in depression: The role and interaction of attachment and social rank in depression. *Journal of Affective Disorders, 74,* 107–121.

Soloff, P., & Millward, J. (1983). Developmental histories of borderline patients. *Comprehensive Psychiatry, 24,* 574–588.

Speltz, M. L., DeKlyen, M., & Greenberg, M. T. (1999). Attachment in boys with early onset conduct problems. *Development and Psychopathology, 11,* 269–285.

Sperry, L., & Mosak, H. H. (1993). Personality disorders. In L. Sperry & J. Carlson (Eds.), *Psychopathology and psychotherapy: From diagnosis to treatment* (pp. 299–367). Philadelphia: Accelerated Development.

Sroufe, L. A. (1983). Infant-caregiver attachment and patterns of adaptation in preschool: The roots of maladaptation and competence. In M. Perlmutter (Ed.), *Minnesota symposia in child psychology* (Vol. 16). Hillsdale, NJ: Lawrence Erlbaum.

Sroufe, L. A., Carlson, E. A., Levy, A. K., & Egeland, B. (1999). Implications of attachment theory for developmental psychopathology. *Development and Psychopathology, 11,* 1–13.

Sroufe, L. A., & Waters, E. (1977). Attachment as an organizational construct. *Child Development, 48,* 1184–1199.

Strober, M., & Humphrey, L. (1987). Familial contributions to the etiology and course of anorexia nervosa and bulimia. *Journal of Consulting and Clinical Psychology, 55,* 654–659.

Strodl, E., & Noller, P. (2003). The relationship of adult attachment dimensions to depression and agoraphobia. *Personal Relationships, 10,* 171–185.

Sund, A. M., & Wichstrom, L. (2002). Insecure attachment as a risk factor for future depressive symptoms in early adolescence. *Journal of the American Academy of Child and Adolescent Psychiatry, 41,* 1478–1486.

Thompson-Pope, S. K., & Turkat, I. D. (1993). Schizotypal, schizoid, paranoid, and avoidant personality disorders. In P. B. Sutker & H. E. Adams (Eds.), *Comprehensive handbook of psychopathology* (2nd ed., pp. 411–434). New York: Plenum Press.

Vertue, F. M. (2003). From adaptive emotion to dysfunction: An attachment perspective on social anxiety disorder. *Personality and Social Psychology Review, 7,* 170–191.

Vivona, J. M. (2000). Parental attachment styles of late adolescents: Qualities of attachment relationships and consequences for adjustment. *Journal of Counseling Psychology, 47,* 316–329.

Ward, A., Ramsay, R., & Treasure, J. (2000). Attachment research in eating disorders. *British Journal of Medical Psychology, 73,* 35–51.

Ward, A., Ramsay, R., Turnbull, S., Benedettini, M., & Treasure, J. (2000). Attachment patterns in eating disorders: Past in present. *International Journal of Eating Disorders, 28,* 370–376.

Ward, A., Ramsay, R., Turnbull, S., Steele, M., Steele, H., & Treasure, J. (2001). Attachment in anorexia nervosa: A transgenerational perspective. *British Journal of Medical Psychology, 74,* 497–505.

Warren, S. L., Huston, L., Egeland, B., & Sroufe, L. A. (1997). Child and adolescent anxiety disorders and early attachment. *Journal of the American Academy of Child and Adolescent Psychiatry, 36,* 637–644.

Waters, E. (1997, April). *The secure base concept in Bowlby's theory and current research.* Paper presented at the Society for Research in Child Development, Washington, DC.

Weinfield, N. S., Sroufe, L. A., Egeland, B., & Carlson, E. A. (1999). The nature of individual differences in infant-caregiver attachment. In J. Cassidy & P. R. Shaver (Eds.), *Handbook of attachment: Theory, research, and clinical applications* (pp. 68–88). New York: Guilford Press.

West, M., & George, C. (2002). Attachment and dysthymia: The contributions of preoccupied attachment and agsency of self to depression in women. *Attachment and Human Development, 4,* 278–293.

West, M., Keller, A., Links, P. S., & Patrick, J. (1993). Borderline disorder and attachment theory. *Canadian Journal of Psychiatry, 38,* 16–22.

West, M., Rose, S., & Sheldon-Keller, A. (1994). Assessment of patterns of insecure attachment in adults and application to dependent and schizoid personality disorders. *Journal of Personality Disorders, 8,* 249–256.

West, M., & Sheldon, A. (1988). Classification of pathological attachment patterns in adults. *Journal of Personality Disorders, 2,* 153–159.

West, M., & Sheldon-Keller, A. E. (1994). *Patterns of relating: An adult attachment perspective.* New York: Guilford Press.

Westen, D. (1991). Cognitive-behavioral interventions in the psychoanalytic psychotherapy of borderline personality disorders. *Clinical Psychology Review, 11,* 211–230.

Zanarini, M. C., Frankenburg, F. R., Hennen, J., & Silk, K. R. (2003). The longitudinal course of borderline psychopathology: 6-year prospective follow-up of the phenomenology of borderline personality disorder. *American Journal of Psychiatry, 160,* 274–283.

Zanarini, M. C., Gunderson, J. G., Marion, M. F., & Schwartz, E. O. (1989). Childhood experiences of borderline patients. *Comprehensive Psychiatry, 30,* 18–25.

Part III

DISORDERS

CHAPTER 10

Depression From Childhood Through Adolescence and Adulthood

A Developmental Vulnerability and Stress Perspective

BENJAMIN L. HANKIN AND JOHN R. Z. ABELA

Depression is one of the most commonly occurring of the major psychopathologies. It is a prototypical multifactorial disorder that profoundly affects individuals' emotions, thoughts, sense of self, behaviors, interpersonal relations, physical functioning, biological processes, work productivity, and overall life satisfaction. Indeed, given the multiple effects that depression has, it has been ranked as the fourth leading cause of disability and premature death worldwide (Murray & Lopez, 1996). There are clearly numerous developmental pathways by which certain individuals have greater liability to experience elevations in depression, including various risk factors such as negative life events, predisposing genetic influences, disturbed family environment, particular personality traits, environmental adversities, other emotional and behavioral symptoms and problems, cognitive influences, interpersonal behaviors, and biological factors. Recently, the importance of combining these disparate risk factors and etiological processes together into a coherent, integrative model has been recognized as various authors have reviewed the diverse risk factors and processes that may culminate in the development of depression over time (see Birmaher et al., 1996; Garber, 2000; Goodyer, 2001a; Hammen & Rudolph, 2003; Hankin & Abramson, 2001, for pertinent, integrative reviews).

In this chapter, we first review recent, relevant facts on the development of depression, including definitions, diagnostic criteria, classification issues, and important epidemiological findings in order to delineate and characterize what depression is over development and how it unfolds descriptively across the life span. Next, we review separately etiological causes, risk factors, and processes for depression, including the influence of stressors and the various individual vulnerabilities discussed in Part II of this book. Last, we present an integrative, coherent theoretical model based on principles of developmental psychopathology (Rutter & Sroufe, 2000) that may explain many of the facts of depression reviewed in the first section.

DEFINITIONS, DIAGNOSTIC CRITERIA, AND CLASSIFICATION ISSUES IN DEPRESSION

According to the official psychiatric classification system (the *Diagnostic and Statistical Manual of Mental Disorders,* 4th edition [*DSM-IV-TR*]; American Psychiatric Association [APA], 2000), an episode of major depression can be diagnosed with the same symptoms in childhood and adolescence as in adulthood, except that irritability can be applied as a mood symptom along with depressed, sad mood and anhedonia in youth. The *DSM-IV-TR* states that dysthymia in youth has the same symptom profile as in adults, but there is a minimum 1-year duration in youth compared with 2 years in adulthood. Other research suggests that there is little difference between major depressive disorder and dysthymia in youth in terms of clinical course, impairment, or demographic factors except that dysthymia tends to precede major depression (Goodman, Schwab-Stone, Lahey, Shaffer, & Jensen, 2000). Thus, it seems that major depression and dysthymia in youth are fairly similar psychiatric disorders, although those youth with "double depression" (both major depression and dysthymia) exhibit greater impairment. Based on this similarity, we will review evidence about the development of depression generally, as opposed to major depressive episodes or dysthymia specifically.

In contrast to the assertion in *DSM-IV-TR* (APA, 2000) that the structure and nature of depression in youth is largely the same as in adults, research by developmental psychopathologists has suggested that depression may differ given the cognitive, social, emotional, and biological changes that transpire over time throughout childhood and adolescence (Cicchetti & Toth, 1998; Weiss & Garber, 2003). The specific symptoms that comprise depression and influence its phenomenological manifestation may differ developmentally because (a) younger children may not have developed the requisite cognitive, social, emotional, or biological capacities to experience certain typical adult depressive symptoms, and (b) the causes or consequences of depression may change across different developmental periods.

It is fundamentally essential to know whether the structure and nature of depression are the same across development, because such knowledge influences our understanding of how vulnerability and stress factors may transact over time to affect the development of depression over the life span. Despite the importance of this question, surprisingly little research has systematically addressed whether the symptoms and structure of depression are the same in children, adolescents, and adults. Indeed, a recent review examining this issue suggested that "it may be premature to conclude that depression is developmentally isomorphic at either the symptom or syndrome level" for children, adolescents, and adults (Weiss & Garber, 2003, p. 423). However, this review and other previous research (e.g., Carlson & Kashani, 1988; Kovacs, 1996; Ryan et al., 1987) suggest that very young children, especially preschoolers, tend not to report depressed mood or hopelessness and that younger children are more likely to describe somatic symptoms of depression. Other symptoms, such as anhedonia and psychomotor retardation, tend to increase and become more prevalent with the transition from childhood into adolescence, whereas the somatic complaints and appearing depressed tend to decrease with age. Still, these studies have not been able to determine conclusively whether the symptoms and structure of depression differ across development. It is essential that further research investigate the critical question of whether depression is the same in children, adolescents, and adults, because the limited existing research suggests that there may be a need for changes or age-appropriate modifications to make the diagnostic criteria for depression developmentally sensitive over the life span. Importantly, though, it is clear that children can be identified who fit adult *DSM-IV-TR* (APA, 2000) diagnostic criteria.

In the developmental literature, distinctions have been made between different terms and meanings of *depression* (Compas, Ey, & Grant, 1993). Depression can be considered as a mood symptom (e.g., sad or unhappy), as a syndrome of mood and other cohering symptoms that statistically go together (e.g., an anxious/depressed syndrome; Achenbach, 1991), and as a disorder with official criteria and duration that must be met for a diagnosis (e.g., a categorical diagnosis of major depression in *DSM-IV-TR*, APA, 2000).

Another important issue regarding the definition and classification of depression is whether the latent structure of depression is best considered as a category or a dimension. When viewed dimensionally, depression differs quantitatively by degree (i.e., individuals are more or less depressed); there is no sharp boundary between individuals as "normal" or abnormally "depressed." When viewed categorically, depression differs in kind in a qualitatively distinct way, such that individuals either are depressed or are not. Despite considerable debate and discussion on this issue (e.g., Flett, Vredenburg, & Krames, 1997), only a few methodologically sophisticated studies have empirically addressed this question with adults (e.g., A. M. Ruscio & J. Ruscio, 2002; J. Ruscio & A. M. Ruscio, 2000) and youth (e.g., Hankin, Fraley, Lahey, & Waldman, in press). For the most part, these studies show that the structure of depression is dimensional in children, adolescents, and adults, although there is some question whether the more extreme forms of depression (e.g., melancholic depression) may be qualitatively different from normal mood (e.g., Ambrosini, Bennett, Cleland, & Haslam, 2002; Beach & Amir, 2003). Thus, the preponderance of extant evidence suggests that depression varies along a continuum of affective severity. Given that the best available evidence supports the dimensional perspective, we consider and review studies on depressed mood, syndrome, and disorder over the life span to further knowledge and theory on vulnerability and stress models of depression.

EPIDEMIOLOGY OF DEPRESSION

Prevalence and Development of Depression Over the Life Course

Numerous studies have examined the prevalence rates of depression in different age groups over the life course and with different methods and samples. In our review, we emphasize community samples, which are preferable for estimating prevalence rates of depression, because samples drawn from psychiatric clinics may be biased in various ways (e.g., actively seeking treatment, exhibiting greater severity, and revealing higher comorbidity). Such biases can inflate artificially the prevalence rates of depression, thus distorting the delineation of a descriptive picture for the development of depression over the life course. Additionally, we focus more on prospective, longitudinal studies over cross-sectional research, because cross-sectional studies often average together individuals from different age groups, so it is difficult to ascertain when the rates of depression are rising throughout the life course. Piecing together different age groups culled from various cross-sectional studies can be misleading, because there are age cohort effects, such that individuals born more recently (e.g., during the Vietnam War era) exhibit higher rates of depression compared with individuals from older generations (e.g., those born during the Great Depression; see Kessler, Avenevoli, & Merikangas, 2001).

Cross-sectional studies of self-reported depressive symptomatology (i.e., less than a clinically significant depressive disorder) indicate that between 20% and 50% (Kessler et al., 2001; Petersen et al., 1993) of adolescents report significant subclinical levels of depressive symptoms. Prospective longitudinal studies of self-reported depressive symptoms show that average levels of depressive mood and symptoms rise substantially, from relatively low levels in childhood to much higher levels starting in middle adolescence (Cole, Martin, Peeke, Seroczynski, & Fier, 1999; Ge, Lorenz, Conger, Elder, & Simons, 1994; Wade, Cairney, & Pevalin, 2002; Wichstrom, 1999). It is important to note that elevated rates of depressed mood or symptoms do not merely indicate typical, benign adolescent "moodiness" or "turmoil" but rather represent a substantial risk for later clinically significant depressive disorder (e.g., Pine, E. Cohen, P. Cohen, & Brook, 1999) and impaired functioning (e.g., Gotlib, Lewinsohn, & Seeley, 1995). Indeed, the fact that depressed mood carries risk for later depression and is associated with impairment is consistent with our perspective, as reviewed above, that depression is best viewed as varying along a continuum (Lewinsohn, Solomon, Seeley, & Zeiss, 2000).

Cross-sectional studies of diagnosed clinical levels of depression show that the rates of depression are generally low in children and increase to near-adult prevalence levels in adolescence. Preadolescent school-age children tend to have low lifetime prevalence rates of depression (less than 3%) (P. Cohen, J. Cohen, Kasen, & Velez, 1993; Costello et al., 1996). Rates of depression among adolescents are generally comparable with those observed among adults. For example, results from the largest representative community study, the National Comorbidity Survey, show that the lifetime prevalence of major depression for 15- to 18-year-olds was 14% and was 11% for minor depression (Kessler et al., 1994). Various prospective, community-based studies (P. Cohen et al., 1993; Costello, Mustillo, Erkanli, Keeler, & Angold, 2003; Fergusson, Horwood, & Lynskey, 1993; Hankin et al., 1998; Reinherz, Giaconia, Lefkowitz, Pakiz, & Frost, 1993; see Kessler et al., 2001; Lewinsohn, Rohde, & Seeley, 1998, for reviews) reveal that the rates of clinical depression are generally low in childhood (e.g., 1%–3%), and then increase dramatically in middle to late adolescence, when they reach rates observed throughout adulthood (up to 17%). Figure 10.1 provides an illustration of a representative prospective birth study for the overall rates of depression from childhood to young adulthood.

Finally, most individuals experience their first depression sometime during late childhood through adolescence. Adult depression is typically preceded by youth depression. In a recent prospective follow-back study (Kim-Cohen et al., 2003) in which an entire birth cohort of individuals was followed for 26 years, of those members of the cohort who had a depressive disorder, the vast majority of adults at age 26 (75%) had already had a depressive disorder in childhood or adolescence, whereas only 25% experienced onset of depression in adulthood (ages 21–26). Similar results have been reported in other large-scale, prospective community studies (e.g., Lewinsohn, Rohde, Seeley, Klein, & Gotlib, 2000).

Gender and Ethnic Differences in Depression

It is important to describe any potential group differences in depression (e.g., gender and ethnic), because such differences can provide an important window into further understanding and revealing the causal mechanisms and vulnerability factors that etiologically contribute to depression (Hankin & Abramson, 2001; Rutter, Caspi, & Moffitt, 2003).

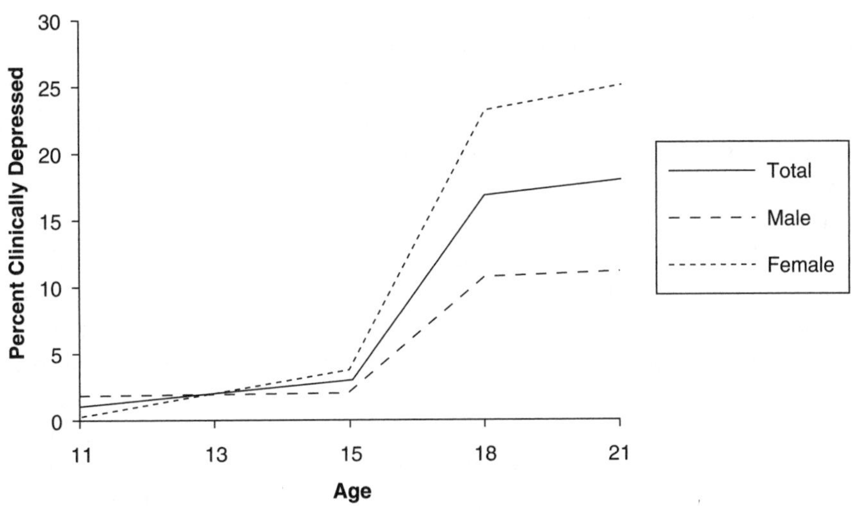

Figure 10.1 Developmental Course of Rates of Clinical Depression by Age and Gender From a Prospective Community Birth Cohort Study

SOURCE: Hankin, B. L., Abramson, L. Y., Moffitt, T. E., Silva, P. A., McGee, R., & Angell, K. A. (1998). Development of depression from preadolescence to young adulthood: Emerging gender differences in a 10-year longitudinal study. *Journal of Abnormal Psychology, 107,* 128–141. Figure reprinted with permission. Copyright 1998 by the American Psychological Association.

NOTE: There is a substantial, sixfold increase in rates of clinical depression from ages 15 to 18. Also, more girls than boys begin to become depressed starting after age 13, and girls become substantially more depressed than boys during middle to late adolescence (ages 15–18).

Approximately 25% to 40% of adolescent girls exhibit high levels of depressed mood, compared with 20% to 35% of adolescent boys (Petersen et al., 1993). Longitudinal community studies have examined the emergence of this gender difference in depressive symptoms and mood and have shown that more girls than boys report depression starting in early adolescence (around ages 12–13) (Angold, Erkanli, Silberg, Eaves, & Costello, 2002; Ge et al., 1994; Wade et al., 2002; Wichstrom, 1999; see Twenge & Nolen-Hoeksema, 2002, for a review). Longitudinal studies have also investigated the emergence of the gender difference at the level of depressive disorder (Costello et al., 2003; Hankin et al., 1998; Reinherz et al., 1993; Weissman, Warner, Wickramaratne, Moreau, & Olfson, 1997). Taken together, these studies show that more boys than girls are depressed in childhood, but more girls than boys begin to become clinically depressed after age 12–13. Further, the gender divergence in clinical depression becomes most noticeable and dramatic in middle to late adolescence. Last, the female preponderance in depression remains at a 2:1 female-to-male ratio from adolescence throughout most of adulthood (Hankin & Abramson, 1999).

Although these studies have clearly established that the gender difference in depression emerges around age 13, age is an ambiguous marker for development and may mask more accurate developmental mechanisms that hold etiological clues for explaining why more girls become depressed than boys. Pubertal development and timing has been studied. Angold, Costello, and Worthman (1998) found the gender difference in depression emerged at Tanner Stage III and was a better predictor than age alone. Moreover, girls who start puberty earlier than their peers are more likely to become depressed (Ge, Conger, & Elder, 1996, 2001; Graber, Lewinsohn, Seeley, & Brooks-Gunn, 1997).

Whereas the findings on the gender divergence in depression are fairly clear, the findings are mixed whether there are distinct ethnic and racial differences in depression. One longitudinal study of adolescents (7th to 12th graders) found that nonwhite youth reported more depressive symptoms than did whites (Rushton, Forcier, & Schectman, 2002). In a more specific examination of race, Costello and colleagues (1996) found few differences in depression levels between European American and African American youth. A large study of children in sixth to eighth grades (R. E. Roberts, C. R. Roberts, & Chen, 1997) found that most ethnic groups exhibited comparable rates of major depression except that youth of Mexican descent had the highest rates of depression. African American girls do not exhibit similar elevations in depressive symptoms from pre- to postpuberty as European American girls do (Hayward, Gotlib, Schraedley, & Litt, 1999). Last, the largest study of ethnic and racial differences among adults showed that African Americans were significantly less depressed compared with whites or Latinos (Kessler et al., 1994). In sum, there is currently no clear consensus on ethnic differences in depression, so continued research is needed to examine how ethnicity influences depression across the life span, to consider separately how different cultural expressions may affect depression, and to explore whether possible ethnic differences in vulnerabilities and stressors influence depression.

Continuity and Recurrence of Depression Over the Life Course

Depressed mood at younger ages carries risk for development of depressive disorder later in life. For example, a prospective community study found that teacher reports at age 6 and youths' self-reports at age 9 of anxious/depressive symptoms predicted occurrence of major depressive disorder at age 21 (Reinherz, Giaconia, Hauf, Wasserman, & Paradis, 2000). However, even though there is evidence that elevations in symptoms or early onset of depression in childhood predicts an increased likelihood for depression later in life, it is important to note that most depressed prepubertal children do not grow up to become adults with major depression (Harrington, Fudge, Rutter, Pickles, & Hill, 1990; Weissman et al., 1997). Compared with the continuity of depression from childhood into adulthood, there is much stronger continuity for depression from adolescence into adulthood (Hankin et al., 1998; Lewinsohn, Allen, Seeley, & Gotlib, 1999; Pine, P. Cohen, Gurley, Brook, & Ma, 1998; Pine et al., 1999; Weissman et al.). In sum, despite documented continuity in depression from childhood into adolescence and adulthood, it appears that there are important differences between depression that arises during childhood compared with depression that develops in adolescence or adulthood (Duggal, Carlson, Sroufe, & Egeland, 2001; Jaffee et al., 2002).

Another related, well-documented fact about depression is that it is a chronic or recurrent disorder. Approximately half of individuals with a diagnosis of depression will experience a recurrence within 2 years, more than 80% within 5–7 years, and individuals who have had more than three lifetime episodes of depression are particularly likely to have another recurrence (Belsher & Costello, 1988; Boland & Keller, 2002; Coryell et al., 1994; Judd; 1997; Solomon, Haaga, & Arnow, 2001). Moreover, once individuals have had multiple recurrences, their time to experience the next recurrence decreases with each additional recurrence. Most adults experience a depressive recurrence within 5 years;

however, not all individuals who experience an episode of depression have a recurrence. Similar results have been found with community adolescents. Approximately 40% of youth will have a depression recurrence over 3–5 years (Lewinsohn, Clarke, Seeley, & Rohde, 1994; Rao, Hammen, & Daley, 1999). So, there clearly are individual differences over the life span in the likelihood of experiencing initial increases in depression as well as later recurrences. These findings for continuity and recurrence strongly suggest that there is vulnerability to depression, and potentially, some individual differences in risk factors may either be the same or different for initial depression onset versus recurrence.

Comorbidity

Depression co-occurs commonly with other disorders, especially anxiety and disruptive behavioral disorders. A meta-analysis of depression comorbidity with other common psychiatric disorders in community samples of youth provides the best evidence to date for this fact (Angold, Costello, & Erkanli, 1999). Depression is associated at greater-than-chance levels with anxiety disorders (median odds ratio = 8.2), conduct/oppositional defiant disorder (median odds ratio = 6.6), and attention deficit/hyperactivity disorder (ADHD; median odds ratio = 5.5).

Additionally, it is important to consider developmental patterns of sequential comorbidity. Children and early adolescents are more likely to have a co-occurring diagnosis of separation anxiety disorder and depression, whereas older adolescents are more likely to exhibit comorbid eating disorders and substance use problems. The well-known comorbidity of depression with anxiety and with attention deficit and externalizing behaviors appears similar throughout childhood and adolescence. In terms of temporal precedence, elevations in symptoms of or a diagnosis of anxiety often precedes the development of depressive symptoms or disorder (Avenevoli, Stolar, Li, Dierker, & Merikangas, 2001; P. Cohen et al., 1993; Cole, Peeke, Martin, Truglio, & Seroczynski, 1998; Kim-Cohen et al., 2003; Pine et al., 1998; Reinherz et al., 1993). With respect to the temporal precedence of depression comorbidity with behavioral problems, earlier externalizing behaviors tend to predict later depressive symptoms, whereas earlier depressive symptoms do not predict later externalizing behaviors (Curran & Bollen, 2001; Kim-Cohen et al.).

This comorbidity of depression with other emotional and behavior symptoms and their sequential developmental unfolding over time has important implications for the diagnostic classification of, the methodological study of, and the clues to the etiology of depression. Methodologically, both depression and its co-occurring symptoms need to be assessed in research in order to examine whether hypothesized vulnerability factors and processes predict the development of depression specifically or general, comorbid problems co-occurring alongside depression. Without measuring depression and other comorbid symptoms, it is impossible to evaluate whether vulnerabilities or stressors actually predict depression or are only associated with depression because of its overlap with other symptoms and disorders. Etiologically, the developmental patterns of comorbidity suggest various plausible causal models, including (a) the common-cause hypothesis, in which some etiological factors may be shared among co-occurring disorders; (b) the etiologically specific-cause hypothesis, in which some etiological vulnerability factors or types of stressors may be relatively specific to a particular disorder; and (c) the disorder causal hypothesis, in which elevations in symptoms of one disorder (e.g., anxiety) may directly contribute to elevations in another disorder (e.g., depression) later in the life course. Importantly for the present chapter, it is vital that coherent vulnerability-stress models of depression be able to explain and account for the comorbidity of depression with other problem behaviors as well as the developmental unfolding of comorbid depression patterns over time.

VULNERABILITY AND STRESS THEORETICAL MODELS FOR THE DEVELOPMENT OF DEPRESSION

We believe that any coherent, integrative theoretical model of depression needs to be able to account for the facts of depression that we just reviewed, including the developmental timeline for the development of depression, gender and ethnicity patterns in depression, and sequential developmental comorbidity patterns of depression. We believe that vulnerability and stress models of depression, grounded in developmental psychopathological principles (e.g., Rutter & Sroufe, 2000), are ideally suited to explain these big facts of depression and are capable of generating novel, testable hypotheses about depression that will advance theory and knowledge on the development of depression over the life course. In sum, there are several major facts of depression that any comprehensive theoretical model of depression should be able to explain. These include (but are not limited to) the following: (a) depression is a common disorder, (b) rates of depression rise dramatically in adolescence, (c) the gender difference in depression emerges in early adolescence and remains throughout adulthood, (d) depression tends to be a continuous and recurrent disorder starting in adolescence, (e) depression is comorbid with many other psychopathological disorders, and (f) the latent structure of depression is dimensional.

In this section, we review major theoretical models for depression vulnerabilities that have been proposed and examined. We discuss stressors first and then review those vulnerabilities that are presented and reviewed in Part II of this book, including genetic, biological, personality, cognitive, interpersonal, and attachment vulnerabilities for depression. It is important to note that we will survey the conceptual models and findings for stressors and each vulnerability separately in this section, even though it is most likely that a developmentally sensitive, integrative theoretical model can and should combine these disparate depression vulnerabilities and stressors together into a coherent vulnerability-stress model of depression. Most of the depression facts that we review are descriptive in nature and as such do not clearly indicate that any single etiological framework (e.g., biological, interpersonal, cognitive, emotional, personality, etc.) will provide a necessary and sufficient causal explanation for the development of depression. Indeed, a complete explanation of depression is likely to be multifactorial and should take a developmental psychopathological focus, given the many developmental facts suggesting that there is both continuity and change in depression over time. At the end of this chapter, we will present and review evidence for one proposed integrative, coherent, expanded vulnerability-transactional stress model (Hankin & Abramson, 2001).

Stressful Negative Life Events

Life events, particularly negative events and stressors, play a substantial contributory role in the development of depression from childhood through adulthood (G. W. Brown & Harris, 1989; Goodyer, 2001b; S. E. Meyer, Chrousos, & Gold, 2001; Monroe & Simons, 1991; see Grant & McMahon, Chapter 1 of this volume). Almost all individuals with a depressive disorder encountered at least one significant negative life event in the month prior to the onset of depression (Goodyer, 2001b). Additionally, longitudinal studies have discovered that experiencing stressors precedes the initial elevation, recurrence, and exacerbation of depression (e.g., Ge et al., 2001; Goodyer, Herbert, Tamplin, & Altham, 2000).

In addition to the perspective that stressors precede and contribute to depression, a complementary perspective suggests that the stress-depression relationship is not a static, unidirectional one, but rather a transactional process. The stress-generation hypothesis (Hammen 1991) suggests that some individuals, because of personality characteristics or behaviors, such as their being depressed, generate stressful circumstances and additional events for themselves, and these can then advance further increases in depression. In the stress-generation model, there is a distinction between independent events (fateful events that occur outside a person's control) and dependent events (those that occur partly as a result of a person's behavior or personality). Various cross-sectional studies have supported this stress-generation mechanism, especially within interpersonal relationships, by showing that depressive symptoms are associated with self-generated stressors (e.g., Rudolph & Hammen, 1999; Williamson, Birmaher, Anderson, Al-Shabbout, & Ryan, 1995). Such research, combined with the evidence that stressors contribute to depression, suggests that negative events may be a consequence as well as a cause of depression.

There are surprisingly few longitudinal studies that have shown that personality characteristics or behaviors prospectively predict the occurrence of later negative events. The available research using two–time point designs supports the hypothesis that depressive symptoms are associated with subsequently occurring negative events (L. H. Cohen, Burt, & Bjorck, 1987; Compas, Howell, Phares, Williams, & Giunta, 1989; Waaktaar, Borge, Fundingsrud, Christie, & Torgersen, 2004; Windle, 1992; Wingate & Joiner, 2004). Further, the results of a 1-year longitudinal study of children (ages 6–14) of affectively ill parents indicated that baseline cognitive and interpersonal vulnerability factors predicted greater number and objective severity of subsequent dependent interpersonal, but not dependent noninterpersonal, independent interpersonal, or independent noninterpersonal, negative events (Abela, Starrs, & Adams, 2004). Last, Daley and colleagues (1997) used a longitudinal method and interviewed late-adolescent women at three time points in 6-month intervals. The study supported the stress-generation model by demonstrating that depression at time 1 predicted an increased number of stressful life events reported at times 2 and 3.

More recent multiwave longitudinal studies provide the strongest support to date for the stress-generation hypothesis. In a three-wave, 1-year longitudinal study of adolescents (8th and 10th graders), Hankin, Roesch, Mermelstein, and Flay (2004) examined the stress-generation hypothesis using structural equation modeling to control for continuity of depression and stressors over time. Results indicated that depressive symptoms at one time point predicted later increases in objectively assessed stressors at the following time point and that stressors at the same time point were concurrently associated with depressive symptoms. Similar results were obtained in a 10-wave, 1-year longitudinal study of children (ages 6–14) of affectively ill parents (Abela, Ho, Nueslovici, & Chan, 2004). Consistent with the stress-generation hypothesis, a bidirectional relationship was found between the occurrence of negative events and increases in depressive symptoms using latent difference score analyses in structural equation modeling.

Recently, the importance of developing a taxonomy of stressors and negative life events has been emphasized (Grant et al., 2003; Grant & McMahon, Chapter 1 of this volume; McMahon, Grant, Compas, Thurm, & Ey, 2003) because not all stressors, their domain, or their context can be treated equivalently or are equally associated with risk for depression. Various subtypes of stressors (including events that are of danger to the self, danger to others, personal disappointments, and loss) have been proposed and are important to consider when examining the relation between events and emotional distress. In particular, it seems that personal disappointment and loss-related stressors are particularly associated with elevated risk for depression (Goodyer, 2001b). Research with adults showed that negative events categorized as humiliating and loss related were specifically linked with onset of depression (Kendler, Hettema, Butera, Gardner, & Prescott, 2003). Others have emphasized stressor domains such as achievement versus interpersonal. Certain types of interpersonal stressors, including romantic relationship breakups (Monroe, Rohde, Seeley, & Lewinsohn, 1999), peer rejection (Panak & Garber, 1992), and disrupted friendships (Rudolph, 2002) have been linked with depression. Other research suggests a potentially stronger association between depression and interpersonal stressors than with achievement stressors (Rudolph & Hammen, 1999).

There are developmental changes that occur in the frequency and types of stressors experienced across the life span. First, there is a developmental rise in the number of uncontrollable negative life events experienced starting after age 13, and this increasing trajectory in stressors closely parallels the rise in depressive symptoms throughout adolescence (Ge et al., 1994). Thus, the fact that stressors appear to be on an increasing trajectory from late childhood into adolescence provides a potentially important mechanism to explain why the levels of depression follow the developmental timeline described earlier. Further, adolescent girls exhibit a significantly greater increase in stressors after age 13 than do boys (Ge et al., 1994; Hankin, Roesch, et al., 2004), and this developmental timeline for the gender difference in stressors matches the emergence of the gender difference in depression. Indeed, girls' increased experience of stressors, particularly interpersonal stressors, was found to partly explain why girls are more depressed than boys (Hankin, Roesch, et al.). Second, preadolescent children tend to report stressors within the family, adolescents frequently report interpersonal and peer-related stressors, and adults tend to report achievement and work-related events (Rudolph & Hammen, 1999; Wagner & Compas, 1990). Last, it is important to consider why the number of stressors would start to rise around early adolescence and seem to peak in middle adolescence (Newcomb, Huba, & Bentler, 1981). It appears that the increasing trajectory of stressors begins around puberty, which is a transitional period in development, and transitions frequently are associated with elevated emotional distress and increases in stress (Caspi & Moffitt, 1991; Ge et al., 2001; Graber, Brooks-Gunn, & Petersen, 1996). It seems likely that as individuals encounter more negative life events as they enter and progress through adolescence, these stressors contribute to the likelihood that they will experience increased depression; this process may be particularly relevant for females.

It is clear that not everyone who experiences negative life events becomes depressed, although the majority of those individuals who are significantly depressed encountered at least one major negative life event prior to the onset of the depression. Indeed, only 20%–50% of individuals who experience severe, major negative life events develop clinically significant levels of depression (e.g., Goodyer et al., 2000; Lewinsohn, R. E. Roberts, et al., 1994). So, whereas research implicates stressors as an important contributory cause of depression, it is clear that negative life events are neither necessary nor sufficient to cause depression without some underlying vulnerability. We now turn to various depression vulnerabilities that may enhance one's risk for depression, especially in the context of stressors.

Genetics and Family History Vulnerability

One of the strongest predictors of depression in childhood or adolescence is having a parent with a history of major depression (Beardslee, Versage, & Gladstone, 1998). However, knowledge of a familial history of depression cannot disentangle whether the risk mechanisms are carried through genetic transmission, psychosocial factors associated with growing up in a family with a depressed parent, or both (Goodman & Gotlib, 2002). Fortunately, behavioral-genetic research (e.g., twin studies) can separate genetic, heritable influences from environmental (both shared and unique environmental) factors. Behavior-genetic studies with children, adolescents, and adults have found depression to be moderately heritable (see Rice, Harold, & Thapar, 2002a; Sullivan, Neale, & Kendler, 2000, for reviews; see also Lemery & Doelger, Chapter 7 of this volume). Heritability estimates for parents' rating of youths' depressive symptoms are modest to high (range 30%–80%), whereas these genetic estimates are lower for youths' own ratings of their depressive symptoms (range 15%–80%) (Rice et al., 2002a). Evidence from twin research also suggests that depressive symptoms are heritable starting in adolescence (after age 11) and continuing throughout adulthood, whereas shared common family environment, but not genetic factors, is linked with depression in childhood (before age 11; Rice et al., 2002a).

In addition to establishing a genetic risk for depression, twin studies with children, adolescents, and adults have found that the genetic vulnerability to depression partly overlaps with the genetic liability for comorbid symptoms. Among youth, the genetic liability for depression is shared with that for externalizing conduct problems (O'Connor, Neiderhiser, Reiss, Hetherington, & Plomin, 1998) and anxiety symptoms (Thapar & McGuffin, 1997). Further, recent twin research with adults (Kendler, Gardner, & Prescott, 2003) shows that the strong overlap between depression and anxiety is due to shared genetic risk, whereas the disorder specificity for anxiety and depression may best be explained by the unique environments that individuals experience. This common genetic liability to depression and overlapping emotional and behavioral problems may largely reflect other vulnerabilities, such as temperament/personality (e.g., neuroticism), which are partially heritable (S. B. Roberts & Kendler, 1999).

In addition to depression being moderately heritable, research also indicates that some of the etiological risk factors for depression are moderately heritable. The concepts of gene-environment correlations and interactions are important here (see Rutter, Pickles, Murray, & Eaves, 2001; Rutter & Silberg, 2002). Simply put, gene-environment correlations reflect the fact that genetic and environmental influences are associated, not independent. As children grow up, they are exposed to environments that are associated with their parents' genetic makeup (i.e., a passive gene-environment correlation), and youth choose particular environmental contexts (e.g., "niche fitting"), through evocative and active person-environment transactions, and these environmental exposures are influenced by the youths' genes as well as their parents' genetic makeup (see Lemery & Doelger, Chapter 7 of this volume, for greater discussion). Consistent with gene-environment correlations, behavioral-genetic research with children and adolescents (Thapar, Harold, & McGuffin, 1998; Silberg et al., 1999) and adults (Kendler, 1995; Kendler, Neale, Kessler, Heath, & Eaves, 1993) shows that the liability to experience negative events is partially heritable. Also, a twin study with adult women (Kendler & Karkowki-Shuman, 1997) found that depression was associated with exposure particularly to interpersonal negative events. Further, consistent with the developmental timeline of depression showing the large surge in depression and the emergence of the gender difference occurring in middle adolescence, a longitudinal twin study (Silberg et al.) reported that genetic vulnerabilities increased the risk for depression and for experiencing stressors for girls after, but not before, puberty. These examples provide evidence for important gene-environment correlations in that the association between depression and stressors is partly accounted for by genetic factors. Thus, depression is moderately heritable, stressors contribute to depression, and the propensity for some individuals to encounter stressors is also partially genetically mediated.

Last, gene-environment interactions refer to the idea that there is differential genetic liability to certain environmental risks. Support for this comes from a recent study reporting a gene-environment interaction between independent negative events and depressive symptoms among female adolescents (Silberg, Rutter, Neale, & Eaves, 2001). The most specific evidence to date for a gene-environment interaction that explains how some individuals, at genetic risk, become depressed in the face of stress, comes from a recent prospective birth cohort study (Caspi et al., 2003). Using molecular genetic techniques, a functional polymorphism in the promoter region of the serotonin transporter gene (*5-HTT*) interacted with the occurrence of stressors over time in adulthood to predict the onset of depression. Specifically, those individuals who had one or two copies of the short-allele form of *5-HTT* (the genetic vulnerability) and encountered more stressors over time experienced the greatest incidence of depression, even compared with adults who experienced equivalent stress levels but were homozygous for the long allele of the *5-HTT* promoter (less genetic risk).

In sum, the research to date clearly supports the perspective that there is a moderate genetic vulnerability to experience depression, but what exactly is inherited and the mechanisms by which genes influence the development of depression are currently not clear. Importantly, though, this recent report (Caspi et al., 2003) provides an important advance by demonstrating how a specific genetic risk (i.e., functional polymorphism on *5-HTT* promoter) can combine with environmental stress in a manner completely consistent with a vulnerability-stress framework.

Personality/ Temperament Vulnerability

As noted in passing above, there is also genetically influenced personality or temperamental vulnerability for depression. Depression has consistently been linked with personality traits subsumed under negative emotionality (L. A. Clark, Watson, & Mineka, 1994; Widiger, Verheul, & van den Brink, 1999). Neuroticism, or negative emotionality, reflects the extent to which an individual perceives and experiences the world as threatening or distressing (Watson, L. A. Clark, & Harkness, 1994; see Tackett & Krueger, Chapter 8 of this volume, for greater discussion). Individuals with high scores on this personality dimension are more likely to report feeling negative emotions (e.g., anxiety, depression, anger) more intensely and frequently; suffer from a wide variety of problems; feel inadequate; and experience more stressors (Watson et al.).

Empirical research indicates that personality traits, neuroticism in particular, may serve as a vulnerability to developing depression among children, adolescents, and adults (Block, Gjerde, & Block, 1991; L. A. Clark et al., 1994; Compas, Connor-Smith, & Jaser, 2004; Hirschfeld et al., 1989; Krueger, 1999, 2000; Krueger, Caspi, Moffit, Silva, & McGee, 1996; Trull & Sher, 1994) and to experiencing more stressors (Kendler, Gardner, et al., 2003; Van Os & Jones, 1999). Individuals who exhibit high neuroticism lack the emotional resilience and strength to overcome daily hassles and more severe uncontrollable traumas (J. Roberts & Monroe, 1994).

Although the majority of personality vulnerability research to date has focused on neuroticism as a predictor of depression, considerably less attention has been paid to how personality traits, such as neuroticism, may interact with other depression vulnerabilities or stressors to provide a more proximal, process-oriented mechanism to explain prospective increases in depression. Kendler and colleagues (1993) found that the strongest predictors of a major depressive episode among adults were negative life events, genetic factors, a previous depressive episode, and neuroticism. Building on this research, a recent prospective study (Lakdawalla & Hankin, 2003) with young adults showed that initial levels of neuroticism predicted the occurrence of additional stressors over a 2-year interval, and these stressors, especially when combined with high levels of cognitive vulnerability, explained the prospective association between baseline neuroticism and elevations in depressive symptoms over the 2 years. Taken together, the corpus of evidence suggests that neuroticism confers vulnerability to develop depression and may contribute to the generation of stressors or to the emergence of other vulnerabilities that more proximally predict depression.

Biological Vulnerability

Numerous aspects of biological vulnerability to depression have been investigated in children, adolescents, and adults (see Kaufman, Martin, King, & Charney, 2001; Thase, Jindal, & Howland, 2002, for reviews; see also Pihl & Nantel-Vivier, Chapter 4 of this volume). Given the multitude of biological risks that have been explored and the voluminous research, we focus our brief review on recent, developmentally informed research highlighting (a) the role of neurotransmitter and neuroendocrine dysregulations in the central nervous system in response to stressors, and (b) putative neurobiological substrates of a dysregulated brain circuit underlying depression.

Humans biologically respond to stressors in environmental context through activation of the hypothalamic-pituitary-adrenal (HPA) axis, and dysregulation of this human stress response has been implicated as a biological vulnerability to depression (Gold, Goodwin, & Chrousos, 1988; S. E. Meyer et al., 2001). In response to the perception or experience of stress, the hypothalamus releases peptides that act on the pituitary, which in turn releases hormones to control the release of cortisol from the adrenal glands. Cortisol is a stress hormone that allows the body to manage stress effectively in the short term, and growth hormone (GH) is released by the pituitary; both hormones have been used to examine whether HPA axis dysfunction is a biological vulnerability for depression. Corticotropin-releasing hormone (CRH) and norepinephrine (NE) are the core central regulators of the HPA axis; activation of CRH and NE increases behavior, arousal, and activity and interferes with vegetative functions (e.g., sleep and eating, which comprise depressive symptoms when impaired).

Most empirical studies of HPA axis dysfunction have been cross-sectional comparisons of youth with clinical depression against youth with other psychiatric symptoms or normal controls. To date, the available research with children suggests that depressed and nondepressed children do not differ on baseline cortisol levels (Ryan, 1998), and the findings are mixed when physiological challenges of the HPA axis system (e.g., dexamethasone suppression test) are used (Dahl, Kaufman, Ryan, & Perel, 1992). The HPA axis likely develops and matures from childhood through adulthood, so developmental changes in HPA axis response may explain some of the equivocal findings to date, because consistently stronger results with adults have been found (Thase et al., 2002). With respect to GH, most studies in children (e.g., W. J. Meyer et al., 1991) and adults (e.g., Dinan, 1998) have found blunted secretion in response to biological challenges. Birmaher and colleagues (2000) have found that offspring of depressed parents, who were at high risk for depression but had not yet experienced clinical depression, exhibited reduced GH response; these studies suggest that GH response may index a biological vulnerability for depression in youth.

In addition to these aspects of the biological response to stress, there are biological substrates that compose a neural circuit in the brain that has been implicated in vulnerability to depression (e.g., Davidson, Pizzagalli, Nitschke, & Putnam, 2002). The amygdala is a subcortical region of the brain that mediates fear, anxiety, and emotional memory. The mesolimbic dopamine system is involved with reward and pleasure. The prefrontal cortex helps control behavioral and affective flexibility and is involved with approach/withdrawal systems. These regions have been found to be abnormal in studies comparing depressed adults with normal controls (Davidson et al.). Also, asymmetry in electrophysiological activity in resting frontal brain activity has been used to assess a neurobiological vulnerability for depression and is probably associated mostly with potential prefrontal cortex dysfunction. Relative left-frontal underactivity compared with right-frontal activity has been associated with depression in adults and may comprise a stable biological vulnerability for depression (Davidson et al.; Tomarken & Keener, 1998). Research shows that child (Tomarken, Simien, & Garber, 1994) and infant (Dawson et al., 1997) offspring of depressed mothers, who are at high risk for depression but not yet depressed, revealed left-frontal underactivity. This suggests another potential biological vulnerability to depression.

In sum, there are theoretically exciting and empirically supported biological vulnerabilities for the development of depression. However, in contrast to some of the other vulnerabilities reviewed in this chapter, there are inconsistencies in findings within and across age, especially for basal cortisol. Also, it is important to note that most of the research has focused on adults and has employed cross-sectional designs. Retrospective, cross-sectional studies cannot disentangle biological factors as a cause, correlate, or consequence of depression, nor can they clearly establish whether putative biological indices (especially HPA axis dysregulation) comprise a relatively stable vulnerability for the development of depression. Developmentally sensitive, prospective studies are sorely needed to examine the etiological status of the neuroendocrine, neurotransmitter biological stress response system and brain-based neural circuitry as vulnerabilities for the onset of depression across the life course.

Cognitive Vulnerability

Although a multitude of vulnerability factors have been posited by cognitive theorists, we will focus our review on the following vulnerability factors, because they have been studied the most extensively across child, early adolescent, adolescent, and adult populations: (a) depressogenic inferential styles about causes, consequences, and the self (Abramson, Metalsky, & Alloy, 1989; Abramson, Seligman, & Teasdale, 1978); (b) dysfunctional attitudes (Beck, 1967, 1983); (c) the tendency to ruminate in response to depressed mood (Nolen-Hoeksema, 1991); and (d) self-criticism (Blatt & Zuroff, 1992). We briefly describe these cognitive vulnerabilities (see Gibb & Coles, Chapter 5 of this volume, for more details). A person with a negative inferential style is likely to attribute negative events to global and stable causes, to catastrophize the consequences of negative events, and to view himself or herself as flawed or deficient following negative events. An individual with dysfunctional attitudes is likely to think his or her self-worth hinges on being perfect or receiving approval from others. For example, the dysfunctional attitude "I'm worthless unless I'm perfect" may be activated if an individual does not excel in class. Rumination describes the cognitive process in which initially mildly dysphoric individuals focus on the meanings and implications of their depressed mood and, as a result, develop enduring and severe depressive symptoms. Finally, individuals high in self-criticism are preoccupied with issues pertaining to self-definition, competence, and worth. Such individuals are prone to view themselves as a failure as well as to feel guilty and experience decreases in self-esteem when not meeting expectations or goals.

Several studies have examined the hypothesis that cognitive factors confer vulnerability to depression among adults, adolescents, and children (see Abramson et al., 2002; Gibb & Coles, Chapter 5 of this volume; Hankin & Abramson, 2001; Ingram, Miranda, & Segal, 1998, for reviews). Given space limitations, we cannot exhaustively review all of the studies from this large body of literature, so instead, we highlight key points about cognitive vulnerability for depression using recent evidence. Moreover, we delve into some greater depth, describing the evidence both supporting and contradicting these theories, because cognitive vulnerability factors have received potentially the most theoretical, methodological, and empirical attention. We believe the knowledge accumulated and the lessons learned from this corpus of theory and research are highly relevant for advancing theory and knowledge for the other vulnerabilities to depression discussed more briefly in this chapter. In particular, we use cognitive vulnerabilities as a focal example to illustrate how research on other vulnerabilities, alone and in combination with stressors, can progress with enhanced emphasis on methodologically strong research (e.g., prospective studies controlling for initial depression to disentangle causes, consequences, and correlates of depression), focus on processes and mechanisms, and pay close attention to developmental issues. We focus our review on prospective studies that control for initial levels of depression, because they provide the most powerful tests of cognitive vulnerability theories.

Prospective research with adults shows that depression is predicted by a negative inferential style (e.g., Alloy et al., 2000; Hankin, Abramson, Miller, & Haeffel, 2004; Hankin, Fraley, & Abela, in press; Metalsky & Joiner, 1992), dysfunctional attitudes (Hankin, Abramson, et al., 2004; Hankin, Fraley, & Abela, in press; Joiner, Metalsky, Lew, & Klocek, 1999; Klocek, Oliver, & Ross, 1997), rumination (Butler & Nolen-Hoeksema, 1994; Keuhner & Weber, 1999; Nolen-Hoeksema & Harrell, 2002; Nolen-Hoeksema & Morrow, 1991), and self-criticism (Blaney & Kutcher, 1991; Zuroff, Igreja, & Mongrain, 1990). Several of these studies have found that cognitive vulnerabilities interact with stressors to predict depressive symptoms (e.g., Hankin, Abramson, et al., 2004; Metalsky & Joiner; Joiner et al., 1999), and initial research has shown that cognitive vulnerabilities, as main effects (e.g., Alloy et al.; Nolen-Hoeksema, 2000) or in interaction with stressors (Hankin, Abramson, et al., 2004), can predict clinically significant depressive episodes.

Research with child and adolescent populations has lagged far behind that of adult populations, yet several studies support cognitive vulnerability theories among youth. Among adolescents, a depressogenic attributional style interacts with subsequently occurring negative events to predict increases in depressive symptoms (Hankin, Abramson, & Siler, 2001; Southall & J. E. Roberts,

2002), dysfunctional attitudes interact with stress to predict clinical depression (Lewinsohn, Joiner, & Rohde, 2001), and rumination is associated with increases in depressive symptoms over time (Schwartz & Koenig, 1996). Among child populations, depression is predicted by a depressogenic inferential style (e.g., Abela, 2001; Brozina & Abela, 2004; Dixon & Ahrens, 1992; Hilsman & Garber, 1995; Panak & Garber, 1992; Robinson, Garber, & Hilsman, 1995), dysfunctional attitudes (Abela, Thompson, & Payne, 2004), rumination (Abela, Brozina, & Haigh, 2002; Abela & Aydin, 2004), and self-criticism (Abela, Taxel, & Sakellaropoulo, in press; Adams, Abela, Auerbach, & Skitch, 2004).

At the same time, other studies have provided mixed support for cognitive vulnerability to depression in adults (e.g., Abela & Seligman, 2000; Sarin, Abela, & Auerbach, in press) and youth (e.g., Abela & D'Alessandro, 2002; Lewinsohn et al., 2001) or lack of support in adults (e.g., Abela, Brozina, & Seligman, 2004; Follette & Jacobson, 1987; Hammen, Marks, DeMayo, & Mayol, 1985; Segal, Shaw, & Vella, 1989; Swendsen, 1998) and youth (Abela & Sarin, 2002; Hammen, Adrian, & Hiroto, 1988). Some of the inconsistencies may relate to gender (e.g., support only for men in Barnett & Gotlib, 1988, 1990, but only for women in Dykmann & Johll, 1998) or age (e.g., support in early adolescence, but not childhood, in Cole & Turner, 1993; Nolen-Hoeksema, Girgus, & Seligman, 1986, 1992; Turner & Cole, 1994, but support in younger but not older children in Conley, Haines, Hilt, & Metalsky, 2001). Highlighting this issue, Abela and Taylor (2003) found that self-criticism interacted with negative events to predict increases in depressive symptoms in third graders and in seventh-grade boys but not in seventh-grade girls.

It is important to note that the degree of support for cognitive vulnerabilities to depression appears to be equal over the life span, because studies have found full support, mixed support, and lack of support among children, early adolescents, adolescents, and adults. Because inconsistent findings exist within the literature examining theories of cognitive vulnerability to depression in all age groups, researchers have attempted to identify factors that can account for such inconsistencies. Although there is clearly more support than lack of support for these cognitive vulnerabilities, it is vital to understand why there are inconsistencies in findings across all age groups, because elucidating these reasons can advance theory and knowledge on how cognitive vulnerabilities operate to contribute to the development of depression.

One possible explanation for past inconsistent findings is that researchers have failed, for the most part, to consider possible relationships among the many risk, vulnerability, and protective factors proposed *across* various theories of vulnerability to depression (cognitive and others reviewed in this chapter). It is unlikely that each vulnerability theory is presenting a distinct etiological pathway leading to the development of depression, unaffected by the various contributory causes of depression proposed by alternative theories. Consequently, the richest examination of vulnerability models will ultimately involve the integration of the various distinct risk, vulnerability, and protective factors proposed by empirically supported theories.

To date, the most common integrative approach has examined whether high levels of self-esteem buffer individuals who possess cognitive vulnerability factors against experiencing increases in depressive symptoms following the occurrence of negative events. Research has generally supported this integrated self-esteem/cognitive vulnerability-stress approach in adults (Metalsky, Joiner, Hardin, & Abramson, 1993; Southall & J. E. Roberts, 2002; for exception, see Ralph & Mineka, 1998), adolescents (Abela, 2002), and children/early adolescents (e.g., Abela & Payne, 2003; Conley et al., 2001; Robinson et al., 1995; for exception, see Abela & Sullivan, 2003). Another example of an integrative approach can be found in a month-long daily-diary study of young adults (Hankin, Fraley, & Abela, in press). Here, dispositional negative inferential style, dysfunctional attitudes, rumination, neuroticism, and daily negative explanations made about the most stressful event of the day were used to predict individual trajectories of daily depressive symptoms over 35 consecutive days. Results showed that dispositional negative inferential style, dysfunctional attitudes, and neuroticism predicted daily depression over time, controlling for other vulnerabilities and initial depression. Moreover, negative explanations made to daily stressors interacted with dispositional negative inferential style and neuroticism, albeit in different ways, to predict individuals' experience of daily depression. On those days when individuals made negative inferences about daily stressors, they exhibited higher depression regardless of their dispositional negative cognitive style, whereas when they made benign or optimistic inferences for a daily stressor, people with a dispositional negative cognitive style, compared with those with a more optimistic cognitive style, reported relatively greater depressive symptoms. In contrast, highly neurotic individuals who made negative explanations for daily stressors reported the greatest elevation in depression. This integrative diary study, along with the integrated self-esteem/cognitive vulnerability research, shows the importance of considering how various vulnerability factors may work together in a more comprehensive manner to explain depression.

A second possible explanation for past inconsistent findings is that researchers have examined the vulnerability and protective factors proposed within specific theories in isolation. For example, the majority of research examining hopelessness theory has examined each of the three inferential styles separately without considering the possible relationships among them. However, using such an approach, inconsistent findings may result, given that some individuals may exhibit one depressogenic inferential style (e.g., negative attributional style) but not others (e.g., negative inferential styles about consequences and the self). Abela and Sarin's (2002) "weakest link" hypothesis posits that an individual is as vulnerable to depression as his or her most depressogenic inferential style makes him or her. In an initial study examining this hypothesis, Abela and Sarin reported that early adolescents' "weakest links," but not their overall negative inferential styles, interacted with subsequently occurring negative events to predict increases in depressive symptoms. Additional research with child samples has replicated this finding (Abela & Payne, 2003; Abela & Richardson, in press; Brozina & Abela, 2004). The weakest link hypothesis highlights important implications for conducting developmentally oriented research across development. Research with adults has shown that the three aspects of a negative inferential style form one latent factor and are not distinguishable empirically (Hankin, Carter, Abela, & Adams, 2003), whereas research with children has shown them to be separable (e.g., Abela, 2001; Adams, Abela, & Hankin, 2004). This suggests that these cognitive vulnerabilities may emerge at different points over development.

A third possible explanation for past inconsistent findings is that cognitive vulnerability factors have been measured insufficiently. Many have posited that cognitive vulnerability factors are typically latent cognitive structures or processes that must be activated or primed in order to be assessed accurately (Ingram et al., 1998; Persons & Miranda, 1992). According to the activation hypothesis, predicting changes in depressive symptoms based on cognitive vulnerability factors depends on whether these vulnerabilities have been activated before they are assessed. Numerous studies, mostly cross-sectional, support this activation hypothesis among adults (see Ingram et al., 1998, for a review) and adolescents (J. E. Roberts & Gamble, 2001; Taylor & Ingram, 1999). The few longitudinal studies provide the most powerful support to date for the activation hypothesis among adults (Abela & Brozina, 2004; Abela, Brozina, et al., 2004; Segal, Gemar, & Williams, 1999). To date, no prospective study has examined this in youth.

Related researchers examining cognitive vulnerabilities with youth samples have tended to assess cognitive vulnerability factors using age-inappropriate measures with poor psychometric properties. The vast majority of studies failing to provide support for attributional style as a cognitive vulnerability in younger children have utilized the Children's Attributional Style Questionnaire (CASQ; Seligman et al., 1984), which has poor internal consistency. In contrast, more consistent support for cognitive vulnerability factors has been found using more reliable measures. For example, Hankin and Abramson (2002) developed a more reliable measure of negative inferential style and found that cognitive vulnerability interacted with stressors to predict depressive symptoms, but not externalizing behaviors. Moreover, they found that negative inferential style explained the adolescent gender difference in depression when assessed reliably, whereas studies with the CASQ have not found this (Thompson, Kaslow, Weiss, & Nolen-Hoeksema, 1998), probably because of poor measurement. Also, in younger children, a depressogenic attributional style interacted with negative events to predict increases in depressive symptoms when using a semistructured interview designed to assess attributional style in younger children (Brozina & Abela, 2003; Conley et al., 2001), whereas this was not obtained with the CASQ in past studies.

It is important to note that a history of poor measurement of cognitive vulnerability factors has likely contributed to inconsistent findings, and as a result, to researchers' development of theoretical modifications to account for such mixed findings. Indeed, given the developmental pattern of findings observed over the past 20 years of research using poor measures of cognitive vulnerability, some researchers have concluded that cognitive vulnerability to depression emerges only during the transition from late childhood to early adolescence when children acquire the ability to engage in abstract reasoning and formal operational thought (Cole & Turner, 1993; Nolen-Hoeksema et al., 1992; Turner & Cole, 1994). According to this "developmental hypothesis," negative cognitions play a role in triggering depressive symptoms in younger children, but such cognitions are viewed as more likely to be a direct consequence of negative events themselves and subsequent environmental feedback rather than the product of a preexisting vulnerability factor (Turner & Cole). Once stable individual differences in personality traits, styles of thinking, and self-views emerge in adolescence, then cognitions may become more of a product of the interaction of vulnerability factors with the environment than of the environment alone (Turner & Cole).

To examine the developmental hypothesis directly, Abela (2001) used more reliable measures of cognitive vulnerability in third graders (when concrete thinking predominates and cognitive vulnerabilities are not supposed to operate) and seventh graders (when formal operational thinking is expected and cognitive vulnerabilities are functioning). Abela (2001) found that a depressogenic attributional style, as assessed by the CASQ, interacted with subsequently occurring negative events to predict increases in depressive symptoms in seventh-grade but not third-grade children. However, contrary to the "developmental hypothesis," a depressogenic inferential style about consequences interacted with negative events to predict increases in depressive symptoms in both third- and seventh-grade children, and a depressogenic inferential style about the self interacted with negative events to predict increases in depressive symptoms in third- and seventh-grade girls but not boys. This pattern of findings suggests that cognitive vulnerabilities may emerge earlier than previously thought. Consistent with this hypothesis, numerous other studies have now examined a wider array of cognitive vulnerabilities, including depressogenic inferential styles (Abela, Oziransky, & Adams, 2004; Abela & Payne, 2003; Abela & Richardson, in press; Conley et al., 2001), dysfunctional attitudes (Abela, Thompson, et al., 2004), self-criticism (Abela, Adams, et al., 2004; Abela & Taylor, 2003; Abela, Wagner, Webb, & Skitch, 2004), and a ruminative response style (Abela & Aydin, 2004; Abela, Brozina, & Haigh, 2002). These cognitive vulnerability factors interacted with the occurrence of negative events to predict increases in depressive symptoms in both children (ages 6–9) and early adolescents (ages 10–14).

In sum, the preponderance of evidence has found strong support for various cognitive vulnerabilities for predicting depression, although inconsistencies remain. We sought briefly to provide several explanations and accompanying evidence that may account for the inconsistencies over the life span. Given that initial support has been obtained for each of the explanations outlined above, additional research is needed to examine these and other potential explanations. At the same time, caution is needed to avoid making overly broad conclusions about either theories of cognitive vulnerability to depression in general or the applicability of such theories to youth.

Interpersonal Vulnerabilities

The majority of research examining the relationship between interpersonal vulnerability factors and depressive symptoms has been cross-sectional in nature. This makes it difficult to draw conclusions about whether such factors play a role in the onset of depressive symptoms or whether they are simply a correlate or consequence of such symptoms. For the purpose of this review, we will focus our attention on interpersonal theories of vulnerability to depression that have captured a fair degree of empirical attention (see also Van Orden, Wingate, Gordon, & Joiner, Chapter 6 of this volume). In addition, we will review only interpersonal vulnerability factors that can be characterized as manifesting themselves within the individual, such as excessive reassurance seeking (Joiner, Metalsky, Katz, & Beach, 1999), dependency (Blatt & Zuroff, 1992), and social support.

The hypothesis of Joiner, Metalsky, Katz, et al. (1999) that excessive reassurance seeking serves as a vulnerability factor to depression has generated a substantial degree of support in adult populations. For example, individuals who exhibit high levels of reassurance seeking have been shown to exhibit higher levels of depressive symptoms than individuals who exhibit low levels of reassurance seeking (e.g., Joiner, 1994; Joiner, Alfano, & Metalsky, 1992, 1993; Joiner & Metalsky, 1995; Joiner & Schmidt, 1998; Katz & Beach, 1997; Katz, Beach, & Joiner, 1998; Potthoff, Holahan, & Joiner, 1995). Excessive reassurance seeking has been found to interact with negative events to predict increases in depressive symptoms over time (e.g., Katz et al., 1998; Joiner & Metalsky, 2001). Last, reassurance seeking has been found to play a role in the social transmission of depression, with individuals who exhibit high levels of reassurance seeking more likely than their low-reassurance-seeking counterparts to develop depression when interacting with a depressed partner or roommate (Joiner, 1994; Katz, Beach, & Joiner, 1999).

Far less research has examined the relationship between excessive reassurance seeking and depressive symptoms in youth. Results from cross-sectional studies have been consistent with the hypotheses of

Joiner, Metalsky, Katz, et al. (1999). Higher levels of reassurance seeking have been found to be associated with higher levels of depressive symptoms in both child and early adolescent populations (Abela, Hankin, et al., in press; Joiner, 1999). Similarly, youth psychiatric inpatients with a primary diagnosis of a depressive disorder have been found to exhibit higher levels of reassurance seeking than those with a primary diagnosis of an externalizing or anxiety disorder (Joiner, Metalsky, F. Gencoz, & T. Gencoz, 2001). Last, high levels of reassurance seeking have been found to predict a past history of clinically significant depressive episodes in children and early adolescents exhibiting an insecure attachment style to their parents, even after controlling for current depressive symptoms (Abela, Hankin, et al., in press).

At the same time, although results from cross-sectional studies have been supportive of the hypotheses of Joiner, Metalsky, Katz, et al. (1999) in both children and early adolescents, results from a recent prospective study suggest that reassurance seeking may serve as a vulnerability factor to depression only in early adolescents. More specifically, using a 1-year multiwave longitudinal design and a sample of children of affectively ill parents (ages 6–14), Abela, Zuroff, Ho, Adams, and Hankin (2004) reported that excessive reassurance seeking was associated with increases in depressive symptoms following increases in either hassles or parental depressive symptoms in older but not younger children. Abela, Zuroff, et al. (2004) hypothesized that reassurance seeking tendencies may be normative and even adaptive in children, leading reassurance seeking to emerge as a vulnerability factor to depression only in early adolescence, when lower levels of reassurance seeking become normative. In line with this hypothesis, older children exhibited lower levels of reassurance seeking. Also consistent with this, age moderated the strength of the association between excessive reassurance seeking and depressive symptoms, with reassurance seeking being more strongly associated with depressive symptoms in older children.

A substantial body of prospective research has accumulated supporting the hypothesis that high levels of dependency are associated with greater increases in depressive symptoms following increases in stress in adult populations (e.g., Hammen, Marks, Mayol, & deMayo, 1985; Hewitt & Flett, 1993; Lakey & Ross, 1994; Rude & Burnham, 1993; Segal, Shaw, & Vella, 1989; Zuroff & Mongrain, 1987; Zuroff et al., 1990; for exceptions see J. D. Brown & Silberschatz, 1989; Segal, Shaw, Vella, & Katz, 1992; Smith, O'Keefe, & Jenkins, 1988). Relatively few studies, however, have examined the relationship between dependency and depressive symptoms in youth. With respect to cross-sectional studies, researchers have reported that higher levels of dependency are associated with higher levels of depressive symptoms in adolescents but not children (Abela, Taxel, et al., in press; Abela & Taylor, 2003; Blatt, Shaffer, Bers, & Quinlan, 1992; Fichman, Koestner, & Zuroff, 1994; Luthar & Blatt, 1993). With respect to prospective studies using child and early adolescent samples, researchers have failed to find a relationship between dependency and increases in depressive symptoms over time (e.g., Abela, Taxel, et al.; Abela & Taylor). Thus, preliminary results from both cross-sectional and prospective research appear to suggest that high levels of dependency may be normative and even adaptive in younger populations, such that dependency may emerge as a vulnerability factor to depression only in adolescence, when low levels of dependency and high levels of autonomy become normative. An alternative explanation for the lack of support for a relationship between dependency and depressive symptoms in children and early adolescents is that dependency is a multidimensional construct with both maladaptive (e.g., excessive fear of other's disapproval or neediness) and adaptive (e.g., preference for affiliation or connectedness) components (D. A. Clark & Beck, 1999). Research in youth examining sociotropy, a related construct, has supported this (Little & Garber, 2000). Thus, a more multidimensional approach toward operationalizing dependency may be needed in youth in order to disentangle its adaptive and maladaptive components.

Social support is widely viewed as a multidimensional concept and is commonly defined as the availability of a network of people on whom a person can rely in times of need. There are different types of social support (e.g., emotional, financial, informational, or enacted support), and a social support network might include family members, friends, significant others, as well as colleagues. Although the context in which social support may optimally operate is not clear, there is evidence that it does buffer against stress. There is evidence of the buffering effects of social support across the developmental spectrum. Kashani, Suarez, Jones, and Reid (1999) reported that depressed, compared with anxious, children had lower satisfaction levels with their social networks; conversely, children who were higher functioning and more competent reported greater social support (Garber & Little, 1999). Adolescent depression is linked to lower levels of family support (Cumsille & Epstein, 1994; Marcotte, Marcotte, & Bouffard, 2002; Patten et al., 1997; Sheeber, Hops, Alpert, Davis, & Andrews, 1997) and lower levels of social support from friends (Klein, Lewinsohn, & Seeley, 1997), with some evidence for gender effects of social support on depression (Schraedley, Gotlib, & Hayward, 1999). Conversely, adolescents who perceived higher family support reported better adjustment (Sim, 2000). Perceptions of family support buffer against marital conflict (Davies & Windle, 2001).

Insecure Attachment as Vulnerability

Numerous cross-sectional studies have demonstrated that insecure attachment is associated with higher levels of depressive symptoms among adults (e.g., Duggan, Sham, Minne, Lee, & Murray, 1998; Enns, Cox, & Larsen, 2000; Haaga et al., 2002; Sakado et al., 2000; Sato et al., 1998; see Blatt & Homann, 1992; see also Davila, Ramsay, Stroud, & Steinberg, Chapter 9 of this volume). The few prospective studies have reported that insecure attachment predicts increases in depressive symptoms over time in adults through the mediating role of both negative cognitions (Hankin, Kassel, & Abela, in press; Reinecke & Rogers, 2001; J. E. Roberts, Gotlib, & Kassel, 1996) and interpersonal stress-generation processes (Hankin, Kassel, et al., in press).

Similarly, several cross-sectional studies have demonstrated that attachment insecurity is associated with depressive symptoms in adolescent samples (e.g., Armsden & Greenberg, 1987; Armsden, McCauley, Greenberg, Burke, & Mitchell, 1990; Burbach, Kashani, & Rosenberg, 1989; Marton & Maharaj, 1993; McFarlane, Bellisimo, & Norman, 1995; Muris, Meesters, van Melick, & Zwambag, 2001; Priel & Shamai, 1995; Vivona, 2000; West, Spreng, Rose, & Adam, 1999). In one of the few prospective studies, Hammen and colleagues (1995) reported that attachment insecurity was associated with increases in depressive symptoms over a 1-year longitudinal follow-up among female high school seniors. In addition, in line with a vulnerability-stress perspective, they reported that the relationship between attachment insecurity and depressive symptoms was moderated by interpersonal stressors. Adolescent females who exhibited attachment insecurity reported increases in depressive symptoms when experiencing high but not low levels of interpersonal stress.

The link between attachment insecurity and depressive symptoms has also been well documented in child populations (e.g., Abela, Hankin, et al., in press; Graham & Easterbrooks, 2000; Haaga et al., 2002; Hortacsu, Cesur, & Oral, 1993; Muris, Mayer, & Meesters, 2000; Stein et al.,

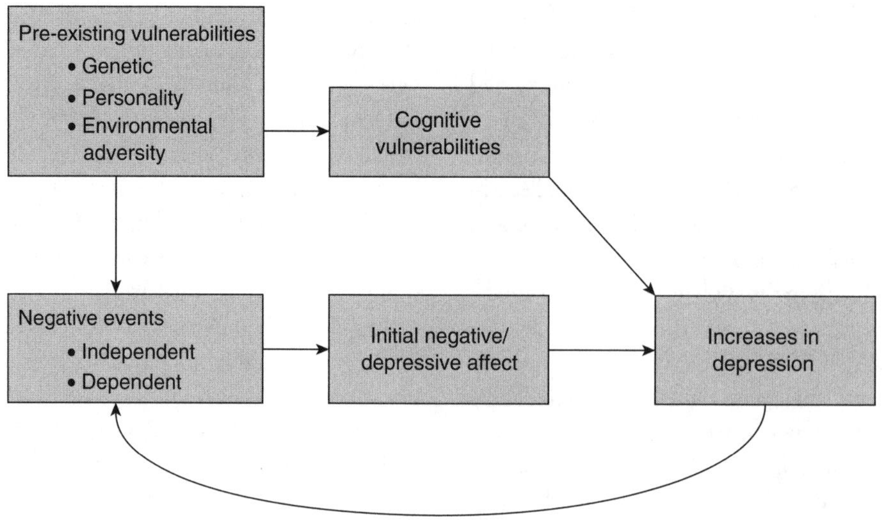

Figure 10.2 The Elaborated Cognitive Vulnerability-Transactional Stress Model of Depression

SOURCE: Hankin, B. L., & Abramson, L. Y. (2001). Development of gender differences in depression: An elaborated cognitive vulnerability-transactional stress theory. *Psychological Bulletin, 127,* 773–796. Figure reprinted with permission. Copyright 2001 by the American Psychological Association.

2000). Preliminary research provides support for a prospective relationship between attachment insecurity and depressive symptoms, particularly within a vulnerability-stress framework. For example, in a 1-year multiwave longitudinal study of children and early adolescents of affectively ill parents, Abela, Adams, Kryger, and Hankin (2004) reported that higher levels of insecure attachment to parents were associated with greater increases in depressive symptoms following increases in parental depressive symptoms.

Developmentally Sensitive, Integrative Vulnerability and Stress Model of Depression

As we noted at the start of the vulnerability and stress section, we believe that a coherent, integrative theory of depression over the life span should incorporate various vulnerabilities and stressors and delineate how these transact together over time to contribute to the development of depression and explain the big facts of depression that we reviewed in the first section of the chapter. Given our review of independent vulnerabilities to depression and stressors, we now briefly present a developmentally informed theoretical integration of a vulnerability and stress model for depression, called the elaborated vulnerability-transactional stress model (Hankin & Abramson, 2001; see Figure 10.2). The model aims to account for the development of depression as a complex multifactorial disorder over time.

As can be seen in Figure 10.2, the causal chain of the elaborated theory begins with the occurrence of a *negative event* (either independent or dependent; see below). This reflects the big fact that stressors often lead to increases in depression. A negative event contributes to elevations in *initial levels of negative affect.* The construct of negative affect includes various negative emotions, including anxious, depressive, and angry affect (Watson, 2000). As demonstrated earlier in the chapter (see also Grant & McMahon, Chapter 1 of this volume), prospective studies have found that negative life events predict later increases in depression, even after controlling for initial levels of negative/depressive affect among children, adolescents, and adults. We also highlight here that various vulnerabilities (e.g., emotional, personality, biological, cognitive) can increase the likelihood that negative affect will be experienced given a stressor and that negative affect will be experienced faster and last longer (e.g., affective style; Davidson et al., 2002).

If the initial negative affect increases and remains, it can lead to increases in depressive symptoms. In contrast to most generic vulnerability-stress models of depression, which state that a negative event contributes to depressive symptoms (especially when moderated by vulnerability), the elaborated model posits that initial negative affect comes between the occurrence of a negative event and later increases in depressive symptoms. This intermediary step of initial negative affect is included in the causal chain for at least two related reasons. First, research examining the temporal relationship between negative events and the rise in depressive symptoms has found that initial elevations of nonspecific negative affect follow the occurrence of a negative event (Grant & McMahon, Chapter 1 of this volume). Further, prospective studies assessing changes in negative affect after a naturally occurring stressor (e.g., academic exam, earthquake) show that negative affect rises initially for most people after the negative event occurs, but that this initial increase in negative affect persists only among vulnerable individuals (e.g., Hankin, Abramson, et al., 2004; Metalsky, Joiner, Hardin, & Abramson, 1993; Nolen-Hoeksema & Morrow, 1991). The second reason for including initial negative affect in the causal chain is to clarify the conundrum of comorbidity commonly observed with depression. As reviewed earlier, depression typically co-occurs with other psychological disorders, especially anxiety and behavioral disorders. Broad negative affect has been identified as the central common factor underlying the association between depression and co-occurring anxiety and externalizing symptoms (e.g., Chorpita, Albano, & Barlow, 1998; L. A. Clark & Watson, 1991; Cole, Truglio, & Peeke, 1997; Mineka, Watson, & L. A. Clark, 1998). By including initial elevations of general negative affect into the elaborated causal chain, the model reflects the reality that depression commonly overlaps with other negative emotions and psychopathological disorders. In this elaborated theory, then, the depression comorbidity issue is addressed, because initial negative affect, common to depression and other disorders, results from the occurrence of a negative event. Depression-specific vulnerabilities are included in the model to explain the development of depression specifically, as opposed to psychopathology in general.

The next step in the elaborated causal chain involves *cognitive vulnerability* factors. These cognitive risk factors enhance the likelihood that an individual ultimately will experience increases in depression. As described in the cognitive vulnerability section, cognitive factors are hypothesized to interact with the occurrence of a negative life event to lead to a greater probability of experiencing eventual depression. In the elaborated model, it is also hypothesized that cognitive factors can interact with the initial negative affect to amplify the affect, which can then contribute to increases in depressive symptoms. An important aspect of the cognitive vulnerability factors posited in the elaborated causal chain is that they are hypothesized to be more depression specific than some other depression vulnerabilities. Research supports the specificity hypothesis with adolescents (Lewinsohn, Seeley, & Gotlib, 1997; Gladstone, Kaslow, Seeley, & Lewinsohn, 1997; Hankin & Abramson, 2002; Robinson et al., 1995; Weiss, Susser, & Catron, 1998), although the specificity among adults is less clear (see Haeffel et al.,

2003; Hankin, Abramson, et al., 2004; Metalsky & Joiner, 1992, for support; see Ralph & Mineka, 1998, for lack of support). Overall, research generally supports the hypothesis that cognitive vulnerability more consistently and more strongly predicts depression compared with other comorbid conditions, but more research is needed to resolve this issue, especially with children.

Taking a developmental perspective, the elaborated model suggests that there may be changes over time in the primary domain of cognitive vulnerability for individuals. For example, Erikson (1974) has emphasized that people confront different tasks at different stages of the life span. Whereas adolescents confront the task of establishing an identity, elderly individuals question whether their lives had meaning. This view suggests that the domains most relevant for cognitive vulnerability may change over the life span. Health may be a more relevant domain for elderly people than for children, whereas the domain of perceived physical attractiveness and body satisfaction may be very motivationally significant for adolescents. For example, dissatisfaction with body image and physical appearance among adolescents is an important domain of vulnerability (e.g., Allgood-Merten, Lewinsohn, & Hops, 1990; Hankin & Abramson, 2002).

There can be a domain match between vulnerability and stressor. As reviewed earlier, there are subtypes or domains of stressors. The elaborated model hypothesizes that a match between stressors and an individual's primary domain of cognitive vulnerability (e.g., physical appearance, interpersonal, or achievement) is particularly likely to lead to depression. In line with this hypothesis, several studies with adults have shown that cognitive vulnerability factors, such as a negative inferential style (Abela, 2002; Abela & Brozina, 2004; Metalsky, Halberstadt, & Abramson, 1987; for exception see Abela & Seligman, 2000) and self-criticism (e.g., Blaney & Kutcher, 1991; Zuroff et al., 1990), interact with domain-congruent, but not domain-incongruent, stressors to predict increases in depressive symptoms. Far less research has examined this congruency hypothesis among children and adolescents. Hammen and Goodman-Brown (1990) found that cognitive vulnerability (a depressogenic schema) interacted with domain-congruent, but not domain-incongruent, stressors to predict increases in depressive symptoms among a mixed sample of children and adolescents. Abela, Taxel, and colleagues (in press) reported that self-criticism interacted with negative achievement, but not interpersonal, events to predict increases in depressive symptoms with early adolescents. Among younger child samples, the limited research to date has failed to provide support for the specific vulnerability hypothesis with self-criticism (Abela, Adams, et al., 2004; Abela & Taylor, 2003; Abela, Wagner, et al., 2004), although other aspects of specific cognitive vulnerability have not been examined in children yet. Developmentally, it may be that younger children's self-concepts are not yet differentiated enough for them to exhibit specific vulnerability. The complexity of children's self-concepts increases considerably during the transition from middle childhood to adolescence (e.g., Abela & Véronneau-McArdle, 2002). As the complexity of children's self-concepts increases, they begin to perceive different domains of their life as separate from one another, leading negative interpersonal and achievement events to become relevant to different self-aspects.

After individuals' experience increases in depressive symptoms, a *transactional stress-generation mechanism* is included as part of the elaborated causal chain, based on work from the interpersonal theories of depression (e.g., Hammen, 1991; Joiner & Coyne, 1999). As we reviewed earlier, and consistent with the model, depression can contribute to the creation of further dependent negative events. In the elaborated model, both independent and dependent negative events lead to elevations in initial negative affect and depression, and increases in depression can lead to more dependent negative life events. In addition, in the elaborated model it is hypothesized that psychopathological symptoms and disorders co-occurring with depression provide another interpersonal mechanism that can contribute to the creation of additional dependent negative events. For example, an individual with depression overlapping with relational aggression (Crick et al., 1999) would likely be creating dependent, interpersonal negative events as she or he is rejected by peers or romantic partners for aggressive behavior within close peer relationships. The net result of this transactional process is the further creation of dependent negative events, and this can restart the process at the beginning of the causal chain, thus leading to increases in and potential maintenance of depression over time.

Up to this point, a general vulnerability-transactional stress depression model has been articulated that likely would apply equally well to both youth and adults. In addition, the model contains particular developmental factors that can influence the elaborated causal chain and help explain why depression rises dramatically during middle adolescence, especially among girls. In the theory, particular developmentally sensitive factors are emphasized, including the influence of preexisting vulnerabilities (e.g., genetic and personality as well as early stressful environmental adversities). The model posits that such distal vulnerabilities and early adversity will enhance the likelihood of encountering more negative events and developing greater vulnerability to depression (e.g., cognitive) throughout childhood and adolescence. Thus, in the model it is hypothesized that various vulnerabilities to depression distally contribute to the development of depression through more proximal stressors and vulnerability mechanisms. The evidence reviewed earlier in the chapter provides initial support for this hypothesis, because these distal vulnerabilities enhance risk for depression. Further research is needed to examine whether preexisting vulnerabilities contribute to depression through more proximal vulnerabilities transacting with stressors. Importantly, initial research has supported this idea. For example, childhood emotional maltreatment has been found to predict cognitive vulnerability (Gibb, 2002; Hankin, 2003) as well as insecure attachment and additional stressors (Hankin), and in turn, these factors predicted prospective increases in depression. Also, baseline neuroticism has been shown to predict prospective increases in stressors, and the interaction between cognitive vulnerabilities and additional stressors explained the association between neuroticism and later depression (Lakdawalla & Hankin, 2003).

We explicitly note that these vulnerability factors likely do not operate as discrete categories but are interconnected and influence each other. For example, behavioral-genetic studies show that factors typically viewed as "environmental adversity," such as family discord, are influenced by genetic factors (Deater-Deckard, Fulker, & Plomin, 1999; Neiderhiser, Reiss, Hetherington, & Plomin, 1999; Reiss et al., 1995; see Lemery & Doelger, Chapter 7 of this volume). Thus, this general, elaborated model is intended to reflect the reality that individuals' propensity to develop psychopathology occurs as part of a complex nature-nurture relationship unfolding over time (Pennington, 2002). Other vulnerabilities reviewed in this chapter, such as early insecure attachment to primary caregivers, could also be included as a distal vulnerability that increases the propensity to experience stressors (cf. Hankin, Fraley, Lahey, et al., in press) and cognitive vulnerability (e.g., Hankin, Fraley, Lahey, et al., in press; J. E. Roberts et al., 1996).

In the elaborated model, as articulated to date, biological vulnerabilities have not been explicitly included. Biological factors have been excluded not because they are unimportant in understanding the development of depression and the major findings (see Pihl & Nantel-Vivier, Chapter 4 of this volume). Instead, biological risk factors have not been included because it is currently unclear whether the major biological factors are *causally* implicated in the development of depression or whether they reflect concurrent biological stress responses (e.g., HPA axis dysfunction) or converge with other vulnerabilities (e.g., behavioral inhibition as a temperament/personality dimension with underlying biological substrates). As noted in the biological vulnerability section (see also Pihl & Nantel-Vivier, Chapter 4 in this volume), prospective longitudinal studies, in which initially nondepressed samples are followed to allow for prediction of future depression, are vitally important to advance knowledge about the etiological status of biological vulnerabilities.

REFERENCES

Abela, J. R. Z. (2001). A test of the diathesis-stress and causal mediation components of the hopelessness theory of depression in third and seventh grade children. *Journal of Abnormal Child Psychology, 29,* 241–254.

Abela, J. R. Z. (2002). Depressive mood reactions to failure in the achievement domain: A test of the integration of the hopelessness and self-esteem theories of depression. *Cognitive Therapy and Research, 26,* 531–552.

Abela, J. R. Z., Adams, P., Kryger, S., & Hankin, B. L. (2004). *Contagious depression: Insecure attachment as a moderator of the relationship between parental depression and child depression.* Manuscript submitted for publication.

Abela, J. R. Z., & Aydin, C. (2004). *Responses to depression in children: Reconceptualizing the relation among response styles.* Manuscript submitted for publication.

Abela, J. R. Z., & Brozina, K. (2004). The use of negative events to prime cognitive vulnerabilities to depression. *Cognitive Therapy and Research, 28,* 209–227.

Abela, J. R. Z., Brozina, K., & Haigh, E. P. (2002). An examination of the response styles theory of depression in third and seventh grade children: A short-term longitudinal study. *Journal of Abnormal Child Psychology, 30,* 513–525.

Abela, J. R. Z., Brozina, K., & Seligman, M. E. P. (2004). A test of the integration of the activation hypothesis and the diathesis-stress component of the hopelessness theory of depression. *British Journal of Clinical Psychology, 43,* 111–128.

Abela, J. R. Z., & D'Alessandro, D. U. (2002). A test of the diathesis-stress and causal mediation components of Beck's cognitive theory of depression. *British Journal of Clinical Psychology, 41,* 111–128.

Abela, J. R. Z., Hankin, B. L., Haigh, E. A. P., Vinokuroff, T., Trayhern, L., & Adams, P. (2005). Interpersonal vulnerability to depressive episodes in high risk children: The role of insecure attachment and reassurance seeking. *Journal of Clinical Child and Adolescent Psychology, 34, 182–192.*

Abela, J. R. Z., Ho, M., Nueslovici, J., & Chan, C. (2004). *A multi-wave longitudinal study of the transactional relations between depressive symptoms, hopelessness, and stress in high-risk youth.* Paper accepted for presentation at the annual convention of the Canadian Association for Child and Adolescent Psychiatry.

Abela, J. R. Z., Oziransky, V., & Adams, P. (2004). *The timing of parent and child depression: A hopelessness theory perspective.* Manuscript submitted for publication.

Abela, J. R. Z., & Payne, A. V. L. (2003). A test of the integration of the hopelessness and self-esteem theories of depression in third and seventh grade children. *Cognitive Therapy and Research, 27,* 519–535.

Abela, J. R. Z., & Richardson, J. (in press). A test of the integration of the hopelessness and self-esteem theories of depression in children of affectively ill parents: A multi-wave longitudinal study. *International Journal of Psychology.*

Abela, J. R. Z., & Sarin, S. (2002). Cognitive vulnerability to hopelessness depression: A chain is only as strong as its weakest link. *Cognitive Therapy and Research, 26,* 811–829.

Abela, J. R. Z., & Seligman, M. E. P. (2000). The hopelessness theory of depression: A test of the diathesis-stress component in the interpersonal and achievement domains. *Cognitive Therapy and Research, 24,* 361–378.

Abela J. R. Z., Starrs, C., & Adams, P. (2004, October). *Predictors of stress generation in children of affectively-ill parents: A one-year longitudinal study.* Paper accepted for presentation at the annual convention of the Canadian Association for Child and Adolescent Psychiatry, Montreal, Quebec, Canada.

Abela, J. R. Z., & Sullivan, C. (2003). A test of Beck's cognitive diathesis-stress theory of depression in early adolescents. *Journal of Early Adolescence, 23,* 384–404.

Abela, J. R. Z., Taxel, E., & Sakellaropoulo, M. (in press). Integrating two subtypes of depression: Psychodynamic theory and its relation to hopelessness depression in schoolchildren. *Journal of Early Adolescence.*

Abela, J. R. Z., & Taylor, G. (2003). Specific vulnerability to depressive mood reactions in schoolchildren: The moderating role of self-esteem. *Journal of Clinical Child and Adolescent Psychology, 32,* 408–418.

Abela, J. R. Z., Thompson, M., & Payne, A. V. L. (2004). *Dysfunctional attitudes as a cognitive vulnerability factor for depression in children of affectively-ill parents: A multi-wave longitudinal study.* Manuscript submitted for publication.

Abela, J. R. Z., & Véronneau-McArdle, M. (2002). The relationship between self-complexity and depressive symptoms in third and seventh grade children: A short-term longitudinal study. *Journal of Abnormal Child Psychology, 30,* 155–166.

Abela, J. R. Z., Wagner, C., Webb, C. A., & Skitch, S. A. (2004). *Self-criticism, depressive symptoms, and the protective role of self-esteem: A multi-wave longitudinal study of children of affectively-ill parents.* Manuscript submitted for publication.

Abela, J. R. Z., Zuroff, D. C., Ho, R., Adams, P., & Hankin, B. L. (2004). *Excessive reassurance seeking, hassles, and depressive symptoms in children of affectively-ill parents: A multi-wave longitudinal study.* Manuscript submitted for publication.

Abramson, L. Y., Alloy, L. B., Hankin, B. L., Haeffel, G. J., MacCoon, D., & Gibb, B. E. (2002). Cognitive vulnerability-stress models of depression in a self-regulatory and psychobiological context. In I. H. Gotlib & C. L. Hammen (Eds.), *Handbook of depression and its treatment* (pp. 268–294). New York: Guilford Press.

Abramson, L. Y., Metalsky, G. I., & Alloy, L. B. (1989). Hopelessness depression: A theory based subtype of depression. *Psychological Review, 96,* 358–372.

Abramson, L. Y., Seligman M. E. P., & Teasdale, J. D. (1978). Learned helplessness in humans: Critique and reformulation. *Journal of Abnormal Psychology, 87,* 49–74.

Achenbach, T. M. (1991). *Manual for the Youth Self-Report and 1991 Profile.* Burlington: University of Vermont, Department of Psychiatry.

Adams, P., Abela, J. R. Z., Auerbach, R., & Skitch, S. (2004). *Personality predispositions to depression in high-risk youth: An experience sampling analysis.* Manuscript submitted for publication.

Adams, P., Abela, J. R. Z., & Hankin, B. L. (2004). *Factorial categorization of depression-related constructs and symptoms in schoolchildren.* Manuscript submitted for publication.

Allgood-Merten, B., Lewinsohn, P. M., & Hops, H. (1990). Sex differences and adolescent depression. *Journal of Abnormal Psychology, 99,* 55–63.

Alloy, L. B., Whitehouse, W. G., Robinson, M. S., Abramson, L. Y., Hogan, M. E., Rose, D. T., et al. (2000). The Temple-Wisconsin Cognitive Vulnerability to Depression Project: Lifetime history of Axis I psychopathology in individuals at high and low cognitive risk for depression. *Journal of Abnormal Psychology, 109,* 403–418.

Ambrosini, P., Bennett, D., Cleland, C. M., & Haslam, N. (2002). Taxonicity of adolescent melancholia: A categorical or dimensional construct? *Journal of Psychiatric Research, 36,* 247–256.

American Psychiatric Association. (2000). *Diagnostic and Statistical Manual of Mental Disorders* (4th ed., text revision). Washington, DC: Author.

Angold, A., Costello, E. J., & Erkanli, A. (1999). Comorbidity. *Journal of Child Psychology and Psychiatry and Allied Disciplines, 40,* 57–87.

Angold, A., Costello, E. J., & Worthman, C. M. (1998). Puberty and depression: The roles of age, pubertal status and pubertal timing. *Psychological Medicine, 28,* 51–61.

Angold, A., Erkanli, A., Silberg, J., Eaves, L., & Costello, E. J. (2002). Depression scale scores in 8–17-year-olds: Effects of age and gender. *Journal of Child Psychology & Psychiatry & Allied Disciplines, 43,* 1052–1063.

Armsden, G. C., & Greenberg, M. T. (1987). The Inventory of Parent and Peer Attachment: Individual differences and their relationship to psychological well being in adolescents. *Journal of Youth and Adolescence, 16,* 427–454.

Armsden, G. C., McCauley, E., Greenberg, M. T., Burke, P. M., & Mitchell, J. R. (1990). Parent and peer attachment in early adolescent depression. *Journal of Abnormal Child Psychology, 18,* 683–697.

Avenevoli, S., Stolar, M., Li, J., Dierker, L., & Merikangas, K. R. (2001). Comorbidity of depression in children and adolescents: Models and evidence from a prospective high-risk family study. *Biological Psychiatry, 49,* 1071–1081.

Barnett, P. A., & Gotlib, I. H. (1988). Psychosocial functioning in depression: Distinguishing among antecedents, concomitants, and consequences. *Psychological Bulletin, 104,* 97–126.

Barnett, P. A., & Gotlib, I. H. (1990). Cognitive vulnerability to depressive symptoms among men and women. *Cognitive Therapy and Research, 14,* 47–61.

Beach, S. R. H., & Amir, N. (2003). Is depression taxonic, dimensional, or both? *Journal of Abnormal Psychology, 112,* 228–236.

Beardslee, W. R., Versage, E. M., & Gladstone, T. R. (1998). Children of affectively ill parents: A review of the past 10 years. *Journal of the Academy of Child and Adolescent Psychiatry, 37,* 1134–1141.

Beck, A. T. (1967). *Depression: Clinical, experimental, and theoretical aspects.* New York: Harper & Row.

Beck, A. T. (1983). Cognitive therapy of depression: New perspectives. In P. J. Clayton & J. E. Barrett (Eds.), *Treatment of depression: Old controversies and new approaches* (pp. 265–290). New York: Raven Press.

Belsher, G., & Costello, C. G. (1988). Relapse after recovery from unipolar depression: A critical review. *Psychological Bulletin, 104,* 84–96.

Birmaher, B., Dahl, R. E., Williamson, D. E., Perel, J. M., Brent, D. A., Axelson, D. A., et al. (2000). Growth hormone secretion in children and adolescents at high risk for major depressive disorder. *Archives of General Psychiatry, 57,* 867–872.

Birmaher, B., Ryan, N. D., Williamson, D. E., Brent, D. A., Kaufman, J., Dahl, R. E., et al. (1996). Childhood and adolescent depression: A review of the past 10 years: Part I. *Journal of the American Academy of Child and Adolescent Psychiatry, 35,* 1427–1439.

Blaney, P. H., & Kutcher, G. S. (1991). Measures of depressive dimensions: Are they interchangeable? *Journal of Personality Assessment, 56,* 502–512.

Blatt, S. J., & Homann, E. (1992). Parent-child interaction in the etiology of dependent and self-critical depression. *Clinical Psychology Review, 12,* 47–91.

Blatt, S. J., Shaffer, C. E., Bers, S. A., & Quinlan, D. M. (1992). Psychometric properties of the depressive experiences questionnaire for adolescents. *Journal of Personality Assessment, 59,* 82–98.

Blatt, S. J., & Zuroff, D. C. (1992). Interpersonal relatedness and self-definition: Two prototypes for depression. *Clinical Psychology Review, 12,* 527–562.

Block, J. H., Gjerde, P. F., & Block, J. H. (1991). Personality antecedents of depressive tendencies in 18-year-olds: A prospective study. *Journal of Personality & Social Psychology, 60,* 726–738.

Boland, R. J., & Keller, M. B. (2002). Course and outcome of depression. In I. H. Gotlib & C. L. Hammen (Eds.), *Handbook of depression* (pp. 43–60). New York: Guilford Press.

Brown, G. W., & Harris, T. O. (1989). Depression. In G. W. Brown & T. O. Harris (Eds.), *Life events and illness* (pp. 49–93). New York: Guilford Press.

Brown, J. D., & Silberschatz, G. (1989). Dependency, self-criticism, and depressive attributional style. *Journal of Abnormal Psychology, 98,* 187–188.

Brozina, K., & Abela, J. R. Z. (2003, November). *The Youth Attributional Style Questionnaire vs. the Children's Attributional Style Questionnaire: A prospective examination of vulnerability to depression.* Poster presented at the meeting of the Association for the Advancement of Behavior Therapy, Boston.

Brozina, K., & Abela, J. R. Z. (2004, November). *Searching for common vulnerabilities to depression and anxiety in children: Inferential styles for causes, consequences, and the self.* Paper presented at the meeting of the Association for the Advancement of Behavior Therapy, New Orleans, LA.

Burbach, D. J., Kashani, J. H., & Rosenberg, T. K. (1989). Parental bonding and depressive disorders in adolescents. *Journal of Child Psychology and Psychiatry and Allied Disciplines, 30,* 417–429.

Butler, L. D., & Nolen-Hoeksema, S. (1994). Gender differences in responses to depressed mood in a college sample. *Sex Roles, 30,* 331–346.

Carlson, G. A., & Kashani, J. (1988). Phenomenology of major depression from childhood through young adulthood: Analysis of three studies. *American Journal of Psychiatry, 145,* 1222–1225.

Caspi, A., & Moffitt, T. E. (1991). Individual differences are accentuated during periods of social change: The sample case of girls at puberty. *Journal of Personality and Social Psychology, 61,* 157–168.

Caspi, A., Sugden, K., Moffit, T. E., Taylor, A., Craig, I. W., & Harrington, H. (2003). Influence of life stress on depression: Moderation by a polymorphism in the 5-HTT gene. *Science, 301,* 386–389.

Chorpita, B. F., Albano, A. M., & Barlow, D. H. (1998). The structure of negative emotions in a clinical sample of children and adolescents. *Journal of Abnormal Psychology, 107,* 74–85.

Cicchetti, D., & Toth, S. L. (1998). The development of depression in children and adolescents. *American Psychologist, 53,* 221–241.

Clark, D. A., & Beck, A. T. (1999). *Scientific foundations of cognitive theory and therapy of depression.* New York: Wiley.

Clark, L. A., & Watson, D. (1991). Tripartite model of anxiety and depression: Psychometric evidence and taxonomic implications. *Journal of Abnormal Psychology, 100,* 316–336.

Clark, L. A., Watson, D., & Mineka, S. (1994). Temperament, personality, and the mood and anxiety disorders. *Journal of Abnormal Psychology, 103,* 103–116.

Cohen, L. H., Burt, C. E., & Bjorck, J. P. (1987). Life stress and adjustment: Effects of life events experienced by young adolescents and their parents. *Developmental Psychology, 23,* 583–592.

Cohen, P., Cohen, J., Kasen, S., & Velez, C. N. (1993). An epidemiological study of disorders in late childhood and adolescence: I. Age and gender specific prevalence. *Journal of Child Psychology and Psychiatry and Allied Disciplines, 34,* 851–867.

Cole, D. A., Martin, J. M., Peeke, L. G., Seroczynski, A. D., & Fier, J. (1999). Children's over and underestimation of academic competence: A longitudinal study of gender differences, depression and anxiety. *Child Development, 70,* 459–473.

Cole, D. A., Peeke, L. G., Martin, J. M., Truglio, R., & Seroczynski, A. D. (1998). A longitudinal look at the relation between depression and anxiety in children and adolescents. *Journal of Consulting & Clinical Psychology, 66,* 451–460.

Cole, D. A., Truglio, R., & Peeke, L. (1997). Relation between symptoms of anxiety and depression in children: A multitrait-multimethod-multigroup assessment. *Journal of Consulting and Clinical Psychology, 65,* 110–119.

Cole, D. A., & Turner, J. E., Jr. (1993). Models of cognitive mediation and moderation in child depression. *Journal of Abnormal Psychology, 102,* 271–281.

Compas, B. E., Connor-Smith, J., & Jaser, S. S. (2004). Temperament, stress reactivity, and coping: Implications for depression in childhood and adolescence. *Journal of Clinical Child & Adolescent Psychology, 33,* 21–31.

Compas, B. E., Ey, S., & Grant, K. E. (1993). Taxonomy, assessment, and diagnosis of depression during adolescence. *Psychological Bulletin, 114,* 323–344.

Compas, B. E., Howell, D. C., Phares, V., Williams, R. A., & Giunta, C. T. (1989). Risk factors for emotional/behavioral problems in young adolescents: A prospective analysis of adolescent and parental stress and symptoms. *Journal of Consulting and Clinical Psychology, 57,* 732–740.

Conley, C. S., Haines, B. A., Hilt, L. M., & Metalsky, G. I. (2001). The children's attributional style interview: Developmental tests of cognitive diathesis-stress theories of depression. *Journal of Abnormal Child Psychology, 29,* 445–463.

Coryell, W., Akiskal, H. S., Leon, A. C., Winokur, G., Maser, J., Mueller, T., et al. (1994). The time course of nonchronic major depressive disorder: Uniformity across episodes and samples. *Archives of General Psychiatry, 51,* 405–410.

Costello, E. J., Angold, A., Burns, B. J., Erkanli, A., Stangl, D. K., & Tweed, D. L. (1996). The Great Smoky Mountains Study of youth: Functional impairment and serious emotional disturbance. *Archives of General Psychiatry, 53,* 1137–1143.

Costello, E. J., Mustillo, S., Erkanli, A., Keeler, G., & Angold, A. (2003). Prevalence and development of psychiatric disorders in childhood and adolescence. *Archives of General Psychiatry, 60,* 837–844.

Crick, N. R., Werner, N. E., Casas, J. F., O'Brien, K. M., Nelson, D. A., Grotpeter, J. K., et al. (1999). Childhood aggression and gender: A new look at an old problem. In D. Bernstein (Ed.), *Gender and motivation: Nebraska Symposium on Motivation* (pp. 75–141). Lincoln: University of Nebraska Press.

Cumsille, P. E., & Epstein, N. (1994). Family cohesion, family adaptability, social support, and adolescent depressive symptoms in outpatient clinic families. *Journal of Family Psychology, 8,* 202–214.

Curran, P. J., & Bollen, K. A. (2001). The best of both worlds: Combining autoregressive and latent curve models. In L. M. Collins & A. G. Sayer (Eds.), *New methods for the analysis of change: Decade of behavior* (pp. 107–135). Washington, DC: American Psychological Association.

Dahl, R. E., Kaufman, J., Ryan, N. D., & Perel, J. M. (1992). The dexamethasone suppression test in children and adolescents: A review and a controlled study. *Biological Psychiatry, 32,* 109–126.

Daley, S., Hammen, C., Burge, D., Davila, J., Paley, B., Lindberg, N., et al. (1997). Predictors of the generation of episodic stress: A longitudinal study of late adolescent women. *Journal of Abnormal Psychology, 106,* 251–259.

Davidson, R. J., Pizzagalli, D., Nitschke, J. B., & Putnam, K. (2002). Depression: Perspectives from affective neuroscience. *Annual Review of Psychology, 53,* 545–574.

Davies, P. T., & Windle, M. (2001). Interparental discord and adolescent adjustment trajectories: The potentiating and protective role of interpersonal attributes. *Child Development, 72,* 1163–1178.

Dawson, G., Frey, K., Panagiotides, H., Osterling, J., & Hessl, D. (1997). Infants of depressed mothers exhibit atypical frontal brain activity: A replication and extension of previous findings. *Journal of Child Psychology & Psychiatry & Allied Disciplines, 38,* 179–186.

Deater-Deckard, K., Fulker, D. W., & Plomin, R. (1999). A genetic study of the family environment in the transition to early adolescence. *Journal of Child Psychology and Psychiatry, 40,* 769–775.

Dinan, T. G. (1998). Psychoneuroendocrinology of depression: Growth hormone. *Psychoneuroendocrinology, 21,* 325–339.

Dixon, J. F., & Ahrens, A. H. (1992). Stress and attributional styles as predictors of self-reported depression in children. *Cognitive Therapy and Research, 16,* 623–634.

Duggal, S., Carlson, E. A., Sroufe, L. A., & Egeland, B. (2001). Depressive symptomatology in childhood and adolescence. *Development & Psychopathology, 13,* 143–164.

Duggan, C., Sham, P., Minne, C., Lee, A., & Murray, R. (1998). Family history as a predictor of poor long-term outcome in depression. *British Journal of Psychiatry, 173,* 527–530.

Dykman, B. M., & Johll, M. (1998). Dysfunctional attitudes and vulnerability to depressive symptoms: A 14-week longitudinal study. *Cognitive Therapy and Research, 22,* 337–352.

Enns, M. W., Cox, B. J., & Larsen, D. K. (2000). Perceptions of parental bonding and symptom severity in adults with depression: Mediation by personality dimensions. *Canadian Journal of Psychiatry, 45,* 263–268.

Erikson, E. H. (1974). *Dimensions of a new identity.* New York: Norton.

Fergusson, D. M., Horwood, J., & Lynskey, M. T. (1993). Prevalence and comorbidity of DSM-III-R diagnoses in a birth cohort of 15 year olds. *Journal of the American Academy of Child & Adolescent Psychiatry, 32,* 1127–1134.

Fichman, L., Koestner, R., & Zuroff, D. C. (1994). Depressive styles in adolescence: Assessment, relation to social functioning, and developmental trends. *Journal of Youth and Adolescence, 23,* 315–330.

Flett, G. L., Vredenburg, K., & Krames, L. (1997). The continuity of depression in clinical and nonclinical samples. *Psychological Bulletin, 121,* 395–416.

Follette, V. M., & Jacobson, N. S. (1987). Importance of attributions as a predictor of how people cope with failure. *Journal of Personality and Social Psychology, 52,* 1205–1211.

Garber, J. (2000). Development and depression. In A. J. Sameroff, M. Lewis, & S. M. Miller (Eds.), *Handbook of developmental psychopathology* (pp. 467–490). New York: Kluwer.

Garber, J., & Little, S. (1999). Predictors of competence among offspring of depressed mothers. *Journal of Adolescent Research, 14,* 44–71.

Ge, X., Conger, R. D., & Elder, G. H. (1996). Coming of age too early: Pubertal influences on girls' vulnerability to psychological distress. *Child Development, 67,* 3386–3400.

Ge, X., Conger, R. D., & Elder, G. H., Jr. (2001). Pubertal transition, stressful life events, and the emergence of gender differences in adolescent depressive symptoms. *Developmental Psychology, 37,* 404–417.

Ge, X., Lorenz, F. O., Conger, R. D., Elder, G. H., & Simons, R. L. (1994). Trajectories of stressful life events and depressive symptoms during adolescence. *Developmental Psychology, 30,* 467–483.

Gibb, B. E. (2002). Childhood maltreatment and negative cognitive styles: A quantitative and qualitative review. *Clinical Psychology Review, 22,* 223–246.

Gladstone, T. G., Kaslow, N. J., Seeley, J. R., & Lewinsohn, P. M. (1997). Sex differences, attributional style, and depressive symptoms among adolescents. *Journal of Abnormal Child Psychology, 25,* 297–305.

Gold, P. W., Goodwin, F. K., & Chrousos, G. P. (1988). Clinical and biochemical manifestations of depression: Relation to the neurobiology of stress. *New England Journal of Medicine, 319,* 348–353.

Goodman, S. H., & Gotlib, I. H. (Eds.). (2002). *Children of depressed parents: Mechanisms of risk and implications for treatment.* Washington, DC: American Psychological Association.

Goodman, S. H., Schwab-Stone, M., Lahey, B. B., Shaffer, D., & Jensen, P. S. (2000). Major depression and dysthymia in children and adolescents: Discriminant validity and differential consequences in a community sample. *Journal of the American Academy of Child & Adolescent Psychiatry, 39,* 761–770.

Goodyer, I. M. (Ed.). (2001a). *The depressed child and adolescent* (2nd ed.). New York: Cambridge University Press.

Goodyer, I. M. (2001b). Life events: Their nature and effects. In I. M. Goodyer (Ed.), *The depressed child and adolescent* (2nd ed., pp. 204–232). New York: Cambridge University Press.

Goodyer, I. M., Herbert, J., Tamplin, A., & Altham, P. M. E. (2000). Recent life events, cortisol, dehydroepiandrosterone and the onset of major depression in high-risk adolescents. *British Journal of Psychiatry, 177,* 499–504.

Gotlib, I. H., Lewinsohn, P. M., & Seeley, J. R. (1995). Symptoms versus a diagnosis of depression: Differences in psychosocial functioning. *Journal of Consulting and Clinical Psychology, 63,* 90–100.

Graber, J. A., Brooks-Gunn, J., & Petersen, A. C. (1996). *Transitions through adolescence: Interpersonal domains and context.* Mahwah, NJ: Lawrence Erlbaum.

Graber, J. A., Lewinsohn, P. M., Seeley, J. R., & Brooks-Gunn, J. (1997). Is psychopathology associated with the timing of pubertal development? *Journal of the American Academy of Child and Adolescent Psychiatry, 36,* 1768–1776.

Graham, C. A., & Easterbrooks, M. A. (2000). School-aged children's vulnerability to depressive symptomatology: The role of attachment security, maternal depressive symptomatology, and economic risk. *Development & Psychopathology, 12,* 201–213.

Grant, K. E., Compas, B. E., Stuhlmacher, A. F., Thurm, A. E., McMahon, S. D., & Halpert, J. A. (2003). Stressors and child and adolescent psychopathology: Moving from markers to mechanisms of risk. *Psychological Bulletin, 129,* 447–466.

Haaga, D. F., Yarmus, M., Hubbard, S., Brody, C., Solomon, A., Kirk, L., et al. (2002). Mood dependency of self-rated attachment style. *Cognitive Therapy & Research, 26,* 57–71.

Haeffel, G. J., Abramson, L. Y., Voelz, Z. R., Metalsky, G. I., Halberstadt, L., Dykman, B. M., et al. (2003). Cognitive vulnerability to depression and lifetime history of Axis I psychopathology: A comparison of negative cognitive styles (CSQ) and dysfunctional attitudes (DAS). *Journal of Cognitive Psychotherapy, 17,* 3–22.

Hammen, C. (1991). The generation of stress in the course of unipolar depression. *Journal of Abnormal Psychology, 100,* 555–561.

Hammen, C. L., Adrian, C., & Hiroto, D. (1988). A longitudinal test of the attributional vulnerability model of depression in children at risk for depression. *British Journal of Clinical Psychology, 27,* 37–46.

Hammen, C. L., Burge, D., Daley, S. E., Davila, J., Paley, B., & Rudolph, K. D. (1995). Interpersonal attachment cognitions and prediction of symptomatic responses to interpersonal stress. *Journal of Abnormal Psychology, 104,* 436–443.

Hammen, C., & Goodman-Brown, T. (1990). Self-schemas and vulnerability to specific life stress in children at risk for depression. *Cognitive Therapy & Research, 14,* 215–227.

Hammen, C., Marks, T., DeMayo, R., & Mayol, A. (1985). Self-schemas and risk for depression: A prospective study. *Journal of Personality and Social Psychology, 49,* 1147–1159.

Hammen, C., Marks, T., Mayol, A., & deMayo, R. (1985). Depressive self-schematas, life-stress, and vulnerability to depression. *Journal of Abnormal Psychology, 94,* 308–319.

Hammen, C., & Rudolph, K. D. (2003). Childhood mood disorders. In E. J. Mash & R. A. Barkley (Eds.), *Child psychopathology* (2nd ed., pp. 233–278). New York: Guilford Press.

Hankin, B. L. (in press). Childhood maltreatment and psychopathology: Prospective tests of attachment, cognitive vulnerability, and stress as mediating processes. *Cognitive Therapy and Research.*

Hankin, B. L., & Abramson, L. Y. (1999). Development of gender differences in depression: Description and possible explanations. *Annals of Medicine, 31,* 372–379.

Hankin, B. L., & Abramson, L. Y. (2001). Development of gender differences in depression: An elaborated cognitive vulnerability-transactional stress theory. *Psychological Bulletin, 127,* 773–796.

Hankin, B. L., & Abramson, L. Y. (2002). Measuring cognitive vulnerability to depression in adolescence: Reliability, validity and gender differences. *Journal of Clinical Child & Adolescent Psychology, 31,* 491–504.

Hankin, B. L., Abramson, L. Y., Miller, N., & Haeffel, G. J. (2004). Cognitive vulnerability-stress theories of depression: Examining affective specificity in the prediction of depression versus anxiety in 3 prospective studies. *Cognitive Therapy and Research, 28,* 309–345.

Hankin, B. L., Abramson, L. Y., Moffitt, T. E., McGee, R., Silva, P. A., & Angell, K. E. (1998). Development of depression from preadolescence to young adulthood: Emerging gender differences in a 10-year longitudinal study. *Journal of Abnormal Psychology, 107,* 128–140.

Hankin, B. L., Abramson, L. Y., & Siler, M. (2001). A prospective test of the hopelessness theory of depression in adolescence. *Cognitive Therapy & Research, 25,* 607–632.

Hankin, B. L., Carter, I. L., Abela, J. R. Z., & Adams, P. (2004). *Factorial categorization of three central cognitive theories of depression: Exploratory and confirmatory factor analyses of hopelessness theory, Beck's theory, and response styles theory.* Manuscript submitted for publication.

Hankin, B. L., Fraley, R. C., & Abela, J. R. Z. (2005). Daily depression and cognitions about stress: Evidence for a trait-like depressogenic cognitive style and the prediction of depressive symptoms trajectories in a prospective daily diary study. *Journal of Personality and Social Psychology.*

Hankin, B. L., Fraley, R. C., Lahey, B. B., & Waldman, I. (in press). Is youth depressive disorder best viewed as a continuum or discrete category? A taxometric analysis of childhood and adolescent depression in a population-based sample. *Journal of Abnormal Psychology.*

Hankin, B. L., Kassel, J. D., & Abela, J. R. Z. (2005). Adult attachment styles and specificity of emotional distress: Prospective investigations of cognitive risk and interpersonal stress generation as mediating mechanisms. *Personality and Social Psychology Bulletin, 31,* 136–151.

Hankin, B. L., Roesch, L., Mermelstein, R., & Flay, B. (2004, July). *Depression, stressors, and gender differences in adolescence: Examination of a transactional stress generation hypothesis in a multi-wave study.* Paper presented at the World Congress of Behavioral and Cognitive Therapies, Kobe, Japan.

Harrington, R. C., Fudge, H., Rutter, M. L., Pickles, A., & Hill, J. (1990). Adult outcomes of childhood and adolescent depression: I. Psychiatric status. *Archives of General Psychiatry, 47,* 465–473.

Hayward, C., Gotlib, I. H., Schraedley, P. K., & Litt, I. F. (1999). Ethnic differences in the association between pubertal status and symptoms of depression in adolescent girls. *Journal of Adolescent Health, 25,* 143–149.

Hewitt, P. L., & Flett, G. L. (1993). Dimensions of perfectionism, daily stress, and depression: A test of the specific vulnerability hypothesis. *Journal of Abnormal Psychology, 102,* 58–65.

Hilsman, R., & Garber, J. (1995). A test of the cognitive diathesis-stress model of depression in children: Academic stressors, attributional style, perceived competence, and control. *Journal of Personality and Social Psychology, 69,* 370–380.

Hirschfeld, R. M., Klerman, G. L., Lavori, P., Keller, M. B., Griffith, P., & Coryell, W. (1989). Premorbid personality assessments of first onset of major depression. *Archives of General Psychiatry, 46,* 345–350.

Hortacsu, N., Cesur, S., & Oral, A. (1993). Relationship between depression and attachment styles in parent- and institution-reared Turkish children. *Journal of Genetic Psychology, 154,* 329–337.

Ingram, R. E., Miranda, J., & Segal, Z. V. (1998). *Cognitive vulnerability to depression.* New York: Guilford Press.

Jaffee, S. R., Moffitt, T. E., Caspi, A., Fombonne, E., Poulton, R., & Martin, J. (2002). Differences in early childhood risk factors for juvenile-onset and adult-onset depression. *Archives of General Psychiatry, 59,* 215–222.

Joiner, T. E. (1994). Contagious depression: Existence, specificity to depressed symptoms, and the role of reassurance seeking. *Journal of Personality and Social Psychology, 67,* 287–296.

Joiner, T. E. (1999). A test of interpersonal theory of depression in youth psychiatric inpatients. *Journal of Abnormal Child Psychology, 27,* 77–85.

Joiner, T. E., Alfano, M. S., & Metalsky, G. I. (1992). When depression breeds contempt: Reassurance seeking, self-esteem, and rejection of depressed college students by their roommates. *Journal of Abnormal Psychology, 101,* 165–173.

Joiner, T. E., Alfano, M. S., & Metalsky, G. I. (1993). Caught in the crossfire: Depression, self-consistency, self-enhancement, and the response of others. *Journal of Social and Clinical Psychology, 12,* 113–134.

Joiner, T., & Coyne, J. C. (1999). *The interactional nature of depression: Advances in interpersonal approaches.* Washington, DC: American Psychological Association.

Joiner, T. E., & Metalsky, G. I. (1995). A prospective test of an integrative interpersonal theory of depression: A naturalistic study of college roommates. *Journal of Personality & Social Psychology, 69,* 778–788.

Joiner, T. E., Jr., & Metalsky, G. I. (2001). Excessive reassurance seeking: Delineating a risk factor involved in the development of depressive symptoms. *Psychological Science, 12,* 371–378.

Joiner, T. E., Metalsky, G. I., Gencoz, F., & Gencoz, T. (2001). The relative specificity of excessive reassurance seeking to depressive symptoms and diagnosis among clinical samples of adults and youth. *Journal of Psychopathology and Behavioral Assessment, 23,* 35–41.

Joiner, T. E., Metalsky, G. I., Katz, J., & Beach, S. R. H. (1999). Depression and excessive reassurance-seeking. *Psychological Inquiry, 10,* 269–278.

Joiner, T. E., Metalsky, G. I., Lew, A., & Klocek, J. (1999). Testing the causal mediation component of Beck's theory of depression: Evidence for specific mediation. *Cognitive Therapy and Research, 23,* 401–412.

Joiner, T. E., Jr., & Schmidt, N. B. (1998). Excessive reassurance seeking predicts depressive but not anxious reactions to acute stress. *Journal of Abnormal Psychology, 107,* 533–537.

Judd, L. L. (1997). The clinical course of unipolar major depressive disorders. *Archives of General Psychiatry, 54,* 989–991.

Kashani, J. H., Suarez, L., Jones, M. R., & Reid, J. C. (1999). Perceived family characteristic differences between depressed and anxious children and adolescents. *Journal of Affective Disorders, 52,* 269–274.

Katz, J., & Beach, S. R. H. (1997). Romance in the crossfire: When do women's depressive symptoms predict partner relationship dissatisfaction? *Journal of Social and Clinical Psychology, 16,* 243–258.

Katz, J., Beach, S. R. H., & Joiner, T. E. (1998). When does partner devaluation predict emotional distress? Prospective moderating effects of reassurance seeking and self-esteem. *Personal Relationships, 5,* 409–421.

Katz, J., Beach, S. R. H., & Joiner, T. E. (1999). Contagious depression in dating couples. *Journal of Social and Clinical Psychology, 18,* 1–13.

Kaufman, J., Martin, A., King, R. A., & Charney, D. (2001). Are child-, adolescent-, and adult-onset depression one and the same disorder? *Biological Psychiatry, 49,* 980–1001.

Kendler, K. S. (1995). Adversity, stress, and psychopathology: A psychiatric genetic perspective. *International Journal of Methods in Psychiatric Research, 5,* 163–170.

Kendler, K. S., Gardner, C. O., & Prescott, C. A. (2003). Personality and the experience of environmental adversity. *Psychological Medicine, 33,* 1193–1202.

Kendler, K. S., Hettema, J. M., Butera, F., Gardner, C. O., & Prescott, C. A. (2003). Life event dimensions of loss, humiliation, entrapment, and danger in the prediction of onsets of major depression and generalized anxiety. *Archives of General Psychiatry, 60,* 789–796.

Kendler, K. S., & Karkowski-Shuman, L. (1997). Stressful life events and genetic liability to major depression: Genetic control of exposure to the environment? *Psychological Medicine, 27,* 539–547.

Kendler, K. S., Neale, M., Kessler, R., Heath, A., & Eaves, L. (1993). A twin study of recent life events and difficulties. *Archives of General Psychiatry, 50,* 789–796.

Kessler, R. C., Avenevoli, S., & Merikangas, K. R. (2001). Mood disorders in children and adolescents: An epidemiologic perspective. *Biological Psychiatry, 49,* 1002–1014.

Kessler, R. C., McGonagle, K. A., Zhao, S., Nelson, C. B., Hughes, M., Eshleman, S., et al. (1994). Lifetime and 12-month prevalence of DSM-III-R psychiatric disorders in the United States: Results from the National Comorbidity Survey. *Archives of General Psychiatry, 51,* 8–19.

Keuhner, C., & Weber, I. (1999). Responses to depression in unipolar depressed patients: An investigation of Nolen-Hoeksema's response style theory. *Psychological Medicine, 29,* 1323–1333.

Kim-Cohen, J., Caspi, A., Moffitt, T. E., Harrington, H., Milne, B. J., & Poulton, R. (2003). Prior juvenile diagnoses in adults with mental disorder: Developmental follow-back of a prospective-longitudinal cohort. *Archives of General Psychiatry, 60,* 709–717.

Klein, D. N., Lewinsohn, P. M., & Seeley, J. R. (1997). Psychosocial characteristics of adolescents with a past history of dysthymic disorder: Comparison with adolescents with past histories of major depressive and non-affective disorders, and never mentally ill controls. *Journal of Affective Disorders, 42,* 127–135.

Klocek, J. W., Oliver, J. M., & Ross, M. J. (1997). The role of dysfunctional attitudes, negative life events, and social support in the prediction of depressive dysphoria: A prospective longitudinal study. *Social Behaviour and Personality, 25,* 123–136.

Kovacs, M. (1996). Presentation and course of major depressive disorder during childhood and later years of the lifespan. *Journal of the American Academy of Child & Adolescent Psychiatry, 35,* 705–715.

Krueger, R. F. (1999). Personality traits in late adolescence predict mental disorders in early adulthood: A prospective-epidemiological study. *Journal of Personality, 67,* 39–65.

Krueger, R. F. (2000). Phenotypic, genetic, and nonshared environmental parallels in the structure of personality: A view from the Multidimensional Personality Questionnaire. *Journal of Personality & Social Psychology, 79,* 1057–1067.

Krueger, R. F., Caspi, A., Moffitt, T. E., Silva, P. A., & McGee, R. (1996). Personality traits are differentially linked to mental disorders: A multitrait-multidiagnosis study of an adolescent birth cohort. *Journal of Abnormal Psychology, 105,* 299–312.

Lakdawalla, Z., & Hankin, B. L. (2003, November). *Personality as a prospective vulnerability to depression: Proposed mechanisms.* Paper presented at the 37th Annual Meeting of the Association for Advancement of Behavior Therapy, Boston.

Lakey, B., & Ross, L. (1994). Dependency and self-criticism as moderators of interpersonal and achievement stress: The role of initial dysphoria. *Cognitive Therapy and Research, 18,* 581–599.

Lewinsohn, P. M., Allen, N. B., Seeley, J. R., & Gotlib, I. H. (1999). First onset versus recurrence of depression: Differential processes of psychosocial risk. *Journal of Abnormal Psychology, 108,* 483–489.

Lewinsohn, P. M., Clarke, G. N., Seeley, J. R., & Rohde, P. (1994). Major depression in community adolescents: Age at onset, episode duration, and time to recurrence. *Journal of the American Academy of Child & Adolescent Psychiatry, 33,* 809–818.

Lewinsohn, P. M., Joiner, T. E., Jr., & Rohde, P. (2001). Evaluation of cognitive diathesis-stress models in predicting major depressive disorder in adolescents. *Journal of Abnormal Psychology, 110,* 203–215.

Lewinsohn, P. M., Roberts, R. E., Seeley, J. R., Rohde, P., Gotlib, I. H., & Hops, H. (1994). Adolescent psychopathology: II. Psychosocial risk factors for depression. *Journal of Abnormal Psychology, 103,* 302–315.

Lewinsohn, P. M., Rohde, P., & Seeley, J. R. (1998). Major depressive disorder in older adolescents: Prevalence, risk factors, and clinical implications. *Clinical Psychology Review, 18,* 765–794.

Lewinsohn, P. M., Rohde, P., Seeley, J. R., Klein, D. N., & Gotlib, I. H. (2000). Natural course of adolescent major depressive disorder in a community sample: Predictors of recurrence in young adults. *American Journal of Psychiatry, 157,* 1584–1591.

Lewinsohn, P. M., Seeley, J. R., & Gotlib, I. H. (1997). Depression related psychosocial variables: Are they specific to depression in adolescents? *Journal of Abnormal Psychology, 106,* 365–375.

Lewinsohn, P. M., Solomon, A., Seeley, J. R., & Zeiss, A. (2000). Clinical implications of "subthreshold" depressive symptoms. *Journal of Abnormal Psychology, 109,* 345–351.

Little, S. A., & Garber, J. (2000). Interpersonal and achievement orientations and specific stressors predicting depressive and aggressive symptoms in children. *Cognitive Therapy & Research, 24,* 651–670.

Luthar, S. S., & Blatt, S. J. (1993). Dependent and self-critical depressive experiences among inner-city adolescents. *Journal of Personality, 61,* 365–386.

Marcotte, G., Marcotte, D., & Bouffard, T. (2002). The influence of familial support and dysfunctional attitudes on depression and delinquency in an adolescent population. *European Journal of Psychology of Education, 17,* 363–376.

Marton, P., & Maharaj, S. (1993). Family factors in adolescent unipolar depression. *Canadian Journal of Psychiatry, 38,* 373–382.

McFarlane, A. H., Bellisimo, A., & Norman, G. R. (1995). Family structure, family functioning, and adolescent well-being: The transcendent influence of parental style. *Journal of Child Psychology and Psychiatry, 36,* 847–864.

McMahon, S. D., Grant, K. E., Compas, B. E., Thurm, A. E., & Ey, S. (2003). Stress and psychopathology in children and adolescents: Is there evidence of specificity? *Journal of Child Psychology & Psychiatry & Allied Disciplines, 44,* 107–133.

Metalsky, G. I., Halberstadt, L. J., & Abramson, L. Y. (1987). Vulnerability to depressive mood reactions: Toward a more powerful test of the diathesis × stress and causal mediation components of the reformulated theory of depression. *Journal of Personality and Social Psychology, 52,* 386–393.

Metalsky, G. I., & Joiner, T. E., Jr. (1992). Vulnerability to depressive symptomatology: A prospective test of the diathesis-stress and causal mediation components of the hopelessness theory of depression. *Journal of Personality and Social Psychology, 63,* 667–675.

Metalsky, G. I., Joiner, T. E., Jr., Hardin, T. S., & Abramson, L. Y. (1993). Depressive reactions to failure in a naturalistic setting: A test of the hopelessness and self-esteem theories of depression. *Journal of Abnormal Psychology, 102,* 101–109.

Meyer, S. E., Chrousos, G. P., & Gold, P. W. (2001). Major depression and the stress system: A life span perspective. *Development and Psychopathology, 13,* 565–580.

Meyer, W. J., Richards, G. E., Cavallo, A., Holt, K. G., Hejazi, M. S., Wigg, C., et al. (1991). Depression and growth hormone. *Journal of the American Academy of Child and Adolescent Psychiatry, 30,* 335.

Mineka, S., Watson, D., & Clark, L. A. (1998). Comorbidity of anxiety and unipolar mood disorders. *Annual Review of Psychology, 49,* 377–412.

Monroe, S. M., Rohde, P., Seeley, J. R., & Lewinsohn, P. M. (1999). Life events and depression in adolescence: Relationship loss as a prospective risk factor for first onset of major depressive disorder. *Journal of Abnormal Psychology, 108,* 606–614.

Monroe, S. M., & Simons, A. D. (1991). Diathesis-stress theories in the context of life stress research: Implications for the depressive disorders. *Psychological Bulletin, 110,* 406–425.

Muris, P., Mayer, B., & Meesters, C. (2000). Self-reported attachment style, anxiety, and depression in children. *Social Behavior & Personality, 28,* 157–162.

Muris, P., Meesters, C., van Melick, M., & Zwambag, L. (2001). Self-reported attachment style, attachment quality, and symptoms of anxiety and depression in young adolescents. *Personality and Individual Differences, 30,* 809–818.

Murray, C. J. L., & Lopez, A. D. (1996). *The global burden of disease.* Cambridge, MA: Harvard University Press.

Neiderhiser, J. M., Reiss, D., Hetherington, E. M., & Plomin, R. (1999). Relationships between parenting and adolescent adjustment over time: Genetic and environmental contributions. *Developmental Psychology, 35,* 680–692.

Newcomb, M. D., Huba, G. J., & Bentler, P. M. (1981). A multidimensional assessment of stressful life events among adolescents: Derivation and correlates. *Journal of Health and Social Behavior, 22,* 400–415.

Nolen-Hoeksema, S. (1991). Responses to depression and their effects on the duration of depressive episodes. *Journal of Abnormal Psychology, 100,* 569–582.

Nolen-Hoeksema, S. (2000). The role of rumination in depressive disorders and mixed anxiety/depressive symptoms. *Journal of Abnormal Psychology, 109,* 504–511.

Nolen-Hoeksema, S., Girgus, J. S., & Seligman, M. E. P. (1986). Learned helplessness in children: A longitudinal study of depression, achievement, and attributional style. *Journal of Personality and Social Psychology, 51,* 435–442.

Nolen-Hoeksema, S., Girgus, J. S., & Seligman, M. E. P. (1992). Predictors and consequences of childhood depressive symptoms: A 5-year longitudinal study. *Journal of Abnormal Psychology, 101,* 405–422.

Nolen-Hoeksema, S., & Harrell, Z. A. (2002). Rumination, depression, and alcohol use: Tests of gender differences. *Journal of Cognitive Psychotherapy, 16,* 391–403.

Nolen-Hoeksema, S., & Morrow, J. (1991). A prospective study of depression and posttraumatic stress symptoms after a natural disaster: The 1989 Loma Prieta earthquake. *Journal of Personality and Social Psychology, 61,* 115–121.

O'Connor, T. G., Neiderhiser, J. M., Reiss, D., Hetherington, E. M., & Plomin, R. (1998). Co-occurrence of depressive symptoms and antisocial behavior in adolescence: A common genetic liability. *Journal of Abnormal Psychology, 10,* 27–38.

Panak, W. F., & Garber, J. (1992). Role of aggression, rejection, and attributions in the prediction of depression in children. *Development and Psychopathology, 4,* 145–165.

Patten, C. A., Gillin, C. J., Farkas, A. J., Gilpin, E. A., Berry, C. G., & Pierce, J. P. (1997). Depressive symptoms in California adolescents: Family structure and parental support. *Journal of Adolescent Health, 20,* 271–278.

Pennington, B. F. (2002). *The development of psychopathology: Nature and nurture.* New York: Guilford Press.

Persons, J. B., & Miranda, J. (1992). Cognitive theories of vulnerability to depression: Reconciling negative evidence. *Cognitive Therapy and Research, 16,* 485–502.

Petersen, A. C., Compas, B. E., Brooks-Gunn, J., Stemmler, M., Ey, S., & Grant, K. E. (1993). Depression in adolescence. *American Psychologist, 48,* 155–168.

Pine, D. S., Cohen, E., Cohen, P., & Brook, J. (1999). Adolescent depressive symptoms as predictors of adult depression: Moodiness or mood disorder? *American Journal of Psychiatry, 156,* 133–135.

Pine, D. S., Cohen, P., Gurley, D., Brook, J., & Ma, Y. (1998). The risk for early-adulthood anxiety and depressive disorders in adolescents with anxiety and depressive disorders. *Archives of General Psychiatry, 55,* 56–64.

Potthoff, J. G., Holahan, C. J., & Joiner, T. E. (1995). Reassurance seeking, stress generation, and depressive symptoms: An integrative model. *Journal of Personality and Social Psychology, 68,* 664–670.

Priel, B., & Shamai, D. (1995). Attachment style and perceived social support: Effects on affect regulation. *Personality and Individual Differences, 19,* 235–241.

Ralph, J. A., & Mineka, S. (1998). Attributional style and self-esteem: The prediction of emotional distress following a midterm exam. *Journal of Abnormal Psychology, 107,* 203–215.

Rao, U., Hammen, C., & Daley, S. E. (1991). Continuity of depression during the transition to adulthood: A 5-year longitudinal study of young women. *Journal of the American Academy of Child & Adolescent Psychiatry, 38,* 908–915.

Reinecke, M. A., & Rogers, G. M. (2001). Dysfunctional attitudes and attachment style among clinically depressed adults. *Behavioural and Cognitive Psychotherapy, 29,* 129–141.

Reinherz, H. Z., Giaconia, R. M., Hauf, A. M. C., Wasserman, M. S., & Paradis, A. D. (2000). General and specific childhood risk factors for depression and drug disorders by early adulthood. *Journal of the American Academy of Child & Adolescent Psychiatry, 39,* 223–231.

Reinherz, H. Z., Giaconia, R. M., Lefkowitz, E. S., Pakiz, B., & Frost, A. K. (1993). Prevalence of psychiatric disorders in a community population of older adolescents. *Journal of the American Academy of Child and Adolescent Psychiatry, 32,* 369–377.

Reiss, D., Howe, G. W., Simmens, S. J., Bussell, D. A., Hetherington, E. M., Henderson, S. H., et al. (1995). Genetic questions for environmental studies: Differential parenting and psychopathology in adolescence. *Archives of General Psychiatry, 52,* 925–936.

Rice, F., Harold, G. T., & Thapar, A. (2002a). Assessing the effects of age, sex and shared environment on the genetic etiology of depression in childhood and adolescence. *Journal of Child Psychology & Psychiatry & Allied Disciplines, 43,* 1039–1051.

Rice, F., Harold, G. T., & Thapar, A. (2002b). The genetic aetiology of childhood depression: A review. *Journal of Child Psychology & Psychiatry & Allied Disciplines, 43,* 65–79.

Roberts, J. E., & Gamble, S. A. (2001). Current mood-state and past depression as predictors of self-esteem and dysfunctional attitudes among adolescents. *Personality & Individual Differences, 30,* 1023–1037.

Roberts, J. E., Gotlib, I. H., & Kassel, J. D. (1996). Adult attachment mediates security and symptoms of depression: Mediating roles of dysfunctional attitudes and low self-esteem. *Journal of Personality and Social Psychology, 70,* 310–320.

Roberts, J., & Monroe, S. M. (1994). A multidimensional model of self-esteem in depression. *Clinical Psychology Review, 14,* 161–181.

Roberts, R. E., Roberts, C. R., & Chen, Y. R. (1997). Ethnocultural differences in prevalence of adolescent depression. *American Journal of Community Psychology, 25,* 95–110.

Roberts, S. B., & Kendler, K. S. (1999). Neuroticism and self-esteem as indices of the vulnerability to major depression in women. *Psychological Medicine, 29,* 1101–1109.

Robinson, N. S., Garber, J., & Hilsman, R. (1995). Cognitions and stress: Direct and moderating effects on depressive versus externalizing symptoms during the junior high transition. *Journal of Abnormal Psychology, 104,* 453–463.

Rude, S. S., & Burnham, B. L. (1993). Do interpersonal and achievement vulnerabilities interact with congruent events to predict depression? Comparison of DEQ, SAS, DAS, and combined scales. *Cognitive Therapy and Research, 17,* 531–548.

Rudolph, K. D. (2002). Gender differences in emotional responses to interpersonal stress during adolescence. *Journal of Adolescent Health, 30,* 3–13.

Rudolph, K. D., & Hammen, C. (1999). Age and gender as determinants of stress exposure, generation, and reactions in youngsters: A transactional perspective. *Child Development, 70,* 660–677.

Ruscio, A. M., & Ruscio, J. (2002). The latent structure of analogue depression: Should the Beck Depression Inventory be used to classify groups? *Psychological Assessment, 14,* 135–145.

Ruscio, J., & Ruscio, A. M. (2000). Informing the continuity controversy: A taxometric analysis of depression. *Journal of Abnormal Psychology, 109,* 473–487.

Rushton, J. L., Forcier, M., & Schectman, R. M. (2002). Epidemiology of depressive symptoms in the National Longitudinal Study of Adolescent Health. *Journal of the American Academy of Child & Adolescent Psychiatry, 41,* 199–205.

Rutter, M., Caspi, A., & Moffitt, T. E. (2003). Using sex differences in psychopathology to study causal mechanisms: Unifying issues and research strategies. *Journal of Child Psychology and Psychiatry, 44,* 1092–1115.

Rutter, M., Pickles, A., Murray, R., & Eaves, L. (2001). Testing hypotheses on specific environmental causal effects on behavior. *Psychological Bulletin, 127,* 291–324.

Rutter, M., & Silberg, J. (2002). Gene-environment interplay in relation to emotional and behavioral disturbance. *Annual Review of Psychology, 53,* 463–490.

Rutter, M., & Sroufe, L. A. (2000). Developmental psychopathology: Concepts and challenges. *Development and Psychopathology, 12,* 265–296.

Ryan, N. (1998). Psychoneuroendocrinology of children and adolescents. *Psychiatric Clinics of North America, 21,* 435–441.

Ryan, N. D., Puig-Antich, J., Ambrosini, P., Rabinovich, H., Robinson, N., Nelson, B., et al. (1987). The clinical picture of major depression in children and adolescents. *Archives of General Psychiatry, 44,* 854–861.

Sakado, K., Kuwabara, H., Sato, T., Uehara, T., Sakado, M., & Someya, T. (2000). The relationship between personality, dysfunctional parenting in childhood, and lifetime depression in a sample of employed Japanese adults. *Journal of Affective Disorders, 60,* 47–51.

Sarin, S., Abela, J. R. Z., & Auerbach, R. P. (in press). The response style theory of depression: A test of specificity and causal mediation. *Cognition and Emotion.*

Sato, T., Sakado, K., Uehara, T., Narita, T., Hirano, S., Nishioka, K., et al. (1998). Dysfunctional parenting as a risk factor to lifetime depression in a sample of employed Japanese adults: Evidence for the "affectionless control" hypothesis. *Psychological Medicine, 28,* 737–742.

Schraedley, P. K., Gotlib, I. H., & Hayward, C. (1999). Gender differences in correlates of depressive symptoms in adolescents. *Journal of Adolescent Health, 25,* 98–108.

Schwartz, A. J. A., & Koenig, L. J. (1996). Response styles and negative affect among adolescents. *Cognitive Therapy and Research, 20,* 13–36.

Segal, Z. V., Gemar, M., & Williams, S. (1999). Differential cognitive response to a mood challenge following successful cognitive therapy or pharmacotherapy for unipolar depression. *Journal of Abnormal Psychology, 108,* 3–10.

Segal, Z. V., Shaw, B. F., & Vella, D. D. (1989). Life stress and depression: A test of the congruency hypothesis for life event content and depressive subtype. *Canadian Journal of Behavioural Science, 21,* 389–400.

Segal, Z. V., Shaw, B. F., Vella, D. D., & Katz, R. (1992). Cognitive and life stress predictors of relapse in remitted unipolar depressed patients: Test of the congruency hypothesis. *Journal of Abnormal Psychology, 101,* 26–36.

Seligman, M. E. P., Peterson, C., Kaslow, N. J., Tenenbaum, R. L., Alloy, L. B., & Abramson, L. Y. (1984). Attributional style and depressive symptoms among children. *Journal of Abnormal Psychology, 93,* 235–241.

Sheeber, L., Hops, H., Alpert, A., Davis, B., & Andrews, J. A. (1997). Family support and conflict: Prospective relations to adolescent depression. *Journal of Abnormal Child Psychology, 25,* 333–344.

Silberg, J. L., Pickles, A., Rutter, M., Hewitt, J., Simonoff, E., Maes, H., et al. (1999). The influence of genetic factors and life stress on depression among adolescent girls. *Archives of General Psychiatry, 56,* 225–232.

Silberg, J., Rutter, M., Neale, M., & Eaves, L. (2001). Genetic moderation of environmental risk for depression and anxiety in adolescent girls. *British Journal of Psychiatry, 179,* 116–121.

Sim, T. N. (2000). Adolescent psychosocial competence: The importance and role of regard for parents. *Journal of Research on Adolescence, 10,* 49–64.

Smith, T. W., O'Keefe, J. C., & Jenkins, M. (1988). Dependency and self-criticism: Correlates of depression or moderators of the effects of stressful life events? *Journal of Personality Disorders, 2,* 160–169.

Solomon, A., Haaga, D. A. F., & Arnow, B. A. (2001). Is clinical depression distinct from subthreshold depressive symptoms? A review of the continuity issue in depression research. *Journal of Nervous and Mental Disease, 189,* 498–506.

Southall, D., & Roberts, J. E. (2002). Attributional style and self-esteem in vulnerability to adolescent depressive symptoms following life stress: A 14-week prospective study. *Cognitive Therapy & Research, 26,* 563–579.

Stein, D., Williamson, D. E., Birmaher, B., Brent, D. A., Kaufman, J., Dahl, R., et al. (2000). Parent-child bonding and family functioning in depressed children and children at high risk and low risk for future depression. *Journal of the American Academy of Child and Adolescent Psychiatry, 39,* 1387–1395.

Sullivan, P. F., Neale, M. C., & Kendler, K. S. (2000). Genetic epidemiology of major depression: Review and meta-analysis. *American Journal of Psychiatry, 157,* 1552–1562.

Swendsen, J. D. (1998). The helplessness-hopelessness theory and daily mood experience: An idiographic and cross-situational perspective. *Journal of Personality and Social Psychology, 74,* 1398–1408.

Taylor, L., & Ingram, R. E. (1999). Cognitive reactivity and depressotypic information processing in children of depressed mothers. *Journal of Abnormal Psychology, 108,* 202–210.

Thapar, A., Harold, G., & McGuffin, P. (1998). Life events and depressive symptoms in childhood—Shared genes or shared adversity? A research note. *Journal of Child Psychology and Psychiatry, 39,* 1153–1158.

Thapar, A., & McGuffin, P. (1997). Anxiety and depressive symptoms in childhood—A genetic study of comorbidity. *Journal of Child Psychology and Psychiatry, 38,* 651–656.

Thase, M. E., Jindal, R., & Howland, R. H. (2002). Biological aspects of depression. In I. H. Gotlib & C. L. Hammen (Eds.), *Handbook of depression* (pp. 192–218). New York: Guilford Press.

Thompson, M., Kaslow, N. J., Weiss, B., & Nolen-Hoeksema, S. (1998). Children's Attributional Style Questionnaire—Revised: Psychometric examination. *Psychological Assessment, 10,* 166–170.

Tomarken, A. J., & Keener, A. D. (1998). Frontal brain asymmetry and depression: A self-regulatory perspective. *Cognition & Emotion, 12,* 387–420.

Tomarken, A. J., Simien, C., & Garber, J. (1994). Resting frontal brain asymmetry discriminates adolescent children of depressed mothers from low risk controls. *Psychophysiology, 3,* S97–S98.

Trull, T. J., & Sher, T. J. (1994). Relationship between the five-factor model of personality and Axis I disorders in a nonclinical sample. *Journal of Abnormal Psychology, 103,* 350–360.

Turner, J. E., & Cole, D. A. (1994). Developmental differences in cognitive diatheses in child depression. *Journal of Abnormal Psychology, 103,* 15–32.

Twenge, J. M., & Nolen-Hoeksema, S. (2002). Age, gender, race, socioeconomic status, and birth cohort difference on the children's depression inventory: A meta-analysis. *Journal of Abnormal Psychology, 111,* 578–588.

Van Os, J., & Jones, P. B. (1999). Early risk factors and adult person-environment relationships in affective disorder. *Psychological Medicine, 29,* 1055–1067.

Vivona, J. M. (2000). Parental attachment styles of late adolescents: Qualities of attachment relationships and consequences for adjustment. *Journal of Counseling Psychology, 47,* 316–329.

Waaktaar, T., Borge, A. I. H., Fundingsrud, H. P., Christie, H. J., & Torgersen, S. (2004). The role of stressful life events in the development of depressive symptoms in adolescence—A longitudinal community study. *Journal of Adolescence, 27,* 153–163.

Wade, T. J., Cairney, J., & Pevalin, D. J. (2002). Emergence of gender differences in depression during adolescence: National panel results from three countries. *Journal of the American Academy of Child & Adolescent Psychiatry, 41,* 190–198.

Wagner, B. M., & Compas, B. E. (1990). Gender, instrumentality, and expressivity: Moderators of the relation between stress and psychological symptoms during adolescence. *American Journal of Community Psychology, 18,* 383–406.

Watson, D. (2000). *Mood and temperament.* New York: Guilford Press.

Watson, D., Clark, L. A., & Harkness, A. R. (1994). Structures of personality and their relevance to psychopathology. *Journal of Abnormal Psychology, 103,* 18–31.

Weiss, B., & Garber, J. (2003). Developmental differences in the phenomenology of depression. *Development & Psychopathology, 15,* 403–430.

Weiss, B., Susser, K., & Catron, T. (1998). Common and specific features of childhood psychopathology. *Journal of Abnormal Psychology, 107,* 118–128.

Weissman, M. M., Warner, V., Wickramaratne, P., Moreau, D., & Olfson, M. (1997). Offspring of depressed parents: 10 years later. *Archives of General Psychiatry, 54,* 932–940.

West, M. L., Spreng, S. W., Rose, S. M., & Adam, K. S. (1999). Relationship between attachment-felt security and history of suicidal behaviours in clinical adolescents. *Canadian Journal of Psychiatry, 44,* 578–582.

Wichstrom, L. (1999). The emergence of gender difference in depressed mood during adolescence: The role of intensified gender socialization. *Developmental Psychology, 35,* 232–245.

Widiger, T. A., Verheul, R., & van den Brink, W. (1999). Personality and psychopathology. In L. Pervin & O. P. John (Eds.), *Handbook of personality: Theory and research* (2nd ed., pp. 347–366). New York: Guilford Press.

Williamson, D. E., Birmaher, B., Anderson, B. P., Al-Shabbout, M., & Ryan, N. D. (1995). Stressful life events in depressed adolescents: The role of dependent events during the depressive episode. *Journal of the American Academy of Child and Adolescent Psychiatry, 34,* 591–598.

Windle, M. (1992). A longitudinal study of stress buffering for adolescent problem behaviors. *Developmental Psychology, 28,* 522–530.

Wingate, L. R., & Joiner, T. (2004). Depression-related stress generation: A longitudinal study of black adolescents. *Behavior Therapy, 35,* 247–261.

Zuroff, D. C., Igreja, I., & Mongrain, M. (1990). Dysfunctional attitudes, dependency, and self-criticism as predictors of depressive mood states: A 12-month longitudinal study. *Cognitive Therapy & Research, 14,* 315–326.

Zuroff, D. C., & Mongrain, M. (1987). Dependency and self-criticism: Vulnerability factors for depressive affective states. *Journal of Abnormal Psychology, 96,* 14–22.

CHAPTER 11

Anxiety Disorders

A Developmental Vulnerability-Stress Perspective

NATHAN L. WILLIAMS, JOHN M. REARDON,
KATHLEEN T. MURRAY, AND TARA M. COLE

Anxiety disorders represent the most common class of psychological disorders in the United States, affecting as many as one in four Americans over their lifetimes (Kessler et al., 1994). Moreover, anxiety disorders are the most financially costly class of mental health problems in the United States, costing an estimated $46.6 billion in 1990 alone in direct and indirect costs (DuPont et al., 1996). Anxiety disorders are associated with heightened co-occurrence of other Axis I disorders (e.g., T. A. Brown, DiNardo, Lehman, & Campbell, 2001), myriad "unexplained" physical symptoms and chronic health conditions (e.g., Roy-Byrne & Katon, 2000), and poorer quality of life (Leon, Portera, & Weissman, 1995). An even larger percentage of the population suffers from subclinical anxiety (e.g., Kessler et al., 1994), which may contribute to a range of social, occupational, and health difficulties, including high blood pressure, heart disease, ulcers, lost productivity, impaired sleep, and interpersonal problems (Schonfeld et al., 1997). Epidemiological studies suggest that although anxiety disorders occur across all age and cultural groups, they occur approximately twice as often in females (Eaton, Dryman, & Weissman, 1991; Kessler et al., 1994). Moreover, studies suggest that anxiety disorders are often long-standing in the absence of effective treatment and consequently are among the most chronic of psychological disorders (e.g., Goisman et al., 1998; Yonkers, Warshaw, Maisson, & Keller, 1996).

Barlow (1988, 2000, 2002) suggests that although fear and anxiety both have defensive motivational functions, they fundamentally differ in their phenomenology, neurobiology, and behavioral expression. Barlow suggests that fear entails an immediate fight-or-flight response, occurring when confronted with present and imminent danger, that enables an immediate behavioral response, such as avoidance. In contrast, Barlow conceptualizes anxiety as a cognitive-affective structure that entails a sense of helplessness and perceived uncontrollability to cope with or prevent possible *future* threats or dangers. Anxiety involves a sense of apprehension toward the future, vigilance for signs of potential threat, and a constant state of preparation and readiness to cope with potential dangers. Because the threats associated with anxiety are typically future oriented and vague, individuals may engage in self-defeating behaviors aimed at warding off anxiety (e.g., worry, thought suppression, behavioral avoidance). Similarly, A. T. Beck and Clark (1997) conceptualize the anxious state as an innate, survival-oriented response to environmental stressors that originally served the purpose of orienting the individual toward life-threatening danger. According to A. T. Beck's initial model, anxiety disorders result when individuals develop overactive danger schemas that lead them to misperceive or exaggerate the presence and magnitude of future threat while simultaneously underestimating their ability to successfully cope with future threat (A. T. Beck & Emery, 1985). These danger schemas are hypothesized to operate automatically and to consistently distort the appraisal of relatively benign situations as potentially threatening or harmful. Thus, anxiety and fear both have some adaptive value through the evolutionarily derived defensive functions that they were designed to serve (Lang, Cuthbert, & Bradley, 1998). In the anxiety disorders, however, heightened expectations of unrealized threat lead to a pervasive sense of dread and helplessness, apprehension about the future, and diminished expectations of personal agency and efficacy to cope with or ward off anticipated dangers.

In this chapter, we present a developmental vulnerability-stress perspective on the ontogenesis of anxiety disorders. In the first section, we present characterizations of seven anxiety disorders along with epidemiological research highlighting the prevalence and phenomenology of these disorders. In the second half of this chapter, we present a review of major identified biological and psychological vulnerabilities to anxiety disorders, as well as a review of the empirical and theoretical study of stress. This section draws from Barlow's (2002) model of tripartite vulnerabilities to anxiety, including generalized biological vulnerabilities, generalized psychological vulnerabilities, and specific psychological vulnerabilities. In the final section, we integrate research on biological and psychological vulnerabilities, stress, and developmental psychopathology to present a developmental vulnerability-stress perspective on the development of anxiety disorders.

CHARACTERIZATION OF THE DISORDERS: DIAGNOSTIC CRITERIA AND EPIDEMIOLOGY

Specific Phobia

Specific phobia refers to an intense and persistent fear of an identifiable and circumscribed object or situation, such that exposure or anticipation of exposure to the feared stimulus almost invariably provokes an anxiety response (American Psychiatric Association [APA], 1994). This fear and anxiety lead to subsequent efforts to avoid the phobic stimulus, or else the stimulus is endured with great distress. To meet diagnostic criteria for specific phobia, adults must also recognize that their fear is excessive or unreasonable and manifest evidence that the phobia leads to clinically significant impairment(s) in functioning. Recently, the necessity of recognizing the excessiveness of one's fears has been questioned as a diagnostic criterion for specific phobia (e.g., Jones & Menzies, 2000). The anxiety response to the phobic stimulus in adults typically takes the form of an acute increase in activation of the sympathetic nervous system (i.e., a situationally bound or predisposed panic attack, or paniclike reaction;

for a review, see Craske, 1991). In some phobias (e.g., blood-injury-injection phobias), however, the anxiety response may take the form of a diphasic response in which initial activation of the sympathetic nervous system triggers the abrupt activation of the parasympathetic nervous system, resulting in a sharp decrease in heart rate and blood pressure and subsequent fainting (i.e., "vasovagal syncope"; Page, 1994).

Although myriad specific phobias have been identified (e.g., Agras, Sylvester, & Oliveau, 1969), the *Diagnostic and Statistical Manual of Mental Disorders,* 4th edition (*DSM-IV*; APA, 1994) identifies four main categories of specific phobias and a residual category: animal type (e.g., spiders, insects, snakes, etc.), natural environment type (e.g., heights, water, storms, etc.), blood-injection-injury (BII) type (e.g., seeing blood, receiving an injection, etc.), situational type (e.g., elevators, bridges, flying, etc.), and other types (e.g., choking, vomiting, loud sounds, etc.). The decision to parse the numerous specific phobias into five types was based on empirical evidence suggesting that the types could be differentiated by age of onset, patterns of covariation with other specific phobias, focus of anxiety, physiological response, and sex ratio. For example, BII phobias are the only types associated with a tendency to faint on exposure to the phobic stimulus (Page, 2003), and BII and animal-type phobias have an earlier age of onset than other types of specific phobias (e.g., Antony, T. A. Brown, & Barlow, 1997). Despite some evidence to support this differentiation, researchers have questioned both the diagnostic utility (Antony et al.) and factorial stability (Curtis, Magee, Eaton, Wittchen, & Kessler, 1998) of the *DSM-IV* phobia subtypes.

Specific phobias and subthreshold fears are prevalent in the general population. The two largest epidemiological studies of anxiety disorders in the United States, the Epidemiological Catchment Area study (ECA; Eaton et al., 1991) and the National Comorbidity Survey (NCS; Kessler et al., 1994), converge in estimating a lifetime prevalence rate of approximately 11% and a 2:1 female-to-male sex ratio for any specific phobias. A smaller epidemiological study of Swedish residents estimated a current prevalence of about 20% for specific phobias, and this study provides evidence for differential sex ratios based on the type of specific phobia (Fredrickson, Annas, Fischer, & Wik, 1996). Specifically, Fredrickson et al. suggest that sex differences are particularly strong for fears of animals, lightning, enclosed places, and darkness, but not significant for fears of heights, flying, injections, injuries, and dentists, leading Davey (1994) and others to propose that sex differences in certain specific phobias may be mediated by sex differences in disgust sensitivity (for a review, see Woody & Teachman, 2000). Follow-up analyses on the NCS data suggest that the most common specific phobias in adults are animals, heights, blood, and enclosed places (Curtis et al., 1998). Moreover, Curtis and colleagues, among others, provide evidence that specific phobias frequently co-occur with other specific phobias and other anxiety disorders in adults. Despite the high prevalence of specific phobias in epidemiological studies, relatively few individuals with specific phobias present for treatment.

The *DSM-IV* diagnostic criteria for specific phobia have been modified somewhat for use with children. Ollendick and Vasey (1999) suggest that these modifications reflect an increased recognition of the developmental nature and course of specific phobias in children. Specifically, phobic children who encounter the feared stimulus may experience a panic attack or may express their anxiety through crying, freezing, clinging, or tantrums. Moreover, children need not view their fears as excessive or unreasonable to meet criteria for a specific phobia but must demonstrate persistent symptoms for at least 6 months. In a recent review of the epidemiology of fears and specific phobias in children, Ollendick, King, and Muris (2002) estimated the prevalence of specific phobias in children at 5% (citing a range in prevalence from 2.6% to 9.1%) and in clinic-referred children for anxiety-related problems at about 15%. Ollendick et al. (2002) also report less comorbidity for specific phobias than for other anxiety disorders in *community* samples of children and adolescents, and they suggest a moderate degree of continuity for specific phobias across intervals ranging from 2 to 5 years. In contrast, Ollendick et al. (2002) suggest substantial comorbidity for specific phobias in *child clinical* populations.

Researchers examining fears and specific phobias within a developmental framework suggest that fears vary somewhat in content and intensity across the life span (Agras et al., 1969; Campbell, 1986; Fredrickson et al., 1996). Campbell suggests that infants demonstrate developmentally appropriate fears of loud and sudden stimuli, loss of support, and height in their first 6 months of life. Fears of strangers and novel or looming objects emerge in their second 6 months of life. Between ages 1 and 4, children typically develop separation anxiety, which peaks around 18 months and remains fairly common through age 4 (Dashiff, 1995). Campbell also suggests that fears of animals, monsters, and the dark are common among toddlers and preschoolers. According to her developmental review, Campbell suggests that the focus of children's fears shifts from early to middle childhood: fears of animals, the dark, and monsters decline, whereas fears of physical danger, natural disasters, and injury increase. Consistent with this developmental progression from early to middle childhood, Ollendick, King, and Frary (1989) provide epidemiological evidence using the Fear Survey Schedule for Children—Revised that the top 10 most commonly endorsed fears in a sample of normal children ages 7 to 16 were similar in content across age groups and gender and were focused on events dealing with physical injury and danger (e.g., being hit by an automobile, suffocation, falling). Further, Ollendick et al. (1989) provide evidence that girls endorse more fears than boys and that young children (ages 7–10) report more fears than older children (ages 11–13 and 14–16). Social and school-achievement fears become more evident in later childhood (i.e., about sixth grade) and are more likely to persist into adulthood (Campbell). Collectively, these findings suggest that some specific fears are developmentally phase appropriate and likely to remit with increased maturity (e.g., fears associated with imaginary creatures), whereas others may persist across the life span. The commonality and early age of onset of specific types of phobias (e.g., animals and BII stimuli) has led some to speculate that humans are biologically "prepared" to acquire fears to certain stimuli faster than others (Seligman, 1971), though this assertion remains equivocal (McNally, 1987).

Social Phobia

Social phobia refers to persistent fears of social or performance situations involving the potential for scrutiny by others and possible embarrassment (APA, 1994). As with specific phobias, exposure, or the anticipation of exposure, to feared social or performance situations almost invariably provokes an anxiety response, which may take the form of a situationally bound or situationally predisposed panic attack. Adults and adolescents must recognize that their fear or anxiety response is disproportional to the situation or unreasonable, whereas children need not evidence such insight to meet diagnostic criteria. Individuals with social phobia avoid or endure with marked distress their feared social or performance situations, and this fear or avoidance causes significant impairment in important areas of life functioning. Starting with *DSM-III-R* (APA, 1987), a generalized subtype has been included in the diagnostic criteria for social phobia if the individual manifests fears across "most social situations." Research on the generalized subtype suggests that it may be associated with more severe anxiety, depression, fear of negative evaluation, avoidance, social inhibition, and an earlier age of onset than more circumscribed social phobias (Heimberg, Holt, Schneier, Spitzer, & Liebowitz, 1993; Turner, Beidel, & Cooley-Quille, 1995). On the other hand, the literature demonstrates a high overlap between generalized social phobia and avoidant personality disorder (APD), leading some to propose a continuum of social anxiety ranging from circumscribed social fears to generalized social phobia with APD (McNeil, 2001).

Epidemiological research suggests that social phobia is both a common and impairing disorder. For example, data from the NCS produced a lifetime prevalence estimate of 13.3% and a 12-month prevalence estimate of 7.9% in the general adult population (Kessler et al., 1994). Results of the NCS suggest that social phobia occurs more frequently in women than men (i.e., a 3:2 sex ratio), whereas clinical studies suggest an equal sex ratio (e.g., Turner et al., 1995). Less severe variants of social phobia, such as social anxiety and shyness, appear to be considerably more prevalent in the general population. Epidemiological studies suggest that the most commonly feared social and performance situations are public speaking, parties, meeting members of the opposite sex, lecture halls, and using public transportation (e.g., Turner, Williams, Beidel, & Mezzich, 1986). A subgroup of individuals with social phobia evidences fears of specific activities, such as eating, drinking, writing, or urinating in public (e.g., Turner et al., 1986).

Social phobia appears to follow a chronic course and results in significant life interference in vocational and social functioning (Rapee, 1995; Schneier et al., 1994). Epidemiological studies suggest that social phobia typically begins in late childhood or early adolescence (Turner & Beidel, 1989), although shyness and social reticence can be observed by age 2 or 3 (i.e., behavioral inhibition; Kagan, Reznick, & Snidman, 1988). Retrospective studies of social phobia indicate that the disorder typically has a gradual onset with no clear precipitants. Until the publication of the *DSM-IV* (APA, 1994), a separate child-specific diagnosis of "avoidant disorder" was indicated for children or adolescents presenting with symptoms of "excessive shrinking from contact with unfamiliar people that is of sufficient severity to interfere with social functioning in peer relationships and that is of at least six months' duration" (APA, 1987, p. 61). Under the current diagnostic system, avoidant disorder has been eliminated, because its symptoms are subsumed under the diagnosis of social phobia. Early epidemiological studies of avoidant disorder suggest a prevalence rate of around 1% (McGee, Feehan, Williams, & Anderson, 1992), although this is likely an underestimate of the prevalence of social phobia in children and adolescents based on the results of large-scale community-based epidemiological studies.

Panic Disorder and Agoraphobia

Panic disorder is characterized by "recurrent, unexpected panic attacks followed by at least 1 month of persistent concern about having another Panic Attack, worry about the possible implications or consequences of the Panic Attacks, or a significant behavioral change related to the attacks" (APA, 1994, p. 397). Panic attacks are characterized as an intense period of fear or discomfort in which the person experiences somatic symptoms of autonomic hyperactivity (e.g., palpitations, sweating, chest pain, nausea, paresthesias, dizziness), fears of losing control or dying, and the behavioral urge to escape (APA, 1994). Because of the subjective sense of fear and terror associated with panic attacks, Barlow (1988) and others have argued that fear and panic are equivalent. By definition, panic attacks develop abruptly and reach their climax within 10 minutes. Panic attacks may be situationally bound (i.e., the attack almost invariably occurs on exposure or in anticipation of exposure to a situational cue), situationally predisposed (i.e., the attack is associated with a situational cue but does not invariably occur immediately after exposure), or "uncued" (i.e., the individual does not associate onset with an internal or external trigger but rather perceives the attack as coming "out of the blue"). Situationally bound or predisposed panic attacks occur in a number of anxiety disorders, but the specific diagnosis of panic disorder requires the presence of *uncued* panic attacks. Research suggests that panic disorder may be differentiated from panic attacks that occur in other anxiety disorders by the presence of catastrophic cognitions associated with panic (e.g., "I'm having a heart attack" or "Something is terribly wrong with me") and by anxiety that is focused on the misinterpretation of bodily sensations (Barlow, 1988; T. A. Brown, Marten, & Barlow, 1996). In addition, panic disorder requires that at least one of the attacks has been preceded by significant worry about the implications or consequences of the attack or a significant behavioral change related to the attacks (APA, 1994).

One such behavioral change that may occur in the context of panic disorder is the phobic condition agoraphobia. Agoraphobia is characterized by the pervasive avoidance, or endurance with anxiety or distress, of situations in which escape might be difficult or help might be unavailable if one were to experience panic (APA, 1994). Typically, agoraphobia involves the avoidance of clusters of feared situations such as being outside the home, entering crowded situations, or using public transportation. Agoraphobia may also involve *introceptive avoidance,* in which the individual avoids activities or substances (e.g., exercise, caffeine) that lead to increased autonomic arousal (Rapee, Craske, & Barlow, 1995). The link between panic disorder and agoraphobia remains equivocal, such that a history of panic does not necessitate the development of agoraphobia, and the magnitude of agoraphobic avoidance varies across patients (Craske & Barlow, 1988).

Epidemiological data suggest that panic disorder is less common than either specific phobias or social phobia. Kessler et al. (1994) reported a lifetime prevalence of 3.5% and a 1-year prevalence of 2.3% for panic disorder in the NCS, whereas Eaton et al. (1991) reported a lifetime prevalence of 1.57% for panic disorder based on *DSM-III* criteria in the ECA study. The prevalence of panic disorder appears to be substantially higher in clinical samples and in medical settings (e.g., APA, 1994). For example, patients with panic disorder frequently present to medical settings with symptoms of chest pain, heart palpitations, irritable bowl syndrome, and unexplained faintness (Roy-Byrne & Katon, 2000) and have high rates of emergency health care service utilization (Markowitz, Weissman, Ouellette, Lish, & Klerman, 1989). Converging epidemiological results from both community and clinical samples suggest that panic disorder is two to three times more common in females than in males. The prevalence of panic disorder with agoraphobia differs depending on the type of sample assessed. Kessler et al. (1994) reported a higher lifetime prevalence for agoraphobia without a history of panic disorder than for panic disorder either with or without agoraphobia in the NCS (e.g., 5.3% vs. 3.5%, respectively), whereas results from clinical samples suggest that treatment-seeking agoraphobics almost always have a precipitating history of panic (Craske, Miller, Rotunda, & Barlow, 1990).

Approximately one third to one half of community-based samples of individuals who meet criteria for panic disorder also have agoraphobia (APA, 1994).

Panic disorder appears to be largely an adult disorder with a relatively chronic course. Panic disorder most commonly develops between late adolescence and the mid-30s, with a median age of onset of 24 years (Burke, Burke, Regier, & Rae, 1990) and an average age of treatment seeking of 34 years (Craske et al., 1990). Panic disorder with or without agoraphobia is less common in older adult (J. G. Beck & Stanley, 1997) and in prepubescent populations (Hayward et al., 1992). In the majority of cases, stress has been identified as a clinical correlate of panic disorder onset and the frequency of subsequent panic symptoms (Craske et al.). Several prospective studies provide evidence for the chronic course of panic disorder. For example, Yonkers et al. (1998) reported a 5-year rate of remission of 39% for panic disorder, whereas Katschnig and Amering (1994) found that only 31% of panic disorder patients experienced sustained remission 2–6 years after completion of pharmacological treatment. In a 22-month prospective study, Hirschfeld (1996) indicated that only 18% of patients with panic disorder with agoraphobia and 43% of patients with panic disorder without agoraphobia recovered after their first episode of panic, compared with 80% recovery for patients with major depressive disorder. Panic disorder is also frequently comorbid with other psychological disorders, including other anxiety, mood, substance-use, and personality disorders (T. A. Brown et al., 2001).

Generalized Anxiety Disorder

Generalized anxiety disorder (GAD) is characterized by excessive and persistent anxiety and worry that occurs for at least 6 months (APA, 1994). The pervasive worry in GAD is typically appraised as uncontrollable, associated with a variety of content areas (e.g., finances, health, social relationships), and frequently about "minor" things. Indeed, the tendency to frequently worry about relatively minor things has been supported in empirical studies as one of the defining features of GAD (Abel & Borkovec, 1995). Unlike anxiety disorders characterized by symptoms of autonomic hyperactivity, the six somatic symptoms currently associated with GAD are more characteristic of a chronic stress reaction (e.g., muscle tension, restlessness, being easily fatigued, irritability, sleep disturbance, and difficulty concentrating). This shift away from somatic symptoms associated with high levels of physiological arousal in GAD was based on empirical findings suggesting that worry serves to reduce physiological arousal (Borkovec & Hu, 1990) and that symptoms of autonomic hyperactivity were less frequently and reliably endorsed by patients with GAD (T. A. Brown, Barlow, & Liebowitz, 1994; Marten et al., 1993). GAD also appears to be associated with considerable impairment in areas of life functioning such as lost productivity at work, interpersonal problems, and increased medical service cost (e.g., Greenberg et al., 1999).

Epidemiological data suggest that GAD is a relatively common disorder with a chronic course and a variable age of onset. For example, results of the NCS suggest a lifetime prevalence of 5.1% and a 1-year prevalence of 1.6% based on *DSM-III-R* criteria (Wittchen, Zhao, Kessler, & Eaton, 1994). The prevalence of GAD seems to be even higher in primary care settings and among high utilizers of medical care (Greenberg et al., 1999). Data from both community and clinical samples suggest that GAD is approximately twice as common in females as in males (e.g., Yonkers et al., 1996). GAD typically has a persistent course (Noyes et al., 1992) with a relatively low rate of remission (Yonkers et al., 1996). The age of onset for GAD varies considerably across studies (e.g., Yonkers et al., 1996), leading some to propose two distinct subtypes of GAD with early and late onset (Hoehn-Saric, Hazlett, & McLeod, 1993). For example, evidence from the ECA study suggested that GAD was most prevalent in the youngest age group, whereas evidence from the NCS suggested that GAD was most common in those older than age 45. Hoehn-Saric et al. found that 64% of their clinical sample reported "early onset" of GAD (i.e., before age 19) associated with a childhood history of fears, avoidance, and inhibition. In contrast, "late-onset" GAD was more likely to be precipitated by an identifiable stressor.

Obsessive-Compulsive Disorder

Obsessive-compulsive disorder (OCD) is characterized by recurrent obsessions or compulsions that cause distress or impairment or that consume more than 1 hour of time daily (APA, 1994). Obsessions are defined as recurrent thoughts, feelings, images, or impulses that are experienced as intrusive and unwanted, and that cause marked anxiety or distress (APA, 1994). Obsessions are typically experienced as alien to the individual, inconsistent with one's values or goals, and as somewhat uncontrollable. Further, individuals with OCD frequently use strategies to neutralize or suppress obsessional thinking, which may lead to paradoxical increases in the frequency of the obsession and the severity of OCD symptoms (e.g., Rachman, 1997; Salkovskis, Shafran, Rachman, & Freestone, 1999). The most common types of obsessions involve contamination fears, excessive self-doubt, aggressive impulses, sexual imagery, and the need to have things in a particular order (Rasmussen & Eisen, 1992). Obsessions may not be excessive worries about real-life situations and are recognized as products of the person's own mind (APA, 1994). Individuals with OCD typically recognize that their obsessions or compulsions are excessive or unreasonable, although the specifier of *poor insight* was added to the *DSM-IV* criteria to account for individuals who persistently overestimate the validity of their obsessions or fail to see the excessiveness of their compulsive behavior. When OCD symptoms present in children, however, insight into the excessive or unreasonable nature of the obsessions or compulsions is not required.

Compulsions represent ritualized patterns of behavior or cognition that the person feels driven to perform to reduce the anxiety or distress associated with an obsession or to prevent some dreaded consequence from occurring (APA, 1994). For example, individuals with contamination obsessions may engage in excessive washing behavior, whereas individuals with doubting obsessions may repeatedly check to ensure that a door is locked or that appliances are turned off. Compulsions are either clearly excessive (e.g., washing one's hands until the skin is raw) or not realistically connected with the obsessions that they are performed to neutralize or prevent (e.g., ritualized counting to neutralize aggressive impulses). The most common compulsions include washing and cleaning, counting, checking, repeating actions, and ordering (Jenike, Baer, Minchiello, Schwartz, & Carey, 1986; Rasmussen & Eisen, 1992). Several studies conducted to examine the relations between different types of obsessions and compulsions converge in suggesting three OCD symptom subtypes: harming/religious/sexual obsessions and checking compulsions; contamination obsessions and washing/cleaning compulsions; and symmetry/ordering/certainty obsessions and counting/repeating/checking compulsions (e.g., Baer, 1994; Mataix-Cols, Rauch, Manzo, Jenike, & Baer, 1999; Summerfelt, Richter, Antony, & Swinson, 1999). Results of these studies also suggest that hoarding compulsions represent a separate symptom not linked to the other OCD subtypes (Mataix-Cols et al.).

Epidemiological studies of OCD have estimated a lifetime prevalence of 1.9% to 2.5% and a 1-year prevalence of 1.1% to 1.8% in adult community samples and a lifetime prevalence of 1% to 2.3% in children and adolescent community samples (Weissman et al., 1994). In addition, some researchers have estimated that OCD may be present in up to 10% of psychiatric outpatients (Abramowitz, 1997). Subclinical variants of OCD such as intrusive thoughts and compulsive behaviors appear to be relatively common in the general population. OCD appears to be most commonly diagnosed in adolescence through early adulthood, though cases have been reported in children as young as age 5 (Jenike et al., 1986). For example, Last, Perrin, Hersen, and Kazdin (1992) found a mean age of onset of 10.8 years and mean age at intake of 12.8 years for OCD, whereas Flament et al. (1988) reported a mean age of onset of 12.8 years and mean age at diagnosis of 16.2 years. Research suggests that boys are twice as likely as girls to be diagnosed with childhood OCD, but that this sex ratio becomes equivalent in adulthood. For example, Bellodi, Sciuto, Diaferia, Ronchi, and Smeraldi (1992) estimate a mean onset range of 14 to 19.5 years for males and of 21 to 22 years for females. In the majority of cases, OCD is associated with a gradual onset and a chronic waxing and waning course that may correspond to fluctuations in stress (e.g., Rachman, 1997). OCD is also frequently comorbid with other Axis I disorders (e.g., other anxiety, mood, and somatoform disorders; Eisen et al., 1999) and with Axis II disorders (e.g., Cluster C personality disorders; Steketee, Chambless, & Tran, 2001).

Posttraumatic Stress Disorder

Posttraumatic stress disorder (PTSD) is characterized by the development of symptoms of persistent reexperiencing, avoidance or numbing, and increased arousal that are present for at least 1 month following exposure to an extreme traumatic stressor (APA, 2000). By definition, an extreme traumatic stressor involves directly experiencing an event that involves actual or threatened death, serious injury, or other threat to one's physical integrity; witnessing such an event happen to another person; or learning about such an event experienced by a significant other (APA, 2000). Several meta-analytic studies support the *DSM-IV-TR*'s (APA, 2000) delineation of three characteristic PTSD symptom clusters: reexperiencing, avoidance, and arousal (e.g., Taylor, Kuch, Koch, Crockett, & Passey, 1998). Symptoms of reexperiencing include recurrent and intrusive recollections, dreams, and flashbacks of the traumatic event; the subjective experience that the event is recurring; and intense distress or physiological reactivity to internal or external cues that resemble the traumatic event. Symptoms of avoidance include emotional numbing, anhedonia, detachment from others, hopelessness or a sense of a foreshortened future, as well as behavioral and cognitive avoidance of stimuli associated with the traumatic event. Finally, symptoms of increased arousal include an exaggerated startle response, hypervigilance, sleep difficulty, difficulty concentrating, and increased irritability or outbursts of anger.

Epidemiological evidence suggests that although exposure to extreme traumatic stressors is relatively common in the general population, only a minority of exposed individuals go on to develop PTSD. For example, Kessler, Sonnega, Bromet, Hughes, and Nelson (1995), in the NCS, found that more than 50% of women and more than 60% of men had been exposed to traumatic events, but that only 7.8% of the overall sample met criteria for PTSD. Rape/sexual assault and combat were the most likely traumatic stressors to produce PTSD, but the sudden death of a loved one resulted in the most cases of PTSD. Children and adolescents are also susceptible to PTSD. For example, studies have estimated that as many as 13% of exposed school-age children met criteria for PTSD 10 months after Hurricane Andrew (La Greca, Silverman, Vernberg, & Prinstein, 1996), and as many as 44% of children who had been sexually abused met criteria for PTSD (McLeer, Deblinger, Henry, & Orvaschel, 1992). Based on a nationally representative sample of adolescents, Kilpatrick and Saunders (1999) estimate the current prevalence of PTSD to be 5%. Across these epidemiological studies, females appear to be approximately twice as likely to develop PTSD. The duration of PTSD appears to vary widely across individuals, with approximately 50% of individuals recovering within 3 months of onset but many others experiencing persistent symptoms over years or even decades (APA, 2000). The best predictors of the likelihood of developing PTSD appear to be the severity, duration, and proximity of an individual's exposure to the traumatic event (e.g., Brewin, Andrews, & Valentine, 2000). Additional risk factors include a preexisting psychiatric illness or a family history of mood, anxiety, or substance use disorders; a history of childhood physical or sexual abuse; a lack of social support; and instability within the family (for reviews, see Brewin et al.; Ozer, Best, Lipsey, & Weiss, 2003).

Separation Anxiety Disorder

Separation anxiety disorder (SAD) is characterized by excessive anxiety or distress about separation from the home or from major attachment figures that is beyond what would be expected given the individual's developmental level and that persists for at least 4 weeks (APA, 2000). Separation anxiety may manifest as excessive worry about harm befalling major attachment figures, school and sleep refusal, avoidance of being alone, separation-themed nightmares, and somatic symptoms when separation occurs or is anticipated (APA, 2000). Since the publication of the *DSM-IV* (APA, 1994), SAD is the only anxiety disorder with child-specific criteria. Research suggests that expression of SAD symptoms varies across development (Francis et al., 1987). Specifically, Francis et al. indicate that young children (ages 5–8) were more likely to report nightmares and worry, older children (ages 9–12) were more likely to report excessive distress upon separation from major attachment figures, and adolescents (ages 12–19) were more likely to report physical symptoms and demonstrate school refusal behaviors. Epidemiological data suggest that the prevalence of SAD ranges from 3% to 12% across studies (Silverman & Ginsburg, 1998), with a reported prevalence of 4% in *DSM-IV* (APA, 1994). Males and females appear to be at equal risk for SAD in clinical samples, but SAD seems to be more prevalent in females in community-based samples (Costello & Angold, 1995; Silverman & Ginsburg).

Epidemiological Summary

The class of anxiety disorders is made up of a heterogeneous set of specific disorders with different symptom profiles (e.g., ranging from acute autonomic arousal to a general state of chronic tension) and different feared stimuli or situations (e.g., heights to internal sensations to diffuse worry across content domains) that are brought together by the common thread of anxious apprehension and avoidance. Anxiety is a fundamental part of human experience. What separates pathological fear/anxiety from anxiety that is part of the normal developmental course appears to be the intensity of the response and subsequent avoidance, rather than the specific focus of one's fear or anxiety. Across the anxiety disorders, there is consensus that a far greater percentage of individuals experience subclinical or transient symptoms (e.g., specific fears, worry, intrusive thoughts, panic attacks) than those who go on to develop a full-blown anxiety disorder. These epidemiological data also highlight the importance of applying a developmental perspective to the understanding of anxiety disorders. Some anxiety disorders appear to emerge most commonly in childhood (e.g., SAD and certain specific phobias, such as fears of animals), others are more likely to emerge in later childhood and adolescence (e.g., social phobia), others only rarely develop in children and are primarily "adult disorders" (e.g., panic disorder), and still others can emerge at any point in the life span (e.g., OCD, GAD, PTSD). Moreover, the symptom expression and phenomenological experience of anxiety disorders may vary across the life span, and consequently, accurate diagnosis requires consideration of developmental context. Finally, these epidemiological data suggest that anxiety disorders are particularly common in adult females by approximately a 2:1 ratio, with the exceptions of OCD and social phobia, but this sex difference may not be as remarkable as was once thought (Costello & Angold, 1995).

VULNERABILITY TO ANXIETY DISORDERS

Vulnerability factors can be conceptualized as relatively stable causal mechanisms that may confer increased risk to the development of anxiety disorders under certain conditions (e.g., Ingram & Price, 2001). Specifically, vulnerability factors are thought to operate in a diathesis-stress framework such that a given vulnerability may remain latent until activated by relevant environmental events or triggers (see Ingram & Luxton, Chapter 2 of this volume). Once activated, such factors may influence the processing of threat-related information, the use of coping styles and strategies, the conditionability to threat stimuli, or the individual's engagement with his or her social support network (e.g., Barlow, 1988, 2000; A. T. Beck & Emery, 1985). Recent research also highlights the reciprocal influence between vulnerability factors and environmental influences, and in so doing has begun to emphasize both the transactional nature of diathesis-stress interactions and the interactions between multiple vulnerability processes, environmental stressors, and developmental context (e.g., Cicchetti & Cohen, 1995; Ingram & Price; Sroufe, 1997). The field of developmental psychopathology provides an integrative paradigm for conceptualizing this dynamic interplay between various vulnerability and protective processes, environmental influences, and developmental course (Cicchetti & Rogosch, 2002).

The study of vulnerability to anxiety disorders dates back to early learning theories that examined ethological models of conditionability to aversive stimuli and "experimental neurosis" (see Mineka & Kihlstrom, 1978, for a review). Since that pioneering early work, there have been multiple levels of inquiry into vulnerability to anxiety disorders including the genetic, cognitive/learning, and social levels of analysis (e.g., Alloy & Riskind, 2002; Barlow, 1988, 2000, 2002; A. T. Beck & Emery, 1985; Ingram & Price, 2001; Zuckerman, 1999). For example, Barlow (1988, 2000, 2002) has advanced a "tripartite" model of vulnerability to anxiety disorders that includes generalized biological vulnerabilities, generalized psychological vulnerabilities, and specific psychological vulnerabilities. Using Barlow's model as a guide, we review evidence regarding identified biological and psychological vulnerability factors to anxiety disorders in the sections that follow and also present a brief review of stress. Because a full review of vulnerabilities to anxiety is beyond the scope of this chapter, the review provided here is intended to highlight major identified vulnerability factors to anxiety and anxiety disorders. Finally, these vulnerabilities are discussed within an integrative developmental vulnerability-stress perspective.

Biological Vulnerability Factors

Biological vulnerability factors are thought to represent heritable dispositional factors that confer increased vulnerability to psychopathology under appropriate activating conditions (see Pihl and Nantel-Vivier, Chapter 4 of this volume). Three lines of inquiry provide evidence for generalized biological vulnerability factors to anxiety disorders, including research on genetic factors, research on behavioral inhibition, and research on the construct of trait-based negative affect (variously referred to as trait anxiety, neuroticism, and negative affectivity).

Genetic Factors

In general, there is evidence to support moderate to modest heritability for the class of anxiety disorders (Zuckerman, 1999; see Lemery & Doelger, Chapter 7 of this volume). Among the anxiety disorders, more circumscribed evidence supports a genetic contribution to panic disorder and specific phobia (Fyer, Mannuzza, Chapman, Martin, & Klein, 1995; Kendler, Myers, Prescott, & Neal, 2001), with weaker but still significant genetic evidence for the other anxiety disorders (Zuckerman). For example, Kendler, Neale, Kessler, Heath, and Eaves (1992) estimated a 40% genetic transmission of panic disorder and agoraphobia, but the specific genes involved and their location remain unknown. In contrast, equivocal evidence for genetic transmission has emerged in studies of GAD, with some studies providing no evidence of differences in concordance rates between monozygotic and dizygotic twins, other studies suggesting a weak genetic contribution, and still other studies suggesting that GAD and major depressive disorder share a common genetic factor (e.g., Kendler et al., 1995). In this same study, Kendler et al. (1995) found modest heritabilities (23%–39%) for all other anxiety disorders except for situational phobias. At the same time, the majority of the variance in the transmission of anxiety disorders was accounted for by environmental factors. There is an emerging consensus that emotional disorders may have a common genetic vulnerability, with environmental factors operating to determine the specific disorder that may develop. Moreover, genetic models are moving from single-gene models to polygenetic models in which multiple genetic effects combine to form a general biological vulnerability to anxiety (Plomin, DeFries, McClearn, & Rutter, 1997). This general biological vulnerability to anxiety may not directly cause anxiety disorders but may exert an indirect influence through the development of temperament and personality traits (e.g., neuroticism).

Behavioral Inhibition

Behavioral inhibition is considered to be a temperament trait, reflected in a characteristic pattern of response with concomitant physiological indices (Kagan, 1989; Kagan et al., 1988; see Tackett & Krueger, Chapter 8 of this volume). Individual differences in behavioral inhibition are found early in development and are considered to be relatively stable. Infants classified as behaviorally inhibited are more reactive, easily aroused, and distressed. Toddlers are described as fearful, wary, and shy with strangers. In early and middle childhood, behavioral inhibition often presents as overly cautious and introverted responding (Pollock, Rosenbaum, Marrs, Miller, & Biederman, 1995). By definition, then, behaviorally inhibited children show a wariness and reluctance to engage with new and novel objects or adults in unfamiliar situations or environments. Kagan and Snidman (1991) have identified characteristics of behavioral inhibition that are quantifiable as early as 4 months of age, namely reacting to novelty with high motor reactivity and distress. Infants classified as behaviorally inhibited at 4 months of age are more likely to be similarly classified at age three and a half. Children who display stable levels of behavioral inhibition also tend to display high levels of negative affect. Kagan and colleagues suggest that approximately 10% to 15% of children may be classified as behaviorally inhibited (Kagan, 1989; Kagan et al., 1988).

The relevance of behavioral inhibition as a vulnerability factor lies in its predictive power for later anxiety disorders. Biederman et al. (1993) found that children classified as behaviorally inhibited had higher rates of multiple anxiety disorders (two or more), avoidant disorder, and phobic disorder later in development. Furthermore, they concluded that a developmental progression from overanxious, phobic, and avoidant disorders in younger children to separation anxiety disorder and agoraphobia in older children was common. Inhibited temperament and anxious symptoms do not appear to be simply variations of the same construct, however, because only 33% of inhibited children classified by Biederman et al. developed later diagnosable anxiety disorders. In a 12-year prospective study, Caspi, Henry, McGee, Moffitt, and Silva (1995) found that girls', but not boys', levels of behavioral inhibition at ages 3 to 5 were predictive of anxious symptoms in later childhood and adolescence. Interestingly, boys', but not girls', approach behaviors (i.e., willingness to explore novel situations) at ages 3 to 5 appeared to buffer against later anxiety. Thus, there is support for the premise that behaviorally inhibited children are at an *increased risk* for later anxiety disorders, but this risk may be differentially associated with the child's sex.

At the same time, not all children who are initially classified as behaviorally inhibited remain so over time. Research suggests that stability of behavioral inhibition is modest, at best. For example, Kagan, Reznick, and Snidman (1987) found that 40% of a sample of children identified as behaviorally inhibited at 21 months of age were less inhibited by 5 and a half years of age. In contrast, fewer than 10% of initially uninhibited children became more inhibited with age, and boys were more likely than girls to become less inhibited with age. Similarly, Fox, Henderson, Rubin, Calkins, and Schmidt (2001) provide evidence that behavioral indicators of behavioral inhibition at 4 months of age modestly predicted behavioral inhibition in toddlers 2 years later and social reticence at age 4. Results of the Fox et al. study suggest that physiological measures of behavioral inhibition may demonstrate more continuity. Specifically, infants classified as continuously inhibited across the first 4 years of life displayed right-frontal electroencephalogram asymmetry as early as 9 months, whereas those who changed in the level of behavioral inhibition did not. Other studies report similar findings regarding the stability of behavioral inhibition: Behavioral inhibition shows both continuity and discontinuity across early and middle childhood (Kagan, Snidman, & Arcus, 1998).

Several factors may influence the extent to which behavioral inhibition remains stable across development. Fox et al. (2001) found that a significant portion of the children who changed in their level of behavioral inhibition across the first 4 years of life experienced nonparental care. Similarly, Rubin, Burgess, and Hastings (2002) found that toddlers who were behaviorally inhibited at age 2 were most likely to be socially reticent at age 4 *only if* their mothers were intrusively controlling or derisive. Thus, these studies suggest that parenting styles may be potential moderators of behavioral inhibition. The apparent stability of behavioral inhibition may also be influenced by the type of assessment paradigm and the indices of behavioral inhibition that are utilized. For example, the Fox et al. (2001) study provides evidence that the manifestation of behavioral inhibition may vary as a function of developmental level and cognitive competencies. Fox et al. explained that as children develop and mature, they come to understand that people, more so than objects, are unpredictable, and consequently manifestations of behavioral inhibition shift from reluctance to engage with novel objects to wariness of unfamiliar people and situations. Given this developmental shift, it seems reasonable that the temporal continuity of behavioral inhibition may vary according to whether assessments are developmentally appropriate.

Although much of the research in this area has been done by only a handful of investigators, these recent findings are promising and function to generate questions for future research. Certain conclusions can be drawn from the research on behavioral inhibition. Behaviorally inhibited children are at a higher risk for later anxiety problems. The degree of risk is debatable, largely because of the modest longitudinal stability of measures of this temperament trait. In examining the stability of this trait, researchers have agreed that presentations of behavioral inhibition may be age dependent. Physiological markers correspond to age-appropriate behavioral measures, suggesting stability in the construct itself, and these markers are related to outcomes of social reticence. Finally, factors other than temperament may contribute to the modest stability of this trait. Additional research is needed to identify antecedents (vulnerabilities and stress) and the developmental pathways that contribute to the etiology of adult anxiety disorders.

Negative Affect

Considerable evidence also supports the heritability of trait-based negative affect, which has been referred to as *neuroticism* (Eysenck, 1967), *trait anxiety* (Gray, 1982; Spielberger, Gorsuch, & Lushene, 1970), and *negative affectivity* (Watson & Clark, 1984; Watson, Clark, & Tellegen, 1988; see Tackett & Krueger, Chapter 8 of this volume). Although there is conceptual overlap between these three constructs, there are also unique components. Negative affectivity (NA, or neuroticism) is conceptualized as a general vulnerability factor to various forms of psychopathology, most notably anxiety and mood disorders. According to Watson and Clark's seminal paper on NA, the construct represents a stable and pervasive individual difference trait, such that high-NA individuals typically report subjective feelings of distress, apprehension, tension, and worry. In contrast, trait anxiety represents an underlying stable personality trait that is intended to be *specific* to anxiety proneness (Spielberger et al.). Individuals high in trait anxiety, as compared with those high in neuroticism, can be differentiated on the specificity of symptoms and reactivity to stress. Specifically, although individuals high on both trait anxiety and neuroticism react in anxious ways to stressful situations, only individuals with high neuroticism exhibit elevated negative affect in the absence of stress (Watson & Clark). Heritability estimates for trait anxiety and neuroticism range from 30% to 50%, with the remaining variance in the development of anxiety and depression attributable to shared and nonshared environmental factors (Legrand, McGue, & Iacono, 1999). For example, Topolski et al. (1997), in a sample of 8- to 16-year-old twins, found that the heritability of trait anxiety ranged from .23 to .45 for boys and from .42 to .57 for girls. More recently, Legrand et al. found evidence that trait anxiety is moderately heritable, with additive genetic effects accounting for 45% of the variance in a sample of 547 twin pairs.

The high comorbidity among anxiety and mood disorders (Zimmerman, McDermut, & Mattia, 2000) and the consistently observed shared variance between self-report measures of anxiety and depression have led to the suggestion of a hierarchical model of emotional disorders, with negative affectivity as an undifferentiated higher-order general distress factor (T. A. Brown, Chorpita, & Barlow, 1998; Zinbarg & Barlow, 1996). Specifically, this model suggests that high negative affectivity is common to both anxious and depressive symptoms; low positive affectivity is specific to depressive symptoms; and autonomic hyperarousal is specific to panic disorder (Clark & Watson, 1991). Research investigating this model in adults has yielded relatively consistent results in cross-sectional studies. For example, neuroticism, negative affectivity, and trait anxiety have been shown to correlate positively with measures of anxiety and anxiety disorders, as well as measures of depression (Bieling, Antony, & Swinson, 1998; T. A. Brown et al., 1998; Clark, Watson, & Mineka, 1994; Trull & Sher, 1994; Zinbarg & Barlow). Further, autonomic hyperarousal has been shown to correlate positively with panic disorder symptoms, but more equivocal results have been obtained for the other anxiety disorders (e.g., T. A. Brown et al., 1998). In addition, recent evidence supports the applicability of this tripartite model to child and adolescent populations (see Laurent & Ettelson, 2001, for a review). On the other hand, results obtained on the tripartite model in older adults suggest a somewhat different factor structure from that of adolescents and adults, thus raising questions about the generalizability of this model to older adults (Shapiro, Roberts, & J. G. Beck, 1999).

Although the majority of studies that have examined trait-based negative affect as a vulnerability to anxiety disorders are descriptive, a number of prospective studies have been conducted in recent years. For example, Gershuny and Sher (1998), in a 3-year longitudinal study of 400 college students, found evidence that neuroticism interacts with introversion to predict residual changes in global ratings of both anxiety and depression. Jorm et al. (2000) attempted to replicate the findings of Gershuny and Sher in both a cross-sectional study of 2,677 community residents (ages 18–79) and a 3- to 4-year longitudinal study of older adults (age 70 or older). Although Jorm and colleagues did not find a similar Neuroticism-by-Introversion interaction, both studies provide evidence that neuroticism was a significant predictor of residual change in both anxious and depressive symptoms. Although these prospective studies provide theoretically consistent evidence that neuroticism predicts changes in both anxious and depressive symptoms, results have been equivocal in providing evidence that trait anxiety is a *specific* predictor of anxious, but not depressive, symptoms (Bieling et al., 1998). For example, Beiling et al. found that the Spielberger Trait Anxiety Inventory assesses both anxious and depressive symptoms, with 13 of the 20 trait anxiety items loading more heavily on a depression content factor. The difficulty associated with psychometrically differentiating trait anxiety from neuroticism/negative affect has led some to propose that trait anxiety and depression may be lower-order factors of negative affect (e.g., Kocovski, Endler, Cox, & Swinson, 2003).

Summary

Taken together, research on genetic factors, behavioral inhibition, and trait-based negative affect provides evidence for a generalized biological vulnerability to emotional disorders (i.e., both anxiety disorders and depression). Specifically, these findings suggest that trait-based negative affect and behavioral inhibition represent general, heritable vulnerability factors to emotional disorders, rather than vulnerability factors specific to anxiety. Moreover, results of empirical investigations of genetic factors converge in suggesting polygenetic models of transmission of a general biological diathesis—one that may confer vulnerability to the development of a behaviorally inhibited temperament or higher baseline levels of trait-based negative affect. Several possible mechanisms exist through which this general biological vulnerability may influence specific risk for anxiety disorders. First, a general biological vulnerability factor may interact with nonspecific psychological vulnerability factors (e.g., parenting styles, social relationships, cognitive processes) under appropriate activating conditions (e.g., stress) to confer increased risk for the development of anxiety disorders. Second, it has been suggested that a general biological vulnerability factor may affect enhanced conditionability to aversive emotional reactions or stimuli (Bouton, Mineka, & Barlow, 2001; Zinbarg & Mohlman, 1998), which could lead to a greater propensity to respond fearfully to one's own anxious symptoms (e.g., anxiety sensitivity, metaworry) or to a greater propensity to acquire anxious/fearful reactions to relatively benign stimuli. In either case, there is converging evidence that biological vulnerability factors likely interact with psychological vulnerabilities, environmental contingencies, and developmental context in influencing specific risk for anxiety disorders.

Psychological Vulnerability Factors

Psychological vulnerability factors parallel the concepts of biological or genetic vulnerability factors in that they are thought to represent ontogenetically acquired individual difference factors that confer increased vulnerability to psychopathology under appropriate activating conditions. That is, just as individuals may inherit a genetic predisposition that increases their likelihood of developing a psychological disorder or physical illness when certain environmental conditions are encountered, individuals may also acquire psychological predispositions to psychopathology as a result of their developmental experiences. In the sections that follow, three *general* psychological vulnerability factors are discussed that have relevance for understanding the ontogenesis of emotional disorders: (a) perceived uncontrollability and unpredictability; (b) parenting styles characterized by excessive control or rejection-neglect, as well as disrupted parental bonding and attachment insecurity; and (c) negative cognitions and information-processing biases. In addition, two more specific psychological vulnerability factors to anxiety disorders are briefly reviewed: anxiety sensitivity and the looming cognitive style.

Perceived Uncontrollability and Unpredictability: The Early Environment

Barlow and colleagues have posited that a perceived sense of unpredictability and uncontrollability, acquired from the individual's early experiences with the environment, plays a pivotal role in the development of anxiety states and disorders (Barlow, 1988, 2000, 2002; Chorpita & Barlow, 1998; see Gibb & Coles, Chapter 5 of this volume). According to their model, early experiences with perceived uncontrollability may lead to the development of a general psychological diathesis (i.e., a generalized sense that the world is uncontrollable and unpredictable) that may confer increased risk for the development of later anxiety states and disorders under appropriate activating conditions (Chorpita & Barlow). They contend that early experiences with uncontrollable or unpredictable stimuli may foster increased negative emotionality, lead to a general lack of perceived self-efficacy, and undermine the acquisition of mastery experiences. Similarly, Costanzo, Miller-Johnson, and Wencel (1995) suggest that children with low perceived sense of control and diminished self-efficacy are more vulnerable to later anxiety and depressive disorders. Early experiences may lead to increased activation of the behavioral inhibition system, a neurobiological system described by Gray (1982; Gray & McNaughton, 1996) as the biological basis of anxiety, and ultimately to increased symptoms of inhibited temperament (i.e., wariness of novel stimuli, cautious and introverted responding, and increased negative affect; e.g., Kagan, 1989).

Chorpita and Barlow (1998) contend that as development progresses and the child acquires increased experiences with uncontrollable and unpredictable stimuli, the individual's cognitive schemata (i.e., acquired bodies of knowledge that guide future information processing) become increasingly inflexible and resistant to change. In this way, a confirmation bias may be established such that early experiences with uncontrollable stimuli lead to a pervasive sense of uncontrollability, which in turn leads individuals to actively select out information or situations that provide evidence that the world is unpredictable and uncontrollable and that generate or maintain negative affect. Chorpita, T. A. Brown, and Barlow (1998) provide evidence using a sample of children with an average age of 11.15 years that a sense of uncontrollability *mediates* the relationship between negative life events and anxious and depressive symptoms in childhood. However, they suggest that in later adolescence and adulthood, uncontrollability may operate as a *moderator* of life stress, such that a lack of perceived control amplifies the experience of stress.

Much of the evidence for the role of perceived uncontrollability and unpredictability in the genesis of anxiety comes from ethological laboratory investigations of conditionability to aversive stimuli and "experimental neurosis." In their seminal review of the literature, Mineka and Kihlstrom (1978) concluded that experimental neurosis (or anxiety) results when environmental conditions become uncontrollable, unpredictable, or both. For example, Maier and Seligman (1976) found that when dogs were exposed to inescapable electric shocks (i.e., they learned that the environment was uncontrollable), they later did not initiate escape responses or were slower to respond when exposed to escapable shocks—a condition described as *learned helplessness*. Mineka, Gunnar, and Champoux (1986) provide additional evidence for the role of perceived uncontrollability in a laboratory investigation of rhesus monkeys reared under different conditions of environmental control. Specifically, monkeys who did not have control over the delivery of reinforcers evidenced fewer exploring behaviors, increased fear, and less effective distress regulation strategies when separated from peers. In a follow-up study of rhesus monkeys, Mineka and Tomarken (1989) provided further evidence for the role of control in the development of anxious behaviors during anxiety-eliciting situations. Specifically, those rhesus monkeys that were yoked to another, and thus had no control over conditions of shock in the experiment, developed debilitating symptoms of anxiety, whereas monkeys that had control did not. Based on this ethological evidence, Chorpita and Barlow (1998) have emphasized the central role of parenting styles in the development of a sense of control.

Parenting Styles and Attachment

Interest in the influence of parenting styles on children's emotional and social development began with Baumrind's (1971) groundbreaking research. Based on her work, research typically identifies two orthogonal dimensions of parenting: control and acceptance. Control can be defined as the extent to which parents exert direct influence over the child's daily activities and behaviors. Acceptance, in turn, is the extent to which parents are receptive to the child's decisions and individuality. Later research (Baumrind, 1973) showed that authoritative parents (those high on both control and acceptance) had children who were better adjusted both emotionally and socially than parents who were either authoritarian (high on control but low on acceptance), or permissive (low on control but high on acceptance). Since then, much research has explored not only the connection between parenting styles and child development, but also the relations between parenting styles and anxiety and depressive disorders.

Parental Control

A number of studies provide evidence that overcontrolling parenting is associated with increased childhood anxiety and depression and vulnerability to later emotional disorders (Baumrind, 1991). Chorpita and Barlow (1998) propose that parents who are more controlling, intrusive, or overprotective may undermine their children's sense of controllability and predictability. Parents who are overcontrolling are found to frequently limit their child's exposure to anxiety-eliciting situations and to reinforce the child for choosing avoidant solutions. Research has shown that exposure is an effective treatment for a wide range of anxiety disorders, and this is explained by classical conditioning theories of extinction. Thus, limiting exposure for a child who tends to be anxious in novel or social situations may limit opportunities for extinction of the anxiety response. Furthermore, research has demonstrated that children of controlling parents are more socially isolated and have less exposure to novel social situations (Bruch, Heimberg, Berger, & Collins, 1989). In addition to limiting children's exposure to new experiences, overcontrolling parents may promote and model avoidant behavioral responses to anxiety-eliciting situations. For example, parents who report behaving fearfully in front of their children and engaging in more avoidant behaviors have children who are more fearful and more avoidant (Muris, Steerneman, Merckelback, & Meesters, 1996). The influence of parental modeling of fearful and avoidant behavior on their child's response to similar situations may be exacerbated by predispositional fearfulness, so that anxious children are more likely to acquire fears from a modeling experience than are less anxious children (Craske, 1997). In turn, avoidance strategies may become self-reinforcing as the child avoids the negative affectivity elicited by novel situations, thereby increasing the probability that the child will continue to employ behavioral avoidance.

Not only do parents of anxious children model anxious and avoidant behavior, but they also may encourage the same responses in their children. Consistent with this, Barrett, Rapee, Dadds, and Ryan (1996) found that anxious children more frequently choose avoidant solutions to hypothetical anxiety-eliciting situations when compared with children with oppositional and defiant behaviors. In a further examination of this finding using a dyadic coding system to assess conversational problem-solving processes, Dadds, Barrett, Rapee, and Ryan (1996) found that mothers of anxious children reinforce and reciprocate more avoidant solutions in conversations regarding anxiety-eliciting situations. In fact, family discussions of hypothetical vignettes magnified the frequency of children's avoidant solutions. Taken together, these findings suggest that parental overcontrol may function to restrict extinction of fearfulness in children by limiting exposure to novel situations, objects, and peers and may function to promote an avoidant behavioral style in those children.

Negative-Rejecting Parenting Styles

In addition to level of control exercised by the parent, the quality of interaction between a parent and child may be related to the development, maintenance, or exacerbation of anxiety, as well as other internalizing problems, in children (Baumrind, 1991; Greco & Morris, 2002). Negative-rejecting parenting is typically characterized by a lack of support, a failure to set developmentally appropriate limits, parental disengagement, and disturbed early attachment relationships. For example, parents of socially withdrawn children are often overtly rejecting (Gerhold, Laucht, Terdorf, Schmidt, & Esser, 2001). Hummel and Gross (2001) found that parents of socially anxious children provide more overall negative feedback and less positive feedback to their children while the child is engaged in a task, potentially increasing the child's anxiety regarding the task and thereby decreasing the capacity to perform as expected. Mills and Rubin (1993) found that parents of anxious or inhibited children tend to direct more anger toward their child while engaged in similar task-oriented activities. In addition to being critical, parents of anxious children often restrict the child's attempts at acquiring new skills. Mills and Rubin report that parents of inhibited children resort to more coercive methods of helping their children to complete tasks, potentially implying that the child is not capable of competently completing the task. As a consequence, the child fails to master the intended skill, potentially establishing a chain of failures and expectations to fail on similar or more complex tasks.

Parental criticism can have additional negative effects. Parents of anxious children may actually reinforce the child's anxieties by responding to the child's behavior in a negative or derogatory evaluative manner (Cobham, Dadds, & Spence, 1999). Similarly, Krohne and Hock (1991) found that negative feedback and parental restriction were related to high levels of anxiety in children. Barrett et al. (1996) found that parents of anxious children expected their child to avoid physically and socially threatening situations in the future rather than risk failure. Similarly, Kendall, Kortlander, and Chansky (1992) found that mothers of anxious children expressed more negative expectations regarding their children's future performances than did mothers of control children. In these ways, parental socialization factors may contribute to the development of an overall pattern of negative cognitions and expectancies for failure in children regarding their abilities when faced with stressful situations. This, in turn, may foster the development of negative cognitive styles that serve as additional vulnerabilities to anxiety and depression.

Attachment and Parental Bonding

Considerable research indicates a critical link between early parent-child interaction variables and later psychological disorders (Davila, Hammen, Burge, Daley, & Paley, 1996; Parker, 1983; Williams & Riskind, 2004). In particular, research on parental bonding (e.g., Parker) and parent-child attachment (e.g., Ainsworth, Blehar, Waters, & Wall, 1978; Bowlby, 1980; see Davila, Ramsay, Stroud, & Steinberg, Chapter 9 of this volume) suggest that disruptions in early parent-child interactions may lead to the development of anxiety and mood disorders. Attachment and parental bonding, though not equivalent processes, emphasize the development of cognitive models of others that are abstracted from the quality of child-caregiver interactions. According to Parker, parental bonding encompasses both parental care (i.e., the provision of nurturance and affection) and parental protection (i.e., the creation of a sense of safety and security). Attachment theory encompasses elements of parental care in the "working model of others" that individuals abstract from early interactions, as well as a "working model of self" that is likely determined in part based on individuals' attributions of the quality of caregiver interactions (e.g., "Am I lovable, worthy, and acceptable to others?") (Bowlby, 1969). Bowlby (1969, 1980) hypothesized that disruptions in early attachment, such as parental separation, loss, neglect, or abuse, are likely to result in the development of negative working models of self and other, as well as deficits in effective emotion regulation. Working models of self and other are thought to be malleable during early development but, once consolidated, become relatively stable across the life span (e.g., Weinfeld, Sroufe, & Egeland, 2000) and can be used to characterize adult romantic and other types of relationships (e.g., Hazan & Shaver, 1987).

Considerable research provides evidence that retrospective perceptions of parents' care as overprotective are associated with current levels of anxiety and depression (Ingram, Miranda, & Segal, 1998). In addition, research also documents a relation between adult and child attachment insecurity and psychopathology (e.g., Davila et al., 1996; Dozier, Stovall, & Albus, 1999; Hankin, Kassel, & Abela, in press; Williams & Riskind, 2004). For example, insecure attachments have been linked to GAD (Cassidy, 1995), social phobia (e.g., Eng, Heimberg, Hart, Schneier, & Liebowitz, 2001), depressive symptoms (e.g., Davila et al.), and increased global ratings of anxiety and depression in young adult samples (Williams & Riskind). In addition, Chorpita and Barlow (1998) have suggested that a sense of uncontrollability may be produced by parents who respond inconsistently—a hallmark sign of insecure attachment. Thus, research and theory on attachment and parental bonding provide evidence that disruptions in parent-child interactions are not relegated to negative consequences in childhood, but rather may continue to affect increased vulnerability to psychopathology across the life span. Disrupted parental bonding, insecure attachments, and maladaptive parenting styles (i.e., parental over control and neglectful-rejecting parenting) appear to create a general psychological diathesis to later psychopathology—rather than a specific vulnerability to anxiety—that may be implicated in the development of a diminished sense of perceived predictability and control.

Negative Cognitions and Information Processing

Cognitive-clinical and information-processing models of anxiety (A. T. Beck & Clark, 1997; A. T. Beck & Emery, 1985) emphasize the appraisal and processing of threat-related information (see Gibb & Coles, Chapter 5 of this volume). These models describe what appear to be stable, "trait-like" patterns (i.e., schemata) of anxious responding, in which surface-level negative cognitions (i.e., automatic thoughts) concerning future threat and danger are thought to signal the existence of more stable danger schemata (A. T. Beck & Emery). According to A. T. Beck and Clark's information-processing model, anxiety is likely an innate, survival-oriented response to environmental stress that serves to orient individuals to perceived danger and prepare them for action. The model contends that anxiety becomes maladaptive when appraisals of threat or danger become misperceived or exaggerated (i.e., when the individual perceives danger in the absence of veridical threat). These biased interpretations represent underlying cognitive schemata that are hypothesized to operate automatically and to consistently distort the appraisal of relatively innocuous situations as being potentially threatening or harmful. Similarly, Kendall (1985) proposed that pathological childhood anxiety results from stable, easily accessible schemata focused on themes of danger and death. According to cognitive theories of anxiety, these cognitive distortions reflect attentional biases to threat information, overestimation of danger and threat, and underestimations of the ability to perform optimally in the face of perceived threat.

Considerable evidence supports the existence of anxiety-related cognitive distortions and information-processing biases in both adult and child populations. In adult samples, systematic lines of research on cognitive bias in anxiety have yielded several conclusions with regard to information processing in anxiety. First, it is now well established that anxiety is associated with heightened vigilance for threat-related information (e.g., MacLeod, 1991; Mogg & Bradley, 1998). Second, anxiety is associated with a tendency to overestimate the magnitude and severity of potential threat (e.g., Butler & Mathews,

1983), including a tendency to habitually interpret ambiguous information in a threatening manner (e.g., Mathews & Mackintosh, 2000). Third, considerable evidence indicates that anxiety is associated with enhanced implicit memory for threatening information in both clinically and nonclinically anxious populations (e.g., MacLeod & McLaughlin, 1995). In contrast, anxiety is not as generally associated with explicit memory (i.e., intentional, facilitated recall) for threat-related information (e.g., MacLeod & Mathews, 1991). In child samples, several studies have shown that anxious children display cognitive information-processing biases toward threat. For example, Vasey, Daleiden, Williams, and L. M. Brown (1995) provide evidence that anxiety-disordered children showed a bias toward threatening stimuli compared with normal controls, 9–14 years of age, using a probe-detection task. Chorpita, Albano, and Barlow (1996) found a significant relation between anxiety levels and biased threat interpretations in ambiguous situations in a sample of normal children. Similarly, Boegels and Zigterman (2000) found that children who were diagnosed with an anxiety disorder were more likely to overestimate danger and underestimate their ability to cope with danger in ambiguous situations when compared with both children with externalizing disorders and normal controls. One of the critical questions that remain, however, is whether these observed information-processing biases are concomitants of anxiety disorders or whether they represent vulnerabilities.

According to the cognitive content specificity hypothesis suggested by A. T. Beck, G. Brown, Eidelson, Steer, and Riskind (1987), anxiety disorders and depression should correspond to different cognitive content (i.e., anxiety to content concerning future threat and danger and depression to content concerning past loss and failure). Research investigating negative cognitions, however, has yielded more equivocal results than information-processing research in both adult and child samples (e.g., R. Beck & Perkins, 2001; Williams & Reardon, 2004). For example, children with diagnosed anxiety disorders appear to report higher levels of both anxious and depressive negative self-statement and self-talk, indicative of a general cognitive diathesis to negative affectivity as opposed to cognitive specificity (e.g., Ronan & Kendall, 1997; Treadwell & Kendall, 1996). There is growing consensus that anxious and depressive disorders are concurrently associated with negative cognitions. However, the evidence for the specificity of these cognitions and whether these cognitions are vulnerabilities or concomitant factors remain equivocal.

Anxiety Sensitivity

Anxiety sensitivity (AS) is the fear of anxiety-related bodily sensations that are postulated to emerge from beliefs that these sensations have harmful somatic, social, or psychological consequences (Reiss & McNally, 1985). For example, one who experiences heart palpitations may erroneously attribute their occurrence to an imminent heart attack and consequently experience an increase in anxiety. Likewise, dizziness or racing thoughts may be appraised as a loss of control or of "losing one's mind," which could lead to a fear of embarrassment. Expectancy theory (Reiss, 1991) posits that an individual holding such beliefs will become anxious when the symptoms are experienced and will attempt to avoid situations or places that might exacerbate the aversive symptoms. AS is recognized as a stable individual difference variable such that some individuals are more inclined to respond fearfully to autonomic arousal (Reiss). The idiographic expression of AS is hypothesized to arise from a combination of genetic influences and specific learning experiences leading to the acquisition of beliefs about the potentially harmful consequences of arousal

(Scher & Stein, 2003; Stein, Jang, & Livesley, 1999; Stewart et al., 2001). Given that AS appears to share many of the cognitive and physiological features of panic (e.g., misinterpretation of bodily sensations leading to hypervigilance of related bodily arousal cues), much of the research attempting to implicate AS as a premorbid vulnerability factor to psychopathology has done so in relation to panic.

Although a comprehensive review of the AS literature is beyond the scope of this chapter (see Taylor, 1999, for a review), an abbreviated review is provided. Several studies utilizing the Anxiety Sensitivity Index (ASI) have demonstrated that panic disorder patients exhibit elevated ASI scores as compared with healthy controls (McNally & Lorenz, 1987). Donnell and McNally (1990) provide evidence that nearly two thirds of high-AS subjects had never experienced a spontaneous panic attack, suggesting that AS may emerge from particular learning experiences or genetic factors rather than simply as the result of a "scar" from a previous panic episode. Recent evidence suggests that AS is moderately heritable, with additive genetic factors accounting for an estimated 45% of the variance in ASI scores but with the largest portion of the variance attributable to environmental factors (Stein et al., 1999). Research also suggests that AS may arise from early learning experiences suggesting that unexplained somatic sensations are dangerous or signals of serious illness (e.g., McNally & Eke, 1996). In addition, research suggests that AS may be learned through observation of parental sick-role behaviors related to panic symptoms (Ehlers, 1993). Follow-up studies on the developmental origins of AS have implicated more experiences of parental reinforcement of sick-role behavior in response to their own anxiety symptoms, more frequent observation of parental sick-role behavior related to parents' anxiety symptoms, and more experiences of parental encouragement of sick-role behavior to their own cold symptoms (Watt, Stewart, & Cox, 1998). Taken together, these findings imply that AS may have some degree of heritability but that AS appears to emerge from a particular set of learning experiences in the early environment that teach the child that somatic symptoms are dangerous or that reinforce sick-role behaviors.

Several large-scale studies have examined the degree to which AS prospectively predicts the development of panic symptoms. For example, Schmidt, Lerew, and Jackson (1997) assessed a large sample of Air Force Academy cadets before and after a highly intensive and stressful 5-week period of basic cadet training (BCT). Results were consistent with predictions that AS would emerge as a predisposing factor to panic. When participants were divided into quartiles based on ASI scores, those scoring in the highest quartile exhibited twice the risk for spontaneous panic during BCT as did those whose scores fell in the bottom three quartiles. In a replication and extension of their first study, Schmidt, Lerew, and Jackson (1999) again found considerable support for AS as a vulnerability factor to spontaneous panic. A median split of ASI scores revealed that participants with elevated ASI scores were nearly three times more likely to report an instance of spontaneous panic during BCT. Also notable, results indicated that AS contributed significantly to the development of panic, even when controlling for a history of panic and trait anxiety. These findings are substantial and provide a cogent retort to researchers who have argued that AS constitutes a lower-order factor of trait anxiety rather than a distinct construct (Lilienfeld, Turner, & Jacob, 1993). Recent studies have begun to examine more complex models of AS in the prospective prediction of panic (e.g., Bouton et al., 2001). For example, Schmidt et al. (2000) have recently examined the relation between AS and a *5-HTT* genotype (associated with serotonergic responses) during CO_2 challenge and found that AS interacted with *5-HTT* genotype in predicting cardiovascular reactivity in response to the challenge task. Although prospective and cross-sectional studies have generally converged in supporting a relation between heightened AS and panic attacks and disorder, research investigating the specificity of AS to anxiety or panic have been equivocal (e.g., Otto, Pollack, Fava, Uccello, & Rosenbaum, 1995). On the one hand, the overlap between symptoms of anxiety and depression may be responsible for the relationship between AS and depressive symptoms. On the other hand, AS may be a predictor of the broader construct of experiential avoidance (i.e., discomfort remaining in contact with negative emotions, thoughts, or bodily sensations; Hayes, Wilson, Gifford, Follette, & Strosahl, 1996) rather than a specific predictor of panic.

Looming Cognitive Style

The looming cognitive style (LCS) has been proposed as a broad and pervasive cognitive tendency to cross-situationally appraise threat as rapidly rising in risk, progressively worsening, or actively accelerating and speeding up (Riskind, 1997; Riskind, Williams, Gessner, Chrosniak, & Cortina, 2000; Williams, Shahar, Riskind, & Joiner, 2005; see Gibb & Coles, Chapter 5 of this volume). The LCS is conceptualized as a schema-driven, evolutionarily based process of threat and harm appraisal that is assumed to systematically bias the ways in which individuals mentally represent the temporal and spatial progression of possible future threat. Moreover, the LCS is posited to represent a unique cognitive risk factor for anxiety *but not depression* that functions as a danger schema (Riskind et al.). The LCS is hypothesized to consist of primarily imagery-based mental representations of the developmental progression(s) of potential threat over time (i.e., dynamic fear-related imagery). Consequently, individuals who develop the LCS are likely to have difficulty habituating to potential threats, demonstrate increased vigilance and anxiety, perceive a sense of time urgency and imperative need for action, and overuse cognitive and behavioral avoidance strategies (see Riskind & Williams, in press, for a review).

The LCS emerged from the "looming vulnerability" model of anxiety, which posits that the distinct cognitive phenomenology of anxiety and anxiety disorders involves mental representations of dynamically intensifying danger and rapidly rising risk (Riskind, 1997; Riskind et al., 2000). According to Riskind and colleagues, a unique feature of the mental scenarios generated by anxious individuals is the perception of threat movement as still unfolding and intensifying as one projects the self into an anticipated future. All individuals are assumed to have the capacity to mentally represent or forecast how potentially threatening situations are likely to develop or play out, as a product of our autonoetic consciousness (i.e., the uniquely human ability to represent past, present, and future; Wheeler, Stuss, & Tulving, 1997). Cognitively vulnerable individuals, however, are assumed to develop mental representations in which anticipated threats are escalating in risk, moving toward the self or toward a dreaded final outcome, and moving through time (i.e., looming).

A number of cross-sectional, experimental, and prospective studies provide support for the LCS as a cognitive vulnerability to anxiety (see Riskind & Williams, in press, for a review). These studies indicate that cognitively vulnerable individuals—that is, those high in the LCS—demonstrate higher levels of general anxious symptoms, as well as higher levels of several correlates of anxiety, including worry, thought suppression, catastrophizing, and behavioral avoidance. In addition, a recent study provides evidence that the LCS is associated with increased levels of symptoms of PTSD, OCD, GAD, specific phobias, and social anxiety in a college student population (Williams et al., 2005). Recent experimental studies have also demonstrated that individuals high in the LCS demonstrate attentional vigilance for threatening visual images, enhanced estimations of environmental threat, and a memory bias for threatening information, even controlling for the effects of current levels of anxious symptoms.

Several studies also provide prospective evidence for the LCS as a distal vulnerability (i.e., cognitive diathesis) that interacts with stress (e.g., negative life events) to confer increased risk for anxiety symptoms and anxiety disorders. For example, a recent study provides evidence that the LCS interacts with negative life events to predict residual change in anxious symptoms over a 2-month time period (Williams, 2002). A growing body of studies also provides evidence for the applicability of the LCS to a variety of different anxiety disorders (see Riskind & Williams, in press, for a review). For example, heightened levels of the LCS have been found in patients with panic disorder, GAD, and social phobia, as well as analog contamination phobics. At the same time, consistent evidence has been obtained for the discriminant validity of the LCS, suggesting that it is psychometrically and conceptually distinct from measures of trait-based negative affect (neuroticism, negative affectivity, and trait anxiety), correlates of anxiety (worry, catastrophizing, and static appraisals of threat), and depressive symptoms. Thus, although research on the LCS is in its relative infancy, initial results for the specificity of this construct as a specific cognitive vulnerability to anxiety have been promising.

Summary

Taken together, research on psychological vulnerabilities provides evidence for several general psychological vulnerability factors to emotional disorders or psychopathology more broadly (e.g., externalizing disorders, substance-use disorders, etc.), as well as two potential circumscribed psychological vulnerability factors that confer risk specifically to anxiety disorders. Evidence on general psychological vulnerability factors suggests that perceived uncontrollability or unpredictability, maladaptive parenting styles or disrupted attachment and parental bonding, and negative cognitions are interdependent, rather than orthogonal constructs. That is, perceived uncontrollability may emerge as a consequence of disrupted attachment or maladaptive parenting styles and may lead to increased negative affectivity and concomitant negative cognitions. Research on specific psychological vulnerabilities to anxiety disorders highlights the role of the mental representation of anticipated future threat (i.e., the looming cognitive style), anxiety-related information-processing biases (i.e., attentional vigilance, misperception or exaggerated appraisals of threat, and implicit memory biases for threat-related information), as well as specific fears of anxiety-related somatic symptoms (i.e., anxiety sensitivity). As with the general psychological vulnerability factors, these circumscribed psychological vulnerability factors and information-processing biases may combine in multiple ways, and may combine as well with general psychological vulnerability factors, to increase specific risk for anxiety. It is notable that numerous disorder-specific psychological vulnerability factors have not been discussed in this section because of space limitations (e.g., metaworry in GAD, exaggerated appraisals of responsibility and the negative significance of intrusive thoughts in OCD). It seems likely, however, that these lower-order, disorder-specific psychological vulnerabilities, as well as specific learning experience, may orient individuals to focus their anxiety or fear on some object or event (e.g., Barlow, 2002; Bouton et al., 2001; Riskind & Williams, in press).

Stress

Throughout the earlier sections of this chapter we have emphasized that vulnerability factors, whether biological or psychological, are typically thought to remain latent until activated by environmental conditions. In this section we elaborate on the nature of those activating conditions and, specifically, examine the nature of stress. Although numerous conceptualizations of stress have been identified, they generally converge in suggesting that stress consists of environmental pressures (subjective or objective) that disrupt the individual's typical physiological, emotional, cognitive, and behavioral functioning and that interfere with adaptive capabilities (see Grant & McMahon, Chapter 1 of this volume). For example, Lazarus and Folkman (1984) emphasize the interaction between an objective stimulus and the individual's subjective appraisal of that stimulus in their definition of stress, whereas Holmes and Rahe (1967) emphasize the occurrence of objective life events in their definition of stress. Within the voluminous stress literature several types of stress have been identified, and several different methods of measuring stress have been employed (e.g., Cohen, Kamarck, & Mermelstein, 1983; Lazarus, 1990; Monroe & Simons, 1991; Seyle, 1978). Distinctions have been made between acute and chronic stressors (Seyle, 1978), between major aversive life events and the accumulation of minor life events or "daily hassles" (Monroe & Simons; Lazarus), and between objective stress and perceived stress (Cohen et al., 1983). Consequently, numerous measures have been developed, including checklists of major life events, chronic stress, daily events, and measures of perceived stress. A comprehensive review of the measurement of stress is provided by Cohen, Kessler, and Underwood (1995).

Models of vulnerability to anxiety (Barlow, 2002; A. T. Beck & Emery, 1985; Riskind, 1997) posit that the types of stress associated with the ontogenesis of anxiety disorders should focus on *future threat or danger*, whereas the stress associated with the development of depression should focus on themes of past loss or failure (e.g., A. T. Beck, 1967). In support of this proposition, G. W. Brown (1993) found that anxiety was primarily associated with anticipated danger, whereas depression was predominantly associated with past loss. Further, recent developments suggest that different types of stress are associated with different anxiety disorders. For example, Ehlers (1993) provides evidence that experiences of unexplained somatic symptoms are associated with the development of panic and anxiety sensitivity. Barrett et al. (1996) provide evidence that social phobia may be associated with early experiences in which the danger of social evaluative concerns is communicated by parents or significant others. Kessler et al. (1995) provide evidence that rape or sexual assault is the most likely traumatic stressor to produce PTSD. Barlow and colleagues (e.g., Chorpita & Barlow, 1998; Chorpita et al., 1998) provide evidence that early experience with stressful events characterized as uncontrollable or unpredictable leads to a general psychological diathesis to view the world as unpredictable and uncontrollable. In addition, recent research has begun to focus on the effects of prolonged exposure to stress to account for the variation in stress-induced pathology across different types of stressors.

In his early work, Cannon (1936) proposed that stress results in the activation of the sympathetic nervous system (e.g., increased heart rate, fast breathing, enhanced adrenal response, and pupil dilation) as the individual prepares for action. Physiological research has generally confirmed Cannon's initial model in suggesting that the stress response is mediated by the hypothalamic-pituitary-adrenal (HPA) axis and entails increased secretion of epinephrine (adrenaline), norepinephrine, and cortisol and decreased immune functioning (see McEwen, 1998, for a review). Specifically, when individuals encounter stress, the hypothalamus releases corticotropin-releasing factor, signaling the adrenal cortex to secrete cortisol, epinephrine, and norepinphrine. Epinephrine and norepinephrine act to mobilize the muscles for action, including increased blood pressure and heart rate. Cortisol acts to replenish cellular energy stores that have been mobilized for action, prepares the body to fight against injury or attack by enhancing the immune system in the short term, and operates a sort of check-and-balance system governing HPA functioning. According to McEwen, when individuals experience severe or chronic stressors the stress response becomes imbalanced, resulting in suppression of the immune system and increased susceptibility to physical ailments ranging from the common cold to sudden death. Interestingly, high levels of anxious arousal, particularly chronic levels as would be expected in GAD, are associated with similar neurobiological processes and physical consequences. Further, ethological studies of the effects of stress suggest that early stressful or traumatic experiences may lead to permanent changes in brain functioning and chronic alterations in the functioning of the HPA axis (Heim & Nemeroff, 1999).

A DEVELOPMENTAL VULNERABILITY-STRESS PERSPECTIVE

Thus far we have reviewed literature on biological and psychological vulnerability factors, the empirical study of stress, and the characterization and epidemiology of the anxiety disorders. In this final section, we integrate across these domains in presenting a developmental vulnerability-stress perspective on the ontogenesis of anxiety disorders. A vulnerability-stress perspective (e.g., Alloy & Riskind, 2002; Barlow, 2000; A. T. Beck & Emery, 1985; Ingram & Luxton, Chapter 2 of this volume) posits that certain dispositional factors, be they biological or psychological, become activated by specific environmental circumstances to confer increased risk for the development of psychopathology. In the absence of appropriate activating events (e.g., stress), these vulnerabilities may remain latent, and the individual may remain unaffected. Once activated, these vulnerabilities may bias the processing of information; enhance conditionability to aversive stimuli; lead to the inflexible use of avoidance-oriented coping strategies; and maintain a continued state of negative affectivity, readiness, and arousal. Moreover, these vulnerabilities may both directly and indirectly influence individuals' experiences of stress (e.g., Kendler et al., 1995) by leading individuals to select or create more threatening environments, by impairing performance in anxiety-provoking situations, and by maintaining the immediate and lingering effects of experiencing a stressful or traumatic event.

Developmental psychopathology provides an integrative paradigm for conceptualizing the dynamic interplay between multiple vulnerabilities, environmental influences, and developmental course across the life span (e.g., Cicchetti & Cohen, 1995; Sroufe, 1997). A developmental perspective holds that at different points in development, individuals are faced with different developmental tasks and challenges (e.g., Sroufe). Extended to the study of stress, a developmental perspective suggests that what constitutes stress should likewise show some correspondence to the developmental level of the individual. A developmental perspective also holds that biological and psychological factors are in continuous interaction with themselves and with environmental demands (e.g., Cicchetti & Rogosch,

2002). For example, a child's temperament may influence a parent's choice of parenting style, which may in turn influence the child's behavior and affect as well as the child's view of self and others. Likewise, a person experiencing high levels of negative affect may engage in behaviors that elicit rejecting responses from others in the environment, thereby generating stress and confirming negative self-evaluative concerns. Finally, developmental models emphasize that multiple developmental pathways may lead to the same outcome or disorder (i.e., equifinality) and that the same vulnerability factor may lead to different outcomes or disorders as a result of individual genetic and ontogenic differences (i.e., multifinality; Cicchetti & Cohen).

Drawing on the vulnerability-stress model and developmental psychopathology, a developmental vulnerability-stress perspective emphasizes that vulnerability-stress interactions are reciprocal, multidetermined, and couched within a developmental context. From this integrative perspective, anxiety disorders are believed to be caused by multiple nonspecific and specific biological and psychological vulnerabilities that are in a continuous state of reciprocal interaction both with themselves and with environmental contingencies. Moreover, different vulnerability-stress interactions and different sources of stress may be important at different points in the life span. For example, behavioral inhibition may pose an early, nonspecific vulnerability to psychopathology that interacts with parenting styles, trait-based negative affectivity, and a child's sense of self and the world. At later points in development, however, temperament may exert little direct influence on vulnerability to anxiety. From this perspective, it also seems critical to examine the multiple pathways by which vulnerabilities may lead to the development of anxiety disorders, as well as the protective factors that may buffer an individual against the development of anxiety. For example, anxiety sensitivity may lead to the development of panic disorder through different pathways for different individuals and at different points in development. For research and theory on vulnerabilities to anxiety to advance to the next level, integrative research that reduces the divide between developmental psychology and vulnerability-stress models is essential.

REFERENCES

Abel, J. L., & Borkovec, T. D. (1995). Generalizability of DSM-III-R generalized anxiety disorder to proposed DSM-IV criteria and cross-validation of proposed changes. *Journal of Anxiety Disorders, 9,* 303–315.

Abramowitz, J. S. (1997). Effectiveness of psychological and pharmacological treatments for obsessive-compulsive disorder: A quantitative review. *Journal of Consulting and Clinical Psychology, 65,* 44–52.

Agras, W. S., Sylvester, D., & Oliveau, D. (1969). The epidemiology of common fears and phobia. *Archives of General Psychiatry, 10,* 151–156.

Ainsworth, M. S., Blehar, M. C., Waters, E., & Wall, S. (1978). *Patterns of attachment: A psychological study of the Strange Situation.* Hillsdale, NJ: Lawrence Erlbaum.

Alloy, L. B., & Riskind, J. H. (2002). *Cognitive vulnerability to emotional disorders.* Mahwah, NJ: Lawrence Erlbaum.

American Psychiatric Association. (1987). *Diagnostic and statistical manual of mental disorders* (3rd ed., rev.). Washington, DC: Author.

American Psychiatric Association. (1994). *Diagnostic and statistical manual of mental disorders* (4th ed.). Washington, DC: Author.

American Psychiatric Association. (2000). *Diagnostic and statistical manual of mental disorders* (4th ed., text revision). Washington, DC: Author.

Antony, M. M., Brown, T. A., & Barlow, D. H. (1997). Heterogeneity among specific phobia types in DSM-IV. *Behaviour Research and Therapy, 35,* 1089–1100.

Baer, L. (1994). Factor analysis of symptom subtypes of obsessive compulsive disorder and their relation to personality and tic disorders. *Journal of Clinical Psychiatry, 55,* 18–23.

Barlow, D. H. (1988). *Anxiety and its disorders: The nature and treatment of anxiety and panic.* New York: Guilford Press.

Barlow, D. H. (2000). Unraveling the mysteries of anxiety and its disorders from the perspective of emotion theory. *American Psychologist, 55,* 1247–1263.

Barlow, D. H. (2002). *Anxiety and its disorders: The nature and treatment of anxiety and panic* (2nd ed.). New York: Guilford Press.

Barrett, P. M., Rapee, R. M., Dadds, M. R., & Ryan, S. M. (1996). Family enhancement of cognitive style in anxious and aggressive children: Threat bias and the fear effect. *Journal of Abnormal Child Psychology, 24,* 187–203.

Baumrind, D. (1971). Current patterns of parental authority. *Developmental Psychology Monographs, 1,* 1–103.

Baumrind, D. (1973). The development of instrumental competence through socialization. In A. D. Pick (Ed.), *Minnesota symposia on child psychology* (Vol. 7, pp. 3–46). Minneapolis: University of Minnesota Press.

Baumrind, D. (1991). Parenting styles and adolescent development. In R. M. Lerner, A. C. Petersen, & J. Brooks-Gunn (Eds.), *Encyclopedia of adolescence* (Vol. 11, pp. 746–758). New York: Guilford Press.

Beck, A. T. (1967). *Depression: Clinical, experimental, and theoretical aspects.* New York: Harper & Row.

Beck, A. T., Brown, G., Eidelson, J. I., Steer, R. A., & Riskind, J. H. (1987). Differentiating anxiety and depression: A test of the cognitive content-specificity hypothesis. *Journal of Abnormal Psychology, 96,* 179–183.

Beck, A. T., & Clark, D. A. (1997). An information-processing model of anxiety: Automatic and strategic processes. *Behavior Research and Therapy, 39,* 40–58.

Beck, A. T., & Emery, G. (1985). *Anxiety disorders and phobias: A cognitive perspective.* New York: Basic Books.

Beck, J. G., & Stanley, M. A. (1997). Anxiety disorders in the elderly: The emerging role of behavior therapy. *Behavior Therapy, 28,* 83–100.

Beck, R., & Perkins, T. S. (2001). Cognitive content-specificity for anxiety and depression: A meta-analysis. *Cognitive Therapy and Research, 25,* 651–663.

Bellodi, L., Sciuto, G., Diaferia, G., Ronchi, P., & Smeraldi, E. (1992). Psychiatric disorders in the families of patients with obsessive compulsive disorder. *Psychiatry Research, 42,* 111–120.

Biederman, J., Rosenbaum, J. F., Bolduc-Murphy, E., Farone, S. V., Chaloff, J., Hirshfeld, D. R., et al. (1993). A three year follow-up of children with and without behavioral inhibition. *Journal of the American Academy of Child and Adolescent Psychiatry, 32,* 814–834.

Bieling, P. J., Antony, M. M., & Swinson, R. P. (1998). The State-Trait Anxiety Inventory, Trait version: Structure and content re-examined. *Behaviour Research and Therapy, 36,* 777–778.

Boegels, S. M., & Zigterman, D. (2000). Dysfunctional cognitions in children with social phobia, separation anxiety disorder, and generalized anxiety disorder. *Journal of Abnormal Child Psychology, 28,* 205–211.

Borkovec, T. D., & Hu, S. (1990). The effect of worry on cardiovascular response to phobic imagery. *Behaviour Research and Therapy, 28,* 69–73.

Bouton, M. E., Mineka, S., & Barlow, D. H. (2001). A modern learning-theory perspective on the etiology of panic disorder. *Psychology Review, 108,* 4–32.

Bowlby, J. (1969). *Attachment and loss: Vol. 1. Attachment.* New York: Basic Books.

Bowlby, J. (1980). *Attachment and loss: Vol. 3. Sadness and depression.* New York: Basic Books.

Brewin, C. R., Andrews, B., & Valentine, J. D. (2000). Meta-analysis of risk factors for posttraumatic stress disorder in trauma-exposed adults. *Journal of Consulting and Clinical Psychology, 68,* 748–766.

Brown, G. W. (1993). Life events and affective disorder: Replications and limitations. *Psychosomatic Medicine, 55,* 248–259.

Brown, T. A., Barlow, D. H., & Liebowitz, M. R. (1994). The empirical basis of generalized anxiety disorder. *American Journal of Psychiatry, 151,* 1272–1280.

Brown, T. A., Chorpita, B. F., & Barlow, D. H. (1998). Structural relationships among dimensions of the DSM-IV anxiety and mood disorders and dimensions of negative affect, positive affect, and autonomic arousal. *Journal of Abnormal Psychology, 107,* 179–192.

Brown, T. A., DiNardo, P. A., Lehman, C. L., & Campbell, L. A. (2001). Reliability of DSM-IV anxiety and mood disorders: Implications for classification of emotional disorders. *Journal of Abnormal Psychology, 110,* 49–58.

Brown, T. A., Marten, P. A., & Barlow, D. H. (1996). Empirical evaluation of the panic symptom ratings in DSM-III-R panic disorder. In T. A. Widiger, A. J. Frances, H. A. Pincus, R. Ross, M. B. First, W. Davis, et al. (Eds.), *DSM-IV sourcebook* (Vol. 4, pp. 209–216). Washington, DC: American Psychiatric Association.

Bruch, M. A., Heimberg, R. G., Berger, P., & Collins, T. M. (1989). Social phobia and perceptions of early parental and personal characteristics. *Anxiety Research, 2,* 57–65.

Burke, K. C., Burke, J. D., Jr., Regier, D. A., & Rae, D. S. (1990). Age at onset of selected mental disorders in five community populations. *Archives of General Psychiatry, 47,* 511–518.

Butler, G., & Mathews, A. (1983). Cognitive processes in anxiety. *Advances in Behaviour Research and Therapy, 5,* 51–62.

Campbell, S. B. (1986). Developmental issues in childhood anxiety. In R. Gittelman (Ed.), *Anxiety disorders of childhood* (pp. 24–57). New York: Guilford Press.

Cannon, W. B. (1936). *Bodily changes in pain, hunger, fear, and rage.* New York: Appleton-Century.

Caspi, A., Henry, B., McGee, R. O., Moffitt, T. E., & Silva, P. A. (1995). Temperamental origins of child and adolescent behavior problems: From age three to age fifteen. *Child Development, 66,* 55–68.

Cassidy, J. (1995). Attachment and generalized anxiety disorder. In D. Cicchetti & S. Toth (Eds.), *Rochester symposium on developmental psychopathology: Emotion, cognition and representation* (pp. 343–370). Rochester, NY: University of Rochester Press.

Chorpita, B. F., Albano, A. M., & Barlow, D. H. (1996). Cognitive processing in children: Relation to anxiety and family influences. *Journal of Clinical Child Psychology, 25,* 170–176.

Chorpita, B. F., & Barlow, D. H. (1998). The development of anxiety: The role of control in the early environment. *Psychological Bulletin, 124,* 3–21.

Chorpita, B. F., Brown, T. A., & Barlow, D. H. (1998). Perceived control as a mediator of family environment in etiological models of childhood anxiety. *Behavior Therapy, 29,* 457–476.

Cicchetti, D., & Cohen, D. (Eds.). (1995). *Developmental psychopathology: Vol. 1. Theory and methods.* New York: Wiley.

Cicchetti, D., & Rogosch, F. A. (2002). A developmental psychopathology perspective on adolescence. *Journal of Consulting and Clinical Psychology, 70,* 6–20.

Clark, L. A., & Watson, D. (1991). Tripartite model of anxiety and depression: Psychometric evidence and taxonomic implications. *Journal of Abnormal Psychology, 100,* 316–336.

Clark, L. A., Watson, D., & Mineka, S. (1994). Temperament, personality, and the mood and anxiety disorders. *Journal of Abnormal Psychology, 103,* 103–116.

Cobham, V. E., Dadds, M. R., & Spence, S. H. (1999). Anxious children and their parents: What do they expect? *Journal of Clinical Child Psychology, 28,* 220–231.

Cohen, S., Kamarck, T., & Mermelstein, R. (1983). A global measure of perceived stress. *Journal of Health and Social Behavior, 24,* 385–396.

Cohen, S., Kessler, R., & Underwood, G. L. (1995). Strategies for measuring stress in studies of psychiatric and physical disorders. In S. Cohen, R. Kessler, & G. L. Underwood (Eds.), *Measuring stress* (pp. 3–28). New York: Oxford University Press.

Costanzo, P., Miller-Johnson, S., & Wencel, H. (1995). Social development. In J. S. March (Ed.), *Anxiety disorders in children and adolescents* (pp. 109–124). New York: Guilford Press.

Costello, E. J., & Angold, A. (1995). Epidemiology. In J. S. March (Ed.), *Anxiety disorders in children and adolescents* (pp. 109–124). New York: Guilford Press.

Craske, M. G. (1991). Phobic fear and panic attacks: The same emotional states triggered by different cues? *Clinical Psychology Review, 11,* 599–620.

Craske, M. G. (1997). Fear and anxiety in children and adolescents. *Bulletin of the Menninger Clinic, 61,* A4–A36.

Craske, M. G., & Barlow, D. H. (1988). A review of the relationship between panic and avoidance. *Clinical Psychology Review, 8,* 667–685.

Craske, M. G., Miller, P. P., Rotunda, R., & Barlow, D. H. (1990). A descriptive report of features of initial unexpected panic attacks in minimal and extensive avoiders. *Behaviour Research and Therapy, 28,* 395–400.

Curtis, G. C., Magee, W. J., Eaton, W. W., Wittchen, H.-U., & Kessler, R. C. (1998). Specific fears and phobias: Epidemiology and classification. *British Journal of Psychiatry, 173,* 212–217.

Dadds, M. R., Barrett, P. M., Rapee, R. M., & Ryan, S. (1996). Family processes and child anxiety and aggression: An observational analysis. *Journal of Abnormal Child Psychology, 24,* 715–734.

Dashiff, C. J. (1995). Understanding separation anxiety disorder. *Journal of Child and Adolescent and Psychiatric Nursing, 8,* 27–38.

Davey, G. C. L. (1994). Self-reported fears of common indigenous animals in adult UK population: The role of disgust sensitivity. *British Journal of Psychology, 85,* 541–554.

Davila, J., Hammen, C., Burge, D., Daley, S. E., & Paley, B. (1996). Cognitive/interpersonal correlates of adult interpersonal problem-solving strategies. *Cognitive Therapy and Research, 20,* 465–480.

Donnell, C. D., & McNally, R. J. (1990). Anxiety sensitivity and panic attacks in a nonclinical population. *Behaviour Research and Therapy, 28,* 83–85.

Dozier, M., Stovall, K. C., & Albus, K. E. (1999). Attachment and psychopathology in adulthood. In J. Cassidy & P. R. Shaver (Eds.), *Handbook of attachment: Theory, research, and clinical applications* (pp. 497–519). New York: Guilford Press.

DuPont, R. L., Rice, D. P., Miller, L. S., Shiraki, S. S., Rowland, C. R., & Harwood, H. J. (1996). Economic costs of anxiety disorders. *Anxiety, 2,* 167–172.

Eaton, W. W., Dryman, A., & Weissman, M. M. (1991). Panic and phobia. In L. N. Robins & D. A. Regier (Eds.), *Psychiatric disorders in America: The Epidemiological Catchment Area study* (pp. 155–179). New York: Free Press.

Ehlers, A. (1993). Somatic symptoms and panic attacks: A retrospective study of learning experiences. *Behaviour Research and Therapy, 31,* 269–278.

Eisen, J. L., Goodman, W. K., Keller, M. B., Warshaw, B. G., DeMarco, L. M., Luce, D. D., et al. (1999). Patterns of remission and relapse in obsessive-compulsive disorder: A 2-year prospective study. *Journal of Clinical Psychiatry, 60,* 346–351.

Eng, W., Heimberg, R. G., Hart, T. A., Schneier, F. R., & Liebowitz, M. R. (2001). Attachment in individuals with social anxiety disorder: The relationship among adult attachment styles, social anxiety, and depression. *Emotion, 1,* 365–380.

Eysenck, H. J. (Ed.). (1967). *The biological basis of personality.* Springfield, IL: Charles C. Thomas.

Flament, M. F., Whitaker, A., Rapoport, J. L., Davies, M., Berg, C. Z., Kalikow, K., et al. (1988). Obsessive compulsive disorder in adolescence: An epidemiological study. *Journal of the American Academy of Child and Adolescent Psychiatry, 27,* 764–771.

Fox, N. A., Henderson, H. A., Rubin, K. H., Calkins, S. D., & Schmidt, L. A. (2001). Continuity and discontinuity of behavioral inhibition and exuberance: Psychophysiological and behavioral influences across the first four years of life. *Child Development, 72,* 1–21.

Francis, G., Last, C. G., & Strauss, C. C. (1987). Expression of separation anxiety disorder: The roles of age and gender. *Child Psychiatry and Human Development, 18,* 82–89.

Fredrickson, M., Annas, P., Fischer, H., & Wik, G. (1996). Gender and age differences in the prevalence of specific fears and phobias. *Behaviour Research and Therapy, 26,* 241–244.

Fyer, A. J., Mannuzza, S., Chapman, T. F., Martin, L. Y., & Klein, D. F. (1995). Specificity in familial aggregation of phobic disorders. *Archives of General Psychiatry, 52,* 564–573.

Gerhold, M., Laucht, M., Terdorf, C., Schmidt, M. H., & Esser, G. (2001). Early mother-infant interaction as a precursor to childhood social withdrawal. *Child Psychiatry and Human Development, 32,* 277–293.

Gershuny, B. S., & Sher, K. J. (1998). The relation between personality and anxiety: Findings from a 3-year prospective study. *Journal of Abnormal Psychology, 107,* 252–262.

Goisman, R. M., Allsworth, J., Rogers, M. P., Warshaw, M. G., Goldenberg, I., Vasile, R. G., et al. (1998). Simple phobia as a comorbid anxiety disorder. *Anxiety and Depression, 7,* 105–112.

Gray, J. A. (1982). *The neuropsychology of anxiety.* New York: Oxford University Press.

Gray, J. A., & McNaughton, N. (1996). The neuropsychology of anxiety: A reprise. In D. A. Hope (Ed.), *Nebraska symposium on motivation: Perspectives on anxiety, panic, and fear* (pp. 61–134). Lincoln: University of Nebraska Press.

Greco, L. A., & Morris, T. L. (2002). Paternal child-rearing and social anxiety: Investigation of child perceptions and actual father behavior. *Journal of Psychopathology and Behavioral Assessment, 24,* 259–267.

Greenberg, P. E., Sisitsky, T., Kessler, R. C., Finkstein, S. N., Berndt, E. R., Davidson, J. R. T., et al. (1999). The economic burden of anxiety disorders in the 1990s. *Journal of Clinical Psychiatry, 60,* 427–435.

Hankin, B. L., Kassel, J. D., & Abela, J. R. Z. (2005). Adult attachment styles and specificity of emotional distress: Prospective investigations of cognitive risk and interpersonal stress generation as mediating mechanisms. *Personality and Social Psychology Bulletin, 31,* 136–151.

Hayes, S. C., Wilson, K. G., Gifford, E. V., Follette, V. M., & Strosahl, K. (1996). Experiential avoidance and behavioral disorders: A functional dimensional approach to diagnosis and treatment. *Journal of Consulting and Clinical Psychology, 64,* 1152–1168.

Hayward, C., Killen, J. D., Hammer, L. D., Litt, I. F., Wilson, D. M., Simmonds, B., et al. (1992). Pubertal stage and panic attack history in sixth- and seventh-grade girls. *American Journal of Psychiatry, 149,* 1239–1243.

Hazan, C., & Shaver, P. R. (1987). Romantic love conceptualized as an attachment process. *Journal of Personality and Social Psychology, 52,* 511–524.

Heim, C., & Nemeroff, C. B. (1999). The impact of early aversive experience on brain systems involved in the pathophysiology of anxiety and affective disorders. *Biological Psychiatry, 46,* 1509–1522.

Heimberg, R. G., Holt, C. S., Schneier, F. R., Spitzer, R. L., & Liebowitz, M. R. (1993). The issue of subtypes in the diagnosis of social phobia. *Journal of Anxiety Disorders, 7,* 249–269.

Hirschfeld, R. M. A. (1996). Placebo response in the treatment of panic disorder. *Bulletin of the Menninger Clinic, 60*(2), A76–A86.

Hoehn-Saric, R., Hazlett, R. L., & McLeod, D. R. (1993). Generalized anxiety disorder with early and late onset of anxiety symptoms. *Comprehensive Psychiatry, 34,* 291–298.

Holmes, T. H., & Rahe, R. H. (1967). The social readjustment rating scale. *Journal of Psychosomatic Research, 11,* 213–218.

Hummel, R. M., & Gross, A. M. (2001). Socially anxious children: An observational study of parent-child interaction. *Child & Family Behavior Therapy, 23,* 19–41.

Ingram, R. E., Miranda, J., & Segal, Z. V. (1998). *Cognitive vulnerability to depression.* New York: Guilford Press.

Ingram, R., & Price, J. M. (2001). *Vulnerability to psychopathology: Risk across the lifespan.* New York: Guilford Press.

Jenike, M. A., Baer, L., Minchiello, W. E., Schwartz, E. E., & Carey, R. J. (1986). Concomitant obsessive-compulsive disorder and schizotypal personality disorders. *American Journal of Psychiatry, 143,* 360–311.

Jones, M. K., & Menzies, R. G. (2000). Danger expectancies, self-efficacy and insight in spider phobia. *Behaviour Research and Therapy, 38,* 585–600.

Jorm, A. F., Christensen, H., Henderson, A. S., Jacomb, P. A., Korten, A. E., & Rodgers, B. (2000). Predicting anxiety and depression from personality: Is there a synergistic effect of neuroticism and extraversion? *Journal of Abnormal Psychology, 109,* 145–149.

Kagan, J. (1989). Temperamental contributions to social behavior. *American Psychologist, 44,* 668–674.

Kagan, J., Reznick, S., & Snidman, N. (1987). The physiology and psychology of behavior inhibition in children. *Development Psychology, 58,* 1459–1473.

Kagan, J., Reznick, S., & Snidman, N. (1988). Biological basis of childhood shyness. *Science, 240,* 167–171.

Kagan, J., & Snidman, N. (1991). Temperamental factors in human development. *American Psychologist, 46,* 856–862.

Kagan, J., Snidman, N., & Arcus, D. (1998). Childhood derivatives of high and low reactivity in infancy. *Child Development, 69,* 1483–1493.

Katschnig, H., & Amering, M. (1994). The long-term course of panic disorder. In B. E. Wolfe & J. D. Maser (Eds.), *Treatment of panic disorder: A consensus development conference* (pp. 73–81). Washington, DC: American Psychiatric Press.

Kendall, P. C. (1985). Toward a cognitive-behavioral model of child psychopathology and a critique of related interventions. *Journal of Abnormal Child Psychology, 13,* 357–372.

Kendall, P. C., Kortlander, E., & Chansky, T. E. (1992). Comorbidity of anxiety and depression in youth: Treatment implications. *Journal of Consulting & Clinical Psychology, 60,* 869–880.

Kendler, K. S., Kessler, R. C., Walters, E. E., MacLean, C., Neale, M. C., Heath, A. C., et al. (1995). Stressful life events, genetic liability, and onset of an episode of major depression in women. *American Journal of Psychiatry, 152,* 833–842.

Kendler, K. S., Myers, J., Prescott, C. A., & Neal, M. C. (2001). The genetic epidemiology of irrational fears and phobias in men. *Archives of General Psychiatry, 58,* 257–265.

Kendler, K. S., Neale, M. C., Kessler, R. C., Heath, A. C., & Eaves, L. J. (1992). Generalized anxiety disorder in women: A population-based twin study. *Archives of General Psychiatry, 49,* 267–272.

Kessler, R. C., McGonagle, K. A., Zhao, S., Nelson, C. B., Hughes, M., Eshleman, S., et al. (1994). Lifetime and 12-month prevalence of DSM-III-R psychiatric disorders in the United States: Results from the National Comorbidity Survey. *Archives of General Psychiatry, 51,* 8–19.

Kessler, R. C., Sonnega, A., Bromet, E., Hughes, M., & Nelson, C. B. (1995). Posttraumatic stress disorder in the National Comorbidity Survey. *Archives of General Psychiatry, 52,* 1048–1060.

Kilpatrick, D. G., & Saunders, B. E. (1999). *Prevalence and consequences of child victimization: Results from the National Survey of Adolescents.* Washington, DC: National Institute of Justice.

Kocovski, N. L., Endler, N. S., Cox, B. J., & Swinson, R. P. (2003). The differential assessment of state-trait anxiety and depression in a clinically anxious sample. *Journal of Psychopathology and Behavioral Assessment, 26,* 165–172.

Krohne, H. W., & Hock, M. (1991). Relationships between restrictive mother-child interactions and anxiety of the child. *Anxiety Research, 4,* 109–124.

La Greca, A. M., Silverman, W. K., Vernberg, E. M., & Prinstein, M. J. (1996). Symptoms of post-traumatic stress in children after Hurricane Andrew: A prospective study. *Journal of Consulting and Clinical Psychology, 64,* 712–723.

Lang, P. J., Cuthbert, B. N., & Bradley, M. M. (1998). Measuring emotion in therapy: Imagery, activation, and feeling. *Behavior Therapy, 29,* 655–674.

Last, C. G., Perrin, S., Hersen, M., & Kazdin, A. E. (1992). DSM-III-R anxiety disorders in children: Sociodemographic and clinical characteristics. *Journal of the American Academy of Child and Adolescent Psychiatry, 31,* 1070–1076.

Laurent, J., & Ettelson, R. (2001). An examination of the tripartite model of anxiety and depression and its application to youth. *Clinical Child and Family Psychology Review, 4,* 209–230.

Lazarus, R. S. (1990). Theory-based stress management. *Psychological Inquiry, 1,* 3–13.

Lazarus, R. S., & Folkman, S. (1984). *Stress, appraisal and coping.* New York: Springer-Verlag.

Legrand, L. N., McGue, M., & Iacono, W. G. (1999). A twin study of state and trait anxiety in childhood and adolescence. *Journal of Child Psychology and Psychiatry, 40,* 953–958.

Leon, A. C., Portera, L., & Weissman, M. M. (1995). The social costs of anxiety disorders. *British Journal of Psychiatry, 166*(Suppl. 27), 19–22.

Lilienfeld, S. O., Turner, S. M., & Jacob, R. G. (1993). Anxiety sensitivity: An examination of theoretical and methodological issues. *Advances in Behavior Research and Therapy, 15,* 147–182.

MacLeod, C. (1991). Clinical anxiety and the selective encoding of threatening information. *International Review of Psychiatry, 3,* 279–292.

MacLeod, C., & Mathews, A. (1991). Cognitive-experimental approaches to the emotional disorders. In P. R. Martin (Ed.), *Handbook of behaviour therapy and psychological science: An integrative approach* (pp. 115–150). New York: Pergamon.

MacLeod, C., & McLaughlin, K. (1995). Implicit and explicit memory bias in anxiety: A conceptual replication. *Behaviour Research and Therapy, 33,* 1–14.

Maier, S. F., & Seligman, M. E. P. (1976). Learned helplessness: Theory and evidence. *Journal of Comparative and Physiological Psychology, 88,* 554–564.

Markowitz, J. S., Weissman, M. M., Ouellette, R., Lish, J. D., & Klerman, G. L. (1989). Quality of life in panic disorder. *Archives of General Psychiatry, 46,* 984–992.

Marten, P. A., Brown, T. A., Barlow, D. H., Borkovec, T. D., Shear, M. K., & Lydiard, R. B. (1993). Evaluation of the ratings comprising the associated symptom criterion of DSM-III-R generalized anxiety disorder. *Journal of Nervous and Mental Disease, 181,* 676–682.

Mataix-Cols, D., Rauch, S. L., Manzo, P. A., Jenike, M. A., & Baer, L. (1999). Use of factor analyzed symptom dimensions to predict outcome with serotonin reuptake inhibitors and placebo in the treatment of obsessive-compulsive disorders. *American Journal of Psychiatry, 156,* 1409–1416.

Mathews, A., & Mackintosh, B. (2000). Induced emotional interpretation bias and anxiety. *Journal of Abnormal Psychology, 109,* 602–615.

McEwen, B. S. (1998). Protective and damaging effects of stress mediators. *New England Journal of Medicine, 338,* 171–179.

McGee, R., Feehan, M., Williams, S., & Anderson, J. (1992). DSM-III disorders from age 11 to age 15 years. *Journal of the American Academy of Child and Adolescent Psychiatry, 31,* 51–59.

McLeer, S. V., Deblinger, E. B., Henry, D., & Orvaschel, H. (1992). Sexually abused children at high risk for post-traumatic stress disorder. *Journal of the American Academy of Child and Adolescent Psychiatry, 31,* 875–879.

McNally, R. J. (1987). Preparedness and phobias: A review. *Psychological Bulletin, 101,* 283–303.

McNally, R. J., & Eke, M. (1996). Anxiety, sensitivity, suffocation fear, and breath holding duration as predictors of response to carbon dioxide challenge. *Journal of Abnormal Psychology, 105,* 146–149.

McNally, R. J., & Lorenz, M. (1987). Anxiety sensitivity in agoraphobics. *Journal of Behavior Therapy and Experimental Psychiatry, 18,* 3–11.

McNeil, D. W. (2001). Terminology and evolution of the constructs. In S. G. Hofman & P. M. DiBartolo (Eds.), *From social anxiety to social phobia: Multiple perspectives* (pp. 8–19). Needham Heights, MA: Allyn & Bacon.

Mills, R. S., & Rubin, K. H. (1993). Socialization factors in the development of social withdrawal. In K. H. Rubin & J. Aspendorf (Eds.), *Social withdrawal, inhibition, and shyness in childhood* (pp. 117–148). Hillsdale, NJ: Lawrence Erlbaum.

Mineka, S., Gunnar, M., & Champoux, M. (1986). Control and early social-emotional development: Infant rhesus monkeys reared in controllable versus uncontrollable environments. *Child Development, 57,* 1241–1256.

Mineka, S., & Kihlstrom, J. (1978). Unpredictable and uncontrollable aversive events. *Journal of Abnormal Psychology, 87,* 256–271.

Mineka, S., & Tomarken, A. J. (1989). The role of cognitive biases in the origins and maintenance of fear and anxiety disorders. In T. Archer & L. Nilsson (Eds.), *Aversion, avoidance, and anxiety: Perspectives on aversively motivated behavior* (pp. 195–221). Hillsdale, NJ: Lawrence Erlbaum.

Mogg, K., & Bradley, B. P. (1998). A cognitive-motivational analysis of anxiety. *Behaviour Research and Therapy, 36,* 809–848.

Monroe, S. M., & Simons, A. D. (1991). Diathesis-stress theories in the context of life stress research: Implications for the depressive disorders. *Psychological Bulletin, 110,* 406–425.

Muris, P., Steerneman, P., Merckelback, H., & Meesters, C. (1996). The role of parental fearfulness and modeling in children's fear. *Behaviour Research and Therapy, 34,* 265–268.

Noyes, R., Woodman, C., Garvey, M. J., Cook, B. L., Suelzer, M., Clancy, J., et al. (1992). Generalized anxiety disorder versus panic disorder: Distinguishing characteristics and patterns of comorbidity. *Journal of Nervous and Mental Disease, 180,* 369–370.

Ollendick, T. H., King, N. J., & Frary, R. B. (1989). Fears in children and adolescents: Reliability and generalizability across gender, age and nationality. *Behaviour Research and Therapy, 27,* 19–26.

Ollendick, T. H., King, N. J., & Muris, P. (2002). Fears and phobias in children: Phenomenology, epidemiology, and aetiology. *Child and Adolescent Mental Health, 3,* 98–106.

Ollendick, T. H., & Vasey, M. W. (1999). Developmental theory and the practice of clinical child psychology. *Journal of Clinical Child Psychology, 28,* 457–466.

Otto, M. W., Pollack, M. H., Fava, M., Uccello, R., & Rosenbaum, J. F. (1995). Elevated anxiety sensitivity index scores in patients with major depression: Correlates and changes with antidepressant treatment. *Journal of Anxiety Disorders, 9,* 117–123.

Ozer, E. J., Best, S. R., Lipsey, T. L., & Weiss, D. S. (2003). Predictors of posttraumatic stress disorder and symptoms in adults: A meta-analysis. *Psychological Bulletin, 129,* 52–73.

Page, A. C. (1994). Blood-injury phobia. *Clinical Psychology Review, 14,* 443–461.

Page, A. C. (2003). The role of disgust in faintness elicited by blood and injection stimuli. *Journal of Anxiety Disorders, 17,* 45–58.

Parker, G. (1983). Parental "affectionless control" as an antecedent to adult depression. *Archives of General Psychiatry, 40,* 956–960.

Plomin, R., DeFries, J. C., McClearn, G. E., & Rutter, M. (1997). *Behavioral genetics: A primer* (3rd ed.). New York: Freeman.

Pollock, R. A., Rosenbaum, J. F., Marrs, A., Miller, B. S., & Biederman, J. (1995). Anxiety disorders of childhood: Implications for adult psychopathology. *Psychiatric Clinics of North America, 18,* 745–766.

Rachman, S. J. (1997). A cognitive theory of obsessions. *Behaviour Research and Therapy, 35,* 793–802.

Rapee, R. M. (1995). Descriptive psychopathology of social phobia. In R. G. Heimberg, M. R. Liebowitz, D. A. Hope, & F. R. Schneier (Eds.), *Social phobia: Diagnosis, assessment, and treatment* (pp. 41–66). New York: Guilford Press.

Rapee, R. M., Craske, M. G., & Barlow, D. H. (1995). Assessment instrument for panic disorder that includes fear of sensation-producing activities: The Albany Panic and Phobia Questionnaire. *Anxiety, 1,* 114–122.

Rasmussen, S., & Eisen, J. L. (1992). The epidemiology and differential diagnosis of obsessive compulsive disorder. *Journal of Clinical Psychiatry, 53,* 4–10.

Reiss, S. (1991). Expectancy model of fear, anxiety, and panic. *Clinical Psychology Review, 11,* 141–153.

Reiss, S., & McNally, R. J. (1985). Expectancy model of fear. In S. Reiss & R. R. Bootzin (Eds.), *Theoretical issues in behavior therapy* (pp. 107–121). San Diego, CA: Academic Press.

Riskind, J. H. (1997). Looming vulnerability to threat: A cognitive paradigm for anxiety. *Behaviour Research and Therapy, 35,* 386–404.

Riskind, J. H., & Williams, N. L. (in press). A unique vulnerability common to all anxiety disorders: The looming maladaptive style. In L. B. Alloy & J. H. Riskind (Eds.), *Cognitive vulnerability to emotional disorders.* Hillsdale, NJ: Lawrence Erlbaum.

Riskind, J. H., Williams, N. L., Gessner, T., Chrosniak, L., & Cortina, J. (2000). A pattern of mental organization and danger schema related to anxiety: The looming maladaptive style. *Journal of Personality and Social Psychology, 79,* 837–852.

Ronan, K. R., & Kendall, P. C. (1997). Self-talk in distressed youth: States-of-mind and content specificity. *Journal of Clinical Child Psychology, 26,* 330–337.

Roy-Byrne, P. P., & Katon, W. (2000). Anxiety management in the medical settings: Rationale, barriers to diagnosis and treatment, and proposed solutions. In D. I. Mostofsky & D. H. Barlow (Eds.), *The management of stress and anxiety in medical disorders* (pp. 1–14). Boston: Allyn & Bacon.

Rubin, K. H., Burgess, K. B., & Hastings, P. D. (2002). Stability and social-behavioral consequences of toddlers' inhibited temperament and parenting behaviors. *Child Development, 73,* 483–495.

Salkovskis, P. M., Shafran, R., Rachman, S., & Freestone, M. H. (1999). Multiple pathways to inflated responsibility beliefs in obsessional problems: Possible origins and implications for therapy and research. *Behaviour Research and Therapy, 37,* 1055–1072.

Scher, C. D., & Stein, M. B. (2003). Developmental antecedents of anxiety sensitivity. *Journal of Anxiety Disorders, 17,* 253–269.

Schmidt, N. B., Lerew, D. R., & Jackson, R. J. (1997). The role of anxiety sensitivity in the pathogenesis of panic: Prospective evaluation of spontaneous panic attacks during acute stress. *Journal of Abnormal Psychology, 106,* 355–364.

Schmidt, N. B., Lerew, D. R., & Jackson, R. J. (1999). Prospective evaluation of anxiety sensitivity in the pathogenesis of panic: Replication and extension. *Journal of Abnormal Psychology, 108,* 532–537.

Schmidt, N. B., Storey, J., Greenberg, B. D., Santiago, H. T., Li, Q. L., & Murphy, D. L. (2000). Evaluating Gene × Psychological Risk Factor effects in the pathogenesis of anxiety: A new model approach. *Journal of Abnormal Psychology, 109,* 308–320.

Schneier, F. R., Heckelman, L. R., Garfinkle, R., Campeas, R., Fallon, B., Gitow, A., et al. (1994). Functional impairment in social phobia. *Journal of Clinical Psychiatry, 55,* 322–331.

Schonfeld, W. H., Verboncoeur, C. J., Fifer, S. K., Lipschutz, R. C., Lubeck, D. P., & Buesching, D. P. (1997). The functioning and well-being of patients with unrecognized anxiety disorders and major depressive disorder. *Journal of Affective Disorders, 43,* 105–119.

Seligman, M. E. P. (1971). Phobias and preparedness. *Behavior Therapy, 2,* 307–320.

Seyle, H. (1978). *The stress of life* (2nd ed.). New York: McGraw-Hill.

Shapiro, A. M., Roberts, J. E., & Beck, J. G. (1999). Differentiating symptoms of anxiety and depression in older adults: Distinct cognitive and affective profiles? *Cognitive Therapy and Research, 23,* 53–74.

Silverman, W. K., & Ginsburg, G. S. (1995). Specific phobias and generalized anxiety disorder. In J. S. March (Ed.), *Anxiety disorders in children and adolescents* (pp. 151–180). New York: Guilford Press.

Spielberger, C. D., Gorsuch, R. L., & Lushene, R. E. (1970). *Manual for the State-Trait Anxiety Inventory.* Palo Alto, CA: Consulting Psychologists Press.

Sroufe, L. A. (1997). Psychopathology as an outcome of development. *Development and Psychopathology, 9,* 251–268.

Stein, M. B., Jang, K. L., & Livesley, W. J. (1999). Heritability of anxiety sensitivity: A twin study. *American Journal of Psychiatry, 156,* 246–251.

Steketee, G., Chambless, D. L., & Tran, G. Q. (2001). Effects of Axis I and Axis II comorbidity on behavior therapy outcome for obsessive compulsive disorder and agoraphobia. *Comprehensive Psychiatry, 42,* 76–86.

Stewart, S. H., Taylor, S., Jang, K. L., Cox, B. J., Watt, M. C., Fedoroff, I. C., et al. (2001). Causal modeling of relations among learning history, anxiety sensitivity, and panic attacks. *Behaviour Research and Therapy, 39,* 443–456.

Summerfelt, L. J., Richter, M. A., Antony, M. M., & Swinson, R. P. (1999). Symptom structure in obsessive-compulsive disorder: A confirmatory factor-analytic study. *Behaviour Research and Therapy, 37,* 297–311.

Taylor, S. (1999). *Anxiety sensitivity: Theory, research and treatment of anxiety.* Mahwah, NJ: Lawrence Erlbaum.

Taylor, S., Kuch, K., Koch, W. J., Crockett, D. J., & Passey, G. (1998). The structure of posttraumatic stress symptoms. *Journal of Abnormal Psychology, 107,* 154–160.

Topolski, T. D., Hewitt, J. K., Eaves, L. J., Silberg, J. L., Meyer, J. M., Rutter, M., et al. (1997). Genetic and environmental influences on child reports of manifest anxiety symptoms and symptoms of separation anxiety and overanxious disorders: A community-based twin study. *Behavior Genetics, 27,* 15–28.

Treadwell, K. R. H., & Kendall, P. C. (1996). Self-talk in youth with anxiety disorders: States of mind, content specificity, and treatment outcome. *Journal of Consulting and Clinical Psychology, 64,* 941–950.

Trull, T. J., & Sher, K. J. (1994). Relationship between the five-factor model of personality and Axis I disorders in a nonclinical sample. *Journal of Abnormal Psychology, 103,* 350–360.

Turner, S. M., & Beidel, D. C. (1989). Social phobia: Clinical syndrome, diagnosis, and comorbidity. *Clinical Psychology Review, 9,* 3–18.

Turner, S. M., Beidel, D. C., & Cooley-Quille, M. R. (1995). Two year follow-up of social phobics treated with Social Effectiveness Therapy. *Behaviour Research and Therapy, 33,* 553–556.

Turner, S. M., Williams, S. L., Beidel, D. C., & Mezzich, J. E. (1986). Panic disorder and agoraphobia with panic attacks: Covariation along with the dimensions of panic and agoraphobic fear. *Journal of Abnormal Psychology, 95,* 384–388.

Vasey, M. W., Daleiden, E. L., Williams, L. L., & Brown, L. M. (1995). Biased attention in childhood anxiety disorders: A preliminary study. *Journal of Abnormal Child Psychology, 23,* 267–279.

Watson, D., & Clark, L. A. (1984). Negative affectivity: The disposition to experience aversive emotional states. *Psychological Bulletin, 96,* 465–490.

Watson, D., Clark, L. A., & Tellegen, A. (1988). Development and validation of brief measures of positive and negative affect: The PANAS scales. *Journal of Personality and Social Psychology, 54,* 1063–1070.

Watt, M. C., Stewart, S. H., & Cox, B. J. (1998). A retrospective study of the learning history origins of anxiety sensitivity. *Behaviour Research and Therapy, 36,* 505–525.

Weinfeld, N. S., Sroufe, L. A., & Egeland, B. (2000). Attachment from infancy to early adulthood in a high-risk sample: Continuity, discontinuity and their correlates. *Child Development, 71,* 695–700.

Wheeler, M. A., Stuss, D. T., & Tulving, E. (1997). Toward a theory of episodic memory: The frontal lobes and autonoetic consciousness. *Psychological Bulletin, 121,* 331–354.

Williams, N. L. (2002). *The cognitive interactional model of appraisal and coping: Implications for anxiety and depression.* Unpublished doctoral dissertation, George Mason University, Fairfax, VA.

Williams, N. L., & Reardon, J. (2004). *A comparison of vulnerabilities to anxiety: The Looming Cognitive Style and anxiety sensitivity.* Manuscript submitted for publication.

Williams, N. L., & Riskind, J. H. (2004). Adult romantic attachment and cognitive vulnerabilities to anxiety and depression: Examining the interpersonal basis of vulnerability models. *Journal of Cognitive Psychotherapy, 18,* 7–24.

Williams, N. L., Shahar, G., Riskind, J. H., & Joiner, T. E. (2005). The looming cognitive style has a general effect on an anxiety disorder symptoms factor: Further support for a cognitive model of vulnerability to anxiety. *Journal of Anxiety Disorders, 19,* 157–175.

Weissman, M. M., Bland, R., Canino, G., Greenwald, S., Hwo, H., Lee, C., et al. (1994). The cross national epidemiology of obsessive compulsive disorder. *Journal of Clinical Psychiatry, 55,* 5–10.

Wittchen, H.-U., Zhao, S., Kessler, R. C., & Eaton, W. W. (1994). DSM-III-R generalized anxiety disorder in the National Comorbidity Survey. *Archives of General Psychiatry, 51,* 355–364.

Woody, S. R., & Teachman, B. (2000). Intersection of disgust and fear: Normative and pathological views. *Clinical Psychology: Science and Practice, 7,* 291–311.

Yonkers, K. A., Warshaw, M. R., Maisson, A. O., & Keller, M. B. (1996). Phenomenology and course of generalised anxiety disorder. *British Journal of Psychiatry, 168,* 308–313.

Yonkers, K. A., Zlotnick, C., Allsworth, J., Warshaw, M., Shea, T., & Keller, M. B. (1998). Is the course of panic disorder the same in men and women? *American Journal of Psychiatry, 155,* 596–602.

Zimmerman, M., McDermut, W., & Mattia, J. I. (2000). Frequency of anxiety disorders in psychiatric outpatients with major depressive disorder. *American Journal of Psychiatry, 157,* 1337–1340.

Zinbarg, R. E., & Barlow, D. H. (1996). Structure of anxiety and the anxiety disorders: A hierarchical model. *Journal of Abnormal Psychology, 105,* 181–193.

Zinbarg, R., & Mohlman, J. (1998). Individual differences in the acquisition of affectively valenced associations. *Journal of Personality and Social Psychology, 74,* 1024–1040.

Zuckerman, M. (1999). *Vulnerability to psychopathology: A biosocial model.* Washington, DC: American Psychological Association.

CHAPTER 12

A Developmental Vulnerability-Stress Model of Eating Disorders

A Cognitive Approach

MYRA COOPER

The aims of this chapter are to briefly introduce eating disorders (EDs), vulnerability, and stress; discuss the relevant theory and literature; and provide an integrated vulnerability-stress account of the development of EDs. The account will cover the major developmental systems, but it will have a cognitive bias and will be integrated with noncognitive research and theory in order to maximize the explanatory power of our current knowledge about vulnerability and stress in the development of EDs. The empirical evidence supporting the new account will also be presented and discussed.

Eating disorders, defined using the criteria outlined by the *Diagnostic and Statistical Manual of Mental Disorders*, 4th edition (*DSM-IV*; American Psychiatric Association [APA], 1994), consist of two well-known types, anorexia nervosa (AN) and bulimia nervosa (BN), and a third group of disorders termed *eating disorder not otherwise specified* (ED-NOS). Binge eating disorder (BED) belongs in the latter category. Relatively little is known about ED-NOS, and this chapter will focus primarily on AN and BN, for which both theory and empirical research are much more advanced. At the same time, information on ED-NOS will be included when available.

Anorexia nervosa is characterized by body weight below a minimal normal level for age and height, intense fear of gaining weight, and disturbed perception of body size or shape. Postmenarcheal females with AN are also amenorrheic. BN is characterized by binge eating, inappropriate compensatory behavior (e.g., self-induced vomiting) to prevent weight gain, and self-evaluation unduly influenced by body weight and shape. Precise criteria for both disorders (e.g., frequency of binge eating in BN) can be found in *DSM-IV* (APA, 1994). ED-NOS includes a broad group of disorders similar to AN and BN but for which one or more of the key criteria for either diagnosis are not met. Only one disorder in this group (BED) is specified in detail, to date, as Draft Research Criteria. The criteria for BED include binge eating (as in BN) but in association with features such as eating more rapidly than normal, and it does not include inappropriate compensatory behavior.

PREVALENCE

A review of BN studies (M. J. Cooper, 2003) suggests that prevalence rates are 1%–2%, similar to the estimate made by Fairburn and Beglin (1990), although there is some evidence that a slight increase may have occurred in recent years (M. J. Cooper, 2003). Another review (Hoek & van Hoeken, 2003) estimates the prevalence at 1% in young women and 0.1% in young men. BN is less common in minority groups and in non-Western and more traditional societies (M. J. Cooper, 2003). AN is less common than BN, with prevalence estimated at 0.3% in young women (Hoek & van Hoeken). As with BN, there is some suggestion that rates, at least of registered cases, have risen over the last century, at least until the 1970s. The female-to-male ratio for AN seems to be at least 10:1 (van Hoeken, Seidell, & Hoek, 2003). AN seems to affect a similar subgroup of the global population as BN. However, there are some differences in key features. For example, AN tends to become evident 3 to 4 years earlier than BN (see Crisp, Hsu, Harding, & Hartshorn, 1980, for AN and Fairburn & P. J. Cooper, 1984, for BN), and some differences in risk factors have been found (see below). The prevalence of ED-NOS and BED is unclear, although clinically significant ED-NOS seems very common (Turner & Bryant-Waugh, 2004). There is relatively little information on how ED-NOS differs from BN (although see Hay & Fairburn, 1998) or AN, and only a small amount of information on the differences between BN and BED (Brody, Walsh, & Devlin, 1994).

DEVELOPMENTAL THEORY

Researchers, and those who have proposed theories that include an account of the development of eating disorders, have long been concerned with the factors that make individuals vulnerable to developing an eating disorder. An edited volume (Smolak, Levine, & Striegel-Moore, 1996) has attempted to place some of these vulnerabilities in eating disorders within a developmental framework, and it offers a useful introduction to the topic. However, the chapters in the Smolak et al. volume, like much of the empirical research, do not attempt to integrate the various vulnerabilities and stressors discussed into a coherent model or to explain how a vulnerability-stress model might operate in relation to the development of EDs. In addition, despite the existence of cognitive theory of eating disorders, the evidence base (including for the efficacy of cognitive therapy) of developmental theory rarely avails itself of this resource.

VULNERABILITY

Vulnerability, by definition, implies causality (Ingram & Luxton, Chapter 2 of this volume) and can be distinguished from risk—or from simple empirical correlation. It informs about mechanisms and thus is particularly useful in developing treatment, notably treatment that is based on a clear, articulated theory of the content, processes, and mechanisms involved in the disorder.

Vulnerability includes features that lead to the onset and maintenance of a disorder as well as contribute to the recovery and postrecovery course of a disorder (Ingram & Luxton, Chapter 2 of this volume). These aspects cannot usually be separated easily, because factors implicated in maintenance also have a cause or developmental history that requires explanation. Vulnerability factors have certain characteristics—these are not always universally true (particularly in eating disorders), but in general, it is probably useful to define them as internal factors or attributes of the person.

Most studies of eating disorders have tackled risk, not vulnerability, and have used a multidimensional or atheoretical framework to examine statistical predictors. Most studies are cross-sectional rather than longitudinal, and many also aim to predict eating-disorder symptoms rather than disorders. The articulation of vulnerability factors, however, implies a theoretical framework. Theories relevant to eating disorders that include a vulnerability perspective include psychodynamic theory (particularly as outlined by Bruch, 1973) and cognitive theory.

Cognitive theories have been well researched, and there is considerable empirical evidence to support them (see review by M. J. Cooper, 1997). They also form the basis of a great deal of treatment, particularly for BN, where extensive research supports their effectiveness (e.g., in a large, multicenter, randomized, controlled trial: Agras, Walsh, Fairburn, Wilson, & Kraemer, 2000). There is also some evidence that cognitive treatments are efficacious for BED (e.g., Wilfley et al., 1993). However, it is important to note that the outcome with standard cognitive behavioral therapy for BN is not always ideal (Fairburn et al., 1995) and that there is no good empirical evidence for its usefulness in AN, or indeed for any other treatment in this disorder (Hay, Bacaltchuk, Claudino, Ben-Tovim, & Yong, 2003).

COGNITIVE THEORIES OF EATING DISORDERS

Several cognitive models of eating disorders now exist, all originally inspired by Garner and Bemis's (1982) model of AN, which drew on Bruch's (1973) work and the cognitive theory of depression as developed by Beck et al. (Beck, Rush, Shaw, & Emery, 1979). Developments include greater specification of the cognitions involved (M. J. Cooper, Wells, & Todd, 2004) and the introduction of general schema theory (M. J. Cooper, 1997; M. J. Cooper et al., 2004; Waller, Kennerley, & Ohanian, in press). These two developments are particularly relevant to the current chapter and will be discussed below.

M. J. Cooper et al. (2004)

This model was developed primarily for BN, but it is also of relevance to AN. An important feature is that it conceptualizes key behaviors. These include binge eating and, in the case of AN, not eating,[1] and thus the model is not necessarily restricted to diagnosed cases but can be applied to the various manifestations of eating disorders as they present, including members of the ED-NOS category and subclinical and atypical disorders. The model uses Beckian terminology to understand and describe key cognitive constructs (e.g., Beck et al., 1979; Beck, Freeman, & Associates, 1990). The term *automatic thoughts* refers to self-talk or moment-to-moment, fleeting thoughts that enter consciousness with minimal volition. The term *underlying assumptions* refers to deeper-level rules or beliefs that apply across situations and reflect general propositions. *Core beliefs* refers to global, absolute beliefs that have usually always been true and that, in eating disorders, often reflect negative beliefs about the self. Assumptions and core beliefs have schematic properties—they both guide and influence the processing of information received and transmitted by individuals. The fashion in which this is achieved reflects certain distinctive styles of information processing, including selective attention and memory. Both assumptions and core beliefs typically develop in the context of negative early experiences, particularly within the family but also in the broader social environment with peers and at school.

In conceptualizing binge eating in BN, four types of automatic thoughts—interwoven with emotional and physiological features—are important. Negative self-beliefs are also involved, and these act with the negative automatic thoughts in the form of a vicious circle to maintain binge eating. More specifically, a trigger activates negative self-beliefs (e.g., "I'm stupid, a failure, useless"). Typical triggers can include events or situations with and without eating, weight, or shape content (e.g., an argument with a partner, actual or perceived criticism of body shape or weight). Positive thoughts about eating then result in eating to cope with the self-belief activated and the associated distress (e.g., "eating will help me feel less upset"). Permissive thoughts (e.g., "one biscuit won't hurt") and thoughts of no control (e.g., "I can't help myself") facilitate eating more and result in a binge. Eating is terminated when negative thoughts about eating predominate (e.g., "I'll get fat"). The patient's degree of conviction in the initial negative self-belief, and in any thoughts associated with the trigger, is thus maintained and reinforced—indeed, the usual experience is that degree of belief in the initial negative self-belief increases after binge eating. Bingeing also serves to decrease arousal linked to the associated distress. The decreased arousal becomes a further factor in reinforcement of the negative self-beliefs that triggered the episode, because these are invariably associated with considerable distress. In AN, not eating (on a day-to-day, moment-to-moment basis) is the key behavior that is most usefully conceptualized in a cognitive model of the disorder. Like binge eating in BN, not eating represents a coping strategy and is designed to cope with any negative self-beliefs and their associated distress that are activated in a trigger situation (e.g., "not eating will help me feel less worthless"). Not eating is characterized by increased belief in control, success, and, importantly, a sense of powerfulness, which reinforce not eating but leave the initial self-belief, and any associated negative automatic thoughts, unchallenged. Both BN and AN are characterized by negative self-beliefs and underlying assumptions about the meaning of weight, shape, and eating, including personal meaning to the patient. Although these beliefs and assumptions have traditionally been assumed to have content that is common to both disorders, some preliminary evidence is beginning to suggest that this may not always be true (see below). As noted above, both schemata and underlying assumptions have schematic properties. Both are also thought to develop relatively early in life as the result of negative experiences, and this is particularly true of negative self-beliefs—thus schema theory in these accounts forms the basis for the development of EDs.

Waller et al. (in press)

Waller also draws on schema theory. Although his analysis has features in common with the model outlined above, a key difference is the suggestion that BN and AN are distinguished by the type of schema avoidance employed, rather than by any differences in the content of schemata. The suggestion arises primarily from work conducted by Waller and colleagues (in press) that finds little or no difference between AN and BN, or other eating disorders, in the content of schemata as measured by the Young Schema Questionnaire (Young, 1994). In this account, AN is characterized by primary avoidance, in which the patient attempts to prevent the distress associated with core belief activation by preventing the belief from occurring. This is manifested behaviorally by, for example, restricting intake to lose weight in order to avoid triggering negative feelings about the self. BN is characterized by secondary avoidance: The belief is activated, intolerable distress is experienced, and the patient seeks to reduce its impact by bingeing and purging—impulsive behaviors designed to reduce or block the affect that has been triggered.

Cognitions are articulated in some detail, particularly for the BN theory (M. J. Cooper et al., 2004), but accompanying stressors are not often well specified, although they may be inferred via knowledge of the literature on risk and vulnerability factors. A definite and detailed developmental framework that takes into account important transitions for children and adolescents is also often lacking, not only in the model of Waller et al. (in press), where it is given scant attention, but also in the model presented by M. J. Cooper et al. (2004), where, although present, it is not articulated in detail. For example, the precise nature of any links between developmental tasks and topics and the cognitions identified in these models, including at the different levels, is not expounded at length. This is particularly true of the proposed link between negative early experiences and the development of negative self- or core beliefs—the mechanism involved here has not been explored in any detail. One of the aims of this chapter is to provide a basic framework for integrating these topics in eating disorders.

Other theories, such as psychodynamic theory, also have an important role to play in understanding vulnerability, especially individual vulnerability, although relatively little empirical evidence exists for their basic tenets. Much of the psychodynamic theory and evidence can be readily "translated" into cognitive constructs and are very relevant to cognitive theory. This is particularly true of ego psychology and object relations theory as articulated by Bruch (1973) for eating disorders in relation to the development of self and identity. It is also true more generally of those interested in attachment theory and concepts such as theory of mind and internal working models and how these might relate to early developmental tasks. Bruch's discussion of "cognitive distortions" in relation to the self, for example, has parallels with the negative self-beliefs and associated schema and information-processing errors described by cognitive theorists. The building blocks of cognitive therapy and theory, such as the ability to identify and label emotions and cognitions (which are often taken for granted in work with adults but which may be particularly problematic in eating disorders), is a topic much discussed in the psychodynamic literature. In particular, psychodynamic theory can help provide a useful and much more detailed perspective on childhood and also on the emotional as well as the cognitive origins of eating disorders than is typically contained in cognitive theory. Psychodynamic theory also includes a lot of relevant detail on transitions in adolescence and early adulthood, providing a wealth of detailed information on later developmental aspects—including adolescent tasks—that are also not always well articulated in cognitive models. Some of this work has the potential to form the basis of a cognitive explanation, linking early experience and cognitive development, as well as early experience and emotional development.

STRESS

The role of stress has been relatively neglected in cognitive accounts of eating disorders, although it is the predominant theme of sociocultural theories. Both early experiences within the family and the role of specific triggers (or stressors) are identified as triggers for episodes of problematic eating behavior in cognitive models, but relatively little is known about them from a cognitive perspective, that is, how they relate or link to the cognitive constructs identified as vulnerability factors. Rather poorly articulated concepts of stress are often employed in cognitive models, and this has included cognitive models of eating disorders. Elsewhere, however, research on life events and daily hassles can help to increase our knowledge of the role of these in cognitive theory. A stress model has been developed (C. L. Cooper & Bagliono, 1998) that incorporates life stress, coping styles, social support, and personality factors in a revised form (Bennett & C. L. Cooper, 1999) as factors that may be involved in the onset and maintenance of eating disorders, but there is as yet no direct empirical research to support it or clear understanding of how its constructs might link to cognition. In contrast to vulnerability factors, stress is usually viewed as an external pressure operating on an individual that strains his or her capacities psychologically or physiologically (see Grant & McMahon, Chapter 1 of this volume), although again this definition is not universally applicable to eating disorders. Although Bennett and C. L. Cooper's revised model, unlike many such models in eating disorders, does include some individual factors (and mentions appraisals of stressors), these have not been integrated in any detail or depth with cognition as a vulnerability factor.

Other theories that have a key role in understanding stressors, with little to say on individual vulnerability, include both sociocultural and feminist theories, in particular those that highlight the role of the family, peers, society, and cultural variables. Sociocultural theories in particular have generated a considerable amount of research, and there is a relatively large body of evidence attesting to the importance of its key constructs. One theory that has generated many important and interesting findings is that of Stice (1994). Like most other sociocultural theories, it focuses primarily on factors external to the individual, although it does consider some internal factors insofar as external stressors are internalized (as in Stice, 1994). However, what the individual brings personally or historically is not considered in any detail. Research based on Stice's (1994) model has proved particularly valuable because, unlike much other sociocultural research, it has examined predictors of eating-disordered behavior such as binge eating and the development of clinical eating disorders rather than simply the prediction of generic collections of eating disorder–related symptoms in otherwise healthy groups (e.g., Stice, 1998, 2002). Importantly, some of the studies based around sociocultural theories have used longitudinal designs, which add considerable validity to the findings (e.g., Paxton, Schutz, Wertheim, & Muir, 1999; Stice, 1998).

KEY ISSUES

Implicit in vulnerability-stress models is often the idea that disorders exist on a continuum. This has been a popular idea in EDs, where dieting has been seen as one end and eating disorders as the other end of a continuum. Although a dimensional (as opposed to a categorical) approach is widely recognized to be useful in the advancement of psychological research and understanding, it has been suggested that the use of this particular dimension in EDs may involve a rather simplistic continuum that may not be particularly helpful in facilitating the development of treatment or the understanding of how normal eating develops into disordered eating (M. J. Cooper, 2003). One problem is that, as currently articulated, the model assumes discontinuity between eating-disordered behavior and normal (i.e., nondieting) eating. As a result, developments in the cognitive control of normal eating have not been applied to eating disorders. This excludes a whole area of theory and research that might be usefully applied to eating disorders—including their development and treatment.

It is extremely important to separate distal and proximal factors that may be involved in vulnerability. For example, although longitudinal studies suggest that dieting is a risk factor for later eating disorder, on a moment-to-moment basis restricting or dieting does not always seem to predict specific eating-disordered behaviors. Thus, the stage of the disorder—precursor, maintaining, or relapse prevention—must be identified to judge and evaluate research adequately, because different behaviors may have different impacts at different stages of the disorder. As suggested above, each stage thus needs examination. More fine-grained analysis is particularly needed at the proximal (moment-to-moment) level to enable more specific prediction of problem behaviors and development of more effective treatments. Some initial attempts to achieve this by more detailed specification of the cognitions involved in maintaining EDs will be reported below.

Stress can occur at any stage of a person's development of an eating disorder and can appear in a multitude of forms. Clinically, vulnerabilities and stressors are unlikely to lead to the development of an ED in a linear fashion, yet little research has been conducted on potential interactions between them (see Ingram & Luxton, Chapter 2 of this volume, for a discussion of different forms of interaction). Similarly, there may be protective factors, or resilience, that interact with both to reduce the possibility that an ED will develop, yet little work has been conducted along these lines. Longitudinal studies examining complex interactions present enormous logistical, resource, and statistical problems. The model presented below may help to provide a first step in guiding the development of any such study by integrating some of the factors involved in the onset (and maintenance) of eating disorders developmentally, and by approaching the issue from a cognitive perspective. This will help suggest theoretically important variables for future research to examine in longitudinal studies.

Vulnerability factors can be found in each of the major developmental systems—thus, it is especially important to look to normal development, and how it goes wrong, in considering why an individual develops a disorder. Unfortunately, there has been relatively little dialogue between clinical researchers and those interested in the development of normal eating and other constructs that are relevant to eating disorders. There has been much discussion of the dimensional link between EDs and dieting but no discussion of the link between EDs and normal eating. This is a rather curious omission and has led some researchers to focus on dieting as a paradigm or analogue for EDs. As suggested above, this may cause confusion in trying to understand eating disorders and how they relate to other eating behavior. For the sake of simplicity and conceptual clarity, this chapter will focus primarily on theory and research that has investigated patients, not dieters or those who score highly on symptom measures.

In the following sections, the chapter will consider each developmental system—cognition, affective, social/behavioral, and biological—and the possible role of vulnerability factors relevant to EDs in each. The potential role of stressors, divided into subsets (e.g., family, sociocultural factors), will then be considered. Relevant empirical evidence will be discussed. Finally, an integrated vulnerability-stress model, based on a detailed and well-articulated cognitive theory, that incorporates many of the factors identified earlier will be outlined. Although this model has been developed primarily for BN, its general themes also have considerable potential for application to AN. Where appropriate, these will be identified, and the content and processes that might be involved in AN will be outlined. As yet, it is important to remember that the latter observations currently lack significant empirical support.

Cognitive

Cognition has been little studied as a potential vulnerability factor in eating disorders. This section will consider schemata, underlying assumptions, and automatic thoughts as well as hunger, satiety, and awareness and expression of emotional states.

Beck's cognitive theory of depression (Beck et al., 1979) and general schema theory postulate schemata as risk factors. Similarly, cognitive theory of BN also postulates schemata as risk or vulnerability factors for eating disorders. It has been suggested, for example, that for an eating disorder to develop, schemata (which may include negative self-beliefs common to many disorders)[2] need to develop in conjunction with disorder-specific assumptions—those concerning weight, shape, and eating (M. J. Cooper, Todd, & Wells, 1998). Some automatic thoughts might be seen to derive directly from basic schemata and assumptions and may be activated in response to stress, but others would seem to require a specific developmental history. Yet others would seem to be examples of normal cognitive development gone awry, for example, when cognitive mechanisms responsible for the control of normal eating acquire unusual meaning. In BN, for example, this may involve beliefs that eating will be useful in coping with or avoiding painful thoughts or emotional distress, that is, in solving psychological problems.[3] Such beliefs may be expressed, for example, as beliefs such as "eating/bingeing will take away my distress" or "it will make me feel less humiliated/rejected."

The evidence linking schemata and eating disorders comes from cross-sectional or between-group studies. The same is true of evidence linking automatic thoughts to eating disorders. There are also some retrospective semi-structured interview studies taking a historical perspective on the content and processes associated with schema, that is, investigating the origins of schemata and their role in maintaining problematic eating-disordered behavior. To date, however, the issue has been little researched. Consequently, longitudinal studies are badly needed, both at a specific and more general level of analysis. One important area to be explored is separating the relative contribution of the different meanings to disordered eating, dieting, and normal eating—an important issue in identifying the specificity of the theory.

It is currently unclear how far other cognitive factors are associated with, or increase vulnerability to, an ED. These are also not explicitly addressed in cognitive models, although it is quite possible to add them in as additional variables that may be important in the development and maintenance of both AN and BN.

Bruch (1973) first drew attention to disturbance in hunger and satiety and also to disturbance in awareness and expression of emotional states. There is empirical evidence, using the Interoceptive Awareness subscale of the Eating Disorder Inventory (EDI; Garner, Olmsted, & Polivy, 1983) and the Toronto Alexithymia Scale (Taylor, Ryan, & Bagby, 1985), for difficulties in both these areas in EDs. These features have not been much studied empirically, and it is currently unclear whether they might be disorders of perception, cognition or interpretation, or expression (M. J. Cooper, 2003). However, they can also be considered as a potential vulnerability factor (for which further empirical evidence and investigation are needed).

Within cognitive models of eating disorders, the cognitive elements discussed above—core beliefs, underlying assumptions, schema processes, and automatic thoughts—create vulnerability to eating disorders, and without the presence of each of these factors it is very unlikely that a person will develop an eating disorder. The role of other cognitive elements is little understood but requires integration with these and other potential vulnerability factors.

Affective

In this section, the role of negative affect, including its control and regulation, will be considered.

Affect has an important role in at least two cognitive models—Fairburn's revised bulimia nervosa model (Fairburn, 1997) and the transdiagnostic model (Fairburn, Z. Cooper, & Shafran, 2003), on which the former is based. The link is relatively simple in these two models—negative affect increases the probability of bingeing and vice versa. In the model of M. J. Cooper et al. (2004), however, negative affect has a fully integrated role with thoughts, behavior, and physiology, which are hypothesized to act together in vicious circles of cause and effect to maintain BN. This theory is consistent with other developments in cognitive theory, particularly for anxiety disorders. Historically, interest in affect as a trigger of binge eating can be found in Heatherton and Baumeister's (1991) escape model, in which negative affect narrows the focus of attention and removes normal barriers to eating, as well as increasing uncritical acceptance of negative and dysfunctional beliefs and thoughts. Irrational or negative and dysfunctional thoughts occur because normal patterns of reasoning are suspended as the focus of attention shifts. Meaningful thought subsequently decreases, and critical evaluation of novel ideas is less effective than usual.

Waller and his colleagues have characterized the affect model as being in competition with the dieting model in relation to the triggering of binge eating (Waters, Hill, & Waller, 2000), arguing that each proposes a different explanation for the maintenance of binge eating. They have urged that the two models should be integrated, providing some preliminary evidence that both mechanisms may be involved in maintaining binge eating (Waters et al.). However, the roles of restraint and negative affect in the triggering of binge eating are not yet fully understood. There is, for example, evidence suggesting that negative affect triggers or precedes binge eating (e.g., Waters et al.), and tests of the dieting/restraint model have not always found a key role for restraint in binge eating (e.g., Byrne & McLean, 2002). However, it is also important to remember that although the evidence on affect and dieting as causal in the maintenance of binge eating is unclear, several studies now confirm that dieting does seem to have a causal role in the development of EDs. This illustrates the potential importance of distinguishing the stage at which triggers may act (i.e., whether proximal or distal) when discussing the precise roles of potential vulnerability factors.

Affect as a vulnerability factor has not been much investigated in eating disorders. However, there is some evidence that ED patients have problems in the control and regulation of affect. For example, they may find self-soothing very difficult (Esplen, Garfinkel, & Gallop, 2000). Nevertheless (as with hunger and satiety awareness), it is not at all clear where the problem might be. For example, do patients experience more intense affect than others or different types of negative affect? The term *emotional regulation* has been applied to EDs, with the suggestion that poor emotional regulation is characteristic of ED patients, but the term has been used in several different and inconsistent ways in the literature (see Chaplin & Cole, Chapter 3 of this volume). Moreover, the validity of the concept of regulation has been questioned insofar as it implies that everyone has certain emotions and that there is an optimal level at which these should be expressed. Instead, it has been suggested that emotions are best conceptualized as becoming organized, not regulated, in relation to the self and the environment, including other people (Oatley & Jenkins, 1996). This emphasizes the systemic and dynamic nature of emotional development rather than the expression of absolute levels or linear relationships between emotion, the self, and the environment (e.g., Lewis & Granic, 2000). Again, although potentially a vulnerability factor, these aspects of affect have not been much studied empirically in EDs, and the use of terms to describe and understand the phenomena needs greater clarification.

Social/Behavioral

Social and behavioral factors might increase vulnerability to EDs. These include poor social skills, coping skills, interpersonal relationships and factors, and attachment styles. In turn, some of these factors, such as attachment style, might well serve as vulnerabilities for other elements in an integrated vulnerability-stress model. Social functioning, coping, interpersonal deficits, attachment, personality features, and temperament will be considered in this section.

Social functioning is often impaired in EDs, including when situation-specific skills are assessed. For example, Grissett and Norvell (1992) found that bulimics were rated as less socially effective by observers unaware of their diagnosis. Poor social functioning may well be the result of a problematic early attachment relationship.

Eating disorders are sometimes viewed as a maladaptive coping strategy, and there is some evidence that ED patients have deficits in normal coping skills, including perception of control. For example, unlike control participants, ED patients appear to use cognitive avoidance and rumination to deal with day-to-day stressors (Troop, Holbrey, & Treasure, 1998). In another study, current and past ED participants were more likely to use escape avoidance as a coping strategy than controls, even when controlling for level of depression (Ghaderi & Scott, 2000). There is some evidence that coping skills improve with treatment, although the skills were still less adequate than those possessed by the controls (Bloks, Spinhoven, Callewaert, Willemse-Koning, & Turksma, 2001).

In some disorders, interpersonal deficits may be a vulnerability factor (see Van Orden, Wingate, Gordon, & Joiner, Chapter 6 of this volume). These include social skills (see above), ability to make relationships, and so forth. There is little work on this in EDs. Some evidence exists that patients with eating disorders are sometimes different from controls in terms of sexuality and nature of intimate relationships (e.g., Morgan, Wiederman, & Pryor, 1995), but as yet there is little knowledge of how these differences relate to disordered eating. Clearly, deficits in these areas could increase vulnerability to a disorder—but equally, the ED could cause problems with relationships.

The importance of attachment (see Davila, Ramsay, Stroud, & Steinberg, Chapter 9 of this volume) in EDs was originally proposed by Bruch (1973) and later by Selvini-Palazzoli (1978). Disturbance in the mother-infant relationship results in ego deficits—that is, the person has no sense of individuation and grows up feeling helpless, confused, and unable to distinguish hunger and satiety from other needs and discomforts. Such persons may maintain a façade of coping until they are forced to rely on self and their own internal cues for making sense of the world. This typically occurs during adolescence, when a lack of self-awareness becomes particularly apparent. It sets the scene for a later eating disorder. There is some evidence that families of ED patients are less cohesive, expressive, and encouraging of personal growth than control families (Latzer, Hochdorf, Bachar, & Canetti, 2002) and that childhood attachment may be insecure (Ward, Ramsay, Turnbull, Benedettini, & Treasure, 2000). A study also found that ED patients reported less childhood mastery and more childhood helplessness than controls (Troop & Treasure, 1997). Another study found that ED patients scored high on individual items involving feeling unwanted, alone, helpless, shame, and guilt and feeling responsible for parental happiness (Chassler, 1997). These findings overlap with those suggesting that certain negative self-beliefs tend to be characteristic of patients with EDs (M. J. Cooper, Todd, & Cohen-Tovee, 1996; Turner & M. J. Cooper, 2002b).

One of the consequences of poor attachment may be alexithymia. This concept includes difficulties in identifying feelings, difficulty distinguishing between feelings and bodily sensations of emotional arousal, and difficulty describing feelings to other people. Several studies find a relationship between EDs and alexithymia (see Corcos et al., 2000, for confirmation of earlier findings). The construct maps onto some of the features Bruch (1973) noted in her patients, including difficulty in identifying feelings and body sensations and difficulty in expressing feelings (e.g., de Groot, Rodin, & Olmsted, 1995).

Several studies of attachment in ED suggest, for example, that patients have disturbed attachments (e.g., they have high scores on measures of Compulsive Care Seeking and Compulsive Self Reliance; Ward et al., 2000). The developmental literature suggests that the relationship with a caregiver in the first few years needs to be synchronized and in tune with the infant's internal state (Stern, 1985). If normal experience does not occur at this stage, later problems in several areas may occur, including problems or disturbance in the development of internal hunger and satiety signals and in emotional and cognitive development. More generally, early attachment experience may also underpin the development of the self and self-identity, including self-concept. There is some empirical evidence, for example, in a nonclinical sample that infant-mother attachment at 1 year predicts children's ability to verbally express an understanding of mixed emotions in hypothetical social and emotional situations (Steele, Steele, Croft, & Fonagy, 1999).

The exact nature of the relationship between early attachment experiences and later cognitive and emotional development is not fully understood. In eating disorder studies, a relatively simple link is often considered in which specific beliefs result from certain experiences, but little detail is provided on how this might occur (M. J. Cooper et al., 2004) or, in the case of primary and secondary avoidance, no detail on a link is provided (Waller et al., in press). A more sophisticated approach has been taken in other fields. For example, Fonagy (2003) describes a model in which early attachment experience creates a mind that is able to generate causal motivational and epistemic mind states. This rich understanding of mind, and its many facets, has not yet been applied to eating disorders, but it would seem to have the potential to explain in detail the different cognitive features that have been described as important in cognitive theory and therapy. These include not only the development of the content of beliefs, but also possible deficiencies in information processing and deficiencies in other psychological aspects of "mind" and self-awareness in these disorders, including the "interpersonal interpretive function" described by Fonagy, which focuses on how the mind works rather than on its content. This approach would appear to have some similarity to the concept of *metacognition* as it is currently being developed in cognitive theory and therapy. This involves study of the processes involved in thinking and extends beyond content of thoughts to the way in which individuals relate to their thoughts. For example, patients with EDs may express metabeliefs such as "If I don't worry about my weight, I'll get fat." The role of such thinking in EDs is not yet understood.

Personality features (see Tackett & Krueger, Chapter 8 of this volume) are not well studied in EDs. There is some evidence that AN, including binge-purge AN, is characterized by loneliness, shyness, and feelings of inferiority in adolescence, but not in early childhood, whereas shyness tends to characterize BN in childhood and adolescence (Troop & Bifulco, 2002). Some of the characteristic personality features can be translated into cognitive equivalents or descriptors. For example, loneliness in AN may be expressed cognitively as a negative self-belief such as "I'm all alone" and inferiority as "I'm a failure."

Perfectionism is regarded as particularly typical of AN, and it has an important role in some recent theories (e.g., Fairburn et al., 2003). Research reports provide evidence for very high levels of perfectionism in AN. Halmi and colleagues (2000) suggest that it forms part of a genetic diathesis stress model, and they characterize it as a phenotype—one of several related phenotypical temperament and personality trait markers that may be involved in expressing genetic vulnerability to AN. Much less is known about perfectionism in BN.

Temperament has not been much investigated in EDs. One study found that BN patients had less general rhythmicity (i.e., a less regular pattern of diurnal activities, including sleep and eating). They also had less attentional focus (less ability to concentrate and persist with activities) than AN patients but were no different from a depressed group (Shaw & Steiner, 1997).

Biological

In this section, genetic (see Lemery & Doelger, Chapter 7 of this volume) as well as neurobiological factors and brain structure and function (see Pihl & Nantel-Vivier, Chapter 4 of this volume) will be considered as vulnerability factors for EDs.

It has been estimated that there is strong evidence for heritable causation in EDs. A recent study estimated that 24%–42% of the variance in AN and 17%–46% in BN is due to nonshared environmental factors (Klump, Wonderlich, Lehoux, Lilenfeld, & Bulik, 2002).

Neurobiology studies also find differences in patients and controls, but it is not clear if these differences are causal or a consequence of having an ED. This applies, for example, to studies that find differences in the hormone histidyl-diketo-piperazine, which is involved in premature feelings of satiety (Steiner et al., 2003).

Work in this area has, however, focused mainly on neuropeptide and monoamine (especially *5-HT* systems), because these are thought to be important in the regulation of eating and weight. With respect to AN, it has been argued that the gene *5-HT2A* may be an important vulnerability factor, having a complex impact on AN (Gorwood, Kipman, & Foulon, 2003). Normal dieting alters *5-HT* function (Cowen, Clifford, Walsh, Williams, & Fairburn, 1996), and this process has been proposed as a possible mechanism (Fairburn & Harrison, 2003).

Brain structure and function have been studied with neuroimaging technology. In a review of AN studies, Kerem and Katzman (2003) concluded that structural brain abnormalities were common, but that some, although not all, reversed with treatment. Functional neuroimaging finds some alteration in brain metabolism, but no consistent abnormality is found. The role of these deficits is still poorly understood. Moreover, most work has taken place with adults, and because EDs typically develop in adolescence, it is not clear how far they affect the developmental processes involved in physiological, intellectual, and emotional growth as the adolescent brain develops. Overall, it is currently unclear whether and to what extent structural and functional brain abnormalities are a consequence of EDs or have a causal role.

It is also not clear how genetic markers link into a cognitively based model or map onto different types of cognitions and cognitive processes. There have been some attempts to derive behavioral phenotypes, based on findings that some personality traits and weight and shape concerns may cluster in families (Woodside et al., 2002), but the role of cognition in this has not been investigated. It seems likely that there may be general and specific cognitive vulnerabilities, corresponding to the presence of core beliefs and to weight and shape concern. Phenotypes for these have not yet been investigated.

A neurodevelopmental model for AN has been proposed (Connan, Campbell, Katzman, Lightman, & Treasure, 2003) integrating genetic and biological data with cognitive and psychosocial models and also taking a developmental perspective. In this model, genetic factors interact with early attachment experiences to modify hypothalamic-pituitary-adrenal axis regulation, leading to protracted and poorly regulated stress responses. These same factors may set up a developmental pathway for maladaptive emotional, cognitive, and social functioning and a limited capacity to cope with and resolve stress.

Stressors can arise from several sources and are often considered to be the result of learning (e.g., modeling, or stimulus response learning), although this is not always true in EDs, where normal maturation and growth can generate stress. Below, some of the key stressors that operate in eating disorders will be examined.

STRESSORS

Stressors can occur at any stage in the genesis and development of an ED. Some may be single "one-off" events, whereas others may be chronic or ongoing (see Grant & McMahon, Chapter 1 of this volume). Stress can originate from several sources and may be usefully considered under the headings often employed to describe potential sources of stress in stress theories (e.g., as in Bennett & Cooper, 1999)—life stress, family environment, social and cultural, and biological sources of stress.

Life Stress

Lifestyle and Work

Occupational or leisure interests may create stress. For example, there is some evidence that EDs are more common than would be expected in certain groups, such as athletes and ballet students, where there are exceptionally high levels of emphasis on appearance, weight, and shape (Sundgot-Borgen, 1996).

Life Events

Patients with EDs often report more stressful life events prior to the onset of the disorder (Raffi, Rondini, Grandi, & Fava, 2000). Both AN and BN patients had experienced either a severe event or marked difficulty before onset, often linked to close family and friends (Schmidt, Tiller, Blanchard, Andrews, & Treasure, 1997). A study investigating BN found more stressful life events in the year preceding onset and found that these concerned disruption of family and social relationships or a threat to physical safety (Welch, Doll, & Fairburn, 1997).

Social Support

There is evidence that ED patients lack social support. For example, ED patients were less likely to have a partner as a support figure, and they reported less actual emotional and practical support than controls. They also set lower ideals for support (Tiller et al., 1997). They had fewer people in their support networks available to provide emotional support and were dissatisfied with the level of emotional support provided by relatives (Rorty, Yager, Buckwalter, & Rossotto, 1999).

Family Environment

Parent-Child Relationship

A key stressor may be family and caregiver behavior in the early years of life. This may result, as suggested above, in poor attachment, which may subsequently lead to low self-worth, the development of negative self-beliefs, and the processes associated with these. At the same time, parental interaction may disrupt the normal development of feeding, appetite, and relationship to food (Steiner, Smith, Rosenkrantz, & Litt, 1991), perhaps through similar mechanisms to the disturbed attachment, and to which its development is likely to be related. A caregiver's inability to respond appropriately and sensitively to appetite and feeding cues in the infant may prevent infants from developing the ability to regulate and manage their eating and food intake normally. Depending on the particular experience (e.g., a parent responds to psychological distress by feeding the child), eating may become controlled not by normal cognitive mechanisms but by those that characterize ED, for example, the idea that eating is an appropriate and effective way to control distressing emotions.

Other experiences within the family may also be important. The family may, for example, model or directly teach disturbed beliefs and behaviors, including modeling or direct teaching of symptoms, behaviors, and thoughts associated with EDs, including perhaps those associated with a negative self-concept. The evidence for this is somewhat limited by the difficulties and lack of longitudinal research in this area. However, there is some evidence that attitudes and behaviors related to eating disorders, for example, distinguish families of ED patients from control and depressives' families (Laliberte, Boland, & Leichner, 1999). The role of the family is considered central to systems theories and to family therapy (Minuchin, Rosman, & Baker, 1978). On a moment-by-moment basis, family hassles also seem to predict bulimic symptoms later that day (Oken, Greene, & Smith, 2003) and thus have a role in maintenance.

Social and Cultural

Peers

General bullying and teasing, or teasing and bullying related to a child's weight or shape, can be a possible stressor. There may be peer pressure to diet or to engage in ED behaviors. Reports of such events are often associated with the development of assumptions related to weight, shape, and eating (Cooper et al., 1998).

Media

Exposure to the media, with its high level of general emphasis on weight, shape, and eating, which is particularly characteristic of Western countries and cultures, may encourage dieting and eating disorders. The pressure placed on women in particular is hypothesized to be important. A cultural account of development of EDs has been explored from a cognitive perspective elsewhere (Cooper, 2001). The link has not been explored in detail in ED patients, largely because of the problems inherent in establishing a suitable longitudinal study. One study found that ED women reported more feminine gender-role stress, but they also reported more masculine role stress and more stress overall (Bekker & Boselie, 2002). A longitudinal study found that some mass-media involvement, including frequent reading of girls' magazines and radio listening, was linked to the development of an ED (Martinez-Gonzalez et al., 2003).

Biological

Puberty

Aspects of puberty can be a stressor for some people and may increase the chances of developing an eating disorder, depending on how they are experienced and handled by the individual (which of course will partly be dependent on that person's previous life experiences). An extreme example is a case report of a teenager developing AN that seemed triggered by the physical, emotional, and cognitive changes associated with pregnancy (Benton-Hardy & Lock, 1998). Indeed, failure to negotiate any important developmental task may create stress.

Pregnancy and Perinatal Factors

It has been suggested that pregnancy and birth complications may play a role in AN, especially chronic AN. A potential link between these and development of the central nervous system (CNS) has been described. The CNS problems are then expressed in various ways, including physical, behavioral, cognitive, and emotional ways (Bakan, Birmingham, & Goldner, 1991). There is also some suggestion that environmental temperature at birth is associated with AN, as well as temperature at conception (Watkins, Willoughby, Waller, Serpell, & Lask, 2002).

RISK STUDIES

It is not clear how far any or many of the vulnerability factors identified above are causal in the development of EDs, because the relevant longitudinal studies have not been conducted. A small number of longitudinal risk factor studies have been conducted. However, these have not been carried out within a theoretical framework—and there has been very little effort to integrate the factors that have been identified as predictors into a coherent story or theory.

Two studies deserve mention here. One study found that low self-esteem, low perceived social support, high levels of body concern, and high use of escape/avoidance coping strategies predicted EDs, as assessed by the Survey for Eating Disorders (Ghaderi & Scott, 2002). A second study (Moorhead et al., 2002) found that an ED group had more serious health problems before age 5, more mother-reported anxiety/depression at age 9, and more behavior problems at 15. The families also had more history of depression, eating problems, and changes in family financial circumstances.

Such studies are typical of the risk factor research. Although they do measure psychological variables prior to the onset of disturbance, the studies are not carried out within a theoretical framework. They provide information on (mainly statistical) predictors but have little to offer those who seek to develop a theory of EDs. Some of the significant relationships found do provide support for the significance of some of the vulnerability factors identified, but there has been very little effort to test the theories related to these.

Below, an integrated vulnerability-stress model based on a cognitive theory of eating disorders is proposed. A cognitive framework is used as a basis for integrating both vulnerability and stress factors. Such a model has the advantage of eliminating overlap, where constructs in different theories are similar but are labeled differently, and it is also designed to provide a more detailed explanation of why people develop these disorders than many existing cognitive theories by incorporating factors identified as important in other areas. Using one coherent framework, rather than the general multifactorial models that are often very popular in studies of EDs, also means that it has clearer and more direct implications for treatment. More specifically, multifactorial approaches are invariably atheoretical, and an absence of a underlying explanation of the disorder provides little guidance on suitable treatment strategies. Use of cognitive theory as the basis for integration is particularly important and appropriate given that psychological approaches, and cognitive therapy in particular, seem to hold most promise in the treatment of EDs, and there is also arguably more empirical evidence for the validity of this theory in EDs than for any other.

A VULNERABILITY-STRESS COGNITIVE MODEL

Cognitions in the framework presented below are treated as a final common pathway. Thus, where possible, constructs will be phased in terms of cognition. The analysis draws on a revised cognitive model of BN (M. J. Cooper et al., 2004) and emerging thinking on cognition in AN.

Two groups of researchers have primarily been interested in investigating schemata or negative core beliefs in eating disorders. Studies conducted by Waller and colleagues (e.g., Waller et al., in press) have focused on the Young Schema Questionnaire (YSQ; Young, 1994), whereas studies by Cooper and colleagues have investigated the Negative Self-Belief subscale of the Eating Disorder Belief Questionnaire (EDBQ; Cooper, Cohen-Tovee, Todd, Wells, & Tovee, 1997).[4]

Like existing cognitive models, the vulnerability-stress cognitive model proposed here predicts that high levels of schemata or negative self-beliefs will be found in patients with eating disorders compared with controls and dieters. Several studies have confirmed this prediction (e.g., M. J. Cooper et al., 1998; Turner & M. J. Cooper, 2000b). Studies of young women (e.g., Waller, Ohanian, Meyer, & Osman, 2000) as well as a mixed sample of women and men (O'Connor, Simmons, & Cooper, 2003) have further found, in cross-sectional designs, that schemata and negative self-beliefs predict eating disorder symptoms. These findings are consistent with the proposed model (although to date such studies have not been conducted with clinical samples).

Of particular significance in a vulnerability-stress cognitive model, core beliefs (particularly negative self-beliefs) develop in the context of early relationships, notably the early attachment relationship. Several studies have found links between negative early experiences and the development of core beliefs in AN and BN (e.g., M. J. Cooper et al., 1998; Somerville, Cooper, & Hackmann, 2004; Turner & M. J. Cooper, 2002a). These experiences often describe attachment-related experiences related to parental or other family relationships or early important figures, such as teachers.

Studies have also found links between early attachment, core beliefs, and eating disorder symptoms in nonclinical groups, in which negative schemata and core beliefs mediate the relationship between parental bonding and eating disorder–related symptoms (Meyer & Gillings, 2004; Turner, Rose, & M. J. Cooper, 2005). These studies provide preliminary empirical evidence for the theoretical suggestion of a link between early attachment experience and cognition in the development of eating disorders (although, as noted above, such studies have not yet been conducted with clinical samples).

Little is known about how early attachment may differ in BN and AN. This research has not yet been conducted, and current theories are not necessarily helpful in making the distinction or in generating useful predictions. Empirical work has found, however, that core beliefs in AN, unlike those in BN, seemed to be distinguished by the presence of an overwhelming sense of powerlessness (Woolrich, M. J. Cooper, & Turner, 2005), a finding that makes intuitive sense given the nature of early stressors they report, that is, a high incidence of early negative events over which they had no control or influence (Woolrich et al.). This finding needs to be replicated, but it leads to various hypotheses about how subtle differences in early attachment experience might be linked to different EDs. For example, it might be hypothesized that experience of control and powerlessness might be relatively more significant or evident in the early attachment experiences of those with AN than in those with BN. The finding also facilitates our understanding of how AN might be maintained (M. J. Cooper, Todd, Wells, Woolrich, & Turner, 2005).

Attachment as traditionally conceptualized may not, of course, be the only factor involved in the development of schemata and negative self-beliefs. Although the possibility has received very little attention in the ED literature, there may also be a role for the direct teaching, modeling, and learning of such beliefs via more traditional learning theory principles. Clearly, these may well occur within the early attachment relationship and may be one aspect of the experience. Their importance in relation to other aspects (e.g., early reciprocity, mutuality) needs further study—it may be that these constructs can be conceptualized as one way in which early attachment is expressed. Such processes might equally be involved in the development of any or all of the cognitive constructs and processes discussed below—from underlying assumptions to negative automatic thoughts. To date, they remain largely unexplored, as does their relationship to traditional attachment constructs.

Schema-driven processes, as well as the content of schemata, may also be affected by failures in the early attachment relationship. The child may grow up with a tendency to maintain schemata through certain patterns of behavior, each of which may also be determined by early attachment experiences. For example, adult avoidance of relationships linked to an unloveability schema may reflect repeated experiences of unmet needs in early life. Again, studies examining mediating factors might provide a useful first step in teasing out these relationships, using the Young-Rygh Avoidance Inventory (Young & Rygh, 2003) and the Young Compensatory Inventory (Young, 2003) as potential mediators between attachment and eating disorder symptoms. Waller has suggested (Waller et al., in press; see above) that AN and BN may be distinguished by different types of schema processing, although there is as yet no empirical evidence for this. Carefully designed mediator studies using Young's inventories would be helpful here.[5]

Some initial work has been conducted on schema-driven processes, particularly by Waller (e.g., Spranger, Waller, & Bryant-Waugh, 2001). This work forms the basis for a schema model in which primary and secondary processes distinguish the type of eating disorder and behaviors that develop (Waller et al., in press). This model is built around the finding that cognitive content, as assessed by the YSQ, does not typically differentiate eating disorders or key symptoms (e.g., Leung, Waller, & Thomas, 1999), although there are differences in the pattern of associations between restrictive and bulimic symptoms and core beliefs. Work conducted in Oxford, however (and noted above), suggests that a key difference between the two disorders is present in content. Unlike BN, anorexics express beliefs of "powerlessness" that are linked to their eating disorder symptoms (Woolrich et al., 2005; Somerville et al., 2004). This is not a belief typically assessed by existing measures (including both the YSQ and EDBQ) and has emerged only in the course of two detailed semi-structured interviews of patients' idiosyncratic beliefs (Woolrich et al.; Somerville et al.). These findings merit further study.

What makes someone vulnerable to poor attachment? Connan et al. (2003) provide an explanation for a link between attachment and (largely inherited) genetic and neurobiological findings. Here we have detailed the more precise nature of the link between attachment and cognition (consistent with our emphasis on cognition), in which attachment serves as a vulnerability factor for later negative self-beliefs and schemata. However, as the work of Connan et al. suggests, attachment can also be analyzed, using a vulnerability-stress model and including genetic or inherited factors. Although this is an area of increasing interest to many developmental psychologists, it is important to remember that the role of these factors and the nature of their relationship to EDs is far from understood at present, and that exactly what is inherited is often very unclear.

Attachment itself may also be analyzed with greater sophistication than has been usual in cognitive theory and therapies, with a greater focus on how the mind and cognition develop. An integration of work in other fields (e.g., incorporating constructs such as the Interpersonal Interpretive Mechanism described by Fonagy, 2003, and eating disorder development) might be fruitful, particularly in understanding how the self, which includes negative self-beliefs and schema-driven processing as one aspect, develops and is involved in eating disorders. More detailed exploration and analysis of how specific details of the attachment process may facilitate the development of the characteristic cognitive profile associated with eating disorders is also needed.

Underlying assumptions develop rather later than negative self-beliefs, in the context of the family and relationships with peers and other significant adults, such as teachers at school. Although there may be some genetic variability here, too (weight and shape concern seems to cluster in families), it is also not clear exactly what is inherited. ED patients may learn, through modeling and direct teaching, that it is important for them not to be fat. Evidence for a link between generations (mothers and daughters) in eating-related symptoms and attitudes exists in a non–eating-disordered population (Pike & Rodin, 1991), although not yet in an eating-disordered one. There is some evidence that specific family climates differ among bulimic, depressed, and control groups (Laliberte et al., 1999), although the link between generations has not been examined. Laliberte et al., for example, found that family concern with weight, shape, and achievement was typical of the families of bulimics but not the families of depressed and control subjects, even after controlling for differences in depression among the three groups. The mass media most likely play an important role in emphasizing and reinforcing familial messages, as well as contributing to their initial development.

Underlying assumptions have also been investigated using two subscales of the EDBQ (those measuring weight and shape as a means to acceptance by self and others). This includes a study that found that the EDBQ subscales were unique predictors of eating disorder–related symptoms compared with the Dysfunctional Attitude Scale (Power et al., 1994), a generic measure of underlying assumptions (O'Connor et al., 2003). Again, no longitudinal studies have been conducted. Studies have also found that although negative self-beliefs distinguish ED patients from dieting and nondieting controls (M. J. Cooper & Hunt, 1998; M. J. Cooper & Turner, 2000), they do not distinguish them from depressed patients (M. J. Cooper & Hunt).

Puberty places stress on the patient—emotionally, psychologically, and physiologically. It may add to any emotional difficulties, as well as place new demands, and may be important in the development of new and the strengthening of any existing cognitive vulnerabilities. For example, someone already vulnerable to difficulties relevant to EDs may find that the issues raised as puberty begins reinforce those concerns and issues, whereas a child without these vulnerabilities finds puberty easier to negotiate successfully. A child with a deficient sense of self is likely to find adolescent identity, autonomy, and independence much more difficult to master than a child in whom the sense of self has developed satisfactorily. Negative self-beliefs formed in early life may be painfully heightened by the trials of adolescent relationships and may generate behavior that serves to reinforce them.

Negative automatic thoughts—especially positive thoughts in BN, and belief that not eating will help make one powerful or in control in AN—may also develop (especially in AN) in the context of early experiences in attachment and may emerge as significant factors during adolescence, when pubertal development creates a sense of powerlessness or is appraised by the patient as such. In BN the belief that eating will help may also develop in the context of modeling—either independently or as an integral part of the impact of parental or early attachment relationships. In both cases it is likely to be a coping strategy—a way to deal with distress and confusion. As such, it can be seen as a misuse of a normal function—eating is normally controlled cognitively (see, e.g., Pinel, 2000)—and ED patients' reasons or explanations for eating may thus be different from those of individuals without eating disorders (and also probably from those of most "normal" dieters) in, for example, content. This possibility needs to be investigated in more detail. Again, direct teaching and learning, as well as modeling, may be important here. As suggested above, these may exert an independent effect or may also be one aspect of early attachment experience.

Finally, some negative automatic thoughts may be a direct expression of possessing certain schemata and underlying assumptions—that is, negative thoughts such as "I'm fat" or "I need to lose weight" may simply be direct expressions of typical negative self- and other beliefs. The same may be true of some control and permissive thoughts.

In AN the belief that not eating will help in dealing with negative emotions and cognitions may also be learned or modeled in the context of an early attachment relationship as well as influenced more directly by the attachment process. It is likely to be reinforced by the media, the sociocultural pressures on women, and individual experience of powerlessness. Underpinning negative automatic thoughts are (both genetically and environmentally determined) emotional and cognitive vulnerabilities. These may include, for example, genetically determined temperament differences and the impact of attachment on emotional development, expression, and regulation.

It is widely accepted in the literature that negative automatic thoughts are typically concerned with weight, shape, food, and eating—and many studies confirm this, using both self-report questionnaires and techniques derived from experimental psychology, such as a thoughts checklist and "thinking aloud" (M. J. Cooper & Fairburn, 1992). Finer distinctions between thoughts have been made. For example, M. J. Cooper et al. (2004) in their cognitive model of BN distinguish permissive thoughts, positive thoughts, thoughts of no control, and negative thoughts, each of which plays a key role in the vicious circle that maintains binge eating in the disorder. As suggested above, these thoughts may arise directly from schemata (particularly the thoughts of no control and negative thoughts), or they may have a specific developmental history (e.g., positive thoughts may be learned as a result of early experiences with food and eating in the context of a disturbed attachment relationship). Our understanding of these links is limited, and much work is required to tease out the relationships involved.

Information-processing errors may be learned, too, or they may result from (genetically and environmentally determined) emotional and cognitive vulnerabilities. These errors have not been the subject of much study in cognitive theory and research, where most interest has focused on the specific content of cognitions. As a result, there is little research on the learning, teaching, or modeling of information-processing styles or on how they may develop from early attachment experience. In operation they resemble schema-driven processes—indeed, they reflect the schematic properties of assumptions. In individuals with eating disorders, they are likely to be manifest in food, eating, and weight arenas, as well as in relation to a range of other issues. The development of emotional regulation is likely to be particularly important in underpinning information-processing errors, because many of these errors reflect or involve attempts to regulate or manage emotional distress. Further attention needs to be given to how these factors might be linked.

Other factors contribute to the development and maintenance of EDs as acute, ongoing, or chronic stressors. Lack of social support, life events, and media and peer pressure all increase stress or reduce coping ability and make it more likely that the person will use maladaptive ways of coping with everyday and additional stressors. The same may be true of the onset of puberty—someone who already has certain vulnerabilities may not manage this transition very well. This might be particularly true when a stressor (whatever its nature) fits or has similarities to the individual's vulnerabilities, for example, when it activates particular dysfunctional or negative core beliefs that the individual already has, whether this is the result of low levels of social support or a high degree of exposure to and internalization of media pressure. Thus there is interaction between stress and vulnerability factors—the effects are not merely additive. For example, lack of social support might be particularly significant for someone who has negative core beliefs such as "I'm isolated, all alone" and the assumptions "if I get fat, no one will like me or want to know me."

The ability to regulate emotion and organize self-related experiences—for example, a sense of identify, self-awareness, as well as hunger and satiety awareness and differentiation—also develop in this context. Both have been identified as potential vulnerability factors, but neither has a particularly key role in existing cognitive theories. A link between attachment and the regulation of emotion, hunger, and satiety awareness and differentiation in eating disorders does not yet appear to have been investigated empirically, but if the integrative model is accurate, such a link might also be expected. The regulation, awareness, and differentiation of emotion, hunger, and satiety require further investigation. The ability to distinguish cognitions and internal states and establish a degree of control over emotion, although widely recognized by some clinicians as important in EDs, has been largely ignored by those interested in cognitive theory and therapy. Failure to address these issues may help explain why cognitive therapy is not helpful to many with BN and seems largely ineffective in AN. Without these basic tools, patients may well be unable to engage in traditional cognitive therapy. A useful first step might be to replicate the mediator studies described above using a measure of awareness and discrimination of internal states (e.g., the Interoceptive Awareness subscale of the EDI) and a measure of self-regulation (e.g., the self-soothing scale). The role of these as potential mediators between attachment relationships and eating disorder symptoms could then be clarified.

The model proposed is not a linear model: Vulnerability and stress interact continuously, each affecting the other. For example, poor attachment might make someone vulnerable to developing negative self-beliefs and dysfunctional styles of information processing—but it may be that only those who also have other vulnerability factors or who experience a specific stressor such as a negative life event (e.g., bullying related to weight and appearance at school) will go on to develop an ED.

Many studies combine AN and BN when investigating risk factors, or indeed vulnerability factors. This has been questioned (Steiner et al., 2003), and a challenge for the future is to identify specific vulnerabilities for the different EDs. Taking a cognitive vulnerability-stress perspective may help achieve this. Work in other fields on attachment and the development of the mind (emotionally, cognitively, and in relation to experience of hunger and satiety) may be a useful resource in the attempt to understand cognition and the mind in EDs.

In conclusion, a complex, nonlinear interplay between group and individual vulnerabilities and stressors creates an ED. Cognitive models, such as those described here, can provide a useful framework for integrating some of the vulnerability factors and stressors that have been identified in various theories and in some of the relevant empirical research.

NOTES

1. We prefer the term *not eating* rather than *dieting* or *restriction* when applied to AN (M. J. Cooper et al., 2004) to avoid confusion with the typical meanings attached to these concepts, which do not, in our view, readily lend themselves to conceptualizing specific instances of key AN behavior.
2. See, however, later discussion of potential differences between AN and BN in core beliefs.
3. Dieting may be an example of a third way in which the meaning of normal eating has gone awry, and one that is distinct from pathological eating as observed in eating disorders.
4. Note that both the YSQ and the Negative Self-Belief subscale of the EDBQ assess the content of schemata rather than the processes associated with them.
5. Given that the Young inventories such as the YSQ are generic measures, there is also likely to be a role for the development of measures that assess these constructs specifically as they apply to EDs. There is, for example, some preliminary evidence that a core belief measure devised specifically for EDs may have advantages over the more generic YSQ in ED research (M. J. Cooper, Rose, & Turner, in press).

REFERENCES

Agras, W. S., Walsh, T., Fairburn, C. G., Wilson, G. T., & Kraemer, H. C. (2000). A multicentre comparison of cognitive behavioural therapy and interpersonal psychotherapy for bulimia nervosa. *Archives of General Psychiatry, 57,* 459–466.

American Psychiatric Association. (1994). *Diagnostic and statistical manual of mental disorders* (4th ed.). Washington, DC: Author.

Bakan, R., Birmingham, C. L., & Goldner, E. M. (1991). Chronicity in anorexia nervosa: Pregnancy and birth complications as risk factors. *International Journal of Eating Disorders, 10,* 631–645.

Beck, A. T., Freeman, A., & Associates. (1990). *Cognitive therapy of personality disorders.* New York: Guilford Press.

Beck, A. T., Rush, A. J., Shaw, B. F., & Emery, G. (1979). *Cognitive therapy of depression.* New York: Guilford Press.

Bekker, M. H. J., & Boselie, K. A. H. M. (2002). Gender and stress: Is gender role stress? A re-examination of the relationship between feminine gender role stress and eating disorders. *Stress and Health: Journal of the International Society for the Investigation of Stress, 18,* 141–149.

Bennett, D. A., & Cooper, C. L. (1999). Eating disturbance as a manifestation of the stress process: A review of the literature. *Stress Medicine, 15,* 167–182.

Benton-Hardy, L. R., & Lock, J., (1998). Pregnancy and early parenthood: Factors in the development of anorexia nervosa? *International Journal of Eating Disorders, 24,* 223–226.

Bloks, H., Spinhoven, P., Callewaert, I., Willemse-Koning, C., & Turksma, A. (2001). Changes in coping styles and recovery after inpatient treatment for severe eating disorders. *European Eating Disorders Review, 9,* 397–415.

Brody, M. L., Walsh, B. T., & Devlin, M. J. (1994). Binge eating disorder: Reliability of a new diagnostic category. *Journal of Consulting and Clinical Psychology, 62,* 381–386.

Bruch, H. (1973). *Eating disorders.* New York: Basic Books.

Byrne, S. M., & McLean, N. J. (2002). The cognitive-behavioural model of bulimia nervosa: A direct evaluation. *International Journal of Eating Disorders, 31,* 17–31.

Chassler, L. (1997). Understanding anorexia nervosa and bulimia nervosa from an attachment perspective. *Clinical Social Work Journal, 25,* 407–423.

Connan, F., Campbell, I. C., Katzman, M., Lightman, S. L., & Treasure, J. (2003). A neurodevelopmental model for anorexia nervosa. *Physiology and Behaviour, 79,* 13–24.

Cooper, C. L., & Bagliono, A. J. (1998). A structural model approach toward the development of the link between stress and mental health. *British Journal of Medical Psychology, 61,* 87–102.

Cooper, M. J. (1997). Cognitive theory in anorexia nervosa and bulimia nervosa: A review. *Behavioural and Cognitive Psychotherapy, 25,* 113–145.

Cooper, M. J. (2001). Eating disorders, culture and cognition. In J. F. Schumaker & T. Ward (Eds.), *Cultural cognition and psychopathology* (pp. 95–106). Westport, CT: Praeger.

Cooper, M. J. (2003). *The psychology of bulimia nervosa: A cognitive perspective.* Oxford, UK: Oxford University Press.

Cooper, M. J., Cohen-Tovee, E., Todd, G., Wells, M., & Tovee, M. (1997). The eating disorder belief questionnaire: Preliminary development. *Behaviour Research and Therapy, 35,* 381–388.

Cooper, M. J., & Fairburn, C. G. (1992). Thoughts about eating, weight and shape in anorexia nervosa and bulimia nervosa. *Behaviour Research and Therapy, 30,* 501–511.

Cooper, M. J., & Hunt, J. (1998). Core beliefs and underlying assumptions in bulimia nervosa and depression. *Behaviour Research and Therapy, 36,* 895–898.

Cooper, M. J., Rose, K. S., & Turner, H. (in press). Core beliefs and the presence or absence of eating disorder symptoms and depressive symptoms in adolescent girls. *International Journal of Eating Disorders.*

Cooper, M. J., Todd, G., Wells, A., Woolrich, R. A., & Turner, H. M. (2005). *A cognitive model of anorexia nervosa.* Manuscript in preparation.

Cooper, M. J., Todd, G., & Cohen-Tovee, E. (1996). Core beliefs in eating disorders. *International Cognitive Therapy Newsletter, 10,* 2–3.

Cooper, M. J., Todd, G., & Wells, A. (1998). Content, origins, and consequences of dysfunctional beliefs in anorexia nervosa and bulimia nervosa. *Journal of Cognitive Psychotherapy, 12,* 213–230.

Cooper, M. J., & Turner, H. (2000). Underlying assumptions and core beliefs in anorexia nervosa and dieting. *British Journal of Clinical Psychology, 39,* 215–218.

Cooper, M. J., Wells, A., & Todd, G. (2004). A cognitive theory of bulimia nervosa. *British Journal of Clinical Psychology, 43,* 1–16.

Corcos, M., Guilbaud, O., Speranza, M., Paterniti, S., Loas, G., Stephan, P., et al. (2000). Alexithymia and depression in eating disorders. *Psychiatry Research, 93,* 263–266.

Cowen, P. J., Clifford, E. M., Walsh, A. E. S., Williams, C., & Fairburn, C. G. (1996). Moderate dieting causes 5-HT2C receptor supersensitivity. *Psychological Medicine, 26,* 1155–1159.

Crisp, A. H., Hsu, L. K. G., Harding, B., & Hartshorn, J. (1980). Clinical features of anorexia nervosa: A study of a consecutive series of 102 female patients. *Journal of Psychosomatic Research, 24,* 179–191.

de Groot, J. M., Rodin, G., & Olmsted, M. P. (1995). Alexithymia, depression, and treatment outcome in bulimia nervosa. *Comprehensive Psychiatry, 36,* 53–60.

Esplen, M. J., Garfinkel, P. E., & Gallop, R. (2000). Relationship between self-soothing, aloneness, and evocative memory in bulimia nervosa. *International Journal of Eating Disorders, 27,* 96–100.

Fairburn, C. G. (1997). Eating disorders. In D. M. Clark & C. G. Fairburn (Eds.), *The science and practice of cognitive behaviour therapy* (pp. 209–241). Oxford, UK: Oxford University Press.

Fairburn, C. G., & Beglin, S. J. (1990). Studies of the epidemiology of bulimia nervosa. *American Journal of Psychiatry, 147,* 401–408.

Fairburn, C. G., & Cooper, P. J. (1984). The clinical features of bulimia nervosa. *British Journal of Psychiatry, 144,* 238–246.

Fairburn, C. G., Cooper, Z., & Shafran, R. (2003). Cognitive behaviour therapy for eating disorders: A transdiagnostic theory and treatment. *Behaviour Research and Therapy, 41,* 509–528.

Fairburn, C. G., & Harrison, P. J. (2003). Eating disorders. *Lancet, 361,* 407–416.

Fairburn, C. G., Norman, P. A., Welch, S. L., O'Connor, M. E., Doll, H. A., & Peveler, R. C. (1995). A prospective study of outcome in bulimia nervosa and the long-term effects of three psychological treatments. *Archives of General Psychiatry, 153,* 386–391.

Fonagy, P. (2003). The development of psychopathology from infancy to adulthood: The mysterious unfolding of disturbance in time. *Infant Mental Health Journal, 24,* 212–239.

Garner, D. M., & Bemis, K. M. (1982). A cognitive-behavioural approach to anorexia nervosa. *Cognitive Therapy and Research, 6,* 123–150.

Garner, D. M., Olmsted, M. P., & Polivy, J. (1983). Development and validation of a multidimensional Eating Disorder Inventory for anorexia nervosa and bulimia. *International Journal of Eating Disorders, 2,* 15–31.

Ghaderi, A., & Scott, B. (2000). Coping in dieting and eating disorders. *Journal of Nervous and Mental Disease, 188,* 273–279.

Ghaderi, A., & Scott, B. (2002). The preliminary reliability and validity of the Survey for Eating Disorders (SEDs): A self report questionnaire for diagnosing eating disorders. *European Eating Disorders Review, 10,* 61–76.

Gorwood, P., Kipman, A., & Foulon, C. (2003). The human genetics of anorexia nervosa. *European Journal of Pharmacology, 480,* 163–170.

Grissett, N. I., & Norvell, N. K. (1992). Perceived social support, social skills, and quality of relationships in bulimic women. *Journal of Consulting and Clinical Psychology, 60,* 293–299.

Halmi, K. A., Sunday, S. R., Strober, R., Kaplan, A., Woodside, D. B., Fichter, M., et al. (2000). Perfectionism in anorexia nervosa: Variation by subtype, obsessionality and pathological eating behaviour. *American Journal of Psychiatry, 157,* 1799–1805.

Hay, P. J., Bacaltchuk, J., Claudino, A., Ben-Tovim, D., & Yong, P. Y. (2003). Individual psychotherapy in the outpatient treatment of adults with anorexia nervosa (Cochrane Review). *Cochrane Library, 4.*

Hay, P. J., & Fairburn, C. G. (1998). The validity of the DSM-IV scheme for classifying bulimic eating disorders. *International Journal of Eating Disorders, 23,* 7–15.

Heatherton, T. F., & Baumeister, R. (1991). Binge eating as escape from self awareness. *Psychological Bulletin, 110,* 86–108.

Hoek, H. W., & van Hoeken, D. (2003). Review of the prevalence and incidence of eating disorders. *International Journal of Eating Disorders, 34,* 383–396.

Kerem, N. C., & Katzman, D. K. (2003). Brain structure and function in adolescents with anorexia nervosa. *Adolescent Medicine, 14,* 109–118.

Klump, K. L., Wonderlich, S., Lehoux, P., Lilenfeld, L. R. R., & Bulik, C. (2002). Does environment matter? A review of nonshared environment and eating disorders. *International Journal of Eating Disorders, 31,* 118–135.

Laliberte, M., Boland, F. J., & Leichner, P. (1999). Family climate factors specific to disturbed eating and bulimia nervosa. *Journal of Clinical Psychology, 55,* 1021–1040.

Latzer, Y., Hochdorf, Z., Bachar, E., & Canetti, L. (2002). Attachment style and family functioning as discriminating factors in eating disorders. *Contemporary Family Therapy: An International Journal, 24,* 581–599.

Leung, N., Waller, G., & Thomas, G. (1999). Core beliefs in anorexic and bulimic women. *Journal of Nervous and Mental Disease, 187,* 736–741.

Lewis, M. D., & Granic, I. (2000). *Emotion, development, and self-organisation.* Cambridge, UK: Cambridge University Press.

Martinez-Gonzalez, M. A., Gual, P., Lahortiga, F., Alonso, Y., de Irala-Estevez, J., & Cervera, S. (2003). Parental factors, mass media influences, and the onset of eating disorders in a prospective, population-based cohort. *Pediatrics, 111,* 315–320.

Meyer, C., & Gillings, K. (2004). Parental bonding and bulimic psychopathology: The mediating role of mistrust/abuse beliefs. *International Journal of Eating Disorders, 35,* 229–233.

Minuchin, S., Rosman, B. L., & Baker, L. (1978). *Psychosomatic families: Anorexia nervosa in context.* Cambridge, MA: Harvard University Press.

Moorhead, D. J., Stashwick, C. K., Reinherz, H. Z., Giaconia, R. M., Striegel-Moore, R. M., & Paradis, A. D. (2002). Child and adolescent predictors for eating disorders in a community population of young adult women. *International Journal of Eating Disorders, 33,* 1–9.

Morgan, C. D., Wiederman, M. W., & Pryor, T. L. (1995). Sexual functioning and attitudes of eating disordered women: A follow up study. *Journal of Sex and Marital Therapy, 21,* 67–77.

Oatley, K., & Jenkins, J. M. (1996). *Understanding emotion.* Oxford, UK: Blackwell.

O'Connor, M., Simmons, T., & Cooper, M. J. (2003). Assumptions and beliefs, dieting and predictors of eating disordered–related symptoms in young women and young men. *Eating Behaviours, 4,* 1–6.

Oken, D. M., Greene, A. L., & Smith, J. E. (2003). Family interactions predict intraindividual symptom variation for adolescents with bulimia. *International Journal of Eating Disorders, 34,* 450–457.

Paxton, S. J., Schutz, H. K., Wertheim, E. H., & Muir, S. L. (1999). Friendship clique and peer influences on body image concerns, dietary restraint, extreme weight loss behaviours, and binge eating in adolescent girls. *Journal of Abnormal Psychology, 108,* 255–266.

Pike, K. M., & Rodin, J. (1991). Mothers, daughters and disordered eating. *Journal of Abnormal Psychology, 100,* 198–204.

Pinel, J. P. J. (2000). *Biopsychology.* Needham Heights, MA: Allyn & Bacon.

Power, M. J., Katz, R., McGuffin, P., Duggan, C. F., Lam. D., & Beck, A. T. (1994). The Dysfunctional Attitude Scale: A comparison of forms a and b and proposals for a new subscaled version. *Journal of Research in Personality, 28,* 263–276.

Raffi, A. R., Rondini, M., Grandi, S., & Fava, G. A. (2000). Life events and prodromal symptoms in bulimia nervosa. *Psychological Medicine, 30,* 727–731.

Rorty, M., Yager, J., Buckwalter, G., & Rossotto, E. (1999). Social support, social adjustment and recovery status in bulimia nervosa. *International Journal of Eating Disorders, 26,* 1–12.

Schmidt, U., Tiller, J., Blanchard, M., Andrews, B., & Treasure, J. (1997). Is there a specific trauma precipitating anorexia nervosa? *Psychological Medicine, 27,* 523–530.

Selvini-Palazzoli, M. (1978). *Self-starvation.* New York: Aronson.

Shaw, R. J., & Steiner, H. (1997). Temperament in juvenile eating disorders. *Psychosomatics, 38,* 126–131.

Smolak, L., Levine, M. P., & Striegel-Moore, R. (1996). *The developmental psychopathology of eating disorders.* Mahwah, NJ: Lawrence Erlbaum.

Somerville, K., Cooper, M. J., & Hackmann, A. (2004, September). *Imagery in bulimia nervosa.* Paper presented at the annual congress of the European Association for Behavioural and Cognitive Therapies, Manchester, UK.

Spranger, S. C., Waller, G., & Bryant-Waugh, R. (2001). Schema avoidance in bulimic and non–eating disordered women. *International Journal of Eating Disorders, 29,* 302–306.

Steele, H., Steele, M., Croft, C., & Fonagy, P. (1999). Infant-mother attachment at one year predicts children's understanding of mixed emotions at six years. *Social Development, 8,* 161–178.

Steiner, H., Kwan, W., Shaffer, T. -G., Walker, S., Miller, S., Sagar, A., et al. (2003). Risk and protective factors for juvenile eating disorders. *European Child and Adolescent Psychiatry, 12,* i38–i46.

Steiner, H., Smith, C., Rosenkrantz, R. T., & Litt, I. (1991). The early care and feeding of anorexics. *Child Psychiatry and Human Development, 2,* 163–167.

Stern, D. (1985). *The interpersonal world of the infant.* New York: Basic Books.

Stice, E. (1994). A review of the evidence for a socio-cultural model of bulimia nervosa and an exploration of the mechanisms of action. *Clinical Psychology Review, 14,* 663–661.

Stice, E. (1998). Modeling of eating pathology and social reinforcement of the thin-ideal predict onset of bulimic symptoms. *Behavior Research and Therapy, 36,* 931–944.

Stice, E. (2002). Risk and maintenance factors for eating pathology: A meta-analytic review. *Psychological Bulletin, 128,* 825–848.

Sundgot-Borgen, J. (1994). Risk and trigger factors for the development of eating disorders in female elite athletes. *Medicine and Science in Sports and Exercise, 26,* 414–419.

Taylor, G. J., Ryan, D., & Bagby, R. M. (1985). Toward the development of a new self-report alexithymia scale. *Psychotherapy and Psychosomatics, 44,* 191–199.

Tiller, J. M., Sloane, G., Schmidt, U., Troop, N., Power, M., & Treasure, J. L. (1997). Social support in patients with anorexia nervosa and bulimia nervosa. *International Journal of Eating Disorders, 21,* 31–38.

Troop, N. A., & Bifulco, A. (2002). Childhood social arena and cognitive sets in eating disorders. *British Journal of Clinical Psychology, 41,* 205–211.

Troop, N. A., Holbrey, A., & Treasure, J. L. (1998). Stress, coping, and crisis support in eating disorders. *International Journal of Eating Disorders, 24,* 157–166.

Troop, N. A., & Treasure, J. L. (1997). Psychosocial factors in the onset of eating disorders: Responses to life events and difficulties. *British Journal of Medical Psychology, 70,* 373–385.

Turner, H., & Bryant-Waugh, R. (2004). Eating disorder not otherwise specified (EDNOS): Profiles of clients presenting at a community eating disorder service. *European Eating Disorder Review, 12,* 18–26.

Turner, H., & Cooper, M. J. (2002a). Cognitions and their origins in women with anorexia nervosa, normal dieters and female controls. *Clinical Psychology and Psychotherapy, 9,* 242–252.

Turner, H., & Cooper, M. J. (2002b). Core beliefs in females with anorexia nervosa. *Cognitive Therapy, 4,* 4–5.

Turner, H., Rose, K., & Cooper, M. J. (2005). Parental bonding and eating disorder symptoms in adolescents: The mediating role of core beliefs. *Eating Behaviors, 6,* 113–118.

van Hoeken, D., Seidell, J. C., & Hoek, H. W. (2003). Epidemiology. In J. L. Treasure, U. Schmidt, & E. F. van Furth (Eds.), *Handbook of eating disorders* (pp. 11–34). Chichester, UK: Wiley.

Waller, G., Kennerley, H., & Ohanian, V. (in press). Schema focussed cognitive behaviour therapy with the eating disorders. In L. P. Riso, D. J. Stein, P. L. du Toit, & J. E. Young (Eds.), *Cognitive schemas and core beliefs in psychological problems: A scientist-practitioner guide.* Washington, DC: American Psychological Association.

Waller, G., Ohanian, V., Meyer, C., & Osman, S. (2000). Cognitive content among bulimic women: The role of core beliefs. *International Journal of Eating Disorders, 28,* 235–241.

Ward, A., Ramsay, R., Turnbull, S., Benedettini, M., & Treasure, J. (2000). Attachment patterns in eating disorders: Past in the present. *International Journal of Eating Disorders, 28,* 370–376.

Waters, A., Hill, A., & Waller, G. (2000). Internal and external antecedents of binge eating episodes in a group of women with bulimia nervosa. *International Journal of Eating Disorders, 29,* 17–22.

Watkins, B., Willoughby, K., Waller, G., Serpell, L., & Lask, B. (2002). Patterns of birth in anorexia nervosa: I. Early onset cases in the United Kingdom. *International Journal of Eating Disorders, 32,* 11–17.

Welch, S. L., Doll, H. A., & Fairburn, C. G. (1997). Life events and the onset of bulimia nervosa: A controlled study. *Psychological Medicine, 27,* 515–522.

Wilfley, D. E., Agras, W. S., Telch, C. F., Rossiter, E. M., Schneider, J. A., Cole, A., et al. (1993). Group cognitive behavioural therapy and group interpersonal psychotherapy for the nonpurging bulimic individual: A controlled comparison. *Journal of Consulting and Clinical Psychology, 61,* 296–305.

Woodside, D. B., Bulik, C. M., Halmi, K. A., Fichter, M. M., Kaplan, A. S., Berrettini, W. H., et al. (2002). Personality, perfectionism, and attitudes toward eating in parents of individuals with eating disorders. *International Journal of Eating Disorders, 31,* 290–299.

Woolrich, R. A., Cooper, M. J., & Turner, H. (2005). Negative self-beliefs in anorexia nervosa: A detailed exploration of their content, origins and functional links to "not eating" and other characteristic behaviours. Manuscript submitted for publication.

Young, J. E. (1994). *Young Schema Questionnaire.* New York: Cognitive Therapy Center. Retrieved November 19, 2004, from http://www.schematherapy.com

Young, J. E. (2003). *Young-Rygh Compensation Inventory.* New York: Cognitive Therapy Center. Retrieved November 19, 2004, from http://www.schematherapy.com

Young, J. E., & Rygh, J. (2003). *Young-Rygh Avoidance Inventory.* New York: Cognitive Therapy Center. Retrieved November 19, 2004, from http://www.schematherapy.com

CHAPTER 13

The Development of Substance Abuse in Adolescence

Correlates, Causes, and Consequences

Jon D. Kassel, Sally Weinstein, Steven A. Skitch, Jennifer Veilleux, and Robin Mermelstein

Drug use among adolescents has become increasingly normative within the last several decades. Indeed, experimentation with drugs (and other "risky" behaviors) can be viewed as a behavioral manifestation of individuation and the seeking of autonomy. Nonetheless, the profound damage directly attributable to drug misuse among youth cannot be denied. Substance abuse is, in many respects, a prototypical psychological disorder in that it affects virtually every aspect of the individual's intrapersonal and interpersonal life. Moreover, and analogous to other disorders of youth (and adulthood, for that matter), there is strong reason to believe that the etiology of substance abuse is complex and multifactorial. Simplistic linear or additive conceptual models can no longer be viewed as adequate to explain the multiple influences that both protect and render one vulnerable to substance-use problems.

Within the past 10 years, greater emphasis has been placed on understanding the etiology and maintenance of drug-use problems from a developmental framework (e.g., Cicchetti & Luthar, 1999). Indeed, delineation of developmental pathways through which individuals progress to substance abuse have proven most instructive to date. As such, burgeoning research within the field of adolescent substance abuse is moving beyond the simple identification of vulnerability factors, toward understanding how such factors operate within developmental, social, and biological contexts.

In this chapter, we first review facts pertaining to the prevalence and operationalization of substance use in adolescence, focusing our review on the processes associated with substance-use problems per se, rather than benign experimentation. We then consider how the period of adolescence itself sets the stage for drug use and abuse. Next, we

Work on this chapter was supported in part by grants CA80266 and CA98262 from the National Cancer Institute and by grant 5R01AA12240-04 from the National Institute on Alcohol Abuse and Alcoholism.

examine etiologic causes, risk factors, and processes associated with the onset and maintenance of substance abuse, emphasizing the characterization of such processes from a multifactorial and dynamic perspective. Acknowledging the complexity associated with the development of substance-abuse problems, we conclude by discussing recent methodological advances in the field that can help shed light on the mechanisms governing substance abuse over time. To be clear, then, our intention is not to provide an exhaustive review of all correlates of adolescent drug use, but rather to emphasize what is known about the etiology of substance abuse from a developmental, interactive perspective.

PREVALENCE OF SUBSTANCE USE

Adolescent substance use remains a major public health concern today and affects the lives of millions of children, their families, and indeed, society at large. Prevalence data from the Monitoring the Future (MTF) Study, a long-term study of licit and illicit substance use among adolescents, college students, and adults nationwide, suggest that the majority of American adolescents experiment with substances, and a smaller—but still considerable—percentage report heavier use. Recent results indicate that 51% of adolescents have used an illegal drug by the end of high school, and 28% have used "harder," illicit drugs other than marijuana (Johnston, O'Malley, Bachman, & Schulenberg, 2004).

Even more widespread is the use of licit substances (cigarettes and alcohol) in adolescence. Among eighth graders in 2003, 28% reported having tried cigarettes, and 10% were current smokers. Additionally, 46% reported having consumed alcohol, with 12% reporting having had five or more consecutive drinks in the previous 2 weeks (a definition of "binge drinking"; Johnston et al., 2004). These figures double among high school seniors. In 2003, 54% of 12th graders reported some experience with cigarettes, 24% were current smokers, 77% had consumed alcohol, and 28% reported having had five or more consecutive drinks in the previous 2 weeks (Johnston et al.).

Analysis of longitudinal trends in rates of adolescent substance use indicates some improvement in recent years. Although varying somewhat across specific drugs, MTF data indicate that annual use of any illicit drug among adolescents first peaked in the early 1980s, steadily decreased until the early 1990s, and peaked again in 1996–1997. Since then, these rates have declined gradually for eighth graders and, beginning in 2001, have declined for high school students as well. Trends in adolescent cigarette and alcohol use have generally mirrored those of illicit drugs. Cigarette use substantially increased in the 1990s, reaching a peak in 1996–1997. Smoking has since declined considerably among adolescents. Alcohol use and binge-drinking rates increased in the early 1990s and remained fairly steady until 2002, at which point rates of use and binge drinking dropped across eighth graders and high school students (Johnston et al., 2004).

Despite these recent declines in overall adolescent substance use, however, current numbers remain unacceptably high. Further, findings indicate that declining trends in the use of certain substances have either halted or reversed in the past few years. More specifically, prevalence of inhalant use among eighth graders increased significantly in 2003, and cocaine use among all adolescents has remained steady since 2001 (Johnston et al., 2004). Finally, of great concern is converging evidence from the MTF and the 2003 national Youth Risk Behavior Survey (YRBS) studies indicating that a substantial proportion of American youth initiates substance use in early adolescence. Of the 15,240 students sampled in the YRBS study, 18.3% reported cigarette use, 27.8% reported consuming alcohol, and 9.9% reported having tried marijuana, all prior to age 13 (Grunbaum et al., 2004). Acknowledging that the prevalence rates of illicit substances such as cocaine, heroin, and others are extremely low among adolescents, we will focus most of our efforts on reviewing and considering the literatures devoted to the use of alcohol, tobacco, and marijuana.

DEFINING ADOLESCENT SUBSTANCE USE

Adolescent substance users comprise a heterogeneous group, ranging from those who minimally experiment with substances to habitual substance users. When substance use is frequent and paired with significant impairment or distress, adolescents may be diagnosed with a substance-use disorder. Traditional diagnostic approaches to substance use, such as the *Diagnostic and Statistical Manual of Mental Disorders,* 4th edition (*DSM-IV*; American Psychiatric Association, 1994), distinguish between two mutually exclusive categories of substance disorders for adolescents as well as adults: substance abuse and the more severe diagnosis of substance dependence. To qualify for the diagnosis of *substance dependence,* an adolescent must exhibit persistent use of substances despite the occurrence of three or more cognitive (e.g., persistent desire for the substance; continued use despite knowledge of substance-related physical or psychological problems), behavioral (e.g., large amounts or long periods of use; amount of time spent to obtain the substance; and reduction or abandonment of activities because of substance use), or physiological consequences (e.g., tolerance; withdrawal) occurring within a 12-month period.

Of lesser severity, *substance abuse* is defined by a pattern of repeated substance use despite occurrence of one or more harmful and recurrent consequences of use within a 12-month period, including failure to fulfill obligations at work, school, or home; substance use in hazardous situations; substance-related legal problems; and interpersonal distress resulting from or exacerbated by substance use. Although the specific symptoms differ slightly, the *DSM-IV* diagnostic criteria for substance abuse and dependence described above are generally applicable across 11 different drug types, including alcohol, amphetamine, caffeine, cannabis, cocaine, hallucinogens, inhalants, nicotine, opioids, phencyclidine, and sedatives. Diagnoses of substance disorders among adolescents, albeit clearly lower than rates of "any use," are still quite high. For example, in a sample of 74,000 Minnesota high school students, Harrison and colleagues (Harrison, Fulkerson, & Beebe, 1998) found that 7% of 9th graders and 16% of 12th graders met criteria for substance abuse, and 4% of 9th graders and 7% of 12th graders met criteria for substance dependence.

Despite near-universal reliance on the *DSM-IV* nosological scheme, several diagnostic questions remain regarding the utility and validity of substance disorders in adolescence as defined by *DSM-IV.* First, whereas adolescent substance disorders are viewed as phenomenologically equivalent to adult substance disorders, strong evidence points to important developmental differences in the manifestation of substance-use problems. Within the adolescent alcohol-use literature, for example, studies of clinical and community samples suggest that several *DSM-IV* symptoms of alcohol abuse and dependence are generally underrepresented among adolescent samples. Specifically, the dependence symptoms of withdrawal and alcohol-related medical problems, as well as the abuse symptoms of hazardous use and alcohol-related legal problems, are relatively uncommon among adolescents (Lewinsohn, Rohde, & Seeley, 1996; Martin, Kaczynski, Maisto,

Bukstein, & Moss, 1995; Winters, Latimer, & Stinchfield, 1999) and are particularly rare in early adolescence (Langenbucher & Martin, 1996). In contrast, the dependence symptom of tolerance may be an insensitive indicator of maladaptive substance use among adolescents. Given adolescents' developmental status, the emergence of tolerance to alcohol is considered normative in adolescence. Indeed, in a study of adolescent drinkers, tolerance was commonly reported across those with and without diagnoses of alcohol dependence (Martin et al., 1995).

Two additional issues limit the utility of the abuse/dependence distinction in adolescence. The first concerns the prevalence of a group of "diagnostic orphans" (Hasin & Paykin, 1998). Research has demonstrated that a substantial portion of adolescent substance users exhibit one or two dependence symptoms but no symptoms of abuse, thus failing to qualify for a *DSM-IV* diagnosis despite regular to heavy substance use (Martin & Winters, 1998; Pollock & Martin, 1999; Winters, 2001). Further, the current diagnostic criteria lack specificity in distinguishing among levels of adolescent substance use. Rather, the one-symptom threshold for the diagnosis of substance abuse—combined with the broad range of possible abuse symptoms—produces a most heterogeneous group of adolescents. As such, normative experimenters and heavier users may be lumped together within the same diagnostic class (Martin & Winters).

A final limitation of *DSM-IV* criteria is the lack of information regarding the onset and progression of problematic substance use. Although substance abuse is considered the milder, and hence prodromal, diagnosis (Winters, 2001), research indicates that alcohol-abuse symptoms do not necessarily precede alcohol-dependence symptoms in adolescents (Martin, Langenbucher, Kaczynski, & Chung, 1996). Taken together, these findings therefore suggest that adolescent substance use is neither well defined nor conceptualized by the traditional abuse/dependence diagnostic categories, because these categories largely ignore developmental and normative considerations unique to this age group.

In contrast to a categorical approach, adolescent substance use may be viewed as falling along a dimension of use severity. Conceptualizing substance use in terms of sequential stages provides greater insight into subclinical substance use and also has the advantage of identifying levels of severity among adolescent substance users. For instance, Winters (2001) outlines six stages of adolescent substance use. The first is *Abstinence,* in which the adolescent has never used any drugs. Within the field of adolescent smoking, this stage has been further categorized into a no-intention substage, in which the youth expresses no intention to smoke, and a contemplation/susceptible substage, in which the youth acknowledges that he or she is considering smoking in the near future (Mayhew, Flay, & Mott, 2000). The second stage, *Experimental Use,* refers to adolescents who have used substances only minimally, with their use generally limited to recreational activities and often involving only alcohol. The third stage, *Early Abuse,* includes more established users: Here, use is more frequent, use tends to involve more than one substance, and adverse consequences of use begin to occur. *Abuse,* the fourth stage, defines those adolescents who regularly and frequently use substances over an extended period of time. Furthermore, such use is often accompanied by the occurrence of adverse consequences. The fifth stage, *Dependence,* involves continued regular use despite the repeated occurrence of adverse consequences. Moreover, adolescents in this stage reliably show signs of tolerance and adjust activities around substance seeking and substance use. Finally, *Recovery* refers to the return to abstinence, although adolescents may relapse and re-cycle through the preceding stages.

In sum, relative to categorical and nosological frameworks, dimensional approaches afford researchers and clinicians alike better opportunities for understanding the developmental unfolding and progression of adolescent substance use, ranging from normative, experimental usage to potentially maladaptive trajectories. Moreover, stage conceptualizations delineate levels of subsyndromal use, leading to important implications in terms of targeting stage-specific prevention and intervention efforts.

ADOLESCENCE: A UNIQUE PERIOD OF VULNERABILITY TO SUBSTANCE USE

As a period of multiple transitional events and developmental challenges (Cicchetti & Rogosch, 2002), adolescence represents a time of heightened risk for emotional and behavioral problems. In light of the tremendous biological, cognitive, emotional, and social changes occurring in adolescence, it is not surprising that most individuals initiate substance use during this developmental period. In this section, we highlight the major intra- and interpersonal transformations encountered by the adolescent that set the stage for maladaptive patterns of substance use.

Recent data from the neuropsychological, brain imaging, and animal literatures have shown that adolescence is a time of neurodevelopmental plasticity and change (Steinberg et al., 2004), such that changes in the structure and function of the brain during this period may significantly affect behavior and psychological functioning (Spear, 2000). Evidence suggests that transformations include alterations in the mesocorticolimbic dopaminergic systems, which have been implicated in modulating the reinforcing properties of drugs and alcohol. In addition, maturation of the prefrontal cortex and the amygdala occurs in adolescence, and these regions are involved in goal-directed behaviors, emotional processing, and emotional reactivity (Spear, 2002). Specific to the prefrontal cortex, research with nonhuman primates indicates that glutamate (an excitatory neurotransmitter) and gamma-aminobutyric acid (an inhibitory neurotransmitter) activity is reduced in the prefrontal cortex in adolescence, whereas dopaminergic activity increases (Lewis, 1997). Although evidence remains inconclusive, some have theorized that the influences of external stressors and individual drug use during this sensitive period of development may also increase dopaminergic activity in the prefrontal cortex and other mesolimbic brain regions, facilitating further drug-seeking behavior (Dawes et al., 2000).

Thus, during adolescence, development takes place in the regions and systems responsible for the regulation of behavior and emotion and cognitions of risk and reward (Steinberg et al., 2004). This neurobiological reorganization renders adolescence a unique period of vulnerability to extreme emotional and drive states; consequently, the propensity to use and misuse substances is increased (Steinberg et al.). Along these lines, research has suggested that sensation- and novelty-seeking behavior is highest during adolescence (Zuckerman, 1994), a temperament risk factor that has been shown to predict cigarette and alcohol use in adolescence (Crawford, Pentz, Chou, Li, & Dwyer, 2003).

The onset of puberty in adolescence and the associated physical, hormonal, and maturational changes accompanying this transition represent another arena of increased vulnerability. Although the specific etiological processes linking pubertal change and adolescent substance use are unclear, the timing of this stage relative to same-age peers may negatively influence the completion of developmental tasks in adolescence (e.g., developing one's identity, autonomy from parents, and forging romantic relationships; Dawes et al., 2000). The inability to complete these stage-salient tasks in turn heightens risk for negative outcomes, such as substance abuse (Cicchetti & Rogosch, 2002). Further, Graber (2003) concludes that early maturation is associated with alcohol, tobacco, and substance use in adolescent females and is linked with alcohol use in adolescent males.

In addition to the biological and cognitive changes that accompany adolescence, emotional lability represents another phenomenological hallmark experienced by most young people. Although adolescence is no longer characterized as a period of universal storm and stress (Hall, 1904), mood disruptions are nonetheless considered a central feature of teenage development (Arnett, 1999). A considerable body of research has demonstrated that levels of dysphoria and emotional instability rise with entry to adolescence (Garber, Keiley, & Martin, 2002; Larson, Moneta, Richards, & Wilson, 2002), and one third to one half of adolescents report feelings of depressed mood (Compas, Hinden, & Gerhardt, 1995). Moreover, adolescence is associated with more frequent negative affect as compared to middle and later adulthood (Cartensen, Pasupathi, Mayr, & Nesselroade, 2000). These documented increases in negative emotion constitute a major risk factor for adolescent substance use. Feelings of distress in adolescence, particularly negative mood, have been linked with, and shown to prospectively predict, cigarette and alcohol use in both cross-sectional and longitudinal studies (e.g., R. A. Brown, Lewinsohn, Seeley, & Wagner, 1996; Chassin, Pillow, Curran, Molina, & Barrera, 1993; Windle & Windle, 2001).

In sum, given the substantial changes occurring across biological and psychological domains of development, adolescence is a period of unique risk for substance use and misuse. However, these factors do not operate in isolation. Rather, it is the complex interactions of these factors, in addition to simultaneous contextual changes, that result in maladaptive trajectories of substance use. In the next section, we elaborate on empirically supported theories that incorporate the interactions and transactions among multiple levels of vulnerability factors to explain the development of substance use in adolescence.

THEORETICAL FRAMEWORKS FOR UNDERSTANDING THE DEVELOPMENT OF SUBSTANCE ABUSE

Over the course of the last 30 years, a great deal of effort has been devoted to the identification of factors that render one vulnerable to substance abuse. Indeed, a vast array of such variables have been identified. Hawkins, Catalano, and Miller (1992), for example, conducted a thorough review of the literature, concluding that the following factors may all play a potentially critical role in the development of substance-use disorders: laws and norms favorable toward drug use; availability of drugs; extreme economic deprivation; neighborhood disorganization; certain psychological characteristics; early and persistent behavior problems, including aggressive behavior in males, other conduct problems, and hyperactivity in childhood and adolescence; a family history of alcoholism and parental use of illegal drugs; poor family management practices; family conflict; low bonding to family; academic failure; lack of commitment to school; early peer rejection; social influences to use drugs; alienation and rebelliousness; attitudes favorable to drug use; and early initiation of drug use (p. 96).

Identification of such disparate, distal factors found to be related to substance-use initiation and escalation certainly represents an important first step toward better understanding the processes through which adolescents progress to problematic use. But ultimately, such factors must be understood within more complex conceptual frameworks that emphasize the intricate interplay among numerous intrapersonal and contextual variables. As such, what is clearly needed are informed theoretical frameworks through which such variables can be organized and understood within a unified, albeit intricate, conceptualization. Moreover, some have argued (e.g., Glantz, 1992) that, at least until fairly recently, most of the prior work with respect to theory building and testing in this area has been devoted to understanding substance use, rather than abuse per se. Thus, another implication for theory building and testing is that, as discussed earlier, substance use should be viewed as falling along a continuum that varies from nonproblematic, experimental use through substance dependence.

DEVELOPMENTAL PSYCHOPATHOLOGY PERSPECTIVES ON SUBSTANCE ABUSE

Recent contributions steeped in the field of developmental psychopathology are proving most instructive in helping shed light on the processes underlying substance abuse among adolescents (e.g., Cicchetti & Luthar, 1999; Glantz & Leshner, 2000; Wills, Sandy, & Yaeger, 2000; Windle & Davies, 1999). Application of a developmental psychopathology approach to the study of adolescent substance abuse fundamentally differs from previous attempts at understanding this problem in several important respects. As alluded to earlier, the simple identification of correlates and precursors of substance-use behavior among adolescents is viewed as an insufficient, albeit necessary, approach. Rather, emphasis is placed on understanding adolescents in the various contexts in which they live, work, and play, and how various vulnerability factors (at the levels of biology, temperament, cognitive factors, family environment, and social environment) interact within these contexts. As such, this way of thinking about substance-use disorders differs dramatically from more simplistic unifactorial theories (e.g., disease models) that emphasize singularity with regard to the role played by prominent risk factors (e.g., genetic and personality), coupled with a more deterministic view of the inevitability of outcome (e.g., possession of one or more risk factors will inevitably lead to substance-abuse outcome). Hence, predisposition is not viewed as destiny (Glantz & Leshner) from a developmental psychopathology perspective. Recent epigenetic approaches to understanding substance-abuse etiology among youth espouse similar sentiments. These emerging theoretical perspectives examine substance abuse from a developmental framework affording the opportunity to characterize the emergence of at-risk phenotypes as a function of numerous reciprocal influences, including social, cultural, behavioral, neural, and genetic (Dawes et al., 2000; Wills et al., 2000).

The hypothetical model presented in Figure 13.1 captures some of the key ideas espoused by a developmental psychopathology framework. The depicted model comprises three main domains, which in reality are not as distinct (nonoverlapping) as suggested here: (a) risk factors (e.g., temperament, psychopathology); (b) contextual factors (e.g., peer group, family, school); and (c) drug use itself. Note that all of these interrelated factors are believed to exert influence over one another. As such, an inherent dynamism and fluidity becomes integral to the developmental perspective. It is also important to remember that these complex relationships and processes all play out against a backdrop of adolescent development and maturation. For example, as shown in Figure 13.1, drug use can both adversely influence and, in turn, be influenced by developmental processes themselves. Correspondingly, drug use is not viewed solely as a dependent variable or outcome variable, but rather as a behavior that can both be affected by and affect other contextual and risk factors.

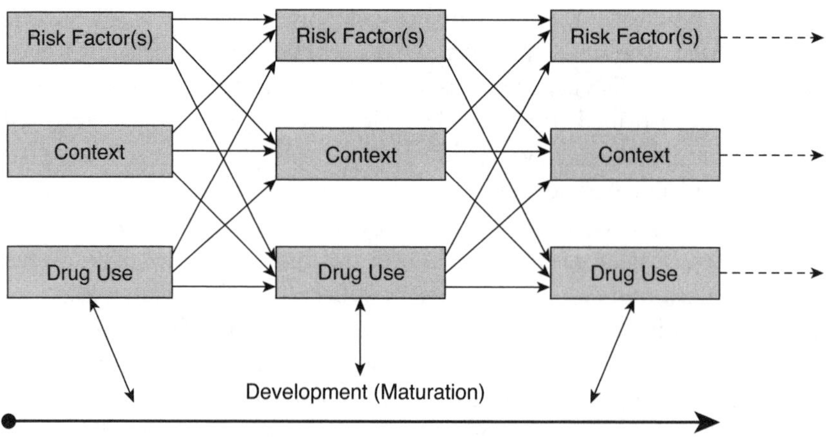

Figure 13.1 A Dynamic Developmental Model of Adolescent Substance Use

As an example, consider an adolescent who possesses several risk factors (high physical activity, anxiety, and family history of alcoholism), lives in a disruptive family, and begins to experiment with drugs. Although on the face of it, such factors may converge to portend an undesirable outcome in terms of both future drug use and overall psychological functioning, such an outcome cannot be viewed as inevitable. In this instance, the child's school becomes aware of the drug use, and a social worker is assigned to the case, offering a diagnosis of attention deficit/hyperactivity disorder (ADHD). Once placed on appropriate medication, the child's behavior in school and home improves, the family receives counseling, and the developmental landscape has shifted dramatically as a result. Although such an outcome might appear "Pollyanna-ish," the point is that the reciprocal influences of risk factors, contextual influences, and drug use allow for myriad outcomes, both positive and maladaptive. Modeling and understanding these processes clearly presents exciting and important challenges to both adolescent substance-abuse researchers and clinicians.

VULNERABILITY FACTORS FOR THE DEVELOPMENT OF ADOLESCENT SUBSTANCE USE

We now focus on specific etiological causes and vulnerability factors associated with the onset and course of adolescent substance-use problems. This review is not meant to be exhaustive or to encompass all theories that have been proposed to explain the development of adolescent substance-use disorders. Rather, we focus on vulnerability factors that have received the most empirical support and attention. Although vulnerability factors are presented separately, it is important to emphasize the interactional nature of the relation, such that vulnerability factors affect the risk for substance-use problems over the course of development.

The Role of Temperament

Whereas research does not support the existence of an "addictive personality," evidence does suggest that certain temperament characteristics may serve as vulnerability markers for later drug abuse. Most often conceptualized from a dimensional perspective, temperament can be defined as constitutionally based characteristics identified in early childhood that manifest as individual differences in emotional and physiological reactivity and self-regulation (Rothbart & Ahadi, 1994). When viewed as antecedents to more cognitively complex personality traits, temperament may be affected by both biological and social forces as experienced through intellectual and emotional development (Rothbert & Ahadi; Wills & Dishion, 2004).

The number and quality of temperament dimensions also vary among conceptual models. One early model posited three temperament dimensions: *physical activity level, emotionality,* and *sociability* (Buss & Plomin, 1984). Whereas others have emphasized the importance of the traits of impulsivity and novelty/sensation seeking (Cloninger, 1987; Henderson, Galen, & DeLuca, 1998; Rothbert & Ahadi, 1994), recent evidence suggests these traits should not be viewed as base-level temperaments because they cannot be empirically validated in young children. Rather, novelty seeking and impulsivity may be better understood as intermediaries between baseline temperament dimensions and risk for substance abuse (Wills & Dishion, 2004). Recent conceptualizations also recommend splitting the dimension of emotionality into two separate dimensions of negative emotionality and positive emotionality, because each has been shown to yield differential effects on substance-use outcome (Wills et al., 2000).

The dimensions of physical activity level and negative emotionality have been consistently identified as predictors of early-onset substance abuse (Wills, DuHamel, & Vaccaro, 1995; Wills et al., 2000). Though perhaps initially counterintuitive as a risk factor, high physical activity, often viewed in the same context as hyperactivity, is implicated in conduct disorder, a known correlate and precursor of drug use and abuse (Wills et al., 1995; Windle, 1991). Indeed, it may be that heightened physical activity level itself plays no direct role in priming children for substance use, but instead precedes development of conduct disorder, which may play a more direct and immediate role in substance-abuse etiology (Tarter, 1988; Tarter et al., 1999). Moreover, hyperactivity and conduct disorder are often linked with high novelty seeking. Working from the behavioral activation model of alcoholism, Cloninger (1987) reported that subjects with a propensity toward novelty seeking had heightened dopaminergic release to alcohol relative to subjects low in novelty seeking. Thus, one interesting interpretation of these findings is that the biological correlates of temperament dimensions may sensitize certain people to the effects of drugs and thereby render them vulnerable to further instances of drug self-administration.

Negative affectivity, characterized by frequent and intense unpleasant moods, also appears to be a significant risk factor for adolescent substance abuse. Negative affectivity is negatively correlated with age of drug-use onset (Henderson et al., 1998; Stice, Myers, & S. A. Brown, 1998) and positively associated with greater substance use and substance-use escalation during adolescence (Myers et al., 2003; Wills & Stoolmiller, 2002). Emotional volatility has been linked to problems in self-regulation, which may represent a higher-order factor influencing young people's decisions to initially experiment with and continue to use drugs and alcohol (Wills et al., 1995).

Recent models also predict that temperament affects the development of intermediary variables such as self-control (Wills et al., 2000). Longitudinal studies of middle school students found significant paths from negative emotionality and physical activity (together termed *difficult temperament*) to poor self-control, and even stronger links between self-control and early-onset substance use (Wills et al., 2000; Wills & Stoolmiller, 2002). Thus, in the context of drug-abuse etiology, temperament may become most relevant when viewed as a vulnerability toward maladaptive socialization processes (Tarter et al., 1999).

In some instances, temperament may also play a protective role against likelihood of substance abuse. The two primary dimensions that have been identified as potential protective influences are positive emotionality and task-attentional orientation (Wills et al., 2000). *Positive emotionality* refers to the tendency to experience positive emotion regularly and without difficulty, whereas *task-attentional orientation* reflects the ability to focus attention on the task at hand. Several studies of middle school students found significant paths from positive emotionality and task-attentional orientation (together called *protective temperament*) to enhanced self-control (Wills et al., 2000; Wills & Stoolmiller, 2002). Indeed, research has shown that children with good self-control tend to avoid substance abuse in adolescence, even after initial experimentation (Wills & Dishion, 2004), and protective temperament may also help promote academic competence and buffer negative social factors such as poor parent-child relationships (Wills, Sandy, Yaeger, & Shinar, 2001). Other candidate personality traits that may also provide protective influences include high harm avoidance and its more pathological correlate, social anxiety (Cloninger, 1987; Myers, Aarons, Tomlinson, & Stein, 2003).

To reiterate, then, the field is moving away from linear models of temperament's influence on substance abuse, in part because of the inevitable interaction between temperament and other important contextual variables. Indeed, no evidence has surfaced pointing to a definitive, inevitable relationship between temperament and drug use. Moreover, it may be that the influence of temperament varies over the developmental life span. For instance, whereas early-onset alcoholics tend to manifest high activity levels and novelty-seeking behaviors, later-onset alcoholics have more characteristic neurotic features, typical of negative emotionality, which are embodied within self-regulation problems, leading to drug and alcohol use as coping mechanisms (Cloninger, 1987).

The Role of Psychopathology

Studies conducted both with clinical populations of adolescent substance abusers (Abrantes, S. A. Brown, & Tomlinson, 2003; Burkstein, Glancy, & Kaminer, 1992) and community samples of adolescents (Kandel et al., 1999; Rohde, Lewinsohn, & Seely, 1996) have indicated that there is substantial comorbidity between substance-use disorders and other psychiatric conditions. In general, it has been found that the development of other psychiatric conditions precedes the onset of adolescent substance-use problems (Armstrong & Costello, 2002; Rohde et al., 1996). Adolescents with psychiatric disorders initiate substance use at a younger age and develop abuse symptoms earlier than adolescents without psychiatric conditions (Costello, Erkanli, Federman, & Angold, 1999). This is particularly worrisome given that earlier onset of substance use is a strong predictor of the development of severe drug-use disorders (Robins & Przybeck, 1993). Therefore, it is essential to consider the role of psychopathology as a risk factor in the development of adolescent substance-use disorders.

Certain types of psychopathology have been found to be associated with increased risk for the development of problematic substance use among adolescents. Disruptive behavior disorders (conduct disorder, ADHD, and oppositional defiant disorder) have been indicated as particularly potent risk factors for the development of substance-use problems in adolescence (for reviews, see Armstrong & Costello, 2002; Flory & Lynam, 2003). Longitudinal studies with community samples of children indicate that preadolescence disruptive behavior symptoms are linked to a pathway involving delinquency and antisocial behaviors that lead to the development of adolescent substance-abuse problems (Clark, Parker, & Lynch, 1999; Loeber, Stouthamer-Loeber, & White, 1999; Lynskey & Fergusson, 1995). Indeed, Problem Behavior Theory (Donovan, R. Jessor, & Costa, 1991; R. Jessor & S. Jessor, 1980) has long espoused the influential notion that drug-use behaviors often co-occur with other unconventional, or deviant, problem behaviors.

Depressive disorders have also been associated with increased risk for substance-use problems in adolescents. In some studies, the early onset of depression has been associated with increased risk for the development of substance-use problems in adolescence, and abuse problems emerge at an earlier age in these depressed adolescents compared with nondepressed adolescent substance abusers (Burke, Burke, & Rae, 1994; Escobedo, Reddy, & Giovino, 1998). However, other studies have found no clear temporal pattern between the onset of depressive disorder and substance-use disorders (e.g., Rohde et al., 1996), or have found that substance-use problems typically precede the development of depression in adolescents (Rohde, Lewinsohn, & Seely, 1991). The mechanism and direction of the causal relationship between depression and substance use in adolescents has not yet been determined.

The presence of anxiety disorders has also been linked to risk for substance-use disorder in adolescence. However, the observed association between anxiety disorders and substance-use disorders tends to be weaker than the association between adolescent substance use and other psychiatric conditions (Armstrong & Costello, 2002; Costello et al., 1999). Longitudinal studies have indicated a prospective relationship between certain anxiety disorders and adolescent substance-use problems, including panic disorders, social phobia, and posttraumatic stress disorder (Giaconia et al, 2000; Sontag, Wittchen, Hofler, Kessler, & Stein, 2000; Zimmerman et al., 2003). Recent findings indicate the relationship between early-onset anxiety disorders and risk for substance-use disorders in adolescence may be primarily due to the influence of comorbid depressive symptoms and peer influences (Goodwin, Fergusson, & Horwood, 2004).

It is important to note that the developmental interrelationships between adolescent substance-use disorders and other Axis I psychiatric conditions are dynamic and reciprocal. Adolescents' substance-use problems affect the etiology and course of the psychiatric conditions that tend to occur with substance use. For example, cigarette smoking and nicotine dependence in adolescence have been associated with increased risk for the development of anxiety and depressive disorders in early adulthood (J. G. Johnson et al., 2000; Kandel, Davies, Karus, & Yamaguchi, 1986). Conduct disorder symptoms are more severe in children and adolescents with substance-use disorders, indicating a potential reciprocal relationship between the two conditions (Reebye, Moretti, & Lessard, 1995). Furthermore, heavy adolescent substance use is a strong predictor of progression from adolescent conduct disorder to antisocial personality disorder in young adulthood (Myers, Stewart, & S. A. Brown, 1998). Generally, adolescent substance misuse predicts later maladjustment and psychopathology in early adulthood beyond the impact of other comorbid adolescent psychiatric disorders (J. S. Brook, Cohen, & D. W. Brook, 1998; R. J. Johnson & Kaplan, 1990). Brook et al. hypothesized that adolescent drug abuse may confer risk for the subsequent development of psychopathology through two mechanisms: (a) the neurotoxic effects of certain drugs, and (b) interpersonal stress generated as a consequence of excessive drug use.

The co-occurrence of substance-use disorders and other psychiatric conditions in adolescence is not necessarily indicative of a causal relationship between any of the disorders. It has been suggested that substance-use disorders and comorbid psychiatric conditions such as disruptive behavior disorders, depressive disorders, and anxiety disorders are associated because of shared etiological factors (J. S. Brook et al., 1998; R. Jessor, 1987). A variety of shared vulnerability factors have been identified and have received research support, including genetic predispositions, family environment, self-esteem, environmental stressors, and personality traits (Conrad, Flay, & Hill, 1992; Krueger et al., 2002; Merikangas, Swendsen, Preisig, & Chazan, 1998; Wills, Sandy, Yaeger, Cleary, & Shinar, 2001). The relationship between substance-use problems and psychopathology is complex and likely to reflect variations in vulnerability factors and stress that evolve over the course of adolescent development.

Family and Peer Influence

Research has reliably demonstrated that families and peers play a critical role in influencing adolescents' decisions to initiate drug and alcohol use. Moreover, peer and family sway may also be determining factors in adolescents' subsequent behavioral trajectories toward rejection of drugs, continued experimentation, or escalation toward abuse (Bauman & Ennett, 1996; Darling & Cumsille, 2003). Whereas the empirical database has clearly documented the existence of these important relationships, it is not yet clearly delineated precisely how these potent interpersonal factors affect drug use, nor how a working knowledge of peer and family influence can ultimately inform adolescent substance-abuse prevention and treatment.

Adolescence marks a developmental shift away from family influence toward rising levels of peer influence. Between the ages of 10 and 18, the amount of time young people spend with their families drops from about 35% to 14% of waking hours, and this family time is replaced, in great part, by time devoted to leisure and peer-related activities (Larson, Richards, Moneta, Holmbeck, & Duckett, 1996). Concurrent with this period of increased peer involvement, many adolescents begin to experiment with smoking and drinking (Flory, Lynam, Milich, Leukefeld, & Clayton, 2004, Sutherland & Shepherd, 2001). This indicates that increased peer involvement may be an important factor in initial experimentation with substance use.

Several influential theories of adolescent substance abuse draw heavily on the notion that peer context and influence are, in fact, the most salient risk factors yet identified with respect to substance-use initiation and escalation. Peer Cluster Theory (e.g., Oetting & Beauvais, 1987) and its more recent iteration, Primary Socialization Theory (e.g., Oetting & Donnermeyer, 1998), argue that normative and deviant behaviors are learned social behaviors that emerge as products of the interaction of social, psychological, and cultural characteristics. Hence, norms for social behaviors, including drug use, are learned predominantly in the context of interactions with primary socialization sources.

To date, numerous studies have revealed strong correlations between: (a) measures assessing the number of a respondent's friends who use drugs, and (b) measures indicating the level of an adolescent's own substance use (e.g., Hawkins et al., 1992). An important, and as yet unanswered, question is the direction of causality underlying this observed relationship, or whether, indeed, another variable may account for this potent correlation. Probably the most predominant assumption is that adolescents initiate or escalate their drug use as a result of peer influence (e.g., Tarter et al., 1999). An alternative etiological explanation, however, is the notion that adolescents choose friendships based on similarities in drug behavior, and that the formation of peer groups around drug behaviors is at least as important as postgroup formation influences (Ennett & Bauman, 1994). Research has shown that friends clearly do influence one another, because most adolescents who use drugs and alcohol report that their friends do, too (Shilts, 1991; Wills, Sandy, Yaeger, Cleary, et al., 2001). Likewise, individuals who are more resistant to peer influence are more likely to manifest later onset of initiation and lower levels of use (Flory et al., 2004). One of the few empirical investigations specifically designed to test the peer-influence versus peer-selection hypotheses reported that, during middle adolescence, initial peer drug use was positively related to rate of change in adolescent use, thus supporting the influence mechanisms (Wills & Cleary, 1999). It is important to remember, however, that whereas such findings have important implications for understanding the etiology of substance use per se, they may tell us little about the transition from experimental use to substance-use problems.

Despite the decreasing influence of family on adolescents as age increases, familial influences are still important. Family effects can be both direct and mediated and, like peer influence, can provide potential prophylactic effects or actually increase the influence of risk factors (Glantz & Leshner, 2000; Sale, Sambrano, Springer, & Turner, 2003). Again, families may exert greater influence on younger children, because the family remains the primary source of contact and support, thereby yielding instrumental effects on a child's process of socialization (Rothbart & Ahadi, 1994). Family influence may also come via its role in teaching proper self-regulation skills (Wills et al., 2000).

One of the most significant family-related predictors of substance use is a family history of drug abuse (Glantz & Leshner, 2000). If family members (particularly parents) abuse drugs or alcohol, a child obtains an early introduction to the substance and derives a sanctioned model of acceptance. Family structure itself can act as a risk factor of sorts, because children from nonintact families have higher rates of substance abuse (Sutherland & Shepherd, 2001; Wills, Sandy, Yaeger, & Shinar, 2001), as do families who experience proportionally more negative life events (Darling & Cumsille, 2003).

On the positive side, higher levels of parental support can also buffer the effects of stress and negative events on substance use (Wills & Cleary, 1996) and may help guide young people toward making friends with positive peer groups (Sale et al., 2003). Parental expectations can influence youth drinking behavior by delaying the age at which a child first uses alcohol (Simons-Morton, 2004). Indeed, research has shown that greater parental involvement, such as monitoring after-school activities and maintaining a positive relationship, can reduce a child's risk for using substances (Cohen, Richardson, & LaBree, 1994).

Finally, it is important to note that peer and family influences on substance abuse are inherently intertwined, because most young people draw upon both peer and family support. It has been posited that families, through higher levels of monitoring and support, can decrease the probability that a young person will fraternize with a deviant peer group (Sale et al., 2003). The mechanisms and mediating variables underlying such social influence are still in the early stages of discovery, but it seems clear that both family and peer influences play a significant role in drug initiation and escalation.

Cognitive Deficits

Evidence has accumulated indicating that deficits in executive cognitive functioning (ECF) are related to increased risk for the development of adolescent substance-use disorders (for review, see Giancola & Tarter, 1999; Pihl, Peterson, & Finn, 1990). ECF involves the planning and control of goal-directed behaviors (Burgess, Alderman, Evans, Emslie, & Wilson, 1998), and deficits in executive functioning are related to dysfunction in the prefrontal areas of the brain (Damasio, 1998). A variety of cognitive abilities are considered to be components of ECF, including attention, abstract thinking, behavioral organization, planning, self-monitoring, working memory, and response inhibition (Giancola & Tarter; Pihl, Paylan, Gentes-Hawn, & Hoaken, 2003).

Deficits in ECF have been found in children and adolescents who are predisposed to develop substance-use disorders. The majority of research in this area has been conducted with the sons of substance-dependent fathers, because this group of children is at a particularly heightened risk for the development of substance-use disorders (Vanyukov & Tarter, 2000). Studies have indicated that children from families with a history of substance abuse have deficits in a variety of executive cognitive abilities, including attention, abstract reasoning, impulse control, hypothesis generation, and working memory (Giancola, Moss, Martin, Kirisci, & Tarter, 1996; Nigg et al., 2004; Tarter, Kirisci, Habeych, Reynolds, & Vanyukov, 2004). There have been few studies examining the developmental relationship between executive cognitive deficits and substance use in females. However, preliminary evidence indicates that female adolescent substance users have deficits in ECF similar to those observed in male adolescent substance users (Giancola, Shoal, & Mezzich, 2001; Shoal & Giancola, 2001).

Longitudinal studies indicate that children with deficits in ECF are more vulnerable to the development of substance-use problems later in adolescence (Giancola & Parker, 2001; Najam, Moss, Kirisci, & Tarter, 1997; Tapert, Baratta, Abrantes, & S. A. Brown, 2002; Tarter et al., 2004). Giancola and Parker found that executive cognitive deficits interacted with a cluster of personality dimensions, including negative affectivity and emotional dysregulation, to predict increased vulnerability to substance-use problems over time. Specifically, they found that deficits in ECF combined with temperamental vulnerability factors to predict increased delinquency and aggression, which in turn predicted later increases in substance use.

Drug-Use Expectancies

A large literature, particularly within the area of alcohol consumption, has shown that individuals' expectations of drug effects can have profound effects on motivational and drug-seeking processes (e.g., Cox & Klinger, 1988; Goldman, Del Boca, & Darkes, 1999). Alcohol expectancies, that is, the beliefs that adolescents hold about the effects that alcohol use will have on them, have been implicated as important factors in the development of adolescent substance-use problems. Adolescents have been found to hold a variety of expectancies about the potential effects of alcohol use, including: (a) will improve overall functioning, (b) will alter social behavior, (c) will improve cognitive and motor functioning, (d) will improve sexual performance, (e) will deteriorate cognitive and motor performance, (f) will increase physiological arousal, and (g) will promote relaxation (Christiansen & Goldman, 1983).

Children and adolescents hold expectancies about the effects of alcohol prior to any alcohol usage based upon modeling from their family and cultural environment (S. A. Brown, Tate, Vik, Haas, & Aarons, 1999; Christiansen, Goldman, & Inn, 1992). However, alcohol expectancies of adolescents are strongly shaped by their initial experiences using alcohol and may change sharply based upon these first experiences (Wiers, Gunning, & Sergeant, 1998). Smith,

Goldman, Greenbaum, and Christiansen (1995) found that as adolescents began to experiment with alcohol, expectancies and alcohol use influenced each other in a reciprocal positive fashion. In their sample, initial positive alcohol expectancies predicted increased alcohol consumption. Heavier drinking then led to stronger expectations about the benefits of alcohol use, which in turn amplified the relationship between expectancies and levels of alcohol use.

Adolescents who hold positive expectancies about the effects of alcohol consumption appear to be at greater risk of developing problems with alcohol use. Cooper, Frone, Russell, and Mudar (1995) found that in a community sample, adolescents who held positive expectations that alcohol consumption would relieve tension were more likely to drink to alleviate negative emotions and more likely to experience alcohol problems. Longitudinal studies have found that expectations that alcohol consumption will improve cognitive and motor functioning are risk factors for the development of problematic patterns of alcohol use in adolescence (Christiansen, Smith, Roehling, & Goldman, 1989; Mann, Chassin, & Sher, 1987; Smith & Goldman, 1995). There is also evidence that positive alcohol expectancies partially mediate the relationship between a family history of alcohol abuse and adolescents' increased risk for alcohol-use problems (Mann et al.).

Within the realm of cigarette smoking, Bauman and Chenoweth (1984) assessed the expected consequences from smoking cigarettes among 1,400 adolescents, only a small proportion of whom had ever smoked. Analyses revealed that the factor regarding expectations of negative physical and social consequences was inversely related to likelihood of smoking initiation. At the same time, expectations of pleasurable effects from smoking (e.g., "smoking will make me feel more relaxed") predicted increased smoking among those who were smokers at the study's onset. In line with this finding, Chassin, Presson, Sherman, and Edwards (1991) found that strong positive beliefs about the psychological consequences of smoking predicted smoking onset during both adolescence and adulthood.

Biologic Vulnerability

Findings indicate that substance-use disorders have a genetic component to their etiology (for reviews, see Hopfer, Crowley, & Hewitt, 2003; Tyndale, 2003; Vanyukov et al., 2003). There is substantial evidence that individuals coming from families with a history of substance-use disorders are at elevated risk of developing a substance-use disorder themselves (Chassin, Rogosch, & Barrera, 1991; Sher, 1991). However, research indicates that intergenerational transmission of vulnerability to substance-use disorders is more typical in cases in which the substance-use disorder has an early rather than late onset and when the affected individual is male (Cloninger, 1987; McGue, Pickens, & Svikis, 1992; van den Bree et al., 1998).

Twin and adoption studies have been employed to determine the relative contribution of genetic vulnerability factors to the development of substance-use problems in the general population. Findings from these studies have demonstrated that for both males and females, whereas substance-use disorders have a large heritable component, environmental factors have a moderating impact on this vulnerability (Kendler & Prescott, 1998a, 1998b; Prescott & Kendler, 1999). Among adolescents, twin and adoption studies have found that genetic factors are most predictive of vulnerability to more severe substance-use problems and dependence rather than experimentation and less problematic usage patterns (Maes et al., 1999; Rhee et al., 2003). Although promising results are emerging, the identification of specific genes involved in the etiology of substance-use disorders is not yet complete (Dick & Foroud, 2003).

There is evidence for genetic vulnerability to the development of substance-use disorders; however, the biological mechanism mediating this relationship is unknown. One mechanism that has been proposed is a genetic predisposition toward behavioral disinhibition and emotional dysregulation (Tarter et al., 2004). Findings have supported this as a potential mechanism underlying genetic vulnerability to the development of substance-use problems (McGue, Iacono, Legrand, & Elkins, 2001; Mustanski, Viken, Kaprio, & Rose, 2003). Importantly, it has also been proposed that individuals who possess genetic vulnerability to the development of substance-use disorders differ from other people in their sensitivity to the pharmacological effects of substance usage (e.g., O. F. Pomerleau, Collins, Shiffman, & C. S. Pomerleau, 1993; Schuckit, Li, Cloninger, & Dietrich, 1985).

Individuals who are genetically predisposed to substance-use problems demonstrate altered autonomic activity in response to stressors and also differ from non–genetically predisposed individuals in their sensitivity to the acute effects of substance usage (for review, see Newlin & Thomson, 1997). Some studies have indicated that children and adolescents from families with a history of substance misuse demonstrate hyperactivity following a stressor (Harden & Pihl, 1995), whereas others have indicated that these children and adolescents demonstrate autonomic hyporeactivity following a stressor (Moss, Vanyukov, & Martin, 1995; Taylor, Carlson, Iacono, Lykken, & McGue, 1999). However, it has been consistently shown that alcohol consumption has a greater stress-dampening effect in individuals with a family history of substance-use disorders compared with individuals not having a family history of substance-use disorders (Levenson, Oyama, & Meek, 1987; Zimmerman, Spring, Kunz-Ebrecht, et al., 2004; Zimmerman, Spring, Wittchen, et al., 2004). That is, genetically predisposed individuals' ingestion of alcohol reduces their autonomic stress response following an aversive stimulus to a greater degree that is observed in non–genetically predisposed individuals. Genetically predisposed people may be more sensitive to the pharmacologically reinforcing qualities of substance use and therefore be more inclined to use these substances heavily relative to non–genetically predisposed people (Newlin & Thomson, 1997). In line with this hypothesis, there is evidence that individuals with a family history of substance-use problems are more sensitive to the stimulating properties of alcohol consumption than individuals without a family history of substance-use problems (Conrod, Peterson, Pihl, & Mankowski, 1997; J. Erblich, Earleywine, B. Erblich, & Bovbjerg, 2003).

Stress-Coping Conceptualizations

Perhaps one of the most theoretically integrative and influential frameworks to appear in the past 20 years is the stress-coping model (Wills & Shiffman, 1985) of drug abuse. The model is integrative, in that it calls upon multiple interacting variables in explaining the etiology and maintenance of substance-use problems. Several important implications emerge from a stress-coping model. First, in the absence of an effective coping repertoire, adolescents are believed to be at heightened risk to engage in drug-use behavior. Indeed, a number of studies have reported that maladaptive coping styles (e.g., emotion-focused coping) are associated with problematic drug-use behavior (Cooper et al., 1995; McKee, Hinson, Wall, & Spriel, 1998). Second, based upon the tenets of the stress-coping model, affective distress (e.g., anxiety, dysphoria) should represent a risk factor in the development of drug-use problems. Consistent with this notion, the results of numerous studies point to a strong association between various indices of subjective stress and drug use and abuse (Hussong & Chassin, 1994; Kassel, Stroud, & Paronis, 2003; Schuckit, 1994). Finally, another implication of the stress-coping model and related motivational models of substance use (e.g., Cooper et al., 1995; Cox & Klinger, 1988) is that individuals' motives for using drugs should be related to drug-use behavior and consequences. People clearly self-administer drugs for a variety of reasons. Of note, those who drink alcohol, for example, as a means of coping with negative mood are more likely to drink heavily and to experience problems indicative of alcohol abuse or dependence relative to those whose drinking is governed by social or affiliative motives (Carey & Correia, 1997; Cooper et al., 1995; Williams & Clark, 1998).

Research on the relationship between coping and substance misuse must be considered in the context of a diathesis-stress model of vulnerability to substance-use problems based on the strong association between various indices of life stress and adolescent substance abuse (e.g., Wills, Sandy, Yaeger, Cleary, et al., 2001). Hence, several questions emerge from this stress-coping perspective: (a) Does stress, in the form of negative life events or other objective indices, exert a main effect on substance-use outcome, regardless of available coping skills? (b) Conversely, is coping style directly related to substance use, irrespective of life stress? (c) Does an interaction model—in which adaptive coping is believed to reduce the impact of a risk factor such as high levels of life stress—best capture the phenomenon of adolescent substance use and abuse? And finally, (d) Do these hypothesized mechanisms operate differentially at the levels of substance-use initiation versus escalation to more problematic use?

Numerous studies have found associations between various indices of psychological stress and smoking uptake. Childhood abuse and household dysfunction (Felitti et al., 1998), adverse childhood experiences (Anda et al., 1999), parental divorce (Patton et al., 1998), negative life events (Koval & Pederson, 1999), acute and chronic stressors (Koval, Pederson, Mills, McGrady, & Carvajal, 2000), and perceived stress (Dugan, Lloyd, & Lucas, 1999) have been found to increase the risk for smoking initiation. Byrne and Mazanov (1999) reported that the impact of different types of stressors on smoking uptake varied by gender, such that overall relationships were generally stronger for girls, particularly with respect to family-related stress and smoking. Importantly, affective distress and negative life events also appear to predict transition from experimental to regular smoking (Hirschman, Leventhal, & Glynn, 1984; Orlando, Ellickson, & Jinnett, 2001). Although the findings of these studies are important and clearly implicate the direct role of stress in promoting smoking initiation and escalation, the conclusions that can be drawn are limited by the lack of concurrent assessment of coping dimensions.

In one of the most rigorous tests of the stress-coping model to date, Wills, Sandy, Yaeger, Cleary, et al. (2001) employed latent growth curve analyses on a cohort followed for 2 years, reporting that behavioral coping (an index of coping engagement) was inversely related to initial level of adolescent substance use and growth over time in peer use. Three indices of disengagement coping (anger coping, helpless coping, and hangout coping) were positively correlated to initial levels of peer use and adolescent use and to growth in adolescent use over time. Life stress was positively related to initial levels for peer use and adolescent use and to growth in adolescent use. Finally, tests of moderation indicated that effects of coping were significantly greater at higher levels of stress. Importantly, these interactions were consistent with the results of previous investigations (e.g., Cooper, Russell, Skinner, Frone, & Mudar, 1992; Sandler, Tein, &

West, 1994). Such findings help to elucidate the mechanisms underlying both drug-use initiation and escalation and, as such, represent an important step in the testing of dynamic, integrative models of adolescent substance use and abuse.

METHODOLOGICAL ADVANCES IN UNDERSTANDING ADOLESCENT SUBSTANCE USE

The concept of a dynamic, developmental model of adolescent substance use requires a relatively complex approach to both data collection and analysis in which researchers need to consider interactions among risk factors, contexts, and substance use as they all change over time and as individuals progress through adolescence and young adulthood. For example, at certain points in adolescence, family influences on substance use may be stronger than peer influences. Or mood may affect progression to dependency, but not initial use. The result of these dynamic interplays is a heterogeneous set of individualized pathways or trajectories of use across adolescence. Both theories and analytic methods need to consider the dynamic interplay among these factors, including identifying mediating and moderating influences and common patterns of use. Fortunately, recent advances in analytical approaches to longitudinal data have allowed researchers to move beyond simple consideration of prospective predictors of substance use from one time point to another, to consideration of factors such as the rate and patterning of change in substance use and predictors of those patterns. Identifying patterns of change or pathways to dependence may ultimately provide better information for tailoring both prevention and intervention programs to high-risk groups of adolescents.

One of the more notable analytical advances has been the use of trajectory analysis (Nagin, 1999) or latent growth mixture modeling (Muthen, 1998) to identify distinct developmental patterns of substance use among heterogeneous samples. These approaches assume that a relatively small set of distinct behavioral patterns is present in the population of interest and that these patterns can be identified statistically. For example, Chassin, Presson, Sherman, and Pitts (2000) identified six smoking trajectory groups using longitudinal data spanning ages 11–31. These groups were: (a) stable abstainers; (b) erratic smokers (relapsers and remitters); (c) an early stable group (relatively early age of onset between 12 and 13 and averaging 1–10 cigarettes a day by age 15); (d) a late stable group (later age of onset, infrequent smoking in high school, but transitioning to weekly smoking at age 18); (e) an experimenter group (similar to the early stable group, but never escalated to heavy smoking); and (f) a quitter group (started midway between early and late groups, and stopped smoking). Of note, Chassin et al. (2000) found that parental smoking was more associated with smoking that persisted into adulthood and less with adolescent experimentation. Colder et al. (2001) used latent growth mixture modeling to identify five distinct longitudinal patterns, including an early rapid escalator group characterized by early escalation (by age 13) that rapidly increased to heavy smoking by age 16. Soldz and Cui (2002) identified a very similar set of six longitudinal patterns of smoking from 6th through 12th grade, and Orlando, Tucker, Ellickson, and Klein (2004) also found six patterns similar to those of these previous groups. However, these six smoking trajectory groups ultimately reduced to two by age 23: low- and high-frequency users. These findings point to critical periods of intervention, such as the transition from high school to young adulthood, when the group of smokers labeled as late increasers was most at risk of progressing into a heavier pattern of use.

Beyond the use of trajectory analyses, there have been other notable advances in approaches to the analysis of longitudinal data that have been of particular note for studying contextual influences on adolescent substance use. As noted earlier in this chapter, adolescent substance use may be influenced by a series of multilevel contexts. For example, most adolescents live in families, attend schools, live in neighborhoods with varying social/economic/political forces, and are exposed to a host of media and peer influences. Thorough understanding of adolescent substance use and its patterns over time requires consideration of the joint influence of these multiple contexts, along with the potential for time-varying covariates and interactions. Statistical models for the analysis of these types of multilevel data have been developed under a variety of names: random-effects models (Laird & Ware, 1982), hierarchical linear models (Bryk & Raudenbush, 1987), and multilevel models (Goldstein, 1987). These approaches also allow for time-varying covariates, thus providing a way to examine questions about the dynamic nature of both explanatory variables and outcomes within a developmental, longitudinal framework.

Finally, methodological advances in data collection techniques also provide new opportunities for addressing questions about contextual influences on substance use in ways that have not been possible before. Substance use among adolescents is highly context dependent. Ecological momentary assessments (EMA), or real-time data capture, can provide an excellent window into the lives of adolescents and a way of examining the specific contextual influences on substance use. EMA allows researchers to capture more accurately than other measurement modalities the frequency, intensity, and tone of social interactions and moods surrounding substance use, as they occur. Nearly all research on adolescent substance use to date has relied heavily on adolescents' retrospective recall of their behavior and the contexts or antecedents of their substance use. EMA allows researchers to assess substance use as it occurs and in the context in which it occurs. Several recent studies have used EMA methods to study adolescent smoking and have demonstrated its feasibility and value in capturing moods and affect surrounding smoking (Mermelstein, Hedeker, Flay, & Shiffman, in press; Whalen, Jamner, Henker, & Delfino, 2001). Thus, EMA may be a valuable tool for studying the microcontextual influences on adolescent substance use.

In sum, there has been a huge surge of developments methodologically and in the analysis of longitudinal data over the past decade that now allow researchers to more effectively address key questions about the dynamic, longitudinal interplay of context, risk factor, and developmental influences on adolescent substance use than has previously been done. Future research will need to incorporate these newer methodological techniques to expand our knowledge of the patterns and processes that lead to the development of dependence and abuse. Understanding more about these patterns and varying influences at different stages in adolescence has the potential to give us leverage points for more targeted and tailored interventions.

REFERENCES

Abrantes, A. M., Brown, S. A., & Tomlinson, K. L. (2003). Psychiatric comorbidity among inpatient substance abusing adolescents. *Journal of Child and Adolescent Substance Abuse, 13,* 83–101.

American Psychiatric Association. (1994). *Diagnostic and statistical manual of mental disorders* (4th ed.). Washington, DC: Author.

Anda, R. F., Croft, J. B., Felitti, V. J., Nordenberg, D., Giles, W. H., Williamson, D. F., et al. (1999). Adverse childhood experiences and smoking during adolescence and adulthood. *Journal of the American Medical Association, 282,* 1652–1658.

Armstrong, T. D., & Costello, E. J. (2002). Community studies on adolescent substance use, abuse, or dependence and psychiatric comorbidity. *Journal of Consulting and Clinical Psychology, 70,* 1224–1239.

Arnett, J. J. (1999). Adolescent storm and stress, reconsidered. *American Psychologist, 54,* 317–326.

Bauman, K. E., & Chenoweth, R. L. (1984). The relationship between the consequences adolescents expect from smoking and their behavior: A factor analysis with panel data. *Journal of Applied Social Psychology, 14,* 28–41.

Bauman, K. E., & Ennett, S. T. (1996). On the importance of peer influence for adolescent drug use: Commonly neglected considerations. *Addiction, 91,* 185–198.

Brook, J. S., Cohen, P., & Brook, D. W. (1998). Longitudinal study of co-occurring psychiatric disorders and substance use. *Journal of the American Academy of Child and Adolescent Psychiatry, 37,* 322–330.

Brown, R. A., Lewinsohn, P. M., Seeley, J. R., & Wagner, E. F. (1996). Cigarette smoking, major depression, and other psychiatric disorders among adolescents. *Journal of the American Academy of Child and Adolescent Psychiatry, 35,* 1602–1610.

Brown, S. A., Tate, S. R., Vik, P. W., Haas, A. L., & Aarons, G. A. (1999). Modeling of alcohol use mediates the effect of family history of alcoholism on adolescent alcohol expectancies. *Experimental & Clinical Psychopharmacology, 7,* 20–27.

Bryk, A. S., & Raudenbush, S. W. (1987). Application of hierarchical linear models to assessing change. *Psychological Bulletin, 101,* 147–158.

Burgess, P. W., Alderman, N., Evans, J., Emslie, H., & Wilson, B. A. (1998). The ecological validity of tests of executive function. *Journal of the International Neuropsychological Society, 4,* 547–558.

Burke, J. F., Burke, K. C., & Rae, D. S. (1994). Increased rates of drug abuse and dependence after onset of mood or anxiety disorders in adolescents. *Hospital and Community Psychiatry, 45,* 451–455.

Burkstein, O. G., Glancy, L. J., & Kaminer, Y. (1992). Patterns of affective comorbidity in a clinical population of dually diagnosed adolescent substance abusers. *Journal of the American Academy of Child and Adolescent Psychiatry, 31,* 1041–1045.

Buss, A., & Plomin, R. (1984). *Temperament: Early developing personality traits.* Hillsdale, NJ: Lawrence Erlbaum.

Byrne, D. G., & Mazanov, J. (1999). Sources of adolescent stress, smoking and the use of other drugs. *Stress Medicine, 15,* 215–227.

Carey, K. B., & Correia, C. J. (1997). Drinking motives predict alcohol-related problems in college students. *Journal of Studies on Alcohol, 58,* 100–105.

Cartensen, L., Pasupathi, M., Mayr, U., & Nesselroade, J. (2000). Emotional experience in everyday life across the adult life span. *Journal of Personality and Social Psychology, 79,* 644–655.

Chassin, L. A., Pillow, D. R., Curran, P. J., Molina, B., & Barrera, M. (1993). Relation of parental alcoholism to early adolescent substance use: A test of three mediating mechanisms. *Journal of Abnormal Psychology, 102,* 3–19.

Chassin, L., Presson, C. C., Sherman, S. J., & Edwards, D. A. (1991). Four pathways to young-adult smoking status: Adolescent social-psychological antecedents in a Midwestern community sample. *Health Psychology, 10,* 409–418.

Chassin, L., Presson, C. C., Sherman, S. J., & Pitts, S. C. (2000). The natural history of cigarette smoking from adolescence to adulthood in a Midwestern community sample: Multiple trajectories and their psychosocial correlates. *Health Psychology, 19,* 223–231.

Chassin, L., Rogosch, R., & Barrera, M. (1991). Substance use symptomatology among adolescent children of alcoholics. *Journal of Abnormal Psychology, 100,* 449–463.

Christiansen, B. A., & Goldman, M. S. (1983). Alcohol-related expectancies versus demographic/background variables in the prediction of adolescent drinking. *Journal of Consulting and Clinical Psychology, 51,* 249–257.

Christiansen, B. A., Goldman, M. S., & Inn, A. (1982). Development of alcohol-related expectancies in adolescents: Separating pharmacological from social-learning influences. *Journal of Consulting and Clinical Psychology, 50,* 336–344.

Christiansen, B. A., Smith, G. T., Roehling, P. V., & Goldman, M. S. (1989). Using alcohol expectancies to predict adolescent drinking behavior after one year. *Journal of Consulting and Clinical Psychology, 57,* 93–99.

Cicchetti, D., & Luthar, S. S. (1999). Developmental approaches to substance use and abuse. *Development and Psychopathology, 11,* 655–656.

Cicchetti, D., & Rogosch, F. A. (2002). A developmental psychopathology perspective on adolescence. *Journal of Consulting and Clinical Psychology, 70,* 6–20.

Clark, D. B., Parker, A. M., & Lynch, K. G. (1999). Psychopathology and substance-related problems during early adolescence: A survival analysis. *Journal of Clinical Child Psychology, 28,* 333–341.

Cloninger, C. R. (1987). Neurogenetic adaptive mechanisms in alcoholism. *Science, 236,* 410–416.

Cohen, D. A., Richardson, J., & LaBree, L. (1994). Parenting behaviors and the onset of smoking and alcohol use: A longitudinal study. *Pediatrics, 94,* 368–375.

Colder, C., Mehta, P., Balanda, K., Campbell, R. T., Mayhew, K., Stanton, W. R., et al. (2001). Identifying trajectories of adolescent smoking: An application of latent growth mixture modeling. *Health Psychology, 20,* 127–135.

Compas, B. E., Hinden, B. R., & Gerhardt, C. A. (1995). Adolescent development: Pathways and processes of risk and resilience. *Annual Review of Psychology, 46,* 265–293.

Conrad, K. M., Flay, B. R., & Hill, D. (1992). Why children start smoking cigarettes: Predictors of onset. *British Journal of Addiction, 87,* 1711–1724.

Conrod, P. J., Peterson, J. B., Pihl, R. O., & Mankowski, S. (1997). Biphasic effects of alcohol on heart rate are influenced by alcoholic family history and rate of alcohol ingestion. *Alcoholism: Clinical and Experimental Research, 21,* 140–149.

Cooper, M. L., Frone, M. R., Russell, M., & Mudar, P. (1995). Drinking to regulate positive and negative emotions: A motivational model of alcohol use. *Journal of Personality and Social Psychology, 69,* 990–1005.

Cooper, M. L., Russell, M., Skinner, J. B., Frone, M. R., & Mudar, P. (1992). Stress and alcohol use: Moderating effects of gender, coping, and alcohol expectancies. *Journal of Abnormal Psychology, 101,* 139–152.

Costello, E. J., Erkanli, A., Federman, E., & Angold, A. (1999). Development of psychiatric comorbidity with substance abuse in adolescents: Effects of timing and sex. *Journal of Clinical Child Psychology, 28,* 298–311.

Cox, W. M., & Klinger, E. (1988). A motivational model of alcohol use. *Journal of Abnormal Psychology, 97,* 168–180.

Crawford, A. M., Pentz, M. A., Chou, C., Li, C., & Dwyer, J. H. (2003). Parallel developmental trajectories of sensation-seeking and regular substance use in adolescents. *Psychology of Addictive Behavior, 17,* 179–192.

Damasio, A. R. (1998). The somatic marker hypothesis and the possible functions of the prefrontal cortex. In A. C. Roberts, T. W. Robbins, & L. Weiskrantz (Eds.), *The prefrontal cortex* (pp. 36–50). Oxford, UK: Oxford University Press.

Darling, N., & Cumsille, P. (2003). Theory, measurement, and methods in the study of family influences on adolescent smoking. *Addiction, 98*(Suppl. 1), 21–36.

Dawes, M. A., Antelman, S. M., Vanyukov, M. M., Giancola, P., Tarter, R. E., Susman, E. J., Mezzich, A., & Clark, D. B. (2000). Developmental sources of variation in liability to adolescent substance use disorders. *Drug and Alcohol Dependence, 61,* 3–14.

Dick, D. M., & Foroud, T. (2003). Candidate genes for alcohol dependence: A review of genetic evidence from human studies. *Alcoholism: Clinical & Experimental Research, 27,* 868–879.

Donovan, J. E., Jessor, R., & Costa, F. M. (1991). Adolescent health behavior and conventionality-unconventionality: An extension of problem-behavior theory. *Health Psychology, 10,* 52–61.

Dugan, S., Lloyd, B., & Lucas, K. (1999). Stress and coping as determinants of adolescent smoking behavior. *Journal of Applied Social Psychology, 29,* 870–888.

Ennett, S. T., & Bauman, K. E. (1994). The contribution of influence and selection to adolescent peer group homogeneity: The case of adolescent cigarette smoking. *Journal of Personality and Social Psychology, 67,* 653–663.

Erblich, J., Earleywine, M., Erblich, B., & Bovbjerg, D. H. (2003). Biphasic stimulant and sedative effects of ethanol: Are children of alcoholics really different. *Addictive Behaviors, 28,* 1129–1139.

Escobedo, L. G., Reddy, M., & Giovino, G. A. (1998). The relationship between depressive symptoms and cigarette smoking in US adolescents. *Addiction, 93,* 433–440.

Felitti, V. J., Anda, R. F., Nordenberg, D., Williamson, D. F., Spitz, A. M., Edwards, V., et al. (1998). Relationship of childhood abuse and household dysfunction to many of the leading causes of death in adults: The Adverse Childhood Experiences (ACE) Study. *American Journal of Preventive Medicine, 14,* 245–258.

Flory, K., & Lynam, D. R. (2003). The relation between attention deficit hyperactivity disorder and substance abuse: What role does conduct disorder play. *Clinical Child and Family Psychology Review, 6,* 1–16.

Flory, K., Lynam, D., Milich, R., Leukefeld, C., & Clayton, R. (2004). Early adolescent through young adult alcohol and marijuana use trajectories: Early predictors, young adult outcomes, and predictive utility. *Development and Psychopathology, 16,* 193–213.

Garber, J., Keiley, M. K., & Martin, N. C. (2002). Developmental trajectories of adolescents' depressive symptoms: Predictors of change. *Journal of Consulting and Clinical Psychology, 70,* 79–95.

Giaconia, R. M., Reinherz, H. Z., Hauf, A. C., Paradis, A. D., Wasserman, M. S., & Langhammer, D. M. (2000). Comorbidity of substance use and post-traumatic stress disorders in a community sample of adolescents. *American Journal of Orthopsychiatry, 70,* 253–262.

Giancola, P., Moss, H., Martin, C., Kirisci, L., & Tarter, R. (1996). Executive cognitive functioning predicts reactive aggression in boys at high risk for substance dependence: A prospective study. *Alcoholism: Clinical and Experimental Research, 20,* 740–744.

Giancola, P. R., & Parker, A. M. (2001). A six-year prospective study of pathways toward drug use in adolescent boys with and without a family history of a substance use disorder. *Journal of Studies on Alcohol, 62,* 166–178.

Giancola, P. R., Shoal, G. D., & Mezzich, A. C. (2001). Constructive thinking, executive functioning, antisocial behavior, and drug use involvement in adolescent females with a substance use disorder. *Experimental & Clinical Psychopharmacology, 9,* 215–227.

Giancola, P. R., & Tarter, R. E. (1999). Executive cognitive functioning and risk for substance abuse. *Psychological Science, 10,* 203–205.

Glantz, M. D. (1992). A developmental psychopathology model of drug abuse vulnerability. In M. D. Glantz & R. Pickens (Eds.), *Vulnerability to drug abuse* (pp. 389–418). Washington, DC: American Psychological Association.

Glantz, M. D., & Leshner, A. I. (2000). Drug abuse and developmental psychopathology. *Development and Psychopathology, 12,* 795–814.

Goldman, M. S., Del Boca, F. K., & Darkes, J. (1999). Alcohol expectancy theory: The application of cognitive neuroscience. In K. E. Leonard & H. T. Blane (Eds.), *Psychological theories of drinking and alcoholism* (pp. 203–246). New York: Guilford Press.

Goldstein, H. (1987). *Multilevel models in educational and social research.* New York: Oxford University Press.

Goodwin, R. D., Fergusson, D. M., & Horwood, L. J. (2004). Association between anxiety disorders and substance use disorders among young persons: Results of a 21-year longitudinal study. *Journal of Psychiatric Research, 38,* 295–304.

Graber, J. A. (2003). Puberty in context. In C. Hayward (Ed.), *Gender differences at puberty* (pp. 307–325). New York: Cambridge University Press.

Grunbaum, J., Kann, L., Kinchen, S., Ross, J., Hawkins, J., Lowry, R., et al. (2004, May 21). Youth Risk Behavior surveillance: United States, 2003. *Centers for Disease Control and Prevention Morbidity and Mortality Weekly Report, 53* (SS02), 1–96.

Hall, G. S. (1904). *Adolescence: Its psychology and its relation to physiology, anthropology, sociology, sex, crime, religion, and education.* Englewood Cliffs, NJ: Prentice Hall.

Harden, P. W., & Pihl, R. O. (1995). Cognitive function, cardiovascular reactivity, and behavior in boys at high risk for alcoholism. *Journal of Abnormal Psychology, 104,* 94–103.

Harrison, P. A., Fulkerson, J. A., & Beebe, T. J. (1998). *DSM-IV* substance use disorder criteria for adolescents: A critical examination based on a statewide school survey. *American Journal of Psychiatry, 155,* 486–492.

Hasin, D., & Paykin, A. (1998). Dependence symptoms but no diagnosis: Diagnostic orphans in a "community" sample. *Drug and Alcohol Dependence, 50,* 19–26.

Hawkins, J. D., Catalano, R. F., & Miller, J. Y. (1992). Risk and protective factors for alcohol and other drug problems in adolescence and early adulthood: Implications for substance abuse prevention. *Psychological Bulletin, 112,* 64–105.

Henderson, M. J., Galen, L. W., & DeLuca, J. W. (1998). Temperament style and substance abuse characteristics. *Substance Abuse, 19*(2), 61–70.

Hirschman, R. S., Leventhal, H., & Glynn, K. (1984). The development of smoking behavior: Conceptualization and supportive cross-sectional survey data. *Journal of Applied Social Psychology, 14,* 184–206.

Hopfer, C. J., Crowley, T. J., & Hewitt, J. K. (2003). Review of twin and adoption studies of adolescent substance use. *Journal of the American Academy of Child & Adolescent Psychiatry, 42,* 710–719.

Hussong, A. M., & Chassin, L. (1994). The stress-negative affect model of adolescent alcohol use: Disaggregating negative affect. *Journal of Studies on Alcohol, 55,* 707–718.

Jessor, R. (1987). Problem-behavior theory, psychosocial development, and adolescent problem drinking. *British Journal of Addiction, 82,* 331–342.

Jessor, R., & Jessor, S. (1980). A social-psychological framework for studying drug use. *NIDA Research Monograph, 30,* 102–109.

Johnson, J. G., Cohen, P., Pine, D. S., Klein, D. F., Kasen, S., & Brook, J. S. (2000). Association between cigarette smoking and anxiety disorders during adolescence and early adulthood. *JAMA: Journal of the American Medical Association, 284,* 2348–2351.

Johnson, R. J., & Kaplan, H. B. (1990). Stability of psychological symptoms: Drug use consequences and intervening processes. *Journal of Health & Social Behavior, 31,* 277–291.

Johnston, L. D., O'Malley, P. M., Bachman, J. G., & Schulenberg, J. E. (2004). *Monitoring the Future national results on adolescent drug use: Overview of key findings, 2003.* Bethesda, MD: National Institute on Drug Abuse.

Kandel, D. B., Davies, M., Karus, D., & Yamaguchi, K. (1986). The consequences in young adulthood of adolescent drug involvement. *Archives of General Psychiatry, 43,* 746–754.

Kandel, D. B., Johnson, J. G., Bird, H. R., Weissman, M. M., Goodman, S. H., Lahey, B. B., et al. (1999). Psychiatric comorbidity among adolescents with substance use disorders: Findings from the MECA study. *Journal of the American Academy of Child and Adolescent Psychiatry, 38,* 693–699.

Kassel, J. D., Stroud, L. R., & Paronis, C. A. (2003). Smoking, stress, and negative affect: Correlation, causation, and context across stages of smoking. *Psychological Bulletin, 129,* 270–304.

Kendler, K. S., & Prescott, C. A. (1998a). Cannabis use, abuse, and dependence in a population-based sample of female twins. *American Journal of Psychiatry, 155,* 1016–1022.

Kendler, K. S., & Prescott, C. A. (1998b). Cocaine use, abuse and dependence in a population-based sample of female twins. *British Journal of Psychiatry, 173,* 343–350.

Koval, J. J., & Pederson, L. J. (1999). Stress-coping and other psychosocial risk factors: A model for smoking in grade 6 students. *Addictive Behaviors, 24,* 207–218.

Koval, J. J., Pederson, L. L., Mills, C. A., McGrady, G. A., & Carvajal, S. C. (2000). Models of the relationship of stress, depression, and other psychosocial factors to smoking behavior: A comparison of a cohort of students in grades 6 and 8. *Preventive Medicine, 30,* 463–477.

Krueger, R. F., Hicks, B. M., Patrick, C. J., Carlson, S. R., Iacono, W. G., & McGue, M. (2002). Etiologic connections among substance dependence, antisocial behavior and personality: Modeling the externalizing spectrum. *Journal of Abnormal Psychology, 111,* 411–424.

Laird, N. M., & Ware, J. H. (1982). Random effects models for longitudinal data. *Biometrics, 38,* 963–974.

Langenbucher, J. W., & Martin, C. S. (1996). Alcohol abuse: Adding content to category. *Alcoholism: Clinical and Experimental Research, 20*(Suppl.), 270A–275A.

Larson, R. W., Moneta, G., Richards, M. H., & Wilson, S. (2002). Continuity, stability and change in daily emotional experience across adolescence. *Child Development, 73,* 1151–1165.

Larson, R. W., Richards, M. H., Moneta, G., Holmbeck, G., & Duckett, E. (1996). Changes in adolescents' daily interactions with their families from ages 10 to 18: Disengagement and transformation. *Developmental Psychology, 32,* 744–754.

Levenson, R. W., Oyama, O. N., & Meek, P. S. (1987). Greater reinforcement from alcohol for those at risk: Parental risk, personality risk, and gender. *Journal of Abnormal Psychology, 96,* 242–253.

Lewinsohn, P. M., Rohde, P., & Seeley, J. R. (1996). Alcohol consumption in high school adolescents: Frequency of use and dimensional structure of associated problems. *Addiction, 91,* 375–390.

Lewis, D. A. (1997). Development of the prefrontal cortex during adolescence: Insights into vulnerable neural circuits in schizophrenia. *Neuropsychopharmacology, 16,* 385–398.

Loeber, R., Stouthamer-Loeber, M., & White, H. R. (1999). Developmental aspects of delinquency and internalizing problems and their association with persistent juvenile substance use between ages 7 and 18. *Journal of Clinical Child Psychology, 28,* 322–332.

Lynskey, M. T., & Fergusson, D. M. (1995). Childhood conduct problems, attention deficit behaviors, and adolescent alcohol, tobacco, and illicit drug use. *Journal of Abnormal Child Psychology, 23,* 281–302.

Maes, H. H., Woodard, C. E., Murrelle, L., Meyer, J. M., Silberg, J. L., Hewitt, J. K., et al. (1999). Tobacco, alcohol and drug use in eight- to sixteen-year-old twins: The Virginia Twin Study of Adolescent Behavioral Development. *Journal of Studies on Alcohol, 60,* 293–305.

Mann, L. M., Chassin, L., & Sher, K. J. (1987). Alcohol expectancies and the risk for alcoholism. *Journal of Consulting & Clinical Psychology, 55,* 411–417.

Martin, C. S., Kaczynski, N. A., Maisto, S. A., Bukstein, O. M., & Moss, H. B. (1995). Patterns of *DSM-IV* alcohol abuse and dependence symptoms in adolescent drinkers. *Journal of Studies on Alcohol, 56,* 672–680.

Martin, C. S., Langenbucher, J. W., Kaczynski, N. A., & Chung, T. (1996). Staging in the onset of *DSM-IV* alcohol abuse and dependence symptoms in adolescent drinkers. *Journal of Studies on Alcohol, 57,* 549–558.

Martin, C. S., & Winters, K. C. (1998). Diagnosis and assessment of alcohol use disorders among adolescents. *Alcohol Health and Research World, 22,* 95–106.

Mayhew, K. P., Flay, B. R., & Mott, J. A. (2000). Stages in the development of adolescent smoking. *Drug and Alcohol Dependence, 59*(Suppl. 1), 61–81.

McGue, M., Iacono, W. G., Legrand, L. N., & Elkins, I. (2001). Origins and consequences of age at first drink: II. Familial risk and heritability. *Alcoholism: Clinical & Experimental Research, 25,* 1166–1173.

McGue, M., Pickens, R. W., & Svikis, D. S. (1992). Sex and age effects on the inheritance of alcohol problems: A twin study. *Journal of Abnormal Psychology, 101,* 3–17.

McKee, S. A., Hinson, R. E., Wall, A. M., & Spriel, P. (1998). Alcohol outcome expectancies and coping styles as predictors of alcohol use in young adults. *Addictive Behaviors, 23*, 17–22.

Merikangas, K. R., Swendsen, J. D., Preisig, M. A., & Chazan, R. Z. (1998). Psychopathology and temperament in parents and offspring: Results of a family study. *Journal of Affective Disorders, 51*, 63–74.

Mermelstein, R., Hedeker, D., Flay, B., & Shiffman, S. (in press). Real time data capture and adolescent cigarette smoking. In A. Stone, S. Shiffman, & A. Atienza (Eds.), *The science of real-time data capture: Self-report in health research*. Oxford, UK: Oxford University Press.

Moss, H. B., Vanyukov, M. M., & Martin, C. S. (1995). Salivary cortisol responses and the risk for substance abuse in prepubertal boys. *Biological Psychiatry, 38*, 546–555.

Mustanski, B. S., Viken, R. J., Kaprio, J., & Rose, R. J. (2003). Genetic influences on the association between personality risk factors and alcohol use and abuse. *Journal of Abnormal Psychology, 112*, 282–289.

Muthen, B. (1998). Second-generation structural equation modeling with a combination of categorical and continuous latent variables: New opportunities for latent class/latent growth modeling. In L. M. Collins & A. Sayer (Eds.), *New methods for the analysis of change* (pp. 291–322). Washington, DC: American Psychological Association.

Myers, M. G., Aarons, G. A., Tomlinson, K., & Stein, M. B. (2003). Social anxiety, negative affectivity, and substance use among high school students. *Psychology of Addictive Behaviors, 17*, 277–283.

Myers, M. G., Stewart, D. G., & Brown, S. A. (1998). Progression from conduct disorder to antisocial personality disorder following treatment for adolescent substance abuse. *American Journal of Psychiatry, 155*, 479–485.

Nagin, D. S. (1999). Analyzing developmental trajectories: A semiparametric group-based approach. *Psychological Methods, 4*, 139–157.

Najam, N., Moss, H. B., Kirisci, L., & Tarter, R. E. (1997). Executive cognitive functioning predicts drug use in youth. *Journal of the Indian Academy of Applied Psychology, 23*, 3–12.

Newlin, D. B., & Thomson, J. B. (1997). Alcohol challenge with sons of alcoholics: A critical review and analysis. In A. G. Marlatt & G. R. VandenBos (Eds.), *Addictive behaviors: Readings on etiology, prevention, and treatment* (pp. 534–578). Washington, DC: American Psychological Association.

Nigg, J. T., Glass, J. M., Wong, M. M., Poon, E., Jester, J. M., Fitzgerald, H. E., et al. (2004). Neuropsychological executive functioning in children at elevated risk for alcoholism: Findings in early adolescence. *Journal of Abnormal Psychology, 113*, 302–314.

Oetting, E. R., & Beauvais, F. (1987). Peer cluster theory, socialization characteristics, and adolescent drug use: A path analysis. *Journal of Counseling Psychology, 34*, 205–213.

Oetting, E. R., & Donnermeyer, J. F. (1998). Primary socialization theory: The etiology of drug use and deviance: I. *Substance Use and Misuse, 33*, 995–1026.

Orlando, M., Ellickson, P. L., & Jinnett, K. (2001). The temporal relationship between emotional distress and cigarette smoking during adolescence and young adulthood. *Journal of Consulting and Clinical Psychology, 69*, 959–970.

Orlando, M., Tucker, J. S., Ellickson, P. L., & Klein, D. J. (2004). Developmental trajectories of cigarette smoking and their correlates from early adolescence to young adulthood. *Journal of Consulting and Clinical Psychology, 72,* 400–410.

Patton, G. C., Carlin, J. B., Coffey, C., Wolfe, R., Hibbert, M., & Bowes, G. (1998). Depression, anxiety, and smoking initiation: A prospective study over 3 years. *American Journal of Public Health, 88,* 1518–1522.

Pihl, R. O., Paylan, S. S., Gentes-Hawn, A., & Hoaken, P. N. S. (2003). Alcohol affects executive cognitive functioning differentially on the ascending versus descending limb of the blood alcohol concentration curve. *Alcoholism: Clinical & Experimental Research, 27,* 773–779.

Pihl, R. O., Peterson, J., & Finn, P. R. (1990). Inherited predisposition to alcoholism: Characteristics of sons of male alcoholics. *Journal of Abnormal Psychology, 99,* 291–301.

Pollock, N. K., & Martin, C. S. (1999). Diagnostic orphans: Adolescents with alcohol symptoms who do not qualify for *DSM-IV* abuse or dependence diagnoses. *American Journal of Psychiatry, 156,* 897–901.

Pomerleau, O. F., Collins, A. C., Shiffman, S., & Pomerleau, C. S. (1993). Why some people smoke and others do not: New perspectives. *Journal of Consulting and Clinical Psychology, 61,* 723–731.

Prescott, C. A., & Kendler, K. S. (1999). Genetic and environmental contributions to alcohol abuse and dependence in a population-based sample of male twins. *American Journal of Psychiatry, 156,* 34–40.

Reebye, P., Moretti, M. M., & Lessard, J. C. (1995). Conduct disorder and substance use disorder: Comorbidity in a clinical sample of preadolescents and adolescents. *Canadian Journal of Psychiatry, 40,* 313–319.

Rhee, S. H., Hewitt, J. K., Young, S. E., Corley, R. P., Crowley, T. J., & Stallings, M. C. (2003). Genetic and environmental influences on substance initiation, use, and problem use in adolescents. *Archives of General Psychiatry, 60,* 1256–1264.

Robins, L. N., & Przybeck, T. R. (1993). Age of onset of drug use as a factor in drug and other disorders. *Drug and Alcohol Dependence, 33,* 129–137.

Rohde, P., Lewinsohn, P. M., & Seeley, J. R. (1991). Comorbidity of unipolar depression: II. Comorbidity with other mental disorders in adolescents and adults. *Journal of Abnormal Psychology, 100,* 214–222.

Rohde, P., Lewinsohn, P. M., & Seeley, J. R. (1996). Psychiatric comorbidity with problematic alcohol use in high school students. *Journal of the American Academy of Child and Adolescent Psychiatry, 35,* 101–109.

Rothbart, M. K., & Ahadi, S. A. (1994). Temperament and the development of personality. *Journal of Abnormal Psychology, 103,* 55–66.

Sale, E., Sambrano, S., Springer, J. F., & Turner, C. W. (2003). Risk, protection, and substance use in adolescents: A multi-site model. *Journal of Drug Education, 33,* 91–105.

Sandler, I. N., Tein, J. Y., & West, S. G. (1994). Coping, stress, and psychological symptoms of children of divorce. *Child Development, 65,* 1744–1763.

Schuckit, M. A. (1994). Alcohol and depression: A clinical perspective. *Acta Psychiatrica Scandinavica, 89,* 28–32.

Schuckit, M. A., Li, T. K., Cloninger, C. R., & Dietrich, R. A. (1985). Genetics of alcoholism. *Alcoholism: Clinical and Experimental Research, 9,* 475–492.

Sher, K. J. (1991). *Children of alcoholics.* Chicago: University of Chicago Press.

Shilts, L. (1991). The relationship of early adolescent substance use to extracurricular activities, peer pressure, and personal attitudes. *Adolescence, 26,* 613–617.

Shoal, G. D., & Giancola, P. R. (2001). Executive cognitive functioning, negative affectivity, and drug use in adolescent boys with and without a family history of a substance use disorder. *Journal of Child & Adolescent Substance Abuse, 10,* 111–121.

Simons-Morton, B. (2004). Prospective association of peer influence, school engagement, drinking expectancies, and parent expectations with drinking initiation among sixth graders. *Addictive Behaviors, 29,* 299–309.

Smith, G. T., & Goldman, M. S. (1995). Alcohol expectancy theory and the identification of high-risk adolescents. In G. M. Boyle, J. Howard, & R. A. Zucker (Eds.), *Alcohol problems among adolescents: Current directions in prevention research* (pp. 85–104). Hillsdale, NJ: Lawrence Erlbaum.

Smith, G. T., Goldman, M. S., Greenbaum, P. E., & Christiansen, B. A. (1995). Expectancy for social facilitation from drinking: The divergent paths of high-expectancy and low-expectancy adolescents. *Journal of Abnormal Psychology, 104,* 32–40.

Soldz, S., & Cui, X. (2002). Pathways through adolescent smoking: A 7-year longitudinal grouping analysis. *Health Psychology, 21,* 495–504.

Sonntag, H., Wittchen, H. U., Hofler, M., Kessler, R. C., & Stein, M. B. (2000). Are social fears and DSM-IV social anxiety disorder associated with smoking and nicotine dependence in adolescents and young adults. *European Psychiatry, 15,* 67–74.

Spear, L. P. (2000). The adolescent brain and age-related behavioral manifestations. *Neuroscience and Biobehavioral Reviews, 24,* 417–463.

Spear, L. P. (2002). Alcohol's effects on adolescents. *Alcohol Research & Health, 26,* 87–91.

Steinberg, L., Dahl, R., Keating, D., Kupfer, D., Masten, A. & Pine, D. (2004). The study of developmental psychopathology in adolescence: Integrating affective neuroscience with the study of context. In D. Cicchetti (Ed.), *Handbook of developmental psychopathology* (pp. 2–46). New York: Wiley.

Stice, E., Myers, M. G., & Brown, S. A. (1998). A longitudinal grouping analysis of adolescent substance use escalation and de-escalation. *Psychology of Addictive Behaviors, 12,* 14–27.

Sutherland, I., & Shepherd, J. P. (2001). Social dimensions of adolescent substance use. *Addiction, 96,* 445–458.

Tapert, S. F., Baratta, M. V., Abrantes, A. M., & Brown, S. A. (2002). Attention dysfunction predicts substance involvement in community youths. *Journal of the American Academy of Child & Adolescent Psychiatry, 41,* 680–686.

Tarter, R. E. (1988). Are there inherited behavioral traits that predispose to substance abuse? *Journal of Consulting and Clinical Psychology, 56,* 189–196.

Tarter, R. E., Kirisci, L., Habeych, M., Reynolds, M., & Vanyukov, M. (2004). Neurobehavior disinhibition in childhood predisposes boys to substance use disorder by young adulthood: Direct and mediated etiologic pathways. *Drug and Alcohol Dependence, 73,* 121–132.

Tarter, R. E., Vanyukov, M., Giancola, P., Dawes, M., Blackson, T., Mezzich, A., et al. (1999). Etiology of early age onset substance use disorder: A maturational perspective. *Development and Psychopathology, 11,* 657–683.

Taylor, J., Carlson, S. R., Iacono, W. G., Lykken, D. T., & McGue, M. (1999). Individual differences in electrodermal responsivity to predictable aversive stimuli and substance dependence. *Psychophysiology, 36,* 193–198.

Tyndale, R. F. (2003). Genetics of alcohol and tobacco use in humans. *Annals of Medicine, 35,* 94–121.

van den Bree, M. B. W., Johnson, E. O., Neale, M. C., Svikis, D. S., McGue, M., & Pickens, R. W. (1998). Genetic analysis of diagnostic systems of alcoholism in males. *Biological Psychiatry, 43,* 139–145.

Vanyukov, M. M., & Tarter, R. E. (2000). Genetic studies of substance abuse. *Drug and Alcohol Dependence, 59,* 101–123.

Vanyukov, M. M., Tarter, R. E., Kirisci, L., Kirillova, G. P., Maher, B. S., & Clark, D. B. (2003). Liability to substance use disorders: 1. Common mechanisms and manifestations. *Neuroscience & Biobehavioral Reviews, 27,* 507–515.

Whalen, C. K., Jamner, L. D., Henker, B., & Delfino, R. J. (2001). Smoking and moods in adolescents with depressive and aggressive dispositions: Evidence from surveys and electronic diaries. *Health Psychology, 20,* 99–111.

Wiers, R. W., Gunning, W. B., & Sergeant, J. A. (1998). Do young children of alcoholics hold more positive or negative alcohol-related expectancies than controls. *Alcoholism: Clinical & Experimental Research, 22,* 1855–1863.

Williams, A., & Clark, D. (1998). Alcohol consumption in university students: The role of reasons for drinking, coping strategies, expectancies, and personality traits. *Addictive Behaviors, 23,* 371–378.

Wills, T. A., & Cleary, S. D. (1996). How are social support efforts mediated? A test with parental support and adolescent substance use. *Journal of Personality and Social Psychology, 71,* 937–952.

Wills, T. A., & Cleary, S. D. (1999). Peer and adolescent substance use among 6th–9th graders: Latent growth analyses of influence versus selection mechanisms. *Health Psychology, 18,* 453–463.

Wills, T. A., & Dishion, T. J. (2004). Temperament and adolescent substance use: A transactional analysis of emerging self-control. *Journal of Clinical Child and Adolescent Psychology, 33,* 69–81.

Wills, T. A., DuHamel, K., & Vaccaro, D. (1995). Activity and mood temperament as predictors of adolescent substance use: Test of a self-regulation mediational model. *Journal of Personality and Social Psychology, 68,* 901–916.

Wills, T. A., Sandy, J. M., & Yaeger, A. (2000). Temperament and adolescent substance use: An epigenetic approach to risk and protection. *Journal of Personality, 68,* 1127–1151.

Wills, T. A., Sandy, J. M., Yaeger, A. M., Cleary, S. D., & Shinar, O. (2001). Coping dimensions, life stress, and adolescent substance use: A latent growth analysis. *Journal of Abnormal Psychology, 110,* 309–323.

Wills, T. A., Sandy, J. M., Yaeger, A., & Shinar, O. (2001). Family risk factors and adolescent substance use: Moderation effects for temperament dimensions. *Developmental Psychology, 37,* 283–297.

Wills, T. A., & Shiffman, S. (1985). Coping and substance use: A conceptual framework. In S. Shiffman & T. A. Wills (Eds.), *Coping and substance use* (pp. 3–24). New York: Academic Press.

Wills, T. A., & Stoolmiller, M. (2002). The role of self-control in early escalation of substance use: A time-varying analysis. *Journal of Consulting and Clinical Psychology, 70,* 986–997.

Windle, M. (1991). The difficult temperament in adolescence: Associations with substance use, family support, and problem behaviors. *Journal of Clinical Psychology, 47,* 310–315.

Windle, M., & Davies, P. T. (1999). Developmental theory and research. In K. E. Leonard & H. T. Blane (Eds.), *Psychological theories of drinking and alcoholism* (pp. 164–202). New York: Guilford Press.

Windle, M., & Windle, R. C. (2001). Depressive symptoms and cigarette smoking among middle adolescents: Prospective associations and intrapersonal and interpersonal influences. *Journal of Consulting and Clinical Psychology, 69,* 215–226.

Winters, K. C. (2001). Assessing adolescent substance use problems and other areas of functioning: State of the art. In P. M. Monti, S. M. Colby, & T. A. O'Leary (Eds.), *Adolescents, alcohol, and substance abuse: Reaching teens through brief interventions* (pp. 80–108). New York: Guilford Press.

Winters, K. C., Latimer, W. W., & Stinchfield, R. D. (1999). *DSM-IV* criteria for adolescent alcohol and cannabis use disorders. *Journal of Studies on Alcohol, 60,* 337–344.

Zimmerman, P., Wittchen, H. U., Fler, H. O., Pfister, H., Kessler, R. C., & Lieb, R. (2003). Primary anxiety disorders and the development of subsequent alcohol use disorders: A 4-year community study of adolescents and young adults. *Psychological Medicine, 33,* 1211–1222.

Zimmerman, U., Spring, K., Kunz-Ebrecht, S. R., Uhr, M., Wittchen, H. U., & Holsboer, F. (2004). Effect of ethanol on hypothalamic-pituitary-adrenal system response to psychosocial stress in sons of alcohol-dependent fathers. *Neuropsychopharmacology, 29,* 1156–1165.

Zimmerman, U., Spring, K., Wittchen, H. U., Himmerich, H., Ladgraf, R., Uhr, M., et al. (2004). Arginine vasopressin and adrenocorticotropin secretion in response to psychosocial stress is attenuated by ethanol in sons of alcohol-dependent fathers. *Journal of Psychiatric Research, 38,* 385–393.

Zuckerman, M. (1994). *Behavioral expressions and biosocial bases of sensation seeking.* New York: Cambridge University Press.

CHAPTER 14

Development of Behavioral Problems Over the Life Course

A Vulnerability and Stress Perspective

BENJAMIN L. HANKIN, JOHN R. Z. ABELA, RANDY P. AUERBACH, CHAD M. MCWHINNIE, AND STEVEN A. SKITCH

In this chapter, we present a vulnerability and stress perspective on the origins of disruptive, behavioral problems with a focus on childhood and adolescence. To start, we review pertinent descriptive findings about the genesis and developmental unfolding of behavioral problems. Next, we evaluate some of the vulnerability and stressor/environmental factors for the origins of behavior problems. Last, we provide empirical examples of how vulnerability and stress factors for behavioral problems can be integrated. Consistent with the general theme and emphasis of this volume and recent commentary (Rutter, 2003), we seek to elucidate the causal mechanisms that are implicated in the development of behavioral problems, rather than merely reiterating well-known indicators of risk status (e.g., low socioeconomic status [SES], ethnicity, sex; see Hinshaw & Lee, 2003, for a recent review). We aim to achieve this goal by focusing on various vulnerabilities that may serve as distal and proximal processes as well as vulnerabilities that may moderate the influence that environmental stressors have on the ontogeny of behavioral problems.

DEFINITIONS, DIAGNOSTIC CRITERIA, AND CLASSIFICATION ISSUES

Before ascertaining and evaluating the causes of behavioral problems, it is first necessary to describe their origins and growth over time. We briefly review next the definitions, diagnostic criteria, classification issues, and epidemiological findings, so that the developmental unfolding of behavioral problems and their pathways over time can be delineated accurately. We have used the broad term *behavioral problems* in the title and will use it throughout this chapter to refer to behaviors that violate important norms or laws. Consistent with the terms *conduct problems* or *externalizing behaviors,* both juvenile crimes and symptoms of conduct disorder (CD) as described in the *Diagnostic and Statistical Manual of Mental Disorders,* 4th edition (*DSM-IV*; American Psychiatric Association [APA], 1994), the official psychiatric classification for these problems, are included in this definition of *behavioral problems.*

In this chapter, we focus primarily on behavioral problems, such as conduct disorder problems, aggression, and delinquency, and provide less emphasis on milder behavior problems, as indicated, for example, by *DSM-IV*'s oppositional defiant disorder (ODD), although we will discuss ODD problems as they relate to the development of behavioral problems more broadly. There is overwhelming evidence that ODD and CD are comorbid (e.g., Angold, Costello, & Erkanli, 1999) and comprise a general "externalizing behavior" dimension (e.g., Lahey, Applegate, Waldman, Hankin, & Rick, 2004), yet there is also evidence that separate, but correlated, dimensions of behavioral problem severity (i.e., more aggressive acts vs. delinquent behaviors) underlie this spectrum (Tackett, Krueger, Sawyer, & Graetz, 2003). Within the broad spectrum of "externalizing behaviors," an important distinction should be made between aggressive, antisocial behaviors and the inattentive/impulsive/overactive symptoms that comprise the core features of attention deficit/hyperactivity disorder (ADHD). Whereas behavioral problems, which are the focus of this chapter, and ADHD symptoms frequently co-occur (e.g., Angold et al.), the distinction between these two broad externalizing problems has been validated (e.g., Jensen, Martin, & Cantwell, 1997; Lahey et al., 2004).

As with ODD problems, ADHD problems not only co-occur frequently with aggressive, delinquent behaviors, but evidence suggests that there may be a developmental pathway—starting with ADHD problems, leading to ODD problems, and culminating in aggression and delinquency—that characterizes the ontogeny of behavioral problems for some, but not all, youth (Lahey, McBurnett, & Loeber, 2000). Indeed, it appears that ODD-like behaviors almost always precede CD, although ODD is not sufficient and does not often predict the development of CD (e.g., see Loeber, Green, Keenan, & Lahey, 1995, for an example of risk factors predicting progression on an antisocial trajectory). We discuss these descriptive developmental pathways, and their implications for understanding the likely causes of behavioral problems from a vulnerability and stress perspective, in greater depth later in the chapter.

Youths with earlier ages of onset of behavioral problems are more likely to meet diagnostic criteria for ADHD and ODD during childhood than youths with later ages of onset of conduct problems (Hinshaw, Lahey, & Hart, 1993; Lahey et al., 1998; Loeber et al., 1995; Moffitt, 1990; Moffitt, Caspi, Dickson, Silva, & Stanton, 1996). There is also increasing evidence that children with early-onset conduct problems and co-occurring ADHD and ODD are more likely to exhibit aggression, to show persistent or worsening conduct problems over time, and to exhibit psychopathic characteristics later in life (Henry, Caspi, Moffitt, & Silva, 1996; Lynam, 1998).

One reason that early-onset conduct problems, ADHD, and ODD often co-occur may be explained by the hypothesis that they reflect the *same* underlying set of vulnerabilities (e.g., temperament/personality and cognitive vulnerabilities, discussed later). In other words, the high-risk profile of temperamental and cognitive vulnerabilities is not specifically associated with conduct/antisocial problems but may be a risk profile for all disruptive behavior disorders. If this is the case, then it is also important to explain why many children exhibit only one or two of these three disorders. There may be at least two reasons. First, differences in the child's transactions with a stressful social environment will determine which children will exhibit which combination of ADHD, ODD, and CD behaviors. Second, variations in the *degree* of variation in each area of vulnerability are expected to be a factor in determining the pattern of disruptive behavioral problems that each child exhibits. Given the strong co-occurrence among ADHD, ODD, and CD as well as theory and evidence that the same set of vulnerabilities may contribute to the development of these behavioral problems, our review of vulnerability and stress factors follows from these facts and focuses on etiological vulnerability and stress processes for the ontogeny of broadly defined behavioral problems. Of course, there are specific vulnerability and stress factors for particular behavioral problems (e.g., CD vs. ADHD), and we discuss appropriate evidence for specific etiologies.

The official psychiatric classification system, *DSM-IV* (APA, 1994), places behavioral problems primarily in the "disruptive behavior disorders" section of disorders diagnosed during childhood. The *DSM-IV*'s definition of CD includes aggressive and antisocial acts that involve status offenses (e.g., running away from home), denying rights to others (e.g., stealing), and inflicting pain (e.g., setting fires, starting fights). ODD, on the other hand, is characterized by age-inappropriate and persistent displays of irritable, defiant, angry, and oppositional behaviors that are less severe than the behaviors classified in CD. *DSM-IV* includes antisocial personality disorder (APD) as the diagnostic category for persistent behavioral problems throughout adulthood.

DSM-IV (APA, 1994) states that each of these disorders is a categorical entity, that is, a diagnosis that an individual either has or does not have. However, the available evidence suggests that problematic behaviors of aggression and delinquency do not form distinct categories that qualitatively separate "conduct-disordered" youth from "normal" youth, but rather are viewed more accurately as the extreme end of the continuum of conduct and behavioral problems (e.g., Bucholz, Hesselbrock, Heath, Kramer, & Schuckit, 2000; Osgood, McMorris, & Potenza, 2002; Vollebergh et al., 2001). Essentially, these studies highlight the idea that the point of demarcation between CD and "normal behavior" reflects a convenient custom rather than a true category in nature (Lahey et al., 1994). In addition, substantial evidence suggests that behavioral problems comprise heterogeneous phenomena with various phenomenological behavioral profiles, causes, developmental pathways and mechanisms, and course over time (Moffitt, 1993; Rutter, Giller, & Hagell, 1998). In other words, the preponderance of data suggests that antisocial behavior problems, which may appear unitary or similar at a particular time point during development, in fact are composed of different subtypes or developmental trajectories when examined longitudinally (Farrington, 1991; Loeber, 1988; Patterson, Reid, & Dishion, 1992). As such, it is vital that integrative accounts of vulnerability and stress factors account for these disparate developmental pathways, which may be differentially relevant for different youth. Our review highlights the different vulnerability and stress factors that lead to the different subtypes of behavioral problems.

Various subtypes of antisocial, aggressive, behavioral problems have been proposed and investigated (see Coie & Dodge, 1998; Hinshaw & Lee, 2003, for reviews), although *DSM-IV* explicitly lists only one subtype based on age of onset. Consideration of potential subtypes or differing developmental pathways and mechanisms is important, because these different forms may be caused by relatively distinct causes (e.g., vulnerabilities) and thus may inform more accurate classification efforts. First, interpersonal aggression can be separated into verbal versus physical forms, and physical aggression typically appears early in development and may be fairly normative throughout preschool years. Second, aggression can be differentiated into two types: instrumental (or goal-directed) versus hostile (or intentional) infliction of pain. Related and similar to this distinction, aggression can be proactive, such as bullying, or reactive. Third, aggression can be distinguished by direct (e.g., verbal, physical) versus indirect, or relational, manifestations. Relational aggression (Crick & Grotpeter, 1995) frequently occurs in interpersonal relationships and involves such indirect aggressive acts as gossiping, excluding peers, sullying peers' reputations, and so forth; it is more typically exhibited by females, whereas males are more likely to be directly aggressive. Last, aggression has been categorized separately as overt (i.e., physically aggressive behaviors) versus covert (i.e., not physically aggressive, involving behaviors such as stealing, lying, truancy, etc.) (see Loeber & Schmaling, 1985). *DSM-IV*, as the official classification system, does not distinguish among these putatively different subtypes with possibly different developmental trajectories and pathways; rather, a diagnosis of CD combines these various forms together. For example, a diagnosis of CD includes both overt (e.g., assault) and covert (e.g., shoplifting) behavioral criteria.

The subtypes that *DSM-IV* does recognize, which have considerable empirical support, are the early-onset and late-onset types, based largely on Moffitt's (1993) developmental taxonomy of life-course-persistent and adolescent-limited behavioral problems. Moffitt proposed a "developmental taxonomy" in which two groups of antisocial youths were distinguished based on their ages of onset and trajectories of conduct problems. She posited that these groups of antisocial youths differ enough to require different causal explanations and to be categorized as truly different subtypes. In her seminal paper, she postulated that the confusing picture seen in the literature on aggression and delinquency, especially inconsistencies in etiological vulnerabilities, processes, correlates, and treatments, could be explained by past investigations that had mixed together these different subtypes in mostly cross-sectional studies. The life-course-persistent subgroup is composed of a relatively small-sized group of youth, and they have onset of aggressive behaviors early in childhood and are at elevated risk for a persistent course of behavioral problems that worsens as the youth progresses through adolescence and into adulthood. In contrast, the adolescent-limited group comprises a larger group of youth who typically initiate milder behavioral problems starting in adolescence and usually ending in early adulthood. The early-onset group is hypothesized to account for a substantial amount of the overall antisocial behavior in society over their life course and to engage in more serious and severe acts.

The corpus of evidence supports Moffitt's (1993) view and shows that youths with the earliest and latest ages of onset of conduct problems tend to be antisocial for different reasons (see Moffitt, 2003; Moffitt, Caspi, Rutter, & Silva, 2001, for reviews), although there is some debate over her hypothesis whether behavioral problems, based on age of onset, fall along a continuum of ages of onset or whether they reflect a true developmental taxonomy of distinct categories (for various viewpoints and evidence, see Lahey et al., 2000; Moffitt, 2003; Nagin & Tremblay, 1999; Rutter et al., 1998). Indeed, empirical findings show that there are more than two age-based subgroups, such as a small subgroup that does not exhibit behavioral problems until young adulthood and a subgroup of early-onset aggressive youth that actually desists over time rather than persisting as originally hypothesized. Moreover, Moffitt (1993) postulated that there are distinct causes and developmental pathways that characterize life-course-persistent versus adolescent-limited types, although it is also debated whether these subtypes have disparate causal mechanisms or whether the same set of causal factors influences behavioral problems emerging at all ages, with a differing strength and pattern of these causal influences that varies along the continuum of the age of onset of conduct problems. Although there continues to be some debate and research over these fine points in Moffitt's (1993) original model, it is clear that her theory emphasizing developmental subgrouping of youth based on age of onset and potentially different causal factors is one of the most empirically supported and accepted.

EPIDEMIOLOGY OF BEHAVIORAL PROBLEMS

Prevalence

Ascertaining the precise prevalence rate of behavioral problems is difficult for numerous reasons, some of which we discuss briefly. First, as reviewed above, the evidence suggests that there is not a categorical "conduct disorder" existing in nature, which some youth "have" and others do not; instead, behavioral problems vary along a continuum upon which various cuts can be made. Thus, depending on where investigators demarcate clinical significance of behavioral problems along this dimension, widely varying prevalence rates can be obtained. Second, based on different demarcations along the behavioral disorder dimension, the diagnostic definitions and criteria for behavioral problems (e.g., ODD and CD) have changed remarkably over the past 25 years since the advent of the *DSM-III* (APA, 1987), so the rates will fluctuate with the changing definitions and criteria because the prevalence rates are highly dependent on these criterion definitions and the samples to which they are applied (Lahey, Miller, et al., 1999). Third, behavioral disorders comprise developmental phenomena and become more prominent as youth age, yet developmentally informed prevalence data are suspect because they are based on piecing together prevalence rates from different cross-sectional studies with youth of various ages. There is no published prospective, representative sample starting with youth at very early ages to establish a solid developmental trajectory of behavioral disorders over time. Despite these difficulties, it is important to provide reasonable prevalence estimates, with lower and upper boundaries, over time to establish roughly how many youth experience such problems and why behavioral problems comprise an important societal concern. Based on child and adolescent samples, the prevalence estimates of ODD range from 1% to 20%, with 3% as the median, and estimates of CD vary from 1% to 10% (Lahey, Miller, et al., 1999).

Sex-Difference Patterns

There are clear sex differences in behavioral disorders, such that more males than females exhibit higher rates of behavioral problems, as these are typically and currently defined. For example, *DSM-IV* states the range for CD as 6%–16% for males and 2%–9% for females (APA, 1994). This sex divergence is substantial in childhood, although it diminishes somewhat in adolescence (Zoccolillo, 1993). However, more recent research suggests that the manifestation of behavioral problems may not be the same for males and females (Keenan, Loeber, & Green, 1999). Indeed, it may be that the difference in average levels of aggression and delinquency are more reflective of the typical definition and criteria of the male manifestation of behavioral problems and that the substantial sex divergence might diminish greatly if sex-specific manifestations and definitions were used instead (see Zahn-Waxler, 1993;

Zocollilo, for a discussion of possible sex-specific changes to definitions and criteria). Indeed, girls seem to exhibit more indirect/relational aggression, whereas boys exhibit more direct/physical aggression (e.g., Crick & Grotpeter, 1995). This brief discussion of sex differences highlights the difficulty of simply establishing prevalence rates because of potentially incorrect definitions, criteria, and classification systems and points to the importance of understanding more deeply the heterogeneity of behavioral problems, the possibility of different subtypes, and potentially disparate causal pathways.

Research examining sex differences in behavioral disorders has become increasingly important in recent years (e.g., Keenan & Shaw, 1997; Keenan et al., 1999; Moffitt et al., 2001; Rutter, Caspi, & Moffitt, 2003). Understanding the nature of this sex difference, as a specific example of a difference between groups, highlights the important issue of homotypic versus heterotypic continuity in developmental psychopathology. The theory of *homotypic continuity* states that the same set of causal processes is operating across all individuals equally over time, whereas the idea of *heterotypic continuity* emphasizes that varying causal processes may contribute to the development of psychopathology differently depending on the particular group of individuals (e.g., boys vs. girls) or across development (e.g., children vs. adolescents). Ultimately, it is vital to explain the origins and development of behavioral problems over time, not merely to describe and document the prevalence rates overall and by different groups (e.g., sex). An emphasis on etiological vulnerability and stress mechanisms reveals that the same underlying cause(s) can explain behavioral problems equally for males and females (i.e., homotypic continuity), or different etiological processes may cause behavioral problems separately by sex (i.e., heterotypic continuity). Still, even with a focus on homotypic versus heterotypic continuity in behavioral problems, research is needed to connect the underlying causes of problematic behaviors with the phenotypic manifestation observed. For example, if the same set of causal processes were found to produce behavioral problems for males and females (i.e., homotypic continuity), then additional research would be required to explain the mean-level sex difference in behavioral problem prevalence and the sex difference in behavioral disorder manifestation.

Continuity and Developmental Progression of Behavioral Problems Over Time

Understanding continuity and developmental progression is a vital process for ascertaining which individuals are most likely to escalate in or desist from aggressive or delinquent behaviors, and thus for elucidating the etiological vulnerability and stress processes implicated in the origins and development of these problems over time. However, determining the degree of continuity in behavioral problems over the life course is difficult because, as we just reviewed, there are different forms of continuity (i.e., homotypic and heterotypic). Nevertheless, there is considerable evidence for both aspects of continuity. With respect to homotypic continuity, or simple stability and consistency in measures of behavioral problems over time, longitudinal data indicate considerable stability over long follow-ups (e.g., Farrington, 1992; Frick & Loney, 1999), and these correlations may be stronger after correcting for measurement error (Moffitt & Caspi, 2001). Consistent with heterotypic continuity, there is also evidence that the underlying causal processes are stable over time despite changes in the surface manifestations of behavior problems (Patterson, 1993; Patterson, Forgatch, Yoerger, & Stoolmiller, 1998).

VULNERABILITY AND STRESS-THEORETICAL MODELS FOR THE ONTOGENY OF BEHAVIORAL PROBLEMS

In this section, we review various vulnerabilities and stressful environmental factors for the development of behavioral problems with a particular emphasis on childhood and adolescence. It is important to state that we cannot comprehensively cover all of the theory and knowledge on vulnerability and stress factors for externalizing problems (see Hinshaw & Lee, 2003; Lahey, Moffitt, & Caspi, 2003; Rutter et al., 1998; Tremblay, 2000, for reviews). Moreover, we do not wish to convey the impression that a complete understanding of behavioral problems can be achieved by reviewing disparate vulnerability factors and stressful contexts in independent subsections of this chapter. Clearly, a true understanding requires a coherent combination of multifaceted vulnerabilities transacting with stressors in environmental contexts over time in a chainlike manner to reveal the underlying developmental processes that culminate into a behavioral-problem pathway over time. Although we seek to advance knowledge toward this end in this chapter by providing empirical examples of how to integrate various vulnerabilities together within a broad vulnerability and stress perspective, we are cognizant that this is a preliminary first step, in a fairly constrained space, to attempt this ambitious understanding.

Gottfredson and Hirschi (1990) proposed that variations in antisocial behavior can be explained by individual differences in *antisocial propensity*. Stressful environmental influences on conduct problems can be strong (see below), yet the origins of behavioral problems cannot be understood without accounting for individual differences in vulnerabilities and how these vulnerabilities interact with stressors and transact with the person's environment. Antisocial propensity is inferred from individual differences in behavioral problems, and it is defined and measured in noncircular, independent terms. Lists of hypothesized components of individual differences in antisocial propensity include lower intelligence and higher levels of impulsivity (Farrington, 1991, 1995; Gottfredson & Hirschi). Our review of individual difference vulnerabilities builds on this conceptual foundation (see also Lahey & Waldman, 2003).

Multiple child factors contribute to antisocial propensity. These factors influence behavioral problems that emerge at all ages, from early childhood through late adolescence, but their influence varies with the age of onset of behavioral problems, because the strength of the various causal influences on behavioral problems affects the age of onset of such problems. For youths with earlier ages of onsets of behavioral problems, it appears that vulnerabilities for antisocial propensity (e.g., high negative emotionality and low cognitive ability) play significant roles, interacting with stressors and working through transactions with a stressful familial and social environment to increase the level of behavioral problems over time. As the age of onset of behavioral problems increases, it is likely that the vulnerabilities that comprise an antisocial propensity become progressively less important, and certain environmental factors (e.g., peer influence and other social factors) play more significant etiological roles. This perspective is consistent with the developmentally based subtypes for behavioral problems (e.g., Moffitt, 1993) reviewed earlier.

In a masterful synthesis of the literature, Loeber and Farrington (2000) classified many childhood risk factors into broad categories, including: (a) child factors, (b) family factors, (c) parents' poor child-rearing practices, (d) school factors, (e) peer factors, and (f) neighborhood factors. Although a very useful categorization of risk factors, it is likely that any subdivision of risks is somewhat arbitrary, and it is unclear whether the particular risks they identified within a broad category are considered best as vulnerabilities or stressors. Here, we subdivide our coverage of vulnerability and stress factors based primarily on those vulnerabilities covered in Part II of this volume.

Also, we will use a broad definition of stressful factors, one that encompasses objective stressors experienced in environmental contexts (e.g., poverty, neighborhoods). The operationalization of stress in this chapter is consistent with that presented in Grant and McMahon's chapter defining stress (Chapter 1 of this volume). Still, it is worth noting that a clear, precise taxonomy of objective, discrete stressors that take place in stressful environmental contexts (e.g., low SES, poverty) seems to be lacking and underresearched generally in the field of behavioral problems. Indeed, we believe it is important to highlight this point, especially for this volume focusing on vulnerability and stress perspectives, because the vast majority of research seeking to understand the etiology and developmental pathways underlying the ontogeny of behavioral problems has tended to focus on either intraindividual vulnerability factors (e.g., temperament, genetics, social-cognitive processing, low intelligence) or on broadly defined stressful environments (e.g., poor neighborhoods). Thus, before reviewing the most prominent theory and evidence on vulnerabilities and stressful contexts for behavioral problems, we emphasize the need and importance for future theory and research to focus more attention on the processes and transactions involved in the emergence of behavioral problems, as understood from a vulnerability and stress perspective. Indeed, this valuable vantage point, emphasizing vulnerability and stress interactions as contributing to externalizing problems, has been successful in further understanding behavioral problems. For example, this perspective is exemplified by a recent paper by Caspi and colleagues (2002) showing that a molecular genetic vulnerability for antisocial behavior propensities interacted with childhood maltreatment to predict the development of serious behavioral problems in adulthood. We believe this vulnerability and stress perspective may be particularly important and salient, because such vulnerability and stress models (see Ingram & Luxton, Chapter 2 of this volume, for specification of such models and how they inform etiological process) can provide important information and understanding for the causal mechanisms, rather than mere risk indicators (see Rutter, 2003; Rutter, Pickles, Murray, & Eaves, 2001), involved in the ontogeny of behavioral problems.

Stressful Environmental Contexts

A clear and strong association has been observed between increased risk for youths' behavioral problems and indicators of broad, environmental adversities. Lower levels of SES are a general risk for behavioral problems (Lahey, Miller, et al., 1999). These SES-linked environmental factors include living in high-crime neighborhoods, attending schools with delinquent peers, and the family's lack of economic resources—each of these may affect access to day care, after-school care, mental health services, and the like (Harnish, Dodge, & Valente, 1995; Kilgore, Snyder, & Lentz, 2000). Other broad environmental factors include poverty, family crowding, poor and unresponsive schools, inner-city environments, and unemployment (Coie & Dodge, 1998). Overall, these environmental circumstances foster the social learning of conduct problems (Caspi, A. Taylor, Moffitt, & Plomin, 2000). On the other hand, part of the association between lower SES and behavioral problems reflects selection effects. There is evidence of downward socioeconomic mobility (or staying at the low SES of their family of origin) among parents who are antisocial or who have mental health and substance-abuse problems (B. P. Dohrenwend & B. S. Dohrenwend, 1974; Miech, Caspi, Moffitt, Wright, & Silva, 1999). In some people, then, individual characteristics contribute to their living in adverse socioeconomic circumstances (selection effects), and these circumstances, in turn, influence their children (causal effects). Consistent with the vulnerability and stress perspective, children with greater vulnerability levels (e.g., those who are affectively, dispositionally, genetically, or cognitively predisposed to develop behavioral problems) will be more influenced by the environmental factors associated with lower SES than other children. Because there are genetic vulnerabilities that influence liability for behavioral problems (see later), we note in passing here that the environmental influences associated with SES influence the child partly through genotype-environment interactions.

A critical question underlying these distal, stressful risk factors is whether such environmental influences directly relate to behavioral problems or indirectly predict externalizing behaviors by increasing the likelihood that vulnerability factors develop or that stressors occur. There is some evidence for direct effects between distal risk factors and the development of externalizing behaviors. For example, stressful neighborhoods have been found to predict increased risk for child behavioral problems that is separable from genetic risk effects or genetic mediation (Caspi et al., 2000). There is also evidence that women who give birth at younger ages are more likely to have children who engage in behavioral problems (e.g., Levine, Pollack, & Comfort, 2001; Nagin, Pogarsky, & Farrington, 1997). This fact appears to reflect both individual vulnerability factors that select certain women into early childbearing and environmental influences on their offspring that are associated with early childbearing (cf. Jaffee, Caspi, Moffitt, & Silva, 2001). However, other stressful environmental contexts have been found to be indirect predictors of behavioral problems. Various studies have shown that the influences of low SES, family transitions, and unemployment on behavioral problems are mediated by poor parenting practices. McLoyd (1990) showed that problematic parenting accounted for the association between poverty and later antisocial behavior development, because poverty increases family stress, lack of resources, and disorganization. In particular, parental harsh discipline, poor parental supervision, and weak parent-child relationships explained most of the association between family poverty and adolescent delinquency (Sampson & Laub, 1997).

One of the clearest examples of an objective stressor as a risk for behavioral problems is physical abuse. Physical abuse within the first 5 years of life has been repeatedly found to be a strong and consistent distal predictor for later aggression and violence in youth (e.g., Dodge, Bates, & Pettit, 1990; see Coie & Dodge, 1998, for review). As with other social, environmental contexts, there can be vulnerability and stress correlations, such that certain stressful experiences are more likely to be experienced when individuals have higher levels of vulnerability. These vulnerability-stress associations can make it difficult to ascertain whether the stressful experience (or a vulnerability) by itself is contributing to the ontogeny of behavioral problems. With respect to physical abuse, the fact that child physical maltreatment strongly predicts later externalizing behaviors could result from the direct effect of physical abuse causing behavioral problems; the indirect effect of genetic risk factors passed from parent to child, increasing the likelihood of both abusive experiences and engagement in antisocial behavior (i.e., a gene-environment correlation); or a combination of both effects. Recently, an environmentally sensitive study examining these competing hypotheses reported that physical abuse is an environmentally mediated process that is directly involved in causally contributing to youths' behavioral problems independent of known genetic risk (Jaffee, Caspi, Moffitt, & A. Taylor, 2004). Additional support for a mediational model has been obtained in research demonstrating that the relationship between familial violence and physical abuse can be explained, at least in part, by social-cognitive information-processing factors developed by youth in response to abusive experiences (Coie & Dodge, 1998). These mediating social-cognitive vulnerabilities are discussed in more depth below (see also Gibb & Coles, Chapter 5 of this volume).

Another factor falling within our broad definition of stressful environmental contexts is that of exposure and influence of media violence as risks for development of behavioral problems, especially aggression and violence. A recent review (Anderson et al., 2004) indicated that there is "unequivocal evidence" that media violence (e.g., violent television, video games, music) enhances the likelihood of behavioral problems in both the short and long term. The processes by which exposure to media violence operates to contribute to aggression and violence appear similar to those found in research with deviant peers. Media violence, in the immediate context, increases aggressive cognitive scripts and representations, enhances physiological arousal, and augments the tendency to copy observed externalizing behaviors. Over the long term, media violence leads to various learning processes and reduces negative reactions to violence. Consistent with the vulnerability and stress perspective, Anderson and colleagues' review revealed that individual differences in vulnerabilities (e.g., social-cognitive vulnerability) and social environments (e.g., degree of parental influence and monitoring) can interact with media violence to moderate how strongly this exposure predicts behavioral problems.

Genetic Vulnerability

Numerous twin and adoption studies have shown that child and adolescent antisocial behavior is influenced by genetic and environmental factors (e.g., Deater-Deckard & Plomin, 1999; Gjone & Stevenson, 1997; O'Connor, Neiderhiser, Reiss, Hetherington, & Plomin, 1998; Rutter, 1997; Rutter et al., 1997; van den Oord, Boomsma, & Verhulst, 1994; see Rhee & Waldman, 2002; Rutter, Silberg, O'Connor, & Simonoff, 1999, for reviews; see Lemery & Doelger, Chapter 7 of this volume, for greater discussion about genetic vulnerability). These include genetic influences on both the onset of conduct problems and their persistence over time (Robinson, Kagan, Reznick, & Corley, 1992; Saudino, Plomin, & DeFries, 1996). Last, there is growing evidence that the genetic influences on conduct problems, ODD, and ADHD overlap to a considerable degree (Coolidge, Thede, & Young, 2000; Eaves et al., 2000; Waldman, Rhee, Levy, & Hay, 2001).

In addition, oppositional and aggressive forms of behavioral problems appear to be influenced more by heritable factors and little by shared environmental factors, whereas delinquency, or covert behavioral problems, is less heritable and exhibits more shared environmental input (Deater-Deckard & Plomin, 1999; van den Oord et al., 1994). A developmental behavioral-genetic study (Waldman et al., 2001) that examined four aspects of behavioral problems that have been identified in factor-analytic research (Frick et al., 1993) showed that heritability was highest for oppositional behaviors and decreased for aggression, property violations, and status violations. A common set of genetic influences contributed to this developmental pattern of heritabilities. Only oppositional behavior demonstrated specific genetic influence, whereas no genetic influences were specific to the other three groups of conduct problems. On the other hand, shared environmental contributions were of the opposite direction, such that oppositional symptoms were lowest and increased successively for aggression, property violations, and status violations. The same set of environmental influences was found to contribute to this increasing shared environmental influence. Specific shared environmental experiences were found for each of the four behavioral problem clusters. These genetic and common environmental influences for each of the four behavior problem clusters are particularly interesting because of the developmental progression of each of these conduct problem factors: The average age of onset increases, starting with oppositional behavior and increasing for aggression, property crimes, and status offenses (Frick et al.). This developmental pattern, combined with the behavioral-genetic evidence, suggests that the magnitude of the genetic influence is inversely associated with the age of onset for behavioral problems, whereas the strength of shared environmental influence is positively associated with age of onset. Youth with earlier-onset behavioral problems tend to be highly oppositional and exhibit all forms of antisocial behavior (aggression, crimes, and status offenses). Finally, it is suggested that genetic factors contribute more strongly to the predisposition for an oppositional trait, but genetic factors have less influence for behavioral problems that develop later in the life course. Consistent with this perspective, stronger heritability has been found for childhood-onset aggression and behavioral problems than for those with adolescent-onset problems (J. Taylor, Iacono, & McGue, 2000). In sum, genetic influences on the propensity toward behavioral problems are not static across development (Jacobson, Prescott, & Kendler, 2002) and vary depending on the form of behavioral problems.

Genetic influences on behavioral problems likely interact with objective stressors (such as peer rejection and academic failure) and operate indirectly through youths' transactions within stressful social environments (such as poor parenting and family socialization) (Lahey, Waldman, et al., 1999). The extent to which heritable early predispositions culminate in the development of behavioral problems likely depends on youths' social environments (Reid & Patterson, 1989). The concept of gene-environment correlations suggests that the moderately heritable disposition that a child brings to the family and the child's family environment are associated for genetic reasons (Rutter et al., 1997). Later in the chapter, we will review temperamental vulnerabilities for behavioral problems (e.g., negative emotionality, daring, and prosociality), but for now we note that these affective dispositions are moderately heritable (Lahey, Waldman, et al., 1999). Earlier in this chapter, we briefly discussed some of the poor parenting practices that have been implicated as a part of a broadly conceived stressful environmental context. But such poor parenting does not appear to operate as a main-effects risk for youth behavioral problems. Consistent with a transactional, developmental pathways approach, research has revealed gene-environment correlations between negative, coercive parenting and child behavioral problems (O'Connor, Deater-Deckard, Fulker, Rutter, & Plomin, 1998). This indicates that children who possess an increased genetic liability to behavioral problems are more likely to grow up in stressful home environments and experience poor parenting. Thus, some youth are more likely to progress forward on an antisocial developmental pathway because such children with a genetic predisposition to behavioral problems often have absent, antisocial fathers and are raised by mothers with significant psychopathology (e.g., antisocial behavior, depression, substance abuse; Lahey et al., 1988; Lahey, Russo, Walker, & Piacentini, 1989). These gene-environment correlations can operate through *passive* (e.g., growing up with parents who exhibit poor parenting skills), *evocative* (e.g., youth's behavior elicits negative parenting), and *active* (e.g., interacting with delinquent peers) mechanisms to contribute to the development of behavioral problems (Rutter, 1997).

In addition to gene-environment correlations, there is also evidence for gene-environment interactions. In particular, we discuss two types of genotype-environment interactions that have been investigated. First, genetic influences on behavioral problems can be diminished by favorable social learning environments. Various adoption studies indicate that behavioral problems in the adopted-away offspring of antisocial parents are less common when they are raised by well-adjusted adoptive parents than by adoptive parents with problems like those of their biological parents (Bohman, 1996; Cadoret, Yates, Troughton, Woodward, & Stewart, 1995). Second, there are individual differences in the manner in which some respond to the social factors that encourage behavioral problems. Importantly, Caspi and colleagues (2002) have provided striking evidence that maltreated children who have one allele of the gene that encodes the neurotransmitter monoamine oxidase A (*MAOA*), which has been found in some studies to be a biological vulnerability for behavioral problems, are more likely to engage in antisocial behavior than maltreated children without this allele. Importantly, this study showed that neither genetic vulnerability (*MAOA*) nor childhood maltreatment predicted ontogeny of behavioral problems on their own as main effects; rather, it was the interactive combination of genetic risk and childhood abuse that predicted adult antisocial problems. Recently, this pattern was replicated in an independent longitudinal study of adolescent boys (Foley et al., 2004): Low *MAOA* activity interacted with familial adversities to predict risk for behavioral problems. In addition to replicating the original report by Caspi and colleagues (2002) in an independent sample, it is also important that the same pattern of findings was obtained while examining the interaction of different stressors in environmental context (interparental violence, parental neglect, and inconsistent discipline in Foley et al.; maternal rejection, loss of primary caregiver, harsh discipline, physical abuse, and sexual abuse in Caspi et al., 2002) alongside the exact same genetic risk (low *MAOA* activity). This suggests that the Genotype × Stress interaction is robust across a variety of childhood adversities and stressors.

Biological Vulnerability

One of the more prominent biological vulnerability models derives from Gray's (1987) theory involving the Behavioral Facilitation (or Activation) System (BFS or BAS) and Behavioral Inhibition System (BIS). The BFS, which involves locomotion, gratification, and reward sensitivity, is based in the mesolimbic dopaminergic pathway. Aggressive behavior tends to produce immediate rewards (despite the potential for long-term negative consequences), so a strong BFS is hypothesized to contribute to chronic instrumental aggression (Quay, 1993). In contrast, the BIS is hypothesized to stop an individual from engaging in behavior when the expectations for the behavior's outcome are negative (e.g., punishment). The BIS allows for effective impulse control, and it has been associated with impulsive aggression. Aspects of the BIS include low cerebrospinal fluid concentrations of serotonin metabolites (5-HIAA; Kruesi, Rapoport, Hamburger, & Hibbs, 1990), low serotonin levels (5-HT; Coccaro, Kavoussi, & Lesser, 1992), and low levels of norepinephrine (Rogeness, Javors, & Pliszka, 1992).

Another consistent finding is that autonomic nervous system activity, comprised of low skin conductance and low resting heart rate (Raine, 1993, 1997), is associated with chronic behavioral problems. Youth with behavioral problems, particularly those with early onset and aggressive features, exhibit low psychophysiological/cortical arousal and low autonomic reactivity. In contrast, nonaggressive or late-onset behavior-disordered youth tend to show the opposite pattern: They have arousal and reactivity responses that typically are elevated above groups of early-onset and normal youth (McBurnett & Lahey, 1994). It is believed that the low arousal and low reactivity make it less likely for a child to become socialized properly, to learn avoidance conditioning, and to respond to punishment (see Fowles & Missel, 1994, for similar research findings with adults).

Other biological vulnerabilities have also been found. Low levels of cortisol (a stress hormone) were shown to characterize boys at greater risk for persistent antisocial behavior (McBurnett, Lahey, Rathouz, & Loeber, 2000). Maternal smoking during pregnancy was associated with youths' later risk for behavioral problems (Wakschlag et al., 1997), even after controlling for SES and maternal age (i.e., risk factors for behavioral problems).

Temperament/Personality Vulnerability

In this section, we use the term *temperament* to refer to substantially heritable and relatively persistent individual differences in global aspects of socioemotional responding that emerge early in childhood and constitute the foundation for many personality traits (Buss & Plomin, 1975, 1984; Caspi, 1998) from childhood through adolescence and adulthood (see Tackett & Krueger, Chapter 8 of this volume, for greater elucidation of combining temperament and personality models throughout the life span). We focus on three dimensions of temperament that have been theorized and examined as vulnerabilities for the ontogeny of behavioral disorders based on the work of Lahey and colleagues (Lahey, Waldman, et al., 1999; Lahey et al., 2003).

First, *negative emotionality,* or neuroticism, is positively correlated with a wide range of mental health problems, including antisocial behavior among adults (e.g., Krueger, 1999; Moffitt et al., 2001). Negative emotionality is defined by experiencing negative emotions frequently, intensely, and with little provocation in most trait models of personality (see reviews by Bouchard & Loehlin, 2001; Zuckerman, Kuhlman, Joireman, Teta, & Kraft, 1993). The existing literature on the relation between negative emotionality and child conduct problems has been inconsistent. A number of studies have found significant concurrent or prospective associations of negative emotionality with child conduct problems (e.g., Eisenberg et al., 1996; Gabrys, 1983; Gjone & Stevenson, 1997; Rowe & Flannery, 1994), whereas other studies have not (e.g., Fonseca & Yule, 1995; Furnham & Thompson, 1991; Heaven, 1996; John, Caspi, Robins, Moffitt, & Stouthamer-Loeber, 1994; Tranah, Harnett, & Yule, 1998). This lack of consistency may reflect differences in the operationalization of negative emotionality across studies, may indicate that the relation between negative emotionality and behavioral problems is complex, or may suggest that stressors are needed to interact with negative emotionality to predict behavioral problems. Indeed, few studies have examined more complex, interactive effects between negative emotionality and stressors in context (for exceptions, see Dodge, 1993); most studies investigate temperament as a main-effect predictor of behavioral problems.

Second, *daring* (also referred to as *sensation seeking,* Zuckerman, 1996, or *novelty seeking,* Cloninger, 1987) youth have been found to be considerably more likely to be chronic criminal offenders during adolescence and adulthood (Farrington & West, 1993).

These constructs have been found to be positively correlated with conduct problems in diverse samples (Arnett, 1996; Daderman, 1999; Daderman, Wirsen, & Hallman, 2001; Goma-I-Freixnet, 1995; Greene, Krcmar, Walters, Rubin, & Hale, 2000; Luengo, Otero, Carrillo-de-la-Pena, & Miron, 1994; Newcomb & McGee, 1991; Simo & Perez, 1991). Inversely related to daring is *disinhibition,* which has been found to predict conduct problems during late childhood and early adolescence in several samples (Biederman et al., 2001; Hirshfeld et al., 1992; Kerr, Tremblay, Pagani-Kurtz, & Vitaro, 1997; Raine et al., 1998; Schwartz, Snidman, & Kagan, 1996). Cloninger also identified an individual differences dimension, termed *harm avoidance,* which may also describe some aspects of the opposite side of the daring dimension. Persons high in harm avoidance are cautious, apprehensive, and inhibited in the face of novel or dangerous situations. Children with higher harm avoidance scores were less likely to engage in significant antisocial behavior in adolescence and young adulthood in longitudinal research (Sigvardsson, Bohman, & Cloninger, 1987; Tremblay, Pihl, Vitaro, & Dobkin, 1994).

Third is the construct of *prosociality.* From preschool through adolescence, youths who exhibit more behavioral problems show less sympathy and concern for others (D. C. Cohen & Strayer, 1996; Eisenberg et al., 1996; Hastings, Zahn-Waxler, Robinson, Usher, & Bridges, 2000; Hughes, White, Sharpen, & Dunn, 2000; Luengo et al., 1994; Miller & Eisenberg, 1988). Haemaelaeinen and Pulkkinen (1996) obtained peer ratings on prosocial behavior at age 8 years and found that it predicted criminal offenses by age 27 years, even after controlling for early conduct problems and school failure. Last, many studies have found that children who have high levels of behavioral problems exhibit little guilt over their misdeeds (e.g., Loeber, Farrington, Stouthamer-Loeber, & Van Kammen, 1998). Related to these findings, Tremblay and colleagues (1994) demonstrated that children scoring high in novelty seeking, low in harm avoidance, and low in reward dependence (Cloninger's, 1987, model of personality) exhibited greater conduct problems during early adolescence. In addition, Tellegen's (1982) personality constructs of higher negative emotionality and lower constraint (a combination of low daring and high prosociality) have been found to predict greater antisocial behavior in adolescence and adulthood (Caspi et al., 1994; Krueger et al., 1994; Moffitt et al., 1996; Moffitt, Caspi, Harrington, & Milne, 2002). A recent study (Moffitt et al., 2002) examining these personality vulnerabilities, assessed in adolescence, showed that males who abstained from antisocial behavior from childhood into adulthood were low in daring, high in prosociality, and low in negative emotionality, whereas boys showing life-course-persistent conduct problems exhibited the opposite pattern. Finally, "undercontrolled" youth exhibited substantially more conduct problems than the other personality types, "resilient" or "overcontrolled" (Asendorpf, Borkenau, Ostendorf, & Van Aken, 2001; Hart, Hofmann, Edelstein, & Keller, 1997; Robins, Johns, Caspi, Moffitt, & Stouthamer-Loeber, 1996).

There is consistent evidence that temperamental vulnerabilities for antisocial propensity are both moderately heritable and contain significant environmental influence (see Caspi, 1998; Lahey et al., 2003, for reviews). Moreover, recent studies provide evidence for a genetic mediation hypothesis (i.e., genetic risk affects ontogeny of behavioral problems partly through the influence of temperament). Schmitz and colleagues (1999) showed that maternal ratings of the negative emotionality of infant and toddler-aged twins prospectively predicted behavioral problems at age 4. Consistent with genetic mediation, most of the correlation between early negative emotionality and later behavioral problems was explained by genetic influences common to both variables. Temperamental constructs similar to negative emotionality and daring, which were measured at age 5, predicted behavior problems at age 7, and genetic influences on age-7 behavioral problems were entirely mediated by age-5 measures (Lemery, Essex, & Smider, 2002). Last, Gjone and Stevenson (1997) showed that parent rating of negative emotionality for twin pairs (5–15 years old at the first assessment) predicted behavioral problems 2 years later. Negative emotionality and aggression shared common genetic influences, but neither common genetic nor shared environmental influences explained the prospective association between temperament and delinquency problems. This finding is consistent with evidence reviewed earlier: Developmentally early behavioral problems, which constitute mostly aggression problems and are found mostly among youths with earlier ages of onset, have stronger genetic influences than delinquency problems (which are also common among youths with later ages of onset).

Attachment Styles

In this section we discuss evidence for the importance of insecure attachment styles as a risk factor for the development of behavior problems in children and adolescents. Attachment styles develop in the context of early parent-child interactions, and insecure attachment styles are thought to confer nonspecific risk for the development of psychopathology (see Davila, Ramsay, Stroud, & Steinberg, Chapter 9 of this volume). Longitudinal studies have found that having an insecure attachment style in early childhood is predictive of increased risk for behavior problems later in development (Lyons-Ruth, Alpern, & Repacholi, 1993; Moss, Cyr, & Dubois-Comtois, 2004; Moss, Parent, Gosselin, Rousseau, & St-Laurent, 1996; Renken, Egeland, Marvinney, Mangelsdorf, & Sroufe, 1989). For example, Lyons-Ruth et al. (1993) found that the strongest predictor of hostile behavior in 5-year-old children from low-income families was having a disorganized attachment style at 18 months of age. At the same time, it is important to note that several other researchers have obtained either mixed (e.g., Speltz, DeKlyen, & Greenberg, 1999) or unsupportive (Bates, Bayles, Bennett, Ridge, & Brown, 1991; Bates, Maslin, & Frankel, 1985; Fagot, 1995; Fagot & Kavanagh, 1990) findings with respect to a direct link between insecure attachment and the development of problematic behavior in childhood.

More recent models (e.g., DeKlyen & Speltz, 2001; Greenberg, Speltz, & DeKlyen, 1993) hypothesize that a direct link between insecure attachment and behavioral problems has not been found but that insecure attachment interacts with other risk factors (e.g., low SES, family environment, and biological factors) to confer vulnerability for the development of behavior problems. In line with this hypothesis, longitudinal studies have indicated that insecure attachment styles interact with a variety of factors to predict the development of behavior problems, including cognitive deficits (Lyons-Ruth, Easterbrooks, & Cibelli, 1997), parental psychopathology (Alpern & Lyons-Ruth, 1993; Shaw, Owens, Vondra, & Keenan, 1996), and negative emotionality (Burgess, Marshall, Rubin, & Fox, 2003; Vondra, Shaw, Swearingen, M. Cohen, & Owens, 2001).

Emotion Vulnerability

In addition to the vulnerabilities we just explicitly discussed, we note briefly in passing here that emotional vulnerability for the development of behavioral problems has been investigated. Aspects of emotion vulnerability include problems with emotion regulation (e.g., Eisenberg et al., 1996; Keenan & Shaw, 2003; see Chaplin & Cole, Chapter 3 of this volume) and affective style (e.g., Davidson, Putnam, & Larson, 2000). The components that make up dysregulated emotional regulation and affective style merit further attention, but limited space does not permit a greater discussion of these emotion vulnerabilities here. Moreover, some of the more developed aspects of emotional vulnerability may be subsumed under other vulnerabilities we have reviewed in greater detail. For example, *temperamental vulnerability,* defined as "persistent individual differences in global aspects of socio-*emotional* responding," already incorporates broad aspects of emotion regulation and affective style. Also, recent integrative models (e.g., Davidson et al.) have focused on the neurobiological underpinnings of dysregulated emotion as a vulnerability for serious behavioral problems, and they have focused on how neural circuitry involving brain areas, such as the prefrontal cortex (e.g., Raine, 1996) and subcortical regions such as the amygdala, are implicated in the ontogeny of behavioral problems. Clearly, as stressors are experienced in particular environmental contexts, individuals with heightened emotional vulnerability (e.g., poor emotion-regulation skills as instantiated biologically with greater amygdala activity and lowered prefrontal cortex activity) are more likely to feel negative emotions (e.g., anger, frustration) more quickly, to experience a longer duration of such negative affect, and to take longer to return to an emotional baseline; as a result, such youth would be more likely to respond behaviorally with greater aggression and more behavioral problems.

Cognitive Vulnerability

In this section, we first review theory and findings for (a) social-cognitive information processing, and (b) intelligence/verbal ability as they relate to the development of behavioral problems.

Cognitive and emotional processes can mediate the relationship between a child or adolescent's aggressive behavior and social cognitions. Dodge's (1993) social information–processing model of aggression posits that cognitive distortions may account for aggressive behavior in children and adolescents. Cues from specific social situations initiate the processing of social information, which occurs in a parallel series, with feedback loops, of five processing operations. The five steps are: (a) detection and encoding of social cues into working memory utilizing sensation, perception, and attention; (b) interpretation of cues in a social situation; (c) generation of possible responses to the situation based on stored social knowledge; (d) response decision, where the response selection is evaluated and based on outcome expectations; and (e) behavioral reaction to the social cue, as the selected response is enacted. Encoding and interpretation of the cues allows the child to comprehensively assess the self, others, past performances, and potential goals. Once the child has interpreted the situation, access to memories of similar past performances assists in generating possible responses, at which point an evaluation is made on how appropriate a response may be, how well a response can be enacted, and what will happen after the response.

Deficits or biases can occur at one or more of the five processing steps, resulting in acts of aggression or antisocial behavior. Deficits for each of the first four steps may include: (a) encoding deficits, such as attending to fewer, more hostile cues and lacking sufficient information about a situation, which can contribute to an aggressive response; (b) interpretation of a threat in a situation that may be neutral, or hostile attributional bias; (c) response-generation deficits, such that possessing less knowledge about the resolution of social situations can result in accessing fewer and more aggressive responses; and (d) response-decision deficits, which lead to the likelihood of aggressive solutions.

Within the framework of Dodge's (1993) social information–processing model, behavioral enactment can be differentiated into two subtypes of aggression: reactive and proactive aggression (Dodge, Lochman, Harnish, Bates, & Pettit, 1997). An immediate aggressive reaction to a situation is associated with the earlier stages of the model, namely encoding, interpretation (hostile attributional biases), and response generation. Aggressive behavior with the intent to obtain a desired goal is more likely to occur in the later stages of the model, when an aggressive reaction may be viewed positively.

Dodge and Pettit (2003) provided a review of empirical findings supporting the social information–processing model and each processing step. Findings suggest that children who act aggressively focus on fewer, more hostile cues (Dodge, Pettit, McClaskey, & Brown, 1986; Gouze, 1987); attribute negative intent to others' behavior (Dodge & Frame, 1982; Waas, 1988) when the intent is unclear and make interpretative errors when the intent is clear (Waldman, 1996); access fewer, more aggressive responses (Asarnow & Callan, 1985); select aggressive responses as socially appropriate to obtain desirable outcomes (Crick & Ladd, 1990; Dodge et al., 1986); and infrequently enact nonaggressive behavioral responses (Dodge et al., 1986).

With respect to cognitive abilities, numerous studies have found that such abilities, particularly verbal abilities, are inversely related to individual differences in behavioral problems (Elkins, Iacono, Doyle, & McGue, 1997; Ge, Donnellan, & Wenk, 2001; Kratzer & Hodgins, 1999; Lynam, Moffitt, & Stouthamer-Loeber, 1993; Moffitt & Silva, 1988; Stattin & Klackenberg-Larsson, 1993). This association cannot be explained away by differences in SES, greater ability of more intelligent youths to avoid detection of their antisocial behaviors, or differences in test motivation (Lynam et al.; Moffitt & Silva). The specific cognitive deficits associated with conduct problems include intelligence, neuropsychological dysfunction, and executive functioning, although these constructs partially overlap. Emerging evidence suggests that a cluster of executive function and language abilities is associated with early-onset conduct problems, even controlling for general intelligence (Giancola, Martin, Tarter, Pelham, & Moss, 1996; Seguin, Boulerice, Harden, Tremblay, & Pihl, 1999). Early deficits in language development are associated with behavioral problems (Baker & Cantwell, 1987; Beitchman et al., 2001; N. J. Cohen et al., 1998; Dery, Toupin, Pauze, Mercier, & Fortin, 1999; Pennington & Ozonoff, 1996). Genetic influences on cognitive ability and the development of language skills are also well documented (Eley, Dale, & Bishop, 2001; Emde et al., 1992; Petrill et al., 1997; Plomin & Petrill, 1997).

Interpersonal Vulnerability

Maladaptive, transactional interpersonal processes are central to several prominent theories of the developmental unfolding of conduct-disordered behaviors (Capaldi & Patterson, 1994; Dishion, French, & Patterson, 1995; Moffitt, 1993; Patterson et al., 1992). The central vulnerability factor in such models is antisocial behavior on the part of the child. How does such antisocial behavior develop? As outlined previously, genetic, biological, and personality factors are likely to play a key role in both shaping the child's problem behavior and constraining family members' reactions to such behavior. At the same time, interpersonal transactional models, such as that created by Patterson and colleagues (Capaldi & Patterson, 1994; Dishion et al., 1995; Patterson et al., 1998), argue that a linear model in which the children's antisocial traits serve as the primary force, exerting their influence by eliciting negative parenting practices, is only one piece of a much broader picture. More specifically, Patterson and colleagues hypothesize that such factors are embedded within a larger interpersonal framework of self-perpetuating, reciprocal, transactional processes embedded within a network involving both parent and peer influences. Central to the model of Patterson and colleagues (Capaldi & Patterson, 1994; Dishion et al., 1995; Patterson et al., 1998) is the notion that the basic training for antisocial behavior takes place in the home, with family members being the primary trainers (Patterson et al., 1998). The vicious cycle commences with a breakdown of effectiveness in parent control strategies. Such a breakdown can result from numerous factors including, but not limited to, inconsistency in the use of disciplinary strategies (Patterson et al., 1992), supervisory and care neglect (Knutson, DeGarmo, & Reid, 2004; Patterson et al., 1992), lack of positive involvement with the child (Capaldi & Patterson, 1996; Patterson et al., 1992), and deficits in family problem solving (Forgatch & Patterson, 1989). As parental control strategies deteriorate, disciplinary confrontations between parents and children increase, setting the stage for the occurrence of coercive interactions between the target child and his or her family members. Patterson (1998) utilizes the term *coercion* to refer to aversive events being used contingently on the behavior of another person (e.g., family members). Within the framework of coercion theory, the child learns that aversive and aggressive behaviors (e.g., temper tantrums, yelling, hitting, and crying) are effective strategies in both eliminating the aversive behaviors of other family members and obtaining positive outcomes. When giving in to the child's inappropriate demands and requests, family members' "surrender behaviors" are negatively reinforced, because they lead to the cessation of the child's inappropriate demands and requests. At the same time, in the long term, enticement into this seductive "reinforcement trap" backfires as "surrendering" on the part of the parents either negatively (e.g., removal of being grounded) or positively (e.g., given a requested positive outcome) reinforces the child's maladaptive interpersonal strategies, which subsequently increases the likelihood they will occur again in the future. This dynamic and reciprocal transactional process is hypothesized to increase in both frequency and intensity over time (e.g., dyadic escalation), laying the groundwork for the development of interpersonal skill deficits on the part of the child. Such deficits are hypothesized to ultimately serve as both a vulnerability factor to later maladaptive developmental outcomes as well as a mechanism for the generation of stressors that will interact with the child's increasingly entrenched maladaptive interpersonal style.

The maladaptive outcomes that are engineered by and consequently interact with the target child's maladaptive interpersonal style intensify in childhood when the target child enters school (Capaldi & Patterson, 1994; Patterson et al., 1998). Antisocial behavior on the part of children impairs the development of healthy peer relationships and academic peer competencies. Children with conduct-disordered behavior are readily identified by their peers as argumentative, anger prone, and deliberately annoying (Kazdin, 1997). As early as the preschool years, such children experience peer rejection as a result of their behaviors—an interpersonal outcome that ultimately leads to further perpetuation and escalation of problem behavior (Capaldi & Patterson, 1994; Coie, Terry, Zakriski, & Lochman, 1995). As target children's maladaptive interpersonal style triggers the occurrence of rejection and isolation from prosocial peers, the gap between their interpersonal skills and those of their peers progressively widens, further increasing vulnerability. Worsening the situation, the development of deficits in academic skills often accompanies such impairment in peer relationships. Coercive techniques learned initially in the home are likely to become generalized to the school setting, with the ultimate outcome being (a) disruptive classroom behavior that interferes with learning, (b) failure to initiate and follow through with difficult tasks, and ultimately (c) avoidance of school and its associated tasks (Capaldi & Patterson, 1994; DeBaryshe, Patterson, & Capaldi, 1993; Patterson et al., 1998). As failures in the peer and academic domains accumulate, risk for the experience of depressive symptomatology increases (Capaldi & Stoolmiller, 1999). Further, as negative feedback is passed from home to school, conflict between the target child and his or her parent is likely to further increase—a mechanism that may ultimately serve to further exacerbate the initial problems.

As Patterson and colleagues (1998) view the development of conduct-disordered behavior as a process of accretion rather than succession, target youth are hypothesized to enter adolescence maintaining the vulnerabilities and adverse environmental circumstances developed during middle childhood. Consequently, vulnerability is hypothesized to continue to increase the risk for the occurrence of adverse outcomes as well as to shape the environmental context in which the youth develops. Of primary importance, maladaptive peer influences are hypothesized to increase during this developmental period (e.g., Dishion, Andrews, & Crosby, 1995). More specifically, whereas youth with externalizing problems are pushed away from prosocial peers during middle childhood, it is hypothesized that they are pulled toward antisocial peers during adolescence. Increasing involvement with deviant peers has been found to be associated with growth in delinquency (Stoolmiller, 1994). Interestingly, research examining the "delinquency training" that takes place during the adolescent period suggests that it is not simply level of peers' delinquency that predicts further exacerbation of conduct-disordered behavior, but rather that quality of peer interactions, including topics of discussion, are also central predictors (e.g., Dishion, Eddy, Haas, Li, & Spracklen, 1997; Shortt, Capaldi, Dishion, Bank, & Owen, 2003). More specifically, research suggests that antisocial talk, and the positive affect associated with it, reinforces ongoing delinquent behavior and encourages the initiation of new forms of delinquent behavior. Such escalating delinquency may result in further escalation of problems, including increased violence as well as the development of comorbid disturbances (e.g., substance abuse).

It is important to note that from the interpersonal perspective, the development of conduct-disordered behavior is typically conceptualized as a time-ordered trajectory in which problem behaviors are expressed as changes over time (Patterson et al., 1998). Patterson and colleagues (1998) propose that a single set of mechanisms can explain both the initiation as well as the progression through the movement along the trajectory. As such, mechanisms that foster antisocial behaviors in children are good predictors of future risk for conduct-disordered behaviors. Disrupted parenting practices, a proximal mechanism, are thought to promote antisocial forms of deviancy that occur while the individual is still a member of the family. During early adolescence, farther down the trajectory, deviant peer groups function as a second proximal mechanism. Both disrupted parenting styles and deviant peer groups are thought to be analogous to a trajectory of increasingly severe symptoms found in some medical disease processes. More specifically, just as patients with lung cancer move through a sequence of progressively more severe symptoms until death, so too does the individual with antisocial behaviors race along a sequence of increasingly more severe forms of antisocial events (Patterson et al., 1998).

TOWARD A VULNERABILITY-STRESS MODEL OF THE EMERGENCE OF BEHAVIORAL PROBLEMS

Clearly, the developmental unfolding of behavioral problems in children and adolescents is multidetermined, with evidence linking genetic, biological, interpersonal, cognitive, attachment, and emotional regulation factors and processes to the emergence of problem behaviors. Although a well-articulated vulnerability-stress model does not currently exist, such a framework may ultimately prove useful in order to organize the diverse array of empirical findings presented into a holistic, integrative model. It is important to note, however, that multiple forms of individual-environment interactions are likely to be implicated in this model because of both the multitude of pathways leading to and the likely existence of distinct subtypes of behavioral problems.

As outlined by Scarr and McCartney (1983), at the most basic level, passive individual-environment effects (e.g., those that occur when an individual has no choice in the selection of his or her environment and consequently has limited ability to affect the environment) set the stage of risk by increasing the likelihood both that vulnerability factors will develop and that environmental stressors relevant to the ontogenesis of behavioral problems will occur. Such effects may include environments provided by caregivers in early childhood, familial history of antisocial behavior, and neighborhood characteristics. At the same time, individual-environment effects may take a more interactive form in which aspects of the individual contribute either to the occurrence of negative chain reactions or to his or her response to environmental risk factors. For example, evocative effects are likely to involve aspects of the individual (e.g., temperament-related variables, coercive interpersonal strategies, or a strong BAS) that increase the likelihood of adverse environmental outcomes occurring. In contrast, reactive effects (e.g., social-cognitive information-processing styles, insecure attachment, or dysregulated emotional regulation styles) are likely to involve individual differences in tendencies to react to environmental events. Finally, active effects, in which an individual selects his or her environment (e.g., deviance training or assortive mating) are likely to complete the process. It is important to note that although the selection of environments is often in line with an individual's characteristics, individual characteristics may influence the range of environmental options available (e.g., an individual who fails to graduate from high school may have limited employment options). Indeed, such a restriction of environmental options is a prevailing consequence of conduct-problem and antisocial behaviors that likely plays a role in the promotion of intergenerational cycles of disadvantage that become self-perpetuating over time (Capaldi & Shortt, 2003).

REFERENCES

Alpern, L., & Lyons-Ruth, K. (1993). Preschool children at social risk: Chronicity and timing of maternal depressive symptoms and child behavior problems at school and at home. *Development and Psychopathology, 5,* 371–387.

American Psychiatric Association. (1987). *Diagnostic and statistical manual of mental disorders* (3rd ed.). Washington, DC: Author.

American Psychiatric Association. (1994). *Diagnostic and statistical manual of mental disorders* (4th ed.). Washington, DC: Author.

Anderson, C. A., Berkowitz, L., Donnerstein, E., Huesmann, L. R., Johnson, J. D., Linz, D., et al. (2004). The influence of media violence on youth. *Psychological Science in the Public Interest, 4,* 81–110.

Angold, A., Costello, E. J., & Erkanli, A. (1999). Comorbidity. *Journal of Child Psychology and Psychiatry and Allied Disciplines, 40,* 57–87.

Arnett, J. J. (1996). Sensation seeking, aggressiveness, and adolescent reckless behavior. *Personality and Individual Differences, 20,* 693–702.

Asarnow, J. R., & Callan, J. W. (1985). Boys with peer adjustment problems: Social cognitive processes. *Journal of Consulting and Clinical Psychology, 53,* 80–87.

Asendorpf, J. B., Borkenau, P., Ostendorf, F., & Van Aken, M. A. G. (2001). Carving personality description at its joints: Confirmation of three replicable personality prototypes for both children and adults. *European Journal of Personality, 15,* 169–198.

Baker, L., & Cantwell, D. P. (1987). A prospective psychiatric follow-up of children with speech/language disorders. *Journal of the American Academy of Child and Adolescent Psychiatry, 26,* 546–553.

Bates, J. E., Bayles, K., Bennett, D. S., Ridge, B., & Brown, M. M. (1991). Origins of externalizing behavior problems at eight years of age. In D. J. Pepler & K. H. Rubin (Eds.), *The development and treatment of childhood aggression* (pp. 93–120). Hillsdale, NJ: Lawrence Erlbaum.

Bates, J. E., Maslin, C. A., & Frankel, K. A. (1985). Attachment security, mother-child interaction, and temperament as predictors of behavior-problem ratings at age three years. *Monographs of the Society for Research in Child Development, 50,* 167–193.

Beitchman, J. H., Wilson, B., Johnson, C. J., Atkinson, L., Young, A., Adlaf, E., et al. (2001). Fourteen-year follow-up of speech/language-impaired and control children: Psychiatric outcome. *Journal of the American Academy of Child and Adolescent Psychiatry, 40,* 75–82.

Biederman, J., Hirshfeld-Becker, D. R., Rosenbaum, J. F., Herot, C., Friedman, D., Snidman, N., et al. (2001). Further evidence of association between behavioral inhibition and social anxiety in children. *American Journal of Psychiatry, 158,* 1673–1679.

Bohman, M. (1996). Predispositions to criminality: Swedish adoption studies in retrospect. In G. R. Bock & J. A. Goode (Eds.), *Genetics of criminal and antisocial behavior* (pp. 99–114). Chichester, UK: Wiley.

Bouchard, T. J., & Loehlin, J. C. (2001). Genes, evolution, and personality. *Behavior Genetics, 31,* 243–273.

Bucholz, K. K., Hesselbrock, V. M., Heath, A. C., Kramer, J. R., & Schuckit, M. A. (2000). A latent class analysis of antisocial personality disorder symptom data from a multi-centre family study of alcoholism. *Addiction, 95,* 553–567.

Burgess, K. B., Marshall, P. J., Rubin, K. H., & Fox, N. A. (2003). Infant attachment and temperament as predictors of subsequent externalizing problems and cardiac physiology. *Journal of Child Psychology and Psychiatry and Allied Disciplines, 44,* 819–831.

Buss, A. H., & Plomin, R. (1975). *A temperament theory of personality development.* New York: Wiley-Interscience.

Buss, A. H., & Plomin, R. (1984). *Temperament: Early developing personality traits.* Hillsdale, NJ: Lawrence Erlbaum.

Cadoret, R. J., Yates, W. R., Troughton, E., Woodward, G., & Stewart, M. A. (1995). Genetic-environmental interaction in the genesis of aggressivity and conduct disorders. *Archives of General Psychiatry, 52,* 916–924.

Capaldi, D. M., & Patterson, G. R. (1994). Interrelated influences of contextual factors on antisocial behavior in childhood and adolescence for males. In D. C. Fowles, P. Sutker, & S. H. Goodman (Eds.), *Progress in experimental personality and psychopathology research* (pp. 165–198). New York: Springer.

Capaldi, D. M., & Patterson, G. R. (1996). Can violent offenders be distinguished from frequent offenders: Predictions from childhood to adolescence. *Journal of Research in Crime & Delinquency, 33,* 206–231.

Capaldi, D. M., & Shortt, J. W. (2003). Understanding conduct problems in adolescence from a lifespan perspective. In G. Adams & M. Berzonsky (Eds.), *Blackwell handbook of adolescence* (pp. 470–493). Malden, MA: Blackwell.

Capaldi, D. M., & Stoolmiller, M. (1999). Co-occurrence of conduct problems and depressive symptoms in early adolescent boys: III. Prediction to young-adult adjustment. *Development and Psychopathology, 11,* 59–84.

Caspi, A. (1998). Personality development across the life course. In N. Eisenberg (Ed.), *Handbook of child psychology* (Vol. 3, 5th ed., pp. 311–388). New York: Wiley.

Caspi, A., McClay, J., Moffitt, T., Mill, J., Martin, J., Craig, I. W., et al. (2002). Role of genotype in the cycle of violence in maltreated children. *Science, 297,* 851–854.

Caspi, A., Moffitt, T. E., Silva, P. A., Stouthamer-Loeber, M., Schmutte, P. S., & Krueger, R. (1994). Are some people crime-prone? Replications of the personality-crime relation across nation, gender, race and method. *Criminology, 32,* 301–333.

Caspi, A., Taylor, A., Moffitt, T. E., & Plomin, R. (2000). Neighborhood deprivation affects children's mental health: Environmental risks identified in a genetic design. *Psychological Science, 11,* 338–342.

Cloninger, C. R. (1987). A systematic method for clinical description and classification of personality variants: A proposal. *Archives of General Psychiatry, 44,* 573–588.

Cocarro, E. F., Kavoussi, R. J., & Lesser, J. C. (1992). Self and other directed human aggression: The role of the central nervous system. *International Clinical Psychopharmacology, 6*(Suppl. 6), 70–83.

Cohen, D. C., & Strayer, J. (1996). Empathy in conduct-disordered and comparison youth. *Developmental Psychology, 32,* 988–998.

Cohen, N. J., Menna, R., Vallance, D. D., Barwick, M. A., Im, N., & Horodezky, N. B. (1998). Language, social cognitive processing, and behavioral characteristics of psychiatrically disturbed children with previously identified and unsuspected language impairments. *Journal of Child Psychology and Psychiatry, 39,* 853–864.

Coie, J. D., & Dodge, K. A. (1998). Aggression and antisocial behavior. In W. Damon (Series Ed.) & N. Eisenberg (Vol. Ed.), *Handbook of child psychology: Vol. 3. Social, emotional, and personality development* (5th ed., pp. 779–862). New York: Wiley.

Coie, J. D., Terry, R., Zakriski, A., & Lochman, J. (1995). Early adolescent social influences on delinquent behavior. In J. McCord (Ed.), *Coercion and punishment in long-term perspectives* (pp. 229–244). New York: Cambridge University Press.

Coolidge, F. L., Thede, L. L., & Young, S. E. (2000). Heritability and the comorbidity of attention deficit hyperactivity disorder with behavioral disorders and executive function deficits: A preliminary investigation. *Developmental Neuropsychology, 17,* 273–287.

Crick, N. R., & Grotpeter, J. K. (1995). Relational aggression, gender, and social-psychological adjustment. *Child Development, 66,* 710–722.

Crick, N. R., & Ladd, G. W. (1990). Children's perceptions of the outcomes of aggressive strategies: Do the ends justify being mean? *Developmental Psychology, 26,* 612–620.

Daderman, A. M. (1999). Differences between severely conduct-disordered juvenile males and normal juvenile males: The study of personality traits. *Personality and Individual Differences, 26,* 827–845.

Daderman, A. M., Wirsen M. A., & Hallman, J. (2001). Different personality patterns in non-socialized (juvenile delinquents) and socialized (air force pilot recruits) sensation seekers. *European Journal of Personality, 15,* 239–252.

Davidson, R. J., Putnam, K. M., & Larson, C. L. (2000). Dysfunction in the neural circuitry of emotion regulation: A possible prelude to violence. *Science, 289,* 591–594.

Deater-Deckard, K., & Plomin, R. (1999). An adoption study of etiology of teacher and parent reports of externalizing behavior problems in middle childhood. *Child Development, 70,* 144–154.

DeBaryshe, B. D., Patterson, G. R., & Capaldi, D. (1993). A performance model for academic achievement in early adolescent boys. *Developmental Psychology, 29,* 795–804.

DeKlyen, M., & Speltz, M. L. (2001). Attachment and conduct disorder. In J. Hill & B. Maughan (Eds.), *Conduct disorder in child and adolescence* (pp. 320–345). New York: Cambridge University Press.

Dery, M., Toupin, J., Pauze, R., Mercier, H., & Fortin, L. (1999). Neuropsychological characteristics of adolescents with conduct disorder: Association with attention-deficit-hyperactivity and aggression. *Journal of Abnormal Child Psychology, 27,* 225–236.

Dishion, T. J., Andrews, D. W., & Crosby, L. (1995). Antisocial boys and their friends in early adolescence: Relationship characteristics, quality, and interactional process. *Child Development, 66,* 139–151.

Dishion, T. J., Eddy, M. J., Haas, E., Li, F., & Spracklen, K. (1997). Friendships and violent behavior during adolescence. *Social Development, 6,* 207–223.

Dishion, T. J., French, D. C., & Patterson, G. R. (1995). The development and ecology of antisocial behavior. *Developmental Psychopathology, 2,* 421–471.

Dodge, K. A. (1993). Social cognitive mechanisms in the development of conduct disorder and depression. *Annual Review of Psychology, 44,* 559–584.

Dodge, K. A., Bates, J. E., & Pettit, G. S. (1990). Mechanisms in the cycle of violence. *Science, 250,* 1678–1683.

Dodge, K. A., & Frame, C. L. (1982). Social cognitive biases and deficits in aggressive boys. *Child Development, 53,* 620–635.

Dodge, K. A., Lochman, J. E., Harnish, J. D., Bates, J. E., & Pettit, G. S. (1997). Reactive and proactive aggression in school children and psychiatrically impaired chronically assaultive youth. *Journal of Abnormal Psychology, 106,* 37–51.

Dodge, K. A., & Pettit, G. S. (2003). A biopsychosocial model of the development of chronic conduct problems in adolescence. *Developmental Psychology, 39,* 349–371.

Dodge, K. A., Pettit, G. S., McClaskey, C. L., & Brown, M. (1986). Social competence in children. *Monographs of the Society for Research in Child Development, 51*(2, Serial No. 213).

Dohrenwend, B. P., & Dohrenwend, B. S. (1974). Social and cultural influences on psychopathology. *Annual Review of Psychology, 25,* 417–452.

Eaves, L., Rutter, M., Silberg, J. L., Shillady, L., Maes, H., & Pickles, A. (2000). Genetic and environmental causes of covariation in interview assessments of disruptive behavior in child and adolescent twins. *Behavior Genetics, 30,* 321–334.

Eisenberg, N., Fabes, R. A., Guthrie, I. K., Murphy, B. C., Maszk, P., Holmgren, R., et al. (1996). The relations of regulation and emotionality to problem behavior in elementary school children. *Development and Psychopathology, 8,* 141–162.

Eley, T. C., Dale, P., & Bishop, D. (2001). Longitudinal analysis of the genetic and environmental influences on components of cognitive delay in preschoolers. *Journal of Educational Psychology, 93,* 698–707.

Elkins, I., Iacono, W., Doyle, A., & McGue, M. (1997). Characteristics associated with the persistence of antisocial behavior: Results from recent longitudinal research. *Aggression and Violent Behavior, 2,* 101–124.

Emde, R. N., Plomin, R., Robinson, J., Corley, R., Fulker, D. W., Reznick, J. S., et al. (1992). Temperament, emotion, and cognition at fourteen months: The MacArthur Longitudinal Twin Study. *Child Development, 63,* 1437–1455.

Fagot, B. I. (1995). Classification of problem behaviors in young children: A comparison of four systems. *Journal of Applied Developmental Psychology, 16,* 95–106.

Fagot, B. I., & Kavanagh, K. (1990). The prediction of antisocial behavior from avoidant attachment classification. *Child Development, 61,* 864–873.

Farrington, D. P. (1991). Antisocial personality from childhood to adulthood. *Psychologist, 4,* 389–394.

Farrington, D. P. (1992). Explaining the beginning, progress, and ending of antisocial behavior from birth to adulthood. In J. McCord (Ed.), *Advances in criminological theory* (pp. 253–286). New Brunswick, NJ: Transaction.

Farrington, D. P. (1995). The development of offending and antisocial behaviour from childhood: Key findings from the Cambridge Study in Delinquent Development. *Journal of Child Psychology and Psychiatry, 6,* 929–964.

Farrington, D. P., & West, D. J. (1993). Criminal, penal and life histories of chronic offenders: Risk and protective factors and early identification. *Criminal Behaviour and Mental Health, 3,* 492–523.

Foley, D. L., Eaves, L. J., Wormley, B., Silberg, J. L., Maes, H. H., Kuhn, J., et al. (2004). Childhood adversity, monoamine oxidase A genotype, and risk for conduct disorder. *Archives of General Psychiatry, 61,* 738–744.

Fonseca, A. C., & Yule, W. (1995). Personality and antisocial behavior in children and adolescents: An enquiry into Eysenck's and Gray's theories. *Journal of Abnormal Child Psychology, 23,* 767–781.

Forgatch, M. S., & Patterson, G. R. (1989). *Parents and adolescents living together: Part 2. Family problem solving.* Eugene, OR: Castalia.

Fowles, D. C., & Missel, K. A. (1994). Electrodermal hyporeactivity, motivation and psychopathy: Theoretical issues. In D. C. Fowles, P. Sutker, & S. H. Goodman (Eds.), *Progress in experimental personality and psychopathology research* (pp. 263–283). New York: Springer.

Frick, P. J., Lahey, B. B., Loeber, R., Tannenbaum, L., VanHorn, Y., Christ, M. A. G., et al. (1993). Oppositional defiant disorder and conduct disorder: A meta-analytic review of factor analyses and cross-validation in a clinic sample. *Clinical Psychology Review, 13,* 319–340.

Frick, P. J., & Loney, B. (1999). Outcomes of children and adolescents with oppositional defiant disorder and conduct disorder. In H. C. Quay & A. E. Hogan (Eds.), *Handbook of disruptive behavior disorders* (pp. 507–524). New York: Plenum Press.

Furnham, A., & Thompson, J. (1991). Personality and self-reported delinquency. *Personality and Individual Differences, 12,* 585–593.

Gabrys, J. B. (1983). Contrasts in social behavior and personality of children. *Psychological Reports, 52,* 171–178.

Ge, X., Donnellan, M. B., & Wenk, E. (2001). The development of persistent criminal offending in males. *Criminal Justice and Behavior, 26,* 731–755.

Giancola, P. R., Martin, C. S., Tarter, R. E., Pelham, W. E., & Moss, H. B. (1996). Executive cognitive functioning and aggressive behavior in preadolescent boys at high risk for substance abuse/dependence. *Journal of Studies on Alcohol, 57,* 352–359.

Gjone, H., & Stevenson, J. (1997). A longitudinal twin study of temperament and behavior problems: Common genetic or environmental influences? *Journal of the American Academy of Child and Adolescent Psychiatry, 36,* 1448–1456.

Goma-I-Freixnet, M. (1995). Prosocial and antisocial aspects of personality. *Personality and Individual Differences, 19,* 125–134.

Gottfredson, M. R., & Hirschi, T. (1990). *A general theory of crime.* Stanford, CA: Stanford University Press.

Gouze, K. R. (1987). Attention and social problem solving as correlates of aggression in preschool males. *Journal of Abnormal Child Psychology, 15,* 181–197.

Gray, J. A. (1987). *The psychology of fear and stress.* Cambridge, UK: Cambridge University Press.

Greenberg, M. T., Speltz, M. L., & DeKlyen, M. (1993). The role of attachment in the early development of disruptive behavior problems. *Development and Psychopathology, 5,* 191–213.

Greene, K., Krcmar, M., Walters, L. H., Rubin, D. L., & Hale, J. L. (2000). Targeting adolescent risk-taking behaviors: The contribution of egocentrism and sensation-seeking. *Journal of Adolescence, 23,* 439–461.

Haemaelaeinen, M., & Pulkkinen, L. (1996). Problem behavior as a precursor of male criminality. *Development and Psychopathology, 8,* 443–455.

Harnish, J. D., Dodge, K. A., & Valente, E. (1995). Mother-child interaction quality as a partial mediator of the roles of maternal depressive symptomatology and socioeconomic status in the development of child conduct problems. *Child Development, 66,* 739–753.

Hart, D., Hofmann, V., Edelstein, W., & Keller, M. (1997). The relation of childhood personality types to adolescent behavior and development: A longitudinal study of Icelandic children. *Developmental Psychology, 33,* 195–205.

Hastings, P. D., Zahn-Waxler, C., Robinson, J., Usher, B., & Bridges, D. (2000). The development of concern for others in children with behavior problems. *Developmental Psychology, 36,* 531–546.

Heaven, P. C. L. (1996). Personality and self-reported delinquency: A longitudinal analysis. *Journal of Child Psychology and Psychiatry, 37,* 747–751.

Henry, B., Caspi, A., Moffitt, T. E., & Silva, P. A. (1996). Temperamental and familial predictors of violent and nonviolent criminal convictions: Age 3 to age 18. *Developmental Psychology, 32,* 614–623.

Hinshaw, S. P., Lahey, B. B., & Hart, E. L. (1993). Issues of taxonomy and comorbidity in the development of conduct disorder. *Development and Psychopathology, 5,* 31–50.

Hinshaw, S. P., & Lee, S. S. (2003). Conduct and oppositional defiant disorders. In E. J. Mash & R. A. Barkley (Eds.), *Child psychopathology* (2nd ed., pp. 144–198). New York: Guilford Press.

Hirshfeld, D. R., Rosenbaum, J. F., Biederman, J., Bolduc, E. A., Faraone, S. V., Snidman, N., et al. (1992). Stable behavioral inhibition and its association with anxiety disorder. *Journal of the American Academy of Child and Adolescent Psychiatry, 31,* 103–111.

Hughes, C., White, A., Sharpen, J., & Dunn, J. (2000). Antisocial, angry, and unsympathetic: "Hard-to-manage" preschoolers' peer problems and possible cognitive influences. *Journal of Child Psychology and Psychiatry, 41,* 169–179.

Jacobson, K. C., Prescott, C. A., & Kendler, K. S. (2002). Sex differences in the genetic and environmental influences on the development of antisocial behavior. *Development and Psychopathology, 13,* 395–416.

Jaffee, S., Caspi, A., Moffitt, T. E., & Silva, P. A. (2001). Why are children born to teen mothers at risk for adverse outcomes in young adulthood? Results from a 20-year longitudinal study. *Development and Psychopathology, 13,* 377–397.

Jaffee, S. R., Caspi, A., Moffitt, T. E., & Taylor, A. (2004). Physical maltreatment victim to antisocial child: Evidence of an environmentally mediated process. *Journal of Abnormal Psychology, 113,* 44–55.

Jensen, P. S., Martin, D., & Cantwell, D. P. (1997). Comorbidity in ADHD: Implications for research, practice, and DSM-V. *Journal of the American Academy of Child and Adolescent Psychiatry, 36,* 377–397.

John, O. P., Caspi, A., Robins, R. W., Moffitt, T. E., & Stouthamer-Loeber, M. (1994). The "little five": Exploring the nomological network of the five-factor model of personality in adolescent boys. *Child Development, 65,* 160–178.

Kazdin, A. (1997). Conduct disorder across the lifespan. In S. S. Luthar, J. A. Burack, D. Cicchetti, & J. R. Weisz (Eds.), *Developmental psychopathology: Perspectives on adjustment, risk, and disorder* (pp. 248–272). Cambridge, UK: Cambridge University Press.

Keenan, K., Loeber, R., & Green, S. (1999). Conduct disorder in girls: A review of the literature. *Clinical Child and Family Psychology Review, 2,* 3–19.

Keenan, K., & Shaw, D. (2003). Starting at the beginning: Exploring the etiology of antisocial behavior in the first years of life. In B. B. Lahey, T. E. Moffitt, & A. Caspi (Eds.), *Causes of conduct disorder and juvenile delinquency* (pp. 153–181). New York: Guilford.

Keenan, K., & Shaw, D. (1997). Developmental and social influences on young girls' early problem behavior. *Psychological Bulletin, 121,* 95–113.

Kerr, M., Tremblay, R. E., Pagani-Kurtz, L., & Vitaro, F. (1997). Boy's behavioral inhibition and the risk of later delinquency. *Archives of General Psychiatry, 54,* 809–816.

Kilgore, K., Snyder, J., & Lentz, C. (2000). The contribution of parental discipline, parental monitoring, and school risk to early-onset conduct problems in African American boys and girls. *Developmental Psychology, 36,* 835–845.

Knutson, J. F., DeGarmo, D. S., & Reid, J. B. (2004). Social disadvantage and neglectful parenting as precursors to the development of antisocial and aggressive child behavior: Testing a theoretical model. *Aggressive Behavior, 30,* 187–205.

Kratzer, L., & Hodgins, S. (1999). A typology of offenders: A test of Moffitt's theory among males and females from childhood to age 30. *Criminal Behaviour and Mental Health, 9,* 57–73.

Krueger, R. F. (1999). Personality traits in late adolescence predict mental disorders in early adulthood: A prospective-epidemiologic study. *Journal of Personality, 67,* 39–65.

Krueger, R., Schmutte, P. S., Caspi, A., Moffitt, T. E., Campbell, K., & Silva, P. A. (1994). Personality traits are linked to crime among males and females: Evidence from a birth cohort. *Journal of Abnormal Psychology, 103,* 328–338.

Kruesi, M., Rapoport, J. L., Hamburger, S., & Hibbs, E. D. (1990). Cerebrospinal fluid monoamine metabolites, aggression, and impulsivity in disruptive behavior disorders of children and adolescents. *Archives of General Psychiatry, 47,* 419–426.

Lahey, B. B., Applegate, B., Barkley, R. A., Garfinkel, B., McBurnett, K., Kerdyk, L., et al. (1994). DSM-IV field trials for oppositional defiant disorder and conduct disorder in children and adolescents. *American Journal of Psychiatry, 151,* 1163–1171.

Lahey, B. B., Applegate, B., Waldman, I., Hankin, B. L., & Rick, J. (2004). The structure of child and adolescent psychopathology: Generating new hypotheses. *Journal of Abnormal Psychology, 113,* 358–385.

Lahey, B. B., Loeber, R., Quay, H. C., Applegate, B., Shaffer, D., Waldman, I., et al. (1998). Validity of DSM-IV subtypes of conduct disorder based on age of onset. *Journal of the American Academy of Child and Adolescent Psychiatry, 37,* 435–442.

Lahey, B. B., McBurnett, K., & Loeber, R. (2000). Are attention-deficit hyperactivity disorder and oppositional defiant disorder developmental precursors to conduct disorder? In A. Sameroff, M. Lewis, & S. Miller (Eds.), *Handbook of developmental psychopathology* (2nd ed., pp. 431–446). New York: Plenum.

Lahey, B. B., Miller, T. L., Gordon, R. A., & Riley, A. (1999). Developmental epidemiology of the disruptive behavior disorders. In H. Quay & A. Hogan (Eds.), *Handbook of the disruptive behavior disorders* (pp. 23–48). New York: Kluwer Academic.

Lahey, B. B., Moffitt, T. E., & Caspi, A. (2003). *Causes of conduct disorder and juvenile delinquency.* New York: Guilford Press.

Lahey, B. B., Piacentini, J. C., McBurnett, K., Stone, P., Hartdagen, S., & Hynd, G. (1988). Psychopathology and antisocial behavior in the parents of children with conduct disorder and hyperactivity. *Journal of the American Academy of Child and Adolescent Psychiatry, 27,* 163–170.

Lahey, B. B., Russo, M. F., Walker, J. L., & Piacentini, J. C. (1989). Personality characteristics of the mothers of children with disruptive behavior disorders. *Journal of Consulting and Clinical Psychology, 57,* 512–515.

Lahey, B. B., & Waldman, I. D. (2003). A developmental propensity model of the origins of conduct problems during childhood and adolescence. In B. B. Lahey, T. E. Moffitt, & A. Caspi (Eds.), *Causes of conduct disorder and juvenile delinquency* (pp. 76–117). New York: Guilford Press.

Lahey, B. B., Waldman, I. D., & McBurnett, K. (1999). The development of antisocial behavior: An integrative causal model. *Journal of Child Psychology and Psychiatry, 40,* 669–682.

Lemery, K. S., Essex, M. J., & Smider, N. A. (2002). Revealing the relationship between temperament and behavior problems by eliminating measurement confounding: Expert ratings and factor analysis. *Child Development, 73,* 867–882.

Levine, J. A., Pollack, H., & Comfort, M. E. (2001). Academic and behavioral outcomes among the children of young mothers. *Journal of Marriage and the Family, 63,* 355–369.

Loeber, R. (1988). Natural histories of conduct problems, delinquency, and associated substance abuse: Evidence for developmental progressions. In B. B. Lahey & A. E. Kazdin (Eds.), *Advances in clinical child psychology* (Vol. 11, pp. 73–124). New York: Plenum.

Loeber, R., & Farrington, D. P. (2000). Young children who commit crime: Epidemiology, developmental origins, risk factors, early interventions, and policy implications. *Development and Psychopathology, 12,* 737–762.

Loeber, R., Farrington, D. P., Stouthamer-Loeber, M., & Van Kammen, W. (1998). *Antisocial behavior and mental health problems: Explanatory factors in childhood and adolescence.* Mahwah, NJ: Lawrence Erlbaum.

Loeber, R., Green, S. M., Keenan, K., & Lahey, B. B. (1995). Which boys will fare worse? Early predictors of the onset of conduct disorder in a six-year longitudinal study. *Journal of the American Academy of Child and Adolescent Psychiatry, 34,* 499–509.

Loeber, R., & Schmaling, K. F. (1985). Empirical evidence for overt and covert patterns of antisocial conduct problems: A meta-analysis. *Journal of Abnormal Child Psychology, 13,* 337–352.

Luengo, M. A., Otero, J. M., Carrillo-de-la-Pena, M. T., & Miron, L. (1994). Dimensions of antisocial behaviour in juvenile delinquency: A study of personality variables. *Psychology, Crime and Law, 1,* 27–37.

Lynam, D. R. (1998). Early identification of the fledgling psychopath: Locating the psychopathic child in the current nomenclature. *Journal of Abnormal Psychology, 107,* 566–575.

Lynam, D., Moffitt, T., & Stouthamer-Loeber, M. (1993). Explaining the relation between IQ and delinquency: Class, race, test motivation, school failure or self-control? *Journal of Abnormal Psychology, 102,* 187–196.

Lyons-Ruth, K., Alpern, L., & Repacholi, B. (1993). Disorganized infant attachment classification and maternal psychosocial problems as predictors of hostile-aggressive behavior in the preschool classroom. *Child Development, 64,* 572–585.

Lyons-Ruth, K., Easterbrooks, M. A., & Cibelli, C. D. (1997). Infant attachment strategies, infant mental lag, and maternal depressive symptoms: Predictors of internalizing and externalizing problems at age 7. *Developmental Psychology, 33,* 681–692.

McBurnett, K., & Lahey, B. B. (1994). Neuropsychological and neuroendocrine correlates of conduct disorder and antisocial behavior in children and adolescents. In D. C. Fowles, P. Sutker, & S. H. Goodman (Eds.), *Progress in experimental personality and psychopathology research* (pp. 199–231). New York: Springer.

McBurnett, K., Lahey, B. B., Rathouz, P. J., & Loeber, R. (2000). Low salivary cortisol and persistent aggression in boys referred for disruptive behavior. *Archives of General Psychiatry, 57,* 38–43.

McLoyd, V. (1990). The impact of economic hardship on black families and children: Psychological distress, parenting, and socioemotional development. *Child Development, 61,* 311–346.

Miech, R. A., Caspi, A., Moffitt, T. E., Wright, B. R. E., & Silva, P. A. (1999). Low socioeconomic status and mental disorders: A longitudinal study of selection and causation during young adulthood. *American Journal of Sociology, 104,* 1096–1131.

Miller, P. A., & Eisenberg, N. (1988). The relation of empathy to aggressive and externalizing/antisocial behavior. *Psychological Bulletin, 103,* 324–344.

Moffitt, T. E. (1990). Juvenile delinquency and attention deficit disorder: Boys' developmental trajectories from age 3 to 15. *Child Development, 61,* 893–910.

Moffitt, T. E. (1993). Adolescence-limited and life-course-persistent antisocial behavior: A developmental taxonomy. *Psychological Review, 100,* 674–701.

Moffitt, T. E. (2003). Life-course persistent and adolescence-limited antisocial behavior: A 10-year research review and a research agenda. In B. B. Lahey, T. E. Moffitt, & A. Caspi (Eds.), *Causes of conduct disorder and juvenile delinquency* (pp. 49–75). New York: Guilford Press.

Moffitt, T. E., & Caspi, A. (2001). Childhood predictors differentiate life-course persistent and adolescence-limited pathways among males and females. *Development & Psychopathology, 13,* 355–375.

Moffitt, T. E., Caspi, A., Dickson, N., Silva, P., & Stanton, W. (1996). Childhood-onset versus adolescent-onset antisocial conduct problems in males: Natural history from ages 3 to 18 years. *Development and Psychopathology, 8,* 399–424.

Moffitt, T. E., Caspi, A., Harrington, H., & Milne, B. J. (2002). Males on the life-course-persistent and adolescence-limited antisocial pathways: Follow-up at age 26 years. *Development and Psychopathology, 14,* 179–207.

Moffitt, T. E., Caspi, A., Rutter, M., & Silva, P. A. (2001). *Sex differences in antisocial behaviour.* Cambridge, UK: Cambridge University Press.

Moffitt, T. E., & Silva, P. A. (1988). IQ and delinquency: A direct test of the differential detection hypothesis. *Journal of Abnormal Psychology, 97,* 330–333.

Moss, E., Cyr, C., & Dubois-Comtois, K. (2004). Attachment at early school age and developmental risk: Examining family contexts and behavior problems of controlling-caregiving, controlling-punitive, and behaviorally disorganized children. *Developmental Psychology, 40,* 519–532.

Moss, E., Parent, S., Gosselin, C., Rousseau, D., & St-Laurent, D. (1996). Attachment and teacher-reported behavior problems during the preschool and early school-age period. *Development and Psychopathology, 8,* 511–525.

Nagin, D. S., Pogarsky, G., & Farrington, D. P. (1997). Adolescent mothers and the criminal behavior of their children. *Law and Society Review, 31,* 137–162.

Nagin D., & Tremblay, R. E. (1999). Trajectories of boys' physical aggression, opposition, and hyperactivity on the path to physically violent and non-violent delinquency. *Child Development, 70,* 1181–1196.

Newcomb, M. D., & McGee, L. (1991). Influence of sensation seeking on general deviance and specific problem behaviors from adolescence to young adulthood. *Journal of Personality and Social Psychology, 61,* 614–628.

O'Connor, T. G., Deater-Deckard, K., Fulker, D., Rutter, M., & Plomin, R. (1998). Genotype-environment correlations in late childhood and early adolescence: Antisocial behavioral problems and coercive parenting. *Developmental Psychology, 34,* 970–981.

O'Connor, T. G., Neiderhiser, J. M., Reiss, D., Hetherington, E. M., & Plomin, R. (1998). Genetic contributions to continuity, change, and co-occurrence of antisocial and depressive symptoms in adolescence. *Journal of Child Psychology & Psychiatry & Allied Disciplines, 39,* 323–336.

Osgood, D. W., McMorris, B. J., & Potenza, M. T. (2002). Analyzing multiple-item measures of crime and deviance: I. Item response theory scaling. *Journal of Quantitative Criminology, 18,* 267–296.

Patterson, G. R. (1993). Orderly change in a stable world: The antisocial trait as a chimera. *Journal of Consulting and Clinical Psychology, 61,* 911–919.

Patterson, G. R. (1998). Coercion as a basis for early age of onset for arrest. In J. McCord (Ed.), *Coercion and punishment in long-term perspectives* (pp. 81–105). New York: Cambridge University Press.

Patterson, G. R., Forgatch, M. S., Yoerger, K. L., & Stoolmiller, M. (1998). Variables that initiate and maintain an early-onset trajectory for juvenile offending. *Development and Psychopathology, 10,* 531–547.

Patterson, G. R., Reid, J. B., & Dishion, T. J. (1992). *Antisocial boys.* Eugene, OR: Castalia.

Pennington, B. F., & Ozonoff, S. (1996). Executive functions and developmental psychopathology. *Journal of Child Psychology & Psychiatry & Allied Disciplines, 37,* 51–87.

Petrill, S. A., Saudino, K., Cherny, S. S., Emde, R. N., Hewitt, J. K., Fulker, D. W., et al. (1997). Exploring the genetic etiology of low general cognitive ability from 14 to 36 months. *Developmental Psychology, 33,* 544–548.

Plomin, R., & Petrill, S. A. (1997). Genetics and intelligence: What's new? *Intelligence, 24,* 53–77.

Quay, H. C. (1993). The psychobiology of undersocialized aggressive conduct disorder: A theoretical perspective. *Development and Psychopathology, 5,* 165–180.

Raine, A. (1993). *The psychopathology of crime: Criminal behavior as a clinical disorder.* San Diego, CA: Academic Press.

Raine, A. (1996). Violence, brain imaging, and neuropsychology. In D. M. Stoff & R. B. Cairns (Eds.), *Aggression and violence: Genetic, neurobiological and biosocial perspectives* (pp. 145–168). Mahwah, NJ: Lawrence Erlbaum.

Raine, A. (1997). Antisocial behavior and psychophysiology: A biosocial perspective and a prefrontal dysfunction hypothesis. In D. Stoff, J. Breiling, & J. D. Maser (Eds.), *Handbook of antisocial behavior* (pp. 289–304). New York: Wiley.

Raine, A., Reynolds, C., Venables, P. H., Mednick, S. A., & Farrington, D. P. (1998). Fearlessness, stimulation-seeking, and large body size at age 3 years as early predispositions to childhood aggression at age 11 years. *Archives of General Psychiatry, 55,* 745–751.

Reid, J. B., & Patterson, G. R. (1989). The development of antisocial behaviour patterns in childhood and adolescence. *European Journal of Personality, 3,* 107–119.

Renken, B., Egeland, B., Marvinney, D., Mangelsdorf, S., & Sroufe, L. A. (1989). Early childhood antecedents of aggression and passive-withdrawal in early elementary school. *Journal of Personality, 57,* 257–281.

Rhee, S. H., & Waldman, I. D. (2002). Genetic and environmental influences on antisocial behavior: A meta-analysis of twin and adoption studies. *Psychological Bulletin, 128,* 490–529.

Robins, R. W., Johns, O. P., Caspi, A., Moffitt, T. E., & Stouthamer-Loeber, M. (1996). Resilient, overcontrolled, and undercontrolled boys: Three replicable personality types. *Journal of Personality and Social Psychology, 70,* 157–171.

Robinson, J. L., Kagan, J., Reznick, J. S., & Corley, R. (1992). The heritability of inhibited and uninhibited behavior: A twin study. *Developmental Psychology, 28,* 1030–1037.

Rogeness, G. A., Javors, M. A., & Pliszka, S. R. (1992). Neuro-chemistry and child and adolescent psychiatry. *Journal of the American Academy of Child and Adolescent Psychiatry, 31,* 765–781.

Rowe, D. C., & Flannery, D. J. (1994). An examination of environmental and trait influences on adolescent delinquency. *Journal of Research in Crime and Delinquency, 31,* 374–389.

Rutter, M. L. (1997). Nature-nurture integration: The example of antisocial behavior. *American Psychologist, 52,* 390–398.

Rutter, M. (2003). Crucial paths from risk indicator to causal mechanism. In B. B. Lahey, T. E. Moffitt, & A. Caspi (Eds.), *Causes of conduct disorder and juvenile delinquency* (pp. 3–26). New York: Guilford Press.

Rutter, M., Caspi, A., & Moffitt, T. E. (2003). Using sex differences in psychopathology to study causal mechanisms: Unifying issues and research strategies. *Journal of Child Psychology and Psychiatry, 44,* 1092–1115.

Rutter, M., Dunn, J., Plomin, R., Siminoff, E., Pickles, A., Maughan, B., et al. (1997). Integrating nature and nurture: Implications of person-environment correlations and interactions for developmental psychopathology. *Development and Psychopathology, 9,* 335–364.

Rutter, M., Giller, H., & Hagell, A. (1998). *Antisocial behavior by young people.* Cambridge, UK: Cambridge University Press.

Rutter, M., Pickles, A., Murray, R., & Eaves, L. (2001). Testing hypotheses on specific environmental causal effects on behavior. *Psychological Bulletin, 127,* 291–324.

Rutter, M., Silberg, J., O'Connor, T., & Simonoff, E. (1999). Genetics and child psychiatry: II. Empirical research findings. *Journal of Child Psychology and Psychiatry, 40,* 19–55.

Sampson, R. J., & Laub, J. H. (1997). Unraveling the social context of physique and delinquency: A new, long-term look at the Gluecks' classic study. In A. Raine & P. A. Brennan (Eds.), *Biosocial bases of violence. NATO ASI series: Series A: Life sciences* (Vol. 292, pp. 175–188). New York: Plenum.

Saudino, K. J., Plomin, R., & DeFries, J. C. (1996). Tester-rated temperament at 14, 20 and 24 months: Environmental change and genetic continuity. *British Journal of Developmental Psychology, 14,* 129–144.

Scarr, S., & McCartney, K. (1983). How people make their own environments: A theory of genotype leading to environment effects. *Child and Development, 54,* 424–435.

Schmitz, S., Fulker, D. W., Plomin, R., Zahn-Waxler, C., Emde, R. N., & DeFries, J. C. (1999). Temperament and problem behavior during early childhood. *International Journal of Behavioral Development, 23,* 333–355.

Schwartz, C. E., Snidman, N., & Kagan, J. (1996). Early childhood temperament as a determinant of externalizing behavior in adolescence. *Developmental Psychopathology, 8,* 527–537.

Seguin, J. R., Boulerice, B., Harden, P. W., Tremblay, R. E., & Pihl, R. O. (1999). Executive functions and physical aggression after controlling for attention deficit hyperactivity disorder, general memory and IQ. *Journal of Child Psychology and Psychiatry, 40,* 1197–1208.

Shaw, D. S., Owens, E. B., Vondra, J. I., & Keenan, K. (1996). Early risk factors and pathways in the development of early disruptive behavior problems. *Development and Psychopathology, 8,* 679–699.

Shortt, J. W., Capaldi, D. M., Dishion, T. J., Bank, L., & Owen, L. D. (2003). The role of adolescent friends, romantic partners, and siblings in the emergence of the adult antisocial lifestyle. *Journal of Family Psychology, 17,* 521–533.

Sigvardsson, S., Bohman, M., & Cloninger, C. R. (1987). Structure and stability of childhood personality: Prediction of later social adjustment. *Journal of Child Psychology and Psychiatry, 28,* 929–946.

Simo, S., & Perez, J. (1991). Sensation seeking and antisocial behaviour in a junior student sample. *Personality and Individual Differences, 12,* 965–966.

Speltz, M. L., DeKlyen, M., & Greenberg, M. T. (1999). Attachment in boys with early onset conduct problems. *Development and Psychopathology, 11,* 269–285.

Stattin, H., & Klackenberg-Larsson, I. (1993). Early language and intelligence development and their relationship to future criminal behavior. *Journal of Abnormal Psychology, 102,* 369–378.

Stoolmiller, M. (1994). Antisocial behavior, delinquent peer association, and unsupervised wandering for boys: Growth and change from childhood to early adolescence. *Multivariate Behavioral Research, 29,* 263–288.

Tackett, J. L., Krueger, R. F., Sawyer, M. G., & Graetz, B. W. (2003). Subfactors of DSM-IV conduct disorder: Evidence and connections with syndromes from the Child Behavior Checklist. *Journal of Abnormal Child Psychology, 31,* 647–654.

Taylor, J., Iacono, W. G., & McGue, M. (2000). Evidence for a genetic etiology of early-onset delinquency. *Journal of Abnormal Psychology, 109,* 634–643.

Tellegen, A. (1982). *Brief manual for the Multidimensional Personality Questionnaire.* Minneapolis: University of Minnesota.

Tranah, T., Harnett, P., & Yule, W. (1998). Conduct disorder and personality. *Personality and Individual Differences, 24,* 741–745.

Tremblay, R. E. (2000). The development of aggressive behaviour during childhood: What have we learned in the past century? *International Journal of Behavioral Development, 24,* 129–141.

Tremblay, R. E., Pihl, R. O., Vitaro, F., & Dobkin, P. L. (1994). Predicting early onset of male antisocial behavior from preschool behavior. *Archives of General Psychiatry, 51,* 732–739.

van den Oord, E. J., Boomsma, D. I., & Verhulst, F. C. (1994). A study of problem behaviors in 10- to 15-year-old biologically related and unrelated international adoptees. *Behavior Genetics, 24,* 193–205.

Vollebergh, W. A. M., Iedema, J., Bijl, R. V., de Graaf, R., Smit, F., & Ormel, J. (2001). The structure and stability of common mental disorders: The NEMESIS study. *Archives of General Psychiatry, 58,* 597–603.

Vondra, J. I., Shaw, D. S., Swearingen, L., Cohen, M., & Owens, E. B. (2001). Attachment stability and emotional and behavioral regulation from infancy to preschool age. *Development and Psychopathology, 13,* 13–33.

Waas, G. A. (1988). Social attributional biases of peer-rejected and aggressive children. *Child Development, 59,* 969–992.

Wakschlag, L. S., Lahey, B. B., Loeber, R., Green, S. M., Gordon, R. A., & Leventhal, B. L. (1997). Maternal smoking during pregnancy and the risk of conduct disorder in boys. *Archives of General Psychiatry, 54,* 670–676.

Waldman, I. D. (1996). Aggressive boys' hostile perceptual and response biases: The role of attention and impulsivity. *Child Development, 67,* 1015–1033.

Waldman, I. D., Rhee, S. H., Levy, F., & Hay, D. A. (2001). Genetic and environmental influences on the covariation among symptoms of attention deficit hyperactivity disorder, oppositional defiant disorder, and conduct disorder. In D. A. Hay & F. Levy (Eds.), *Attention, genes, and ADHD* (pp. 115–138). Hillsdale, NJ: Lawrence Erlbaum.

Zahn-Waxler, C. (1993). Warriors and worriers: Gender and psychopathology. *Development and Psychopathology, 5,* 79–89.

Zoccolillo, M. (1993). Gender and the development of conduct disorder. *Development and Psychopathology, 5,* 65–78.

Zuckerman, M. (1996). The psychobiological model for impulsive unsocialized sensation seeking: A comparative approach. *Neuropsychobiology, 34,* 125–129.

Zuckerman, M., Kuhlman, D. M., Joireman, J., Teta, P., & Kraft, M. (1993). A comparison of three structural models for personality: The big three, the big five, and the alternative five. *Journal of Personality and Social Psychology, 65,* 757–768.

CHAPTER 15

The Developmental Psychopathology of Personality Disorders

JEFFREY G. JOHNSON, PAMELA G. MCGEOCH, VANESSA P. CASKEY, SOTOODEH G. ABHARY, JOEL R. SNEED, AND ROBERT F. BORNSTEIN

It is widely recognized among clinicians, researchers, and theorists that interpersonal experiences during childhood, adolescence, and to a lesser extent during adulthood play an important role in personality development. Because every aspect of human existence is profoundly affected by social interaction, and because our lives are defined and structured by our relationships with other people, personality itself is widely viewed as being determined or shaped by these relationships. Personality development is generally understood to take place predominantly during childhood and adolescence, and personality disorders (PDs) accordingly tend to become evident by adolescence or early adulthood (American Psychiatric Association [APA], 1968, 1980, 1987, 2000). Epidemiological studies have indicated that personality disorders are fairly prevalent. To a substantial degree, maladaptive personality traits and PDs are likely to result, in part, from disturbances in interpersonal relationships that take place during the formative years of childhood and adolescence.

PD prevalence estimates, based on the diagnostic criteria from the *Diagnostic and Statistical Manual of Mental Disorders,* 4th edition, text revision (*DSM-IV-TR*; APA, 2000), have ranged from approximately 7% to 15% of the adult population and from 6% to 17% of the adolescent population, depending on the diagnostic procedure and the range of PDs assessed (Grant et al., 2004; Johnson, Bromley, Bornstein, & Sneed, in press; Samuels et al., 2002; Torgersen, Kringlen, & Cramer, 2001). There are 10 official *DSM-IV* PDs (antisocial, avoidant, borderline, dependent, histrionic, narcissistic, paranoid, obsessive-compulsive, schizoid, and schizotypal), and 2 additional PD diagnostic criteria sets included for further study (depressive PD and passive-aggressive or negativistic PD). Each of these PDs has been found in most studies to affect 0.5% to 3% of the adults in the general population, although prevalence estimates have varied significantly from study to study.

Numerous studies have shown that adolescents and adults with PDs are more likely than those without PDs to report a history of childhood adversities, including abuse, neglect, maladaptive parenting, parental loss, and other traumatic life events (e.g., Brodsky, Cloitre, & Dulit, 1995; Goldman, D'Angelo, & DeMaso, 1992; Herman, Perry, & van der Kolk, 1989; Johnson, Quigley, & Sherman, 1997; Klonsky, Oltmanns, Turkheimer, & Fiedler, 2000; Ludolph, Westen, & Misle, 1990; Norden, D. N. Klein, Donaldson, Pepper, & L. M. Klein, 1995; Raczek, 1992; Shearer, Peters, Quaytman, & Ogden, 1990; Weaver & Clum, 1993; Westen, Ludolph, Block, Wixom, & Wiss, 1990). However, although retrospective studies have provided substantial evidence in support of this hypothesis, such findings are often not conclusive given the possibility of biased recall and inaccurate reporting of childhood adversities. Prospective longitudinal findings have only recently become available, and it has not been possible to rule out the alternative hypotheses that the association of childhood adversities with maladaptive personality traits is attributable to recall bias or to preexisting childhood traits that may contribute to the onset of some types of childhood adversities (Maughan & Rutter, 1997; Paris, 1997).

Although there have been findings supporting the validity of retrospective reports of childhood adversities (e.g., Bifulco, Brown, & Lillie, 1997; Robins et al., 1985), and although retrospective studies have promoted the formulation of developmental hypotheses, it is nevertheless problematic to make strong causal inferences about the impact of adverse childhood experiences on the development of personality disorders based on retrospective data. Retrospective studies cannot rule out the alternative hypotheses that the association of childhood adversities with maladaptive personality traits is attributable to recall bias or to preexisting childhood traits that may contribute to the onset of some types of childhood adversities (Maughan & Rutter, 1997; Paris, 1997). Both of these alternative hypotheses have presented significant challenges to researchers in this field.

CHILDHOOD ADVERSITY AND A VULNERABILITY-STRESS APPROACH TO PDs

The Need for a Vulnerability-Stress or Interactionist Model of Personality Development

A number of studies have supported the hypotheses that genetic and prenatal factors may play an important role in the development of behavioral and emotional problems that may become evident during childhood (Livesley, Jang, Jackson, & Vernon, 1993; Neugebauer, Hoek, & Susser, 1999; Thomas & Chess, 1984). In addition, research has indicated that maladaptive childhood traits may have an adverse influence on parenting behavior, potentially increasing risk for childhood maltreatment (Kendler, 1996). Such findings have contributed to skepticism in some quarters about the hypothesis that childhood adversities play an important role in the development of maladaptive personality traits and PDs. Other clinicians and researchers who have noted the significance of these challenging findings have recognized the importance of developing an interactionist or vulnerability-stress theory of PD development (e.g., Caspi et al., 2002; Foley et al., 2004).

The field of PD research is currently in the earliest stages of developing an empirically based interactionist or vulnerability-stress model of personality development. Research has provided clear indications that both stressful or traumatic life events and a range of vulnerability factors, ranging from biological to interpersonal diatheses, are likely to contribute to the development of abnormal personality traits (Caspi et al., 2002; Foley et al., 2004). However, researchers and theorists have not yet begun to develop a truly comprehensive and integrated model that incorporates both vulnerability and stress factors (Andersen, 2003). It is important to recognize that, because research on PDs as operationally defined in the *DSM-III* (1980) and beyond is still in its infancy, it is likely that many years or decades of research will be required before a fully adequate model of PD development can be developed.

It is important to note that early life experiences, such as childhood adversities, may be conceptualized as "vulnerability" factors or as "stress" factors (see Johnson et al., 2002).[1] For example, early childhood attachment failure, which may be partially attributable to problematic experiences with key attachment figures, may contribute to an enduring attachment style that interferes with healthy socialization (Brennan & Shaver, 1998; Fossati et al., 2003; see Davila, Ramsay, Stroud, & Steinberg, Chapter 9 of this volume). Thus, enduring attachment difficulties, which are generally viewed as constituting a vulnerability factor for subsequent disorder, may result, in part, from problematic or inadequate parent-child interaction (Brennan & Shaver; Fossati et al.). It is not yet possible to distinguish reliably between vulnerability factors that may have a biological basis (e.g., genetic predisposition toward anxiety and anxious attachment style) and vulnerability factors that may result from highly problematic or abusive interactions between parent and child beginning in early infancy.

Research, including genetic epidemiology, has confirmed that childhood maltreatment is associated with elevated risk for a wide range of psychiatric symptoms, including maladaptive personality traits (see Kendler et al., 2000). However, until better markers are developed for genetic factors, for other biological vulnerability factors, and for vulnerability factors that stem from problematic childhood experiences, it will not be possible to determine with confidence how vulnerability factors and subsequent life experiences combine to bring about the development of maladaptive personality traits. Thus, one of the goals of current and ongoing research is the development of improved and more reliable markers of vulnerability. As more specific indicators of vulnerability are developed, new lines of research will become possible, and this research will hold the potential of promoting the development of a truly comprehensive and systematic theory of PD development.

It is important to recognize that a sizable body of research has confirmed that there are important individual differences in temperament during early childhood, and that these are likely to be due at least in part to a biological (e.g., genetic, prenatal) predisposition (Thomas & Chess, 1984). The extent to which temperamental characteristics predict, influence, or determine subsequent personality development is a topic of ongoing investigation. Although several studies have shown that early childhood temperament or personality predicts subsequent functioning during adolescence or adulthood (e.g., Bernstein, Cohen, Skodol, Bezirganian, & Brook, 1996; Caspi, Moffitt, Newman, & Silva, 1996), it has not yet been possible to disentangle the biological and experiential determinants of early childhood temperament.

Temperamental characteristics (which are themselves likely to be influenced by both biological and experiential factors) are likely to interact in complex ways with other determinants of behavior and personality development. To some extent, enduring and temperament-related diatheses present in early childhood may elicit behaviors from parents (see Kendler, 1996) and others that may help "crystallize" these traits, thereby increasing the likelihood of a similar pattern of behavior that may endure into adolescence and adulthood. In addition, temperamental vulnerability factors may interact with stressful or traumatic life events, including childhood maltreatment, resulting in the development of PD or a maladaptive attachment or personality style. For example, it may be hypothesized that young children who have a relatively anxious, shy, or inhibited temperament may be especially likely to develop a Cluster C (i.e., avoidant, dependent, obsessive-compulsive) PD if they are emotionally neglected during their formative years. Young children with an outgoing, gregarious temperament may be most likely to develop a Cluster B PD (i.e., antisocial, borderline, narcissistic, and histrionic PDs) if physically, sexually, or emotionally abused. Research has clearly suggested that different types of childhood maltreatment and other childhood adversities may contribute to increased risk for the development of different types of PD traits (see Tables 1 through 12). However, it is important to recognize that children adapt and respond in different ways to adversities, depending on their strengths (e.g., coping skills), vulnerabilities, and interpersonal resources (e.g., social support, availability of health care).

It is also important to note that PDs and other chronic mental disorders (e.g., dysthymic disorder) may themselves be conceptualized as vulnerability factors. For example, PD may be conceptualized as a complex of interpersonal deficits, stemming in large measure from problematic interpersonal experiences during childhood, and increasing risk for subsequent mental health problems (Johnson et al., 1997). Although this chapter is principally concerned with risk factors that may contribute to the development of PD, there is abundant evidence indicating that individuals with PD are at substantially elevated long-term risk for adverse mental health outcomes (Daley et al., 1999; Johnson et al., 1996; Johnson, Cohen, Brown, Smailes, & Bernstein, 1999; Kwon et al., 2000). Further, PDs and PD traits have been found to be particularly associated with risk for Axis I disorders in the context of stressful life events (Johnson & Bornstein, 1991).

Recent Evidence Permitting Stronger Inferences Regarding Childhood Adversities and PDs

In recent years, investigations utilizing a number of different research paradigms have provided new and compelling evidence in support of the hypothesis that childhood experiences have an important influence on personality development. Research has indicated that maladaptive personality traits are likely to be caused by the interaction of genetic and environmental risk factors (Caspi et al., 2002; Foley et al., 2004). In addition, maternal behavior, health, and environmental characteristics affecting prenatal development have been found to have a lasting impact on offspring traits and mental health (Neugebauer et al., 1999; Ward, 1991). Epidemiological studies and co-twin analyses that have controlled for genetic factors have indicated that childhood abuse is likely to be causally related to an increased risk for a broad spectrum of psychiatric symptoms (Kendler et al., 2000). Neurobiological studies have provided considerable evidence suggesting that childhood maltreatment may cause persistent deficits in brain activity, and that these deficits are associated with the development of a wide range of psychiatric symptoms, including maladaptive personality traits (Teicher et al., 2003).[2] Prospective longitudinal studies and investigations that obtained evidence of childhood maltreatment from official records have supported the hypothesis that childhood abuse and neglect may contribute to increased risk for the development of PDs (e.g., Drake et al., 1988; Guzder, Paris, & Zelkowitz, 1996; Johnson, Cohen, Brown, et al., 1999; Johnson, Cohen, Kasen, Smailes, & Brook,

2001; Johnson, Cohen, Smailes, et al., 2000; Johnson, Cohen, Smailes, et al., 2001; Luntz & Widom, 1994). The findings of these studies, and of the studies that have provided relevant retrospective data, are described in greater detail below.

The results of these prospective longitudinal studies and studies that obtained evidence of childhood maltreatment from archival records have provided stronger evidence of a possible causal link between childhood maltreatment and risk for personality disorders. These studies have indicated that childhood abuse, neglect, and maladaptive parenting are indeed associated with elevated risk for personality disorders during adolescence and adulthood (e.g., Cohen, 1996; Cohen, Brown, & Smailes, 2001; Drake et al., 1988; Guzder et al., 1996; Johnson, Cohen, Brown, et al., 1999; Johnson, Cohen, Kasen, et al., 2001; Johnson, Cohen, Smailes, et al., 2001; Johnson, Smailes, et al., 2000; Ludolph et al., 1990; Luntz & Widom, 1994). Moreover, several of these investigations specifically indicate that physical, sexual, and verbal or psychological abuse are independently associated with risk for personality disorders (Guzder et al.; Ludolph et al.; Johnson, Cohen, Brown, et al., 1999; Johnson, Cohen, Kasen, et al., 2001; Johnson, Cohen, Smailes, et al., 2001; Johnson, Rabkin, et al., 2000).

Hypotheses Regarding How Childhood Adversities May Contribute to PD Development

There are many possible ways in which chronic adversities such as maladaptive parenting and childhood abuse negatively affect personality development, increasing risk for developing personality disorders during adolescence and adulthood. One possibility proposed by Linehan (1993) is the interaction between a biological vulnerability to emotion dysregulation indicated by high sensitivity and high reactivity to painful affects, as well as a slow return to emotional baseline after arousal, and an invalidating environment. Invalidating environments are characterized by caregivers who: (a) respond erratically or inappropriately to private emotional experiences, (b) are insensitive to people's emotional states, (c) have a tendency to over- or underreact to emotional experiences, (d) emphasize rigid control over negative emotions, and (e) have a tendency to trivialize painful experiences or to attribute such experiences to negative traits (e.g., lack of motivation or discipline). The interaction between emotional vulnerability and invalidating environments, it is hypothesized, results in the inability to label and modulate emotions, tolerate and manage emotional or interpersonal distress, and trust private experiences as valid.

Research supporting this hypothesis has indicated that childhood neglect and maladaptive parenting are independently associated with elevated risk for personality disorder even after childhood abuse and parental psychiatric disorders are accounted for (Guzder et al., 1996; Johnson, Cohen, Brown, et al., 1999; Johnson, Cohen, Kasen, et al., 2001; Johnson, Smailes, et al., 2000; Ludolph et al., 1990). In addition, research has suggested that traumatic experiences including childhood abuse; excessively harsh punishment; and other forms of victimization such as assault, bullying, and intimidation may contribute to the onset of personality disorder traits. Traumatic events may promote the development of affective dysregulation, aggressive behavior, dissociative symptoms, interpersonal withdrawal, and profound mistrust of others (Johnson, 1993; van der Kolk, Hostetler, Herron, & Fisler, 1994). Research confirms that youths who are victims of aggressive or abusive behavior are at elevated risk for the development of PD traits and symptoms (e.g., Johnson, Cohen, Brown, et al., 1999;

Johnson, Cohen, Kasen, et al., 2001; Johnson, Cohen, Smailes, et al., 2001).

Childhood adversities may also have an adverse impact on personality development because they interfere with or alter the normative socialization process that extends beyond the immediate family (Cohen, 1999; Johnson, Cohen, Kasen, et al., 2001). Healthy personality development requires continuous socialization throughout childhood and adolescence, as the child's behavior is molded and refined through day-to-day interactions with parents, teachers, and peers. Although every child has unique temperament characteristics that may be evident from early infancy (Thomas & Chess, 1984), and although these characteristics have an enduring impact on personality development (Hart, Hofmann, Edelstein, & Keller, 1997), socialization and other life experiences also modify these traits and determine the manner in which they are expressed (Cohen, 1999). Cohen's (1999) study suggests that, regardless of the child's temperament, parents, teachers, and other adult supervisors are likely to play an important role in the development of social skills, impulse control, coping strategies, and other characteristics.

In addition, maladaptive parental attachment styles have also been found to influence the personality development of the offspring; the offspring of parents with dysfunctional attachment styles are at elevated risk for a broad array of psychiatric symptoms (Rosenstein & Horowitz, 1996; Sroufe, Carlson, Levy, & Egeland, 1999; see Davila et al., Chapter 9 of this volume). A large literature has emerged linking the development of personality disorders to maladaptive adult attachment patterns, which are theorized to recapitulate one's interpersonal relationship with primary caregivers in childhood. For example, Fossati et al. (2003) used canonical correlation and found that avoidant, depressive, paranoid, and schizotypal PDs significantly correlate with avoidance attachment (attachment characterized by the simultaneous desire for and fear of intimacy) and that dependent, histrionic, and borderline PDs significantly correlate with anxious attachment (attachment characterized by a positive view of others and a negative view of the self). West, Rose, and Sheldon-Keller (1994) showed that preoccupied (enmeshed) and dismissing (detached) attachment styles successfully differentiate between dependent and schizoid PD, respectively. In a nonclinical sample of 1,407 undergraduate students, Brennan and Shaver (1998) used discriminant function analysis to predict belongingness to attachment dimensions based on PD symptoms and found that paranoid, schizotypal, avoidant, self-defeating, borderline, narcissistic, and obsessive-compulsive PD symptoms loaded significantly on the secure-fearful dimension, whereas dependent, schizoid, and histrionic symptoms loaded significantly on the preoccupied-dismissing dimension.

Leading personality theorists such as Erik Erikson (1963) have theorized that personality development consists of a series of psychosocial crises that, depending on the unique interaction among the biopsychosocial forces at work, can be either successfully or unsuccessfully resolved. For example, it is the early experience of the child with his or her primary caregivers that contributes to the child's capacity to develop a sense of basic trust, which forms the basis for his or her capacity to venture forth in the world (autonomy), take risks (initiative), and develop a cohesive sense of self (identity). Interpersonal experiences during childhood that disrupt this basic developmental sequence create conditions for maladaptive thought and behavior patterns. For example, caregivers who invalidate the child's emotional reactions to the world or are insensitive to the child's emotional states run the risk of undermining the communicative function of emotion, which may lead to the child's inability to trust his or her emotional experience of the world (Linehan,

1993). According to Erikson, this basic sense of mistrust creates conditions that foster shame and doubt, inhibit the child's willingness to takes risks because of guilt, and lead to identity confusion in adolescence. In other words, negative childhood experiences—particularly with primary caregivers—are hypothesized to contribute directly to the development of maladaptive personality traits and personality disorders.

Despite evidence that childhood adversities such as abuse and neglect significantly increase the likelihood of developing personality disorders, it should also be noted that personality disorder traits tend to decrease in prevalence over time among children, adolescents, and adults in clinical and community settings (Bernstein et al., 1993; Black, Baumgard, & Bell, 1995; Farrington, 1991; Garnet, Levy, Mattanah, Edell, & McGlashan, 1994; Grilo & Masheb, 2002; Johnson et al., 1997; Johnson, Cohen, Kasen, et al., 2000; Korenblum, Marton, Golombek, & Stein, 1987; Lenzenweger, 1999; Mattanah, Becker, Levy, Edell, & McGlashan, 1995; Orlandini et al., 1997; Ronningstam, Gunderson, & Lyons, 1995; Trull et al., 1998; P. Vaglum, Friis, Karterud, Mehlum, & S. Vaglum, 1993; Vetter & Koller, 1993). Cross-sectional findings have similarly indicated that the prevalence of personality disorder traits declines with age among adolescents and adults (e.g., Johnson, Cohen, Kasen, et al., 2000; Kessler et al., 1994; Robins & Regier, 1991; Samuels et al., 2002). These findings may indicate that most youths and adults eventually learn to inhibit the expression of maladaptive personality traits because these traits are associated with negative consequences (Black et al.; Farrington; Johnson, Cohen, Kasen, et al., 2000; Korenblum et al.; Robins, 1966).

A variety of factors, including parenting, mentoring, biological maturation, societal enforcement of adult role expectations, and other normative socialization experiences, appear to contribute to declines in personality disorder traits from childhood through early adulthood (Stein, Newcomb, & Bentler, 1986). According to this developmental hypothesis, expressed implicitly in *DSM-II, -III,* and *-IV* (APA, 1968, 1980, 1987, 1994, 2000), personality disorder traits and other maladaptive personality traits should peak in prevalence during childhood or early adolescence and then diminish steadily among most individuals throughout adolescence and early adulthood. Although little longitudinal evidence is currently available regarding the prevalence of personality disorders from childhood through adulthood, research has supported the hypothesis that personality disorder traits decline gradually in prevalence from late childhood through early adulthood (Abrams & Horowitz, 1996; Johnson, Cohen, Kasen, et al., 2000). These findings are consistent with the assertion in *DSM-II* (APA, 1968) and *DSM-III-R* (APA, 1987) that personality disorders "are often recognizable by adolescence or earlier" and with the statements in *DSM-IV-TR* that personality disorders "can be traced back at least to adolescence or early adulthood" (APA, 2000, p. 689) and that "the traits of a Personality Disorder that appear in childhood will often not persist unchanged into adult life" (APA, 2000, p. 687).

In addition to the studies cited above, many other studies have yielded findings that are consistent with the hypothesis that personality disorder traits tend to develop during childhood or early adolescence and then decline gradually throughout adolescence and adulthood. Community-based longitudinal studies indicate that many maladaptive personality traits originate during childhood and persist into adolescence and adulthood (Caspi & Roberts, 2001; Charles, Reynolds, & Gatz, 2001; Cohen, 1999; McGue, Bacon, & Lykken, 1993; Roberts & DelVecchio, 2000; Shiner, 2000; Shiner, Masten, & Tellegen, 2002). Complementing the aforementioned studies is the fact that behavioral and emotional problems during childhood are often associated with personality disorder traits during adolescence and adulthood (Bernstein et al., 1996; Cohen, 1999; Drake et al., 1988; Hart et al., 1997; Newman, Caspi, Moffitt, & Silva, 1997). Indirect support for the hypothesis that personality disorder traits tend to decline during adolescence and adulthood has been provided by cross-sectional studies indicating that overall psychiatric symptom levels tend to be higher among adolescents than among adults in the community (Derogatis, 1983; Pancoast & Archer, 1992).

Clinical and Public Health Implications of Research on Childhood Adversities and Risk for PD

Findings suggesting that maladaptive parenting may play a significant role in the development of personality disorder traits have potentially important clinical and public health implications. It may be possible to prevent the onset of chronic personality disorders by providing high-risk parents with educational and social services that assist them in developing more adaptive parenting behaviors. Research has indicated that it is possible to reduce the likelihood that children will develop psychiatric symptoms by helping parents to learn more effective child-rearing techniques (Irvine, Biglan, Smolkowski, Metzler, & Ary, 1999; Redmond, Spoth, Shin, & Lepper, 1999; Spoth, Lopez, Redmond, & Shin, 1999). In addition, because maladaptive parenting may be associated with parental psychiatric disorders, and because parents with psychiatric disorders who receive treatment may be less likely to engage in maladaptive parenting, it may be possible to reduce offspring risk for personality disorders by improving the recognition and treatment of psychiatric disorders among parents in the community (Chilcoat, Breslau, & Anthony, 1996; Johnson, Cohen, Kasen, et al., 2001).

CHILDHOOD ADVERSITIES ASSOCIATED WITH RISK FOR SPECIFIC PERSONALITY DISORDERS

In the following sections we summarize findings regarding the childhood adversities associated with each *DSM-IV* PD, including two diagnostic criteria sets that have been studied extensively with respect to this issue (i.e., depressive PD, passive-aggressive PD).

Childhood Adversities Associated With Risk for Antisocial Personality Disorder

Antisocial personality disorder is "a pervasive pattern of disregard for and violation of the rights of others, occurring since age 15, and a history of conduct disorder by age 15" (APA, 2000). Individuals with antisocial PD, which is diagnosed among individuals who are at least 18 years of age, tend to have long histories of violating the rights of others over their life span, including being aggressive and indifferent to others' needs. Our review of the literature identified nine studies that examined the association between childhood maltreatment and risk for the development of antisocial PD. As seen in Table 15.1, evidence from retrospective studies (Bernstein, Stein, & Handelsman, 1998; Fondacaro, Holt, & Powell, 1999; Norden et al., 1995; Ogata et al., 1990; Pollock, Briere, & Schneider, 1990; Ruggiero, Bernstein, & Handelsman, 1999; Shearer et al., 1990) has indicated that individuals with antisocial PD are more likely than patients with other personality disorders to report a history of childhood physical abuse, sexual abuse, and emotional neglect. Other studies have provided findings indicating that reports of low levels of parental affection during childhood were associated with

Table 15.1 Findings From Studies of Associations Between Specific Types of Childhood Maltreatment and Antisocial Personality Disorder (PD) Traits

Type of Childhood Maltreatment											
PA	*SA*	*EA*	*SN*	*PN*	*EN*	*AN*	*Study*	*N*	*Sample*	*Other Types of Childhood Maltreatment Controlled Statistically*	*Other Covariates That Were Controlled Statistically*
PC[a]						PC[a]	Johnson, Cohen, Brown, et al. (1999)	639	Prospective community-based longitudinal study of parents and their children (SA, PA, AN); data regarding child abuse obtained from state records and retrospective reports by offspring	PA, SA, AN	Co-occurring PD symptoms; child age and gender; parental education, income, and psychiatric disorders
	R						Fondacaro et al. (1999)	211	86 male prisoners with childhood SA and 125 male prisoners without history of SA	—	—
R							Pollock et al. (1990)	201	131 men with alcoholic fathers, 70 matched controls	—	Paternal alcoholism
R				R			Bernstein et al. (1998)	339	Patients with alcohol or drug dependence	—	—
					R		Carter et al. (1999)	248	Depressed outpatients	—	—
R					R		Norden et al. (1995)	90	Psychiatric outpatients	—	—

(Continued)

Table 15.1 (Continued)

Type of Childhood Maltreatment										*Other Types of Childhood Maltreatment Controlled Statistically*	*Other Covariates That Were Controlled Statistically*
PA	*SA*	*EA*	*SN*	*PN*	*EN*	*AN*	*Study*	*N*	*Sample*		
	R						Ruggiero et al. (1999)	200	Male inpatient veterans with substance dependence	—	—
R							Shearer et al. (1990)	40	Female inpatients with borderline PD	—	—
D						D	Widom (1989)	1,575	Prospective study of 908 court-documented cases of abuse and neglect and 667 matched (nonabused) controls	—	Age, sex, race
Summary of Significant Associations											
PC[a]R	R			R	R	PC[a]D					

NOTES: PA = childhood physical abuse; SA = childhood sexual abuse; EA = childhood emotional abuse (verbal abuse is classified as emotional abuse); SN = childhood supervision neglect; PN = childhood physical neglect; EN = childhood emotional neglect; CN = childhood cognitive neglect; AN = any childhood neglect; AM = any childhood maltreatment; P = prospective epidemiological findings, based on documented evidence of childhood maltreatment, were significant after controlling for co-occurring PD symptoms, parental education, and parental psychiatric symptoms; C = combined prospective and retrospective reports of childhood physical abuse, sexual abuse, or any childhood neglect yielded significant findings after controlling for co-occurring PD symptoms, parental education, and parental psychiatric symptoms; R = retrospective clinical studies have obtained a significant association after covariates were controlled statistically; D = individuals with a documented history of physical abuse or neglect were significantly more likely than controls to be diagnosed with antisocial PD; MDD = major depressive disorder.

a. Association remained significant after controlling for other types of childhood abuse and neglect the development of antisocial PD symptoms (Carter, Joyce, Mulder, Luty, & Sullivan, 1999; Norden et al.). Findings of the only study that has reported findings based on both retrospective and prospective data (Johnson, Cohen, Brown, et al., 1999) suggested that childhood physical abuse and any childhood neglect may contribute to elevated risk for the development of antisocial PD.

In addition, problematic parenting has been found to be associated with elevated offspring risk for a broad array of behavior problems, including aggressive and antisocial behavior (Frick et al., 1992; Loeber et al., 2000; Loeber & Farrington, 2000; Reiss et al., 1995; Shaw, Owens, Giovannelli, & Winslow, 2001). Research has also indicated that the association between parental criminality and offspring delinquency may be accounted for, in part, by intervening family processes (Sampson & Laub, 1993, 1994; see Rowe & Farrington, 1997).

Childhood Adversities Associated With Risk for Avoidant Personality Disorder

Avoidant personality disorder is "a pervasive pattern of social inhibition, feelings of inadequacy, and hypersensitivity to negative evaluation" (APA, 2000). Individuals with avoidant PD often have low self-esteem, fear rejection, and have limited friendships. Our review of the literature identified eight studies that obtained evidence of an association between childhood maltreatment and risk for the development of avoidant PD. As seen in Table 15.2, evidence from retrospective studies (Arbel & Stravynski, 1991; Carter et al., 1999; Gauthier, Stollak, Messé, & Aronoff, 1996; Grilo & Masheb, 2002; Ruggiero et al., 1999; Shea, Zlotnick, & Weisberg, 1999) has indicated that individuals with avoidant PD are more likely than those with other personality disorders to report a history of childhood physical abuse, sexual abuse, emotional abuse, emotional neglect, or any childhood neglect.

Other studies have provided findings indicating that shaming, guilt engendering, and intolerant parenting were more likely to be reported among individuals with avoidant PD symptoms than among normal control subjects (Stravynski, Elie, & Franche, 1989), and that patients with avoidant PD reported low levels of parental affection during childhood (Carter et al., 1999; Norden et al., 1995). Prospective studies (Johnson, Cohen, Brown, et al., 1999; Johnson, Smailes, et al., 2000) have provided evidence indicating that childhood emotional neglect and any childhood neglect were significantly associated with risk for the development of avoidant PD. Findings of the only study that has reported both retrospective and prospective data (Johnson, Cohen, Brown, et al., 1999) suggested that childhood neglect may contribute to elevated risk for the development of avoidant PD.

Childhood Adversities Associated With Risk for Borderline Personality Disorder

Borderline personality disorder is "a pervasive pattern of instability of interpersonal relationships, self-image, and affects and marked impulsivity" (APA, 2000). Our review of the literature identified 18 studies that obtained evidence of an association between childhood maltreatment and risk for the development of borderline PD. As seen in Table 15.3, retrospective studies have indicated that individuals with borderline PD are more likely than other patients to report a history of childhood physical abuse, sexual abuse, emotional abuse, emotional neglect, physical neglect, supervision neglect, and any childhood neglect (Brown & Anderson, 1991; Carter et al., 1999; Dubo, Zanarini, Lewis, & Williams, 1997; Goldman et al., 1992; Herman et al., 1989; Laporte &

(Text continues on page 434)

Table 15.2 Findings From Studies of Associations Between Specific Types of Childhood Maltreatment and Avoidant Personality Disorder (PD) Traits

Type of Childhood Maltreatment											
PA	*SA*	*EA*	*SN*	*PN*	*EN*	*AN*	*Study*	*N*	*Sample*	*Other Types of Childhood Maltreatment Controlled Statistically*	*Other Covariates That Were Controlled Statistically*
					R		Carter et al. (1999)	248	Depressed outpatients	—	—
R						R	Gauthier et al. (1996)	518	College undergraduates	PA, AN	—
		R					Grilo & Masheb, (2002)	116	Outpatients with binge eating disorder	PA, SA, EA, EN, PN	—
						PC[a]	Johnson, Cohen, Brown, et al. (1999)	639	Community-based prospective longitudinal study of parents and their children (SA, PA, AN); childhood maltreatment data obtained from state records and retrospective reports by offspring.	PA, SA, AN	Co-occurring PD symptoms; child age and gender; parental education, income, and psychiatric disorders
					P[a]	P[a]	Johnson, Smailes, et al. (2000)	738	Community-based prospective longitudinal study of parents and their children; data regarding childhood neglect were obtained from state records and maternal reports during the child-rearing years	PA, SA, EN, SN, PN, CN	Co-occurring PD symptoms, child age and gender

Type of Childhood Maltreatment							Study	N	Sample	Other Types of Childhood Maltreatment Controlled Statistically	Other Covariates That Were Controlled Statistically
PA	*SA*	*EA*	*SN*	*PN*	*EN*	*AN*					
	R					R	Ruggiero et al. (1999)	200	Male inpatient veterans with substance dependence	—	—
	R						Shea et al. (1999)	140	Female inpatient and outpatient childhood sexual abuse, comparison samples of veteran, OCD, bipolar, panic, bulimia, and MDD	—	—
					R		Arbel & Stravynski (1991)	45	23 patients attending psychiatric research center and comparison group of 22 matched normal controls	—	—
Summary of Significant Associations											
R	R	R			P^aR	P^aC^aR					

NOTES: PA = childhood physical abuse; SA = childhood sexual abuse; EA = childhood emotional abuse (verbal abuse is classified as emotional abuse); SN = childhood supervision neglect; PN = childhood physical neglect; EN = childhood emotional neglect; CN = childhood cognitive neglect; AN = any childhood neglect; AM = any childhood maltreatment; P = prospective epidemiological findings, based on documented evidence of childhood maltreatment, were significant after controlling for co-occurring PD symptoms, parental education, and parental psychiatric symptoms; C = combined prospective and retrospective reports of childhood physical abuse, sexual abuse, or any childhood neglect yielded significant findings after controlling for co-occurring PD symptoms, parental education, and parental psychiatric symptoms; R = retrospective clinical studies have obtained a significant association after covariates were controlled statistically; D = individuals with a documented history of physical abuse or neglect were significantly more likely than controls to be diagnosed with antisocial PD; OCD = obsessive-compulsive disorder; MDD = major depressive disorder.

a. Association remained significant after controlling for other types of childhood abuse and neglect.

Table 15.3 Findings From Studies of Associations Between Specific Types of Childhood Maltreatment and Borderline Personality Disorder (PD) Traits

Type of Childhood Maltreatment											
PA	*SA*	*EA*	*SN*	*PN*	*EN*	*AN*	*Study*	*N*	*Sample*	*Other Types of Childhood Maltreatment Controlled Statistically*	*Other Covariates That Were Controlled Statistically*
R	R						Brown & Anderson (1991)	947	Inpatient military members and dependents (673 active duty, 346 civilians)	SA, PA	—
					R		Carter et al. (1999)	248	Outpatients with MDD	—	—
R							Goldman et al. (1992)	144	44 outpatient children with BPD and 100 outpatient comparison children	—	—
R	R						Herman et al. (1989)	55	Longitudinal study, borderline, schizotypal, antisocial, and bipolar II affective disorders	—	—
C[a]	PC[a]					P[a]C[a]	Johnson, Cohen, Brown, et al. (1999)	639	Community-based prospective longitudinal study of parents and their children (SA, PA, AN); childhood maltreatment data obtained from state records and retrospective reports by offspring.	PA, SA, AN	Co-occurring PD symptoms; child age and gender; parental education, income, and psychiatric disorders

Type of Childhood Maltreatment											
PA	*SA*	*EA*	*SN*	*PN*	*EN*	*AN*	*Study*	*N*	*Sample*	*Other Types of Childhood Maltreatment Controlled Statistically*	*Other Covariates That Were Controlled Statistically*
		P[a]					Johnson, Cohen, Smailes, et al. (2001)	793	Community-based prospective longitudinal study (maternal verbal abuse), assessed by maternal reports during the child-rearing years	PA, SA, AN	Child temperament, physical punishment, co-occurring psychiatric disorders, parental education and psychiatric disorders
			P[a]			P[a]	Johnson, Smailes, et al. (2000)	738	Community-based prospective longitudinal study of parents and their children; data regarding childhood neglect were obtained from state records and maternal reports during the child-rearing years	PA, SA, EN, SN, PN, CN	Co-occurring PD symptoms, child age and gender
R	R	R					Laporte & Guttman (1996)	751	366 patients with borderline PD, 385 patients with other PDs	—	—
	R						Norden et al. (1995)	90	Psychiatric outpatients	—	—
	R						Ogata et al. (1990)	42	24 adult inpatients with BPD and 18 depressed control subjects	—	—

(Continued)

Table 15.3 (Continued)

Type of Childhood Maltreatment											
PA	*SA*	*EA*	*SN*	*PN*	*EN*	*AN*	*Study*	*N*	*Sample*	*Other Types of Childhood Maltreatment Controlled Statistically*	*Other Covariates That Were Controlled Statistically*
R							Oldham et al. (1996)	50	44 inpatients with BPD, 6 inpatients with other PDs	—	—
	R						Paris (1994)	150	Outpatient women, 78 with BPD and 72 with other PDs	—	—
	R						Shea et al. (1999)	140	Female inpatient and outpatient childhood sexual abuse; comparison samples of veteran, OCD, bipolar, panic, bulimia, and MDD	—	—
R	R						Steiger et al. (1996)	61	Outpatients with bulimia nervosa: 14 with BPD, 30 with other PDs, 17 with no PD	—	—
	R						Weaver & Clum (1993)	36	Female inpatients with diagnosed depressive disorder: 17 BPD, 19 non-BPD	PA	Co-occurring psychiatric symptoms and disorders, family environment

Type of Childhood Maltreatment							*Study*	*N*	*Sample*	*Other Types of Childhood Maltreatment Controlled Statistically*	*Other Covariates That Were Controlled Statistically*
PA	*SA*	*EA*	*SN*	*PN*	*EN*	*AN*					
	R						Yen et al. (2002)	653 105	Longitudinal study: 86 schizotypal, 167 borderline, 153 avoidant, and 153 obsessive-compulsive PDs; 94 MDD with no PD	—	Co-occurring PDs and MDD
	R	R					Zanarini et al. (1989)	467	50 outpatients with BPD, 29 with antisocial PD, and 26 with other PDs and comorbid dysthymia	—	—
R	R	R	R	R	R	R	Zanarini et al. (1997)		358 inpatients with BPD, 109 inpatients with other PDs	—	—
Summary of Significant Associations											
C[a]R	PC[a]R	P[a]R	P[a]	R	P[a]C[a]R						

NOTES: PA = childhood physical abuse; SA = childhood sexual abuse; EA = childhood emotional abuse (verbal abuse is classified as emotional abuse); SN = childhood supervision neglect; PN = childhood physical neglect; EN = childhood emotional neglect; CN = childhood cognitive neglect; AN = any childhood neglect; AM = any childhood maltreatment; P = prospective epidemiological findings, based on documented evidence of childhood maltreatment, were significant after controlling for co-occurring PD symptoms, parental education, and parental psychiatric symptoms; C = combined prospective and retrospective reports of childhood physical abuse, sexual abuse, or any childhood neglect yielded significant findings after controlling for co-occurring PD symptoms, parental education, and parental psychiatric symptoms; R = retrospective clinical studies have obtained a significant association after covariates were controlled statistically; D = individuals with a documented history of physical abuse or neglect were significantly more likely than controls to be diagnosed with antisocial PD; BPD = borderline personality disorder; OCD = obsessive-compulsive disorder; MDD = major depressive disorder.

a. Association remained significant after controlling for other types of childhood abuse and neglect.

Guttman, 1996; Norden et al., 1995; Oldham, Skodol, Gallagher, & Kroll, 1996; Paris, 1994; Shea et al., 1999; Steiger, Jabalpurwala, & Champagne, 1996; Weaver & Clum, 1993; Yen et al., 2002; Zanarini, Gunderson, Marino, Schwartz, & Frankenburg, 1989; Zanarini et al., 1997). These results are particularly compelling because they were obtained in large samples of patients and community members with contrasting demographics. Other studies have indicated that reports of low childhood parental affection were associated with the development of borderline PD symptoms (Carter et al., 1999; Norden et al., 1995).

Prospective studies (Johnson, Cohen, Brown, et al., 1999; Johnson, Cohen, Smailes, et al., 2001; Johnson, Smailes, et al., 2000) have provided evidence indicating that childhood physical abuse, sexual abuse, emotional abuse, supervision neglect, and any childhood neglect were associated significantly with risk for the development of borderline PD. Findings of the only study that has reported findings based on both retrospective and prospective data (Johnson, Cohen, Brown, et al., 1999) suggested that childhood physical abuse, sexual abuse, and any childhood neglect may contribute to increased risk for the development of borderline PD.

Childhood Adversities Associated With Risk for Dependent Personality Disorder

Dependent personality disorder is "a pervasive and excessive need to be taken care of that leads to submissive and clinging behavior and fears of separation" (APA, 2000). Individuals with dependent PD tend to have a need to be taken care of, have difficulty making decisions, and fear abandonment. Our review of the literature identified six studies that obtained evidence of an association between childhood maltreatment and risk for the development of dependent PD. As seen in Table 15.4, evidence from retrospective studies (Carter et al., 1999; Drake & Vaillant, 1988) has indicated that individuals with dependent PD are more likely than patients with other personality disorders to report a history of childhood emotional neglect and any childhood neglect. In addition, individuals with dependent PD have been found to report that the family of origin was characterized by a high level of parental control and parental overprotectiveness and low levels of family expressiveness and offspring independence (Baker, Capron, & Azorlosa, 1996; Bornstein, in press; Head, Baker, & Williamson, 1991). Patients with dependent PD have also been found to be particularly likely to report a history of low parental affection during childhood (Carter et al.; Norden et al., 1995). Further, research has indicated that dependent PD is often associated with a history of insecure attachment with parents throughout childhood (Pincus & Wilson, 2001), a pattern that pervades later relationships (e.g., friendships, romantic relationships) as well (Sperling & Berman, 1991).

Prospective studies (Johnson, Cohen, Brown, et al., 1999; Johnson, Smailes, et al., 2000) have provided evidence indicating that childhood physical abuse and any childhood neglect were significantly associated with risk for the development of dependent PD. Findings of the only study that has reported findings based on both retrospective and prospective data (Johnson, Cohen, Brown, et al., 1999) suggest that childhood physical abuse and any childhood neglect may contribute to elevated risk for the development of dependent PD.

Childhood Adversities Associated With Risk for Depressive Personality Disorder

Depressive personality disorder is "a pervasive pattern of depressive cognitions and behaviors" (APA, 2000). Individuals with depressive PD will tend to have long histories

Table 15.4 Findings From Studies of Associations Between Specific Types of Childhood Maltreatment and Dependent Personality Disorder (PD) Traits

Type of Childhood Maltreatment											
PA	*SA*	*EA*	*SN*	*PN*	*EN*	*AN*	*Study*	*N*	*Sample*	*Other Types of Childhood Maltreatment Controlled Statistically*	*Other Covariates That Were Controlled Statistically*
					R		Carter et al. (1999)	248	Depressed outpatients	—	—
						R	Drake & Vaillant (1988)	307	Longitudinal study of 307 middle-aged men	—	—
PC[a]						P[a]C[a]	Johnson, Cohen, Brown, et al. (1999)	639	Community-based prospective longitudinal study of parents and their children (SA, PA, AN); childhood maltreatment data obtained from state records and retrospective reports by offspring	PA, SA, AN	Co-occurring PD symptoms; child age and gender; parental education, income, and psychiatric disorders

(Continued)

Table 15.4 (Continued)

Type of Childhood Maltreatment											
PA	*SA*	*EA*	*SN*	*PN*	*EN*	*AN*	*Study*	*N*	*Sample*	*Other Types of Childhood Maltreatment Controlled Statistically*	*Other Covariates That Were Controlled Statistically*
						P	Johnson, Smailes, et al. (2000)	738	Community-based prospective longitudinal study of parents and their children; data regarding childhood neglect were obtained from state records and maternal reports during the child-rearing years	PA, SA, EN, SN, PN, CN	Co-occurring PD symptoms, child age and gender
Summary of Significant Associations											
PC[a]					R	P[a]C[a]R					

NOTES: PA = childhood physical abuse; SA = childhood sexual abuse; EA = childhood emotional abuse (verbal abuse is classified as emotional abuse); SN = childhood supervision neglect; PN = childhood physical neglect; EN = childhood emotional neglect; CN = childhood cognitive neglect; AN = any childhood neglect; AM = any childhood maltreatment; P = prospective epidemiological findings, based on documented evidence of childhood maltreatment, were significant after controlling for co-occurring PD symptoms, parental education, and parental psychiatric symptoms; C = combined prospective and retrospective reports of childhood physical abuse, sexual abuse, or any childhood neglect yielded significant findings after controlling for co-occurring PD symptoms, parental education, and parental psychiatric symptoms; R = retrospective clinical studies have obtained a significant association after covariates were controlled statistically; D = individuals with a documented history of physical abuse or neglect were significantly more likely than controls to be diagnosed with antisocial PD.

a. Association remained significant after controlling for other types of childhood abuse and neglect.

of negative mood and have negative views about the self. Our review of the literature identified four studies that obtained evidence of an association between childhood maltreatment and risk for the development of depressive PD. As seen in Table 15.5, evidence from retrospective studies (Briere & Runtz, 1990; Mullen, Martin, & Anderson, 1996) has indicated that individuals with depressive PD are more likely than patients with other personality disorders to report a history of childhood sexual abuse and emotional abuse. Prospective studies (Johnson, Cohen, Brown, et al., 1999; Johnson, Smailes, et al., 2000) have provided evidence indicating that childhood physical abuse, sexual abuse, and any childhood neglect were significantly associated with risk for the development of depressive PD. Findings of the only study that has reported findings based on both retrospective and prospective data (Johnson, Cohen, Brown, et al., 1999) suggest that childhood physical and sexual abuse contribute to increased risk for the development of depressive PD.

Childhood Adversities Associated With Risk for Histrionic Personality Disorder

Histrionic personality disorder is "a pervasive pattern of excessive emotionality and attention seeking" (APA, 2000). Individuals with histrionic PD tend to be overly dramatic and theatrical, to express emotions in exaggerated ways, and to often feel uncomfortable when they are not the center of attention. Our review of the literature identified three studies that obtained evidence of an association between childhood maltreatment and risk for the development of histrionic PD. Unfortunately, this relatively modest data pool limits the conclusions that may be drawn in this area (see Table 15.6). Norden et al. (1995) reported retrospective findings indicating that individuals with histrionic PD were more likely than patients with other PDs were to report a history of sexual abuse. Patients with histrionic PD have also been found to report a high level of parental control, achievement orientation, intellectual-cultural orientation, and a low level of family cohesion (Baker et al., 1996). Prospective data (Johnson, Smailes, et al., 2000) indicate that childhood supervision neglect was significantly associated with risk for the development of histrionic PD. Findings of the only study that has reported findings based on both retrospective and prospective data (Johnson, Cohen, Brown, et al., 1999) suggest that childhood sexual abuse may contribute to elevated risk for the development of histrionic PD.

Childhood Adversities Associated With Risk for Narcissistic Personality Disorder

Narcissistic personality disorder is "a pervasive pattern of grandiosity (in fantasy or behavior), need for admiration, and lack of empathy" (APA, 2000). Individuals with narcissistic PD tend to have long histories of thinking very highly of themselves, such that they believe they should be treated differently than others and deserve special treatment. They often are very occupied with themselves, to the point that they lack sensitivity and compassion for others; when confronted with other successful people, they can often be envious or arrogant or feel depressed. Our review of the literature identified four studies that obtained evidence of an association between childhood maltreatment and risk for the development of narcissistic PD (see Table 15.7). Norden et al. (1995) reported that psychiatric outpatients with narcissistic PD were more likely than patients with other personality disorders to report a history of sexual abuse. Prospective studies (Johnson, Cohen, Brown, et al., 1999; Johnson, Cohen, Smailes, et al., 2001; Johnson, Smailes, et al., 2000) have provided evidence indicating that childhood emotional abuse, physical neglect, emotional

(Text continues on page 444)

Table 15.5 Findings From Studies of Associations Between Specific Types of Childhood Maltreatment and Depressive Personality Disorder (PD) Traits

Type of Childhood Maltreatment											
PA	*SA*	*EA*	*SN*	*PN*	*EN*	*AN*	*Study*	*N*	*Sample*	*Other Types of Childhood Maltreatment Controlled Statistically*	*Other Covariates That Were Controlled Statistically*
		R					Briere & Runtz (1990)	277	Female undergraduate students	PA, SA, EA	—
P	C[a]						Johnson, Cohen, Brown, et al. (1999)	639	Community-based prospective longitudinal study of parents and their children (SA, PA, AN); childhood maltreatment data obtained from state records and retrospective reports by offspring	PA, SA, AN	Co-occurring PD symptoms; child age and gender; parental education, income, and psychiatric disorders
						P	Johnson, Smailes, et al. (2000)	738	Community-based prospective longitudinal study of parents and their children; data regarding childhood neglect were obtained from state records and maternal reports during the child-rearing years	PA, SA, EN, SN, PN, CN	Co-occurring PD symptoms, child age and gender

Type of Childhood Maltreatment											
PA	*SA*	*EA*	*SN*	*PN*	*EN*	*AN*	*Study*	*N*	*Sample*	*Other Types of Childhood Maltreatment Controlled Statistically*	*Other Covariates That Were Controlled Statistically*
	R	R					Mullen et al. (1996)	497	Community sample of women (107 abused and 390 nonabused women)	PA, SA, EA	Other developmental adversities
Summary of Significant Associations											
P	C[a]R	R				P					

NOTES: PA = childhood physical abuse; SA = childhood sexual abuse; EA = childhood emotional abuse (verbal abuse is classified as emotional abuse); SN = childhood supervision neglect; PN = childhood physical neglect; EN = childhood emotional neglect; CN = childhood cognitive neglect; AN = any childhood neglect; AM = any childhood maltreatment; P = prospective epidemiological findings, based on documented evidence of childhood maltreatment, were significant after controlling for co-occurring PD symptoms, parental education, and parental psychiatric symptoms; C = combined prospective and retrospective reports of childhood physical abuse, sexual abuse, or any childhood neglect yielded significant findings after controlling for co-occurring PD symptoms, parental education, and parental psychiatric symptoms; R = retrospective clinical studies have obtained a significant association after covariates were controlled statistically; D = individuals with a documented history of physical abuse or neglect were significantly more likely than controls to be diagnosed with antisocial PD.

a. Association remained significant after controlling for other types of childhood abuse and neglect.

Table 15.6 Findings From Studies of Associations Between Specific Types of Childhood Maltreatment and Histrionic Personality Disorder (PD) Traits

Type of Childhood Maltreatment											
PA	*SA*	*EA*	*SN*	*PN*	*EN*	*AN*	*Study*	*N*	*Sample*	*Other Types of Childhood Maltreatment Controlled Statistically*	*Other Covariates That Were Controlled Statistically*
	C[a]						Johnson, Cohen, Brown, et al. (1999)	639	Community-based prospective longitudinal study of parents and their children (SA, PA, AN); childhood maltreatment data obtained from state records and retrospective reports by offspring	PA, SA, AN	Co-occurring PD symptoms; child age and gender; parental education, income, and psychiatric disorders
			P				Johnson, Smailes, et al. (2000)	738	Community-based prospective longitudinal study of parents and their children; data regarding childhood neglect were obtained from state records and maternal reports during the child-rearing years	PA, SA, EN, SN, PN, CN	Co-occurring PD symptoms, child age and gender

Type of Childhood Maltreatment							*Study*	*N*	*Sample*	*Other Types of Childhood Maltreatment Controlled Statistically*	*Other Covariates That Were Controlled Statistically*
PA	*SA*	*EA*	*SN*	*PN*	*EN*	*AN*					
	R						Norden et al. (1995)	90	Psychiatric outpatients	—	—
Summary of Significant Associations											
	C[a] R		P								

NOTES: PA = childhood physical abuse; SA = childhood sexual abuse; EA = childhood emotional abuse (verbal abuse is classified as emotional abuse); SN = childhood supervision neglect; PN = childhood physical neglect; EN = childhood emotional neglect; CN = childhood cognitive neglect; AN = any childhood neglect; AM = any childhood maltreatment; P = prospective epidemiological findings, based on documented evidence of childhood maltreatment, were significant after controlling for co-occurring PD symptoms, parental education, and parental psychiatric symptoms; C = combined prospective and retrospective reports of childhood physical abuse, sexual abuse, or any childhood neglect yielded significant findings after controlling for co-occurring PD symptoms, parental education, and parental psychiatric symptoms; R = retrospective clinical studies have obtained a significant association after covariates were controlled statistically; D = individuals with a documented history of physical abuse or neglect were significantly more likely than controls to be diagnosed with antisocial PD.

a. Association remained significant after controlling for other types of childhood abuse and neglect.

Table 15.7 Findings From Studies of Associations Between Specific Types of Childhood Maltreatment and Narcissistic Personality Disorder (PD) Traits

Type of Childhood Maltreatment											
PA	*SA*	*EA*	*SN*	*PN*	*EN*	*AN*	*Study*	*N*	*Sample*	*Other Types of Childhood Maltreatment Controlled Statistically*	*Other Covariates That Were Controlled Statistically*
						PC[a]	Johnson, Cohen, Brown, et al. (1999)	639	Community-based prospective longitudinal study of parents and their children (SA, PA, AN); childhood maltreatment data obtained from state records and retrospective reports by offspring	PA, SA, AN	Co-occurring PD symptoms; child age and gender; parental education, income, and psychiatric disorders
		P[a]					Johnson, Cohen, Smailes, et al. (2001)	793	Community-based prospective longitudinal study (maternal verbal abuse), assessed by maternal reports during the child-rearing years	PA, SA, AN	Child temperament, physical punishment, co-occurring psychiatric disorders, parental education and psychiatric disorders

Type of Childhood Maltreatment											
PA	*SA*	*EA*	*SN*	*PN*	*EN*	*AN*	*Study*	*N*	*Sample*	*Other Types of Childhood Maltreatment Controlled Statistically*	*Other Covariates That Were Controlled Statistically*
						P	Johnson, Smailes, et al. (2000)	738	Community-based prospective longitudinal study of parents and their children; data regarding childhood neglect were obtained from state records and maternal reports during the child-rearing years	PA, SA, EN, SN, PN, CN	Co-occurring PD symptoms, child age and gender
	R						Norden et al. (1995)	90	Psychiatric outpatients	—	—
Summary of Significant Associations											
	R	P[a]				PC[a]					

NOTES: PA = childhood physical abuse; SA = childhood sexual abuse; EA = childhood emotional abuse (verbal abuse is classified as emotional abuse); SN = childhood supervision neglect; PN = childhood physical neglect; EN = childhood emotional neglect; CN = childhood cognitive neglect; AN = any childhood neglect; AM = any childhood maltreatment; P = prospective epidemiological findings, based on documented evidence of childhood maltreatment, were significant after controlling for co-occurring PD symptoms, parental education, and parental psychiatric symptoms; C = combined prospective and retrospective reports of childhood physical abuse, sexual abuse, or any childhood neglect yielded significant findings after controlling for co-occurring PD symptoms, parental education, and parental psychiatric symptoms; R = retrospective clinical studies have obtained a significant association after covariates were controlled statistically; D = individuals with a documented history of physical abuse or neglect were significantly more likely than controls to be diagnosed with antisocial PD.

a. Association remained significant after controlling for other types of childhood abuse and neglect.

neglect, and any childhood neglect were significantly associated with risk for the development of narcissistic PD. Findings of the only study that has reported findings based on both retrospective and prospective data (Johnson, Cohen, Brown, et al., 1999) suggest that childhood neglect may contribute to increased risk for the development of narcissistic PD.

Childhood Adversities Associated With Risk for Obsessive-Compulsive Personality Disorder

Obsessive-compulsive personality disorder is "a pervasive pattern of preoccupation with orderliness, perfectionism, and mental and interpersonal control, at the expense of flexibility, openness, and efficiency" (APA, 2000). Individuals with obsessive-compulsive PD tend to have long histories of being persistently preoccupied with details, are fixated on having things "done right," and often fail to complete tasks as a result of their perfectionism and rigidity. Our review of the literature identified two studies that obtained evidence of an association between childhood maltreatment and risk for the development of obsessive-compulsive PD (see Table 15.8). Prospective studies (Johnson, Cohen, Brown, et al., 1999; Johnson, Cohen, Smailes, et al., 2001) have provided evidence indicating that childhood emotional abuse and any childhood neglect were significantly associated with risk for the development of obsessive-compulsive PD. Because these data are based entirely on community samples, however, the degree to which these patterns generalize to other populations (e.g., psychiatric inpatients) remains unaddressed.

Childhood Adversities Associated With Risk for Paranoid Personality Disorder

Paranoid personality disorder is "a pervasive distrust and suspiciousness of others such that their motives are interpreted as malevolent" (APA, 2000). Individuals with paranoid PD tend to have long histories of being very distrustful and suspicious of others with little justification. Our review of the literature identified six studies that obtained evidence of an association between childhood maltreatment and risk for the development of paranoid PD. As seen in Table 15.9, evidence from retrospective studies (Carter et al., 1999; Ruggiero et al., 1999; Shea et al., 1999) has indicated that individuals with paranoid PD are more likely than those with other personality disorders to report a history of childhood sexual abuse and emotional neglect. Other studies have shown that reports of low childhood parental affection were found to be associated with the development of paranoid PD symptoms (Carter et al.; Norden et al., 1995). Prospective studies (Johnson, Cohen, Brown, et al., 1999; Johnson, Cohen, Smailes, et al., 2001; Johnson, Smailes, et al., 2000) have provided evidence indicating that the association between childhood emotional abuse, supervision neglect, emotional neglect, and any childhood neglect and paranoid PD development remained significant even after controlling for other types of childhood abuse and neglect.

Childhood Adversities Associated With Risk for Passive-Aggressive Personality Disorder

Passive-aggressive personality disorder is "a pervasive pattern of negativistic attitudes and passive resistance to demands for adequate performance in social and occupational situations" (APA, 2000). Individuals with passive-aggressive PD tend to have long histories of resisting others' routine requests and expectations as they adopt a negative, subtly aggressive attitude. Our review of the literature identified four studies—which involved both community and clinical samples—that obtained evidence of an association between

(Text continues on page 448)

Table 15.8 Findings From Studies of Associations Between Specific Types of Childhood Maltreatment and Obsessive-Compulsive Personality Disorder (PD) Traits

Type of Childhood Maltreatment											
PA	*SA*	*EA*	*SN*	*PN*	*EN*	*AN*	*Study*	*N*	*Sample*	*Other Types of Childhood Maltreatment Controlled Statistically*	*Other Covariates That Were Controlled Statistically*
						P	Johnson, Cohen, Brown, et al. (1999)	639	Community-based prospective longitudinal study of parents and their children (SA, PA, AN); childhood maltreatment data obtained from state records and retrospective reports by offspring	PA, SA, AN	Co-occurring PD symptoms; child age and gender; parental education, income, and psychiatric disorders
		P[a]					Johnson, Cohen, Smailes, et al. (2001)	793	Community-based prospective longitudinal study (maternal verbal abuse), assessed by maternal reports during the child-rearing years	PA, SA, AN	Child temperament, physical punishment, co-occurring psychiatric disorders, parental education and psychiatric disorders
Summary of Significant Associations											
		P[a]				P					

NOTES: PA = childhood physical abuse; SA = childhood sexual abuse; EA = childhood emotional abuse (verbal abuse is classified as emotional abuse); SN = childhood supervision neglect; PN = childhood physical neglect; EN = childhood emotional neglect; CN = childhood cognitive neglect; AN = any childhood neglect; AM = any childhood maltreatment; P = prospective epidemiological findings, based on documented evidence of childhood maltreatment, were significant after controlling for co-occurring PD symptoms, parental education, and parental psychiatric symptoms; C = combined prospective and retrospective reports of childhood physical abuse, sexual abuse, or any childhood neglect yielded significant findings after controlling for co-occurring PD symptoms, parental education, and parental psychiatric symptoms; R = retrospective clinical studies have obtained a significant association after covariates were controlled statistically; D = individuals with a documented history of physical abuse or neglect were significantly more likely than controls to be diagnosed with antisocial PD.

a. Association remained significant after controlling for other types of childhood abuse and neglect.

Table 15.9 Findings From Studies of Associations Between Specific Types of Childhood Maltreatment and Paranoid Personality Disorder (PD) Traits

Type of Childhood Maltreatment											
PA	*SA*	*EA*	*SN*	*PN*	*EN*	*AN*	*Study*	*N*	*Sample*	*Other Types of Childhood Maltreatment Controlled Statistically*	*Other Covariates That Were Controlled Statistically*
					R		Carter et al. (1999)	248	Outpatients with MDD	—	—
						P[a]	Johnson, Cohen, Brown, et al. (1999)	639	Community-based prospective longitudinal study of parents and their children (SA, PA, AN); childhood maltreatment data obtained from state records and retrospective reports by offspring	PA, SA, AN	Co-occurring PD symptoms; child age and gender; parental education, income, and psychiatric disorders
		P[a]					Johnson, Cohen, Smailes, et al. (2001)	793	Community-based prospective longitudinal study (maternal verbal abuse), assessed by maternal reports during the child-rearing years	PA, SA, AN	Child temperament, physical punishment, co-occurring psychiatric disorders, parental education and psychiatric disorders
			P[a]		P[a]	P	Johnson, Smailes, et al. (2000)	738	Community-based prospective longitudinal study of parents and their children; data regarding childhood neglect were obtained from state records and maternal reports during the child-rearing years	PA, SA, EN, SN, PN, CN	Co-occurring PD symptoms, child age and gender

Type of Childhood Maltreatment											
PA	*SA*	*EA*	*SN*	*PN*	*EN*	*AN*	*Study*	*N*	*Sample*	*Other Types of Childhood Maltreatment Controlled Statistically*	*Other Covariates That Were Controlled Statistically*
	R						Ruggiero et al. (1999)	200	Male inpatient veterans with substance dependence	—	—
	R						Shea et al. (1999)	140	Female inpatients and outpatients with childhood sexual abuse; comparison samples of veteran, OCD, bipolar, panic, bulimia, and MDD	—	—
Summary of Significant Associations											
	R	P[a]	P[a]		P[a]R	P[a]					

NOTES: PA = childhood physical abuse; SA = childhood sexual abuse; EA = childhood emotional abuse (verbal abuse is classified as emotional abuse); SN = childhood supervision neglect; PN = childhood physical neglect; EN = childhood emotional neglect; CN = childhood cognitive neglect; AN = any childhood neglect; AM = any childhood maltreatment; P = prospective epidemiological findings, based on documented evidence of childhood maltreatment, were significant after controlling for co-occurring PD symptoms, parental education, and parental psychiatric symptoms; C = combined prospective and retrospective reports of childhood physical abuse, sexual abuse, or any childhood neglect yielded significant findings after controlling for co-occurring PD symptoms, parental education, and parental psychiatric symptoms; R = retrospective clinical studies have obtained a significant association after covariates were controlled statistically; D = individuals with a documented history of physical abuse or neglect were significantly more likely than controls to be diagnosed with antisocial PD; OCD = obsessive-compulsive disorder; MDD = major depressive disorder.

a. Association remained significant after controlling for other types of childhood abuse and neglect.

childhood maltreatment and risk for the development of passive-aggressive PD. As seen in Table 15.10, evidence from retrospective studies (Drake & Vaillant, 1988; Ruggiero et al., 1999) has indicated that individuals with passive-aggressive PD are more likely than patients with other personality disorders to report a history of sexual abuse and any childhood neglect. Prospective studies (Johnson, Cohen, Brown, et al., 1999; Johnson, Smailes, et al., 2000) have provided evidence indicating that childhood physical abuse, supervision neglect, and any childhood neglect were associated significantly with risk for the development of passive-aggressive PD. Findings of the only study that has reported findings based on both retrospective and prospective data (Johnson, Cohen, Brown, et al., 1999) suggest that childhood physical abuse and any childhood neglect may contribute to elevated risk for the development of passive-aggressive PD.

Childhood Adversities Associated With Risk for Schizoid Personality Disorder

Schizoid personality disorder is "a pervasive pattern of detachment from social relationships and a restricted range of expression of emotions in interpersonal settings" (APA, 2000). Individuals with schizoid PD often do not want or enjoy close interpersonal relationships, and as a result, they appear cold and detached. Our review of the literature identified six studies that obtained evidence of an association between childhood maltreatment and risk for the development of schizoid PD. As seen in Table 15.11, retrospective studies have provided evidence indicating that individuals with schizoid PD are more likely than patients with other personality disorders to report a history of sexual abuse or childhood emotional neglect (Bernstein et al., 1998; Norden et al., 1995; Ruggiero et al., 1999). Other studies have obtained findings indicating that reports of low childhood parental affection were associated with the development of schizoid PD symptoms (Carter et al., 1999). Prospective studies (Johnson, Cohen, Brown, et al., 1999; Johnson, Cohen, Smailes, et al., 2001; Johnson, Smailes, et al., 2000) have provided evidence indicating that childhood physical abuse, emotional abuse, supervision neglect, physical neglect, emotional neglect, and any childhood neglect were significantly associated with risk for the development of schizoid PD.

Childhood Adversities Associated With Risk for Schizotypal Personality Disorder

Schizotypal personality disorder is "a pervasive pattern of social and interpersonal deficits marked by acute discomfort with, and reduced capacity for, close relationships as well as by cognitive or perceptual distortions and eccentricities of behavior" (APA, 2000). Individuals with schizotypal PD tend to be socially isolated, to act and think in unusual and bizarre ways (e.g., ideas of reference and magical thinking), and to be suspicious of others. Our review of the literature identified seven studies that obtained evidence of an association between childhood maltreatment and risk for the development of schizotypal PD (see Table 15.12). Evidence from retrospective studies has indicated that individuals with schizotypal PD are more likely than patients with other personality disorders to report a history of childhood physical abuse, sexual abuse, or neglect (Norden et al., 1995; Ruggiero et al., 1999; Shea et al., 1999; Yen et al., 2002). Prospective studies (Johnson, Cohen, Brown, et al., 1999; Johnson, Cohen, Smailes, et al., 2001; Johnson, Smailes, et al., 2000) have provided evidence indicating that childhood physical abuse, emotional abuse, physical neglect, emotional neglect, and any childhood neglect were significantly associated with risk for the

(Text continues on page 455)

Table 15.10 Findings From Studies of Associations Between Specific Types of Childhood Maltreatment and Passive-Aggressive Personality Disorder (PD) Traits

Type of Childhood Maltreatment											
PA	*SA*	*EA*	*SN*	*PN*	*EN*	*AN*	*Study*	*N*	*Sample*	*Other Types of Childhood Maltreatment Controlled Statistically*	*Other Covariates That Were Controlled Statistically*
						R	Drake & Vaillant (1988)	307	Longitudinal study of 307 nonalcoholic middle-aged men	—	—
PC[a]						PC[a]	Johnson, Cohen, Brown, et al. (1999)	639	Community-based prospective longitudinal study of parents and their children (SA, PA, AN); childhood maltreatment data obtained from state records and retrospective reports by offspring	PA, SA, AN	Co-occurring PD symptoms; child age and gender; parental education, income, and psychiatric disorders
			P[a]			P	Johnson, Smailes, et al. (2000)	738	Community-based prospective longitudinal study of parents and their children; data regarding childhood neglect were obtained from state records and maternal reports during the child-rearing years	PA, SA, EN, SN, PN, CN	Co-occurring PD symptoms, child age, and gender

(Continued)

Table 15.10 (Continued)

Type of Childhood Maltreatment							*Study*	*N*	*Sample*	*Other Types of Childhood Maltreatment Controlled Statistically*	*Other Covariates That Were Controlled Statistically*
PA	*SA*	*EA*	*SN*	*PN*	*EN*	*AN*					
	R						Ruggiero et al. (1999)	200	Male inpatient veterans with substance dependence	—	—
Summary of Significant Associations											
PC[a]	R	P[a]				PC[a]R					

NOTES: PA = childhood physical abuse; SA = childhood sexual abuse; EA = childhood emotional abuse (verbal abuse is classified as emotional abuse); SN = childhood supervision neglect; PN = childhood physical neglect; EN = childhood emotional neglect; CN = childhood cognitive neglect; AN = any childhood neglect; AM = any childhood maltreatment; P = prospective epidemiological findings, based on documented evidence of childhood maltreatment, were significant after controlling for co-occurring PD symptoms, parental education, and parental psychiatric symptoms; C = combined prospective and retrospective reports of childhood physical abuse, sexual abuse, or any childhood neglect yielded significant findings after controlling for co-occurring PD symptoms, parental education, and parental psychiatric symptoms; R = retrospective clinical studies have obtained a significant association after covariates were controlled statistically; D = individuals with a documented history of physical abuse or neglect were significantly more likely than controls to be diagnosed with antisocial PD.

a. Association remained significant after controlling for other types of childhood abuse and neglect.

Table 15.11 Findings From Studies of Associations Between Specific Types of Childhood Maltreatment and Schizoid Personality Disorder (PD) Traits

Type of Childhood Maltreatment											
PA	*SA*	*EA*	*SN*	*PN*	*EN*	*AN*	*Study*	*N*	*Sample*	*Other Types of Childhood Maltreatment Controlled Statistically*	*Other Covariates That Were Controlled Statistically*
					R		Bernstein et al. (1998)	339	Patients with alcohol or drug dependence	—	—
P							Johnson, Cohen, Brown, et al. (1999)	639	Community-based prospective longitudinal study of parents and their children (SA, PA, AN); childhood maltreatment data obtained from state records and retrospective reports by offspring	PA, SA, AN	Co-occurring PD symptoms; child age and gender; parental education, income, and psychiatric disorders
		P[a]					Johnson, Cohen, Smailes, et al. (2001)	793	Community-based prospective longitudinal study (maternal verbal abuse), assessed by maternal reports during the child-rearing years	PA, SA, AN	Child temperament, physical punishment, co-occurring psychiatric disorders, parental education and psychiatric disorders

(Continued)

Table 15.11 (Continued)

Type of Childhood Maltreatment											
PA	*SA*	*EA*	*SN*	*PN*	*EN*	*AN*	*Study*	*N*	*Sample*	*Other Types of Childhood Maltreatment Controlled Statistically*	*Other Covariates That Were Controlled Statistically*
			P	P	P	P	Johnson, Smailes, et al. (2000)	738	Community-based prospective longitudinal study of parents and their children; data regarding childhood neglect were obtained from state records and maternal reports during the child-rearing years	PA, SA, EN, SN, PN, CN	Co-occurring PD symptoms, child age and gender
					R		Norden et al. (1995)	90	Psychiatric outpatients	—	—
	R					R	Ruggiero et al. (1999)	200	Male inpatient veterans with substance dependence	—	—
Summary of Significant Association											
P	R	P[a]	P	P	PR	PR					

NOTES: PA = childhood physical abuse; SA = childhood sexual abuse; EA = childhood emotional abuse (verbal abuse is classified as emotional abuse); SN = childhood supervision neglect; PN = childhood physical neglect; EN = childhood emotional neglect; CN = childhood cognitive neglect; AN = any childhood neglect; AM = any childhood maltreatment; P = prospective epidemiological findings, based on documented evidence of childhood maltreatment, were significant after controlling for co-occurring PD symptoms, parental education, and parental psychiatric symptoms; C = combined prospective and retrospective reports of childhood physical abuse, sexual abuse, or any childhood neglect yielded significant findings after controlling for co-occurring PD symptoms, parental education, and parental psychiatric symptoms; R = retrospective clinical studies have obtained a significant association after covariates were controlled statistically; D = individuals with a documented history of physical abuse or neglect were significantly more likely than controls to be diagnosed with antisocial PD.

a. Association remained significant after controlling for other types of childhood abuse and neglect.

Table 15.12 Findings From Studies of Associations Between Specific Types of Childhood Maltreatment and Schizotypal Personality Disorder (PD) Traits

Type of Childhood Maltreatment											
PA	*SA*	*EA*	*SN*	*PN*	*EN*	*AN*	*Study*	*N*	*Sample*	*Other Types of Childhood Maltreatment Controlled Statistically*	*Other Covariates That Were Controlled Statistically*
C[a]						C[a]	Johnson, Cohen, Brown, et al. (1999)	639	Community-based prospective longitudinal study of parents and their children (SA, PA, AN); childhood maltreatment data obtained from state records and retrospective reports by offspring	PA, SA, AN	Co-occurring PD symptoms; child age and gender; parental education, income, and psychiatric disorders
		P[a]					Johnson, Cohen, Smailes, et al. (2001)	793	Community-based prospective longitudinal study (maternal verbal abuse), assessed by maternal reports during the child-rearing years	PA, SA, AN	Child temperament, physical punishment, co-occurring psychiatric disorders, parental education and psychiatric disorders
				P		P	Johnson, Smailes, et al. (2000)	738	Community-based prospective longitudinal study of parents and their children; data regarding childhood neglect were obtained from state records and maternal reports during the child-rearing years	PA, SA, EN, SN, PN, CN	Co-occurring PD symptoms, child age and gender

(Continued)

Table 15.12 (Continued)

Type of Childhood Maltreatment							*Study*	*N*	*Sample*	*Other Types of Childhood Maltreatment Controlled Statistically*	*Other Covariates That Were Controlled Statistically*
PA	*SA*	*EA*	*SN*	*PN*	*EN*	*AN*					
	R						Norden et al. (1995)	90	Psychiatric outpatients	—	—
	R					R	Ruggiero et al. (1999)	200	Male inpatient veterans with substance dependence	—	—
	R						Shea et al. (1999)	140	Female inpatients and outpatients with childhood sexual abuse; comparison samples of veteran, OCD, bipolar, panic, bulimia, and MDD	—	—
R							Yen et al. (2002)	653	Longitudinal study: 86 schizotypal, 167 borderline, 153 avoidant, and 153 obsessive-compulsive PDs; 94 MDD with no PD	PA, SA	Co-occurring PDs, MDD
Summary of Significant Association											
C^aR	R	P^a		P^a	PC^a	P^aC^aR					

NOTES: PA = childhood physical abuse; SA = childhood sexual abuse; EA = childhood emotional abuse (verbal abuse is classified as emotional abuse); SN = childhood supervision neglect; PN = childhood physical neglect; EN = childhood emotional neglect; CN = childhood cognitive neglect; AN = any childhood neglect; AM = any childhood maltreatment; P = prospective epidemiological findings, based on documented evidence of childhood maltreatment, were significant after controlling for co-occurring PD symptoms, parental education, and parental psychiatric symptoms; C = combined prospective and retrospective reports of childhood physical abuse, sexual abuse, or any childhood neglect yielded significant findings after controlling for co-occurring PD symptoms, parental education, and parental psychiatric symptoms; R = retrospective clinical studies have obtained a significant association after covariates were controlled statistically; D = individuals with a documented history of physical abuse or neglect were significantly more likely than controls to be diagnosed with antisocial PD; OCD = obsessive-compulsive disorder; MDD = major depressive disorder.

a. Association remained significant after controlling for other types of childhood abuse and neglect.

development of schizotypal PD. Findings of the only study that has reported findings based on both retrospective and prospective data (Johnson, Cohen, Brown, et al., 1999) suggest that childhood physical abuse and any childhood neglect may contribute to elevated risk for the development of schizotypal PD.

HYPOTHESIZED ASSOCIATIONS OF SPECIFIC TYPES OF CHILDHOOD MALTREATMENT WITH RISK FOR THE DEVELOPMENT OF SPECIFIC PDs

Research on the association between childhood maltreatment and PDs has advanced significantly in recent years. Current findings suggest that specific combinations of childhood emotional abuse, physical abuse, sexual abuse, emotional neglect, physical neglect, and supervision neglect may be associated with the development of specific PD syndromes. Although much research remains to be done, evidence from retrospective studies and from prospective studies that have controlled for co-occurring childhood maltreatment and PD symptoms, supports the following hypotheses: (a) Youths that experience physical abuse and one or more types of childhood neglect may be at particularly elevated risk for antisocial PD. (b) Those that experience emotional neglect may be at elevated risk for avoidant PD. (c) Youths that experience sexual abuse and either emotional abuse, physical abuse, or one or more types of childhood neglect may be at particularly elevated risk for borderline PD. (d) Youths that experience one or more types of childhood neglect in the absence of other forms of abuse may be at elevated risk for dependent PD. (e) Those that experience physical abuse, sexual abuse, or both may be at elevated risk for poor self-esteem and other traits associated with depressive PD. (f) Youths that experience sexual abuse alone may be at elevated risk for histrionic PD. (g) Those that experience emotional abuse and one or more types of childhood neglect may be at particularly elevated risk for narcissistic PD. (h) Childhood emotional abuse may contribute to the development of obsessive-compulsive PD. (i) Childhood emotional abuse, in combination with emotional or supervision neglect, may contribute to the development of paranoid PD. (j) Youths that experience physical abuse, supervision neglect, or both may be at elevated risk for passive-aggressive PD. (k) Those that experience any emotional abuse and one or more other types of childhood maltreatment may be at particularly elevated risk for schizoid PD. (l) Youths that experience emotional abuse, physical abuse, or physical neglect may be at elevated risk for schizotypal PD.

CONCLUSIONS

A substantial body of research evidence has indicated that individuals with PDs are more likely than other individuals to report a history of childhood adversities, including abuse, neglect, maladaptive parenting, and traumatic life events. Retrospective studies have also provided considerable evidence suggesting that specific combinations of childhood adversities may be differentially associated with risk for the development of specific types of PDs. Although strong inferences regarding causality are not possible based on retrospective data, prospective longitudinal studies have provided additional evidence supporting the hypothesis that specific combinations of childhood adversities are differentially associated with risk for specific PDs. These results dovetail with an accumulating body of evidence from genetic and neurobiological studies supporting the overall hypothesis that childhood abuse contributes to elevated risk for the development of PDs.

However, many questions regarding the association between the childhood adversities and risk for PDs remain unanswered.

As noted above, retrospective studies have provided most of the evidence that is currently available regarding these associations, and many associations between specific combinations of childhood adversities and specific PDs have not yet been investigated in a systematic manner. Thus, although there have been noteworthy advances in recent years, scientific understanding of the role that childhood adversities may play in the development of PDs remains somewhat limited. The evidence that is currently available suggests that childhood adversities may play an important role in the development of PDs and that certain combinations of childhood adversities may be differentially associated with risk for specific types of PDs. Increasingly, it will be important for future studies to investigate how childhood adversities may interact with genetic, prenatal, and other vulnerability factors to promote the development of PD symptoms. Researchers have recently begun to make important strides in this direction (e.g., Caspi et al., 2002; Foley et al., 2004), but much more work of this kind needs to be done. In addition to investigating the interaction of genetic and environmental factors, it will be important to investigate the three-way interaction of genetic, prenatal, and environmental factors. Such studies hold the promise of improving our understanding of the etiology of PDs and promoting advances in the prevention and treatment of these chronic and debilitating disorders.

NOTES

1. For example, the interpersonal theory of suicide holds that those with a history of highly problematic interpersonal relationships during childhood may be particularly associated with risk for suicidal behavior later in life, if there have been repeated interpersonal difficulties during adolescence and adulthood (see Johnson, Rabkin, et al., 2000).

2. These investigations have suggested that, because life experiences have a profound effect on the development of neuronal interconnections in the brain throughout childhood and beyond, most mental disorders, even those caused by maltreatment and other adversities, may be viewed as having an important biological or neuropsychological component. Thus, biological vulnerabilities detected as deficits in neurological or neuropsychological functioning may stem at least in part from a history of chronic or severe adversity, ranging from childhood maltreatment to traumatic life events that may take place throughout the life span.

REFERENCES

Abrams, R. C., & Horowitz, S. V. (1996). Personality disorders after age 50: A meta-analysis. *Journal of Personality Disorders, 10,* 271–281.

American Psychiatric Association. (1968). *Diagnostic and statistical manual of mental disorders* (2nd ed.). Washington, DC: Author.

American Psychiatric Association. (1980). Diagnostic and statistical manual of mental disorders (3rd ed.). Washington, DC: Author.

American Psychiatric Association. (1987). *Diagnostic and statistical manual of mental disorders* (3rd ed., rev.). Washington, DC: Author.

American Psychiatric Association. (1994). *Diagnostic and statistical manual of mental disorders* (4th ed.). Washington, DC: Author.

American Psychiatric Association. (2000). *Diagnostic and statistical manual of mental disorders* (4th ed., text revision). Washington, DC: Author.

Andersen, S. L. (2003). Trajectories of brain development: Point of vulnerability or window of opportunity? *Neuroscience and Biobehavioral Reviews, 27,* 3–18.

Arbel, N., & Stravynski, A. (1991). A retrospective study of separation in the development of adult avoidant personality disorder. *Acta Psychiatrica Scandinavica, 83,* 174–178.

Baker, J. D., Capron, E. W., & Azorlosa, J. (1996). Family environment characteristics of persons with histrionic and dependent personality disorders. *Journal of Personality Disorders, 10,* 82–87.

Bernstein, D. P., Cohen, P., Skodol, A., Bezirganian, S., & Brook, J. S. (1996). Childhood antecedents of adolescent personality disorders. *American Journal of Psychiatry, 153,* 907–913.

Bernstein, D. P., Cohen, P., Velez, N., Schwab-Stone, M., Siever, L. J., & Shinsato, L. (1993). Prevalence and stability of the DSM-III-R personality disorders in a community-based survey of adolescents. *American Journal of Psychiatry, 150,* 1237–1243.

Bernstein, D. P., Stein, J. A., & Handelsman, L. (1998). Predicting personality pathology among adult patients with substance use disorders: Effects of childhood maltreatment. *Addictive Behavior, 23,* 855–868.

Bifulco, A., Brown, G. W., & Lillie, A. (1997). Memories of childhood neglect and abuse: Corroboration in a series of sisters. *Journal of Child Psychology and Psychiatry, 38,* 365–374.

Black, D. W., Baumgard, C. H., & Bell, S. E. (1995). A 16- to 45-year follow-up of men with antisocial personality disorder. *Comprehensive Psychiatry, 36,* 130–140.

Bornstein, R. F. (in press). *The dependent patient: A practitioner's guide.* Washington, DC: American Psychological Association.

Brennan, K. A., & Shaver, P. R. (1998). Attachment styles and personality disorders: Their connections to each other and to parental divorce, parental death, and perceptions of parental caregiving. *Journal of Personality, 66,* 835–878.

Briere, J., & Runtz, M. (1990). Differential adult symptomatology associated with three types of child abuse histories. *Child Abuse & Neglect, 14,* 357–364.

Brodsky, B. S., Cloitre, M., & Dulit, R. A. (1995). Relationship of dissociation to self-mutilation and childhood abuse in borderline personality disorder. *American Journal of Psychiatry, 152,* 1788–1792.

Brown, G. R., & Anderson, B. (1991). Psychiatric morbidity in adult inpatients with childhood histories of sexual and physical abuse. *American Journal of Psychiatry, 148,* 55–61.

Carter, J. D., Joyce, P. R., Mulder, R. T., Luty, S. E., & Sullivan, P. F. (1999). Early deficient parenting in depressed outpatients is associated with personality dysfunction and not with depression subtypes. *Journal of Affective Disorders, 54,* 29–37.

Caspi, A., McClay, J., Moffitt, T. E., Mill, J., Martin, J., Craig, I. W., et al. (2002). Role of genotype in the cycle of violence in maltreated children. *Science, 297,* 851–854.

Caspi, A., Moffitt, T. E., Newman, D. L., & Silva, P. A. (1996). Behavioral observations at age 3 years predict adult psychiatric disorders: Longitudinal evidence from a birth cohort. *Archives of General Psychiatry, 53,* 1033–1039.

Caspi, A., & Roberts, B. W. (2001). Personality development across the life course: The argument for change and continuity. *Psychological Inquiry, 12,* 49–66.

Charles, S. T., Reynolds, C. A., & Gatz, M. (2001). Age-related differences and change in positive and negative affect over 23 years. *Journal of Personality & Social Psychology, 80,* 136–151.

Chilcoat, H. D., Breslau, N., & Anthony, J. C. (1996). Potential barriers to parent monitoring: Social disadvantage, marital status, and maternal psychiatric disorder. *Journal of the American Academy of Child and Adolescent Psychiatry, 35,* 1673–1682.

Cohen, P. (1996). Childhood risks for young adult symptoms of personality disorder: Method and substance. *Multivariate Behavioral Research, 31*(1), 121–148.

Cohen, P. (1999). Personality development in childhood: Old and new findings. In C. R. Cloninger (Ed.), *Personality and psychopathology* (pp. 101–127). Washington, DC: American Psychiatric Press.

Cohen, P., Brown, J., & Smailes, E. (2001). Child abuse and neglect and the development of mental disorders in the general population. *Development and Psychopathology, 13,* 981–999.

Daley, S. E., Hammen, C., Burge, D., Davila, J., Paley, B., Lindberg, N., et al. (1999). Depression and Axis II symptomatology in an adolescent community sample: Concurrent and longitudinal associations. *Journal of Personality Disorders, 13,* 47–59.

Derogatis, L. R. (1983). *SCL-90-R administration, scoring, & procedures manual.* Towson, MD: Clinical Psychometric Research.

Drake, R. E., Adler, D. A., & Vaillant, G. E. (1988). Antecedents of personality disorders in a community sample of men. *Journal of Personality Disorders, 2,* 60–68.

Drake, R. E., & Vaillant, G. E. (1988). Introduction: Longitudinal views of personality disorder. *Journal of Personality Disorders, 2,* 44–48.

Dubo, E. D., Zanarini, M. C., Lewis, R. E., & Williams, A. A. (1997). Childhood antecedents of self-destructiveness in borderline personality disorder. *Canadian Journal of Psychiatry, 42,* 63–69.

Erikson, E. H. (1963). *Childhood and society* (2nd ed.). New York: Norton.

Farrington, D. P. (1991). Antisocial personality from childhood to adulthood. *The Psychologist: Bulletin of the British Psychological Society, 4,* 389–394.

Foley, D. L., Eaves, L. J., Wormley, B., Silberg, J. L., Maes, H. H., Kuhn, J., et al. (2004). Childhood adversity, monoamine oxidase A genotype, and risk for conduct disorder. *Archives of General Psychiatry, 61,* 738–744.

Fondacaro, K. M., Holt, J. C., & Powell, T. A. (1999). Psychological impact of childhood sexual abuse on male inmates: The importance of perception. *Child Abuse & Neglect, 23,* 361–369.

Fossati, A., Feeney, J. A., Donati, D., Donini, M., Novella, L., Bagnato, M., et al. (2003). Personality disorders and adult attachment dimensions in a mixed psychiatric sample: A multivariate study. *Journal of Nervous & Mental Disease, 191,* 30–37.

Frick, P. J., Lahey, B. B., Loeber, R., Stouthamer-Loeber, M., Christ, M. A. G., & Hanson, K. (1992). Familial risk factors to oppositional defiant disorder and conduct disorder: Parental psychopathology and maternal parenting. *Journal of Consulting and Clinical Psychology, 60,* 49–55.

Garnet, K. E., Levy, K. N., Mattanah, J. J. F., Edell, W. S., & McGlashan, T. H. (1994). Borderline personality disorder in adolescents: Ubiquitous or specific? *American Journal of Psychiatry, 151,* 1380–1382.

Gauthier, L., Stollak, G., Messé, L., & Aronoff, J. (1996). Recall of childhood neglect and physical abuse as differential predictors of current psychological functioning. *Child Abuse and Neglect, 20,* 549–559.

Goldman, S. J., D'Angelo, E. J., & DeMaso, D. R. (1992). Physical and sexual abuse histories among children with borderline personality disorder. *American Journal of Psychiatry, 149,* 1723–1726.

Grant, B. F., Hasin, H. S., Stinson, F. S., Dawson, D. A., Chou, S. P., Ruan, W. J., et al. (2004). Prevalence, correlates, and disability of personality disorders in the United States: Results from the National Epidemiologic Survey on Alcohol and Related Conditions. *Journal of Clinical Psychiatry, 65,* 948–958.

Grilo, C., & Masheb, R. M. (2002). Childhood maltreatment and personality disorders in adult patients with binge eating disorder. *Acta Psychiatrica Scandinavica, 106,* 183–188.

Guzder, J., Paris, J., & Zelkowitz, P. (1996). Risk factors for borderline pathology in children. *Journal of the American Academy of Child and Adolescent Psychiatry, 35,* 26–33.

Hart, D., Hofmann, V., Edelstein, W., & Keller, M. (1997). The relation of childhood personality types to adolescent behavior and development: A longitudinal study of Icelandic children. *Developmental Psychology, 33,* 195–205.

Head, S. B., Baker, J. D., & Williamson, D. A. (1991). Family environment characteristics and dependent personality disorder. *Journal of Personality Disorders, 5,* 256–263.

Herman, J. L., Perry, J. C., & van der Kolk, B. A. (1989). Childhood trauma in borderline personality disorder. *American Journal of Psychiatry, 146,* 490–495.

Irvine, A. B., Biglan, A., Smolkowski, K., Letzler, C. W., & Ary, D. V. (1999). The effectiveness of a parenting skills program for parents of middle school students in small communities. *Journal of Consulting and Clinical Psychology, 67,* 811–825.

Johnson, J. G. (1993). Relationships between psychosocial development and personality disorder symptomatology in late adolescents. *Journal of Youth & Adolescence, 22,* 33–42.

Johnson, J. G., & Bornstein, R. F. (1991). PDQ-R personality disorder scores and negative life events independently predict changes in SCL-90 psychopathology scores. *Journal of Psychopathology and Behavioral Assessment, 13,* 61–72.

Johnson, J. G., Bromley, E., Bornstein, R. F., & Sneed, J. (in press). Adolescent personality disorders. In D. A. Wolfe & E. J. Mash (Eds.), *Behavioral and emotional disorders in children and adolescents: Nature, assessment, & treatment.* New York: Guilford Press.

Johnson, J. G., Cohen, P., Brown, J., Smailes, E. M., & Bernstein, D. P. (1999). Childhood maltreatment increases risk for personality disorders during early adulthood. *Archives of General Psychiatry, 56,* 600–606.

Johnson, J. G., Cohen, P., Dohrenwend, B. P., Link, B. G., & Brook, J. S. (1999). A longitudinal investigation of social causation and social selection processes involved in the association between socioeconomic status and psychiatric disorders. *Journal of Abnormal Psychology, 108,* 490–499.

Johnson, J. G., Cohen, P., Gould, M. S., Kasen, S., Brown, J., & Brook, J. S. (2002). Childhood adversities, interpersonal difficulties, and risk for suicide attempts during late adolescence and early adulthood. *Archives of General Psychiatry, 59,* 741–749.

Johnson, J. G., Cohen, P., Kasen, S., Skodol, A. E., Hamagami, F., & Brook, J. S. (2000). Age-related change in personality disorder trait levels between early adolescence and adulthood: A community-based longitudinal investigation. *Acta Psychiatrica Scandinavica, 102,* 265–275.

Johnson, J. G., Cohen, P., Kasen, S., Smailes, E. M., & Brook, J. S. (2001). Association of maladaptive parental behavior with psychiatric disorder among parents and their offspring. *Archives of General Psychiatry, 58,* 453–460.

Johnson, J. G., Cohen, P., Skodol, A. E., Oldham, J. M., Kasen, S., & Brook, J. S. (1999). Personality disorders in adolescence and risk of major mental disorders and suicidality during adulthood. *Archives of General Psychiatry, 56,* 805–811.

Johnson, J. G., Cohen, P., Smailes, E. M., Kasen, S., Oldham, J. M., & Skodol, A. E. (2000). Adolescent personality disorders associated with violence and criminal behavior during adolescence and early adulthood. *American Journal of Psychiatry, 157,* 1406–1412.

Johnson, J. G., Cohen, P., Smailes, E. M., Skodol, A. E., Brown, J., & Oldham, J. M. (2001). Childhood verbal abuse and risk for personality disorders during adolescence and early adulthood. *Comprehensive Psychiatry, 42,* 16–23.

Johnson, J. G., Quigley, J. F., & Sherman, M. F. (1997). Adolescent personality disorder symptoms mediate the relationship between perceived parental behavior and Axis I symptomatology. *Journal of Personality Disorders, 11,* 381–390.

Johnson, J. G., Rabkin, J. G., Williams, J. B. W., Remien, R. H., & Gorman, J. M. (2000). Difficulties in interpersonal relationships associated with personality disorders and Axis I disorders: A community-based longitudinal investigation. *Journal of Personality Disorders, 14,* 42–56.

Johnson, J. G., Smailes, E. M., Cohen, P., Brown, J., & Bernstein, D. P. (2000). Associations between four types of childhood neglect and personality disorder symptoms during adolescence and early adulthood: Findings of a community-based longitudinal study. *Journal of Personality Disorders, 14,* 171–187.

Johnson, J. G., Williams, J. B. W., Goetz, R. R., Rabkin, J. G., Remien, R. H., Lipsitz, J. D., et al. (1996). Personality disorders predict onset of Axis I disorders and impaired functioning among homosexual men with and at risk for HIV infection. *Archives of General Psychiatry, 53,* 350–357.

Kendler, K. S. (1996). Parenting: A genetic-epidemiologic perspective. *American Journal of Psychiatry, 153,* 11–20.

Kendler, K. S., Bulik, C. M., Silberg, J., Hettema, J. M., Myers, J., Prescott, C. A. (2000). Childhood sexual abuse and adult psychiatric and substance use disorders in women: An epidemiological and co-twin control analysis. *Archives of General Psychiatry, 57,* 953–959.

Kessler, R. C., McGonagle, K. A., Zhao, S. Y., Nelson, C. B., Hughes, M., Eshleman, S., et al. (1994). Lifetime and 12-month prevalence of DSM-III-R psychiatric disorders in the United States: Results from the National Comorbidity Study. *Archives of General Psychiatry, 51,* 8–19.

Klonsky, E. D., Oltmanns, T. F., Turkheimer, E., & Fiedler, E. R. (2000). Recollections of conflict with parents and family support in the personality disorders. *Journal of Personality Disorders, 14,* 327–338.

Korenblum, M., Marton, P., Golombek, H., & Stein, B. (1987). Disturbed personality functioning: Patterns of change from early to middle adolescence. In S. C. Feinstein & P. L. Giovacchini (Eds.), *Adolescent psychiatry* (Vol. 14, pp. 407–416). Chicago: University of Chicago Press.

Kwon, J. S., Kim, Y. M., Chang, C. G., Park, B. J., Yoon, D. J., Han, W. S., et al. (2000). Three-year follow-up of women with the sole diagnosis of depressive personality disorder: Subsequent development of dysthymia and major depression. *American Journal of Psychiatry, 157,* 1966–1972.

Laporte, L., & Guttman, H. (1996). Traumatic childhood experiences as risk factors for borderline and other personality disorders. *Journal of Personality Disorders, 10,* 247–259.

Lenzenweger, M. F. (1999). Stability and change in personality disorder features: The longitudinal study of personality disorders. *Archives of General Psychiatry, 56,* 1009–1015.

Linehan, M. M. (1993). *Cognitive-behavioral treatment of borderline personality disorder.* New York: Guilford Press.

Livesley, W. J., Jang, K. L., Jackson, D. N., & Vernon, P. A. (1993). Genetic and environmental contributions to dimensions of personality disorder. *American Journal of Psychiatry, 150,* 1826–1831.

Loeber, R., Drinkwater, M., Yin, Y., Anderson, S. J., Schmidt, L. C., & Crawford, A. (2000). Stability of family interaction from ages 6 to 18. *Journal of Abnormal Child Psychology, 28,* 353–369.

Loeber, R., & Farrington, D. P. (2000). Young children who commit crime: Epidemiology, developmental origins, risk factors, early interventions, and policy implications. *Development and Psychopathology, 12,* 737–762.

Ludolph, P. S., Westen, D., & Misle, B. (1990). The borderline diagnosis in adolescents: Symptoms and developmental history. *American Journal of Psychiatry, 147,* 470–476.

Luntz, B. K., & Widom, C. S. (1994). Antisocial personality disorder in abused and neglected children grown up. *American Journal of Psychiatry, 151,* 670–674.

Mattanah, J. J. F., Becker, D. F., Levy, K. N., Edell, W. S., & McGlashan, T. H. (1995). Diagnostic stability in adolescents followed up to 2 years after hospitalization. *American Journal of Psychiatry, 152,* 889–894.

Maughan, B., & Rutter, M. (1997). Retrospective reporting of childhood adversity: Issues in assessing long-term recall. *Journal of Personality Disorders, 11,* 19–33.

McGue, M., Bacon, S., & Lykken, D. T. (1993). Personality stability and change in early adulthood: A behavioral genetic analysis. *Developmental Psychology, 29,* 96–106.

Mullen, P. E., Martin, J. L., & Anderson, J. C. (1996). The long-term impact of the physical, emotional and sexual abuse of children: A community study. *Child Abuse & Neglect, 20,* 7–21.

Neugebauer, R., Hoek, H. W., & Susser, E. (1999). Prenatal exposure to wartime famine and development of antisocial personality disorder in early adulthood. *Journal of the American Medical Association, 282,* 455–462.

Newman, D. L., Caspi, A., Moffitt, T. E., & Silva, P. A. (1997). Antecedents of adult interpersonal functioning: Effects of individual differences in age 3 temperament. *Developmental Psychology, 33,* 206–217.

Norden, K. A., Klein, D. N., Donaldson, S. K., Pepper, C. M., & Klein, L. M. (1995). Reports of the early home environment in DSM-III-R personality disorders. *Journal of Personality Disorders, 9,* 213–223.

Ogata, S. N., Silk, K. R., Goodrich, S., Lohr, N. E., Westen, D., & Hill, E. M. (1990). Childhood sexual and physical abuse in adult patients with borderline personality disorder. *American Journal of Psychiatry, 147,* 1008–1013.

Oldham, J. M., Skodol, A. E., Gallagher, P. E., & Kroll, M. E. (1996). Relationship of borderline symptoms to histories of abuse and neglect: A pilot study. *Psychiatric Quarterly, 67,* 287–295.

Orlandini, A., Fontana, S., Clerici, S., Fossati, A., Fiorilli, M., Negri, G., et al. (1997, June). *Personality modifications in adolescence: A three-year follow-up study.* Paper presented at the Fifth International Congress on the Disorders of Personality, Vancouver, Canada.

Pancoast, D. L., & Archer, R. P. (1992). MMPI response patterns of college students: Comparisons to adolescents and adults. *Journal of Clinical Psychology, 48,* 47–53.

Paris, J. (1994). *Borderline personality disorder: A multidimensional approach.* Washington, DC: American Psychiatric Association.

Paris, J. (1997). Childhood trauma as an etiological factor in the personality disorders. *Journal of Personality Disorders, 11,* 34–49.

Pincus, A. L., & Wilson, K. R. (2001). Interpersonal variability in dependent personality. *Journal of Personality, 69,* 223–251.

Pollock, V. E., Briere, J., & Schneider, L. (1990). Childhood antecedents of antisocial behavior: Parental alcoholism and physical abusiveness. *American Journal of Psychiatry, 147,* 1290–1293.

Raczek, S. W. (1992). Childhood abuse and personality disorders. *Journal of Personality Disorders, 6,* 109–116.

Redmond, C., Spoth, R., Shin, C., & Lepper, H. S. (1999). Modeling long-term parent outcomes of two universal family-focused preventive interventions: One-year follow-up results. *Journal of Consulting and Clinical Psychology, 67,* 975–984.

Reiss, D., Hetherington, M., Plomin, R., Howe, G. W., Simmens, S. J., Henderson, S. H., et al. (1995). Genetic questions for environmental studies: Differential parental behavior and psychopathology in adolescence. *Archives of General Psychiatry, 52,* 925–936.

Roberts, B. W., & DelVecchio, W. F. (2000). The rank-order consistency of personality traits from childhood to old age: A quantitative review of longitudinal studies. *Psychological Bulletin, 126,* 3–25.

Robins, L. N. (1966). *Deviant children grow up: A sociological and psychiatric study of sociopathic personality.* Baltimore: Williams & Wilkins.

Robins, L. N., & Regier, D. (1991). *Psychiatric disorders in America: The Epidemiological Catchment Area study.* New York: Free Press.

Robins, L. N., Schoenberg, S. P., Holmes, S. J., Ratcliff, K. S., Benham, A., & Works, J. (1985). Early home environment and retrospective recall: A test for concordance between siblings with and without psychiatric disorders. *American Journal of Orthopsychiatry, 55,* 27–41.

Ronningstam, E., Gunderson, J., & Lyons, M. (1995). Changes in pathological narcissism. *American Journal of Psychiatry, 152,* 253–257.

Rosenstein, D. S., & Horowitz, H. A. (1996). Adolescent attachment and psychopathology. *Journal of Consulting and Clinical Psychology, 64,* 244–253.

Rowe, D. C., & Farrington, D. P. (1997). The familial transmission of criminal convictions. *Criminology, 35,* 177–201.

Ruggiero, J., Bernstein, D. P., Handelsman, L. (1999). Traumatic stress in childhood and later personality disorders: A retrospective study of male patients with substance dependence. *Psychiatric Annals, 29,* 713–721.

Sampson, R. J., & Laub, J. H. (1993). *Crime in the making: Pathways and turning points through life.* Cambridge, MA: Harvard University Press.

Sampson, R. J., & Laub, J. H. (1994). Urban poverty and the family context of delinquency: A new look at structure and process in a classic study. *Child Development, 65,* 523–540.

Samuels, J., Eaton, W. W., Bienvenu, O. J., III, Brown, C. H., Costa, P. T., Jr., & Nestadt, G. (2002). Prevalence and correlates of personality disorders in a community sample. *British Journal of Psychiatry, 180,* 536–542.

Shaw, D. S., Owens, E. B., Giovannelli, J., & Winslow, E. B. (2001). Infant and toddler pathways leading to early externalizing disorders. *Journal of the American Academy of Child and Adolescent Psychiatry, 40,* 36–43.

Shea, M. T., Zlotnick, C., & Weisberg, R. B. (1999). Commonality and specificity of personality disorder profiles in subjects with trauma histories. *Journal of Personality Disorders, 13,* 199–210.

Shearer, S. L., Peters, C. P., Quaytman, M. S., & Ogden, R. L. (1990). Frequency and correlates of childhood sexual and physical abuse histories in adult female borderline inpatients. *American Journal of Psychiatry, 147,* 214–216.

Shiner, R. L. (2000). Linking childhood personality with adaptation: Evidence for continuity and change across time into late adolescence. *Journal of Personality and Social Psychology, 78,* 310–325.

Shiner, R. L., Masten, A. S., & Tellegen, A. (2002). A developmental perspective on personality in emerging adulthood: Childhood antecedents and concurrent adaptation. *Journal of Personality and Social Psychology, 83,* 1165–1177.

Sperling, M. B., & Berman, W. H. (1991). An attachment classification of desperate love. *Journal of Personality Assessment, 56,* 45–55.

Spoth, R. R., Lopez, M., Redmond, C., & Shin, C. (1999). Assessing a public health approach to delay onset and progression of adolescent substance abuse: Latent transition and log-linear analyses of longitudinal family preventive intervention outcomes. *Journal of Consulting & Clinical Psychology, 67,* 619–630.

Sroufe, L. A., Carlson, E. A., Levy, A. K., & Egeland, B. (1999). Implications of attachment theory for developmental psychopathology. *Development and Psychopathology, 11,* 1–13.

Steiger, H., Jabalpurwala, S., & Champagne, J. (1996). Axis II comorbidity and developmental adversity in bulimia nervosa. *Journal of Nervous and Mental Disease, 184,* 555–560.

Stein, J. A., Newcomb, M. D., & Bentler, P. M. (1986). Stability and change in personality: A longitudinal study from early adolescence to young adulthood. *Journal of Research in Personality, 20,* 276–291.

Stravynski, A., Elie, R., & Franche, R. L. (1989). Perception of early parenting by patients diagnosed with avoidant personality disorder: A test of the overprotection hypothesis. *Acta Psychiatrica Scandinavica, 80,* 415–420.

Teicher, M. H., Andersen, S. L., Polcari, A., Anderson, C. M., Navalta, C. P., & Kim, D. M. (2003). The neurobiological consequences of early stress and childhood maltreatment. *Neuroscience and Biobehavioral Reviews, 27,* 33–44.

Thomas, A., & Chess, S. (1984). Genesis and evolution of behavioral disorders: From infancy to early adult life. *American Journal of Orthopsychiatry, 141,* 1–9.

Torgersen, S., Kringlen, E., & Cramer, V. (2001). The prevalence of personality disorders in a community sample. *Archives of General Psychiatry, 58,* 590–596.

Trull, T. J., Useda, J. D., Doan, B. T., Vieth, A. Z., Burr, R. M., Hanks, A. A., et al. (1998). Two-year stability of borderline personality measures. *Journal of Personality Disorders, 12,* 187–197.

Vaglum, P., Friis, S., Karterud, S., Mehlum, L., & Vaglum, S. (1993). Stability of the severe personality disorder diagnosis: A 2- to 5-year prospective study. *Journal of Personality Disorders, 7,* 348–353.

van der Kolk, B. A., Hostetler, A., Herron, N., & Fisler, R. E. (1994). Trauma and the development of borderline personality disorder. *Psychiatric Clinics of North America, 17,* 715–730.

Vetter, P., & Koller, O. (1993). Stability of diagnoses in various psychiatric disorders: A study of long-term course. *Psychopathology, 26,* 173–180.

Ward, A. J. (1991). Prenatal stress and childhood psychopathology. *Child Psychiatry & Human Development, 22,* 97–110.

Weaver, T. L., & Clum, G. A. (1993). Early family environments and traumatic experiences associated with borderline personality disorder. *Journal of Consulting and Clinical Psychology, 61,* 1068–1075.

West, M., Rose, S. M., & Sheldon-Keller, A. (1994). Assessment of patterns of insecure attachment in adults and application to dependent and schizoid personality disorders. *Journal of Personality Disorders, 8,* 249–256.

Westen, D., Ludolph, P., Block, M. J., Wixom, J., & Wiss, F. C. (1990). Developmental history and object relations in psychiatrically disturbed adolescent girls. *American Journal of Psychiatry, 147,* 1061–1068.

Widom, C. S. (1989). The cycle of violence. *Science, 244,* 160–166.

Yen, S., Shea, M. T., Battle, C. L., Johnson, D. M., Zlotnick, C., Dolan-Sewell, R., et al. (2002). Traumatic exposure and posttraumatic stress disorder in borderline, schizotypal, avoidant and obsessive-compulsive personality disorders: Findings from the collaborative longitudinal personality disorders study. *Journal of Nervous and Mental Disease, 190,* 510–518.

Zanarini, M. C., Gunderson, J. G., Marino, M. F., Schwartz, E. O., & Frankenburg, F. R. (1989). Childhood experiences of borderline patients. *Comprehensive Psychiatry, 30,* 18–25.

Zanarini, M. C., Williams, A. A., Lewis, R. E., Reich, R. B., Vera, S. C., Marino, M. F., et al. (1997). Reported pathological childhood experiences associated with the development of borderline personality disorder. *American Journal of Psychiatry, 154,* 1101–1106.

Author Index

Page numbers followed by *t* refer to tables.

Subject Index

About the Editors

Benjamin L. Hankin is currently an Assistant Professor of Psychology at the University of South Carolina after being on the faculty at the University of Illinois at Chicago. He received his BA in psychology from Northwestern University and his PhD in clinical psychology from the University of Wisconsin. He is a developmental psychopathologist interested in vulnerability and stress models. His research expertise lies in studying the etiology and development of depression over the life span, especially during childhood and adolescence; understanding the emergence of the sex difference in depression; and investigating the common and specific aspects of symptoms and disorders comorbid with depression. He has published widely on these topics and has received funding from the National Institute of Mental Health and the National Cancer Institute to conduct his research. He has served on the editorial boards of various psychology journals, including *Journal of Abnormal Child Psychology, Journal of Research in Personality,* and *Cognitive Therapy and Research.* He has received awards from the Society for Research in Psychopathology and has received the New Researcher Award from the Association of the Advancement of Behavior Therapy.

John R. Z. Abela, PhD, is Associate Professor in the Department of Psychology at McGill University, Associate Professor in the Department of Psychiatry at McGill University Medical School, and Director of the Cognitive Behavior Therapy Clinic at the Montreal Children's Hospital. He received a BA in psychology from Brown University and a PhD in clinical psychology from the University of Pennsylvania. He completed his predoctoral internship at Harvard Medical School and McLean Hospital. His research focuses on cognitive and interpersonal vulnerability to depression in children, adolescents, and adults. He is a two-time recipient of a Young Investigator Award from the National Alliance for Research on Schizophrenia and Depression. His research has also been funded by the Canada Foundation for Innovation, the Social Sciences and Research Council of Canada, and the Canadian Psychiatric Research Foundation. He has received New Researcher Awards from the Canadian Psychological Association, the Association of the Advancement of Behavior Therapy, the International Congress of Psychology, and the Canadian National Research Council for the International Union of Psychological Science. He has also received McGill University's Principal's Prize for Excellence in Teaching and the Faculty of Science's Leo Yaffe Award for Excellence in Teaching.

About the Contributors

Sotoodeh Abhary is a medical doctor currently working as an intern at Flinders Medical Centre and graduated from Adelaide University in 2004 with a degree in Bachelor of Medicine, Bachelor of Surgery. She was the student representative for the University of Adelaide Psychiatry Departmental Committee for 2002–2004. Her systematic review focusing on childhood trauma and borderline personality disorder won her the South Australian Medical Women's Society Student Research Prize in 2003. She coauthored "Psychiatric Aspects of Detention: Illustrative Case Studies" (*Australian and New Zealand Journal of Psychiatry*, 2004), "An Interdisciplinary Course for Trainee Psychiatrists: Feedback and Implications" (in press), and the German book chapter "Personlichkeitsstorungen und fruhe Stresserfahrungen" (Schattauer, 2004).

Randy P. Auerbach is a doctoral candidate in the Clinical Psychology program at McGill University in Montreal. His doctoral research focuses on the relationships among depression, stress, and risky behaviors in adolescents. He is a graduate of Cornell University, where he received his BA in English, and he completed his Postbaccalaureate in psychology at Columbia University. He is the recipient of the McGill Graduate Studies Fellowship.

Robert F. Bornstein received his PhD in clinical psychology from the State University of New York at Buffalo in 1986, and he is now Professor of Psychology at Gettysburg College. His research interests center on personality disorders, unconscious processes, and the empirical study of psychoanalytic constructs. He wrote *The Dependent Personality* (Guilford, 1993) and *The Dependent Patient: A Practitioner's Guide* (American Psychological Association, 2005); coauthored (with Mary Languirand) *When Someone You Love Needs Nursing Home Care* (Newmarket Press, 2001); and coedited (with Joseph Masling) six volumes of the *Empirical Studies of Psychoanalytic Theories* book series. His research has been funded by grants from the National Institute of Mental Health and the National Science Foundation, and he received the Society for Personality Assessment's 1995, 1999, and 2003 Awards for Distinguished Contributions to the Personality Assessment Literature.

Vanessa P. Caskey is a first-year graduate student pursuing a doctoral degree in clinical psychology at Long Island University. She assists Dr. Jeffrey G. Johnson (Columbia University/New York State Psychiatric Institute) in his research on childhood maltreatment and personality disorders. She has a bachelor's degree in psychology with a concentration in neuroscience from Williams College. From 2001 through 2004, she worked for the Administration for Children's Services in New York City as a child welfare specialist counseling at-risk adolescents, where she received a certificate of appreciation for excellence in her work in the field.

Tara M. Chaplin, PhD, is a postdoctoral researcher in the Psychology Department at the University of Pennsylvania. She earned a BA in psychology from the University of Delaware and a PhD in clinical psychology with a developmental psychology minor from the Pennsylvania State University. She completed her predoctoral clinical internship at the University of Medicine and Dentistry of New Jersey. Her research focuses on relations between emotion regulation and the development of psychopathology, with specific interests in the role of emotion in the emergence of gender differences in depression during adolescence.

Pamela M. Cole, PhD, is Professor of Psychology and Human Development and Family Studies at Pennsylvania State University. She earned a BA in psychology from Mercy College, an MA in general-experimental psychology from the College of William and Mary, and a PhD in clinical and developmental psychology from Pennsylvania State University. She completed her predoctoral internship at the University of Colorado Health Sciences Center. Her research focuses on emotional development in early childhood, with specific interests in the relations between emotional functioning and mental health risk and social and cultural influences on emotional development in early childhood. Her research has been funded by the National Institute of Mental Health, the National Science Foundation, and the MacArthur Foundation, and she was the recipient of a Fulbright Senior Scholar Award.

Tara M. Cole is a third-year graduate student in the Clinical Psychology PhD Program at the University of Arkansas, Fayetteville. She received a bachelor's degree in psychology from Henderson State University. She assists Dr. Kathleen Murray in her research on effortful control and the origins of internalizing disorders in children.

Meredith E. Coles, PhD, is an Assistant Professor in the Department of Psychology at Binghamton University. She received a BA in psychology and fine arts from Dickinson College and a PhD in clinical psychology from Temple University. Her research focuses on the etiology and maintenance of anxiety in children and adults, with particular emphasis on obsessive-compulsive disorder and social phobia. She is a member of the Obsessive Compulsive Cognitions Working Group and has received awards from the Anxiety Disorders Association of America, the Association for Advancement of Behavior Therapy, the American Psychological Association, and the Society for a Science of Clinical Psychology.

Myra Cooper, DPhil, is Senior Research Tutor on the Clinical Psychology Doctoral Programme at the University of Oxford and Consultant Clinical Psychologist at the Warneford Hospital, Oxford. She received an MA from Edinburgh University and a DPhil from Oxford University. Her clinical training was completed at Edinburgh University, where she received an MPhil in clinical psychology. Her research focuses primarily on cognition in eating disorders. Her clinical and research training was funded by awards from the Medical Research Council and two University of Edinburgh overseas study awards. Her latest book is *The Psychology of Bulimia Nervosa,* published in 2003 by Oxford University Press, and she is currently working with colleagues on a treatment book that integrates many of her recent research findings. She has published widely in the field and has presented her work at numerous international conferences.

Joanne Davila is an Associate Professor of Psychology at Stony Brook University. She received her PhD in psychology from UCLA. Her expertise lies in the areas of adolescent and adult psychopathology and interpersonal functioning. She has published widely on these topics and has received funding from the National Institute of Mental Health and the National Science Foundation to conduct her research. She is the Director of the Relationship Development Center at Stony Brook University, where she and her research team are conducting projects on the development of romantic competence in adolescence, associations between interpersonal functioning and psychopathology, and the development and course of attachment security in relationships over time. She has served on the editorial boards of numerous psychology journals and is currently an Associate Editor at the *Journal of Consulting and Clinical Psychology*. She is a licensed psychologist and is interested in interventions that attempt to remediate or prevent interpersonal dysfunction and depression.

Lisa Doelger is a doctoral student in the Developmental Psychology program at Arizona State University. She received a BA in psychology from Saint Louis University. Her research interests involve using genetically informative designs to investigate temperament and parenting as risk factors for mood and behavioral disorders in children.

Brandon E. Gibb, PhD, is an Assistant Professor in the Department of Psychology at Binghamton University. He received a BA in psychology from the University of Georgia and a PhD in clinical psychology from Temple University. He completed his predoctoral internship at the Brown University Clinical Psychology Training Consortium. His research focuses on cognitive vulnerability-stress theories of depression among children and adults, with a particular emphasis on the development of cognitive vulnerability to depression.

Kathryn H. Gordon, MS, is a graduate student in clinical psychology at Florida State University. She is currently studying risk factors for eating disorders and suicidal behavior, with a focus on impulsivity and interpersonal risk factors.

Kathryn E. Grant is an Associate Professor of Clinical Child Psychology at DePaul University. She received her PhD from the University of Vermont and completed her clinical internship at Cook County Hospital in Chicago. Her research focuses on the relation between stressors and psychological symptoms in adolescents. She has been selected as a William T. Grant Foundation Faculty Scholar and has received a National Alliance for Research on Schizophrenia and Depression Young Investigator Award, a National Institute of Mental Health B-START Award, and several DePaul University research awards.

Rick E. Ingram is currently Professor of Psychology at the University of Kansas. He previously taught at San Diego State University and was a core faculty member in the SDSU/USCD Joint Doctoral Program in Clinical Psychology. His research program focuses on cognitive functioning in emotional disorders and the association between cognitive functioning and vulnerability to depression. He is currently Editor of *Cognitive Therapy and Research* and an Associate Editor for the *Journal of Consulting and Clinical Psychology*. Along with Jeanne Miranda and Zindel Segal he is coauthor of *Cognitive Vulnerability to Depression,* and with C. R. Snyder he is the coeditor of the *Handbook of Psychological Change: Psychotherapy Processes and Practices for the 21st Century*. He is a recipient of the New Researcher Award of the Association for the Advancement of Behavior Therapy, and he also received the Distinguished Scientific Award of the American Psychological Association for Early Career Contributions to Psychology.

Jeffrey G. Johnson, PhD, is Associate Professor in the Department of Psychiatry,

College of Physicians and Surgeons, Columbia University, and a Research Scientist at the New York State Psychiatric Institute. He received a BA in psychology from Oakland University, an MA in clinical psychology from Temple University, and a PhD in experimental psychology with a concentration in experimental psychopathology. He completed a postdoctoral fellowship in behavioral psychopharmacology at Johns Hopkins University and a postdoctoral fellowship in psychiatric epidemiology at Columbia University. His research has been funded by the Aaron Diamond Foundation, the National Institute of Mental Health, the National Institute on Drug Abuse, and the National Institute of Justice. His research focuses on the psychiatric epidemiology of anxiety, eating, mood, personality, and substance-use disorders among children, adolescents, and adults. He has been the primary author of more than 50 publications, including articles in *JAMA, Science,* the *Archives of General Psychiatry,* the *American Journal of Psychiatry,* the *Journal of Abnormal Psychology,* and the *Journal of Consulting and Clinical Psychology.*

Thomas E. Joiner, PhD, is the Bright-Burton Professor of Psychology at Florida State University. Author of more than 200 peer-reviewed journal articles on the psychology and neurobiology of depression, suicide, anxiety, and eating disorders, he received the Guggenheim Fellowship, the Distinguished Scientific Award for Early Career Achievement from the American Psychological Association (APA), the Shneidman Award for Excellence in Suicide Research from the American Association for Suicidology, the Young Investigator Award from the National Alliance for Research on Schizophrenia and Depression, the Shakow Award for Early Career Achievement from the Division of Clinical Psychology of the APA, as well as research grants from the National Institute of Mental Health, the Borderline Personality Disorder Research Foundation, and the Obsessive Compulsive Foundation.

Jon D. Kassel, PhD, is Associate Professor in the Department of Psychology and Codirector of Clinical Training at the University of Illinois at Chicago. He received a BS in psychology from the University of Minnesota and a PhD in clinical psychology from the University of Pittsburgh. He completed his predoctoral internship at Brown University Clinical Psychology Internship Consortium. His research focuses on drug effects on emotion and cognition, as well as on developmental trajectories of adolescent smoking behavior. He is a two-time recipient of a Young Investigator Award from the Society for Research on Nicotine and Tobacco, from whom he also received the Ove Ferno Innovative Research on Nicotine and Tobacco Award. His research has been funded by the National Institute on Alcohol Abuse and Alcoholism and the National Cancer Institute. He has received New Researcher Awards from the Society of Behavioral Medicine and the American Psychological Association's Division 50 on Addictions.

Robert F. Krueger, PhD, is Associate Professor of Clinical Psychology, Personality Psychology, and Differential Psychology/ Behavior Genetics in the Department of Psychology, and Adjunct Associate Professor of Child Psychology in the Institute of Child Development, at the University of Minnesota, Twin Cities. In 2004, he was awarded the McKnight Presidential Fellowship. He obtained his PhD from the University of Wisconsin at Madison and completed his clinical internship at Brown University. He is currently an Associate Editor of the *Journal of Personality,* and incoming Associate Editor of the *Journal of Abnormal Psychology.* He has served on the editorial boards of the

European Journal of Personality, Journal of Abnormal Psychology, Journal of Research in Personality, Journal of Personality and Social Psychology: Personality Processes and Individual Differences, and *Psychological Assessment.* His major interests lie at the intersection of research on personality, psychopathology, disorders of personality, behavior genetics, and quantitative methods, and he has more than 50 publications in these areas. He was the recipient of a 1997 J. S. Tanaka award for outstanding dissertation in personality psychology and a 2003 Early Career Award from the International Society for the Study of Individual Differences. He currently serves as a Core Working Group Member of the American Psychiatric Association/National Institute of Mental Health DSM/ICD Research Planning Conference on Personality Disorders.

Kathryn S. Lemery is Assistant Professor of Psychology at Arizona State University and codirector of the Wisconsin Twin Project at the Waisman Center on Developmental Disabilities and Human Development. She received a BA in psychology from the Robert D. Clark Honors College at the University of Oregon in 1994, and a PhD in developmental psychology from the University of Wisconsin at Madison in 1999. Her research focuses on early biological and environmental risk and protective factors for later mental and physical health. She is currently funded by the National Institute of Mental Health and is studying young twins with *DSM-IV* diagnoses of mood and behavioral disorders longitudinally.

David D. Luxton, MS, is currently a PhD graduate student in clinical psychology at the University of Kansas. He received his BA in psychology from St. Edward's University and an MS in experimental psychology from the University of Texas at San Antonio. His research primarily involves cognitive vulnerability toward depression, with an emphasis on vulnerable self-esteem and mental control. He also has research interests that focus on the physical health implications of stress and depression.

Pamela G. McGeoch, MA, is a clinical psychology intern at Creedmoor Psychiatric Institute and a doctoral candidate in clinical psychology at the New School University, New York. She received a BA in international relations at the University of Virginia, an MA in psychology at the New School University, and an MA in anthropology at the University of Connecticut. She has been involved in psychiatric research at Beth Israel Medical Center, New York, for 4 years and has coauthored seven publications. She is currently conducting her dissertation research, which focuses on the differential relationships between specific subtypes of childhood maltreatment and adult personality disorders.

Susan D. McMahon, PhD, is an Associate Professor in the Department of Psychology at DePaul University. She received her BS in psychology at the University of Iowa and her MA and PhD at DePaul University in clinical and community psychology. She is currently the Director of the doctoral program in Community Psychology and the Chair of the Institutional Review Board at DePaul University. Her research focuses on understanding the risk and protective factors that urban, at-risk youth experience. Her action-oriented research also focuses on implementing and evaluating school-based interventions designed to improve educational experiences and reduce negative psychosocial outcomes among youth. She is interested in how specific environmental and contextual stressors, such as exposure to violence, influence specific psychological and behavioral outcomes, such as aggression. Her violence prevention work in public housing development communities has been featured in a documentary on anger produced by the Australian Broadcasting Company.

Chad M. McWhinnie is a doctoral student in the Clinical Psychology program at McGill University. He received a BA in psychology from the University of Arizona. His research interests focus on adolescent depression and positive psychology. He is the recipient of McGill University's Richard H. Tomlinson Recruitment Fellowship for doctoral students.

Robin Mermelstein is Professor of Psychology, Director of the Center for Health Behavior Research, and Deputy Director of the Institute for Health Research and Policy at the University of Illinois at Chicago. She holds a PhD in clinical and community psychology from the University of Oregon. Her research interests fall broadly in the area of tobacco use, with studies ranging from longitudinal examinations of the etiology of youth smoking to cessation interventions for adult smokers. She has been the principal investigator on several grants from the National Cancer Institute investigating trajectories of adolescent smoking, with a focus on social and emotional contextual factors. In addition, she has been funded by the Centers for Disease Control and Prevention to examine factors related to youth smoking, and by the National Heart, Lung, and Blood Institute and National Cancer Institute (NCI) for studies of adult smoking cessation. She has also been the Director of the Robert Wood Johnson Foundation's (RWJF) Program Office, Partners With Tobacco Use Research Centers: A Transdisciplinary Approach to Advancing Science and Policy Studies. As part of this program, the RWJF has collaborated with both NCI and the National Institute on Drug Abuse in funding the Transdisciplinary Tobacco Use Research Centers.

Kathleen T. Murray, PhD, is an Assistant Professor in the Department of Psychology at the University of Arkansas. She received her PhD in clinical psychology from the University of Iowa. Her research has focused on the role of temperament in psychopathology, specifically the role of behavioral inhibition and effortful control in the development of emotion regulation.

Amélie Nantel-Vivier is a PhD candidate in clinical psychology at McGill University. She received her BA in psychology from McGill University, where she developed research interests in the fields of interpersonal relationships and child development. Her current doctoral research focuses on the development of children's prosocial behaviors and its link with the development of other types of behaviors, such as aggression, anxiety, and depression. Special attention is given to how serotonergic functioning may be contributing to the development of prosociality and aggression. A student member of the Research Unit on Children's Psychosocial Maladjustment in Montreal, she is a two-time recipient of the Fond Québecois de Recherche Société et Culture scholarship awards for graduate students.

Robert O. Pihl, PhD, is a Professor of Psychology and Psychiatry at McGill University in Montreal. He received a BA from Lawrence University and an MA and PhD from Arizona State University. His clinical internship was completed at Barrow Neurological Institute in Phoenix, Arizona. His recent work has focused on motivational models for substance use/abuse and aggression. He is the recipient of the Heinz Lehmann award from the Canadian College of Neuropsychopharmacology.

Melissa Ramsay is a PhD student in clinical psychology at Stony Brook University. She is currently involved in studying the course and predictors of short- and long-term change in attachment security in close romantic relationships, as well as the development of romantic competence for adolescent girls. She is especially interested in exploring individual factors that influence interpersonal functioning.

John M. Reardon, MA, is a doctoral student in the Clinical Psychology PhD Program at the University of Arkansas, Fayetteville. He received his BS in psychology from Louisiana State University and his MA in clinical psychology from the University of Harford. He has conducted research on cognitive-behavioral treatments for pain, and currently his research focuses on cognitive vulnerabilities for mood and anxiety disorders under the direction of Dr. Nathan Williams.

Steven A. Skitch is a doctoral candidate in clinical psychology at McGill University. His doctoral research focuses on the relationship between depression and substance abuse in adolescents. Particular focus is given to how diathesis-stress models of vulnerability can be used to explain the interrelationship between the two disorders. He is a graduate of the University of Calgary, Department of Psychology, where he researched issues related to the development of problem gambling among university students. He is the recipient of a Social Sciences and Humanities Research Council of Canada scholarship award for graduate students.

Joel R. Sneed, PhD, is a Geriatric Neuropsychiatry Research Fellow at Columbia University and New York State Psychiatric Institute, Department of Biological Psychiatry. He received a BS in psychology from New York University and a PhD in clinical psychology from the University of Massachusetts at Amherst. He completed his predoctoral internship at New York University/Bellevue Hospital. He completed a 2-year postdoctoral fellowship in Mental Health Statistics, where he focused on longitudinal methods for the analysis of change. His substantive research interest lies in the development of personality and psychopathology across the life span. He has particularly focused on identity and how older adults negotiate identity-discrepant experiences. His current research interests lie at the intersection of phenomenology, neuropsychology, and neuroimaging in the study of vascular depression.

Sara Steinberg is a PhD student at Stony Brook University. She received her MA in psychology from Stony Brook University and is currently working on her dissertation. Her research interests focus on the role of family relationships in the development of psychopathology and interpersonal functioning among adolescents and adults. She has presented several conference presentations and posters on these topics and has papers both published and under review. She is active in the Relationship Development Center at Stony Brook University, where she is collaborating on conducting projects that examine the development of romantic competence in adolescence, associations between interpersonal functioning and psychopathology among adolescents and adults, and the development and course of attachment security in relationships over time.

Catherine B. Stroud is a PhD candidate in the Clinical Psychology program at SUNY–Stony Brook. She received her BA from the University of Wisconsin–Madison in 2002. Her interests include depression, adolescent romantic relationships, personality, and adolescent psychopathology.

Jennifer L. Tackett, MA, is a PhD student in the clinical science and psychopathology research program at the University of Minnesota, Twin Cities. She is a graduate of the Texas Academy of Mathematics and Science and received her BS, summa cum laude, from Texas A&M University. Her research pursuits focus on the relationship between personality and psychopathology across the life span. Additional research interests include assessment and classification of childhood psychopathology, childhood antisocial behavior, and behavioral genetics.

Kimberly Van Orden is a doctoral candidate in clinical psychology at Florida State

University. She is currently studying interpersonal factors involved in the development and maintenance of depression and suicidality. She is particularly interested in the interface of clinical and social psychology, including how an understanding of such concepts as the self, interpersonal functioning, and self-regulation may inform our understanding of psychopathology.

Jennifer C. Veilleux is a graduate student in the Clinical Psychology PhD program at the University of Illinois at Chicago. She is a graduate of Macalester College in St. Paul, Minnesota, where she received her BA in Dramatic Arts, and she completed her Postbaccalaureate in Psychology at the University of Minnesota. She currently assists Dr. Jon Kassel in his research on emotional and cognitive factors involved with smoking and alcohol use.

Sally M. Weinstein is a doctoral student in Clinical Psychology at the University of Illinois at Chicago. She received a BS in Psychology from Duke University (2001) and an MA in Clinical Psychology from the University of Illinois at Chicago (2004). Her research focuses on developmental changes in adolescent mood patterns and the influences of social factors on these mood patterns. In addition, she is involved in research examining the relationship between mood, contextual factors, and smoking in adolescence under the direction of Dr. Robin Mermelstein.

Nathan L. Williams, PhD, is an Assistant Professor of Psychology at the University of Arkansas, Fayetteville. He received a BA in psychology from the Pennsylvania State University and a PhD in clinical psychology at George Mason University. He completed his predoctoral internship in the Department of Psychiatry and Behavioral Sciences at Duke University Medical Center in the Behavior Research and Therapy Program. He is a Fellow of the Academy of Cognitive Therapy and serves on the editorial boards of *Journal of Cognitive Psychotherapy, Journal of Social and Clinical Psychology,* and *Cognitive Therapy and Research.* His research focuses on vulnerability-stress models of anxiety disorders, mood disorders, and eating disorders, with a particular emphasis on the cognitive differentiation of anxiety and depression.

LaRicka R. Wingate, MS, is a doctoral candidate in clinical psychology at Florida State University. She is currently studying risk factors for depression and suicide, with a focus on interpersonal risk factors. She is also interested in positive psychology and the relationship between mental health and cultural influences.